Ornithological Biography Or An Account Of The Habits Of The Birds Of The United States Of America (etc.)

ORNITHOLOGICAL BIOGRAPHY.

ORNITHOLOGICAL BIOGRAPHY,

OR AN ACCOUNT OF THE HABITS OF THE

BIRDS OF THE UNITED STATES OF AMERICA;

ACCOMPANIED BY DESCRIPTIONS OF THE OBJECTS REPRESENTED
IN THE WORK ENTITLED

THE BIRDS OF AMERICA,

AND INTERSPERSED WITH DELINEATIONS OF AMERICAN
SCENERY AND MANNERS.

BY JOHN JAMES AUDUBON, F.R.SS. L. & E.

FELLOW OF THE LINNEAN AND ZOOLOGICAL SOCIETIES OF LONDON; MEMBER OF THE LYCEUM
AND LINNEAN SOCIETY OF NEW YORK, OF THE NATURAL HISTORY SOCIETY OF PARIS, THE
WERNERIAN NATURAL HISTORY SOCIETY OF EDINBURGH; HONORARY MEMBER OF THE
SOCIETY OF NATURAL HISTORY OF MANCHESTER, AND OF THE SCOTTISH ACADEMY OF
PAINTING, ARCHITECTURE, AND SCULPTURE, &c.

EDINBURGH:

ADAM BLACK, 55. NORTH BRIDGE, EDINBURGH;

R. HAVELL JUN., ENGRAVER, 77. OXFORD STREET, AND LONGMAN, REES,
BROWN, & GREEN, LONDON; GEORGE SMITH, TITHEBARR STREET,
LIVERPOOL; T. SOWLER, MANCHESTER; MRS ROBINSON, LEEDS;
F. CHARNLEY, NEWCASTLE; POOL & BOOTH, CHESTER; AND BEILBY,
KNOTT, & BEILBY, BIRMINGHAM.

MDCCCXXXI.

NEILL & CO. PRINTERS,
Old Fishmarket, Edinburgh.

INTRODUCTORY ADDRESS.

KIND READER,—Should you derive from the perusal of the following pages, which I have written with no other wish than that of procuring one favourable thought from you, a portion of the pleasure which I have felt in collecting the materials for their composition, my gratification will be ample, and the compensation for all my labours will be more than, perhaps, I have a right to expect from an individual to whom I am as yet unknown, and to whom I must therefore, in the very outset, present some account of my life, and of the motives which have influenced me in thus bringing you into contact with an American Woodsman.

I received life and light in the New World. When I had hardly yet learned to walk, and to articulate those first words always so endearing to parents, the productions of Nature that lay spread all around, were constantly pointed out to me. They soon became my playmates; and before my ideas were sufficiently formed to enable me to estimate the difference between the azure tints of the sky, and the emerald hue of the bright foliage, I felt that an intimacy with them, not consisting of friendship merely, but bordering on phrenzy, must accompany my steps through life;—and now, more than ever, am I persuaded of the power of those early impressions. They laid such hold upon me, that, when removed from the woods, the prairies, and the brooks, or shut up from the view of the wide Atlantic, I experienced none of those pleasures most congenial to my mind. None but aërial companions suited my fancy. No roof seemed so secure to me as that formed of the dense foliage under which the feathered tribes were seen to resort, or the caves and fissures of the massy rocks to which the dark-winged Cormorant and the Curlew retired to rest, or to protect themselves from the fury of the tempest. My father generally accompanied my steps, procured birds and flowers for me with great eagerness,—pointed out the elegant movements of the former, the beauty and softness of their plumage, the manifestations of their pleasure or sense of danger,—and the always perfect forms and splendid attire of the latter. My valued preceptor would then speak of the departure and return of birds with the seasons, would describe their haunts, and, more wonderful than all, their change of livery; thus exciting me to study them, and to raise my mind toward their great Creator.

A vivid pleasure shone upon those days of my early youth, attended with a calmness of feeling, that seldom failed to rivet my attention for hours, whilst I gazed in ecstacy upon the pearly and shining eggs, as they lay imbedded in the softest down, or among dried leaves and twigs, or were exposed upon the burning sand or weather-beaten rock of our Atlantic shores. I was taught to look upon them as flowers yet in the bud. I watched their opening, to see how Nature had provided each different species with eyes, either open at birth, or closed for some time after; to trace the slow progress of the young birds toward perfection, or admire the celerity with which some of them, while yet unfledged, removed themselves from danger to security.

I grew up, and my wishes grew with my form. These wishes, kind reader, were for the entire possession of all that I saw. I was fervently desirous of becoming acquainted with nature. For many years, however, I was sadly disappointed, and for ever, doubtless, must I have desires that cannot be gratified. The moment a bird was dead, however beautiful it had been when in life, the pleasure arising from the possession of it became blunted; and although the greatest cares were bestowed on endeavours to preserve the appearance of nature, I looked upon its vesture as more than sullied, as requiring constant attention and repeated mendings, while, after all, it could no longer be said to be fresh from the hands of its Maker. I wished to possess all the productions of nature, but I wished life with them. This was impossible. Then what was to be done? I turned to my father, and made known to him my disappointment and anxiety. He produced a book of *Illustrations*. A new life ran in my veins. I turned over the leaves with avidity; and although what I saw was not what I longed for, it gave me a desire to copy nature. To Nature I went, and tried to imitate her, as in the days of my childhood I had tried to raise myself from the ground and stand erect, before nature had imparted the vigour necessary for the success of such an undertaking.

How sorely disappointed did I feel for many years, when I saw that my productions were worse than those which I ventured (perhaps in silence) to regard as bad, in the book given me by my father! My pencil gave birth to a family of cripples. So maimed were most of them, that they resembled the mangled corpses on a field of battle, compared with the integrity of living men. These difficulties and disappointments irritated me, but never for a moment destroyed the desire of obtaining perfect representations of nature. The worse my drawings were, the more beautiful did I see the originals. To have been torn from the study would have been as death to me. My time was entirely occupied with it. I produced hundreds of these rude sketches annually; and for a long time, at my request, they made bonfires on the anniversaries of my birth-day.

Patiently, and with industry, did I apply myself to study, for, although I felt the impossibility of giving life to my productions, I did not abandon the idea of representing nature. Many plans were successively adopted, many masters guided my hand. At the age of seventeen, when I returned from France, whither I had gone to receive the rudiments of my education, my drawings had assumed a form. DAVID had guided my hand in tracing objects of large size. Eyes and noses belonging to giants, and heads of horses represented in ancient sculpture, were my models. These, although fit subjects for men intent on pursuing the higher branches of the art, were immediately laid aside by me. I returned to the woods of the New World with fresh ardour, and commenced a collection of drawings, which I henceforth continued, and which is now publishing, under the title of " THE BIRDS OF AMERICA."

To these Illustrations I shall often refer you, good-natured reader, in the sequel, that you may judge of them yourself. Should you discover any merit in them, happy would the expression of your approbation render me, for I should feel that I had not spent my life in vain. You can best ascertain the truth of these delineations. I am persuaded that you love nature—that you admire and study her. Every individual, possessed of a sound heart, listens with delight to the love-notes of the woodland warblers. He never casts a glance upon their lovely forms without proposing to himself questions respecting them; nor does he look on the trees which they frequent, or the flowers over which they glide, without admiring their grandeur, or delighting in their sweet odours or their brilliant tints.

In Pennsylvania, a beautiful State, almost central on the line of our Atlantic shores, my father, in his desire of proving my friend through life, gave me what Americans call a beautiful " plantation," refreshed during the summer heats by the waters of the Schuylkil River, and traversed by a creek named Perkioming. Its fine woodlands, its extensive fields, its hills crowned with evergreens, offered many subjects to my pencil. It was there that I commenced my simple and agreeable studies, with as little concern about the future as if the world had been made for me. My rambles invariably commenced at break of day; and to return wet with dew, and bearing a feathered prize, was, and ever will be, the highest enjoyment for which I have been fitted.

Yet think not, reader, that the enthusiasm which I felt for my favourite pursuits was a barrier opposed to the admission of gentler sentiments. Nature, which had turned my young mind toward the bird and the flower, soon proved her influence upon my heart. Be it enough to say, that the object of my passion has long since blessed me with the name of husband. And now let us return, for who cares to listen to the love-tale of a naturalist, whose feelings may be supposed to be as light as the feathers which he delineates !

For a period of nearly twenty years, my life was a succession of vicissitudes. I tried various branches of cómmerce, but they all proved unprofitable, doubtless because my whole mind was ever filled with my passion for rambling and admiring those objects of nature from which alone I received the purest gratification. I had to struggle against the will of all who at that period called themselves my friends. I must here, however, except my wife and children. The remarks of my other friends irritated me beyond endurance, and, breaking through all bonds, I gave myself entirely up to my pursuits. Any one unacquainted with the extraordinary desire which I then felt of seeing and judging for myself, would doubtless have pronounced me callous to every sense of duty, and regardless of every interest. I undertook long and tedious journeys, ransacked the woods, the lakes, the prairies, and the shores of the Atlantic. Years were spent away from my family. Yet, reader, will you believe it, I had no other object in view, than simply to enjoy the sight of nature. Never for a moment did I conceive the hope of becoming in any degree useful to my kind, until I accidentally formed acquaintance with the PRINCE of MUSIGNANO at Philadelphia, to which place I went, with the view of proceeding eastward along the coast.

I reached Philadelphia on the 5th April 1824, just as the sun was sinking beneath the horizon. Excepting the good Dr MEASE, who had visited me in my younger days, I had scarcely a friend in the city; for I was then unacquainted with HARLAN, WETHERELL, MACMURTRIE, LESUEUR, or SULLY.

I called on him, and showed him some of my drawings.   He
presented me to the celebrated CHARLES LUCIAN BONA-
PARTE, who in his turn introduced me to the Natural History
Society of Philadelphia.   But the patronage which I so much
needed, I soon found myself compelled to seek elsewhere.   I
left Philadelphia, and visited New York, where I was received
with a kindness well suited to elevate my depressed spirits;
and afterwards, ascending that noble stream the Hudson, glided over our broad lakes, to seek the wildest solitudes of the
pathless and gloomy forests.

It was in these forests that, for the first time, I communed
with myself as to the possible event of my visiting Europe
again; and I began to fancy my work under the multiplying
efforts of the graver.   Happy days, and nights of pleasing
dreams!   I read over the catalogue of my collection, and
thought how it might be possible for an unconnected and un-
aided individual like myself to accomplish the grand scheme.
Chance, and chance alone, had divided my drawings into three
different classes, depending upon the magnitude of the objects
which they represented; and, although I did not at that time
possess all the specimens necessary, I arranged them as well as
I could into parcels of five plates, each of which now forms a
Number of my Illustrations.   I improved the whole as much as
was in my power; and as I daily retired farther from the haunts
of man, determined to leave nothing undone, which my labour,
my time, or my purse, could accomplish.

Eighteen months elapsed.   I returned to my family, then
in Louisiana, explored every portion of the vast woods around,
and at last sailed towards the Old World.   But before we visit
the shores of hospitable England, I have the wish, good-natured

reader, to give you some idea of my mode of executing the original drawings, from which the Illustrations have been taken; and I sincerely hope that the perusal of these lines may excite in you a desire minutely to examine them.

Merely to say, that each object of my Illustrations is of the size of nature, were too vague—for to many it might only convey the idea that they are so, more or less, according as the eye of the delineator may have been more or less correct in measurement simply obtained through that medium; and of avoiding error in this respect I am particularly desirous. Not only is every object, as a whole, of the natural size, but also every portion of each object. The compass aided me in its delineation, regulated and corrected each part, even to the very foreshortening which now and then may be seen in the figures. The bill, the feet, the legs, the claws, the very feathers as they project one beyond another, have been accurately measured. The birds, almost all of them, were killed by myself, after I had examined their motions and habits, as much as the case admitted, and were regularly drawn on or near the spot where I procured them. The positions may, perhaps, in some instances, appear *outré*; but such supposed exaggerations can afford subject of criticism only to persons unacquainted with the feathered tribes; for, believe me, nothing can be more transient or varied than the attitudes or positions of birds. The Heron, when warming itself in the sun, will sometimes drop its wings several inches, as if they were dislocated; the Swan may often be seen floating with one foot extended from the body; and some Pigeons, you well know, turn quite over, when playing in the air. The flowers, plants, or portions of trees which are attached to the principal objects, have been chosen from amongst those in the vicinity of which the birds were found, and are not, as some persons have thought, the trees or plants upon which they always feed or perch.

An accident which happened to two hundred of my original drawings, nearly put a stop to my researches in ornithology. I shall relate it, merely to show you how far enthusiasm—for by no other name can I call the persevering zeal with which I laboured—may enable the observer of nature to surmount the most disheartening obstacles. I left the village of Henderson, in Kentucky, situated on the bank of the Ohio, where I resided for several years, to proceed to Philadelphia on business. I looked to all my drawings before my departure, placed them carefully in a wooden box, and gave them in charge to a relative, with injunctions to see that no injury should happen to them. My absence was of several months; and when I returned, after having enjoyed the pleasures of home for a few days, I inquired after my box, and what I was pleased to call my treasure. The box was produced, and opened;—but, reader, feel for me—a pair of Norway rats had taken possession of the whole, and had reared a young family amongst the gnawed bits of paper, which, but a few months before, represented nearly a thousand inhabitants of the air! The burning heat which instantly rushed through my brain was too great to be endured, without affecting the whole of my nervous system. I slept not for several nights, and the days passed like days of oblivion,—until the animal powers being recalled into action, through the strength of my constitution, I took up my gun, my note-book, and my pencils, and went forth to the woods as gaily as if nothing had happened. I felt pleased that I might now make much better drawings than before, and, ere a period not exceeding three years had elapsed, I had my portfolio filled again.

America being my country, and the principal pleasures of my life having been obtained there, I prepared to leave it with deep sorrow, after in vain trying to publish my Illustrations in the United States. In Philadelphia, WILSON's principal en-graver, amongst others, gave it as his opinion to my friends, that my drawings could never be engraved. In New York, other difficulties presented themselves, which determined me to carry my collections to Europe.

As I approached the coast of England, and for the first time beheld her fertile shores, the despondency of my spirits became very great. I knew not an individual in the country; and, although 1 was the bearer of letters from American friends, and statesmen of great eminence, my situation appeared preca-rious in the extreme. I imagined that every individual whom I was about to meet, might be possessed of talents superior to those of any on our side of the Atlantic! Indeed, as I for the first time walked on the streets of Liverpool, my heart nearly failed me, for not a glance of sympathy did I meet in my wan-derings, for two days. To the woods I could not betake myself, for there were none near.

But how soon did all around me assume a different aspect! How fresh is the recollection of the change! The very first letter which I tendered procured me a world of friends. The RATHBONES, the ROSCOES, the TRAILLS, the CHORLEYS, the MELLIES, and others, took me by the hand; and so kind and beneficent, nay, so generously kind, have they all been to-wards me, that I can never cancel the obligation. My draw-ings were publicly exhibited, and publicly praised. Joy swelled

my heart. The first difficulty was surmounted. Honours,
which, on application being made through my friends, Philadelphia had refused, Liverpool freely accorded.

I left that emporium of commerce, with many a passport,
bent upon visiting fair Edina, for I longed to see the men
and the scenes immortalized by the fervid strains of BURNS,
and the glowing eloquence of SCOTT and WILSON. I arrived
at Manchester; and here, too, the GREGGS, the LLOYDS, the
SERGEANTS, the HOLMES, the BLACKWALLS, the BENTLEYS,
and many others, rendered my visit as pleasing as it was profitable to me. Friends pressed me to accompany them to the
pretty villages of Bakewell, Mattlock, and Buxton. It was a
jaunt of pure enjoyment. Nature was then at her best, at least
such was the feeling of our whole party; the summer was full
of promise.

My journey to Scotland was performed along the north-
western shores of England. I passed in view of Lancaster
Castle, and through Carlisle. I had by this time much altered
my ideas of this Island and its inhabitants. I found her
churches all hung with her glories, and her people all alive to
the kindest hospitality. I saw Edinburgh, and was struck with
the natural pictorial elegance of her site; and I soon found
that her inhabitants were as urbane as those whom I had left
behind me. The principal scientific and literary characters of
the ancient metropolis of Scotland received me as a brother.
It is impossible for me to mention all the individuals from
whom I received the kindest attention; but gratitude forbids
my omitting the names of Professors JAMESON, GRAHAM,
RUSSEL, WILSON, BROWN, and MONRO, Sir WALTER
SCOTT, Captain HALL, Dr BREWSTER, Dr GREVILLE,

Mr JAMES WILSON, Mr NEILL, Mr HAY, Mr COMBE, Mr HAMILTON, the WITHAMS, the LIZARSES, the SYMES, and the NICHOLSONS. The Royal Society, the Wernerian Natural History Society, the Society of Scottish Antiquaries, the Society of Useful Arts, and the Scottish Academy of Painting, Sculpture, and Architecture, spontaneously and gratuitously enrolled me among their members.

In this capital commenced the publication of my ILLUS-TRATIONS, and there it might have been accomplished, had not unexpected difficulties come in the way. My engraver, Mr W. H. LIZARS, advised me to seek an artist in London. There, after many fruitless inquiries, I became acquainted with Mr ROBERT HAVELL junior, who has ever since continued to be employed by me, and who, I am happy in saying, has given general satisfaction to my patrons.

Four years have passed. One volume of my Illustrations, containing one hundred plates, is before the public. You may easily see, good-natured reader, that to Britain I owe nearly all my success. She has furnished the artists through whom my labours were to be presented to the world; she has granted me the highest patronage and honours;—in a word, she has thus far supported the prosecution of my Illustrations. To Britain, therefore, I shall ever be grateful.

Two objections have been made to the mode in which my work is published : the great size of the paper upon which the representations are offered to you, and the length of time necessary for their completion.

As to the size of the paper, which has been complained of by some, it could not be avoided without giving up the desire of presenting to the world those my favourite objects in nature, of the size which nature has given to them. As one of the first ornithologists of the age, who kindly reviewed a few numbers of the Plates, has spoken upon this subject in a manner which I cannot here use, I refer you to his observations. The name of SWAINSON is, doubtless, well known to you. Permit me also to lead you, for a defence of my resolution in this matter, to one, who, being the centre of zoological science, is well entitled to your deference in a question relating to Ornithology. You will readily apprehend that I allude to the great, the immortal CUVIER.

Secondly, As to the time necessary for finishing my Work, I have only to observe, that it will be less than the period frequently given by many persons to the maturation of certain wines placed in their cellars, several years previous to the commencement of my work, and which will not be considered capable of imparting their full relish until many years after the conclusion of the "Birds of America."

Since I became acquainted with Mr ALEXANDER WILSON, the celebrated author of the well-known and duly appreciated work on American Birds, and subsequently with my excellent friend CHARLES LUCIAN BONAPARTE, I have been aware of the keenness with which every student of Natural History presses forward to describe an object of his own discovery, or that may have occurred to travellers in distant countries. There seems to be a pride, a glory in doing this, that thrusts aside every other consideration; and I really believe that the ties of friendship itself would not prevent some naturalists from even robbing an old acquaintance of the merit of first describing a previously unknown object. Although I have certainly felt very great pleasure, when, on picking up a bird, I discovered it to be

B

new to me, yet I have never known the desire above alluded to.
This feeling I still cherish; and in spite of the many injunctions which I have received from naturalists far more eminent
than I can ever expect to be, I have kept, and still keep,
unknown to others, the species, which, not finding portrayed
in any published work, I look upon as new, having only given
in my Illustrations a number of them proportionate to the
drawings of already known species that have been engraved.
Attached to the descriptions of these, you will find the place
and date of their discovery.   I do not, however, intend to claim
any merit for these discoveries, and should have liked as well
that the objects of them had been previously known, as this
would have saved some unbelievers the trouble of searching for
them in books, and the disappointment of finding them actually
new.   I assure you, good reader, that, even at this moment, I
should have less pleasure in presenting to the scientific world
a new bird, the knowledge of whose habits I do not possess,
than in describing the peculiarities of one long since discovered.

There are persons whose desire of obtaining celebrity induces them to suppress the knowledge of the assistance which
they have received in the composition of their works.   In many
cases, in fact, the real author of the drawings or the descriptions
in books on Natural History is not so much as mentioned,
while the pretended author assumes to himself all the merit
which the world is willing to allow him.   This want of can-
dour I never could endure.   On the contrary, I feel pleasure
in here acknowledging the assistance which I have received from
a friend, Mr WILLIAM MACGILLIVRAY, who being possessed
of a liberal education and a strong taste for the study of the
Natural Sciences, has aided me, not in drawing the figures of

my Illustrations, nor in writing the book now in your hand, although fully competent for both tasks, but in completing the
scientific details, and smoothing down the asperities of my
Ornithological Biographies.

I do not present to you the objects of which my work consists in the order adopted by systematic writers. Indeed, I can
scarcely believe that yourself, good-natured reader, could wish
that I should do so; for although you and I, and all the world besides, are well aware that a grand connected chain does exist in
the Creator's sublime system, the subjects of it have been left at
liberty to disperse in quest of the food best adapted for them,
or the comforts that have been so abundantly scattered for each
of them over the globe, and are not in the habit of following
each other, as if marching in regular procession to a funeral or
a merry-making. He who would write a general ornithology
of the world, and is possessed of knowledge adequate to such a
task, is the only one by whom the ordination of birds could be
made truly useful. When this work is completed, and when
the results of my observations have been duly weighed and arranged, I shall reduce the whole to an order corresponding with
the improvements recently made in ornithological science, and
present to you a Synopsis of the Birds of the United States,
including the ordinal, generic and specific characters, with the
distinctive habits of each species, and references to the descriptions of other writers.

I shall therefore simply offer you the results of my own observation with respect to each of the species, in the order in
which I have published the representations of them. Nor do I
intend to annoy you with long descriptions, including the number and shape of the feathers, particularly in cases where the

species are well known. Tables of synonyms I have also judged superfluous. Indeed, the technical descriptions and references you will find as appendages to the more generally interesting descriptions of the habits of each species; so that you may read them or not, just as you please. Yet, should you be inclined to enter into these matters, I trust you will find in these appendages descriptions constructed according to the strictest rules of science.

Should you, good-natured reader, be a botanist, I hope you will find pleasure while looking at the flowers, the herbs, the shrubs, and the trees, which I have represented; the more so, I imagine, if you have seen them in their native woods. Should you not, the sight of them in my Illustrations may, for aught I know, tempt you to go and partake of the hospitality of our brethren the Aborigines of America.

Permit me now to address a few words to the Critic, who I fervently hope is a good-natured reader too. This I do with much deference. He has seen my Illustrations, and has judged favourably of them; he has passed his keen eye over this page; he knows the very moderate strength of my talents; and I have only to add, with my compliments, that ever since I have known that such a person as himself exists, I have laboured harder, with more patience and with more care, to gain his good will, indulgence, and support.

JOHN J. AUDUBON.

EDINBURGH,   }
March 1831. }

TABLE OF CONTENTS.

ORNITHOLOGICAL BIOGRAPHY.

THE WILD TURKEY.

Meleagris Gallopavo, Linn.

PLATE I. Male.

The great size and beauty of the Wild Turkey, its value as a delicate and highly prized article of food, and the circumstance of its being the origin of the domestic race now generally dispersed over both continents, render it one of the most interesting of the birds indigenous to the United States of America.

The unsettled parts of the States of Ohio, Kentucky, Illinois, and Indiana, an immense extent of country to the north-west of these districts, upon the Mississippi and Missouri, and the vast regions drained by these rivers from their confluence to Louisiana, including the wooded parts of Arkansas, Tennessee, and Alabama, are the most abundantly supplied with this magnificent bird. It is less plentiful in Georgia and the Carolinas, becomes still scarcer in Virginia and Pennsylvania, and is now very rarely seen to the eastward of the last mentioned States. In the course of my rambles through Long Island, the State of New York, and the country around the Lakes, I did not meet with a single individual, although I was informed that some exist in those parts. Turkeys are still to be found along the whole line of the Alleghany Mountains, where they have become so wary as to be approached only with extreme difficulty. While, in the Great Pine Forest, in 1829, I found a single feather that had been dropped from the tail of a female, but saw no bird of the kind. Farther eastward, I do not think they are now to be found. I shall describe the manners of this bird as observed in the countries where it is most abundant, and having resided for many years in Kentucky and Louisiana, may be understood as referring chiefly to them.

A

The Turkey is irregularly migratory, as well as irregularly gregarious.   With reference to the first of these circumstances, I have to state,
that whenever the *mast* * of one portion of the country happens greatly
to exceed that of another, the Turkeys are insensibly led toward that
spot, by gradually meeting in their haunts with more fruit the nearer
they advance towards the place where it is most plentiful.   In this manner flock follows after flock, until one district is entirely deserted, while
another is, as it were, overflowed by them.   But as these migrations are
irregular, and extend over a vast expanse of country, it is necessary that
I should describe the manner in which they take place.

About the beginning of October, when scarcely any of the seeds and
fruits have yet fallen from the trees, these birds assemble in flocks, and gradually move towards the rich bottom lands of the Ohio and Mississippi.
The males, or, as they are more commonly called, the *gobblers*, associate in
parties of from ten to a hundred, and search for food apart from the
females ; while the latter are seen either advancing singly, each with its
brood of young, then about two-thirds grown, or in connexion with other
families, forming parties often amounting to seventy or eighty individuals, all intent on shunning the old cocks, which, even when the young
birds have attained this size, will fight with, and often destroy them by
repeated blows on the head.   Old and young, however, all move in the
same course, and on foot, unless their progress be interrupted by a river,
or the hunter's dog force them to take wing.   When they come upon a
river, they betake themselves to the highest eminences, and there often
remain a whole day, or sometimes two, as if for the purpose of consultation.   During this time, the males are heard *gobbling*, calling, and
making much ado, and are seen strutting about, as if to raise their
courage to a pitch befitting the emergency.   Even the females and
young assume something of the same pompous demeanour, spread out
their tails, and run round each other, *purring* loudly, and performing
extravagant leaps.   At length, when the weather appears settled, and all
around is quiet, the whole party mounts to the tops of the highest trees,
whence, at a signal, consisting of a single *cluck*, given by a leader, the
flock takes flight for the opposite shore.   The old and fat birds easily
get over, even should the river be a mile in breadth ; but the younger
and less robust frequently fall into the water,—not to be drowned, how-

* In America, the term *mast* is not confined to the fruit of the beech, but is used as a
general name for all kinds of forest fruits, including even grapes and berries.

ever, as might be imagined. They bring their wings close to their body, spread out their tail as a support, stretch forward their neck, and, striking out their legs with great vigour, proceed rapidly towards the shore ; on approaching which, should they find it too steep for landing, they cease their exertions for a few moments, float down the stream until they come to an accessible part, and by a violent effort generally extricate themselves from the water. It is remarkable, that immediately after thus crossing a large stream, they ramble about for some time, as if bewildered. In this state, they fall an easy prey to the hunter.

When the Turkeys arrive in parts where the mast is abundant, they separate into smaller flocks, composed of birds of all ages and both sexes, promiscuously mingled, and devour all before them. This happens about the middle of November. So gentle do they sometimes become after these long journeys, that they have been seen to approach the farm-houses, associate with the domestic fowls, and enter the stables and corn-cribs in quest of food. In this way, roaming about the forests, and feeding chiefly on mast, they pass the autumn and part of the winter.

As early as the middle of February, they begin to experience the impulse of propagation. The females separate, and fly from the males. The latter strenuously pursue, and begin to gobble or to utter the notes of exultation. The sexes roost apart, but at no great distance from each other. When a female utters a call-note, all the gobblers within hearing return the sound, rolling note after note with as much rapidity as if they intended to emit the last and the first together, not with spread tail, as when fluttering round the females on the ground, or practising on the branches of the trees on which they have roosted for the night, but much in the manner of the domestic turkey, when an unusual or unexpected noise elicits its singular hubbub. If the call of the female comes from the ground, all the males immediately fly towards the spot, and the moment they reach it, whether the hen be in sight or not, spread out and erect their tail, draw the head back on the shoulders, depress their wings with a quivering motion, and strut pompously about, emitting at the same time a succession of puffs from the lungs, and stopping now and then to listen and look. But whether they spy the female or not, they continue to puff and strut, moving with as much celerity as their ideas of ceremony seem to admit. While thus occupied, the males often encounter each other, in which case desperate battles take place,

A 2

ending in bloodshed, and often in the loss of many lives, the weaker falling under the repeated blows inflicted upon their head by the stronger.

I have often been much diverted, while watching two males in fierce conflict, by seeing them move alternately backwards and forwards, as either had obtained a better hold, their wings drooping, their tails partly raised, their body-feathers ruffled, and their heads covered with blood. If, as they thus struggle, and gasp for breath, one of them should lose his hold, his chance is over, for the other, still holding fast, hits him violently with spurs and wings, and in a few minutes brings him to the ground. The moment he is dead, the conqueror treads him under foot, but, what is strange, not with hatred, but with all the motions which he employs in caressing the female.

. When the male has discovered and made up to the female (whether such a combat has previously taken place or not), if she be more than one year old, she also struts and gobbles, turns round him as he continues strutting, suddenly opens her wings, throws herself towards him, as if to put a stop to his idle delay, lays herself down, and receives his dilatory caresses. If the cock meet a young hen, he alters his mode of procedure. He struts in a different manner, less pompously and more energetically, moves with rapidity, sometimes rises from the ground, taking a short flight around the hen, as is the manner of some Pigeons, the Red-breasted Thrush, and many other birds, and on alighting, runs with all his might, at the same time rubbing his tail and wings along the ground, for the space of perhaps ten yards. He then draws near the timorous female, allays her fears by purring, and when she at length assents, caresses her.

When a male and a female have thus come together, I believe the connexion continues for that season, although the former by no means confines his attentions to one female, as I have seen a cock caress several hens, when he happened to fall in with them in the same place, for the first time. After this the hens follow their favourite cock, roosting in his immediate neighbourhood, if not on the same tree, until they begin to lay, when they separate themselves, in order to save their eggs from the male, who would break them all, for the purpose of protracting his sexual enjoyments. The females then carefully avoid him, excepting during a short period each day. After this the males become clumsy and slovenly, if one may say so, cease to fight with each other, give up gobbling or calling so frequently, and assume so careless a habit, that the hens are obliged to make all the advances themselves. They *yelp* loudly and almost continually for the cocks, run up to them, caress them, and employ various means to rekindle their expiring ardour.

Turkey-cocks when at roost sometimes strut and gobble, but I have more generally seen them spread out and raise their tail, and emit the pulmonic puff, lowering their tail and other feathers immediately after. During clear nights, or when there is moonshine, they perform this action at intervals of a few minutes, for hours together, without moving from the same spot, and indeed sometimes without rising on their legs, especially towards the end of the love-season. The males now become greatly emaciated, and cease to gobble, their *breast-sponge* becoming flat. They then separate from the hens, and one might suppose that they had entirely deserted their neighbourhood. At such seasons I have found them lying by the side of a log, in some retired part of the dense woods and cane thickets, and often permitting one to approach within a few feet. They are then unable to fly, but run swiftly, and to a great distance. A slow turkey-hound has led me miles before I could flush the same bird. Chases of this kind I did not undertake for the purpose of killing the bird, it being then unfit for eating, and covered with ticks, but with the view of rendering myself acquainted with its habits. They thus retire to recover flesh and strength, by purging with particular species of grass, and using less exercise. As soon as their condition is improved, the cocks come together again, and recommence their rambles. Let us now return to the females.

About the middle of April, when the season is dry, the hens begin to look out for a place in which to deposit their eggs. This place requires to be as much as possible concealed from the eye of the Crow, as that bird often watches the Turkey when going to her nest, and, waiting in the neighbourhood until she has left it, removes and eats the eggs. The nest, which consists of a few withered leaves, is placed on the ground, in a hollow scooped out, by the side of a log, or in the fallen top of a dry leafy tree, under a thicket of sumach or briars, or a few feet within the edge of a cane-brake, but always in a dry place. The eggs, which are of a dull cream colour, sprinkled with red dots, sometimes amount to twenty, although the more usual number is from ten to fifteen. When depositing her eggs, the female always approaches the nest with extreme caution, scarcely ever taking the same course twice ; and when about to leave them, covers them carefully with leaves, so that it is very difficult for a person who may have seen the bird to discover the nest. Indeed, few Turkeys' nests are found, unless the female has been suddenly started from them, or a cunning Lynx, Fox, or Crow has sucked the eggs and left their shells scattered about.

Turkey hens not unfrequently prefer islands for depositing their eggs and rearing their young, probably because such places are less frequented by hunters, and because the great masses of drifted timber which usually accumulate at their heads, may protect and save them in cases of great emergency. When I have found these birds in such situations, and with young, I have always observed that a single discharge of a gun made them run immediately to the pile of drifted wood, and conceal themselves in it. I have often walked over these masses, which are frequently from ten to twenty feet in height, in search of the game which I knew to be concealed in them.

When an enemy passes within sight of a female, while laying or sitting, she never moves, unless she knows that she has been discovered, but crouches lower until he has passed. I have frequently approached within five or six paces of a nest, of which I was previously aware, on assuming an air of carelessness, and whistling or talking to myself, the female remaining undisturbed; whereas if I went cautiously towards it, she would never suffer me to approach within twenty paces, but would run off, with her tail spread on one side, to a distance of twenty or thirty yards, when assuming a stately gait, she would walk about deliberately, uttering every now and then a cluck. They seldom abandon their nest, when it has been discovered by men; but, I believe, never go near it again, when a snake or other animal has sucked any of the eggs. If the eggs have been destroyed or carried off, the female soon yelps again for a male; but, in general, she rears only a single brood each season. Several hens sometimes associate together, I believe for their mutual safety, deposit their eggs in the same nest, and rear their broods together. I once found three sitting on forty-two eggs. In such cases, the common nest is always watched by one of the females, so that no Crow, Raven, or perhaps even Pole-cat, dares approach it.

The mother will not leave her eggs, when near hatching, under any circumstances, while life remains. She will even allow an enclosure to be made around her, and thus suffer imprisonment, rather than abandon them. I once witnessed the hatching of a brood of Turkeys, which I watched for the purpose of securing them together with the parent. I concealed myself on the ground within a very few feet, and saw her raise herself half the length of her legs, look anxiously upon the eggs, cluck with a sound peculiar to the mother on such occasions, carefully remove each half-empty shell, and with her bill caress and dry the young birds, that already stood tottering and attempting to make their way out of the nest. Yes, I have seen this, and have left mother and young to better care than mine could have proved,—to the care of their Creator and mine. I have seen them all emerge from the shell, and, in a few moments after, tumble, roll, and push each other forward, with astonishing and inscrutable instinct.

Before leaving the nest with her young brood, the mother shakes herself in a violent manner, picks and adjusts the feathers about her belly, and assumes quite a different aspect. She alternately inclines her eyes obliquely upwards and sideways, stretching out her neck, to discover hawks or other enemies, spreads her wings a little as she walks, and softly clucks to keep her innocent offspring close to her. They move slowly along, and as the hatching generally takes place in the afternoon, they frequently return to the nest to spend the first night there. After this, they remove to some distance, keeping on the highest undulated grounds, the mother dreading rainy weather, which is extremely dangerous to the young, in this tender state, when they are only covered by a kind of soft hairy down, of surprising delicacy. In very rainy seasons, Turkeys are scarce, for if once completely wetted, the young seldom recover. To prevent the disastrous effects of rainy weather, the mother, like a skilful physician, plucks the buds of the spice-wood bush, and gives them to her young.

In about a fortnight, the young birds, which had previously rested on the ground, leave it and fly, at night, to some very large low branch, where they place themselves under the deeply curved wings of their kind and careful parent, dividing themselves for that purpose into two nearly equal parties. After this, they leave the woods during the day, and approach the natural glades or prairies, in search of strawberries, and subsequently of dewberries, blackberries and grasshoppers, thus obtaining abundant food, and enjoying the beneficial influence of the sun's rays. They roll themselves in deserted ants' nests, to clear their growing feathers of the loose scales, and prevent ticks and other vermin from attacking them, these insects being unable to bear the odour of the earth in which ants have been.

The young Turkeys now advance rapidly in growth, and in the month of August are able to secure themselves from unexpected attacks of Wolves, Foxes, Lynxes, and even Cougars, by rising quickly from the ground, by the help of their powerful legs, and reaching with ease the highest branches of the tallest trees. The young cocks shew the tuft on the breast about this time, and begin to gobble and strut, while the young hens pur and leap, in the manner which I have already described.

The old cocks have also assembled by this time, and it is probable that all the Turkeys now leave the extreme north-western districts, to remove to the Wabash, Illinois, Black River, and the neighbourhood of Lake Erie.

Of the numerous enemies of the Wild Turkey, the most formidable, excepting man, are the Lynx, the Snowy Owl, and the Virginian Owl. The Lynx sucks their eggs, and is extremely expert at seizing both young and old, which he effects in the following manner. When he has discovered a flock of Turkeys, he follows them at a distance for some time, until he ascertains the direction in which they are proceeding. He then makes a rapid circular movement, gets in advance of the flock, and lays himself down in ambush, until the birds come up, when he springs upon one of them by a single bound, and secures it. While once sitting in the woods, on the banks of the Wabash, I observed two large Turkey-cocks on a log, by the river, pluming and picking themselves. I watched their movements for a while, when of a sudden one of them flew across the river, while I perceived the other struggling under the grasp of a lynx. When attacked by the two large species of Owl above mentioned, they often effect their escape in a way which is somewhat remarkable. As Turkeys usually roost in flocks, on naked branches of trees, they are easily discovered by their enemies, the owls, which, on silent wing, approach and hover around them, for the purpose of reconnoitring. This, however, is rarely done without being discovered, and a single *cluck* from one of the Turkeys announces to the whole party the approach of the murderer. They instantly start upon their legs, and watch the motions of the Owl, which, selecting one as its victim, comes down upon it like an arrow, and would inevitably secure the Turkey, did not the latter at that moment lower its head, stoop, and spread its tail in an inverted manner over its back, by which action the aggressor is met by a smooth inclined plane, along which it glances without hurting the Turkey ; immediately after which the latter drops to the ground, and thus escapes, merely with the loss of a few feathers.

The Wild Turkeys cannot be said to confine themselves to any particular kind of food, although they seem to prefer the pecan-nut and winter-grape to any other, and, where these fruits abound, are found in the greatest numbers. They eat grass and herbs of various kinds, corn, berries, and fruit of all descriptions. I have even found beetles, tadpoles, and small lizards in their crops.

Turkeys are now generally extremely shy, and the moment they observe a man, whether of the red or white race, instinctively move from him. Their usual mode of progression is what is termed walking, during which they frequently open each wing partially and successively, replacing them again by folding them over each other, as if their weight were too great. Then, as if to amuse themselves, they will run a few steps, open both wings and fan their sides, in the manner of the common fowl, and often take two or three leaps in the air and shake themselves. Whilst searching for food among the leaves or loose soil, they keep their head up, and are unremittingly on the lookout ; but as the legs and feet finish the operation, they are immediately seen to pick up the food, the presence of which, I suspect, is frequently indicated to them through the sense of touch in their feet, during the act of scratching. This habit of scratching and removing the dried leaves in the woods, is pernicious to their safety, as the spots which they thus clear, being about two feet in diameter, are seen at a distance, and, if fresh, shew that the birds are in the vicinity. During the summer months they resort to the paths or roads, as well as the ploughed fields, for the purpose of rolling themselves in the dust, by which means they clear their bodies of the ticks which at that season infest them, as well as free themselves of the moschettoes, which greatly annoy them, by biting their heads.

When, after a heavy fall of snow, the weather becomes frosty, so as to form a hard crust on the surface, the Turkeys remain on their roosts for three or four days, sometimes much longer, which proves their capability of continued abstinence. When near farms, however, they leave the roosts, and go into the very stables and about the stacks of corn, to procure food. During melting snow-falls, they will travel to an extraordinary distance, and are then followed in vain, it being impossible for hunters of any description to keep up with them. They have then a dangling and straggling way of running, which, awkward as it may seem, enables them to outstrip any other animal. I have often, when on a good horse, been obliged to abandon the attempt to put them up, after following them for several hours. This habit of continued running, in rainy or very damp weather of any kind, is not peculiar to the Wild Turkey, but is common to all gallinaceous birds. In America, the different species of Grouse exhibit the same tendency.

In spring, when the males are much emaciated, in consequence of their attentions to the females, it sometimes happens that, on plain and open ground, they may be overtaken by a swift dog, in which case they squat, and allow themselves to be seized, either by the dog, or the hunter who has followed on a good horse. I have heard of such occurrences, but never had the pleasure of seeing an instance of them.

Good dogs scent the Turkeys, when in large flocks, at extraordinary distances,—I think I may venture to say half a mile. Should the dog be well trained to this sport, he sets off at full speed, and in silence, until he sees the birds, when he instantly barks, and pushing as much as possible into the centre of the flock, forces the whole to take wing in different directions. This is of great advantage to the hunter, for should the Turkeys all go one way, they would soon leave their perches and run again. But when they separate in this manner, and the weather happens to be calm and lowering, a person accustomed to this kind of sport finds the birds with ease, and shoots them at pleasure.

When Turkeys alight on a tree, it is sometimes very difficult to see them, which is owing to their standing perfectly motionless. Should you discover one, when it is down on its legs upon the branch, you may approach it with less care. But if it is standing erect, the greatest precaution is necessary, for should it discover you, it instantly flies off, frequently to such a distance that it would be vain to follow.

When a Turkey is merely winged by a shot, it falls quickly to the ground in a slanting direction. Then, instead of losing time by tumbling and rolling over, as other birds often do when wounded, it runs off at such a rate, that unless the hunter be provided with a swift dog, he may bid farewell to it. I recollect coming on one shot in this manner, more than a mile from the tree where it had been perched, my dog having traced it to this distance, through one of those thick canebrakes that cover many portions of our rich alluvial lands near the banks of our western rivers. Turkeys are easily killed if shot in the head, the neck, or the upper part of the breast; but if hit in the hind parts only, they often fly so far as to be lost to the hunter. During winter many of our *real* hunters shoot them by moonlight, on the roosts, where these birds will frequently stand a repetition of the reports of a rifle, although they would fly from the attack of an owl, or even perhaps from his presence. Thus sometimes nearly a whole flock is secured by men capable of using these guns in such circumstances. They are often destroyed in great numbers when most worthless, that is, early in the fall or autumn, when many are killed in their attempt to cross the rivers, or immediately after they reach the shore.

Whilst speaking of the shooting of Turkeys, I feel no hesitation in relating the following occurrence, which happened to myself. While in search of game, one afternoon late in autumn, when the males go together, and the females are by themselves also, I heard the clucking of one of the latter, and immediately finding her perched on a fence, made towards her. Advancing slowly and cautiously, I heard the yelping notes of some gobblers, when I stopped and listened in order to ascertain the direction in which they came. I then ran to meet the birds, hid myself by the side of a large fallen tree, cocked my gun, and waited with impatience for a good opportunity. The gobblers continued yelping in answer to the female, which all this while remained on the fence. I looked over the log and saw about thirty fine cocks advancing rather cautiously towards the very spot where I lay concealed. They came so near that the light in their eyes could easily be perceived, when I fired one barrel, and killed three. The rest, instead of flying off, fell a strutting around their dead companions, and had I not looked on shooting again as murder without necessity, I might have secured at least another. So I shewed myself, and marching to the place where the dead birds were, drove away the survivors. I may also mention, that a friend of mine shot a fine hen, from his horse, with a pistol, as the poor thing was probably returning to her nest to lay.

Should you, good-natured reader, be a sportsman, and now and then have been fortunate in the exercise of your craft, the following incident, which I shall relate to you as I had it from the mouth of an honest farmer, may prove interesting. Turkeys were very abundant in his neighbourhood, and, resorting to his corn fields, at the period when the maize had just shot up from the ground, destroyed great quantities of it. This induced him to swear vengeance against the species. He cut a long trench in a favourable situation, put a great quantity of corn in it, and

having heavily loaded a famous duck gun of his, placed it so as that he
could pull the trigger by means of a string, when quite concealed from
the birds. The Turkeys soon discovered the corn in the trench, and
quickly disposed of it, at the same time continuing their ravages in the
fields. He filled the trench again, and one day seeing it quite black with
the Turkeys, whistled loudly, on which all the birds raised their heads,
when he pulled the trigger by the long string fastened to it. The explosion followed of course, and the Turkeys were seen scampering off in
all directions, in utter discomfiture and dismay. On running to the trench,
he found nine of them extended in it. The rest did not consider it expedient to visit his corn again for that season.

  · During spring, Turkeys are *called*, as it is termed, by drawing the air
in a particular way through one of the second joint bones of a wing of
that bird, which produces a sound resembling the voice of the female, on
hearing which the male comes up, and is shot. In managing this, however, no fault must be committed, for Turkeys are quick in distinguish-
ing counterfeit sounds, and when *half civilized* are very wary and cunning. I have known many to answer to this kind of call, without moving a step, and thus entirely defeat the scheme of the hunter, who dared
not move from his hiding-place, lest a single glance of the gobbler's eye
should frustrate all further attempts to decoy him. Many are shot when
at roost, in this season, by answering with a rolling gobble to a sound in
imitation of the cry of the Barred Owl.

  But the most common method of procuring Wild Turkeys, is by means
of *pens*. These are placed in parts of the woods where Turkeys have
been frequently observed to roost, and are constructed in the following
manner. Young trees of four or five inches diameter are cut down, and
divided into pieces of the length of twelve or fourteen feet. Two of these
are laid on the ground parallel to each other, at a distance of ten or
twelve feet. Two other pieces are laid across the ends of these, at right
angles to them ; and in this manner successive layers are added, until
the fabric is raised to the height of about four feet. It is then covered
·with similar pieces of wood, placed three or four inches apart, and loaded
with one or two heavy logs to render the whole firm. This done, a trench
about eighteen inches in depth and width is cut under one side of the
·cage, into which it opens slantingly and rather abruptly. It is continued
on its outside to some distance, so as gradually to attain the level of the
surrounding ground. Over the part of this trench within the pen, and

close to the wall, some sticks are placed so as to form a kind of bridge about a foot in breadth. The trap being now finished, the owner places a quantity of Indian corn in its centre, as well as in the trench, and as he walks off drops here and there a few grains in the woods, sometimes to the distance of a mile. This is repeated at every visit to the trap, after the Turkeys have found it. Sometimes two trenches are cut, in which case the trenches enter on opposite sides of the trap, and are both strewn with corn. No sooner has a Turkey discovered the train of corn, than it communicates the circumstance to the flock by a cluck, when all of them come up, and searching for the grains scattered about, at length come upon the trench, which they follow, squeezing themselves one after another through the passage under the bridge. In this manner the whole flock sometimes enters, but more commonly six or seven only, as they are alarmed by the least noise, even the cracking of a tree in frosty weather. Those within, having gorged themselves, raise their heads, and try to force their way through the top or sides of the pen, passing and repassing on the bridge, but never for a moment looking down, or attempting to escape through the passage by which they entered. Thus they remain until the owner of the trap arriving, closes the trench, and secures his captives. I have heard of eighteen Turkeys having been caught in this manner at a single visit to the trap. I have had many of these pens myself, but never found more than seven in them at a time. One winter I kept an account of the produce of a pen which I visited daily, and found that seventy-six had been caught in it, in about two months. When these birds are abundant, the owners of the pens sometimes become satiated with their flesh, and neglect to visit the pens for several days, in some cases for weeks. The poor captives thus perish for want of food; for, strange as it may seem, they scarcely ever regain their liberty, by descending into the trench, and retracing their steps. I have, more than once, found four or five, and even ten, dead in a pen, through inattention. Where Wolves or Lynxes are numerous, they are apt to secure the prize before the owner of the trap arrives. One morning, I had the pleasure of securing in one of my pens, a fine Black Wolf, which, on seeing me, squatted, supposing me to be passing in another direction.

Wild Turkeys often approach and associate with tame ones, or fight with them, and drive them off from their food. The cocks sometimes pay their addresses to the domesticated females, and are generally received by them with great pleasure, as well as by their owners, who are well aware of the advantages resulting from such intrusions, the half-breed being much more hardy than the tame, and, consequently, more easily reared.

While at Henderson, on the Ohio, I had, among many other wild birds, a fine male Turkey, which had been reared from its earliest youth under my care, it having been caught by me when probably not more than two or three days old. It became so tame that it would follow any person who called it, and was the favourite of the little village. Yet it would never roost with the tame Turkeys, but regularly betook itself at night to the roof of the house, where it remained until dawn. When two years old, it began to fly to the woods, where it remained for a considerable part of the day, to return to the enclosure as night approached. It continued this practice until the following spring, when I saw it several times fly from its roosting place to the top of a high cotton-tree, on the bank of the Ohio, from which, after resting a little, it would sail to the opposite shore, the river being there nearly half a mile wide, and return towards night. One morning I saw it fly off, at a very early hour, to the woods, in another direction, and took no particular notice of the circumstance. Several days elapsed, but the bird did not return. I was going towards some lakes near Green River to shoot, when, having walked about five miles, I saw a fine large gobbler cross the path before me, moving leisurely along. Turkeys being then in prime condition for the table, I ordered my dog to chase it, and put it up. The animal went off with great rapidity, and as it approached the Turkey, I saw, with great surprise, that the latter paid little attention. Juno was on the point of seizing it, when she suddenly stopped, and turned her head towards me. I hastened to them, but you may easily conceive my surprise when I saw my own favourite bird, and discovered that it had recognised the dog, and would not fly from it; although the sight of a strange dog would have caused it to run off at once. A friend of mine happening to be in search of a wounded deer, took the bird on his saddle before him, and carried it home for me. The following spring it was accidentally shot, having been taken for a wild bird, and brought to me on being recognised by the red ribbon which it had around its neck. Pray, reader, by what word will you designate the recognition made by my favourite Turkey of a dog which had been long associated with it in the yard and grounds? Was it the result of instinct, or of reason,—an unconsciously revived impression, or the act of an intelligent mind?

1

At the time when I removed to Kentucky, rather more than a fourth of a century ago, Turkeys were so abundant, that the price of one in the market was not equal to that of a common barn-fowl now. I have seen them offered for the sum of three pence each, the birds weighing from ten to twelve pounds. A first-rate Turkey, weighing from twenty-five to thirty pounds avoirdupois, was considered well sold when it brought a quarter of a dollar.

The weight of Turkey hens generally averages about nine pounds avoirdupois. I have, however, shot barren hens in strawberry season, that weighed thirteen pounds, and have seen a few so fat as to burst open on falling from a tree when shot. Male Turkeys differ more in their bulk and weight. From fifteen to eighteen pounds may be a fair estimate of their ordinary weight. I saw one offered for sale in the Louisville market, that weighed thirty-six pounds. Its pectoral appendage measured upwards of a foot.

Some closet naturalists suppose the hen Turkey to be destitute of the appendage on the breast, but this is not the case in the full-grown bird. The young males, as I have said, at the approach of the first winter, have merely a kind of protuberance in the flesh at this part, while the young females of the same age have no such appearance. The second year, the males are to be distinguished by the hairy tuft, which is about four inches long, whereas in the females that are not barren, it is yet hardly apparent. The third year, the male Turkey may be said to be adult, although it certainly increases in weight and size for several years more. The females at the age of four are in full beauty, and have the pectoral appendage four or five inches long, but thinner than in the male. The barren hens do not acquire it until they are very old. The experienced hunter knows them at once in the flock, and shoots them by preference. The great number of young hens destitute of the appendage in question, has doubtless given rise to the idea that it is wanting in the female Turkey.

The long downy *double* feathers * about the thighs and on the lower parts of the sides of the Wild Turkey, are often used for making tippets,

---

* The peculiarities in the structure of the plumage of different species of birds might, if duly attended to, prove of essential service to the systematic ornithologist, as conducing, along with other circumstances, to the elucidation of the natural affinities of birds. On this subject, I would refer the system-makers to the valuable observations of Mr MAC-GILLIVRAY in the Edinburgh New Philosophical Journal for 1828.

by the wives of our squatters and farmers. These tippets, when properly made, are extremely beautiful as well as comfortable.

A long account of the habits of this remarkable bird has already been given in Bonaparte's American Ornithology, vol. i. As that account was in a great measure derived from notes furnished by myself, you need not be surprised, good reader, to find it often in accordance with the above.

Having now said all that I have thought it might be agreeable to you to know of the history and habits of the Wild Turkey, I proceed to the technical description of that interesting bird.

MELEAGRIS GALLOPAVO, *Linn.* Syst. Nat. vol. i. p. 268—*Lath.* Ind. Ornith. p. 618. —*Ch. Bonaparte*, Synops. of Birds of the United States, p. 122.

WILD TURKEY, *Ch. Bonaparte*, Americ. Ornith. vol. i. p. 79. Pl. ix. Male and Female.

AMERICAN TURKEY, *Lath.* Synops. vol. ii. p. 670.

Adult Male. Plate I.

Bill shortish, robust, slightly arched, rather obtuse, the base covered by a bare membrane; upper mandible with the dorsal outline arched, the sides convex, the edges overlapping, the tip a little declinate; under mandible somewhat bulging towards the tip, the sides convex. Nostrils situated in the basal membrane, oblique, linear, covered above by a cartilage. Head small, flattened above, with a conical pendulous, erectile caruncle on the forehead. Neck slender. Body robust. Feet longish and strong; tarsus covered anteriorly with numerous transverse scutella, scaly on the sides, scutellate behind : toes scutellate above, scabrous, papillar and flat beneath; hind toe elevated, half the length of the lateral toes, which are nearly equal, and much shorter than the middle toe; claws slightly arched, strong, convex above, obtuse, flat beneath. A conical, rather obtuse spur on the tarsus, about two-thirds down.

Conical papilla of the forehead rugose, sparsely covered with bristles. Head bare, and corrugated, the skin irregularly raised, and covered with a few scattered bristles. External ear margined with short and slender thin feathers. Neck also bare, corrugated, beset anteriorly and below with a series of oblong, irregular, cavernous caruncles, interspersed with small bristly feathers. Plumage in general compact, glossy, with metallic reflections. Feathers double, as in other gallinaceous birds, generally oblong and truncated. A pendulous tuft of long bristles from the upper part of the breast. Wings shortish, convex, rounded, the fourth and fifth quills longest. Tail rather long, ample, rounded, consisting of eighteen broad rounded feathers; capable of being erected and expanded in a permanent manner, when the bird is excited, and reaching nearly to the ground, when the bird stands erect.

Bill yellowish-brown. Frontal caruncle blue and red. Rugose and carunculated skin of the head and neck of various tints of blue and purple, the pendulous anterior caruncles of the latter, or the *wattles*, bright red, changing to blue. Iris hazel. Legs and toes bright purplish-red; claws brown. Upper part of the back and wings brownish-yellow, with metallic lustre, changing to deep purple, the truncated tips of the feathers broadly margined with velvet-black. On the middle and lower back, the black terminal bands of the feathers almost conceal the bronze colour. The large quill-coverts are of the same colour as the back, but more bronzed, with purple reflections. Quills brownish-black, the primaries banded with greyish-white, the secondaries with brownish-white, gradually becoming deeper towards the proximal feathers, which are similar to the coverts. The lower part of the back and the tail-coverts are deep chestnut, banded with green and black. The tail-feathers are of the same colour, undulatingly barred and minutely sprinkled with black, and having a broad blackish bar towards the tip, which is pale brown and minutely mottled. The under parts are duller. Breast of the same colours as the back, the terminal black band not so broad; sides dark-coloured; abdomen and thighs brownish-grey; under tail-coverts blackish, glossed with bronze, and at the tip bright reddish-brown.

Length 4 feet 1 inch, extent of wings 5 feet 8 inches; beak 1½ inches along the ridge, 2 along the gap; tarsus 7½; middle toe 5, hind toe 2; pectoral appendage 1 foot. Such were the dimensions of the individual represented in the plate, which, I need not say, was a fine specimen.

THE YELLOW-BILLED CUCKOO.

COCCYZUS AMERICANUS. BONAP.

PLATE II. MALE AND FEMALE.

Were I inclined, like many persons who write on Natural History, to criticise the figures given by other students, I should find enough to be censured ; but as my object is simply to communicate the result of studies to which I have devoted the greater part of my life, I shall content myself with merely recommending to those intent on the advancement of that most interesting science, to bestow a little more care on their representations of the bills, legs and feet of the species which they bring into notice, and let it be seen that they indeed borrow from nature.

From Nature !—How often are these words used, when at a glance he who has seen the perfect and beautiful forms of birds, quadrupeds or other objects, as they have come from the hand of Nature, discovers that the representation is not that of *living* Nature ! But I am deviating from the track which I wish to follow, my desire being simply to give you an opportunity, good reader, of judging for yourself as to the truth of my delineations, and to present you with the results of my observations made in those very woods where the subjects have been found and depicted.

The flight of the bird now before you is rapid, silent, and horizontal, as it moves from one tree to another, or across a field or river, and is generally continued amongst the branches of the trees in our woods. When making its way among the branches, it occasionally inclines the body to either side, so as alternately to shew its whole upper or under parts. During its southward migration, it flies high in the air, and in such loose flocks that the birds might seem to follow each other, instead of their keeping company together. On the other hand, early in March, the greater number enter our southern boundaries singly, the males arriving first, and the females a few weeks after. They do not fly in a continued line, but in a broad front, as, while travelling with great rapidity in a steam-boat, so as to include a range of a hundred miles in one day, I have observed this Cuckoo crossing the Mississippi at many different points on the same day. At this season, they resort to the deepest shades of the forests, and intimate their presence by the frequent repetition of their dull and unmusical notes, which are not unlike those of the young Bull-Frog. These notes may be represented by the word *cow*, *cow*, repeated eight or ten times with increasing rapidity. In fact, from the resemblance of its notes to that word, this Cuckoo is named *Cow Bird* in nearly every part of the Union. The Dutch farmers of Pennsylvania know it better by the name of *Rain Crow*, and in Louisiana the French settlers call it *Coucou*.

It robs smaller birds of their eggs, which it sucks on all occasions, and is cowardly and shy, without being vigilant. On this latter account, it often falls a prey to several species of Hawks, of which the Pigeon Hawk (*Falco columbarius*) may be considered as its most dangerous enemy. It prefers the Southern States for its residence, and when very mild winters occur in Louisiana, some individuals remain there, not finding it necessary to go farther south.

This bird is not abundant anywhere, and yet is found very far north. I have met with it in all the low grounds and damp places in Massachusetts, along the line of Upper Canada, pretty high on the Mississippi and Arkansas, and in every state between these boundary lines. Its appearance in the State of New York seldom takes place before the beginning of May, and at Green Bay not until the middle of that month. A pair here and there seem to appropriate certain tracts to themselves, where they rear their young in the midst of peace and plenty. They feed on insects, such as caterpillars and butterflies, as well as on berries of many kinds, evincing a special predilection for the mulberry. In autumn they eat many grapes, and I have seen them supporting themselves by a momentary motion of their wings opposite a bunch, as if selecting the ripest, when they would seize it and return to a branch, repeating their visits in this manner until satiated. They now and then descend to the ground, to pick up a wood-snail or a beetle. They are extremely awkward at walking, and move in an ambling manner, or leap along sidewise, for which the shortness of their legs is ample excuse. They are seldom seen perched conspicuously on a twig, but on the contrary are generally to be found amongst the thickest boughs and foliage, where they emit their notes until late in autumn, at which time they discontinue them.

The nest is simple, flat, composed of a few dry sticks and grass, formed much like that of the Common Dove, and, like it, fastened to a horizontal branch, often within the reach of man, who seldom disturbs it.

It makes no particular selection as to situation or the nature of the tree, but settles any where indiscriminately. The eggs are four or five, of a rather elongated oval form, and bright green colour. They rear only one brood in a season, unless the eggs are removed or destroyed. The young are principally fed with insects during the first weeks. Towards autumn they become very fat, and are fit for being eaten, although few persons, excepting the Creoles of Louisiana, shoot them for the table.

The branch, among the foliage of which you see the male and female winging their way, is one of the Papaw, a tree of small size, seldom more than from twenty to thirty feet in height, with a diameter of from three to seven inches. It is found growing in all rich grounds, to which it is peculiar, from the southern line of our States to central Pennsylvania, seldom farther eastward, here and there only along the alluvial shores of the Ohio and Mississippi. In all other places of like nature you may meet with groves of Papaw trees, covering an acre or more of ground. The fruit, which is represented in the plate, consists of a pulpy and insipid substance, within which are found several large, hard, and glossy seeds. The rind is extremely thin. The wood is light, soft, brittle, and almost useless. The bark, which is smooth, may be torn off from the foot of the tree to the very top, and is frequently used for making ropes, after it has been steeped in water sufficiently to detach the outer part, when the fibres are obtained, which, when twisted, are found to be nearly as tough and durable as hemp. The numerous islands of the Ohio and all the other western rivers are generally well stocked with this tree.

COCCYZUS AMERICANUS, *Ch. Bonaparte*, Synops. of Birds of the United States, p. 42.
CUCULUS AMERICANUS, *Linn.* Syst. Nat. vol. i. p. 170.—*Lath.* Ind. Ornith. vol. i. p. 219.
CAROLINA CUCKOO, *Lath.* Synopsis, vol. ii. p. 527.
YELLOW-BILLED CUCKOO, CUCULUS CAROLINENSIS. *Wils.* Americ. Ornith. vol. iv. p. 13. Pl. 28. fig. 1.

Adult Male.   Plate II. Fig. 1.

Bill as long as the head, compressed, slightly arched, acute, scarcely more robust than in many Sylviæ; upper mandible carinated above, its margins acute and entire; lower mandible carinated beneath, acute. Nostrils basal, lateral, linear-elliptical, half closed by a membrane. Feet short; tarsus scutellate before and behind; toes two before, separated;

two behind, one of which is versatile, the sole flat; claws slender, compressed, arched.

Plumage blended, slightly glossed. Wings long, the first quill short, the third longest, the primaries tapering. Tail long, graduated, of ten feathers, which are rather narrow and rounded.

Upper mandible brownish-black; yellow on the margin towards the base; under mandible yellow. Iris hazel. Feet greyish-blue. The general colour of the upper parts, including the wing-coverts and two middle tail-feathers, is light greenish-brown, deeper anteriorly. Primary quills with the inner webs brownish-orange. Tail-feathers, excepting the two middle ones, black, the next two entirely black, the rest broadly tipped with white, the outermost white on the outer web. The under parts are greyish-white.

Length 12½ inches, extent of wings 16; bill along the ridge 1, along the gap 1¼.

Adult Female. Plate II. Fig. 2.

The female differs very little from the male in colouring.

THE PAPAW TREE.

Porcelia triloba, *Pursh,* Flor. Amer. vol. ii. p. 383. Anona triloba, *Willd.* Sp. Pl. vol. ii. p. 1267. *Mich.* Arbr. Forest. de l'Amer. Sept. vol. iii. p. 162. Pl. 9. —Polyandria Polygynia, *Linn.* Anonæ, *Juss.*

Leaves obovato-cuneate, acuminate, smoothish; outer petals orbiculate; fruits oblong, large, and fleshy. The leaves are from six to ten inches long; the flowers of a rich dark purple.

THE PROTHONOTARY WARBLER.

Sylvia Protonotarius, Lath.

PLATE III. MALE AND FEMALE.

I never saw this pretty bird in any of our eastern districts, and rarely farther up the Ohio than Louisville, in the neighbourhood of which place it rears its young. Louisiana seems in fact better suited to its habits than any other state, on account of its numerous lakes, creeks and lagoons, overshadowed by large trees, and which are favourite places of resort for this species. It is fond of flying over the water of these creeks and lagoons, and is seldom seen in the woods. Its flight is rapid, and more steady than is usual in birds of its genus; and as it moves along, the brightness of its colours attracts the eye. On alighting, it moves rapidly along the twigs, partly sidewise, frequently turning about and extending its neck to look under the leaves, from which it picks various kinds of insects. It often perches upon the rank grasses and water plants, in quest of minute molluscous animals which creep upon them, and which, together with small land snails, I have found in its stomach. It does not perform *sorties*, or sally forth after flying insects, as many other Warblers are in the habit of doing. It has a few notes for its song, which possess no interest. The males, when chasing each other, keep up a creaking noise, until the little battle is over, when they perch and balance their body with much grace and liveliness.

I have observed their arrival in Louisiana to take place, according to the state of the weather, from the middle of March to the first of April. At Henderson, in Kentucky, they do not arrive until a month later. They remain until October, but, I am inclined to believe, rear only a single brood in a season. The nest is fixed in the fork of a small twig bending over the water, and is constructed of slender grasses, soft mosses, and fine fibrous roots. The number of eggs is from four to six. I could never ascertain whether the male assists in incubation, as the difference of plumage in the sexes is not perceptible when the bird is at large, and indeed can hardly be traced when one has procured the male and the female for comparison. It cannot be called a plentiful species. To search for them on the high lands, or at any considerable distance from the places mentioned, would prove quite useless.

The plant on which you see these birds, grows in swampy places, but is extremely rare, and I have not been able to procure any scientific appellation for it. In Louisiana, it is called the *Cane Vine.* It bears a small white flower in clusters. The berries are bitter and nauseous. The stem, which runs up and over trees, resembles that of other climbing plants, is extremely elastic, and as tough as a cord. The leaves, of which you see the form and colour, are also tough and thick.

SYLVIA PROTONOTARIUS, *Lath.* Ind. Ornith. vol. ii. p. 542.—*Ch. Bonaparte,* Synops. of Birds of the United States, p. 86.

PROTHONOTARY WARBLER, SYLVIA PROTONOTARIUS, *Wilson,* Americ. Ornith. vol. iii. p. 72. Pl. xxiv. fig. 3.

Adult Male. Plate III. Fig. 1.

Bill nearly as long as the head, slender, tapering, nearly straight, as deep as broad at the base. Nostrils basal, lateral, elliptical, half closed by a membrane. Head rather small. Neck short. Body rather slender. Feet of ordinary length, slender; tarsus longer than the middle toe, covered anteriorly with a few scutella, the uppermost long: toes scutellate above, the inner free, the hind toe of moderate size; claws slender, compressed, acute, arched.

Plumage soft, blended, tufty. Wings of ordinary length, acute, the first and second quills longest. Tail nearly even, of twelve straight, rather narrow feathers. Bill brownish-black. Iris hazel. Feet and claws greyish-blue. Head all round, neck and under parts generally, of a bright rich pure yellow, paler on the abdomen, and passing into white on the under tail-coverts. Fore part of the back and lesser wing-coverts yellowish-green. Lower back and wings light greyish-blue. Inner webs of the quills blackish. Inner webs of the tail-feathers bluish-grey at the base, then white to near the tip, which is black, as well as the outer webs. The two middle feathers blackish, tinged with greyish-blue.

Length 5¼ inches, extent of wings 8½; beak along the ridge $\frac{7}{12}$, along the gap ¾; tarsus $\frac{11}{12}$.

Adult Female. Plate III. Fig. 2.

The differences which the female exhibits are so slight as scarcely to be describable, the tints being merely a little duller.

THE PURPLE FINCH.

FRINGILLA PURPUREA, GMEL.

PLATE IV. MALE AND FEMALE.

FROM the beginning of November until April, flocks of the Purple Finch, consisting of from six to twenty individuals, are seen throughout the whole of Louisiana and the adjoining States. They fly compactly, with an undulating motion, similar to that of the Common Greenfinch of Europe. They alight all at once, and after a moment of rest, and as if frightened, all take to wing again, make a circuit of no great extent, and return to the tree from which they had thus started, or settle upon one near it. Immediately after this, every individual is seen making its way toward the extremities of the branches, husking the buds with great tact, and eating their internal portion. In doing this, they hang like so many Titmice, or stretch out their necks to reach the buds below. Although they are quite friendly among themselves during their flight, or while sitting without looking after food, yet, when they are feeding, the moment one goes near another, it is strenuously warned to keep off by certain unequivocal marks of displeasure, such as the erection of the feathers of the head and the opening of the mouth. Should this intimation be disregarded, the stronger or more daring of the two drives off the other to a different part of the tree. They feed in this manner principally in the morning, and afterwards retire to the interior of the woods. Towards sunset they reappear, fly about the skirts of the fields and along the woods, until, having made choice of a tree, they alight, and, as soon as each bird has chosen a situation, stand still, look about them, plume themselves, and make short sallies after flies and other insects, but without interfering with each other. They frequently utter a single rather mellow *clink*, and are seen occupied in this manner until near sunset, when they again fly off to the interior of the forest. I one night surprised a party of them roosting in a small holly tree, as I happened to be brushing by it. In their consternation they suddenly started all together, and in the same direction, when, not knowing what birds they were, I shot at them and brought down two.

It is remarkable that, at this season, males in full beauty of plumage

are as numerous as during the summer months in far more northern
parts, where they breed; and you may see different gradations of plumage, from the dingy greenish-brown of the female and young to the
richest tints of the oldest and handsomest male; while along with these
there are others which, by my habit of examining birds, I knew to be
old, and which are of a yellowish-green, neither the colour of the young
males, nor that of the females, but a mixture of all.

The song of the Purple Finch is sweet and continued, and I have enjoyed it much during the spring and summer months, in the mountainous parts of Pennsylvania, where it occasionally breeds, particularly
about the Great Pine Forest, where, although I did not find any nests,
I saw pairs of these birds flying about and feeding their young, which
could not have been many days out, and were not fully fledged. The
food which they carried to their young consisted of insects, small berries,
and the juicy part of the cones of the spruce pine.

They frequently associate with the Common Cross-bills, feeding on the
same trees, and like them are at times fond of alighting against the mud
used for closing the log-houses. They are seldom seen on the ground,
although their motions there are by no means embarrassed. They are
considered as destructive birds by some farmers, who accuse them of
committing great depredations on the blossoms of their fruit-trees. I
never observed this in Louisiana, where they remain long after the peach
and pear trees are in full bloom. I have eaten many of them, and consider their flesh equal to that of any other small bird, excepting the Rice
Bunting.

FRINGILLA PURPUREA, *Gmel.* Syst. vol. i. p. 923.—*Lath.* Ind. Ornith. vol. i. p. 446.
PURPLE FINCH, FRINGILLA PURPUREA, *Wilson,* Americ. Ornith. vol. i. p. 119,
Pl. 7, fig. 4. Adult Male; and vol. v. p. 87, Pl. 42, fig. 3. Male.

Adult Male. Plate IV. Fig. 1, 2.

Bill shortish, robust, bulging, conical, acute; upper mandible with
its dorsal outline a little convex, under mandible with its outline also
slightly convex, both broadly convex transversely, the edges straight to
near the base, where they are a little deflected. Nostrils basal, roundish,
open, partially concealed by the feathers. Head rather large. Neck
short and thick. Body full. Legs of moderate size; tarsus of the same
length as the middle toe, covered anteriorly with a longitudinal plate

above and a few transverse scutella below, posteriorly with an acutely angular longitudinal plate; toes scutellate above, free, the lateral ones nearly equal; claws slender, arched, compressed, acute, that of the hind toe not much larger.

Plumage compact above, blended beneath, wings of moderate length, third and fourth primaries longest, second and first very little shorter. Tail forked. The lateral feathers curved outwards toward the tip.

Bill deep brown above, paler and tinged with blue beneath. Iris blackish-brown. Feet and claws brown. Head, neck, breast, back, and upper tail-coverts of a rich deep lake, approaching to crimson on the head and neck, and fading into rose-colour on the belly. Fore part of the back streaked with brown. Quills and larger coverts deep brown, margined externally and tipped with red, Tail feathers deep brown, similarly margined. A narrow band of cream-colour across the forehead margining the base of the upper mandible.

Length 6 inches, extent of wings 9, beak along the ridge $\frac{5}{12}$, along the gap $\frac{7}{12}$, tarsus $\frac{3}{4}$.

Female. Plate IV. Fig. 3.

The young bird so closely resembles the adult female, that the same description will answer for both. The general colour of the upper parts is brownish-olive, streaked with dark brown. There is a broadish white line over the eye, and another from the commissure of the gap backwards. The under parts are greyish white, the sides streaked with brown. The quills and tail-feathers are dark brown, margined with olive.

THE RED LARCH.

LARIX AMERICANA, *Pursh*, Fl. Amer. vol. ii. p. 645. *Mich.* Arbr. Forest. de l'Amer. Sept. vol. iii. p. 137. Pl. 4.—MONŒCIA POLYANDRIA, *Linn.* CONIFERÆ, *Juss.*

This species of larch, which is distinguished by its short, deciduous, fasciculate leaves, and short ovate cones, occurs in the more northern parts of the United States, and in the mountainous regions of the middle states. It attains a height of sixty feet, and a diameter sometimes of two feet. The wood is highly esteemed on account of its excellent qualities.

BONAPARTE'S FLY-CATCHER.

MUSCICAPA BONAPARTII.

PLATE V. MALE.

WHILST I have the pleasure of honouring this beautiful new species with the name of so distinguished a naturalist as CHARLES LUCIEN BONAPARTE, Prince of Musignano, I regret that I am unable to give any account of its habits, or even of its manner of flight, and must therefore confine my remarks upon it within very brief space. The following extract from my journal contains all that I have to say respecting it.

" Monday, August 18th 1821.—Louisiana.—On arriving at the Cypress Swamp (about five miles from St Francisville), I saw a great number of small birds of different species, and as I looked at them I observed two engaged in a fight or quarrel. I shot at them, but only one fell. On reaching the spot, I found the bird was only wounded, and saw it standing still and upright as if stupified by its fall. When I approached it to pick it up, it spread its tail, opened its wings, and snapped its bill about twenty times sharply and in quick succession, as birds of the genus do when seizing insects on wing. I carried it home, and had the pleasure of drawing it while alive and full of spirit. It often made off from my hand, by starting suddenly, and then would hop round the room as quickly as a Carolina Wren, uttering its *tweet, tweet, tweet* all the while, and snapping its bill every time I took it up. I put it into a cage for a few minutes, but it obstinately thrust its head through the lower parts of the wires. I relieved it from this sort of confinement, and allowed it to go about the room. Next day it was very weak and ruffled up, so I killed it and put it in spirits." To this account I have only to add, that I have not seen another individual since.

MUSCICAPA BONAPARTII. Plate V.

Bill of moderate length, straight, subtrigonal, depressed at the base, acute, upper mandible slightly notched and a little inflected at the tip, lower mandible straight. Nostrils basal, lateral, roundish, partly covered by the frontal feathers. Head and neck moderate. Eyes large. Body slender. Legs of ordinary size; tarsus a little longer than the middle toe; inner toe a little united at the base; claws compressed, acute, arched.

Plumage ordinary, blended. Wings rather long, somewhat acute, second primary longest. Tail rather long, nearly even, straight. Basirostral feathers bristly and directed outwards.

Bill brown above, yellowish beneath, orbits yellow. Iris deep brown. Feet and claws flesh-colour. The upper parts of a light greyish-blue, the quills dusky, their outer webs blue, the two first margined with white. Under parts and forehead ochre-yellow, under tail-coverts whitish; a few dark spots on the upper part of the breast.

Length 5¼ inches; bill along the ridge $\frac{5}{12}$, along the gap $\frac{3}{4}$; tarsus $\frac{5}{6}$.

THE GREAT MAGNOLIA.

MAGNOLIA GRANDIFLORA, *Wild.* Sp. Pl. vol. ii. p. 1255. *Pursh*, Flor. Amer. vol. ii. p. 380. *Mich.* Arbr. Forest. de l'Amer. Sept. vol. iii. p. 71. Pl. i.— POLYANDRIA POLYGYNIA, *Linn.* MAGNOLIÆ, *Juss.*

The magnificent tree, of which a twig, with a cone of ripe fruit, is represented in the plate, attains a height of a hundred feet or even more. The bright red bodies are the seeds, suspended by a filament for some time after the capsules have burst. The trunk is often very straight, from two to four feet in diameter at the base, with a greyish smooth bark. The leaves which remain during the winter are stiff and leathery, smooth, elliptical, tapering at the base. The flowers are white, and seven or eight inches in diameter. It is known by the names of *Large Magnolia*, *Big Laurel* and *Bay-tree*, and occurs abundantly in some parts of Carolina, Georgia, the Floridas and Louisiana.

THE OHIO.

To render more pleasant the task which you have imposed upon your-self, of following an author through the mazes of descriptive ornithology, permit me, kind reader, to relieve the tedium which may be apt now and then to come upon you, by presenting you with occasional descriptions of the scenery and manners of the land which has furnished the objects that engage your attention. The natural features of that land are not less remarkable than the moral character of her inhabitants; and I cannot find a better subject with which to begin, than one of those magnificent rivers that roll the collected waters of her extensive territories to the ocean.

WHEN my wife, my eldest son (then an infant), and myself were re-turning from Pennsylvania to Kentucky, we found it expedient, the waters being unusually low, to provide ourselves with a *skiff*, to enable us to proceed to our abode at Henderson. I purchased a large, commo-dious, and light boat of that denomination. We procured a mattress, and our friends furnished us with ready prepared viands. We had two stout Negro rowers, and in this trim we left the village of Shippingport, in expectation of reaching the place of our destination in a very few days.

It was in the month of October. The autumnal tints already deco-rated the shores of that queen of rivers, the Ohio. Every tree was hung with long and flowing festoons of different species of vines, many loaded with clustered fruits of varied brilliancy, their rich bronzed car-mine mingling beautifully with the yellow foliage, which now predomi-nated over the yet green leaves, reflecting more lively tints from the clear stream than ever landscape painter portrayed or poet imagined.

The days were yet warm. The sun had assumed the rich and glow-ing hue which at that season produces the singular phenomenon called there the " Indian Summer." The moon had rather passed the meri-dian of her grandeur. We glided down the river, meeting no other ripple of the water than that formed by the propulsion of our boat. Leisurely we moved along, gazing all day on the grandeur and beauty of the wild scenery around us.

Now and then, a large cat-fish rose to the surface of the water in pur-suit of a shoal of fry, which starting simultaneously from the liquid element, like so many silvery arrows, produced a shower of light, while the pursuer with open jaws seized the stragglers, and, with a splash of his tail, disappeared from our view. Other fishes we heard uttering beneath our bark a rumbling noise, the strange sounds of which we discovered to proceed from the white perch, for on casting our net from the bow we caught several of that species, when the noise ceased for a time.

Nature, in her varied arrangements, seems to have felt a partiality towards this portion of our country. As the traveller ascends or descends the Ohio, he cannot help remarking that alternately, nearly the whole length of the river, the margin, on one side, is bounded by lofty hills and a rolling surface, while on the other, extensive plains of the richest alluvial land are seen as far as the eye can command the view. Islands of varied size and form rise here and there from the bosom of the water, and the winding course of the stream frequently brings you to places where the idea of being on a river of great length changes to that of floating on a lake of moderate extent. Some of these islands are of considerable size and value; while others, small and insignificant, seem as if intended for contrast, and as serving to enhance the general interest of the scenery. These little islands are frequently overflowed during great *freshets* or floods, and receive at their heads prodigious heaps of drifted timber. We foresaw with great concern the alterations that cultivation would soon produce along those delightful banks.

As night came, sinking in darkness the broader portions of the river, our minds became affected by strong emotions, and wandered far beyond the present moments. The tinkling of bells told us that the cattle which bore them were gently roving from valley to valley in search of food, or returning to their distant homes. The hooting of the Great Owl, or the muffled noise of its wings as it sailed smoothly over the stream, were matters of interest to us; so was the sound of the boatman's horn, as it came winding more and more softly from afar. When daylight returned, many songsters burst forth with echoing notes, more and more mellow to the listening ear. Here and there the lonely cabin of a squatter struck the eye, giving note of commencing civilization. The crossing of the stream by a deer foretold how soon the hills would be covered with snow.

Many sluggish flat-boats we overtook and passed: some laden with produce from the different head-waters of the small rivers that pour their tributary streams into the Ohio; others, of less dimensions, crowded with emigrants from distant parts, in search of a new home. Purer pleasures I never felt; nor have you, reader, I ween, unless indeed you have felt the like, and in such company.

The margins of the shores and of the river were at this season amply supplied with game. A Wild Turkey, a Grouse, or a Blue-winged Teal, could be procured in a few moments; and we fared well, for, whenever we pleased, we landed, struck up a fire, and provided as we were with the necessary utensils, procured a good repast.

Several of these happy days passed, and we neared our home, when, one evening, not far from Pigeon Creek (a small stream which runs into the Ohio, from the State of Indiana), a loud and strange noise was heard, so like the yells of Indian warfare, that we pulled at our oars, and made for the opposite side as fast and as quietly as possible. The sounds increased, we imagined we heard cries of " murder ;" and as we knew that some depredations had lately been committed in the country by dissatisfied parties of Aborigines, we felt for a while extremely uncomfortable. Ere long, however, our minds became more calmed, and we plainly discovered that the singular uproar was produced by an enthusiastic set of Methodists, who had wandered thus far out of the common way, for the purpose of holding one of their annual camp meetings, under the shade of a beech forest. Without meeting with any other interruption, we reached Henderson, distant from Shippingport by water about two hundred miles.

When I think of these times, and call back to my mind the grandeur and beauty of those almost uninhabited shores; when I picture to myself the dense and lofty summits of the forest, that everywhere spread along the hills, and overhung the margins of the stream, unmolested by the axe of the settler; when I know how dearly purchased the safe navigation of that river has been by the blood of many worthy Virginians; when I see that no longer any Aborigines are to be found there, and that the vast herds of elks, deer and buffaloes which once pastured on these hills and in these valleys, making for themselves great roads to the several salt-springs, have ceased to exist; when I reflect that all this grand portion of our Union, instead of being in a state of nature, is now more or less covered with villages, farms, and towns, where the din of hammers and machinery is constantly heard; that the woods are fast disappearing under the axe by day, and the fire by night; that hundreds of steam-boats are gliding to and fro, over the whole length of the

majestic river, forcing commerce to take root and to prosper at every
spot; when I see the surplus population of Europe coming to assist
in the destruction of the forest, and transplanting civilization into its
darkest recesses;—when I remember that these extraordinary changes
have all taken place in the short period of twenty years, I pause, wonder,
and, although I know all to be fact, can scarcely believe its reality.

. Whether these changes are for the better or for the worse, I shall not
pretend to say; but in whatever way my conclusions may incline, I feel
with regret that there are on record no satisfactory accounts of the state
of that portion of the country, from the time when our people first settled in it. This has not been because no one in America is able to accomplish such an undertaking. Our IRVINGS and our COOPERS have
proved themselves fully competent for the task. It has more probably
been because the changes have succeeded each other with such rapidity,
as almost to rival the movements of their pen. However, it is not too
late yet; and I sincerely hope that either or both of them will ere long
furnish the generations to come with those delightful descriptions which
they are so well qualified to give, of the original state of a country that
has been so rapidly forced to change her form and attire under the influence of increasing population. Yes; I hope to read, ere I close my
earthly career, accounts from those delightful writers of the progress of
civilization in our western country. They will speak of the CLARKS,
the CROGHANS, the BOONS, and many other men of great and daring
enterprise. They will analyze, as it were, into each component part, the
country as it once existed, and will render the picture, as it ought to be,
immortal.

1

THE WILD TURKEY.

MELEAGRIS GALLOPAVO, LINN.

PLATE VI. FEMALE AND YOUNG.

THE Male Turkey has already been described, and you have seen that magnificent bird roaming in the forests, approaching the haunts of man, and performing all the offices for which he is destined in the economy of nature. Here you have his mate, now converted into a kind and anxious parent, leading her young progeny, with measured step and watchful eye, through the intricacies of the forest. The chickens, still covered with down, are running among her feet in pursuit of insects. One is picking its sprouting plumelets, while another is ridding itself of a tick which has fastened upon its little wing.

In addition to what has already been said respecting the manners of the Wild Turkey, I have a few circumstances to mention, which relate chiefly to both sexes. Its flight is powerful and rapid, and is composed of strong flappings, which enable it to rise with ease to the highest branches of the largest forest trees. When it starts from the ground, it generally leaves marks which are made by the first motions of its wings, which are so powerful as raise the withered leaves around it. When the ground is covered with snow, the impressions are so distinctly defined as to imitate the form of the pinions. When it leaves its perch, it flaps its wings only a few times at the outset, and then sails for many hundred yards, balancing itself as it proceeds, with great steadiness, until it reaches the ground. If it has flown from its perch with the view of reaching another, it repeats the flappings at intervals of a hundred yards or so. On coming to the ground, it is obliged to run for a few yards, its great weight rendering this necessary to prevent its body from being injured.

The great strength of a full grown Turkey-cock renders it no easy matter to hold it when but slightly wounded; and once or twice I have thought myself in jeopardy, when on entering a pen in which six or seven large cocks had imprisoned themselves, their flutterings and struggles rendered it extremely difficult to secure them.

The Female Turkey, which is considerably inferior in size to the

c

male, differs further from him in wanting the spurs and pendulous wattles, in having the frontal papilla much smaller, the naked space of the
neck less, and the colours much duller, although similar in distribution.
The naked parts of the head and neck are more furnished with bristly
feathers, and are of a light blue colour, with reddish tints interspersed.
The bill, the eyes, and the feet, are of the same colour as in the male,
the latter considerably paler.   There is a line of short bristly dark-coloured feathers down the back of the neck.   The general colour of the
upper and under parts is greyish-brown, with metallic bronzed reflections, each feather terminated by a band of black.   On the lower back
the brown tints become brighter, and on the rump and upper tail-coverts
change into bright chestnut, with transverse bands of brown.   The
ground colour of the tail is pale yellowish-brown, transversely barred
and mottled as in the male, and with a broad subterminal band of brownish-black, beyond which the feathers are mottled, and finally terminated
by uniform light brown.   The abdominal region is dull brownish-grey.
The primary quills are greyish-white, barred with brownish-black ; the
secondaries brownish-grey, similarly barred.   The wing-coverts are similar to the feathers of the back.

Length 3 feet 1 inch, extent of wings 4 feet 6 inches; bill 1 inch
along the ridge, 1¾ along the gap ; tarsus 6 ; middle toe 3¾, hind toe 1½,
pectoral appendage 4 inches.

The young, a few days old, are pale brownish-yellow above, pale yellowish-grey beneath, the top of the head brighter, marked in the middle
with a longitudinal pale brown band, the back and wings spotted with
brownish-black, excepting the lesser wing-coverts, which are uniformly
dull brown.   Iris yellowish-brown ; bill and feet flesh-coloured.

PURPLE GRAKLE OR COMMON CROW-BLACKBIRD.

QUISCALUS VERSICOLOR, VIEILL.

PLATE VII. MALE AND FEMALE.

I COULD not think of any better mode of representing these birds than that which I have adopted, as it exhibits them in the exercise of their nefarious propensities. Look at them : The male, as if full of delight at the sight of the havoc which he has already committed on the tender, juicy, unripe corn on which he stands, has swelled his throat, and is calling in exultation to his companions to come and assist him in demolishing it. The female has fed herself, and is about to fly off with a well-loaded bill to her hungry and expectant brood, that, from the nest, look on their plundering parents, joyously anticipating the pleasures of which they shall ere long be allowed to participate. See how torn the husk is from the ear, and how nearly devoured the grains of corn already are ! This is the tithe our Blackbirds take from our planters and farmers ; but it was so appointed, and such is the will of the beneficent Creator.

These birds are constant residents in Louisiana. I say they are so, because a certain number of them, which in some countries would be called immense, is found there at all seasons of the year. No sooner has the cotton or corn planter begun to turn his land into brown furrows, than the Crow-Blackbirds are seen sailing down from the skirts of the woods, alighting in the fields, and following his track along the ridges of newly-turned earth, with an elegant and elevated step, which shews them to be as fearless and free as the air through which they wing their way. The genial rays of the sun shine on their silky plumage, and offer to the ploughman's eye such rich and varying tints, that no painter, however gifted, could ever imitate them. The coppery bronze, which in one light shews its rich gloss, is, by the least motion of the bird, changed in a moment to brilliant and deep azure, and again, in the next light, becomes refulgent sapphire or emerald-green.

The bird stops, spreads its tail, lowers its wings, and, with swelled throat and open bill, sounds a call to those which may chance to be passing near. The stately step is resumed. Its keen eye, busily engaged on either side, is immediately attracted by a grub, hastening to hide itself

c 2

from the sudden exposure made by the plough.   In vain does it hurry, for the Grakle has seen and marked it for its own, and it is snatched up and swallowed in a moment.

Thus does the Grakle follow the husbandman as he turns one furrow after another, destroying a far worse enemy to the corn than itself, for every worm which it devours would else shortly cut the slender blade, and thereby destroy the plant when it would perhaps be too late to renew it by fresh seed.   Every reflecting farmer knows this well, and refrains from disturbing the Grakle at this season.   Were he as merciful at another time, it would prove his grateful recollection of the services thus render-ed him.   But man is too often forgetful of the benefit which he has re-ceived ; he permits his too commonly weak and selfish feelings to prevail over his reason ; and no sooner does the corn become fit for his own use, than he vows and executes vengeance on all intruders.   But to return to our Blackbird.

The season of love has arrived.   Each male having, by assiduity, va-lour, or good fortune, received the affectionate regards of a faithful mate, unites with her in seeking a safe and agreeable retreat.   The lofty dead trees left standing in our newly cultivated fields, have many holes and cavities, some of which have been bored by woodpeckers, and others caused by insects or decay.   These are visited and examined in succes-sion, until a choice being made, and a few dry weeds and feathers collect-ed, the female deposits her eggs, which are from four to six in number, of a bluish tint, blotched and streaked with brown and black.   She sits upon them while her valiant mate and guardian mounts to the summit of a broken branch, pours forth his rude notes, and cheers and watches her with the kindest and most unremitting care.   I think I see him plunging through the air and overtaking the Red-headed or the Golden-winged Woodpecker, which, in search of their last year's nest, have imprudently alighted at the entrance of the already chosen and oc-cupied hole.   The conflict is but momentary ; the creeping bird is forced to yield, and after whirling round in the air as it defends itself, and very nearly comes to the ground, makes the best of its way off, well knowing that there its opponent is more formidable than even in the air.

This over, the Grakle roams in quest of food.   Little heaps of grubs, with a few grains of corn, afford delicious repasts to himself and his mate. They thus share the labours of incubation, and see the time pass in eager and pleasant expectation.   And now the emerging brood shake off the shell that so long enclosed them; their tottering heads are already raised toward their mother, while she, with intense anxiety, dries and cherishes them. They grow up day after day. The hole becomes nearly filled with their increased bulk. The vigilance and industry of the parents also augment apace. I wish, good-natured reader, you would seek out such a sight: it would gladden your heart, for the rearing of such a family is worthy of your contemplation.

It is with regret that I must turn from this picture. I have already told you that the Grakles are at least as fond of corn as the lords of the land are. Hark to the sound of rattles, and the hallooing of the farmer's sons and servants, as they spread over the field! Now and then the report of a gun comes on the ear. The Grakles have scarcely a single moment of quiet; they are chased, stolen upon, and killed in great numbers, all the country round; but the hungry birds heed not the slaughter of their brethren. They fly in flocks from place to place, and, in spite of all that the farmer has done or threatens to do, continue their depredations. Food must be had. Grubs and worms have already retired to their winter quarters within the earth; no beech-nuts or acorns have yet fallen from the trees; corn is now their only resource, and the quantity of it which they devour is immense.

Now gloomy November brings up its cold blasts from the north, and drives before it the Grakles from the Eastern States. They reach Louisiana and all the Southern States when autumn has not yet retired, when the weather is still mild and serene, and the yellow foliage of the wide woods gives shelter to myriads of birds. The Grakles, congregated in prodigious flocks, alight on the trees that border the vast forests, covering every twig and bough in such astonishing masses, that the most unskilful or most avaricious gunner finds no difficulty in satisfying his wish for sport or game. This is the time to listen to their choruses. They seem to congratulate each other on their escape, and vociferate at such a rate as to make one imagine their number double what it is.

Beech-nuts and acorns are now abundant in the woods, having by this time fallen from the trees, and the Grakles roam in quest of them in immense bodies, rising on wing when disturbed, uttering at the same time a tremendous noise, then making a few rounds, and alighting again. They thus gradually clear away the mast, in the same manner as the wild pigeons are wont to do. As the weather becomes colder, they frequent the farms, and even resort to the cattle pens, where, from among the litter and refuse straw, they pick the scattered grains that have fallen from the stores with which the farmer has supplied his stock. They remain about the farms until the commencement of spring. They are easily caught in traps, and shew little fear when seized, biting so severely as often to draw blood, and laying hold with their claws in a very energetic manner.

During the winter of 1821, I caught a number of them, as well as many other birds, for the purpose of sending them alive to Europe. The whole of my captives were confined together in a large cage, where they were well fed and watered, and received all necessary attention. Things went on favourably for several days, and I with pleasure saw them becoming daily more gentle. An unexpected change, however, soon took place, for as the Grakles became reconciled to confinement, they began to attack the other birds, beating and killing one after another so fast that I was obliged to remove them from the cage. Even this did not prevent further breach of the peace, for the strong attacked and killed the weak of their own race, so that only a few remained in the end. The Grakles thus mangled, killed and partially devoured several Cardinal Grosbeaks, Doves, Pigeons, and Blue Jays. I look upon this remarkable instance of ferocity in the Grakle with the more amazement, as I never observed it killing any bird when in a state of freedom.

What I have said respecting the Purple Grakle (which by some is improperly named the Boat-tailed Grakle) refers particularly to the habits of those in the south, where some of them are found at all seasons. I shall now speak of those of the Western and Middle States. Most of these birds leave the south about the middle of February, setting out in small detached flocks. They reach the State of New York in this straggling manner about the middle of May. Their migratory flight is performed in short undulating lines, resembling small segments of very large circles. It may be explained in this manner. Supposing the bird poised in the air and intent on moving forwards, it propels itself by a strenuous flap of the wings, which carries it forward in a curve, along which it ascends until it attains the level of its original point of departure, when it flaps its wings again, and performs another curve. In this form of flight they pursue their long journey, during which they keep up a continual low chattering, as if they were discussing some important question. When they reach Pennsylvania, they commence the avocations which I have already described, and are seen following the plough, while their kindred that have been left in Louisiana are probably by this time feeding their young, as the difference of climate between these latitudes leaves the northern states a month later in their seasons than the southern.

In the Northern States these birds construct their nests in a much more perfect, and therefore more natural manner. A pine tree, whenever it occurs in a convenient place, is selected by preference, its dense foliage and horizontal branches being well adapted for nidification. There the Grakle forms a nest, which from the ground might easily be mistaken for that of our Robin, the *Turdus migratorius*, were it less bulky. But it is much larger, and instead of being placed by itself, is associated with others, often to the number of a dozen or more, on the horizontal arms of the pine, forming tier above tier, from the lowest to the highest branches. The centre of the nest is what I would call *saddled* on the bough, the materials being laid so that the nest is thinner in its middle part and thicker at the two opposite sides, so as to have a firm hold. It is about six inches in diameter outside, and four inches within, the depth being the same, and is composed of grass, slender roots and mud, lined with hair and finer grasses. I had a white pine-tree in one of my fields on Mill Grove Farm, on which many of these birds bred every spring, when some mischievous lads frequently amused themselves with beating down the nests with long fishing-rods, to my great annoyance. Some of the Pennsylvanian farmers, from a very laudable motive, have given out that Grakles are fond of pulling up the garlic plant, so injurious to the pastures of the Middle States; but I am sorry to say this assertion is by no means correct, and were these good people to look to the Grakles for the clearing of their fields from that evil, they might wait long enough.

The flesh of the Purple Grakle is little better than that of the Crow, being dry and ill-flavoured, notwithstanding which it is frequently used, with the addition of one or two Golden-winged Woodpeckers or Redwings, to make what is here called *pot pie*, even amidst a profusion of so many better things. The eggs, on the contrary, are very delicate, and I am astonished that those who are so anxious for the destruction of these birds do not gratify their wishes by eating them while yet in embryo in the egg. In some parts of Louisiana, the farmers, or, as they are styled, the planters, steep the seed corn for a few hours in a solution of Glauber's salt, to deter the Grakles and other birds from eating the grains when just *planted*, as we term it in America, the word *sow* being seldom employed there to denote the act of depositing in the earth even the smallest seed.

The Purple Grakle travels very far north. I have found it everywhere during my peregrinations, and in one or two instances have seen it form its nest in the fissures of rocks.

QUISCALUS VERSICOLOR, *Vieill.* Nouv. Dict. d'Hist. Nat. vol. xxviii. p. 488.—*Ch. Bonaparte*, Synopsis of Birds of the United States, p. 54. ; and Americ. Ornith. vol. i. p. 42, Pl. v. fig. 1. Female.

GRACULA BARITA, *Gmel.* Syst. vol. i. p. 396 —*Lath.* Ind. Ornith. p. 191.

PURPLE GRAKLE, *Lath.* Synops. vol. ii. p. 462.

BOAT-TAILED GRAKLE, *Lath.* Synops. vol. ii. p. 460.—*Wilson,* Americ. Ornith. vol. iii. p. 44, Pl. xxi. fig. 4. Male.

Adult Male. Plate VII. Fig. 1.

Bill longish, straight, tapering, compressed from the base ; upper mandible prolonged on the forehead, forming an acute angle there, a little declinate at the tip, its dorsal outline slightly convex, as are the sides ; under mandible nearly straight in its lower outline, convex on the sides, acute at the tip ; edges of both acute, of the lower inflected ; the gap line deflected at the base, reaching to beneath the eye. Nostrils basal, oval, half closed by a membrane. Head large, rounded above. Neck of moderate length, thick. Body rather robust. Feet of moderate length, strong ; tarsus considerably longer than the middle toe, covered anteriorly with longish scutella, shorter below, laterally with two longitudinal plates, meeting behind at an acute angle ; lateral toes nearly equal, the outer connected at the base by a membrane ; claws strong, arched, compressed, acute.

Plumage soft, silky, glossy, blended. Wings of ordinary length ; second, third and fourth quills longest, first and fifth nearly equal and little shorter. Tail longish, of twelve feathers, much rounded, concave along the middle above, or what is termed boat-shaped.

Bill, feet and claws black. Iris bright-yellow. Head, neck, and upper part of the breast blackish, with vivid reflections of violet, steel-blue, and green. General colour of the body black, with bright-green, purple and bronze-coloured reflections above, dull beneath. Quills and tail-feathers black, the latter with purple and green reflections ; secondaries and wing-coverts tinged with brown.

Length 13 inches, extent of wings 19 ; beak $1\frac{1}{4}$ along the ridge, $1\frac{1}{4}$ along the gap ; tarsus $1\frac{3}{4}$, middle toe $1\frac{1}{4}$.

Adult Female.   Plate VII.   Fig. 2.

The female differs from the male in being smaller, in having the tail less hollow above, and in the less brilliant reflections of its plumage, which has more of a brown tint.

Length 11 inches, extent of wings 16 ; bill 1 along the ridge, 1¼ along the gap.

The Maize or Indian Corn.

Zea Mays, *Willd.* Sp. Pl. vol. iv. p. 200.   *Pursh*, Flor. Americ. p. 46.—Monœcia Triandria, *Linn.*   Gramineæ, *Juss.*

This very important plant is abundantly cultivated in all parts of America.   As it is generally known, and as I shall have occasion to speak of it elsewhere, it is unnecessary for me to describe it here.

THE WHITE-THROATED SPARROW.

FRINGILLA PENNSYLVANICA, LATH.

PLATE VIII. MALE AND FEMALE.

THIS pretty little bird is a visitor of Louisiana and all the southern districts, where it remains only a very short time. Its arrival in Louisiana may be stated to take place in the beginning of November, and its departure in the first days of March. In all the Middle States it remains longer. How it comes and how it departs are to me quite unknown. I can only say, that, all of a sudden, the hedges of the fields bordering on creeks or swampy places, and overgrown with different species of vines, sumach bushes, briars, and the taller kinds of grasses, appear covered with these birds. They form groups, sometimes containing from thirty to fifty individuals, and live together in harmony. They are constantly moving up and down among these recesses, with frequent jerkings of the tail, and uttering a note common to the tribe. From the hedges and thickets they issue one by one in quick succession, and ramble to the distance of eight or ten yards, hopping and scratching, in quest of small seeds, and preserving the utmost silence. When the least noise is heard, or alarm given, and frequently, as I thought, without any alarm at all, they all fly back to their covert, pushing directly into the very thickest part of it. A moment elapses, when they become reassured, and ascending to the highest branches and twigs, open a little concert, which, although of short duration, is extremely sweet. There is much plaintive softness in their note, which I wish, kind reader, I could describe to you ; but this is impossible, although it is yet ringing in my ear, as if I were in those very fields where I have so often listened to it with delight. No sooner is their music over than they return to the field, and thus continue alternately sallying forth and retreating during the greater part of the day. At the approach of night, they utter a sharper and shriller note, consisting of a single *twit*, repeated in smart succession by the whole group, and continuing until the first hooting of some owl frightens them into silence. Yet, often during fine nights, I have heard the little creatures emit here and there a twit, as if to assure each other that " all's well."

During the warmer days, they remove partially to the woods, but never out of reach of their favourite briar thickets, ascend the tops of hollies, or such other trees as are covered with tangled vines, and pick either a berry or a winter grape. Their principal enemies in the day-time, are the little Sparrow Hawk, the Slate-coloured or Sharp-shinned Hawk, and above all, the Hen-harrier or Marsh Hawk. The latter passes over their little coteries with such light wings, and so unlooked for, that he seldom fails in securing one of them.

No sooner does spring return, when our woods are covered with white blossoms, in gay mimicry of the now melted snows, and the delighted eye is attracted by the beautiful flowers of the Dog-wood tree, than the White-throated Sparrow bids farewell to these parts, not to return till winter. Where it spends the summer I know not, but I should think not within the States.

It is a plump bird, fattening almost to excess, whilst in Louisiana, and affords delicious eating, for which purpose many are killed with *blow-guns*. These instruments—should you not have seen them—are prepared by the Indians, who cut the straightest canes, perforating them by forcing a hickery rod through the internal partitions which intersect this species of bamboo, and render them quite smooth within by passing the rod repeatedly through. The cane is then kept perfectly straight, and is well dried, after which it is ready for use. Splints of wood, or more frequently of cane, are then worked into tiny arrows, quite sharp at one end, and at the other, instead of being feathered, covered with squirrel hair or other soft substances, in the manner of a bottle-brush, so as to fill the tube and receive the impulse imparted by a smart puff of breath, which is sufficient to propel such an arrow with force enough to kill a small bird at the distance of eight or ten paces. With these blow-guns or pipes, several species of birds are killed in large quantities; and the Indians sometimes procure even squirrels by means of them.

The Dog-wood, of which I have represented a twig in early spring, is a small tree found nearly throughout the Union, but generally preferring such lands as with us are called of second quality, although it occasionally makes its appearance in the richest alluvial deposits. Its height seldom exceeds twenty feet, or its diameter ten inches. It is scarcely ever straight to any extent, but the wood, being extremely hard and compact, is useful for turning, when well dried and free of wind-shakes, to which it is rather liable. Its berries are eaten by various species of birds,

and especially by our different kinds of Squirrels, all of which shew great
partiality to them.   Its flowers, although so interesting in early spring,
are destitute of odour, and of short duration.   The bark is used by the
inhabitants in decoction as a remedy for intermittent fevers, and the
berries are employed by the housewife for dyeing black.

FRINGILLA PENNSYLVANICA, *Lath.* Ind. Ornith. vol. i. p. 445.—*Ch. Bonaparte,*
    Synopsis of Birds of the United States, p. 108.
WHITE-THROATED SPARROW, FRINGILLA ALBICOLLIS, *Wils.* Americ. Ornith. vol. iii.
    p. 51, Pl. xxxi. fig. 5.   Male.
WHITE-THROATED FINCH, *Lath.* Synops. vol. iii. p. 443.

Adult Male.   Plate VIII. Fig. 1.

Bill short, robust, conical, acute ; upper mandible broader than the
lower, scarcely declinate at the tip, almost straight in its dorsal outline,
as is the lower, both being rounded on the sides, and the lower with inflected, acute edges ; the gap line nearly straight, a little deflected at the
base, and not extending to beneath the eye.   Nostrils basal, roundish,
open, partially concealed by the feathers.   Head rather large.   Neck
shortish.   Body robust.   Legs of moderate length, slender ; tarsus longer
than the middle toe, covered anteriorly with a few longish scutella ; toes
scutellate above, free, the lateral ones nearly equal ; claws slender, arched,
compressed, acute, that of the hind toe rather large.

Plumage compact above, soft and blended beneath.   Wings short
and curved, rounded, the third and fourth quills longest, the first much
shorter, the secondaries long.   Tail longish, forked, the lateral feathers
curved outwards towards the tip.

Upper mandible dark brown, its edges and the lower mandible light
blue.   Iris hazel.   Feet flesh-coloured, claws light brown.   Upper part
of the head black, with a narrow white stripe from the forehead to the
upper part of the neck.   A broader white stripe, anteriorly passing into
bright orange, over each eye, margined by a narrow black stripe extending from the eye down the neck.   Upper part of the back, and the lesser
wing-coverts, bright bay, variegated with black ; lower back and tail-
coverts brownish-grey.   Quills and large coverts blackish, margined with
bay, the latter, as well as the next series, tipped with white, forming two
conspicuous bands on the wing.   Tail dusky brown.   Throat white ;

sides and fore-part of the neck and breast bluish-grey; the rest of the under parts greyish-white.

Length 6¼ inches, extent of wings 9; bill ⁶⁄₁₂ along the ridge, ⁷⁄₁₂ along the gap; tarsus 1¼, middle toe 1.

Adult Female.   Plate VIII. Fig. 2.

In the female, the colours are similarly arranged, but much duller, the bright bay of the male being changed into reddish-brown, the black into dark brown, and the white into greyish-white.   The white streak above the eye is narrower, shorter, and anteriorly less yellow, the greyish-blue of the breast paler, and the white spot on the throat less defined.

Length 6¼ inches, extent of wings 8½; bill ½ along the ridge, ½ along the gap.

Dog-wood.

Cornus florida, *Willd.* Sp. Plant. vol. i. p. 661.   *Michaux*, Abr. Forest. de l'Amer. Sept. t. iii. p. 138, Pl. lii.   *Pursh*, Flora Americ. p. 108.—Tetrandria Mono-gynia, *Linn.*   Caprifolia, *Juss.*

A beautiful small tree, generally about twenty feet in height, with very hard wood; dark grey bark, cracked into squarish compartments; ovate-elliptical, acuminate leaves, which are light green above, whitish beneath; large, obcordate involucral leaves; and bright-red oval berries.

SELBY'S FLY-CATCHER.

MUSCICAPA SELBII.

PLATE IX. MALE.

THE works of every student of nature are always pleasing to me, and it is with delight that I see the number of such students daily increasing; but when I meet with one who, regardless of the labour attending upon figuring in their full size the objects from which he has derived his knowledge, my heart expands, and I hail his name with enthusiasm. Mr SELBY's great work is so well known to the scientific world, that I need only here mention the favour which its accomplished author has conferred upon me by permitting me to decorate one of my pages with his name, in quality of foster-father to a beautiful and hitherto unknown species of Fly-catcher.

As this bird, to the day on which my engraving of it appeared, had not been described, or, in as far as I know, obtained by any other person than myself, notwithstanding the great number of individuals who have of late years been searching our States for new and rare species, it must be considered as of very unfrequent occurrence, and probably as seldom going farther north or east than the place where I discovered it. Moreover, it is so scarce even there, that in all my walks I only shot three individuals, in the course of nine years. In no instance have I been able to cultivate its society longer than a few minutes, as, before it might escape from me, I was obliged to shoot it, in order to satisfy myself that it was indeed a different bird from any figured or described in books.

My journal, under the date of 1st July 1821, contains the following statement :—" I found this bird about three miles from St Francisville in Louisiana, whilst engaged in searching for a Turkey, which I had wounded. It was afternoon, and the heat oppressive. I saw it innocently approaching us until within a few yards, anxiously looking, as if trying to discover our intentions; but as we stood motionless, it once came so near that I could easily have reached it with my gun barrel. It moved nimbly among the twigs of the low bushes, making now and then short dashes at flies, which it swallowed after killing them under foot, as many other Fly-catchers are in the habit of doing, then peeping at us, and again setting off in pursuit of flies. The snapping of its bill when seizing an insect, was sharp, and as distinct as if the bird had been in my hand. At length, fearing that it might escape, I desired my young friend JOSEPH MASON to retire further from it, that we might shoot it."

On the 4th July, while searching with care about the same place, to find its nest or the female, I shot another of these birds, which I found to be a female. It differed only in being rather smaller, darker above, and paler beneath. On the 27th September of the same year, I shot a second male in beautiful plumage, six or seven miles off, in a different direction, in the same State. Finding the pretty flower on which the bird is drawn, in the immediate neighbourhood, and growing wild, although I am assured it is originally from Europe, I have represented it, thinking it might contrast well with the Fly-catcher in its richly coloured flowers, and be assimilated to it in that of its stem and leaves. This flower is found in damp places, in Louisiana only, at least I have not met with it in the woods of any other State.

SELBY'S FLY-CATCHER, MUSCICAPA SELBII.

Adult Male. Plate X.

Bill longish, depressed, tapering to a sharp point, very broad at the base, the gap reaching to nearly under the eye; upper mandible slightly notched and inflected at the tip; lower straight. Nostrils basal, lateral, linear. Head and neck of moderate size. Body somewhat slender. Feet moderately long, slender; tarsus covered with short scutella above, with a longitudinal keeled plate behind, longer than the middle toe; toes slender, unconnected; claws small, weak, slightly arched, compressed, acute.

Plumage blended, soft and glossy. The beak margined at the base with long spreading bristles. Wings of moderate length, third quill longest, second and first little shorter, the other quills graduated. Tail rather long, forked when closed, rounded when spread, the feathers acuminate.

Bill brown, horn-colour above, passing into dark flesh-colour below. Iris dark brown. Legs, feet, and claws very light flesh-colour. The whole upper parts dark olive; wings black, the feathers margined externally with light olive, internally with white. The whole under parts, including the tail-coverts, and a broad line over the eyes, rich yellow. The three external feathers of the tail marked internally with white, the first more so than the second, and the third less than the latter. Shafts of the quills and tail-feathers deep brownish-black. Basirostral bristles black.

Length $5\frac{1}{4}$ inches, extent of wings $7\frac{1}{4}$; bill along the ridge $\frac{7}{12}$, along the gap $\frac{11}{12}$; tarsus 1, middle toe $\frac{5}{6}$.

The female, as has been said, is nearly similar, the distribution of the colours being the same.

FLOS-ADONIS.

ADONIS AUTUMNALIS, *Linn.* Sp. Pl. p. 771. *Willd.* Sp. Pl. vol. ii. p. 1304. *Smith.* Engl. Fl. vol. iii. p. 43.—POLYANDRIA PENTAGYNIA, *Linn.* RANUNCULACEÆ, *Juss.*

This plant, vulgarly named Pheasant's-eye, grows in Europe in corn-fields. It has an erect, branched stem, with copiously pinnatifid, alternate, sessile, dark green leaves, the segments of which are linear and acute, and deep crimson flowers, having a black spot near the claw of each of the petals, which vary from six to ten.

2

THE BROWN TITLARK.

ANTHUS SPINOLETTA. BONAP.

PLATE X. MALE AND FEMALE.

ALTHOUGH this species is met with in every portion of the United States which I have visited, I have not seen it anywhere during the summer months, or heard of it breeding with us. It is one of the birds that I should call gifted with a double set of habits, for, like a very few others that are strictly named land birds, it occurs not only in the fields in the interior of the country, but also on the borders of rivers, and even on the shores of the Atlantic.

Its flight is extremely easy, and what I would call of a beautiful and delicate nature. In other words, these birds pass and repass through the air, performing numberless evolutions, as if it did not cost them the least labour to fly. When in the interior of the country, they resort to the old fields, and the vast prairies, as well as the ploughed lands, seldom in flocks of less than ten or a dozen, and not unfrequently by hundreds. Now, they are seen high, loosely moving in short reiterated undulations, inspecting the ground below ; now, they come sweeping over and close to it, and seem about to alight, when, on the contrary, their ranks close in an instant, they wheel about, and rise again into the air. These feats are often repeated six or seven times, when at last, satisfied as to their safety, or the abundance of food in the spot, they alight, and immediately run about in quest of food. They run briskly, and as lightly as birds usually called Larks are wont to do, but with this difference, that they suffer their tails to vibrate whenever they stop running. Again, instead of squatting partially down, as true Larks do, to pick up their food, they move their body upon the upper joints of the legs, in the manner of Thrushes and other birds. Another habit seldom found in the Lark genus is that of settling on fences and trees, and walking along them with apparent ease. In fact, the bird, although called a Lark by WILSON and others, belongs to the Pipit or Titlark family.

Whilst residing among the meadows and ploughed fields, these birds feed on insects and small seeds, picking up some gravel at the same time. Along the rivers, or on the sea-shores, they are fond of running as near

THE GREAT PINE SWAMP.

I LEFT Philadelphia, at four of the morning, by the coach, with no other accoutrements than I knew to be absolutely necessary for the jaunt which I intended to make. These consisted of a wooden box, containing a small stock of linen, drawing paper, my journal, colours and pencils, together with 25 pounds of shot, some flints, the due quantum of cash, my gun *Tear-jacket*, and a heart as true to nature as ever.

Our coaches are none of the best, nor do they move with the velocity of those of some other countries. It was eight, and a dark night, when I reached Mauch Chunk, now so celebrated in the Union for its rich coal mines, and eighty-eight miles distant from Philadelphia. I had passed through a very diversified country, part of which was highly cultivated, while the rest was yet in a state of nature, and consequently much more agreeable to me. On alighting, I was shewn to the travellers' room, and on asking for the landlord, saw coming towards me a fine-looking young man, to whom I made known my wishes. He spoke kindly, and offered to lodge and board me at a much lower rate than travellers who go there for the very simple pleasure of being dragged on the railway. In a word, I was fixed in four minutes, and that most comfortably.

No sooner had the approach of day been announced by the cocks of the little village, than I marched out with my gun and note-book, to judge for myself of the wealth of the country. After traversing much ground, and crossing many steep hills, I returned, if not wearied, at least much disappointed at the extraordinary scarcity of birds. So I bargained to be carried in a cart to the central parts of the Great Pine Swamp, and, although a heavy storm was rising, ordered my conductor to proceed. We winded round many a mountain, and at last crossed the highest. The weather had become tremendous, and we were thoroughly drenched, but my resolution being fixed, the boy was obliged to continue his driving. Having already travelled about fifteen miles or so, we left the turnpike, and struck up a narrow and bad road, that seemed merely cut out to enable the people of the Swamp to receive the necessary supplies from the village which I had left. Some mistakes were made, and it was almost dark, when a post directed us to the habitation of a Mr JEDIAH IRISH, to whom I had been recommended. We now rattled down a steep declivity, edged on one side by almost perpendicular rocks, and on the other by a noisy stream, which seemed grumbling at the approach of strangers. The ground was so overgrown by laurels and tall pines of different kinds, that the whole presented only a mass of darkness.

At length we got to the house, the door of which was already opened, the sight of strangers being nothing uncommon in our woods, even in the most remote parts. On entering, I was presented with a chair, while my conductor was shewn the way to the stable, and on expressing a wish that I should be permitted to remain in the house for some weeks, I was gratified by receiving the sanction of the good woman to my proposal, although her husband was then from home. As I immediately fell a-talking about the nature of the country, and inquired if birds were numerous in the neighbourhood, Mrs IRISH, more *au fait* to household affairs than ornithology, sent for a nephew of her husband's, who soon made his appearance, and in whose favour I became at once prepossessed. He conversed like an educated person, saw that I was comfortably disposed of, and finally bade me good-night in such a tone as made me quite happy.

The storm had rolled away before the first beams of the morning sun shone brightly on the wet foliage, displaying all its richness and beauty. My ears were greeted by the notes, always sweet and mellow, of the Wood Thrush and other songsters. Before I had gone many steps, the woods echoed to the report of my gun, and I picked from among the leaves a lovely Sylvia, long sought for, but until then sought for in vain. I needed no more, and standing still for awhile, I was soon convinced that the Great Pine Swamp harboured many other objects as valuable to me.

The young man joined me, bearing his rifle, and offered to accompany me through the woods, all of which he well knew. · But I was anxious to transfer to paper the form and beauty of the little bird I had in my hand ; and requesting him to break a twig of blooming laurel, we returned to the house, speaking of nothing else than the picturesque beauty of the country around.

A few days passed, during which I became acquainted with my hostess and her sweet children, and made occasional rambles, but spent the greater portion of my time in drawing. One morning, as I stood near the window of my room, I remarked a tall and powerful man alight from his horse, loose the girth of the saddle, raise the latter with one hand, pass the bridle over the head of the animal with the other, and move towards the house, while the horse betook himself to the little brook to drink. I heard some movements in the room below, and again the same tall person walked towards the mills and stores, a few hundred yards from the house.

In America, business is the first object in view at all times, and right it is that it should be so. Soon after my hostess entered my room, accompanied by the fine-looking woodsman, to whom, as Mr JEDIAH IRISH, I was introduced. Reader, to describe to you the qualities of that excellent man were vain; you should know him, as I do, to estimate the value of such men in our sequestered forests. He not only made me welcome, but promised all his assistance in forwarding my views.

The long walks and long talks we have had together I never can forget, or the many beautiful birds which we pursued, shot, and admired. The juicy venison, excellent bear flesh, and delightful trout that daily formed my food, methinks I can still enjoy. And then, what pleasure I had in listening to him as he read his favourite Poems of BURNS, while my pencil was occupied in smoothing and softening the drawing of the bird before me! Was not this enough to recall to my mind the early impressions that had been made upon it by the description of the golden age, which I here found realized?

The Lehigh about this place forms numerous short turns between the mountains, and affords frequent falls, as well as below the falls deep pools, which render this stream a most valuable one for mills of any kind. Not many years before this date, my host was chosen by the agent of the Lehigh Coal Company, as their mill-wright, and manager for cutting down the fine trees which covered the mountains around. He was young, robust, active, industrious, and persevering. He marched to the spot where his abode now is, with some workmen, and by dint of hard labour first cleared the road mentioned above, and reached the river at the centre of a bend, where he fixed on erecting various mills. The pass here is so narrow that it looks as if formed by the bursting asunder of the mountain, both sides ascending abruptly, so that the place where the settlement was made is in many parts difficult of access, and the road then newly cut was only sufficient to permit men and horses to come to the spot where JEDIAH and his men were at work. So great, in fact, were the difficulties of access, that, as he told me, pointing to a spot about 150 feet above us, they for many months slipped from it their barrelled provisions, assisted by ropes, to their camp below. But no sooner was the first saw-mill erected, than the axemen began their devastations. Trees one after another were, and are yet, constantly heard falling, during the days; and in calm nights, the greedy mills told the sad tale, that in a century the noble forests around should exist no more. Many mills were erected, many dams raised, in defiance of the impetuous Lehigh. One full third of the trees

have already been culled, turned into boards, and floated as far as Philadelphia.

In such an undertaking, the cutting of the trees is not all. They have
afterwards to be hauled to the edge of the mountains bordering the river,
launched into the stream, and led to the mills over many shallows and
difficult places. Whilst I was in the Great Pine Swamp, I frequently
visited one of the principal places for the launching of logs. To see them
tumbling from such a height, touching here and there the rough angle of
a projecting rock, bouncing from it with the elasticity of a foot-ball, and at
last falling with awful crash into the river, forms a sight interesting in the
highest degree, but impossible for me to describe. Shall I tell you that I
have seen masses of these logs heaped above each other to the number of
five thousand ? I may so tell you, for such I have seen. My friend IRISH
assured me that at some seasons, these piles consisted of a much greater
number, the river becoming in those places completely choked up.

When *freshets* (or floods) take place, then is the time chosen for forwarding the logs to the different mills. This is called a *Frolic*. JEDIAH
IRISH, who is generally the leader, proceeds to the upper leap with his men,
each provided with a strong wooden handspike, and a short-handled axe.
They all take to the water, be it summer or winter, like so many New-
foundland spaniels. The logs are gradually detached, and, after a
time, are seen floating down the dancing stream, here striking against
a rock and whirling many times round, there suddenly checked in dozens
by a shallow, over which they have to be forced with the handspikes.
Now they arrive at the edge of a dam, and are again pushed over. Certain numbers are left in each dam, and when the party has arrived at the
last, which lies just where my friend IRISH's camp was first formed, the
drenched leader and his men, about sixty in number, make their way home,
find there a healthful repast, and spend the evening and a portion of the
night in dancing and frolicking, in their own simple manner, in the most
perfect amity, seldom troubling themselves with the idea of the labour
prepared for them on the morrow.

That morrow now come, one sounds a horn from the door of the store-
house, at the call of which each returns to his work. The sawyers, the
millers, the rafters and raftsmen are all immediately busy. The mills are all
going, and the logs, which a few months before were the supporters of broad
and leafy tops, are now in the act of being split asunder. The boards are
then launched into the stream, and rafts are formed of them for market.

During the summer and autumnal months, the Lehigh, a small river of itself, soon becomes extremely shallow, and to float the rafts would prove impossible, had not art managed to provide a supply of water for this express purpose. At the breast of the lower dam is a curiously constructed lock, which is opened at the approach of the rafts. They pass through this lock with the rapidity of lightning, propelled by the water that had been accumulated in the dam, and which is of itself generally sufficient to float them to Mauch Chunk, after which, entering regular canals, they find no other impediments, but are conveyed to their ultimate destination.

Before population had greatly advanced in this part of Pennsylvania, game of all descriptions found within that range was extremely abundant. The Elk itself did not disdain to browse on the shoulders of the mountains, near the Lehigh. Bears and the Common Deer must have been plentiful, as, at the moment when I write, many of both kinds are seen and killed by the resident hunters. The Wild Turkey, the Pheasant and the Grouse, are also tolerably abundant ; and as to trout in the streams —Ah, reader, if you are an angler, do go there, and try for yourself. For my part, I can only say, that I have been made weary with pulling up from the rivulets the sparkling fish, allured by the struggles of the common grasshopper.

A comical affair happened with the bears, which I shall relate to you, good reader. A party of my friend IRISH's raftsmen, returning from Mauch Chunk, one afternoon, through sundry short cuts over the mountains, at the season when the huckle-berries are ripe and plentiful, were suddenly apprised of the proximity of some of these animals, by their snuffing the air. No sooner was this perceived than, to the astonishment of the party, not fewer than eight bears, I was told, made their appearance. Each man, being provided with his short-handled axe, faced about, and willingly came to the scratch ; but the assailed soon proved the assailants, and with claw and tooth drove off the men in a twinkling. Down they all rushed from the mountain ; the noise spread quickly ; rifles were soon procured and shouldered ; but when the spot was reached, no bears were to be found ; night forced the hunters back to their homes, and a laugh concluded the affair.

I spent six weeks in the Great Pine Forest—Swamp it cannot be called—where I made many a drawing. Wishing to leave Pennsylvania, and to follow the migratory flocks of our birds to the south, I bade adieu

to the excellent wife and rosy children of my friend, and to his kind nephew.   JEDIAH IRISH, shouldering his heavy rifle, accompanied me, and
trudging directly across the mountains, we arrived at Mauch Chunk in
good time for dinner.   Shall I ever have the pleasure of seeing that good,
that generous man again ?

At Mauch Chunk, where we both spent the night, Mr WHITE, the ci-
vil engineer, visited me, and looked at the drawings which I had made
in the Great Pine Forest.   The news he gave me of my sons, then in
Kentucky, made me still more anxious to move in their direction, and,
long before day-break, I shook hands with the goodman of the forest,
and found myself moving towards the capital of Pennsylvania, having as
my sole companion a sharp frosty breeze.   Left to my thoughts, I felt
amazed that such a place as the Great Pine Forest should be so little
known to the Philadelphians, scarcely any of whom could direct me towards it.   How much is it to be regretted, thought I, that the many
young gentlemen who are there so much at a loss how to employ their
leisure days, should not visit these wild retreats, valuable as they are to
the student of nature.   How differently would they feel, if, instead of
spending weeks in smoothing a useless bow, and walking out in full dress,
intent on displaying the make of their legs, to some rendezvous where
they may enjoy their wines, they were to occupy themselves in contemplating the rich profusion which nature has poured around them, or even
in procuring some desiderated specimen for their *Peale's Museum*, once
so valuable and so finely arranged?   But alas ! no : they are none of
them aware of the richness of the Great Pine Swamp, nor are they likely
to share the hospitality to be found there.

Night came on, as I was thinking of such things, and I was turned out
of the coach in the streets of the fair city, just as the clock struck ten.
I cannot say that my bones were much rested, but not a moment was to
be lost.   So I desired a porter to take up my little luggage, and leading
him towards the nearest wharf, I found myself soon after gliding across
the Delaware, towards my former lodgings in the Jerseys.   The lights
were shining from the parallel streets as I crossed them, all was tranquil
and serene, until there came the increasing sound of the Baltimore
steamer, which, for some reason unknown to me, was that evening later
than usual in its arrival.   My luggage was landed, and carried home by
means of a bribe.   The people had all retired to rest, but my voice was
instantly recognised, and an entrance was afforded to me.

THE BIRD OF WASHINGTON.

FALCO WASHINGTONII.

PLATE XI. MALE.

IT was in the month of February 1814, that I obtained the first sight of this noble bird, and never shall I forget the delight which it gave me. Not even HERSCHEL, when he discovered the planet which bears his name, could have experienced more rapturous feelings. We were on a trading voyage, ascending the Upper Mississippi. The keen wintry blasts whistled around us, and the cold from which I suffered had, in a great degree, extinguished the deep interest which, at other seasons, this magnificent river has been wont to awake in me. I lay stretched beside our patroon. The safety of the cargo was forgotten, and the only thing that called my attention was the multitude of ducks, of different species, accompanied by vast flocks of swans, which from time to time passed us. My patroon, a Canadian, had been engaged many years in the fur trade. He was a man of much intelligence, and, perceiving that these birds had engaged my curiosity, seemed anxious to find some new object to divert me. An eagle flew over us. " How fortunate !" he exclaimed ; " this is what I could have wished. Look, sir ! the Great Eagle, and the only one I have seen since I left the lakes." I was instantly on my feet, and having observed it attentively, concluded, as I lost it in the distance, that it was a species quite new to me. My patroon assured me that such birds were indeed rare ; that they sometimes followed the hunters, to feed on the entrails of animals which they had killed, when the lakes were frozen over, but that when the lakes were open, they would dive in the daytime after fish, and snatch them up in the manner of the Fishing Hawk ; and that they roosted generally on the shelves of the rocks, where they built their nests, of which he had discovered several by the quantity of white dung scattered below.

Convinced that the bird was unknown to naturalists, I felt particularly anxious to learn its habits, and to discover in what particulars it differed from the rest of its genus. My next meeting with this bird was a few years afterwards, whilst engaged in collecting crayfish on one of those flats which border and divide Green River, in Kentucky, near its junction with the Ohio. The river is there bordered by a range of high cliffs, which, for some distance, follow its windings. I observed on the rocks, which, at that place, are nearly perpendicular, a quantity of white ordure, which I attributed to owls that might have resorted thither. I mentioned the circumstance to my companions, when one of them, who lived within a mile and a half of the place, told me it was from the nest of the Brown Eagle, meaning the White-headed Eagle (*Falco leucocephalus*) in its immature state. I assured him this could not be, and remarked that neither the old nor the young birds of that species ever build in such places, but always in trees. Although he could not answer my objection, he stoutly maintained that a brown eagle of some kind, above the usual size, had built there; and added that he had espied the nest some days before, and had seen one of the old birds dive and catch a fish. This he thought strange, having, till then, always observed that both Brown Eagles and Bald Eagles procured this kind of food by robbing the fish-hawks. He said that if I felt particularly anxious to know what nest it was, I might soon satisfy myself, as the old birds would come and feed their young with fish, for he had seen them do so before.

In high expectation, I seated myself about a hundred yards from the foot of the rock. Never did time pass more slowly. I could not help betraying the most impatient curiosity, for my hopes whispered it was a Sea Eagle's nest. Two long hours had elapsed before the old bird made his appearance, which was announced to us by the loud hissings of the two young ones, which crawled to the extremity of the hole to receive a fine fish. I had a perfect view of this noble bird as he held himself to the edging rock, hanging like the Barn, Bank, or Social Swallow, his tail spread, and his wings partly so. I trembled lest a word should escape from my companions. The slightest murmur had been treason from them. They entered into my feelings, and, although little interested, gazed with me. In a few minutes the other parent joined her mate, and from the difference in size (the female of rapacious birds being much larger), we knew this to be the mother bird. She also had brought a fish; but, more cautious than her mate, she glanced her quick and piercing eye around, and instantly perceived that her abode had been discovered. She dropped her prey, with a loud shriek communicated the alarm to the male, and, hovering with him over our heads, kept up a growling cry, to intimidate us from our suspected design. This watch-

ful solicitude I have ever found peculiar to the female :—must I be understood to speak only of birds ?

The young having concealed themselves, we went and picked up the
fish which the mother had let fall. It was a white perch, weighing about
5¼ lb. The upper part of the head was broken in, and the back torn
by the talons of the eagle. We had plainly seen her bearing it in the
manner of the Fish-Hawk.

This day's sport being at an end, as we journeyed homewards, we
agreed to return the next morning, with the view of obtaining both the
old and young birds ; but rainy and tempestuous weather setting in, it
became necessary to defer the expedition till the third day following,
when, with guns and men all in readiness, we reached the rock. Some
posted themselves at the foot, others upon it, but in vain. We passed
the entire day, without either seeing or hearing an eagle, the sagacious
birds, no doubt, having anticipated an invasion, and removed their young
to new quarters.

I come at last to the day which I had so often and so ardently desired.
Two years had gone by since the discovery of the nest, in fruitless excursions ; but my wishes were no longer to remain ungratified. In returning from the little village of Henderson, to the house of Doctor
RANKIN, about a mile distant, I saw an eagle rise from a small enclosure
not a hundred yards before me, where the Doctor had a few days before
slaughtered some hogs, and alight upon a low tree branching over the
road. I prepared my double-barrelled piece, which I constantly carry,
and went slowly and cautiously towards him. Quite fearlessly he await-
ed my approach, looking upon me with undaunted eye. I fired and he
fell. Before I reached him he was dead. With what delight did I survey the magnificent bird ! Had the finest salmon ever pleased him as he
did me ?—Never. I ran and presented him to my friend, with a pride
which they alone can feel, who, like me, have devoted themselves from
their earliest childhood to such pursuits, and who have derived from them
their first pleasures. To others I must seem to " prattle out of fashion."
The Doctor, who was an experienced hunter, examined the bird with
much satisfaction, and frankly acknowledged he had never before seen or
heard of it.

The name which I have chosen for this new species of Eagle, " The
Bird of Washington," may, by some, be considered as preposterous and

unfit ; but as it is indisputably the noblest bird of its genus that has yet
been discovered in the United States, I trust I shall be allowed to honour
it with the name of one yet nobler, who was the saviour of his country,
and whose name will ever be dear to it.   To those who may be curious
to know my reasons, I can only say, that, as the new world gave me birth
and liberty, the great man who ensured its independence is next to my
heart.   He had a nobility of mind, and a generosity of soul, such as are
seldom possessed.   He was brave, so is the eagle ; like it, too, he was the
terror of his foes ; and his fame, extending from pole to pole, resembles
the majestic soarings of the mightiest of the feathered tribe.   If America
has reason to be proud of her Washington, so has she to be proud of her
Great Eagle.

In the month of January following, I saw a pair of these eagles flying
over the Falls of the Ohio, one in pursuit of the other.   The next day I
saw them again.   The female had relaxed her severity, had laid aside
her coyness, and to a favourite tree they continually resorted.   I pursued them unsuccessfully for several days, when they forsook the place.

The flight of this bird is very different from that of the White-headed
Eagle.   The former encircles a greater space, whilst sailing keeps nearer
to the land and the surface of the water, and when about to dive for fish
falls in a spiral manner, as if with the intention of checking any retreating movement which its prey might attempt, darting upon it only when
a few yards distant.   The Fish-hawk often does the same.   When rising
with a fish, the Bird of Washington flies to a considerable distance, forming, in its line of course, a very acute angle with the surface line of the
water.   My last opportunity of seeing this bird, was on the 15th of November 1821, a few miles above the mouth of the Ohio, when two passed
over our boat, moving down the river with a gentle motion.   In a letter
from a kind relative, Mr W. BAKEWELL, dated, " Falls of the Ohio, July
1819," and containing particulars relative to the Swallow-tailed Hawk
(*Falco furcatus*), that gentleman says :—" Yesterday, for the first time,
I had an opportunity of viewing one of those magnificent birds, which
you call the Sea Eagle, as it passed low over me, whilst fishing.   I shall
be really glad when I can again have the pleasure of seeing your drawing of it."

Whilst in Philadelphia, about twelve months ago, I had the gratification of seeing a fine specimen of this Eagle at Mr BRANO's museum.   It
was a male in fine plumage, and beautifully preserved.   I wished to pur-

chase it with a view to carry it to Europe, but the price put upon it was above my means.

My excellent friend RICHARD HARLAN, M. D. of that city, speaking of this bird in a letter dated "Philadelphia, August 19, 1830," says, " That fine specimen of *Washington Eagle*, which you noticed in BRANO's museum, is at present in my possession. I have deposited it in the Academy, where it will most likely remain." I saw the specimen alluded to, which, in as far as I could observe, agreed in size and markings exactly with my drawing, to which, however, I could not at the time refer, as it was, with the whole of my collection, deposited in the British Museum, under the care of my ever kind and esteemed friend J. G. CHILDREN, Esq. of that Institution.

The glands containing the oil used for the purpose of anointing the surface of the plumage were, in the specimen represented in the plate, extremely large. Their contents had the appearance of hog's lard, which had been melted and become rancid. This bird makes more copious use of that substance than the White-headed Eagle, or any of the tribe to which it belongs, excepting the Fish-hawk, the whole plumage looking, upon close examination, as if it had received a general coating of a thin clear dilution of gum-arabic, and presenting less of the downy gloss exhibited in the upper part of the White-headed Eagle's plumage. The male bird weighs 14½ lb. avoirdupois, and measures 3 feet 7 inches in length, and 10 feet 2 inches in extent.

FALCO WASHINGTONII.

Adult Male.   Plate XI.

Bill shortish, very deep, compressed ; upper mandible with the dorsal outline forming the third of a circle, rounded above, sloping and flattish on the sides, nearly straight with a slight obtuse process, on the acute, overlapping edges, the tip deflected, trigonal, acute, at its lower part perpendicular to the gap line ; lower mandible convex in its dorsal outline, with inflected acute edges, which are deflected at the end. A naked cere, in the fore part of which are the oblong, oblique, nearly dorsal, open nostrils, which have a process from the anterior margin. Head rather large, flat above. Neck robust, of ordinary length. Body ovate. Feet rather short, with the leg long, the tarsus short, rounded, anteriorly covered with transversely narrow scutella, posteriorly with large, laterally with small tuberculous scales ; toes robust, free, scutellate above, papillar and scabrous beneath, with large tubercles; claws curved, rounded, marginate beneath, very acute.

Plumage compact, imbricated, glossy ; feathers of the head, neck and breast narrow and pointed ; of the back, breast and belly, ovate, distinct, acute; the wing-coverts narrow, acute, compact. Space between the beak and eye barish, being sparsely covered with feathers consisting of a shaft, downy at the base, prolonged into a hair. Eyebrow bare, and greatly projecting. Wings long, second quill longest, first considerably shorter. Tail of ordinary length, rounded, extending considerably beyond the tips of the wings, of twelve broad acute feathers. Tarsus feathered one-third down.

Bill bluish-black, the edges pale, the soft margin towards the commissure, and the base of the under mandible yellow. Cere yellowish-brown. Lore light greenish-blue. Iris chestnut-brown. Feet deep yellow ; claws bluish-black. Upper part of the head, hind neck, back, scapulars, rump, tail-coverts, and posterior tibial feathers blackish-brown, glossed with a coppery tint. Throat, fore-neck, breast and belly light brownish-yellow, each feather marked along the centre with blackish-brown. Wing-coverts light greyish-brown, those next the body becoming darker and approaching the colour of the back. Primary quills dark brown, deeper on their inner webs ; secondaries lighter, and on their outer webs of nearly the same light tint as their coverts. Tail uniform dark brown. Anterior tibial feathers greyish-brown.

Length 3 feet 7 inches, extent of wings 10 feet 2 inches. Bill 3¼ inches along the back ; along the gap, which commences directly under the eye, to the tip of the lower mandible 3½, and 1¾ deep. Length of wing when folded 32 inches ; length of tail 15 inches ; tarsus 4½, middle 4¾, hind claw 2½.

The two stomachs large and baggy. Their contents in the individual described were fish, fishes' scales, and entrails of various kinds. Intestines large, but thin and transparent.

Passing over the affinity of this bird to the young of the White-headed Eagle (*Falco leucocephalus*), which WILSON has described and figured under the name of Sea Eagle (*Falco Ossifragus* Linn.), I shall institute a comparison between it and the true Sea Eagle or Cinereous Eagle (*Falco Albicilla*), which bears so strong a resemblance to the Bird of Washington, that by a superficial observer they might be confounded, at least were he to view them separately.

The White-tailed or Cinereous Eagle (*Falco Albicilla* of LINNÆUS), has, when full grown, the bill and iris yellow, the general colour of the upper parts pale greyish-brown, passing into wood-brown, the belly and thighs chocolate-brown, some of the upper tail-coverts, and the whole of the tail, white. In this state, it is sufficiently different from our bird, at least in colouring, but the young has a different appearance. In the bird just fully fledged, the bill is deep brown, tinged with blue, its base and the cere greenish-yellow; the iris dark brown; the feet gamboge-yellow; the head deep brown, the bases of all the feathers of the body white; on the hind neck the whole feathers white, excepting the ends which are deep brown; the upper and middle back light brown, the tips umber; the lower back white, with umber tips; the tail greyish at its origin, deep brown, with an irregular brownish-white patch along the inner webs, the fore-neck and upper breast brownish-white, spotted with umber, the tips being of the latter colour; the belly pale brown, spotted with umber; the thighs brown; the under tail-coverts whitish, tipped with deep brown. In this state, and until nearly full grown, it has been described as a distinct species, under the name of Sea Eagle or Osprey (*Falco Ossifragus*, LINN.).

The principal changes which take place in regard to colour as the bird advances, are these: the bill first becomes bluish-black, and ultimately yellow, the cere becomes brighter, the iris assumes more of yellow, the white at the base of the plumage gradually disappears, the tail becomes lighter, the general colour of the plumage at first darker, but ultimately paler. At the age of two years, the only period when the bird much resembles ours, it is as follows:—and here I shall make the description correspond in its arrangement with that of the Bird of Washington, that the two may be more satisfactorily compared.

The bill corresponds with that of our bird, only that it is *not so deep*, and proportionally *more elongated*. The other circumstances mentioned in the first paragraph of the description of the Bird of Washington are the same in the Sea Eagle.

Plumage compact, imbricated, glossy; feathers of the head, neck and breast, narrow and pointed; of the back, breast and belly, ovate, distinct, acute; the wing-coverts ovate and pointed. Space between the beak and eye barish, being sparsely covered with bristly feathers. Eyebrow pro-

1

jecting and bare on the edge. Wings long, *fourth and fifth quills longest*, the first considerably shorter. Tail of ordinary length, rounded, of the same length as the closed wing, and consisting of twelve broad acute feathers. Tarsus feathered one-third down.

Bill bluish-black, brownish at the tip of the upper mandible, and along the greater part of the under; yellowish at the edges of the lower. Cere greenish-yellow. Lore of the same colour. Iris darkish brown. Head and hind neck dark brown, the latter still *marked with white*. Fore neck and breast *brownish white,* longitudinally marked with deep brown. Upper parts in general pale brown, spotted with deeper, some of the scapulars glossed with purple. Lower back *white*, the tips umber. Tail-coverts brownish-grey. Base, outer webs and tips of tail-feathers deep brown; inner webs and part of outer near the tip *brownish-white*. Belly pale brown spotted with umber. Primaries brownish-black, secondaries greyish-brown.

Length 3 feet, extent of wings 6 feet 9 inches; bill 3½ inches along the back, 1¼ deep.

All circumstances duly considered, the Bird of Washington stands forth as the champion of America, *sui speciei*, and henceforth not to be confounded with any of its rivals or relatives. If ornithologists are proud of describing new species, I may be allowed to express some degree of pleasure in giving to the world the knowledge of so majestic a bird.

THE BALTIMORE ORIOLE.

ICTERUS BALTIMORE. DAUD.

PLATE XII. MALE IN DIFFERENT STATES OF PLUMAGE, AND NEST.

No traveller who is at all gifted with the faculty of observation, can ascend that extraordinary river, the Mississippi, in the first days of autumn, without feeling enchanted by the varied vegetation which adorns its alluvial shores :—The tall Cotton-tree descending to the very margin of the stream, the arrow-shaped Ash mixing its branches with those of the Pecan and Black Walnut, immense Oaks and numerous species of Hickory, covering with their foliage the densely tangled Canes, from amongst which, at every step, Vines of various kinds shoot up, winding round the stems and interlacing their twigs and tendrils, stretching from one branch to another, until they have reached and overspread the whole, like a verdant canopy, forming one solid mass of richest vegetation, in the fore ground of the picture ; whilst, wherever the hills are in view, the great Magnolias, the Hollies, and the noble Pines, are seen gently waving their lofty heads to the breeze.

The current becomes rapid, and ere long several of the windings of the great stream have been met and passed, and with these new scenes present themselves to the view. The forest at this place, as if in doleful mourning at the sight of the havock made on its margin by the impetuous and regardless waters, has thrown over her a ragged veil, produced by the long dangling masses that spread from branch to branch over the cypress trees. The dejected Indian's camp lies in your sight. He casts a melancholy glance over the scene, and remembers that he is no longer the peaceful and sole possessor of the land. Islands, one after another, come in sight, and at every winding of the stream you see boats propelled by steam ascending the river, and others, without such aid, silently gliding with the current.

Much might the traveller find to occupy his mind, and lead him into speculations regarding the past, the present, and the future, were he not attracted by the clear mellow notes, that issue from the woods, and gratified by the sight of the brilliant Oriole now before you. In solitudes like these, the traveller might feel pleased with any sound, even the howl of the wolf, or the still more dismal bellow of the alligator.   Then how delightful must it be to hear the melody resulting from thousands of musical voices that come from some neighbouring tree, and which insensibly leads the mind, with whatever it may previously have been occupied, first to the contemplation of the wonders of nature, and then to that of the Great Creator himself.

Now we have ascended the mighty river, have left it, and entered the still more enchanting Ohio, and yet never for a day have we been without the company of the Oriole.   Here, amongst the pendulous branches of the lofty Tulip-trees, it moves gracefully up and down, seeking in the expanding leaves and opening blossoms the caterpillar and the green beetle, which generally contribute to its food.   Well, reader, it was one of these pendulous twigs which I took when I made the drawing before you. But instead of having cut it on the banks of the Ohio, I found it in the State of Louisiana, to which we shall return.

The Baltimore Oriole arrives from the south, perhaps from Mexico, or perhaps from a more distant region, and enters Louisiana as soon as spring commences there.   It approaches the planter's house, and searches amongst the surrounding trees for a suitable place in which to settle for the season.   It prefers, I believe, the trees that grow on the sides of a gentle declivity. · The choice of a twig being made, the male Oriole becomes extremely conspicuous.   He flies to the ground, searches for the longest and driest filaments of the moss, which in that State is known by the name of Spanish Beard, and whenever he finds one fit for his purpose, ascends to the favourite spot where the nest is to be, uttering all the while a continued chirrup, which seems to imply that he knows no fear, but on the contrary fancies himself the acknowledged king of the woods.   This sort of chirruping becomes louder, and is emitted in an angry tone, whenever an enemy approaches, or the bird is accidentally surprised, the sight of a cat or a dog being always likely to produce it.   No sooner does he reach the branches, than with bill and claws, aided by an astonishing sagacity, he fastens one end of the moss to a twig, with as much art as a sailor might do, and takes up the other end, which he secures also, but to another twig a few inches off, leaving the thread floating in the air like a swing, the curve of which is perhaps seven or eight inches from the twigs.   The female comes to his assistance with another filament of moss, or perhaps some cotton thread, or other fibrous substance, inspects the work which her mate has done, and immediately commences her operations, placing

ᴇ 2

each thread in a contrary direction to those arranged by her lordly mate, and making the whole cross and recross, so as to form an irregular network. Their love increases daily as they see the graceful fabric approaching perfection, until their conjugal affection and faith become as complete as in any species of birds with which I am acquainted.

The nest has now been woven from the bottom to the top, and so secured that no tempest can carry it off without breaking the branch to which it is suspended. Remark what follows. This nest contains no warming substance, such as wool, cotton, or cloth, but is almost entirely composed of the Spanish moss, interwoven in such a manner that the air can easily pass through it. The parents no doubt are aware of the intense heat which will exist ere long in this part of the world, and moreover take especial care to place their nest on the north-east side of the trees. On the contrary, had they gone as far as Pennsylvania or New York, they would have formed it of the warmest and softest materials, and have placed it in a position which would have left it exposed to the sun's rays, the changes in the weather during the early period of incubation being sometimes so great there, that the bird looks on these precautions as necessary to ensure the life of its brood against intense cold, should it come, while it knows that the heat in these northern latitudes will not be so great as to incommode them. I have observed these sensible differences in the formation and position of the nests of the Baltimore Oriole, a great many times, as no doubt have other persons. The female lays from four to six eggs, and in Louisiana frequently rears two broods in a season. The period of incubation is fourteen days. The eggs are about an inch in length, rather broadly ovate, pale brown, dotted, spotted, and tortuously lined with dark brown.

The movements of these birds as they run among the branches of trees differ materially from those of almost all others. They cling frequently by the feet in order to reach an insect at such a distance from them as to require the full extension of their neck, body, and legs, without letting go their hold. They sometimes glide, as it were, along a small twig, and at other times move sidewise for a few steps. Their motions are elegant and stately. Their song consists of three or four, or at most eight or ten, loud, full, and mellow notes, extremely agreeable to the ear.

A day or two before the young are quite able to leave the nest, they often cling to the outside, and creep in and out of it like young Woodpeckers. After leaving the nest, they follow the parents for nearly a fortnight, and are fed by them. As soon as the mulberries and figs become ripe, they resort to these fruits, and are equally fond of sweet cherries, strawberries, and others. During spring, their principal food is insects, which they seldom pursue on the wing, but which they search for with great activity, among the leaves and branches. I have seen the young of the first brood out early in May, and of the second in July. As soon as they are fully able to take care of themselves, they generally part from each other, and leave the country, as their parents had come, that is, singly.

During migration, the flight of the Baltimore Oriole is performed high above all the trees, and mostly during day, as I have usually observed them alighting, always singly, about the setting of the sun, uttering a note or two, and darting into the lower branches to feed, and afterwards to rest. To assure myself of this mode of travelling by day, I marked the place where a beautiful male had perched one evening, and on going to the spot next morning, long before dawn, I had the pleasure of hearing his first notes as light appeared, and saw him search a while for food, and afterwards mount in the air, making his way to warmer climes. Their flight is straight and continuous.

This beautiful bird is easily kept in cages, and may be fed on dried figs, raisins, hard-boiled eggs, and insects. When shot they will often clench the twig so firmly as to remain hanging fast to it until dislodged by another shot or a blow against the twig.

The plumage of the male bird is not mature until the third spring, and I have therefore in my drawing represented the males of the first, second, and third years. The female will form the subject of another plate. The male of the first year was taken for a female by my engraver, during my absence, and marked as such, although some of the plates were corrected the moment I saw the mistake.

The Baltimore Oriole, although found throughout the Union, is so partial to particular sections or districts, that of two places not twenty miles distant from each other, while none are to be seen in the one, a dozen pairs or more may be in the neighbourhood of the other. They are fondest of hilly grounds, refreshed by streams.

ICTERUS BALTIMORE, *Ch. Bonaparte*, Synopsis of Birds of the United States, p. 51.
ORIOLUS BALTIMORE, *Linn.* Syst Nat. p. 162.—*Gmel.* Syst. vol. i. p. 389.—*Lath.*
     Ind. Ornith. vol. i. p. 180.
BALTIMORE ORIOLE, ORIOLUS BALTIMORE, *Wilson*, Amer. Ornith. vol. i. p. 23.
     Pl. i. fig. 3. Male ; and vol. vi. p. 83. Pl. 53. fig. 4. Female.
BALTIMORE BIRD, *Lath.* Synops. vol. ii. p. 432.

Adult Male, three years old, in spring.   Plate XII. Fig. 1.

Bill conical, slender, longish, compressed, a little curved, very acute, with inflected acute margins ; upper mandible obtuse above, lower broadly obtuse beneath.   Nostrils oval, covered by a membrane, basal.   Head and neck of ordinary size.   Body rather slender.   Feet of ordinary length ; tarsus a little longer than the middle toe ; inner toe little shorter than the outer ; claws arched, compressed, acute, that of the hind toe twice the size of the others.

Plumage blended, glossy.   Wings longish, somewhat rounded, the first quill being almost as long as the second and third, which are the longest. Tail longish, rounded, and slightly forked, the feathers rather narrow, and acuminate.

Bill and feet light blue.   Iris orange.   Head, throat, back part of the neck, fore part of the back, quills and larger secondaries, black, as are the two middle tail-feathers, and the base of all the rest.   The whole under parts, the lesser wing-coverts, and the posterior part of the back, bright orange, deeply tinged with vermilion on the breast and neck.   The tips of the two middle tail-feathers, and the terminal ends of the others, of a duller orange.   Quills, excepting the first, margined with white.

Length 7¾ inches, extent of wings 12 ; bill ⅝ along the ridge, 1⅛ along the gap ; tarsus ¼, toe 1.

Male, two years old, in spring.   Plate XII. Fig. 2.

The distribution of the colours is the same as in the adult male, but the yellow is less vivid, the upper mandible is brownish-black above, and the iris is light-brown.

Young Male, one year old, in spring.   Plate XII. Fig. 1.

The bill is dark brown above, pale blue beneath.   Iris brown.   Feet light blue.   The general colour is dull brownish-yellow, tinged with olive on the head and back.   The wings are blackish-brown, the quills and

large coverts margined and tipped with white. The lesser coverts are
olivaceous, the tail destitute of black, and the under parts paler than in
the adult, without any approach to the vivid orange tints displayed on it.
Length 7½ inches.

The Tulip-Tree.

LIRIODENDRON TULIPIFERA, *Willd.* Sp. Plant. vol. ii. p. 1254. *Pursh.* Flora Americ. p. 382. *Mich.* Abr. Forest. de l'Amer. Sept. t. iii. p. 202, Pl. v.—POLYAN-
DRIA POLYGYNIA, *Linn.* MAGNOLIÆ, *Juss.*

This tree is one of the most beautiful of those indigenous to the United
States, and attains a height of seventy, eighty, or even a hundred feet.
The flowers are yellow and bright red, mixed with green, and upwards
of three inches in diameter. The leaves are ovate at the base, truncato-
bilobate at the end, with one or two lobes on each side, all the lobes acuminate. It is generally distributed, but prefers rich soils. Its bark is
smooth on the branches, cracked and fissured on the stems. The wood
is yellow, hard, but easily wrought, and is employed for numerous purposes, particularly in the construction of houses, and for charcoal. The
Indians often form their canoes of it, for which purpose it is well adapted,
the trunk being of great length and diameter, and the wood light. In
different parts of the United States, it receives the names of Poplar, White
Wood, and Cane Wood.

THE SNOW BIRD.

FRINGILLA HYEMALIS. LINN.

PLATE XIII. MALE AND FEMALE.

THIS is one of our winter visitants from the north, which, along with many others, makes its appearance in Louisiana about the beginning of November, to remain a few months, and again, when spring returns, fly off, to seek in higher latitudes a place in which to nestle and rear its young. So gentle and tame does it become on the least approach of hard weather, that it forms, as it were, a companion to every child. Indeed, there is not an individual in the Union who does not know the little Snow Bird, which, in America, is cherished as the Robin is in Europe. I have seen it fed by persons from the " Old Country," and have always been pleased by such a sight. During fine weather, however, it becomes more timorous, and keeps aloof, resorting to the briar patches and the edges of the fences ; but even then it is easily approached, and will suffer a person on horseback to pass within a few feet of the place where it may be searching for food on the road, or the rails of the fences on which it is perched.

Although the Snow Birds live in little families, consisting of twenty, thirty, or more individuals, they seem always inclined to keep up a certain degree of etiquette among themselves, and will not suffer one of their kind, or indeed any other bird, to come into immediate contact with them. To prevent intrusions of this kind, when a stranger comes too near, their little bills are instantly opened, their wings are extended, their eyes are seen to sparkle, and they emit a repelling sound peculiar to themselves on such occasions.

They are aware of the advantages to be derived by them from larger birds scratching the earth, and in some degree keep company with Partridges, Wild Turkeys, and even Squirrels, for the purpose of picking up such food as these animals may deem beneath their notice. This habit is more easily observed in those which frequent the farm-yards, where the domestic fowls prove regular purveyors to them. The report of a gun, or the unexpected barking of a dog, cause the little flock to rise and perch either on the fences or an adjoining tree, where, however, they remain only for a few minutes, after which they return to their avocations. They are particularly fond of grass-seeds, to procure which they often leap up from the ground, and dexterously seize the bending panicles.

It is a true hopping bird, and performs its little leaps without the least appearance of moving either feet or legs, in which circumstance it resembles the Sparrows. Another of its habits, also indicative of affinity to these birds, is it resorting at night, during cold weather, to stacks of corn or hay, in which it forms a hole that affords a snug retreat during the continuance of such weather, or its recurrence through the winter. In fine weather, however, it prefers the evergreen foliage of the holly, the cedar or low pines, among which to roost. Its flight is easy, and as spring approaches, and its passions become excited by the increased temperature, the males chase each other on wing, when their tails being fully expanded, the white and black colours displayed in them present a quite remarkable contrast.

The migration of these birds is performed by night, as they are seen in a district one day, and have disappeared the next. Early in March, the Snow Bird is scarcely to be seen in Louisiana, but may be followed, as the season advances, retreating towards the mountains of the middle districts, where many remain during the summer and breed. Although I have never had the good fortune to find any of their nests, yet I have seen them rear their young in such places, and particularly in the neighbourhood of the Great Pine Forest, where many persons told me they had often seen their nests.

During the period when the huckleberries are ripe, they feed partially upon them, being found chiefly on the poorest mountain lands, in which that shrub grows most abundantly. I have seen the Snow Birds far up the Arkansas, and in the province of Maine, as well as on our Upper Lakes. I have been told of their congregating so as to form large flocks of a thousand individuals, but have never seen so many together. Their flesh is extremely delicate and juicy, and on this account small strings of them are frequently seen in the New Orleans market, during the short period of their sojourn in that district. Towards the spring, the males have a tolerably agreeable song.

The twig on which you see them is one of the Tupelo, a tree of great magnitude, growing in the low grounds of the state of Louisiana, and on one of which I happened to shoot the pair represented in the plate.

FRINGILLA HYEMALIS, *Linn.* Syst. Nat. Ed. 10. p. 183.—*Ch. Bonaparte*, Synopsis of
    Birds of the United States, p. 109.
EMBERIZA HYEMALIS, *Linn.* Syst. Nat. Ed. 12. p. 308.
SNOW BIRD, FRINGILLA NIVALIS, *Wilson*, American Ornithology, vol. ii. p. 129.
    Pl. 16. fig. 6.

Adult Male.   Plate XIII.   Fig. 1.

Bill short, rather small, conical, very acute; upper mandible a little
broader than the lower, very slightly declinate at the tip, rounded on the
sides, as is the lower, which has the edges inflected and acute; the gap
line straight, not extending to beneath the eye. Nostrils basal, roundish,
concealed by the feathers. Head rather large. Neck short. Body full.
Legs of moderate length, slender; tarsus longer than the middle toe,
covered anteriorly with a few longish scutella; toes scutellate above, free,
the lateral ones nearly equal; claws very slender, greatly compressed,
acute and slightly arched, that of the hind toe little larger.

Plumage soft and blended. Wings shortish, curved, rounded, the
third and fourth quills longest, the second nearly as long, the first little
shorter. Tail long, forked, the lateral feathers curved outwards a little
towards the tip.

Bill white, tinged with red, dark coloured at the tip. Iris blackish-
brown. Feet and claws flesh-coloured. Head, neck, fore part of the
breast, back, wings and upper part of the sides, blackish-grey, deeper on
the head. Quills margined with whitish; tail of the same dark colour as
the wings, excepting the two outer feathers on each side, which are white,
as are the lower breast and abdomen.

Length 6¼ inches, extent of wings 9; beak ½ along the ridge, ½ along
the gap; tarsus ⅘, middle toe ½.

Adult Female.   Plate XIII.   Fig. 2.

The female differs from the male in being of a lighter grey, tinged on
the back with brown. Length 5½ inches.

The Large Tupelo.

Nyssa tomentosa, *Willd.* Sp. Pl. vol. iv. p. 1113. *Pursh*, Flora Americ. p. 177.
———— grandidentata, *Michaux*, Arbr. Forest. de l'Amer. Sept. t. ii. p. 252. Pl. 19.
Polygamia Diœcia, *Linn.* Elœagni, *Juss.*

This species, which occurs in the Southern States only, growing in low and marshy grounds, attains a height of from seventy to eighty feet, with a diameter of eighteen or twenty inches some feet above the ground, although at the very base it is sometimes five or six feet. The leaves are five or six inches in length, elliptical, acuminate, distantly toothed, when young very downy, but finally smooth. The fruit is oblong, and of a dark purple colour. The wood is remarkably light and soft.

THE PRAIRIE WARBLER.

SYLVIA DISCOLOR. VIEILL.

PLATE XIV. MALE AND FEMALE.

THIS little bird has no song, at least I never heard any from it, excepting a delicate soft *whirr,* ejaculated whilst it stands erect on the top of some rank weed or low bush. Its nest, which forms by far the most interesting part of its history, is uncommonly small and delicate. Its eggs I have uniformly found to be four in number, and of a white colour, with a few brownish spots near the larger end. The nest is sometimes attached to three or four blades of tall grass, or hangs between two small sprigs of a slender twig. At first sight, it seems to be formed like that of the Humming Bird, the external parts being composed of delicate grey lichens and other substances, and skins of black caterpillars, and the interior finished with the finest fibres of dried vines. Two broods are reared each season.

In Louisiana I found this bird amongst our cotton fields, where it easily procures the small insects and flies of which its food is entirely composed. It is also found in the prairies along the skirts of the woodlands. I have shot several within a few miles of Philadelphia, in the Jerseys, in a large opening where the woods had been cut down, and were beginning to spring up again. Its flight is light and short, it making an effort to rise to the height of eight or ten yards, and immediately sinking down to the grass or bushes. Whilst on the ground, where it remains a good deal, it searches amongst the leaves slowly and carefully, differing in this respect from all the *true* warblers with which I am acquainted. They go singly, and far apart, scarcely more than three or four being ever seen on an extent of twenty or thirty acres. It is one of the first birds that arrives in spring in Louisiana, and one of the first to depart, being rarely found after the first week of September. I never saw it farther east than on the ridges of the Broad Mountain, about twelve miles from Mauch Chunk; but I have seen it on the Arkansas River, and high up on the Mississippi, as well as along the southern borders of Lake Erie. The young are apt to leave the nest if discovered when unable to fly, and follow their parents through the grass to be fed.

The plant on which a pair of Prairie Warblers are represented, is commonly called Buffalo Grass, and is found all along the edges of our extensive prairies, in the barrens of Kentucky, and in Louisiana, excepting in the swamps, it being more inclined to grow in dry soil and stiff grounds.

SYLVIA DISCOLOR, *Ch. Bonaparte,* Synops. of Birds of the United States, p. 83.
PRAIRIE WARBLER, SYLVIA MINUTA, *Wils.* Americ. Ornith. vol. iii. p. 87. Pl. 25. fig. 4. Male.

Adult Male. Plate XIV. Fig. 1.

Bill of ordinary length, slender, nearly straight, acute, as deep as broad at the base, slightly declinate at the tip. Nostrils oval, basal, lateral, half closed by a membrane. Head rather small, elongated. Neck and body slender. Feet of ordinary length, slender ; tarsus longer than the middle toe, covered anteriorly by a few scutella, the upper long ; toes scutellate above, the inner free, the hind toe of moderate size ; claws slender, compressed, acute, arched.

Plumage soft, blended, tufty. A few short bristles at the base of the upper mandible. Wings of ordinary length, the second quill longest. Tail longish, rounded.

Bill brown, paler at the margin. Iris dark hazel. Feet and claws dark brown. The upper parts are light olive, the back spotted with brownish-red. The under parts, a line over the eye, and the cheeks, dull ochrey yellow, the sides of the neck and breast spotted with brownish-black. Lore, and a curved streak under the eye, black. Quills and tail-feathers deep brown, the former margined with pale yellow ; larger coverts margined and tipped with the same, the second row almost entirely yellow, the three outer tail-feathers with a broad oblique band of white.

Length 5 inches, extent of wings 7 ; beak along the ridge $\frac{1}{3}$, along the gap $\frac{1}{2}$; tarsus $\frac{5}{8}$, middle toe $\frac{1}{2}$.

Adult Female. Plate XIV. Fig. 2.

The female is nearly of the same size, and is coloured in the same manner, but wants the black markings about the eye, and has only two of the lateral tail-feathers white in the middle. The spots on the sides of the neck and breast are also much paler.

Length 4$\frac{3}{4}$.

THE BLUE YELLOW-BACKED WARBLER.

SYLVIA AMERICANA, LATH.

PLATE XV. MALE AND FEMALE.

THIS pretty species enters Louisiana from the south as early as spring appears, at the period when most insects are found closer to the ground, and more about water-courses, than shortly after, when a warmer sun has invited every leaf and blossom to hail the approach of that season when they all become as brilliant as nature intended them to be. The little fellow under your eye is then seen flitting over damp places, such as the edges of ponds, lakes, and rivers, chasing its prey with as much activity and liveliness as any other of the delicate and interesting tribe to which it belongs. It alights on every plant in its way, runs up and down it, picks here and there a small winged insect, and should one, aware of its approach, fly off, pursues it and snatches it in an instant.

I have placed a pair of these Warblers on a handsome species of Iris. This plant grows in the water, and in the neighbourhood of New Orleans, a few miles below that city, where I found it abundantly, and in bloom, in the beginning of April. Several flowers are produced upon the same stem. I have not met with it anywhere else, and the name of *Louisiana Flag* is the one commonly given it.

As soon as the foliage of the forests begins to expand, the Blue Yellow-backed Warbler flies to the tops of the trees, and there remains during the season, gleaning amongst the leaves and branches, in the same active manner as it employed when nearer the ground, not leaving off its quick and short pursuit of small insects on the wing. When on the branches, it frequently raises its body (which is scarcely larger when stripped of its feathers than the first joint of a man's finger) upwards to the full length of its legs and toes, and is thus enabled to seize insects otherwise beyond its reach.

Its flight is that of a true Sylvia. It ascends for a while in a very zigzag manner, and returns suddenly to nearly the same place, as if afraid to encounter the dangers of a prolonged excursion. I do not think it ever flies to the ground. It hops sidewise as well as straight forward, hangs like a Titmouse, and searches the cups of even the smallest flowers for its favourite insects.

I am inclined to think that it raises two broods in a season, having seen and shot the young on the trees, in Louisiana, early in May, and again in the beginning of July. The nest is small, formed of lichens, beautifully arranged on the outside, and lined with the cottony substances found on the edges of different mosses. It is placed in the fork of a small twig, and so far towards the extremity of the branches as to have forced me to cut them ten or fifteen feet from it, to procure one. On drawing in the branch carefully to secure the nest, the male and female always flew toward me, exhibiting all the rage and animosity befitting the occasion. The eggs are pure white, with a few reddish dots at the larger end, and were in two instances four in number. It was several years before I discovered one of these nests, so small are they, and so difficult to be seen from the ground.

This species is found throughout the United States, and may be considered as one of the most beautiful of the birds of those countries. It has no song, but merely a soft, greatly prolonged twitter, repeated at short intervals. It returns southward, out of the Union, in the beginning of October.

SYLVIA AMERICANA, *Lath*. Ind. Ornith. vol. ii. p. 520.—*Ch. Bonaparte*, Synops. of Birds of the United States, p. 33.

YELLOW-BACKED WARBLER, *Lath*. Synops. vol. iv. p. 440.

BLUE YELLOW-BACK WARBLER, SYLVIA PUSILLA, *Wils*. Americ. Ornith. vol. iv. p. 17. Pl. 28. fig. 3. Male.

Adult Male. Plate XV. Fig. 1.

Bill longish, depressed at the base, nearly straight, tapering to a point. Nostrils basal, oval, half concealed by the feathers. Feet of ordinary length, slender; tarsus compressed, covered anteriorly with a few long scutella, acute behind, longer than the middle toe; toes scutellate above, free; claws arched, slender, compressed, acute.

Plumage blended, glossy. Wings longish, little curved, the first quill longest. Tail slightly forked, of ordinary length, the twelve feathers rather narrow and obtuse. A few longish bristles at the base of the upper mandible.

Bill brownish-black above, yellow beneath. Iris dark brown. Feet and claws dusky. Front and lore black. Head and back part of the neck bright rich blue, including the eye, above and beneath which is a slight streak of white. Back yellowish-green; rump pale blue. Quills blackish, margined externally with bright blue, of which colour are the wing-coverts, the tips of the first two rows of which are white, forming two bands of that colour on the wings. Tail-feathers blackish, the outer webs blue, a white spot on the inner webs of the three outer, towards the end. Throat whitish, spotted with yellow; a lunulated blackish spot on the lower neck in front; breast yellow, spotted with orange; the rest of the under parts yellowish, fading into white on the abdomen and under tail coverts.

Length 4½ inches, extent of wings 6½; bill along the ridge ⅓, along the gap ½; tarsus ⅝.

Adult Female. Plate XV. Fig. 2.

Beak and feet of the same colour. Upper parts similarly coloured but paler, the frontal band wanting. Throat, fore neck and breast, yellow, without the orange spots, or black lunule. The other parts as in the male, but fainter.

Length 4 inches.

The Coppery Iris, or Louisiana Flag.

Iris cuprea, *Pursh*, Fl. Amer. vol. i. p. 30.—Triandria Monogynia, *Linn.* Irides. *Juss.*

" Beardless, the stem equal in height to the leaves, which are broadly ensiform, the stigmas linear and short, all the petals emarginate, reflected, and obovate, the inner shorter, the capsules large and hexagonal. Found on the banks of the Mississippi near New Orleans. Flowers of a beautiful copper colour, veined with purple."

THE PRAIRIE.

On my return from the Upper Mississippi, I found myself obliged to cross one of the wide Prairies, which, in that portion of the United States, vary the appearance of the country. The weather was fine, all around me was as fresh and blooming as if it had just issued from the bosom of nature. My napsack, my gun, and my dog, were all I had for baggage and company. But, although well moccassined, I moved slowly along, attracted by the brilliancy of the flowers, and the gambols of the fawns around their dams, to all appearance as thoughtless of danger as I felt myself.

My march was of long duration; I saw the sun sinking beneath the horizon long before I could perceive any appearance of woodland, and nothing in the shape of man had I met with that day. The track which I followed was only an old Indian trace, and as darkness overshaded the prairie, I felt some desire to reach at least a copse, in which I might lie down to rest. The Night-hawks were skimming over and around me, attracted by the buzzing wings of the beetles which form their food, and the distant howling of wolves, gave me some hope that I should soon arrive at the skirts of some woodland.

I did so, and almost at the same instant a fire-light attracting my eye, I moved towards it, full of confidence that it proceeded from the camp of some wandering Indians. I was mistaken:—I discovered by its glare that it was from the hearth of a small log cabin, and that a tall figure passed and repassed between it and me, as if busily engaged in household arrangements.

I reached the spot, and presenting myself at the door, asked the tall figure, which proved to be a woman, if I might take shelter under her roof for the night. Her voice was gruff, and her attire negligently thrown about her. She answered in the affirmative. I walked in, took a wooden stool, and quietly seated myself by the fire. The next object that attracted my notice was a finely formed young Indian, resting his head between his hands, with his elbows on his knees. A long bow rested against the log wall near him, while a quantity of arrows and two or three raccoon skins lay at his feet. He moved not; he apparently breathed not. Accustomed to the habits of the Indians, and knowing that they pay little attention

F

to the approach of civilized strangers (a circumstance which in some countries is considered as evincing the apathy of their character), I addressed
him in French, a language not unfrequently partially known to the people
in that neighbourhood.   He raised his head, pointed to one of his eyes
with his finger, and gave me a significant glance with the other.   His face
was covered with blood.   The fact was, that an hour before this, as he
was in the act of discharging an arrow at a raccoon in the top of a tree, the
arrow had split upon the cord, and sprung back with such violence into
his right eye as to destroy it for ever.

Feeling hungry, I inquired what sort of fare I might expect.   Such
a thing as a bed was not to be seen, but many large untanned bear and
buffalo hides lay piled in a corner.   I drew a fine time-piece from my
breast, and told the woman that it was late, and that I was fatigued.
She had espied my watch, the richness of which seemed to operate upon
her feelings with electric quickness.   She told me that there was plenty
of venison and jerked buffalo meat, and that on removing the ashes I
should find a cake.   But my watch had struck her fancy, and her curiosity had to be gratified by an immediate sight of it.   I took off the gold
chain that secured it from around my neck, and presented it to her.   She
was all ecstacy, spoke of its beauty, asked me its value, and put the chain
round her brawny neck, saying how happy the possession of such a watch
should make her.   Thoughtless, and, as I fancied myself, in so retired a
spot, secure, I paid little attention to her talk or her movements.   I
helped my dog to a good supper of venison, and was not long in satisfying the demands of my own appetite.

The Indian rose from his seat, as if in extreme suffering.   He passed
and repassed me several times, and once pinched me on the side so violently, that the pain nearly brought forth an exclamation of anger.   I
looked at him.   His eye met mine ; but his look was so forbidding, that
it struck a chill into the more nervous part of my system.   He again
seated himself, drew his butcher-knife from its greasy scabbard, examined
its edge, as I would do that of a razor suspected dull, replaced it, and
again taking his tomahawk from his back, filled the pipe of it with tobac-
co, and sent me expressive glances whenever our hostess chanced to have
her back toward us.

Never until that moment had my senses been awakened to the
danger which I now suspected to be about me.   I returned glance for

glance to my companion, and rested well assured that, whatever enemies I might have, he was not of their number.

I asked the woman for my watch, wound it up, and under pretence of wishing to see how the weather might probably be on the morrow, took up my gun, and walked out of the cabin. I slipped a ball into each barrel, scraped the edges of my flints, renewed the primings, and returning to the hut, gave a favourable account of my observations. I took a few bear-skins, made a pallet of them, and calling my faithful dog to my side, lay down, with my gun close to my body, and in a few minutes was, to all appearance, fast asleep.

A short time had elapsed, when some voices were heard, and from the corner of my eyes I saw two athletic youths making their entrance, bearing a dead stag on a pole. They disposed of their burden, and asking for whisky, helped themselves freely to it. Observing me and the wounded Indian, they asked who I was, and why the devil that rascal (meaning the Indian, who, they knew, understood not a word of English) was in the house. The mother—for so she proved to be, bade them speak less loudly, made mention of my watch, and took them to a corner, where a conversation took place, the purport of which it required little shrewdness in me to guess. I tapped my dog gently. He moved his tail, and with indescribable pleasure I saw his fine eyes alternately fixed on me and raised towards the trio in the corner. I felt that he perceived danger in my situation. The Indian exchanged a last glance with me.

The lads had eaten and drunk themselves into such condition, that I already looked upon them as *hors de combat*; and the frequent visits of the whisky bottle to the ugly mouth of their dam I hoped would soon reduce her to a like state. Judge of my astonishment, reader, when I saw this incarnate fiend take a large carving-knife, and go to the grindstone to whet its edge. I saw her pour the water on the turning machine, and watched her working away with the dangerous instrument, until the cold sweat covered every part of my body, in despite of my determination to defend myself to the last. Her task finished, she walked to her reeling sons, and said, " There, that'll soon settle him ! Boys, kill you————, and then for the watch."

I turned, cocked my gun-locks silently, touched my faithful companion, and lay ready to start up and shoot the first who might attempt my life. The moment was fast approaching, and that night might have been

my last in this world, had not Providence made preparations for my
rescue. All was ready. The infernal hag was advancing slowly, probably contemplating the best way of despatching me, whilst her sons
should be engaged with the Indian. I was several times on the eve of
rising, and shooting her on the spot :—but she was not to be punished
thus. The door was suddenly opened, and there entered two stout travellers, each with a long rifle on his shoulder. I bounced up on my feet,
and making them most heartily welcome, told them how well it was for
me that they should have arrived at that moment. The tale was told in
a minute. The drunken sons were secured, and the woman, in spite of
her defence and vociferations, shared the same fate. The Indian fairly
danced with joy, and gave us to understand that, as he could not sleep for
pain, he would watch over us. You may suppose we slept much less than
we talked. The two strangers gave me an account of their once having
been themselves in a somewhat similar situation. Day came, fair and rosy,
and with it the punishment of our captives.

They were now quite sobered. Their feet were unbound, but their
arms were still securely tied. We marched them into the woods off the
road, and having used them as Regulators were wont to use such delinquents, we set fire to the cabin, gave all the skins and implements to the
young Indian warrior, and proceeded, well pleased, towards the settlements.

During upwards of twenty-five years, when my wanderings extended
to all parts of our country, this was the only time at which my life was
in danger from my fellow creatures. Indeed, so little risk do travellers
run in the United States, that no one born there ever dreams of any to be
encountered on the road ; and I can only account for this occurrence by
supposing that the inhabitants of the cabin were not Americans.

Will you believe, good-natured reader, that not many miles from the
place where this adventure happened, and where fifteen years ago, no habitation belonging to civilized man was expected, and very few ever seen,
large roads are now laid out, cultivation has converted the woods into
fertile fields, taverns have been erected, and much of what we Americans
call comfort is to be met with. So fast does improvement proceed in our
abundant and free country.

THE GREAT-FOOTED HAWK.

FALCO PEREGRINUS, GMEL.

PLATE XVI. ADULT MALE AND FEMALE.

THE French and Spaniards of Louisiana have designated all the species of the genus Falco by the name of " *Mangeurs de Poulets ;*" and the farmers in other portions of the Union have bestowed upon them, according to their size, the appellations of " Hen Hawk," " Chicken Hawk," " Pigeon Hawk," &c. This mode of naming these rapacious birds is doubtless natural enough, but it displays little knowledge of the characteristic manners of the species. No bird can better illustrate the frequent inaccuracy of the names bestowed by ignorant persons than the present, of which on referring to the plate, you will see a pair enjoying themselves over a brace of ducks of different species. Very likely, were tame ducks as plentiful on the plantations in our States, as wild ducks are on our rivers, lakes and estuaries, these hawks might have been named by some of our settlers " *Mangeurs de Canards.*"

Look at these two pirates eating their *déjeuné à la fourchette*, as it were, congratulating each other on the savouriness of the food in their grasp. One might think them real epicures, but they are in fact true gluttons. The male has obtained possession of a Green-winged Teal, while his mate has procured a Gadwal Duck. Their appetites are equal to their reckless daring, and they well deserve the name of " Pirates," which I have above bestowed upon them.

The Great-footed Hawk, or Peregrine Falcon, is now frequently to be met with in the United States, but within my remembrance it was a very scarce species in America. I can well recollect the time when, if I shot one or two individuals of the species in the course of a whole winter, I thought myself a fortunate mortal; whereas of late years I have shot two in one day, and perhaps a dozen in the course of a winter. It is quite impossible for me to account for this increase in their number, the more so that our plantations have equally increased, and we have now three gunners for every one that existed twenty years ago, and all of them ready to destroy a hawk of any kind whenever an occasion presents itself.

The flight of this bird is of astonishing rapidity. It is scarcely ever seen sailing, unless after being disappointed in its attempt to secure the prey which it has been pursuing, and even at such times it merely rises with a broad spiral circuit, to attain a sufficient elevation to enable it to reconnoitre a certain space below. It then emits a cry much resembling that of the Sparrow Hawk, but greatly louder, like that of the European Kestrel, and flies off swiftly in quest of plunder. The search is often performed with a flight resembling that of the tame pigeon, until perceiving an object, it redoubles its flappings, and pursues the fugitive with a rapidity scarcely to be conceived. Its turnings, windings and cuttings through the air are now surprising. It follows and nears the timorous quarry at every turn and back-cutting which the latter attempts. Arrived within a few feet of the prey, the Falcon is seen protruding his powerful legs and talons to their full stretch. His wings are for a moment almost closed; the next instant he grapples the prize, which, if too weighty to be carried off directly, he forces obliquely toward the ground, sometimes a hundred yards from where it was seized, to kill it, and devour it on the spot. Should this happen over a large extent of water, the Falcon drops his prey, and sets off in quest of another. On the contrary, should it not prove too heavy, the exulting bird carries it off to a sequestered and secure place. He pursues the smaller Ducks, Water-hens, and other swimming birds, and if they are not quick in diving, seizes them, and rises with them from the water. I have seen this Hawk come at the report of a gun, and carry off a Teal not thirty steps distant from the sportsman who had killed it, with a daring assurance as surprising as unexpected. This conduct has been observed by many individuals, and is a characteristic trait of the species. The largest duck that I have seen this bird attack and grapple with on the wing is the Mallard.

The Great-footed Hawk does not however content himself with waterfowl. He is generally seen following the flocks of Pigeons and even Blackbirds, causing great terror in their ranks, and forcing them to perform various aerial evolutions to escape the grasp of his dreaded talons. For several days I watched one of them that had taken a particular fancy to some tame pigeons, to secure which it went so far as to enter their house at one of the holes, seize a bird, and issue by another hole in an instant, causing such terror among the rest as to render me fearful that they would abandon the place. However, I fortunately shot the depredator.

They occasionally feed on dead fish that have floated to the shores or sand bars. I saw several of them thus occupied while descending the Mississippi on a journey undertaken expressly for the purpose of observing and procuring different specimens of birds, and which lasted four months, as I followed the windings of that great river, floating down it only a few miles daily. During that period, I and my companion counted upwards of fifty of these Hawks, and killed several, among which was the female represented in the plate now before you, and which was found to contain in its stomach bones of birds, a few downy feathers, the gizzard of a Teal, and the eyes and many scales of a fish. It was shot on on the 26th December 1820. The ovary contained numerous eggs, two of which were as large as pease.

Whilst in quest of food, the Great-footed Hawk will frequently alight on the highest dead branch of a tree in the immediate neighbourhood of such wet or marshy grounds as the Common Snipe resorts to by preference. His head is seen moving in short starts, as if he were counting every little space below; and while so engaged, the moment he spies a Snipe, down he darts like an arrow, making a rustling noise with his wings that may be heard several hundred yards off, seizes the Snipe, and flies away to some near wood to devour it.

It is a cleanly bird, in respect to feeding. No sooner is the prey dead than the Falcon turns its belly upward, and begins to pluck it with his bill, which he does very expertly, holding it meantime quite fast in his talons; and as soon as a portion is cleared of feathers, tears the flesh in large pieces, and swallows it with great avidity. If it is a large bird, he leaves the refuse parts, but, if small, swallows the whole in pieces. Should he be approached by an enemy, he rises with it and flies off into the interior of the woods, or if he happens to be in a meadow, to some considerable distance, he being more wary at such times than when he has alighted on a tree.

The Great-footed Hawk is a heavy, compact, and firmly built bird for its size, and when arrived at maturity, extremely muscular, with very tough flesh. The plumage differs greatly according to age. I have seen it vary in different individuals, from the deepest chocolate-brown to light grey. Their grasp is so firm, that should one be hit while perched, and not shot quite dead, it will cling to the branch until life has departed.

Like most other Hawks, this is a solitary bird, excepting during the breeding season, at the beginning of which it is seen in pairs. Their season of breeding is so very early, that it might be said to be in winter. I have seen the male caressing the female as early as the first days of December.

This species visits Louisiana during the winter months only; for although I have observed it mating then, it generally disappears a few days after, and in a fortnight later none can be seen. It is scarce in the Middle States, where, as well as in the Southern Districts, it lives along water-courses, and in the neighbourhood of the shores of the sea and inland lakes. I should think that they breed in the United States, having shot a pair in the month of August near the Falls of Niagara. It is extremely tenacious of life, and if not wounded in the wings, though mortally so in the body, it flies to the last gasp, and does not fall until life is extinct. I never saw one of them attack a quadruped, although I have frequently seen them perched within sight of squirrels, which I thought they might easily have secured, had they been so inclined.

Once when nearing the coast of England, being then about a hundred and fifty miles distant from it, in the month of July, I obtained a pair of these birds, which had come on board our vessel, and had been shot there. I examined them with care, and found no difference between them and those which I had shot in America. They are at present scarce in England, where I have seen only a few. In London, some individuals of the species resort to the cupola of St Paul's Cathedral, and the towers of Westminster Abbey, to roost, and probably to breed. I have seen them depart from these places at day dawn, and return in the evening.

The achievements of this species are well known in Europe, where it is even at the present day trained for the chase. Whilst on a visit at Dalmahoy, the seat of the Earl of Morton, near Edinburgh, I had the pleasure of seeing a pair of these birds hooded, and with small brass bells on their legs, in excellent training. They were the property of that nobleman.

These birds sometimes roost in the hollows of trees. I saw one resorting for weeks every night to a hole in a dead sycamore, near Louisville in Kentucky. It generally came to the place a little before sunset, alighted on the dead branches, and in a short time after flew into the hollow, where it spent the night, and from whence I saw it issuing at dawn.

I have known them also retire for the same purpose to the crevices of high cliffs, on the banks of Green River in the same state. One winter, when I had occasion to cross the Homochitta River, in the State of Mississippi, I observed these Hawks in greater numbers than I had ever before seen.

Many persons believe that this Hawk, and some others, never drink any other fluid than the blood of their victims; but this is an error. I have seen them alight on sand bars, walk to the edge of them, immerse their bills nearly up to the eyes in the water, and drink in a continued manner, as Pigeons are known to do.

FALCO PEREGRINUS, *Gmel.* Syst. vol. L p. 272.—*Lath.* Ind. Ornith. vol. L p. 33.—
    Ch. Bonaparte, Synopsis of Birds of the United States, p. 27.
PEREGRINE FALCON, *Lath.* Synopsis, vol. L p. 73, and Suppl. p. 18.
GREAT-FOOTED HAWK, *Wilson,* Americ. Ornith. vol. ix. p. 120, Pl. 76.

Adult Male. Plate XVI. Fig. 1.

Bill shortish, as broad as deep, the sides convex, the dorsal outline convex from the base; upper mandible cerate, the edges blunt, slightly inflected, with a process towards the curvature on either side with a hollow, the tip trigonal, descending obliquely, acute; lower mandible involute at the edges, truncate at the end, with a notch near it, corresponding to the process above. Nostrils round, lateral, with a soft papilla in the centre, connected with the upper edge. Head rather large and round Neck shortish. Body ovate, anteriorly broad. Legs robust, short roundish; tarsi covered all round with imbricated scales, the anterior largest, broad, and subhexagonal, the posterior small and rounded. Toes robust, covered above with broad scutella, scabrous and tubercular below; middle and outer toes connected by a membrane; claws roundish, strong and curved, acute, marginate beneath.

Plumage ordinary, compact, imbricated. Feathers of the back rounded, of the neck and breast anteriorly broad and rounded; of the sides long, all acuminate; of the thighs long and rounded. Space between the bill and eye covered only with bristly feathers. Feathers of the forehead with bristly points. Wings long; primary quills moderately broad, attenuated; first quill notched near the end; secondaries curved inwards, broad, obtuse, with an acumen. Tail-feathers broadish, rounded, the tail rather long, and nearly even.

Bill blackish-blue at the tip, pale green at the base, cere oil-green; bare orbital space orange. Iris hazel. Feet lemon-yellow; claws brownish-black. Head and hind neck greyish-black, tinged with blue; the rest of the upper parts dark bluish-grey, indistinctly barred with deep brown. Quills blackish-brown, the inner webs marked with transverse elliptical spots of reddish-white. Tail greyish-brown, marked with about twelve bars, the last of which is broad, the rest diminishing in size and intensity of tint. Throat and fore-neck white; a broad band of blackish-blue from the angle of the mouth downwards; cheeks whitish-grey; sides, breast and thighs reddish-white, transversely marked with dark brown spots in longitudinal series. Under wing feathers whitish, transversely barred.

Length 16½ inches, extent of wings 30; bill 1½ along the ridge; tarsus 1⅞, middle toe 2¼.

The figure represents a male in full vigour. When the bird gets older, the colours of the upper parts acquire a lighter tint in the male, and sometimes the back is ash-grey; but in the female, they gradually assume a deeper hue.

Adult Female. Plate XVI. Fig. 2.

The colour of the upper parts is more brown; tips of the secondary quills more or less whitish, tail tipped with brownish-white; throat and fore neck yellowish-white; the latter longitudinally marked with gutti-form spots; general colour beneath yellowish-white, marked with longitudinal broad spots. Vent-feathers reddish; under tail-coverts marked with narrow bars.

Length 19½ inches, extent of wings 36; beak 1½ along the ridge; tarsus 2, middle toe 3¼.

THE CAROLINA TURTLE DOVE.

COLUMBA CAROLINENSIS, LINN.

PLATE XVII. MALE AND FEMALE.

I HAVE tried, kind reader, to give you a faithful representation of two as gentle pairs of Turtles as ever cooed their loves in the green woods. I have placed them on a branch of Stuartia, which you see ornamented with a profusion of white blossoms, emblematic of purity and chastity.

Look at the female, as she assiduously sits on her eggs, embosomed among the thick foliage, receiving food from the bill of her mate, and listening with delight to his assurances of devoted affection. Nothing is wanting to render the moment as happy as could be desired by any couple on a similar occasion.

On the branch above, a love scene is just commencing. The female, still coy and undetermined, seems doubtful of the truth of her lover, and virgin-like resolves to put his sincerity to the test, by delaying the gratification of his wishes. She has reached the extremity of the branch, her wings and tail are already opening, and she will fly off to some more sequestered spot, where, if her lover should follow her with the same assiduous devotion, they will doubtless become as blessed as the pair beneath them.

The Dove announces the approach of spring. Nay, she does more :— she forces us to forget the chilling blasts of winter, by the soft and melancholy sound of her cooing. Her heart is already so warmed and so swelled by the ardour of her passion, that it feels as ready to expand as the buds on the trees are, under the genial influence of returning heat.

The flight of this bird is extremely rapid, and of long duration. Whenever it starts from a tree or the ground, on being unexpectedly approached, its wings produce a whistling noise, heard at a considerable distance. On such occasions, it frequently makes several curious windings through the air, as if to prove its capability of efficient flight. It seldom rises far above the trees, and as seldom passes through dense woods or forests, but prefers following their margins, or flying about the fences and fields. Yet, during spring, and particularly whilst the female is sitting on her eggs, the male rises as if about to ascend to a great height in the air, flapping his wings, but all of a sudden comes downwards again, describing a large circle, and sailing smoothly with wings and tail expanded, until in this manner he alights on the tree where his mate is, or on one very near it. These manœuvres are frequently repeated during the days of incubation, and occasionally when the male bird is courting the female. No sooner do they alight than they jerk out their tail in a very graceful manner, and balance their neck and head. Their migrations are not so extensive as those of the Wild Pigeon *(Columba migratoria)* ; nor are they performed in such numbers, two hundred and fifty or three hundred doves together being considered a large flock.

On the ground, along the fences, or on the branches of trees, the Carolina Turtle walks with great ease and grace, frequently jerking its tail. It is able to run with some swiftness when searching for food in places where it is scarce. It seldom bathes, but drinks by swallowing the water in long draughts, with the bill deeply immersed, frequently up to the eyes.

They breed in every portion of the United States that I have visited, and according to the temperature of different localities, rear either one or two broods in the season. In Louisiana, they lay eggs early in April, and sometimes in the month of March, and have there two broods. In the State of Connecticut, they seldom begin to lay before the middle of May, and as seldom have more than one brood. On the borders of Lake Superior, they are still later. They lay two eggs of a pure white colour, and having some degree of translucency. They make their nest in any kind of tree, on horizontal branches or twigs. It is formed of a few dry sticks, so loosely put together as to appear hardly sufficient to keep the eggs or young from falling.

The roosting places which the Carolina Turtles prefer are among the long grasses found growing in abandoned fields, at the foot of dry stalks of maize, or on the edges of meadows, although they occasionally resort to the dead foliage of trees, as well as that of different species of evergreens. But in all these places they rise and fly at the approach of man, however dark the night may be, which proves that the power of sight which they then possess is very great. They seldom place themselves very near each other when roosting on the ground, but sometimes the individuals of a flock appear diffused pretty equally over a whole field. In this particular, they greatly differ from our Common Wild Pigeon, which settles in compact masses on the limbs of trees during the night. The Doves, however, like the Pigeons, are fond of returning to the same roosting grounds from considerable distances. A few individuals sometimes mix with the Wild Pigeons, as do the latter sometimes with the Doves.

The Turtle Dove may with propriety be considered more as a gleaner than as a reaper of the husbandman's fields, scarcely ever committing any greater depredation than the picking up a few grains in seed-time, after which it prefers resorting to those fields from which the grain has been cut and removed. It is a hardy bird, and stands the severest winters of our Middle States, where some remain the whole year.

The flesh of these birds is remarkably fine, when they are obtained young and in the proper season. Such birds become extremely fat, are tender and juicy, and in flavour equal in the estimation of some of my friends, as well as in my own, to that of the Snipe or even the Woodcock; but as taste in such matters depends much on circumstances, and perhaps on the whim of individuals, I would advise you, reader, to try for yourself. These birds require good shooting to bring them down, when on wing, for they fly with great swiftness, and not always in a direct manner. It is seldom that more than one can be killed at a shot when they are flying, and rarely more than two or three when on the ground, on account of their natural propensity to keep apart.

In winter, they approach the farm-houses, feed among the Poultry, Sparrows, Grakles, and many other birds, and appear very gentle; but no sooner are they frequently disturbed or shot at, than they become extremely shy. When raised from the nest, they are easily tamed. I have even known some instances of their breeding in confinement. When caught in traps and cooped, they feed freely, and soon become fat, when they are excellent for the table.

When shot, or taken alive in the hand, this and our other species of Pigeon, lose the feathers on the slightest touch, a circumstance peculiar to the genus, and to certain gallinaceous birds.

The *Stuartia Malacodendron,* on which I have placed the two pairs alluded to at the commencement of this article, is a tree of small height, which grows in rich grounds at the foot of hills not far from water-courses. The wood is brittle and useless, the flower destitute of scent, but extremely agreeable to the eye. Little clusters of twenty or thirty of these trees are dispersed over the southernmost of the United States. I have never met with it in the Middle, Western or Northern Districts.

COLUMBA CAROLINENSIS, *Linn.* Syst. Nat. vol. i. p. 286.—*Lath.* Ind. Ornith. vol. ii. p. 613.—*Ch. Bonaparte,* Synops. of Birds of the United States, p. 119.

CAROLINA PIGEON, *Lath.* Syn. vol. iv. p. 663.

CAROLINA PIGEON, OR TURTLE DOVE, COLUMBA CAROLINENSIS, *Wils.* Amer. Ornith. vol. v. p. 91. Pl. xliii. fig. 1.

Adult Male.   Plate XVII. Fig. 1, 1.

Bill straight, of ordinary length, rather slender, broader than deep at the base, with a tumid fleshy covering, compressed towards the end, rather obtuse; upper mandible slightly declinate at the tip; edges involute. Head small. Neck slender. Body rather full. Legs short and strong; tarsus covered anteriorly with scutella, rather rounded; toes scutellate, slightly webbed at the base; claws short, depressed, obtuse.

Plumage compact on the back, blended and soft on the head, neck and under parts. Wings long, second quill longest. Tail wedge-shaped, long, of fourteen feathers, the middle ones tapering, the rest obtuse.

Bill blackish, at the base carmine-purple. Iris hazel; orbit greenish-blue. Feet carmine-purple; claws dusky. Crown of the head, and upper part of the neck, bright greenish-blue; the rest of the upper parts, including the wing-coverts, light yellowish-brown, tinged with light blue, of which colour are the edges of the wings, and the outer webs of the quills towards the base. Some of the proximal wing-coverts spotted with black. Forehead, and sides of the head brownish-yellow, which colour predominates on the under parts, the breast and neck tinged with blue, and the abdomen and under tail-coverts paler. Quills dusky, margined externally with whitish, the last secondaries light brown and spotted with black. The two middle tail-feathers, and the outer webs of the next five on each side like the back; all the feathers, excepting the middle ones, have a spot of black about an inch from their extremity, the space between which and the base is bright greenish-blue, that beyond it being paler and tinged with brown, excepting in the three outer feathers, where it is white, as is the outer web of the outermost.

Length 12 inches, extent of wings 17; bill along the ridge $\frac{7}{12}$, along the gap $\frac{3}{4}$.

Adult Female.   Plate XVII. Fig. 2, 2.

The female is somewhat duller in the tints of the plumage; the bright blue of the head is wanting, that part being coloured like the back; the neck and breast have less blue, and the white of the tail is less pure.

Length 11 inches, extent of wings 15½; bill as in the male.

THE WHITE-FLOWERED STUARTIA.

STUARTIA MALACODENDRON, *Willd.* Sp. Pl. vol. iii. p. 840. STUARTIA VIRGINICA, *Pursh*, Fl. Amer. vol. ii. p. 451.—MONADELPHIA POLYANDRIA, *Linn.*

A small tree, with smooth spreading branches; ovate-acute leaves, generally entire at the margins; axillar flowers, which are solitary, or two together; large white corollas, of five rounded petals, and reddish-purple stamina. The leaves vary in being sometimes serrated, and more or less downy. It flowers from June to September.

BEWICK'S WREN.

TROGLODYTES BEWICKII.

PLATE XVIII. MALE.

THE bird represented under the name of Bewick's Wren I shot on the 19th October 1821, about five miles from St Francisville, in the State of Louisiana. It was standing as nearly as can be represented in the position in which you now see it, and upon the prostrate trunk of a tree not far from a fence. My drawing of it was made on the spot. Another individual was shot a few days after, by a young friend, JOSEPH R. MASON, who accompanied me on my rambles. In the month of November 1829, I had the pleasure of meeting with another of the same species, about fifteen miles from the place above mentioned, and as it was near the house at which I was then on a visit, I refrained from killing it, in order to observe its habits. For several days, during which I occasionally saw it, it moved along the bars of the fences, with its tail generally erect, looking from the bar on which it stood towards the one next above, and caught spiders and other insects, as it ran along from one pannel of the fence to another in quick succession, now and then uttering a low *twitter*, the only sound which I heard it emit. It occasionally hopped sidewise, now with its head towards me, and again in the contrary direction, at times descending to the ground, to inspect the lowest bar, but only for a few moments. At other times, it would fly to a peach or apple-tree close to the fence, ascend to its top branches, always with hopping movements, and, as if about to sing, would for an instant raise its head, and lower its tail, but without giving utterance to any musical notes. It would then return to the fence, and continue its avocations as already described. I shot the bird, and have it preserved in spirits.

In shape, colour and movements, it nearly resembles the Great Carolina Wren, and forms a kind of link between that bird and the House Wren, an account of which you will find in this volume. It has not the quickness of motion, nor the liveliness, of either of these birds. Where it comes from, and whither it goes to breed, are quite unknown to me.

I have honoured this species with the name of BEWICK, a person too

1

well known for his admirable talents as an engraver on wood, and for his beautiful work on the Birds of Great Britain, to need any eulogy of mine. I enjoyed the pleasure of a personal acquaintance with that gentleman, and found him at all times a most agreeable, kind, and benevolent friend.

The little twig on which the Wren is perched, is from the tree commonly called the Iron-wood Tree, a species of Elm, the wood of which is very hard and of close texture. The branches, and sometimes the stem, are ornamented with longitudinal expansions, resembling cork in their nature, but much harder.

TROGLODYTES BEWICKII.

Adult Male. Plate XVIII.

Bill nearly as long as the head, subulato-conical, acute, slightly arched, compressed. Mandibles of equal breadth, with acute margins, the gap line a little arched, and slightly deflected at the base. Nostrils basal, oval, half closed by a membrane. Feet longish, proportionally rather robust; tarsus anteriorly scutellate, compressed, acute behind, longer than the middle toe; toes free, scutellate above, the lateral ones nearly equal, the posterior long; claws slender, compressed, acute, arched, that of the hind toe much larger.

Plumage rather compact above, blended beneath. Wings short, very convex, rounded; first quill short, third and fourth longest. Tail erect, long, of ten feathers, much rounded, the outer feather not more than half the length of the middle one, all rounded at the end.

Bill blackish-brown above, pale blue beneath. Iris brown. Feet and claws pale brown. The general colour of the upper parts is rusty brown, that of the lower greyish-blue. Quills and wing-coverts barred with rusty brown and black, as are the two middle tail-feathers. Outer web of the lateral tail-feather, and the terminal portion of that of the others, whitish, barred with black, their middle parts black, toward the base barred with rusty brown. A line of pale brownish-yellow extending from the upper mandible, over the eye, to half way down the neck. The rump feathers white towards their base, with central spots.

Length 5 inches, extent of wings $6\frac{1}{2}$; beak along the ridge $\frac{1}{2}$, along the gap $\frac{2}{3}$; tarsus $\frac{7}{12}$, middle toe $\frac{1}{2}$, hind toe $\frac{7}{12}$.

THE IRON-WOOD TREE, OR WAHOO.

ULMUS ALATA, *Pursh.* Flor. Amer. vol. i. p. 200.   *Mich.* Arbr. Forest. de l'Amer.
Sept. vol. vi. p. 275. Pl. 5.—PENTANDRIA DIGYNIA, *Linn.*   AMENTACEÆ, *Juss.*

Twigs winged on two opposite sides with a corky substance ; leaves
oblongo-oval, acute, nearly equal at the base ; fruit downy and ciliated.
This species of Elm occurs only in the Southern States, where it grows
by the sides of rivers and in marshes.   It attains a height of from thirty
to forty feet.

THE LOUISIANA WATER THRUSH.

TURDUS LUDOVICIANUS.

PLATE XIX. MALE.

MUCH and justly as the song of the Nightingale is admired, I am inclined, after having often listened to it, to pronounce it in no degree superior to that of the Louisiana Water Thrush. The notes of the latter bird are as powerful and mellow, and at times as varied.

This bird is a resident of the low lands of the States of Louisiana and Mississippi, and is to be found at all seasons in the deepest and most swampy of our cane brakes, from which its melodies are heard to a considerable distance, its voice being nearly as loud as that of the Wood Thrush. The bird may be observed perched on a low bough scarcely higher than the tops of the canes, in an erect attitude, swelling its throat, and repeating several times in succession sounds so approaching the whole two octaves of a good piano-forte, as almost to induce the hearer to imagine that the keys of that instrument are used on the occasion. The bird begins on the upper key, and progressively passes from one to another, until it reaches the base note, this last frequently being lost when there is the least agitation in the air. Its song is heard even in the winter, when the weather is calm and warm.

I have taken the liberty of naming this first songster of our groves after the country which has afforded me my greatest pleasures, not, however, as I trust I shall prove in the sequel, without having assured myself that in *habits*, and somewhat in colour, it differs from its kinsman the Common Water Thrush.

The Common Water Thrush is at all times, and in every situation, shy even to wildness. The Louisiana Water Thrush is so gentle and unsuspicious as to allow a person to approach within a few yards of it. The species met with in the Eastern and Northern Districts during the spring months only, has its feet of a clear and transparent flesh-colour, and its tail even. The Southern bird, on the contrary, has the feet of a deep bluish-brown, and the tail forked. Never have I seen it wade through water, although it is always near and over it; while in the bird of the Northern Districts this is a prominent habit. I may add, that I never heard the latter species sing, but merely utter a single smart *twit*, when started by surprise. It moreover frequently feeds on minute water-insects, none of which I have ever been able to discover on dissecting the present species.

The flight of this bird is easy, and continued amongst the trees, just above the canes, or closer over the ground, when it is passing along their skirts, gliding smoothly through the air. When alighted, its body is continually vibrating, the tail being at the same time alternately jerked out and closed again. It walks prettily along the branches, or on the ground, but never *hops*. It feeds on insects and larvæ, often pursuing the former on wing, as well as on the ground, yet in seizing them it does not produce the clicking sound heard from the bill of Flycatchers.

I think its proper station in a general system would be between the Golden-crowned Thrush and the Water Thrush. Its location, however, I leave to the consideration of better ornithologists than myself.

The nest of this species is commenced in the first days of April. I may here remark, that I am not aware that the Common Water Thrush breeds in the United States. It is placed at the foot and amongst the roots of a tree, or by the side of a decayed log, and is so easily discovered at times that my eyes have once or twice been attracted by it, whilst walking about in search of something else. The outer parts are formed of dry leaves and mosses, the inner of fine grasses, with a few hairs, or the dried fibres of the Spanish Moss, which so much resemble horse-hair as scarcely to be distinguished from it. The female lays four or five eggs, and takes fourteen days to hatch them. When disturbed on her nest at an early period of incubation, she merely flies off; but if discovered towards the conclusion of that period, she is seen tumbling and rolling about, spreading her wings and tail, as if in the last agonies of despair, uttering all the while a most piteous tone, to entice the intruder to follow her.

The young leave the nest in about ten days, and follow the parent from place to place, on the ground, where they are fed until able to fly. I have not been able to ascertain whether this bird rears more than one brood in a season, but am inclined to believe that it does not. The eggs are flesh-coloured, sprinkled with darker red on the large end.

During winter, this bird becomes so plump as to be a pure mass of fat, and furnishes extremely delicate eating. I have never seen this species farther eastward than Georgia, nor higher on the Ohio than the cane brakes about Henderson.

The plant on which I have placed a male (the sexes being so nearly alike as to offer no external distinctive characters) is commonly called the Indian Turnip. It grows abundantly in the places frequented by this bird. The root, which is like a small potato, is extremely pungent.

TURDUS LUDOVICIANUS.

Adult Male. Plate XIX.

Bill of ordinary length, straight, slender, tapering to a point, broadish at the base, compressed toward the end ; upper mandible with the edges sharp, and destitute of a notch. Nostrils basal, rounded, half closed by a membrane. Feet of ordinary length, rather slender ; tarsus a little longer than the middle toe ; toes free ; claws slender, much compressed, arched, acute, the hind one not much larger than that of the middle toe.

Plumage ordinary, soft, slightly glossy ; a few bristles at the base of the upper mandible. Wings of ordinary length ; first quill longest. Tail shortish, a little notched, the feathers rather obtuse.

Bill deep brown above, black at the tip, flesh-coloured beneath. Iris deep brown. Feet and claws brown, tinged with blue. The general colour of the upper parts is dull greenish-brown, that of the under parts yellowish-white. A streak of the latter colour over the eye, from the base of the upper mandible, and another from the base of the lower, curving upwards behind the ear-coverts. Fore-neck and breast marked with sagittiform spots of blackish-brown ; sides under the wings streaked with the same colour.

Length 5¾ inches, extent of wings 9½ ; bill along the ridge ½, along the gap ¾ ; tarsus ⅞.

The female, as has been said, hardly differs from the male in appearance.

THE INDIAN TURNIP.

ARUM TRIPHYLLUM, *Willd.* Sp. Pl. vol. iv. p. 480. *Pursh,* Flor. Amer. vol. i. p. 399. —POLYANDRIA POLYGYNIA, *Linn.* AROIDEÆ, *Juss.*

Somewhat caulescent ; leaves ternate, with ovate acuminate leaflets ; spadix clavate ; flowers monœcious. The flowers are green and purple, and the roots are used by the Indians as a remedy for colic.

THE BLUE-WINGED YELLOW WARBLER.

SYLVIA SOLITARIA, WILS.

PLATE XX. MALE AND FEMALE.

THIS pretty little Warbler is migratory, and arrives in Louisiana from the south, in the beginning of spring. It is found in open woods, as well as in the vicinity of ponds overgrown with low bushes and rank weeds. Along with a pair of Blue-winged Yellow Warblers, I have represented a species of Hibiscus, which grows on the edges of these ponds. Its flowers are handsome, but unfortunately have no pleasant odour.

The species which now occupies our attention is a busy, active bird, and is seen diligently searching among the foliage and grasses for the small insects on which it feeds, mounting now and then towards the tops of the bushes, to utter a few weak notes, which are in no way interesting.

Its nest, which is singularly constructed, and of an elongated inversely conical form, is attached to several stalks or blades of tall-grass by its upper edge. The materials of which it is formed are placed obliquely from its mouth to the bottom. The latter part is composed of dried leaves, and is finished within with fine grass and lichens. The female lays from four to six eggs, of a pure white colour, with a few pale red spots at the larger end. The first brood is out about the middle of May, the second in the middle of July. The young disperse as soon as they are able to provide for themselves, this bird being of solitary habits.

It leaves Louisiana in the beginning of October. I have never seen the species farther eastward than the State of Jersey, where I killed several within a few miles of Philadelphia, not however until my last visit to that State in 1829. It is frequent in the barrens of Kentucky, and up the Mississippi, as far at least as St Genevieve, where I shot two individuals many years ago.

Its flight is short, undetermined, and is performed in zig-zag lines, as in most of its tribe. It sometimes ascends twenty or thirty yards in the air, as if with an intention of going to a great distance, but still moving in a zig-zag manner, when it suddenly turns about, and comes down near the place from which it set out. It does not chase insects on wing, but feeds in a great measure on the smaller kinds of spiders, not neglecting, however, to seize other insects when they come within reach. It remains almost constantly among the bushes, and is seldom seen on trees of any size.

SYLVIA SOLITARIA, *Ch. Bonaparte*, Synops. of Birds of the United States, p. 87.
BLUE-WINGED YELLOW WARBLER, *Wils.* Amer. Ornith. vol. ii, p. 109. Pl. 15. Fig.4.

Adult Male. Plate XX. Fig. 1.

Bill nearly as long as the head, straightish, subulato-conical, acute, as deep as broad at the base, the edges acute, the gap line a little deflected at the base. Nostrils basal, lateral, elliptical, half-closed by a membrane. Head rather small. Neck short. Body slender. Feet of ordinary length, slender; tarsus longer than the middle toe, covered anteriorly by a few scutella, the uppermost long; toes scutellate above, the inner free, the hind toe of moderate size; claws slender, compressed, acute, arched.

Plumage soft, blended, tufty. Wings of ordinary length, acute, the second quill longest. Tail longish, rounded when expanded, slightly forked when closed.

Bill black, with a pale margin. Iris dark brown. Feet and claws flesh-colour, tinged with yellow. Forehead, crown, and under parts of a rich bright-yellow. Back of the head and neck, the back and upper tail coverts bright grass-green. Lore black. Wings greyish-blue, slightly margined with paler, the first two rows of coverts tipped with whitish. Four middle tail-feathers greyish-blue, the outer webs of the rest, and an oblique portion of the outer feather at the end, of the same colour, their inner webs white..

Length $4\frac{3}{4}$ inches, extent of wings 7; bill along the ridge $\frac{1}{2}$, along the gap 1.

Adult Female. Plate XX. Fig. 2.

The female scarcely differs from the male in appearance, and is of nearly the same dimensions.

LARGE-FLOWERED HIBISCUS, COTTON ROSE, OR WILD ALTHÆA.

HIBISCUS GRANDIFLORUS, *Mich.* Fl. Amer. vol. ii. p. 46. *Pursh.* Fl. Amer. p. 455.—
MONADELPHIA POLYANDRIA, *Linn.* MALVACEÆ, *Juss.*

This beautiful species of Hibiscus, which does not precisely agree with any that I have seen described, although it is probably the above, is characterised by its ovato-cordate, obtusely and irregularly serrated, acute, venous tough leaves, and its large rose-coloured flowers, which are deep-red at the base, and streaked with the same colour. The corolla is about five inches in diameter, the anthers yellow. The stem and leaves are smooth. It grows in salt marshes, and by the edges of pools.

THE REGULATORS.

THE population of many parts of America is derived from the refuse of every other country. I hope I shall elsewhere prove to you, kind reader, that even in this we have reason to feel a certain degree of pride, as we often see our worst denizens becoming gradually freed from error, and at length changing to useful and respectable citizens. The most depraved of these emigrants are forced to retreat farther and farther from the society of the virtuous, the restraints imposed by which they find incompatible with their habits and the gratification of their unbridled passions. On the extreme verge of civilization, however, their evil propensities find more free scope, and the dread of punishment for their deeds, or the infliction of that punishment, are the only means that prove effectual in reforming them.

In those remote parts, no sooner is it discovered that an individual has conducted himself in a notoriously vicious manner, or has committed some outrage upon society, than a conclave of the honest citizens takes place, for the purpose of investigating the case, with a rigour without which no good result could be expected. These honest citizens, selected from among the most respectable persons in the district, and vested with powers suited to the necessity of preserving order on the frontiers, are named *Regulators*. The accused person is arrested, his conduct laid open, and if he is found guilty of a first crime, he is warned to leave the country, and go farther from society, within an appointed time. Should the individual prove so callous as to disregard the sentence, and remain in the same neighbourhood, to commit new crimes, then wo be to him; for the Regulators, after proving him guilty a second time, pass and execute a sentence, which, if not enough to make him perish under the infliction, is at least for ever impressed upon his memory. The punishment inflicted is generally a severe castigation, and the destruction by fire of his cabin. Sometimes, in cases of reiterated theft or murder, death is considered necessary; and, in some instances, delinquents of the worst species have been shot, after which their heads have been stuck on poles, to deter others from following their example. I shall give you an account of one of these desperadoes, as I received it from a person who had been instrumental in bringing him to punishment.

The name of Mason is still familiar to many of the navigators of the Lower Ohio and Mississippi. By dint of industry in bad deeds he became a notorious horse-stealer, formed a line of worthless associates from the eastern parts of Virginia (a State greatly celebrated for its fine breed of horses) to New Orleans, and had a settlement on Wolf Island, not far from the confluence of the Ohio and Mississippi, from which he issued to stop the flat-boats, and rifle them of such provisions and other articles as he and his party needed. His depredations became the talk of the whole Western Country; and to pass Wolf Island was not less to be dreaded than to anchor under the walls of Algiers. The horses, the negroes, and the cargoes, his gang carried off and sold. At last, a body of Regulators undertook, at great peril, and for the sake of the country, to bring the villain to punishment.

Mason was as cunning and watchful as he was active and daring. Many of his haunts were successively found out and searched, but the numerous spies in his employ enabled him to escape in time. One day, however, as he was riding a beautiful horse in the woods, he was met by one of the Regulators, who immediately recognised him, but passed him as if an utter stranger. Mason, not dreaming of danger, pursued his way leisurely, as if he had met no one. But he was dogged by the Regulator, and in such a manner as proved fatal to him. At dusk, Mason having reached the lowest part of a ravine, no doubt well known to him, hoppled (tied together the fore-legs of) his stolen horse, to enable it to feed during the night without chance of straying far, and concealed himself in a hollow log to spend the night. The plan was good, but proved his ruin.

The Regulator, who knew every hill and hollow of the woods, marked the place and the log with the eye of an experienced hunter, and as he remarked that Mason was most efficiently armed, he galloped off to the nearest house, where he knew he should find assistance. This was easily procured, and the party proceeded to the spot. Mason, on being attacked, defended himself with desperate valour; and as it proved impossible to secure him alive, he was brought to the ground with a rifle ball. His head was cut off, and stuck on the end of a broken branch of a tree, by the nearest road to the place where the affray happened. The gang soon dispersed, in consequence of the loss of their leader, and this infliction of merited punishment proved beneficial in deterring others from following a similar predatory life.

The punishment by castigation is performed in the following manner. The individual convicted of an offence is led to some remote part of the woods, under the escort of sometimes forty or fifty Regulators. When arrived at the chosen spot, the criminal is made fast to a tree, and a few of the Regulators remain with him, whilst the rest scour the forest, to assure themselves that no strangers are within reach, after which they form an extensive ring, arranging themselves on their horses, well armed with rifles and pistols, at equal distances and in each other's sight. At a given signal that " all's ready," those about the culprit, having provided themselves with young twigs of hickory, administer the number of lashes prescribed by the sentence, untie the sufferer, and order him to leave the country immediately.

One of these castigations which took place more within my immediate knowledge, was performed on a fellow who was neither a thief nor a murderer, but who had misbehaved otherwise sufficiently to bring himself under the sentence with mitigation. He was taken to a place where nettles were known to grow in great luxuriance, completely stripped, and so lashed with them, that although not materially hurt, he took it as a hint not to be neglected, left the country, and was never again heard of by any of the party concerned.

Probably at the moment when I am copying these notes respecting the early laws of our frontier people, few or no Regulating Parties exist, the terrible examples that were made having impressed upon the new settlers a salutary dread, which restrains them from the commission of flagrant crimes.

THE MOCKING BIRD.

TURDUS POLYGLOTTUS, LINN.

PLATE XXI. MALE AND FEMALE.

IT is where the Great Magnolia shoots up its majestic trunk, crowned with evergreen leaves, and decorated with a thousand beautiful flowers, that perfume the air around ; where the forests and fields are adorned with blossoms of every hue ; where the golden Orange ornaments the gardens and groves ; where Bignonias of various kinds interlace their climbing stems around the White-flowered Stuartia, and mounting still higher, cover the summits of the lofty trees around, accompanied with innumerable Vines, that here and there festoon the dense foliage of the magnificent woods, lending to the vernal breeze a slight portion of the perfume of their clustered flowers ; where a genial warmth seldom forsakes the atmosphere ; where berries and fruits of all descriptions are met with at every step ;—in a word, kind reader, it is where Nature seems to have paused, as she passed over the Earth, and opening her stores, to have strewed with unsparing hand the diversified seeds from which have sprung all the beautiful and splendid forms which I should in vain attempt to describe, that the Mocking Bird should have fixed its abode, there only that its wondrous song should be heard.

But where is that favoured land ?—It is in that great continent to whose distant shores Europe has sent forth her adventurous sons, to wrest for themselves a habitation from the wild inhabitants of the forest, and to convert the neglected soil into fields of exuberant fertility. It is, reader, in Louisiana that these bounties of nature are in the greatest perfection. It is there that you should listen to the love-song of the Mocking Bird, as I at this moment do. See how he flies round his mate, with motions as light as those of the butterfly ! His tail is widely expanded, he mounts in the air to a small distance, describes a circle, and, again alighting, approaches his beloved one, his eyes gleaming with delight, for she has already promised to be his and his only. His beautiful wings are gently raised, he bows to his love, and again bouncing upwards, opens his bill, and pours forth his melody, full of exultation at the conquest which he has made.

They are not the soft sounds of the flute or of the hautboy that I hear, but the sweeter notes of Nature's own music. The mellowness of the song, the varied modulations and gradations, the extent of its compass, the great brilliancy of execution, are unrivalled. There is probably no bird in the world that possesses all the musical qualifications of this king of song, who has derived all from Nature's self. Yes, reader, all !

No sooner has he again alighted, and the conjugal contract has been sealed, than, as if his breast was about to be rent with delight, he again pours forth his notes with more softness and richness than before. He now soars higher, glancing around with a vigilant eye, to assure himself that none has witnessed his bliss. When these love-scenes, visible only to the ardent lover of nature, are over, he dances through the air, full of animation and delight, and, as if to convince his lovely mate that to enrich her hopes he has much more love in store, he that moment begins anew, and imitates all the notes which nature has imparted to the other songsters of the grove.

For a while, each long day and pleasant night are thus spent; but at a peculiar note of the female he ceases his song, and attends to her wishes. A nest is to be prepared, and the choice of a place in which to lay it is to become a matter of mutual consideration. The Orange, the Fig, the Pear-tree of the gardens are inspected ; the thick briar patches are also visited. They appear all so well suited for the purpose in view, and so well does the bird know that man is not his most dangerous enemy, that instead of retiring from him, they at length fix their abode in his vicinity, perhaps in the nearest tree to his window. Dried twigs, leaves, grasses, cotton, flax, and other substances, are picked up, carried to a forked branch, and there arranged. The female has laid an egg, and the male redoubles his caresses. Five eggs are deposited in due time, when the male having little more to do than to sing his mate to repose, attunes his pipe anew. Every now and then he spies an insect on the ground, the taste of which he is sure will please his beloved one. He drops upon it, takes it in his bill, beats it against the earth, and flies to the nest to feed and receive the warm thanks of his devoted female.

When a fortnight has elapsed, the young brood demand all their care and attention. No cat, no vile snake, no dreaded hawk, is likely to visit their habitation. Indeed the inmates of the next house have by this time become quite attached to the lovely pair of Mocking Birds, and

take pleasure in contributing to their safety.   The dew-berries from the
fields, and many kinds of fruit from the gardens, mixed with insects, supply the young as well as the parents with food.   The brood is soon seen
emerging from the nest, and in another fortnight, being now able to fly
with vigour, and to provide for themselves, they leave the parent birds,
as many other species do.

The above account does not contain all that I wish you to know of
the habits of this remarkable songster ; so, I shall shift the scene to the
woods and wilds, where we shall examine it more particularly.

The Mocking Bird remains in Louisiana the whole year.   I have observed with astonishment, that towards the end of October, when those
which had gone to the Eastern States, some as far as Boston, have returned, they are instantly known by the " southrons," who attack them
on all occasions.   I have ascertained this by observing the greater shyness exhibited by the strangers for weeks after their arrival.   This shyness, however, is shortly over, as well as the animosity displayed by the
resident birds, and during the winter there exists a great appearance of
sociality among the united tribes.

In the beginning of April, sometimes a fortnight earlier, the Mocking Birds pair, and construct their nests.   In some instances they are so
careless as to place the nest between the rails of a fence directly by the
road.   I have frequently found it in such places, or in the fields, as well
as in briars, but always so easily discoverable that any person desirous of
procuring one, might do so in a very short time.   It is coarsely constructed on the outside, being there composed of dried sticks of briars,
withered leaves of trees, and grasses, mixed with wool.   Internally it is
finished with fibrous roots disposed in a circular form, but carelessly arranged.   The female lays from four to six eggs the first time, four or
five the next, and when there is a third brood, which is sometimes the
case, seldom more than three, of which I have rarely found more than
two hatched.   The eggs are of a short oval form, light green, blotched
and spotted with umber.   The young of the last brood not being able to
support themselves until late in the season, when many of the berries and
insects have become scarce, are stunted in growth ;—a circumstance which
has induced some persons to imagine the existence in the United States of
two species of Mocking Bird, a larger and a smaller.   This, however, in
as far as my observation goes, is not correct.   The first brood is frequently brought to the bird-market in New Orleans as early as the middle

of April. A little farther up the country, they are out by the fifteenth of May. The second brood is hatched in July, and the third in the latter part of September.

The nearer you approach to the sea-shores, the more plentiful do you find these birds. They are naturally fond of loose sands, and of districts scantily furnished with small trees, or patches of briars, and low bushes.

During incubation, the female pays such precise attention to the position in which she leaves her eggs, when she goes to a short distance for exercise and refreshment, to pick up gravel, or roll herself in the dust, that, on her return, should she find that any of them has been displaced, or touched by the hand of man, she utters a low mournful note, at the sound of which the male immediately joins her, and they are both seen to condole together. Some people imagine that, on such occasions, the female abandons the nest ; but this idea is incorrect. On the contrary, she redoubles her assiduity and care, and scarcely leaves the nest for a moment ; nor is it until she has been repeatedly forced from the dear spot, and has been much alarmed by frequent intrusions, that she finally and reluctantly leaves it. Nay, if the eggs are on the eve of being hatched, she will almost suffer a person to lay hold of her.

Different species of snakes ascend to their nests, and generally suck the eggs or swallow the young ; but on all such occasions, not only the pair to which the nest belongs, but many other Mocking Birds from the vicinity, fly to the spot, attack the reptiles, and, in some cases, are so fortunate as either to force them to retreat, or deprive them of life. Cats that have abandoned the houses to prowl about the fields, in a half wild state, are also dangerous enemies, as they frequently approach the nest unnoticed, and at a pounce secure the mother, or at least destroy the eggs or young, and overturn the nest. Children seldom destroy the nests of these birds, and the planters generally protect them. So much does this feeling prevail throughout Louisiana, that they will not willingly permit a Mocking Bird to be shot at any time.

In winter, nearly all the Mocking Birds approach the farm-houses and plantations, living about the gardens or outhouses. They are then frequently seen on the roofs, and perched on the chimney-tops ; yet they always appear full of animation. Whilst searching for food on the ground, their motions are light and elegant, and they frequently open their wings as butterflies do when basking in the sun, moving a step or two, and again throwing out their wings. When the weather is mild,

the old males are heard singing with as much spirit as during the spring
or summer, while the younger birds are busily engaged in practising,
preparatory to the love season.   They seldom resort to the interior of
the forest either during the day or by night, but usually roost among
the foliage of evergreens, in the immediate vicinity of houses in Louisiana, although in the Eastern States they prefer low fir trees.

The flight of the Mocking Bird is performed by short jerks of the
body and wings, at every one of which a strong twitching motion of the
tail is perceived.   This motion is still more apparent while the bird is
walking, when it opens its tail like a fan and instantly closes it again.
The common *cry* or *call* of this bird is a very mournful note, resembling
that uttered on similar occasions by its first cousin the *Turdus rufus*, or,
as it is commonly called, the " *French Mocking Bird*."   When travelling, this flight is only a little prolonged, as the bird goes from tree to
tree, or at most across a field, scarcely, if ever, rising higher than the top
of the forest.   During this migration, it generally resorts to the highest
parts of the woods near water-courses, utters its usual mournful note, and
roosts in these places.   It travels mostly by day.

Few hawks attack the Mocking Birds, as on their approach, however
sudden it may be, they are always ready not only to defend themselves
vigorously and with undaunted courage, but to meet the aggressor half
way, and force him to abandon his intention.   The only hawk that occasionally surprises it is the *Falco Stanleii*, which flies low with great
swiftness, and carries the bird off without any apparent stoppage.
Should it happen that the ruffian misses his prey, the Mocking Bird in
turn becomes the assailant, and pursues the Hawk with great courage,
calling in the mean time all the birds of its species to its assistance ; and
although it cannot overtake the marauder, the alarm created by their
cries, which are propagated in succession among all the birds in the vicinity, like the watchwords of sentinels on duty, prevents him from succeeding in his attempts.

The musical powers of this bird have often been taken notice of by
European naturalists, and persons who find pleasure in listening to the
song of different birds whilst in confinement or at large.   Some of these
persons have described the notes of the Nightingale as occasionally fully
equal to those of our bird.   I have frequently heard both species in confinement, and in the wild state, and without prejudice, have no hesitation
in pronouncing the notes of the European Philomel equal to those of a

soubrette of taste, which, could she study under a MOZART, might perhaps in time become very interesting in her way. But to compare her essays to the finished talent of the Mocking Bird, is, in my opinion, quite absurd.

The Mocking Bird is easily reared by hand from the nest, from which it ought to be removed when eight or ten days old. It becomes so very familiar and affectionate, that it will often follow its owner about the house. I have known one raised from the nest kept by a gentleman at Natchez, that frequently flew out of the house, poured forth its melodies, and returned at sight of its keeper. But notwithstanding all the care and management bestowed upon the improvement of the vocal powers of this bird in confinement, I never heard one in that state produce any thing at all approaching in melody to its own natural song.

The male bird is easily distinguished in the nest, as soon as the brood is a little fledged, it being larger than the female, and shewing more pure white. It does not shrink so deep in the nest as the female does, at the sight of the hand which is about to lift it. Good singing birds of this species often bring a high price. They are long-lived, and very agreeable companions. Their imitative powers are amazing, and they mimic with ease all their brethren of the forests or of the waters, as well as many quadrupeds. I have heard it asserted that they possess the power of imitating the human voice, but have never met with an instance of the display of this alleged faculty.

TURDUS POLYGLOTTUS, *Linn.* Syst. Nat. vol. i. p. 293.—*Lath.* Ind. Ornith. vol. i.
   p. 339.—*Ch. Bonaparte,* Synopsis of Birds of the United States, p. 74.
MIMIC THRUSH, *Lath.* Synops. vol. iii. p. 40.
MOCKING BIRD, TURDUS POLYGLOTTUS, *Wils.* Americ. Ornith. vol. ii. p. 14.
   Pl. x. fig. 1.

Adult Male. Plate XXI. Fig. 1, 1.

Bill of moderate length, rather weak, compressed, straightish; upper mandible slightly arched in its dorsal outline, little declinate at the tip; lower mandible nearly straight, acute. Nostrils basal, oblong, half-closed by a membrane. Head of ordinary size. Neck and body rather slender. Feet longish, rather strong; tarsus compressed, acute behind, covered anteriorly with a few long scutella; toes scutellate above, the middle one hardly shorter than the tarsus; inner toe free; hind toe rather robust; claws compressed, acute, arched.

Plumage soft and blended. Wings of moderate length, rounded; third and fourth primaries longest, first short. Tail long, much rounded, of twelve nearly straight, rather narrow, rounded feathers.

Bill brownish-black. Iris pale yellow. Feet and claws dark brown. Upper parts of the head, neck and body dark grey, tinged with brown on the forehead and sides of the head. Under parts brownish-white. Quills brownish-black; primaries white in their proximal part, forming a large spot of that colour on the wing, concealed on the first three, and on the last reaching to near the tip. Large primary coverts white, with a line of black at the tip. Secondary coverts and second row tipped with white. Outer tail-feather white, excepting a light streak of dusky near the tip; the next two also white, but with a longitudinal streak of black on the outer web, larger and broader on the third. The rest brownish-black tinged with grey, and, excepting the middle ones, tipped with white.

Length $9\frac{1}{4}$ inches, extent of wings $13\frac{1}{2}$; bill along the ridge $\frac{7}{12}$, along the gap 1; tarsus $1\frac{1}{2}$, middle toe 1.

Adult Female.   Plate XXI.   Fig. 2, 2.

The female differs very little from the male. The plumage is slightly duller, with more brown, the lateral tail-feathers have more black, and the white parts are less pure. The dimensions are nearly the same.

THE FLORIDA JESSAMINE.

GELSEMINUM NITIDUM, *Mich.* Flor. Amer. vol. i. p. 120. *Pursh.* Flor. Amer. vol. i. p. 184.—PENTANDRIA DIGYNIA, *Linn.* APOCINEÆ, *Juss.*

A climbing shrub, with smooth lanceolate leaves, axillary clusters of yellow flowers, which are funnel-shaped, with the limb spreading and nearly equal, the calyx five-toothed, the capsule two-celled and two-valved. It grows along the sea-coast, especially near rivers, from Virginia to Florida, flowering through the summer. The flowers are fragrant. It is also named *Carolina Jessamine* and *Yellow Jessamine*.

THE PURPLE MARTIN

HIRUNDO PURPUREA, LINN.

PLATE XXII. MALE AND FEMALE.

THE Purple Martin makes its appearance in the City of New Orleans from the 1st to the 9th of February, occasionally a few days earlier than the first of these dates, and is then to be seen gambolling through the air, over the city and the river, feeding on many sorts of insects, which are there found in abundance at that period.

It frequently rears three broods whilst with us. I have had several opportunities, at the period of their arrival, of seeing prodigious flocks moving over that city or its vicinity, at a considerable height, each bird performing circular sweeps as it proceeded, for the purpose of procuring food. These flocks were loose, and moved either eastward, or towards the north-west, at a rate not exceeding four miles in the hour, as I walked under one of them with ease for upwards of two miles, at that rate, on the 4th of February 1821, on the bank of the river below the city, constantly looking up at the birds, to the great astonishment of many passengers, who were bent on far different pursuits. My Fahrenheit's thermometer stood at 68°, the weather being calm and drizzly. This flock extended about a mile and a half in length, by a quarter of a mile in breadth. On the 9th of the same month, not far above the *Battle-ground*, I enjoyed another sight of the same kind, although I did not think the flock so numerous.

At the Falls of the Ohio, I have seen Martins as early as the 15th of March, arriving in small detached parties of only five or six individuals, when the thermometer was as low as 28°, the next day at 45°, and again, in the same week, so low as to cause the death of all the Martins, or to render them so incapable of flying as to suffer children to catch them. By the 25th of the same month, they are generally plentiful about that neighbourhood.

At St Genevieve, in the State of Missouri, they seldom arrive before the 10th or 15th of April, and sometimes suffer from unexpected returns of frost. At Philadelphia, they are first seen about the 10th of April.

H 2

They reach Boston about the 25th, and continue their migration much farther north, as the spring continues to open.

On their return to the Southern States, they do not require to wait for warmer days, as in spring, to enable them to proceed, and they all leave the above-mentioned districts and places about the 20th of August. They assemble in parties of from fifty to a hundred and fifty, about the spires of churches in the cities, or on the branches of some large dead tree about the farms, for several days before their final departure. From these places they are seen making occasional sorties, uttering a general cry, and inclining their course towards the west, flying swiftly for several hundred yards, when suddenly checking themselves in their career, they return in easy sailings to the same tree or steeple. They seem to act thus for the purpose of exercising themselves, as well as to ascertain the course they are to take, and to form the necessary arrangements for enabling the party to encounter the fatigues of their long journey. Whilst alighted, during these days of preparation, they spend the greater part of the time in dressing and oiling their feathers, cleaning their skins, and clearing, as it were, every part of their dress and body from the numerous insects which infest them. They remain on their roosts exposed to the night air, a few only resorting to the boxes where they have been reared, and do not leave them until the sun has travelled an hour or two from the horizon, but continue, during the fore part of the morning, to plume themselves with great assiduity. At length, on the dawn of a calm morning, they start with one accord, and are seen moving due west or south-west, joining other parties as they proceed, until there is formed a flock similar to that which I have described above. Their progress is now much more rapid than in spring, and they keep closer together.

It is during these migrations, reader, that the power of flight possessed by these birds can be best ascertained, and more especially when they encounter a violent storm of wind. They meet the gust, and appear to slide along the edges of it, as if determined not to lose one inch of what they have gained. The foremost front the storm with pertinacity, ascending or plunging along the skirts of the opposing currents, and entering their undulating recesses, as if determined to force their way through, while the rest follow close behind, all huddled together into such compact masses as to appear like a black spot. Not a twitter is then to be heard from them by the spectator below; but the instant the farther edge of the current is doubled, they relax their efforts, to refresh themselves, and twitter in united accord, as if congratulating each other on the successful issue of the contest.

The usual flight of this bird more resembles that of the *Hirundo urbica* of LINNÆUS, or that of the *Hirundo fulva* of VIEILLOT, than the flight of any other species of Swallow; and, although graceful and easy, cannot be compared in swiftness with that of the Barn Swallow. Yet the Martin is fully able to distance any bird not of its own genus. They are very expert at bathing and drinking while on the wing, when over a large lake or river, giving a sudden motion to the hind part of the body, as it comes into contact with the water, thus dipping themselves in it, and then rising and shaking their body, like a water spaniel, to throw off the water. When intending to drink, they sail close over the water, with both wings greatly raised, and forming a very acute angle with each other. In this position, they lower the head, dipping their bill several times in quick succession, and swallowing at each time a little water.

They alight with comparative ease on different trees, particularly willows, making frequent movements of the wings and tail as they shift their place, in looking for leaves to convey to their nests. They also frequently alight on the ground, where, notwithstanding the shortness of their legs, they move with some ease, pick up a goldsmith or other insect, and walk to the edges of puddles to drink, opening their wings, which they also do when on trees, feeling as if not perfectly comfortable.

These birds are extremely courageous, persevering, and tenacious of what they consider their right. They exhibit strong antipathies against cats, dogs, and such other quadrupeds as are likely to prove dangerous to them. They attack and chase indiscriminately every species of Hawk, Crow, or Vulture, and on this account are much patronized by the husbandman. They frequently follow and tease an Eagle, until he is out of sight of the Martin's box; and to give you an idea of their tenacity, when they have made choice of a place in which to rear their young, I shall relate to you the following occurrences.

I had a large and commodious house built and fixed on a pole, for the reception of Martins, in an enclosure near my house, where for some years several pairs had reared their young. One winter I also put up several small boxes, with a view to invite Blue-birds to build nests in them. The Martins arrived in the spring, and imagining these smaller apartments more agreeable than their own mansion, took possession of them, after forcing the lovely Blue-birds from their abode. I witnessed the different conflicts, and observed that one of the Blue-birds was possessed of as much courage as his antagonist, for it was only in consequence of the more powerful blows of the Martin, that he gave up his house, in which a nest was nearly finished, and he continued on all occasions to annoy the usurper as much as lay in his power. The Martin shewed his head at the entrance, and merely retorted with accents of exultation and insult. I thought fit to interfere, mounted the tree on the trunk of which the Blue-bird's box was fastened, caught the Martin, and clipped his tail with scissars, in the hope that such mortifying punishment might prove effectual in inducing him to remove to his own tenement. No such thing; for no sooner had I launched him into the air, than he at once rushed back to the box. I again caught him, and clipped the tip of each wing in such a manner that he still could fly sufficiently well to procure food, and once more set him at liberty. The desired effect, however, was not produced, and as I saw the pertinacious Martin keep the box in spite of all my wishes that he should give it up, I seized him in anger, and disposed of him in such a way that he never returned to the neighbourhood.

At the house of a friend of mine in Louisiana, some Martins took possession of sundry holes in the cornices, and there reared their young for several years, until the insects which they introduced to the house induced the owner to think of a reform. Carpenters were employed to clean the place, and close up the apertures by which the birds entered the cornice. This was soon done. The Martins seemed in despair; they brought twigs and other materials, and began to form nests wherever a hole could be found in any part of the building; but were so chased off that after repeated attempts, the season being in the mean time advanced, they were forced away, and betook themselves to some Woodpeckers' holes on the dead trees about the plantation. The next spring, a house was built for them. The erection of such houses is a general practice, the Purple Martin being considered as a privileged pilgrim, and the harbinger of spring.

The note of the Martin is not melodious, but is nevertheless very pleasing. The twitterings of the male while courting the female are more interesting. Its notes are among the first that are heard in the morning, and are welcome to the sense of every body. The industrious farmer rises from his bed as he hears them. They are soon after mingled with those of many other birds, and the husbandman, certain of a fine day, renews his peaceful labours with an elated heart. The still more inde-

pendent Indian is also fond of the Martin's company. He frequently
hangs up a calabash on some twig near his camp, and in this cradle the
bird keeps watch, and sallies forth to drive off the vulture that might
otherwise commit depredations on the deer-skins or pieces of venison exposed to the air to be dried. The humbled slave of the Southern States
takes more pains to accommodate this favourite bird. The calabash is
neatly scooped out, and attached to the flexible top of a cane, brought
from the swamp, where that plant usually grows, and placed close to his
hut. It is, alas! to him a mere memento of the freedom which he once
enjoyed; and, at the sound of the horn which calls him to his labour, as
he bids farewell to the Martin, he cannot help thinking how happy he
should be, were he permitted to gambol and enjoy himself day after day,
with as much liberty as that bird. Almost every country tavern has a
Martin box on the upper part of its sign-board; and I have observed that
the handsomer the box, the better does the inn generally prove to be.

All our cities are furnished with houses for the reception of these
birds; and it is seldom that even lads bent upon mischief disturb the favoured Martin. He sweeps along the streets, here and there seizing a
fly, hangs to the eaves of the houses, or peeps into them, as he poises himself in the air in front of the windows, or mounts high above the city,
soaring into the clear sky, plays with the string of the child's kite, snapping at it, as he swiftly passes, with unerring precision, or suddenly
sweeps along the roofs, chasing off grimalkin, who is probably prowling
in quest of his young.

In the Middle States, the nest of the Martin is built, or that of the
preceding year repaired and augmented, eight or ten days after its arrival, or about the 20th of April. It is composed of dry sticks, willow-
twigs, grasses, leaves, green and dry, feathers, and whatever rags he meets
with. The eggs, which are pure white, are from four to six. Many
pairs resort to the same box to breed, and the little fraternity appear to
live in perfect harmony. They rear two broods in a season. The first
comes forth in the end of May, the second about the middle of July. In
Louisiana, they sometimes have three broods. The male takes part of
the labour of incubation, and is extremely attentive to his mate. He is
seen twittering on the box, and frequently flying past the hole. His notes
are at this time emphatical and prolonged, low and less musical than even
his common *pews*. Their food consists entirely of insects, among which
are large beetles. They seldom seize the honey-bee.

The circumstance of their leaving the United States so early in autumn, has inclined me to think that they must go farther from them than any of our migratory land birds. This, however, is only conjecture, of which, kind reader, you may better judge when you have read my account of the Cliff Swallow.

HIRUNDO PURPUREA, *Linn.* Syst. Nat. vol. i. p. 844.—*Lath.* Ind. Ornith. vol. ii.
    p. 578.—*Ch. Bonaparte,* Synopsis of Birds of the United States, p. 64.
PURPLE MARTIN, HIRUNDO PURPUREA, *Wils.* Americ. Ornith. p. 58, Pl. xxxix.
    fig. 1. Male ; fig. 2. Female.

Adult Male.   Plate XXII. Fig 1, 1.

Bill short, rather robust, much depressed and very broad at the base; compressed towards the tip; upper mandible notched near the tip, which is rather obtuse and a little declinate; lower mandible nearly straight ; gap as wide as the head, and extending to beneath the eye. Nostrils basal, lateral, roundish. Head large. Neck short. Body rather elongated and depressed. Feet very short ; tarsus and toes scutellate anteriorly, lateral toes nearly equal, the outer united to the second joint ; claws short, weak, arched, rather obtuse.

Plumage silky, shining, and blended. Wings very long and slender, sickle-shaped when closed, the first primary longest. Tail of ordinary length, shorter than the wings, forked, when spread even, of twelve straight, narrowish feathers.

Bill deep brownish-black. Iris dark brown. Feet purplish-black. The plumage is generally of a deep blackish-blue, with intense purplish-blue reflections; the quills and tail-feathers brownish-black.

Length 7½ inches, extent of wings 16 ; bill along the back ⅓, along the gap 1, width of the gap ⅔ ; tarsus ¾, middle toe the same.

Adult Female.   Plate XXII. Fig. 2, 2.

Fore and upper part of the head brownish-grey, mottled with black ; upper parts generally of the same tints as the male, with more grey. Throat, fore neck, and upper breast, dark grey, transversely lined with black. The rest of the under parts lightish grey, longitudinally streaked with blackish, darker and transversely streaked on the sides, and under the tail nearly white, with slight lines.

1

THE YELLOW-BREASTED WARBLER, OR MARYLAND YELLOW-THROAT.

SYLVIA TRICHAS, LATH.

PLATE XXIII. MALE AND FEMALE.

THE notes of this little bird render it more conspicuous than most of its genus, for although they cannot be called very musical, they are far from being unpleasant, and are uttered so frequently during the day, that one, in walking along the briary ranges of the fences, is almost necessarily brought to listen to its *whititee*, repeated three or four times every five or six minutes, the bird seldom stopping expressly to perform its music, but merely uttering the notes after it has picked an insect from amongst the leaves of the low bushes which it usually inhabits. It then hops a step or two up or down, and begins again.

Although timid, it seldom flies far off at the approach of man, but instantly dives into the thickest parts of its favourite bushes and high grass, where it continues searching for food either along the twigs, or among the dried leaves on the ground, and renews its little song when only a few feet distant.

Its nest is one of those which the Cow Bunting *(Icterus pecoris)* selects, in which to deposit one of its eggs, to be hatched by the owners, that bird being similar in this respect to the European Cuckoo. The nest, which is placed on the ground, and partly sunk in it, is now and then covered over in the form of an oven, from which circumstance children name this warbler the *Oven-bird.* It is composed externally of withered leaves and grass, and is lined with hair. The eggs are from four to six, of a white colour, speckled with light brown, and are deposited about the middle of May. Sometimes two broods are reared in a season. I have never observed the egg of the Cow Bunting in the nests of the second brood. It is less active in its motions than most of the Sylviæ, but makes up this deficiency by continued application, it being, to appearance, busily employed during the whole of the day. It does not chase insects by flying after them, but secures them by surprise. Caterpillars and spiders form its principal food.

Although this species is found throughout the Union, the Middle

States seem to attract and detain more individuals, during the breeding season, than any others. Very few breed in Louisiana. In Kentucky, however, many breed in the barrens. The neighbourhood of swamps and such places is their favourite ground, but every field provided with briar patches or tall weeds harbours some of them. It leaves the Central Districts about the middle of September. The male bird does not attain its full colouring until the first spring, being for several months of the same tints as the female.

The twig on which the male is seen, is commonly called in Louisiana the Wild Olive. The tree is small, brittle and useless. It bears an acid fruit, which is sometimes employed as a pickle, and eaten when ripe by some people.

The female is perched on a twig of the Bitter-wood Tree, the wood of which is hard, and resembles that of the Crab. This is also a small tree, and grows along fences, amongst the briars, where the birds are found. Both these trees I have seen in Louisiana only.

SYLVIA TRICHAS, *Lath.* Ind. Ornith. vol. ii. p. 519.

TURDUS TRICHAS, *Linn.* Syst. Nat. vol. i. p. 293.

SYLVIA MARILANDICA, *Ch. Bonaparte,* Synops. of Birds of the United States, p. 85.

YELLOW-BREASTED WARBLER, *Lath.* Synops. vol. iv. p. 438.

MARYLAND YELLOW-THROAT, SYLVIA MARILANDICA, *Wilson,* Americ. Ornith. vol. i. p. 88. Pl. 6. fig. 1. Male; and vol. ii. p. 163. Pl. 18. fig. 4. Female.

Adult Male.   Plate XXIII. Fig. 1.

Bill of ordinary length, tapering, slender, nearly straight, acute. Nostrils basal, lateral, elliptical, half-closed by a membrane. Head and neck of ordinary size, the latter short. Body rather short. Feet longish, slender; tarsus longer than the middle toe, covered anteriorly with a few scutella, the uppermost long; toes scutellate above, the inner free, the hind toe of moderate size; claws slender, compressed, acute, arched.

Plumage loose, blended. Wings very short, the first quill longest. Tail rounded.

Bill dark brown. Iris dark hazel. Feet flesh colour. A broad band of black across the forehead, including the eyes, and terminating in a pointed form half-way down the neck; behind which is a narrower band of very pale blue; a slender white streak under the eye. Fore part of the neck bright ochre-yellow, the rest of the under parts pale brownish-yellow, fading into white on the abdomen and under tail-coverts. Upper parts dull greyish-olive, on the head tinged with red.   Inner webs of the quills deep brown.

Length $5\frac{1}{4}$ inches, extent of wings $6\frac{1}{2}$; bill along the ridge $\frac{5}{12}$; along the gap $\frac{3}{8}$; tarsus $\frac{11}{12}$;

Adult Female.   Plate XXIII. Fig. 2.

The female has the upper parts lighter, the under parts tinged with reddish-brown, and wants the two bands on the head, which is of a pale brownish red colour.

THE SNOW-DROP TREE, SILVER-BELL TREE, OR WILD OLIVE.

HALESIA TETRAPTERA, *Willd.* Sp. Pl. vol. ii. p. 840. *Pursh,* Flor. Amer. vol. ii. p. 448.—MONADELPHIA DECANDRIA, *Linn.* GUAIACANÆ, *Juss.*

Leaves ovate, acuminate, serrate ; flowers with twelve stamina ; the fruit rhomboidal.   It grows in shady woods, generally near rivers.

THE BITTER-WOOD TREE.

VIBURNUM PRUNIFOLIUM, *Willd.* Sp. Pl. vol. i. p. 1847. *Pursh,* Flor. Amer. vol. i. p. 201.—PENTANDRIA DYGYNIA, *Linn.* CAPRIFOLIA, *Juss.*

Glabrous ; the branches spreading ; the leaves roundish ; crenato-serrate ; the petioles smooth ; the cymes sessile ; the fruit round.   The flowers are white, the berries dark purplish-blue.

ROSCOE'S YELLOW-THROAT.

SYLVIA ROSCOE.

PLATE XXIV. MALE.

THE many kind attentions which I have received from the celebrated author of the Life of Leo the Tenth, joined to the valuable advice with which I have been favoured by that excellent gentleman, has induced me to honour the little bird before you with his name.

I shot it in a deep swamp not far from the River Mississippi, in the State bearing the same name, in September 1821. It was flitting amongst the top branches of a high Cypress, when I first observed it, moving sideways, searching for insects, and occasionally following one on the wing. It uttered a single *twit* repeated at short intervals. It having unexpectedly flown to a distant tree of the species on a branch of which you now see it, I followed it and shot it. It was the only one of the kind I have ever seen, although I went to the same swamp for several days in succession. It proved a male, and was to all appearance in perfect plumage. The gizzard was nearly filled with very minute red insects, found on Cypresses and Pines, the wings of different flies, and the heads of red ants.

In general appearance, this species so much resembles the preceding, that had not its habits differed so greatly from those of the Maryland Yellow-throat, I might have been induced to consider it as merely an accidental variety. On examining it more closely, however, and on comparing it with that bird, I felt, as I now feel, fully confident of its being different.

The species of Oak, on a twig of which it stands, is commonly called the *Swamp Oak*. It grows to a large size, always near the edges of damp or watery places. The height is from fifty to sixty feet, its diameter from two to three. The branches come off from the trunk at a height of eight feet from the ground, nearly at right angles. The twigs have a similar disposition. The wood is extremely hard and close in the texture, heavier than that of either the Red or the White Oak, and sinks when thrown into water. The Southern States appear to be those in which it thrives best.

SYLVIA ROSCOE.

Adult Male.   Plate XXIV.

Bill of ordinary length, tapering, slender, nearly straight, acute.
Nostrils basal, lateral, elliptical, half-closed by a membrane.   Head and
neck of ordinary size, the latter short.   Body rather short.   Feet of ordinary length, slender ; tarsus scarcely longer than the middle toe, covered
anteriorly with a few scutella, the uppermost 'long ; toes scutellate above,
the inner free, the hind toe of moderate size ; claws slender, compressed,
acute, arched.

Plumage loose, blended.   Wings very short, the first quill longest.
Tail rounded.

Bill dark flesh-colour, brown at the tip.   Iris light brown.   Feet flesh-
colour.   General colour of the upper parts very dark olive, the feathers
edged with lighter.   The inner webs of the quills dark brown.   A
slender white streak over the eye and close to it ; a broad band of black
from the eye downwards.

Length $5\frac{1}{2}$ inches, extent of wings $6\frac{1}{4}$; bill along the ridge $\frac{5}{12}$, along
the gap $\frac{3}{8}$; tarsus $\frac{1}{2}$.

THE SWAMP OAK.

QUERCUS AQUATICA, WATER OAK, *Mich.* Arb. Forest. vol. ii. p. 90. Pl. 17.—Mo-
NŒCIA POLYANDRIA, *Linn.* AMENTACEÆ, *Juss.*

Leaves oblongo-cuneate, tapering at the base, rounded or apiculate,
sometimes three-lobed.

THE SONG SPARROW.

FRINGILLA MELODIA, WILS.

PLATE XXV. MALE AND FEMALE.

THE Song Sparrow is one of the most abundant of its tribe in Louisiana, during winter. This abundance is easily accounted for by the circumstance that it rears three broods in the year :—six, five, and three young at each time, making fourteen per annum from a single pair. Supposing a couple to live in health, and enjoy the comforts necessary for the bringing up of their young families, for a period of only ten years, which is a moderate estimate for birds of this class, you will readily conceive how a whole flock of Song Sparrows may in a very short time be produced by them.

Among the many desiderata connected with the study of nature, there is one which, long felt by me, is not less so at the present moment. I have never been able to conceive why a bird which produces more than one brood in a season, should abandon its first nest to construct a new one, as is the case with the present species ; while other birds, such as the Ospreys, and various species of Swallows, rear many broods in the first nest which they have made, and to which they return, after their long annual migrations, to repair it, and render it fit for the habitation of the young brood. There is another fact which renders the question still more difficult to be solved. I have generally found the nests of this Sparrow cleaner and more perfect after the brood raised in them have made their departure, than the nests of the other species of birds mentioned above are on such occasions ; a circumstance which would render it unnecessary for the Song Sparrow to repair its nest. You are aware of the cleanliness of birds with respect to their nests during the whole period occupied in rearing their young. You know that the parents remove the excrements to a distance from them, so long as these excrements are contained in a filmy kind of substance, of which the old bird lays hold with its bill for that express purpose, frequently carrying them off to a distance of forty or fifty yards, or even more. Well, the Song Sparrow is among the cleanest of the clean. I have often watched the young birds leaving the nest ; and after their departure, have found it as well fitted for the reception of a fresh set of eggs as the new nest which the bird constructs. I am unable to understand the reason why a new nest is formed. Can you, reader, solve the question?

I have at all times been very partial to the Song Sparrow; for although its attire is exceedingly plain, it is pleasing to hear it, in the Middle States, singing earlier in spring, and later in autumn, than almost any other bird. Its song is sweet, of considerable duration, and performed at all hours of the day. It nestles sometimes on trees, and sometimes on the ground. I have imagined that the old birds, finding by experience the insecurity of their ordinary practice of nestling on the ground, where the eggs are often devoured by Crows, betake themselves to the bushes to conceal their nests from their enemies. But whatever may be the reason, the fact certainly exists, and the nests of the Song Sparrow occur in both kinds of situation. The nest for the first brood is prepared, and the eggs laid, sometimes as early as the 15th of April. The young are out by the first week of May. The third brood is seen by the middle of September. The nest, when on the ground, is well sunk in the earth, and is placed at the roots of tall grasses. It is made of fine grass, and lined with hair, principally horse-hair. The number of eggs is from five to seven, usually from four to six, excepting those for the last brood, which I have seldom found to exceed three. They are of a very broad ovate form, light greenish-white, speckled with dark umber, the specks larger toward the greater end. The male assists in the process of incubation, during which one of the birds feeds the other in succession. At this time the male is often to be observed singing on the top of a neighbouring bush, low tree, or fence-rail.

The flight of the Song Sparrow is short, and much undulated, when the bird is high in the air, but swifter and more level when it is near the ground. They migrate by night, singly or in straggling troops. Some of them remain the whole winter in the Middle Districts, where they are not unfrequently heard to sing, if the weather prove at all pleasant. The greater part, however, seek the Southern States, where myriads of Sparrows of different kinds are everywhere to be seen in low swampy situations, such as they at all periods prefer. It is a fine plump bird, and becomes very flat and juicy. It is picked up in great numbers by the Hen-harriers, which visit us for the purpose of feeding on the different kinds of Sparrows that resort to these States in winter from the Middle Districts. In Louisiana, they are frequently seen to ascend to the tops of large trees, and there continue for some time singing their agreeable chant, after which they dive again into the low bushes, or amongst the rank weeds which grow wherever a stream is to be found. They feed on grass seeds, some berries and insects, especially grasshoppers, and now and then pursue flies on the wing. On the ground their motions are lively. They continue running about with great nimbleness and activity, and sometimes cross shallow waters leg-deep. To the eastward, they often frequent orchards and large gardens, but seldom approach houses.

I have placed a pair of them on a twig of the Huckleberry Bush in blossom. This species sometimes grows to the height of six or seven feet, and produces a fine berry in great abundance. Huckleberries of every sort are picked by women and children, and sold in the eastern markets in great profusion. They are used for tarts, but in my opinion are better when eaten fresh.

FRINGILLA MELODIA, *Ch. Bonaparte,* Synops. of Birds of the United States, p. 108.
SONG SPARROW, FRINGILLA MELODIA, *Wilson,* Americ. Ornith. vol. ii. p. 125.
PL xvi. fig. 4.

Adult Male. Plate XXV. Fig. 1.

Bill short, robust, conical, a little bulging, straight, acute; upper mandible broader, slightly declinate at the tip; gap line a little declinate at the base. Nostrils basal, roundish, concealed by the frontal feathers. Feet of moderate length; tarsus longer than the middle toe; toes free, the lateral ones nearly equal; claws compressed, arched, acute.

Plumage rather compact above, soft and blended beneath. Wings short, rounded, the third and fourth quills longest. Tail longish, even, the feathers narrow and acute.

Bill deep brown above, bluish beneath. Iris hazel. Feet and claws pale brown. Upper part of the head reddish-brown, mottled with dark brown, with a broad line of bluish-grey down the middle. Back grey, streaked with reddish-brown and dusky. Lower back bluish-grey; tail-coverts tinged with light brown. Sides of the head bluish-grey; a broad line of brown from the eye backwards, and another from the commissure of the mouth. Under parts white, tinged on the sides with grey, and posteriorly with reddish-brown, the neck and breast spotted with dark brown, and the lateral under tail-coverts streaked with the same. Wings dark brown, the quills margined externally with reddish-brown, the coverts margined and tipped with whitish. Tail-feathers uniformly dull brown.

Length 6 inches, extent of wings $8\frac{1}{2}$; bill along the ridge $\frac{1}{2}$, along the gap $\frac{1}{2}$; tarsus 1, middle toe $\frac{5}{8}$, hind toe $\frac{3}{8}$.

Adult Female. Plate XXV. Fig. 2.

The female hardly differs in colour from the male.

THE HUCKLE-BERRY OR BLUE-TANGLES.

VACCINIUM FRONDOSUM, *Wild.* Sp. Pl. vol. ii. p. 352. *Pursh,* Flor. Amer. vol. i. p. 285.—DECANDRIA MONOGYNIA, *Linn.* ERICÆ, *Juss.*

Leaves deciduous, ovato-oblong or lanceolate, entire, smooth, glaucous beneath, resinous; racemes lax, bracteate; pedicels long, filiform, bracteolate; corollas ovato-companulate, with acute laciniæ and included anthers. The flower is white, the calyx green, the berry globular and of a bluish-black colour. It varies greatly in the form of the leaves, as well as in stature, sometimes attaining a height of six or seven feet.

Huckle-berries form a portion of the food of many birds, as well as of various quadrupeds. Of the former, I may mention in particular the Wild Turkey, several species of Grouse, the Wild Pigeon, the Turtle Dove, some Loxias, and several Thrushes. Among the latter, the Black Bear stands pre-eminent, although Raccoons, Foxes, Opossums, and others destroy great quantities. When the season is favourable, these berries are so thickly strewn on the twigs, that they may be gathered in large quantities, and as they become ripe, numerous parties resort to the grounds in which they are found, by way of frolicking, and spend the time in a very agreeable manner.

IMPROVEMENTS IN THE NAVIGATION OF THE MISSISSIPPI.

I HAVE so frequently spoken of the Mississippi, that an account of the progress of navigation on that extraordinary stream may be interesting even to the student of nature. I shall commence with the year 1808, at which time a great portion of the western country, and the banks of the Mississippi River, from above the City of Natchez particularly, were little more than a waste, or, to use words better suited to my feelings, remained in their natural state. To ascend the great stream against a powerful current, rendered still stronger wherever islands occurred, together with the thousands of sand-banks, as liable to changes and shiftings as the alluvial shores themselves, which at every deep curve or *bend* were seen giving way, as if crushed down by the weight of the great forests that everywhere reached to the very edge of the water, and falling and sinking in the muddy stream, by acres at a time, was an adventure of no small difficulty and risk, and which was rendered more so by the innumerable logs, called *sawyers* and *planters*, that everywhere raised their heads above the water, as if bidding defiance to all intruders. Few white inhabitants had yet marched towards its shores, and these few were of a class little able to assist the navigator. Here and there a solitary encampment of native Indians might be seen, but its inmates were as likely to prove foes as friends, having from their birth been made keenly sensible of the encroachments of the white men upon their lands.

Such was then the nature of the Mississippi and its shores. That river was navigated principally in the direction of the current, in small canoes, pirogues, keel-boats, some flat-boats, and a few barges. The canoes and pirogues being generally laden with furs from the different heads of streams that feed the great river, were of little worth after reaching the market of New Orleans, and seldom reascended, the owners making their way home through the woods, amidst innumerable difficulties. The flat-boats were demolished and used as fire-wood. The keel-boats and barges were employed in conveying produce of different kinds besides furs, such as lead, flour, pork, and other articles. These returned laden with sugar, coffee, and dry goods suited for the markets of St Genevieve and St Louis on the Upper Mississippi, or branched off and ascended the Ohio to the foot of the Falls near Louisville in Kentucky.   But, reader, follow their movements, and judge for yourself of the fatigues, troubles and risks of the men employed in that navigation.   A keel-boat was generally manned by ten hands, principally Canadian French, and a patroon or master. These boats seldom carried more than from twenty to thirty tons.   The barges frequently had forty or fifty men, with a patroon, and carried fifty or sixty tons.   Both these kinds of vessels were provided with a mast, a square-sail, and coils of cordage, known by the name of *cordelles*.   Each boat or barge carried its own provisions.   We shall suppose one of these boats under way, and, having passed Natchez, entering upon what were called the difficulties of their ascent.   Wherever a point projected, so as to render the course or bend below it of some magnitude, there was an eddy, the returning current of which was sometimes as strong as that of the middle of the great stream.   The bargemen therefore rowed up pretty close under the bank, and had merely to keep watch in the bow, lest the boat should run against a planter or sawyer.   But the boat has reached the point, and there the current is to all appearance of double strength, and right against it.   The men, who have all rested a few minutes, are ordered to take their stations, and lay hold of their oars, for the river must be crossed, it being seldom possible to double such a point and proceed along the same shore.   The boat is crossing, its head slanting to the current, which is however too strong for the rowers, and when the other side of the river has been reached, it has drifted perhaps a quarter of a mile.   The men are by this time exhausted, and, as we shall suppose it to be twelve o'clock, fasten the boat to the shore or to a tree.   A small glass of whisky is given to each, when they cook and eat their dinner, and after repairing their fatigue by an hour's repose, recommence their labours.   The boat is again seen slowly advancing against the stream.   It has reached the lower end of a large sand-bar, along the edge of which it is propelled by means of long poles, if the bottom be hard.   Two men called bowsmen remain at the prow, to assist, in concert with the steers-man, in managing the boat, and keeping its head right against the current.   The rest 'place themselves on the land side of the footway of the vessel, put one end of their poles on the ground, the other against their shoulders, and push with all their might.   As each of the men reaches the stern, he crosses to the other side, runs along it, and comes again to the landward side of the bow, when he recommences operations. The barge in the mean time is ascending at a rate not exceed-ing one mile in the hour.

The bar is at length passed, and as the shore in sight is straight on both sides of the river, and the current uniformly strong, the poles are laid aside, and the men being equally divided, those on the river side take to their oars, whilst those on the land side lay hold of the branches of willows, or other trees, and thus slowly propel the boat. Here and there, however, the trunk of a fallen tree, partly lying on the bank, and partly projecting beyond it, impedes their progress, and requires to be doubled. This is performed by striking it with the iron points of the poles and gaff-hooks. The sun is now quite low, and the barge is again secured in the best harbour within reach. The navigators cook their supper, and betake themselves to their blankets or bear-skins to rest, or perhaps light a large fire on the shore, under the smoke of which they repose, in order to avoid the persecutions of the myriads of moschettoes which occur during the whole summer along the river. Perhaps, from dawn to sunset, the boat may have advanced fifteen miles. If so, it has done well. The next day, the wind proves favourable, the sail is set, the boat takes all advantages, and meeting with no accident, has ascended thirty miles, perhaps double that distance. The next day comes with a very different aspect. The wind is right a-head, the shores are without trees of any kind, and the canes on the banks are so thick and stout, that not even the cordelles can be used. This occasions a halt. The time is not altogether lost, as most of the men, being provided with rifles, betake themselves to the woods, and search for the deer, the bears, or the turkeys, that are generally abundant there. Three days may pass before the wind changes, and the advantages gained on the previous fine day are forgotten. Again the boat proceeds, but in passing over a shallow place runs on a log, swings with the current, but hangs fast, with her lee-side almost under water. Now for the poles ! All hands are on deck, bustling and pushing. At length towards sunset, the boat is once more afloat, and is again taken to the shore, where the wearied crew pass ano-ther night.

I shall not continue this account of difficulties, it having already be-come painful in the extreme. I could tell you of the crew abandoning the boat and cargo, and of numberless accidents and perils; but be it enough to say, that, advancing in this tardy manner, the boat that left New Orleans on the first of March, often did not reach the Falls of the

Ohio until the month of July,—nay, sometimes not until October ; and after all this immense trouble, it brought only a few bags of coffee, and at most 100 hogsheads of sugar. Such was the state of things in 1808. The number of barges at that period did not amount to more than 25 or 30, and the largest probably did not exceed 100 tons burden. To make the best of this fatiguing navigation, I may conclude by saying, that a barge which came up in three months had done wonders, for I believe, few voyages were performed in that time.

If I am not mistaken, the first steam-boat that went down out of the Ohio to New Orleans was named the " Orleans," and if I remember right, was commanded by Captain OGDEN. This voyage, I believe was performed in the spring of 1810. It was, as you may suppose, looked upon as the *ne plus ultra* of enterprise. Soon after, another vessel came from Pittsburg, and before many years elapsed, to see a vessel so propelled became a common occurrence. In 1826, after a lapse of time that proved sufficient to double the population of the United States of America, the navigation of the Mississippi had so improved both in respect to facility and quickness, that I know no better way of giving you an idea of it, than by presenting you with an extract of a letter from my eldest son, which was taken from the books of N. BERTHOUD, Esq. with whom he at that time resided.

" You ask me in your last letter for a list of the arrivals and departures here. I give you an abstract from our list of 1826, shewing the number of boats which plied each year, their tonnage, the trips which they performed, and the quantity of goods landed here from New Orleans and intermediate places.

" 1823, from Jan. 1. to Dec. 31. 42 boats, measuring 7,860 tons. 98 trips. 19,453 tons.
1824,   do. 1. Nov. 25. 36   do.   6,393 do. 118 do. 20,291 do.
1825,   do. 1. Aug. 15. 42   do.   7,484 do. 140 do. 24,102 do.
1826,   do. 1. Dec. 31. 51   do.   9,388 do. 182 do. 28,914 do.

" The amount for the present year will be much greater than any of the above. The number of flat-boats and keels is beyond calculation. The number of steam-boats above the Falls I cannot say much about, except that one or two arrive at and leave Louisville every day. Their passage from Cincinnati is commonly 14 or 16 hours. The Tecumseh, a boat which runs between this place and New Orleans, and which measures 210 tons, arrived here on the 10th instant, in 9 days 7 hours, from port to port ; and the Philadelphia, of 300 tons, made the passage in 9 days 9½ hours, the computed distance being 1650 miles. These are the quickest trips made. There are now in operation on the waters west of the Alleghany Mountains 140 or 145 boats. We had last spring (1826), a very high freshet, which came 4½ feet deep in the counting-room. The rise was 57 feet 3 inches perpendicular."

The whole of the steam-boats of which you have an account did not perform voyages to New Orleans only, but to all points on the Mississippi, and other rivers which fall into it. I am certain that since the above date the number has increased, but to what extent I cannot at present say.

When steam-boats first plied between Shippingport and New Orleans, the cabin passage was a hundred dollars, and a hundred and fifty dollars on the upward voyage. In 1829, I went down to Natchez from Shippingport for twenty-five dollars, and ascended from New Orleans on board the Philadelphia, in the beginning of January 1830, for sixty dollars, having taken two state-rooms for my wife and myself. On that voyage we met with a trifling accident, which protracted it to fourteen days ; the computed distance being, as mentioned above, 1650 miles, although the real distance is probably less. I do not remember to have spent a day without meeting with a steam-boat, and some days we met several. I might here be tempted to give you a description of one of these steamers of the western waters, but the picture having been often drawn by abler hands, I shall desist.

THE CAROLINA PARROT.

PSITTACCUS CAROLINENSIS, LINN.

PLATE XXVI. MALE, FEMALE AND YOUNG.

DOUBTLESS, kind reader, you will say, while looking at the seven figures of Parakeets represented in the plate, that I spared not my labour. I never do, so anxious am I to promote your pleasure.

These birds are represented feeding on the plant commonly named the *Cockle-bur.* It is found much too plentifully in every State west of the Alleghanies, and in still greater profusion as you advance towards the Southern Districts. It grows in every field where the soil is good. The low alluvial lands along the Ohio and Mississippi are all supplied with it. Its growth is so measured that it ripens after the crops of grain are usually secured, and in some rich old fields it grows so exceedingly close, that to make one's way through the patches of it, at this late period, is no pleasant task. The burs stick so thickly to the clothes, as to prevent a person from walking with any kind of ease. The wool of sheep is also much injured by them ; the tails and manes of horses are converted into such tangled masses, that the hair has to be cut close off, by which the natural beauty of these valuable animals is impaired. To this day, no useful property has been discovered in the Cockle-bur, although in time it may prove as valuable either in medicine or chemistry as many other plants that had long been considered of no importance.

Well, reader, you have before you one of these plants, on the seeds of which the parrot feeds. It alights upon it, plucks the bur from the stem with its bill, takes it from the latter with one foot, in which it turns it over until the joint is properly placed to meet the attacks of the bill, when it bursts it open, takes out the fruit, and allows the shell to drop. In this manner, a flock of these birds, having discovered a field ever so well filled with these plants, will eat or pluck off all their seeds, returning to the place day after day until hardly any are left. The plant might thus be extirpated, but it so happens that it is reproduced from the ground, being perennial, and our farmers have too much to do in securing their crops, to attend to the pulling up the cockle-burs by the roots, the only effectual way of getting rid of them.

The Parrot does not satisfy himself with Cockle-burs, but eats or destroys almost every kind of fruit indiscriminately, and on this account is always an unwelcome visitor to the planter, the farmer, or the gardener. The stacks of grain put up in the field are resorted to by flocks of these birds, which frequently cover them so entirely, that they present to the eye the same effect as if a brilliantly coloured carpet had been thrown over them. They cling around the whole stack, pull out the straws, and destroy twice as much of the grain as would suffice to satisfy their hunger. They assail the Pear and Apple-trees, when the fruit is yet very small and far from being ripe, and this merely for the sake of the seeds. As on the stalks of Corn, they alight on the Apple-trees of our orchards, or the Pear-trees in the gardens, in great numbers ; and, as if through mere mischief, pluck off the fruits, open them up to the core, and, disappointed at the sight of the seeds, which are yet soft and of a milky consistence, drop the apple or pear, and pluck another, passing from branch to branch, until the trees which were before so promising, are left completely stripped, like the ship water-logged and abandoned by its crew, floating on the yet agitated waves, after the tempest has ceased. They visit the Mulberries, Pecan-nuts, Grapes, and even the seeds of the Dog-wood, before they are ripe, and on all commit similar depredations. The Maize alone never attracts their notice.

Do not imagine, reader, that all these outrages are borne without severe retaliation on the part of the planters. So far from this, the Parakeets are destroyed in great numbers, for whilst busily engaged in plucking off the fruits or tearing the grain from the stacks, the husbandman approaches them with perfect ease, and commits great slaughter among them. All the survivors rise, shriek, fly round about for a few minutes, and again alight on the very place of most imminent danger. The gun is kept at work; eight or ten, or even twenty, are killed at every discharge. The living birds, as if conscious of the death of their companions, sweep over their bodies, screaming as loud as ever, but still return to the stack to be shot at, until so few remain alive, that the farmer does not consider it worth his while to spend more of his ammunition. I have seen several hundreds destroyed in this manner in the course of a few hours, and have procured a basketful of these birds at a few shots, in order to make choice of good specimens for drawing the figures by which this species is represented in the plate now under your consideration.

The flight of the Parakeet is rapid, straight, and continued through the forests, or over fields and rivers, and is accompanied by inclinations of the body which enable the observer to see alternately their upper and under parts. They deviate from a direct course only when impediments occur, such as the trunks of trees or houses, in which case they glance aside in a very graceful manner, merely as much as may be necessary. A general cry is kept up by the party, and it is seldom that one of these birds is on wing for ever so short a space without uttering its cry. On reaching a spot which affords a supply of food, instead of alighting at once, as many other birds do, the Parakeets take a good survey of the neighbourhood, passing over it in circles of great extent, first above the trees, and then gradually lowering until they almost touch the ground, when suddenly re-ascending they all settle on the tree that bears the fruit of which they are in quest, or on one close to the field in which they expect to regale themselves.

They are quite at ease on trees or any kind of plant, moving sidewise, climbing or hanging in every imaginable posture, assisting themselves very dexterously in all their motions with their bills. They usually alight extremely close together. I have seen branches of trees as completely covered by them as they could possibly be. If approached before they begin their plundering, they appear shy and distrustful, and often at a single cry from one of them, the whole take wing, and probably may not return to the same place that day. Should a person shoot at them, as they go, and wound an individual, its cries are sufficient to bring back the whole flock, when the sportsman may kill as many as he pleases. If the bird falls dead, they make a short round, and then fly off.

On the ground these birds walk slowly and awkwardly, as if their tail incommoded them. They do not even attempt to run off when approached by the sportsman, should he come upon them unawares; but when he is seen at a distance, they lose no time in trying to hide, or in scrambling up the trunk of the nearest tree, in doing which they are greatly aided by their bill.

Their roosting-place is in hollow trees, and the holes excavated by the larger species of Woodpeckers, as far as these can be filled by them. At dusk, a flock of Parakeets may be seen alighting against the trunk of a large Sycamore or any other tree, when a considerable excavation exists within it. Immediately below the entrance the birds all cling to the bark, and crawl into the hole to pass the night. When such a hole does not prove sufficient to hold the whole flock, those around the entrance hook themselves on by their claws, and the tip of the upper mandible, and look as if hanging by the bill. I have frequently seen them in such positions by means of a glass, and am satisfied that the bill is not the only support used in such cases.

When wounded and laid hold of, the Parakeet opens its bill, turns its head to seize and bite, and, if it succeed, is capable of inflicting a severe wound. It is easily tamed by being frequently immersed in water, and eats as soon as it is placed in confinement. Nature seems to have implanted in these birds a propensity to destroy, in consequence of which they cut to atoms pieces of wood, books, and, in short, every thing that comes in their way. They are incapable of articulating words, however much care and attention may be bestowed upon their education; and their screams are so disagreeable as to render them at best very indifferent companions. The woods are the habitation best fitted for them, and there the richness of their plumage, their beautiful mode of flight, and even their screams, afford welcome intimation that our darkest forests and most sequestered swamps are not destitute of charms.

They are fond of sand in a surprising degree, and on that account are frequently seen to alight in flocks along the gravelly banks about the creeks and rivers, or in the ravines of old fields in the plantations, when they scratch with bill and claws, flutter and roll themselves in the sand, and pick up and swallow a certain quantity of it. For the same purpose, they also enter the holes dug by our Kingsfisher. They are fond of saline earth, for which they visit the different Licks interspersed in our woods.

Our Parakeets are very rapidly diminishing in number; and in some districts, where twenty-five years ago they were plentiful, scarcely any are now to be seen. At that period, they could be procured as far up the tributary waters of the Ohio as the Great Kenhawa, the Scioto, the heads of the Miami, the mouth of the Manimee at its junction with Lake Erie, on the Illinois River, and sometimes as far north-east as Lake Ontario, and along the eastern districts as far as the boundary line between Virginia and Maryland. At the present day, very few are to be found higher than Cincinnati, nor is it until you reach the mouth of the Ohio that Parakeets are met with in considerable numbers. I should think that along the Mississippi there is not now half the number that existed fifteen years ago.

Their flesh is tolerable food, when they are young, on which account many of them are shot. The skin of their body is usually much covered with the mealy substances detached from the roots of the feathers. The head especially is infested by numerous minute insects, all of which shift from the skin to the surface of the plumage, immediately after the bird's death. Their nest, or the place in which they deposit their eggs, is simply the bottom of such cavities in trees as those to which they usually retire at night. Many females deposit their eggs together. I am of opinion that the number of eggs which each individual lays is two, although I have not been able absolutely to assure myself of this. They are nearly round, and of a light greenish white. The young are at first covered with soft down, such as is seen on young Owls. During the first season, the whole plumage is green; but towards autumn a frontlet of carmine appears. Two years, however, are passed before the male or female are in full plumage. The only material differences which the sexes present externally are, that the male is rather larger, with more brilliant plumage. I have represented a female with two supernumerary feathers in the tail. This, however, is merely an accidental variety.

PSITTACUS CAROLINENSIS, *Linn.* Syst. Nat. vol. i. p. 141.—*Lath.* Ind. Orn. vol. i. p. 93.—*Ch. Bonaparte*, Synops. of Birds of the United States, p. 41.

CAROLINA PARROT, *Lath.* Synops. vol. i. p. 227.—*Wils.* Amer. Ornith. vol. iii. p. 89. Pl. 26. fig. 1.

Adult Male. Plate XXVI. Fig. 1, 1, 1.

Bill short, bulging, very strong and hard, deeper than broad, convex above and below, with a cere at the base; upper mandible curved from the base, convex on the sides, the margin overlapping, with an angular process, the tip trigonal, acute, declinate, much exceeding the under mandible, which is very short, broadly convex on the back, truncate at the extremity. Nostrils basal, round, open, placed in the cere. Head very large. Neck robust. Body rather elongated. Feet short and robust; tarsus scaly all round; toes scutellate above, flat beneath, two behind and two before, the latter united at the base; claws curved, acute.

Plumage compact and imbricated on the back, blended on the head, neck, and under parts. Orbital space bare. Wings long, second and third quills longest. Tail long, wedge-shaped, of twelve, narrow, tapering feathers.

Bill white. Iris hazel. Bare orbital space whitish. Feet pale flesh-colour, claws dusky. Fore part of the head and the cheeks bright scarlet, that colour extending over and behind the eye, the rest of the head and the neck pure bright yellow: the edge of the wing bright yellow, spotted with orange. The general colour of the other parts is emerald-green, with light blue reflections, lighter beneath. Primary coverts deep bluish-green; secondary coverts greenish-yellow. Quills bluish-green on the outer web, brownish-red on the inner, the primaries bright yellow at the base of the outer web. Two middle tail-feathers deep green, the rest of the same colour externally, their inner webs brownish-red. Tibial feathers yellow, the lowest deep orange.

Length 14 inches, extent of wings 22; bill along the ridge $1\frac{1}{2}$, gap, measured from the tip of the lower mandible, $\frac{1}{4}$; tarsus $\frac{5}{8}$, middle toe $1\frac{1}{4}$.

Adult Female. Plate XXVI. Fig. 2, 2, 2.

The female is similar to the male in colour. The upper figure represents a kind of occasional variety, with fourteen tail-feathers. The specimen from which the drawing was taken was shot at Bayou Sara, in Louisiana.

Young Bird. Plate XXVI. Fig. 3.

The young bird is known by the comparative shortness of the tail, and the uniform green colour of the head.

THE COCKLE-BUR.

XANTHIUM STRUMARIUM, *Willd.* Sp. Pl. vol. iv. p. 373. *Pursh.* Flor. Amer. vol. ii. p. 581. *Smith,* Engl. Fl. vol. iv. p. 136.—MONŒCIA PENTANDRIA, *Linn.* CO-RYMBIFERÆ, *Juss.*

Root fibrous; stem solitary, erect, branched, from three to six feet high, furrowed, downy; leaves on long petioles, cordate, lobed, serrate, scabrous, three-nerved at the base; clusters axillar, of four or five fertile, and one or two barren flowers, which are green; nuts densely armed, and furnished with two beaks.

THE RED-HEADED WOODPECKER.

PICUS ERYTHROCEPHALUS, LINN.

PLATE XXVII. MALE, FEMALE, AND YOUNG.

You have now, kind reader, under consideration a family of Wood-peckers, the general habits of which are so well known in our United States, that, were I assured of your having traversed the woods of America, I should feel disposed to say little about them.

The *Red-heads* (by which name this species is usually designated) may be considered as residents of the United States, inasmuch as many of them remain in the Southern Districts during the whole winter, and breed there in summer. The greater number, however, pass to countries farther south. Their migration takes place under night, is commenced in the middle of September, and continues for a month or six weeks. They then fly very high above the trees, far apart, like a disbanded army, propelling themselves by reiterated flaps of the wings, at the end of each successive curve which they describe in their flight. The note which they emit at this time is different from the usual one, sharp and easily heard from the ground, although the birds may be out of sight. This note is continued, as if it were necessary for keeping the straggling party in good humour. At dawn of day, the whole alight on the tops of the dead trees about the plantations, and remain in search of food until the approach of sunset, when they again, one after another, mount the air, and continue their journey.

With the exception of the Mocking Bird, I know no species so gay and frolicksome. Indeed, their whole life is one of pleasure. They find a superabundance of food everywhere, as well as the best facilities for raising their broods. The little labour which they perform is itself a source of enjoyment, for it is undertaken either with an assurance of procuring the nicest dainties, or for the purpose of excavating a hole for the reception of themselves, their eggs, or their families. They do not seem to be much afraid of man, although they have scarcely a more dangerous enemy. When alighted on a fence-stake by the road, or in a field, and one approaches them, they gradually move sidewise out of sight, peeping now and then to discover your intention; and when you are quite close and opposite, lie still until you are past, when they hop to the top of the stake, and rattle upon it with their bill, as if to congratulate themselves on the success of their cunning. Should you approach within arm's length, which may frequently be done, the Woodpecker flies to the next stake or the second from you, bends his head to peep, and rattles again, as if to provoke you to a continuance of what seems to him excellent sport. He alights on the roof of the house, hops along it, beats the shingles, utters a cry, and dives into your garden to pick the finest strawberries which he can discover.

I would not recommend to any one to trust their fruit to the Red-heads; for they not only feed on all kinds as they ripen, but destroy an immense quantity besides. No sooner are the cherries seen to redden, than these birds attack them. They arrive on all sides, coming from a distance of miles, and seem the while to care little about the satisfaction you might feel in eating some also. Trees of this kind are stripped clean by them. When one has alighted and tasted the first cherry, he utters his call-note, jerks his tail, nods his head, and at it again in an instant. When fatigued, he loads his bill with one or two, and away to his nest, to supply his young.

It is impossible to form any estimate of the number of these birds seen in the United States during the summer months; but this much I may safely assert, that an hundred have been shot upon a single cherry-tree in one day. Pears, Peaches, Apples, Figs, Mulberries, and even Pease, are thus attacked. I am not disposed to add to these depredations those which they commit upon the Corn, either when young and juicy, or when approaching maturity, lest I should seem too anxious to heap accusations upon individuals, who, although culprits, are possessed of many undeniably valuable qualities.

But to return:—They feed on apples as well as on other fruit, and carry them off by thrusting into them their sharp bills when open, with all their force, when they fly away to a fence-stake or a tree, and devour them at leisure. They have another bad habit, which is that of sucking the eggs of small birds. For this purpose, they frequently try to enter the boxes of the Martins or Blue-birds, as well as the pigeon-houses, and are often successful. The corn, as it ripens, is laid bare by their bill, when they feed on the top parts of the ear, and leave the rest either to the Grakles or the Squirrels, or still worse, to decay, after a shower has fallen upon it.

All this while the Red-heads are full of gaiety. No sooner have they satisfied their hunger, than small parties of them assemble on the tops and branches of decayed trees, from which they chase different insects that are passing through the air, launching after them for eight or ten yards, at times performing the most singular manœuvres, and, on securing their victim, return to the tree, where, immediately after, a continued cry of exultation is uttered. They chase each other on wing in a very amicable manner, in long, beautifully curved sweeps, during which the remarkable variety of their plumage becomes conspicuous, and is highly pleasing to the eye. When passing from one tree to another, their flight resembles the motion of a great swing, and is performed by a single opening of the wings, descending at first, and rising towards the spot on which they are going to alight with ease, and in the most graceful manner. They move upwards, sidewise, or backwards, without apparent effort, but seldom with the head downwards, as Nuthatches and some smaller species of Woodpeckers are wont to do.

Their curving from one tree to another, in the manner just described, is frequently performed as if they intended to attack a bird of their own species; and it is amusing to see the activity with which the latter baffles his antagonist, as he scrambles sidewise round the tree with astonishing celerity, in the same manner in which one of these birds, suspecting a man armed with a gun, will keep winding round the trunk of a tree, until a good opportunity presents itself of sailing off to another. In this manner a man may follow from one tree to another over a whole field, without procuring a shot, unless he watches his opportunity and fires while the bird is on wing. On the ground, this species is by no means awkward, as it hops there with ease, and secures beetles which it had espied whilst on the fence or a tree.

It is seldom that a nest newly perforated by these birds is to be found, as they generally resort to those of preceding years, contenting themselves with working them a little deeper. These holes are found not only in every decaying tree, but often to the number of ten or a dozen in a single trunk, some just begun, others far advanced, and others ready to receive the eggs. The great number of these holes, thus left in different stages, depends upon the difficulties which the bird may experience in finishing them; for whenever it finds the wood hard and difficult to be bored, it tries another spot. So few green or living trees are perforated by *this* species, that I cannot at the present moment recollect having seen a single instance of such an occurrence.

All Woodpeckers are extremely expert at discovering insects as they lie under the bark of trees. No sooner have they alighted, than they stand for a few moments motionless and listening. If no motion is observed in the bark, the Woodpecker gives a smart rap with its bill, and bending its neck sidewise lays its head close to it, when the least crawling motion of a beetle or even a larva is instantly discovered, and the bird forthwith attacks the tree, removes the bark, and continues to dig until it reaches its prey, when it secures and swallows it. This manner of obtaining food is observed particularly during the winter, when few forest fruits are to be found. Should they, at this season, discover a vine loaded with grapes, they are seen hanging to the branches by their feet, and helping themselves with their bill. At this time they also resort to the corn-cribs, and feed on the corn gathered and laid up by the farmers.

In Louisiana and Kentucky, the Red-headed Woodpecker rears two broods each year; in the Middle Districts more usually only one. The female lays from two to six eggs, which are pure white and translucent, sometimes in holes not more than six feet from the ground, at other times as high as possible. The young birds have at first the upper part of the head grey; but towards autumn the red begins to appear. During the first winter, the red is seen richly intermixed with the grey feathers, and, at the approach of spring, scarcely any difference is perceptible between the sexes.

The Red-headed Woodpecker is found in all parts of the United States. Its flesh is tough, and smells strongly of ants and other insects, so as to be scarcely eatable.

A European friend of mine, on seeing some of these birds for the first time, as he was crossing the Alleghanies, wrote me, on reaching Pittsburg, that he had met with a beautiful species of Jay, the plumage of which was red, black and white, and its manners so gentle, that it suffered him to approach so near as the foot of a low tree on which it was.

On being wounded in the wing, they cry as they fall, and continue to do so for many minutes after being taken, pecking at their foe with great vigour. If not picked up, they make to the nearest tree, and are soon out of reach, as they can climb by leaps of considerable length faster than can be imagined. The number of insects of all sorts destroyed by this bird alone is incalculable, and it thus affords to the husbandman a full return for the mischief which it commits in his garden and fields.

In Kentucky and the Southern States, many of these birds are killed

2

in the following manner. As soon as the Red-heads have begun to visit a Cherry or Apple tree, a pole is placed along the trunk of the tree, passing up amongst the central branches, and extending six or seven feet beyond the highest twigs. The Woodpeckers alight by preference on the pole, and while their body is close to it, a man standing at the foot of the pole gives it a smart blow with the head of an axe, on the opposite side to that on which the Woodpecker is, when, in consequence of the sudden and violent vibration produced in the upper part, the bird is thrown off dead.

PICUS ERYTHROCEPHALUS, *Linn.* Syst. Nat. vol. i. p. 174.—*Lath.* Ind. Ornith. vol. i. p. 227.—*Ch. Bonaparte,* Synops. of Birds of the United States, p. 45.

RED-HEADED WOODPECKER, PICUS ERYTHROCEPHALUS, *Wilson,* Amer. Ornith. vol. i. p. 142. Pl. ix. fig. 1.—*Lath.* Synops. vol. ii. p. 561.

Adult Male. Plate XXVII. Fig. 1.

Bill longish, straight, strong, compressed toward the tip, which is vertically acute; upper mandible with the dorsal outline nearly straight, the edges acute and overlapping; under mandible with acute, slightly inflected edges. Nostrils basal, elliptical, direct, open. Head rather large; neck short; body robust. Feet short; tarsus and toes scutellate; two toes before and two behind, the inner hind toe shortest; claws strong, arched, acute.

Plumage glossy, generally blended, on the back and wings compact. Wings longish, third and fourth quills longest. Tail much rounded, of twelve decurved stiff feathers, worn by rubbing to an acute, ragged point. Palpebral region bare.

Bill light blue, dark at the tip. Feet of the same colour. Iris dark hazel, palpebral region bluish. Head and neck bright crimson. Back wing-coverts, primaries and tail-feathers black, with blue reflections; rump and secondaries white, the shafts of the latter black. Breast and abdomen white, tinged with yellowish-brown; an irregular transverse narrow band of black at the junction of the red of the fore-neck and the white of the breast.

Length 9 inches, extent of wings 17; bill along the ridge 1, along the gap 1½; tarsus 1.

Adult Female. Plate XXVII. Fig. 2.

K

The female differs from the male only in being smaller, and in having the tints of the plumage somewhat less vivid.

Length 8½ inches.

Young Birds.   Plate XXVII.   Fig. 3, 3, 3.

The young when fully fledged have the bill and iris dark brown, the feet bluish.   The head and neck are dark brownish-grey, mottled with small streaks of dark brown; the back and wing-coverts of the same colour, spotted with darker; the primaries brownish-black, margined with whitish, the secondaries yellowish-white, barred with black; the tail brownish-black, tipped with white; the rump and under parts greyish-white.

THE SOLITARY FLY-CATCHER, OR VIREO.

VIREO SOLITARIUS, VIEILL.

PLATE XXVIII. MALE AND FEMALE.

THIS, reader, is one of the scarce birds that visit the United States from the south, and I have much pleasure in being able to give you an account of it, as hitherto little or nothing has been known of its history.

It is an inhabitant of Louisiana during the spring and summer months, when it resorts to the thick cane-brakes of the alluvial lands near the Mississippi, and the borders of the numberless swamps that lie in a direction parallel to that river. It is many years since I discovered it, but as I am not at all anxious respecting priority of names, I shall not insist upon this circumstance. In the month of May 1809, I killed a male and a female of this species, near the mouth of the Ohio, while on a shooting expedition after young swans. The following spring, I killed a female near Henderson in Kentucky. In 1821, I again procured a pair, with their nest and eggs, near the mouth of Bayou La Fourche, on the Mississippi, and since that period have killed eight or ten pairs.

The nest is prettily constructed, and fixed in a partially pensile manner between two twigs of a low bush, on a branch running horizontally from the main stem. It is formed externally of grey lichens, slightly put together, and lined with hair, chiefly from the deer and raccoon. The female lays four or five eggs, which are white, with a strong tinge of flesh-colour, and sprinkled with brownish-red dots at the larger end. I am inclined to believe that the bird raises only one brood in a season.

The manners of this bird are not those of the Titmouse, Fly-catcher, or Warbler, but partake of those of all three. It has the want of shyness exhibited in the Red-eyed and Yellow-throated Fly-catchers. It hangs to bunches of small berries, feeding upon them as a Titmouse does on buds of trees; and again searches amongst the leaves and along the twigs of low bushes, like most of the Warblers. On the other hand, it differs from all these in their principal habits. Thus, it never snaps at insects on the wing, although it pursues them; it never attacks small birds and kills them by breaking in their skulls, as the Titmouse does; nor does it

K 2

hold its prey under its foot in the way of the Yellow-throated Fly-catcher or Vireo, a habit which allies the latter to the Shrikes.   On account of all these circumstances, I look upon this bird as deserving the attention of systematic writers, who probably will find its proper place in the general arrangement.

The flight of this bird is performed by a continued *tremor* of the wings, as if it were at all times angry.   It seldom rises high above its favourite cane-brakes, but is seen hopping up and down about the stems of low bushes and the stalks of the canes, silently searching for food, more in the manner of the Worm-eating Warbler than in that of any other bird known to me.   Their confidence at the approach of man is very remarkable.   They look on without moving until you are within a few feet, and retire only in proportion as you advance towards them.   In this respect it resembles the White-eyed Fly-catcher.

When wounded by a shot, it remains quite still on the ground, opens its bill when you approach it, and bites with all its might when laid hold of, although its strength is not sufficient to enable it to inflict a wound. I have never heard it utter a note beyond that of a querulous low murmuring sound, when chasing another bird from the vicinity of its nest. The young all leave the nest, if once touched, and hide among the grass and weeds, where the parents continue to feed them.   I once attempted to feed some young birds of this species, but they rejected the food, which consisted of flies, worms, and hard-boiled eggs, and died in three days without ever uttering a note.   In 1829, I shot one of these birds, a fine male, in the Great Pine Swamp.   This was the only individual I ever saw to the eastward of Henderson on the Ohio.   As this happened in the beginning of September, it is probable that some migrate to a considerable distance north-east; but I am at the same time of opinion that very few of these birds enter the United States.

I have represented a pair of them killed near a nest in a cane-brake. A general description of the American Cane will be found in the present volume.

VIREO SOLITARIUS, *Ch. Bonaparte.* Synops. of Birds of the United States, p. 70.

SOLITARY FLY-CATCHER, MUSCICAPA SOLITARIA, *Wils.* Amer. Ornith. vol. ii. p. 143. Pl. xvii. fig. 6.

Adult Male.   Plate XXVIII. Fig. 1.

Bill rather short, broad and depressed at the base, strong, nearly

straight ; upper mandible with the sides convex, the edges overlapping
and notched near the tip, which is suddenly decurved ; lower mandible a
little shorter, convex on the sides and back. Nostrils basal, roundish.
Head and neck large. Body ovate. Feet of ordinary length, rather
strong ; tarsus compressed, covered anteriorly with transverse scutella ;
toes free, scutellate above, the lateral ones nearly equal ; claws arched,
compressed, acute.

Plumage blended, tufty. Bristle-pointed feathers at the base of the
bill. Wings of ordinary length, the third quill longest. Tail slightly
forked, of twelve feathers.

Bill black above, light blue beneath. Iris dark brown. Feet and
claws light blue. Head and back light olive-green ; cheeks of the same
colour. A band of white on the forehead, passing over the eye, and
nearly encircling it, leaving the loral space dark green. Rump and upper tail-coverts greenish-brown. Quills blackish-brown, margined externally with brownish-yellow ; two first rows of coverts blackish-brown,
largely tipped with white, forming two bands on the wing. Tail brownish-black, margined externally with yellowish-white. Under parts brownish-grey, fading posteriorly into white.

Length $5\frac{1}{4}$ inches, extent of wings $8\frac{1}{4}$; bill along the ridge $\frac{9}{12}$, along
the gap $\frac{1}{2}$; tarsus $\frac{2}{3}$.

Adult Female. Plate XXVIII. Fig. 2.

The female is considerably duller. The colouring is generally similar, but the head is brownish-grey, and the band on the forehead and
round the eyes narrower and tinged with grey.

Length $5\frac{1}{4}$.

THE AMERICAN CANE.

MIEGIA MACROSPERMA, *Pursh.* Fl. Amer. vol. l. p. 59. ARUNDINARIA MACROS-
PERMA, *Mich.* Fl. Amer. vol. l. p. 74.—TRIANDRIA MONOGYNIA, *Linn.* GRA-
MINEÆ, *Juss.*

As the Cane is elsewhere described, it is unnecessary to speak particularly of it here.

THE TOWHE BUNTING.

FRINGILLA ERYTHROPHTHALMA, LINN.

PLATE XXIX. MALE AND FEMALE.

THE flight of the Towhe Bunting is short, low, and performed from one bush or spot to another, in a hurried manner, with repeated strong jerks of the tail, and such quick motions of the wings, that one may hear their sound, although the bird should happen to be out of sight. On the ground, where it is more usually to be seen, it hops lightly, without moving the tail more than the Common Sparrow of Europe. It is a diligent bird, spending its days in searching for food and gravel, amongst the dried leaves and in the earth, scratching with great assiduity, and every now and then uttering the notes *tow-hee*, from which it has obtained its name. At other times, it ascends to the top of a small tree, or its favourite low bushes and briars, on which it sings very sweetly a few continued mellow notes.

This species constructs a larger nest than birds of its size usually do, and scoops out a place for its foundation in the earth, sometimes in an open spot, more commonly at the foot of a small sapling or large bunch of tall grass. The nest is sunk into the ground, so as to be level with it at top, and is composed of dried leaves and the bark of vines, lined with grasses of fine texture, as well as fibrous roots. The female lays from four to six eggs, and rears two, sometimes three, broods each season. If disturbed while sitting, she moves off apparently in great agony, but with more celerity than most other birds, by which means she generally prevents her nest being discovered. Snakes, however, suck the eggs, as does the Crow. The young leave the nest long before they are able to fly, and follow the mother about on the ground for several days. Some of the nests of this species are so well concealed, that in order to discover them, one requires to stand quite still on the first appearance of the mother. I have myself several times had to regret not taking this precaution.

The favourite haunts of the Towhe Buntings are dry barren tracts, but not, as others have said, low and swampy grounds, at least during the season of incubation. In the Barrens of Kentucky they are found in the greatest abundance.

Their migrations are performed by day, from bush to bush, and they seem to be much at a loss when a large extent of forest is to be traversed by them. They perform these journeys almost singly. The females set out before the males in autumn, and the males before the females in spring, the latter not appearing in the Middle Districts until the end of April, a fortnight after the males have arrived. Many of them pass the confines of the United States in their migrations southward and north-ward.

Although these birds are abundant in all parts of the Union, they never associate in flocks, but mingle during winter with several species of Sparrow. They generally rest on the ground at night, when many are caught by weasels and other small quadrupeds. None of them breed in Louisiana, nor indeed in the State of Mississippi, until they reach the open woods of the Choctaw Indian Nation.

I have represented the male and female moving through the twigs of the Common Briar, usually called the *Black Briar.* It is a plump bird, and becomes very fat in winter, in consequence of which it is named *Grasset* in Louisiana, where many are shot for the table by the French planters.

FRINGILLA ERYTHROPHTHALMA, *Linn.* Syst. Nat. vol. i. p. 318.—*Ch. Bonaparte,* Synops. of Birds of the United States, p. 112.
EMBERIZA ERYTHROPHTHALMA, *Lath.* Ind. Ornith. vol. i. p. 413.
TOWHE BUNTING, EMBERIZA ERYTHROPHTHALMA, *Wils.* Amer. Ornith. vol. ii. p. 35. Pl. 10. fig. 5. Male; vol. vi. p. 90. Pl. 53. fig. 5. Female.—*Lath.* Synops. vol. iii. p. 199.

Adult Male. Plate XXIX. Fig. 1.

Bill short, robust, narrower than the head, regularly conical, acute ; upper mandible almost straight in its dorsal outline, as is the lower, both having inflected edges ; the gap line nearly straight, a little deflected at the base. Nostrils basal, roundish, open, partially concealed by the feathers. Head rather large, neck shortish, body robust. Legs of moderate length, rather robust ; tarsus longer than the middle toe, covered anteriorly with a few longish scutella ; toes scutellate above, free, the lateral ones nearly equal ; claws slender, arched, compressed, acute, that of the hind toe long.

Plumage rather compact above, soft and blended beneath. Wings of ordinary length, the third and fourth quills longest, the first much shorter, the secondaries short. Tail long, rounded, the lateral feathers slightly curved outwards towards the tip.

Bill black. Iris bright red. Legs and claws pale yellowish-brown. Head, neck, and upper parts generally, deep black. A white band across the primaries, partly concealed by their coverts; outer edge of first quill white; margins of the last secondaries brownish-white. Lateral tail-feathers white, excepting at the base, and a longitudinal streak towards the tip, on the outer web; the next two white on the inner web, towards the end. Breast white, abdomen pale red; sides and lateral parts of the breast brownish-red.

Length 8½ inches, extent of wings 12; beak along the ridge ½, along the gap ⅜; tarsus 1½, middle toe 1, hind toe ⅝.

Adult Female.   Plate XXIX. Fig. 2.

The female is scarcely smaller, and differs from the male in having the parts which in him are of a deep black, reddish-brown, excepting the bill, which is almost entirely light blue, the ridge of the upper mandible only being dark brown.

Length 8¼ inches.

In the adult bird the iris is bright red, but in the young it is frequently brown, and sometimes yellowish-white. In some instances, one eye is brown and the other red.

THE BLACKBERRY.

RUBUS VILLOSUS, *Willd.* Sp. Pl. vol. ii. p. 1085. *Pursh,* Fl. Amer. vol. i. p. 346.— ICOSANDRIA POLYGYNIA, *Linn.* ROSACEÆ, *Juss.*

Pubescent, prickly, with angular twigs; the leaves ternate or quinate, with ovato-oblong, serrate, acuminate leaflets, downy on both sides; the calycine leaves short, acuminate; and a loose raceme of white flowers. The berry is black. This species grows abundantly in old fields and by fences.

VIGORS'S WARBLER.

SYLVIA VIGORSII.

PLATE XXX. MALE.

I REGRET that I am unable to give any account of the habits of a species which I have honoured with the name of a naturalist whose merits are so well known to the learned world. The individual represented in the plate I shot upwards of twenty years ago, and have never met with another of its kind. It was in the month of May, on a small island of the Perkioming Creek, forming part of my farm of Mill Grove, in the State of Pennsylvania. The bird was flittering amongst grasses, uttering an often repeated *cheep*.

The plant on which it is represented is that on which it was perched when I shot it, and is usually called *Spider-wort*. It grows in damp and shady places, as well as sometimes in barren lands, near the banks of brooks.

SYLVIA VIGORSII.

Male. Plate XXX.

Bill of ordinary length, rather robust, depressed at the base, straight, acute; upper mandible notched, slightly deflected at the tip; lower shorter. Head of ordinary size, neck short, body ovate. Legs of ordinary length, slender; tarsus compressed, anteriorly covered with a few long scutella, toes free, the lateral ones nearly equal, the middle toe much longer; claws weak, much compressed, acute, slightly arched.

Plumage soft, tufty, blended. Wings of ordinary size, the second quill longest. Tail longish, a little forked, of twelve feathers. A few small basirostral bristles.

Bill brownish-black. Iris dark brown. Feet flesh-coloured. Head and back light greenish-brown. Wings blackish-brown, the first two rows of coverts tipped with white. Tail of the some colour, the outer feather white. Throat pale grey, lower neck and breast ochre-yellow, abdomen yellowish-white.

Length 6 inches, extent of wings 9; bill along the ridge $\frac{4}{12}$, along the gap $\frac{7}{12}$; tarsus $\frac{5}{6}$, middle toe $\frac{6}{8}$.

The Virginian Spider-wort.

Tradescantia virginica, *Willd.* Sp. Pl. vol. ii. p. 16. *Pursh,* Fl. Amer. vol. i. p. 218.—Hexandria Monogynia, *Linn.* Junci, *Juss.*

This species is distinguished by its erect, succulent stem; elongated, lanceolate, smooth leaves; and umbellate, subsessile flowers, which are of a deep purple colour, with yellow anthers.

A FLOOD.

MANY of our larger streams, such as the Mississippi, the Ohio, the Illinois, the Arkansas and the Red River, exhibit at certain seasons the most extensive overflowings of their waters, to which the name of *floods* is more appropriate than the term *freshets*, usually applied to the sudden risings of smaller streams. If we consider the vast extent of country through which an inland navigation is afforded by the never-failing supply of water furnished by these wonderful rivers, we cannot suppose them exceeded in magnitude by any other in the known world. It will easily be imagined what a wonderful spectacle must present itself to the eye of the traveller, who for the first time views the enormous mass of waters, collected from the vast central regions of our continent, booming along, turbid and swollen to overflowing, in the broad channels of the Mississippi and Ohio, the latter of which has a course of more than a thousand miles, and the former of several thousands.

To give you some idea of a *Booming Flood* of these gigantic streams, it is necessary to state the causes which give rise to it. These are, the sudden melting of the snows on the mountains, and heavy rains continued for several weeks. When it happens that, during a severe winter, the Alleghany Mountains have been covered with snow to the depth of several feet, and the accumulated mass has remained unmelted for a length of time, the materials of a flood are thus prepared. It now and then happens that the winter is hurried off by a sudden increase of temperature, when the accumulated snows melt away simultaneously over the whole country, and the south-easterly wind which then usually blows, brings along with it a continued fall of heavy rain, which, mingling with the dissolving snow, deluges the alluvial portions of the western country, filling up the rivulets, ravines, creeks and small rivers. These delivering their waters to the great streams, cause the latter not merely to rise to a surprising height, but to overflow their banks, wherever the land is low. On such occasions, the Ohio itself presents a splendid, and at the same time an appalling spectacle; but when its waters mingle with those of the Mississippi, then, kind reader, is the time to view an American flood in all its astonishing magnificence.

At the foot of the Falls of the Ohio, the water has been known to rise

upwards of sixty feet above its lowest level. The river, at this point, has
already run a course of nearly seven hundred miles, from its origin at Pittsburg, in Pennsylvania, during which it has received the waters of its numberless tributaries, and overflowing all the bottom lands or valleys, has
swept along the fences and dwellings which have been unable to resist its
violence. I could relate hundreds of incidents which might prove to you
the dreadful effects of such an inundation, and which have been witnessed
by thousands besides myself. I have known, for example, of a cow
swimming through a window, elevated at least seven feet from the
ground, and sixty-two feet above low-water mark. The house was then
surrounded by water from the Ohio, which runs in front of it, while the
neighbouring country was overflowed; yet the family did not remove
from it, but remained in its upper portion, having previously taken off
the sashes of the lower windows, and opened the doors. But let us return to the Mississippi.

There the overflow is astonishing; for no sooner has the water reached the upper part of the banks, than it rushes out and overspreads the
whole of the neighbouring swamps, presenting an ocean overgrown with
stupendous forest-trees. So sudden is the calamity, that every individual, whether man or beast, has to exert his utmost ingenuity to enable
him to escape from the dreaded element. The Indian quickly removes
to the hills of the interior, the cattle and game swim to the different
stripes of land that remain uncovered in the midst of the flood, or attempt to force their way through the waters until they perish from
fatigue. Along the banks of the river, the inhabitants have rafts ready
made, on which they remove themselves, their cattle and their provisions,
and which they then fasten with ropes or grape-vines to the larger trees,
while they contemplate the melancholy spectacle presented by the current,
as it carries off their houses and wood-yards piece by piece. Some who
have nothing to lose, and are usually known by the name of *Squatters*,
take this opportunity of traversing the woods in canoes, for the purpose
of procuring game, and particularly the skins of animals, such as the
deer and bear, which may be converted into money. They resort to the
low ridges surrounded by the waters, and destroy thousands of deer,
merely for their skins, leaving the flesh to putrefy.

The river itself, rolling its swollen waters along, presents a spectacle
of the most imposing nature. Although no large vessel, unless propelled
by steam, can now make its way against the current, it is seen covered

by boats, laden with produce, which running out from all the smaller streams, float silently towards the City of New Orleans, their owners meanwhile not very well assured of finding a landing-place even there. The water is covered with yellow foam and pumice, the latter having floated from the Rocky Mountains of the north-west. The eddies are larger and more powerful than ever. Here and there tracts of forest are observed undermined, the trees gradually giving way, and falling into the stream. Cattle, horses, bears and deer are seen at times attempting to swim across the impetuous mass of foaming and boiling water ; whilst here and there a Vulture or an Eagle is observed perched on a bloated carcass, tearing it up in pieces, as regardless of the flood, as on former occasions it would have been of the numerous *sawyers* and *planters*, with which the surface of the river is covered, when the water is low. Even the steamer is frequently distressed. The numberless trees and logs that float along break its paddles and retard its progress. Besides, it is on such occasions difficult to procure fuel to maintain its fires ; and it is only at very distant intervals that a wood-yard can be found which the water has not carried off.

Following the river in your canoe, you reach those parts of the shores that are protected against the overflowing of the waters, and are called *Levees*. There you find the whole population of the district at work repairing and augmenting those artificial barriers, which are several feet above the level of the fields. Every person appears to dread the opening of a *crevasse*, by which the waters may rush into his fields. In spite of all exertions, however, the crevasse opens, the water bursts impetuously over the plantations, and lays waste the crops which so lately were blooming in all the luxuriance of spring. It opens up a new channel, which, for aught I know to the contrary, may carry its waters even to the Mexican Gulf.

I have floated on the Mississippi and Ohio when thus swollen, and have in different places visited the submersed lands of the interior, propelling a light canoe by the aid of a paddle. In this manner I have traversed immense portions of the country overflowed by the waters of these rivers, and, particularly whilst floating over the Mississippi bottomlands, I have been struck with awe at the sight. Little or no current is met with, unless when the canoe passes over the bed of a bayou. All is silent and melancholy, unless when the mournful bleeting of the hemmed in Deer reaches your ear, or the dismal scream of an Eagle or a

Raven is heard, as the foul bird rises, disturbed by your approach, from the carcass on which it was allaying its craving appetite. Bears, Cougars, Lynxes, and all other quadrupeds that can ascend the trees, are observed crouched among their top branches. Hungry in the midst of abundance, although they see floating around them the animals on which they usually prey, they dare not venture to swim to them. Fatigued by the exertions which they have made in reaching the dry land, they will there stand the hunter's fire, as if to die by a ball were better than to perish amid the waste of waters. On occasions like this, all these animals are shot by hundreds.

Opposite the City of Natchez, which stands on a bluff bank of considerable elevation, the extent of inundated land is immense, the greater portion of the tract lying between the Mississippi and the Red River, which is more than thirty miles in breadth, being under water. The mail-bag has often been carried through the immersed forests, in a canoe, for even a greater distance, in order to be forwarded to Natchitochez.

But now, kind reader, observe this great flood gradually subsiding, and again see the mighty changes which it has effected. The waters have now been carried into the distant ocean. The earth is everywhere covered by a deep deposit of muddy loam, which in drying splits into deep and narrow chasms, presenting a reticulated appearance, and from which, as the weather becomes warmer, disagreeable, and at times noxious, exhalations arise, and fill the lower stratum of the atmosphere as with a dense fog. The banks of the river have almost everywhere been broken down in a greater or less degree. Large streams are now found to exist, where none were formerly to be seen, having forced their way in direct lines from the upper parts of the bends. These are by the navigator called *short-cuts*. Some of them have proved large enough to produce a change in the navigation of the Mississippi. If I mistake not, one of these, known by the name of the *Grand Cut-off*, and only a few miles in length, has diverted the river from its natural course, and has shortened it by fifty miles. The upper parts of the islands present a bulwark consisting of an enormous mass of floated trees of all kinds, which have lodged there. Large sand-banks have been completely removed by the impetuous whirls of the waters, and have been deposited in other places. Some appear quite new to the eye of the navigator, who has to mark their situation and bearings in his log-book. The trees on the margins of the banks have in many parts given way. They are seen bending over the stream, like the grounded arms of an overwhelmed army of giants. Everywhere are heard the lamentations of the farmer and planter, whilst their servants and themselves are busily employed in repairing the damages occasioned by the floods. At one crevasse an old ship or two, dismantled for the purpose, are sunk, to obstruct the passage opened by the still rushing waters, while new earth is brought to fill up the chasms. The squatter is seen shouldering his rifle, and making his way through the morass, in search of his lost stock, to drive the survivors home, and save the skins of the drowned. New fences have everywhere to be formed; even new houses must be erected, to save which from a like disaster, the settler places them on an elevated platform supported by pillars made of the trunks of trees. The lands must be ploughed anew, and if the season is not too far advanced, a crop of corn and potatoes may yet be raised. But the rich prospects of the planter are blasted. The traveller is impeded in his journey, the creeks and smaller streams having broken up their banks in a degree proportionate to their size. A bank of sand, which seems firm and secure, suddenly gives way beneath the traveller's horse, and the next moment the animal has sunk in the quicksand, either to the chest in front, or over the crupper behind, leaving its master in a situation not to be envied.

Unlike the mountain-torrents and small rivers of other parts of the world, the Mississippi rises but slowly during these floods, continuing for several weeks to increase at the rate of about an inch in the day. When at its height, it undergoes little fluctuation for some days, and after this subsides as slowly as it rose. The usual duration of a flood is from four to six weeks, although, on some occasions, it is protracted to two months.

Every one knows how largely the idea of floods and cataclysms enters into the speculations of the geologist. If the streamlets of the European Continent afford illustrations of the formation of strata, how much more must the Mississippi, with its ever-shifting sand-banks, its crumbling shores, its enormous masses of drift timber, the source of future beds of coal, its extensive and varied alluvial deposits, and its mighty mass of waters rolling sullenly along, like the flood of eternity!

THE WHITE-HEADED EAGLE.

FALCO LEUCOCEPHALUS, Linn.

PLATE XXXI. Male.

The figure of this noble bird is well known throughout the civilized world, emblazoned as it is on our national standard, which waves in the breeze of every clime, bearing to distant lands the remembrance of a great people living in a state of peaceful freedom. May that peaceful freedom last for ever!

The great strength, daring, and cool courage of the White-headed Eagle, joined to his unequalled power of flight, render him highly conspicuous among his brethren. To these qualities did he add a generous disposition towards others, he might be looked up to as a model of nobility. The ferocious, overbearing, and tyrannical temper which is ever and anon displaying itself in his actions, is, nevertheless, best adapted to his state, and was wisely given him by the Creator to enable him to perform the office assigned to him.

To give you, kind reader, some idea of the nature of this bird, permit me to place you on the Mississippi, on which you may float gently along, while approaching winter brings millions of water-fowl on whistling wings, from the countries of the north, to seek a milder climate in which to sojourn for a season. The Eagle is seen perched, in an erect attitude, on the highest summit of the tallest tree by the margin of the broad stream. His glistening but stern eye looks over the vast expanse. He listens attentively to every sound that comes to his quick ear from afar, glancing now and then on the earth beneath, lest even the light tread of the fawn may pass unheard. His mate is perched on the opposite side, and should all be tranquil and silent, warns him by a cry to continue patient. At this well known call, the male partly opens his broad wings, inclines his body a little downwards, and answers to her voice in tones not unlike the laugh of a maniac. The next moment, he resumes his erect attitude, and again all around is silent. Ducks of many species, the Teal, the Wigeon, the Mallard and others, are seen passing with great rapidity, and following the course of the current; but the Eagle heeds them not: they are at that time beneath

1

his attention. The next moment, however, the wild trumpet-like sound of a yet distant but approaching Swan is heard. A shriek from the female Eagle comes across the stream,—for, kind reader, she is fully as alert as her mate. The latter suddenly shakes the whole of his body, and with a few touches of his bill, aided by the action of his cuticular muscles, arranges his plumage in an instant. The snow-white bird is now in sight: her long neck is stretched forward, her eye is on the watch, vigilant as that of her enemy; her large wings seem with difficulty to support the weight of her body, although they flap incessantly. So irksome do her exertions seem, that her very legs are spread beneath her tail, to aid her in her flight. She approaches, however. The Eagle has marked her for his prey. As the Swan is passing the dreaded pair, starts from his perch, in full preparation for the chase, the male bird, with an awful scream, that to the Swan's ear brings more terror than the report of the large duck-gun.

Now is the moment to witness the display of the Eagle's powers. He glides through the air like a falling star, and, like a flash of lightning, comes upon the timorous quarry, which now, in agony and despair, seeks, by various manœuvres, to elude the grasp of his cruel talons. It mounts, doubles, and willingly would plunge into the stream, were it not prevented by the Eagle, which, long possessed of the knowledge that by such a stratagem the Swan might escape him, forces it to remain in the air by attempting to strike it with his talons from beneath. The hope of escape is soon given up by the Swan. It has already become much weakened, and its strength fails at the sight of the courage and swiftness of its antagonist. Its last gasp is about to escape, when the ferocious Eagle strikes with his talons the under side of its wing, and with unresisted power forces the bird to fall in a slanting direction upon the nearest shore.

It is then, reader, that you may see the cruel spirit of this dreaded enemy of the feathered race, whilst, exulting over his prey, he for the first time breathes at ease. He presses down his powerful feet, and drives his sharp claws deeper than ever into the heart of the dying Swan. He shrieks with delight, as he feels the last convulsions of his prey, which has now sunk under his unceasing efforts to render death as painfully felt as it can possibly be. The female has watched every movement of her mate; and if she did not assist him in capturing the Swan, it was not from want of will, but merely that she felt full assurance that the power

L

and courage of her lord were quite sufficient for the deed. She now sails
to the spot where he eagerly awaits her, and when she has arrived, they
together turn the breast of the luckless Swan upwards, and gorge themselves with gore.

At other times, when these Eagles, sailing in search of prey, discover
a Goose, a Duck, or a Swan, that has alighted on the water, they accomplish its destruction in a manner that is worthy of your attention. The
Eagles, well aware that water-fowl have it in their power to dive at their
approach, and thereby elude their attempts upon them, ascend in the air
in opposite directions over the lake or river, on which they have observed
the object which they are desirous of possessing. Both Eagles reach a
certain height, immediately after which one of them glides with great
swiftness towards the prey; the latter, meantime, aware of the Eagle's intention, dives the moment before he reaches the spot. The pursuer then
rises in the air, and is met by its mate, which glides toward the water-
bird, that has just emerged to breathe, and forces it to plunge again beneath the surface, to escape the talons of this second assailant. The first
Eagle is now poising itself in the place where its mate formerly was, and
rushes anew to force the quarry to make another plunge. By thus alternately gliding, in rapid and often repeated rushes, over the ill-fated bird,
they soon fatigue it, when it stretches out its neck, swims deeply, and
makes for the shore, in the hope of concealing itself among the rank
weeds. But this is of no avail, for the Eagles follow it in all its motions, and the moment it approaches the margin, one of them darts
upon it, and kills it in an instant, after which they divide the spoil.

During spring and summer, the White-headed Eagle, to procure sustenance, follows a different course, and one much less suited to a bird
apparently so well able to supply itself without interfering with other
plunderers. No sooner does the Fish-Hawk make its appearance along
our Atlantic shores, or ascend our numerous and large rivers, than the
Eagle follows it, and, like a selfish oppressor, robs it of the hard-earned
fruits of its labour. Perched on some tall summit, in view of the ocean,
or of some water-course, he watches every motion of the Osprey while on
wing. When the latter rises from the water, with a fish in its grasp,
forth rushes the Eagle in pursuit. He mounts above the Fish-Hawk,
and threatens it by actions well understood, when the latter, fearing perhaps that its life is in danger, drops its prey. In an instant, the Eagle,
accurately estimating the rapid descent of the fish, closes his wings, fol-

lows it with the swiftness of thought, and the next moment grasps it. The prize is carried off in silence to the woods, and assists in feeding the ever-hungry brood of the Eagle.

This bird now and then procures fish himself, by pursuing them in the shallows of small creeks. I have witnessed several instances of this in the Perkioming Creek in Pennsylvania, where, in this manner, I saw one of them secure a number of *Red-fins*, by wading briskly through the water, and striking at them with his bill. I have also observed a pair scrambling over the ice of a frozen pond, to get at some fish below, but without success.

It does not confine itself to these kinds of food, but greedily devours young pigs, lambs, fawns, poultry, and the putrid flesh of carcasses of every description, driving off the vultures and carrion-crows, or the dogs, and keeping a whole party at defiance until it is satiated. It frequently gives chase to the vultures, and forces them to disgorge the contents of their stomachs, when it alights and devours the filthy mass. A ludicrous instance of this took place near the city of Natchez, on the Mississippi. Many Vultures were engaged in devouring the body and entrails of a dead horse, when a White-headed Eagle accidentally passing by, the vultures all took to wing, one among the rest with a portion of the entrails partly swallowed, and the remaining part, about a yard in length, dangling in the air. The Eagle instantly marked him, and gave chase. The poor vulture tried in vain to disgorge, when the Eagle, coming up, seized the loose end of the gut, and dragged the bird along for twenty or thirty yards, much against its will, until both fell to the ground, when the Eagle struck the vulture, and in a few moments killed it, after which he swallowed the delicious morsel.

I have heard of several attempts made by this bird to destroy children, but have never witnessed any myself, although I have little doubt of its having sufficient daring to do so.

The flight of the White-headed Eagle is strong, generally uniform, and protracted to any distance, at pleasure. Whilst travelling, it is entirely supported by equal easy flappings, without any intermission, in as far as I have observed it, by following it with the eye or the assistance of a glass. When looking for prey, it sails with extended wings, at right angles to its body, now and then allowing its legs to hang at their full length. Whilst sailing, it has the power of ascending in circular sweeps, without a single flap of the wings, or any apparent motion either of them or of the tail ; and in this manner it often rises until it disappears from the view, the white tail remaining longer visible than the rest of the body.   At other times, it rises only a few hundred feet in the air, and sails off in a direct line, and with rapidity.   Again, when thus elevated, it partially closes its wings, and glides downwards for a considerable space, when, as if disappointed, it suddenly checks its career, and reassumes its former steady flight.   When at an immense height, and as if observing an object on the ground, it closes its wings, and glides through the air with such rapidity as to cause a loud rustling sound, not unlike that produced by a violent gust of wind passing amongst the branches of trees. Its fall towards the earth can scarcely be followed by the eye on such occasions, the more particularly that these falls or glidings through the air usually take place when they are least expected.

This bird has the power of raising from the surface of the water any floating object not heavier than itself.   In this manner it often robs the sportsman of ducks which have been killed by him.   Its audacity is quite remarkable.   While descending the Upper Mississippi, I observed one of these Eagles in pursuit of a Green-winged Teal.   It came so near our boat, although several persons were looking on, that I could perceive the glancings of its eye.   The Teal, on the point of being caught, when not more than fifteen or twenty yards from us, was saved from the grasp of its enemy, one of our party having brought the latter down by a shot, which broke one of its wings.   When taken on board, it was fastened to the deck of our boat by means of a string, and was fed with pieces of cat-fish, some of which it began to eat on the third day of its confinement. But, as it became a very disagreeable and dangerous associate, trying on all occasions to strike at some one with its talons, it was killed and thrown overboard.

When these birds are suddenly and unexpectedly approached or surprised, they exhibit a great degree of cowardice.   They rise at once and fly off very low, in zig-zag lines, to some distance, uttering a hissing noise, not at all like their usual disagreeable imitation of a laugh.   When not carrying a gun, one may easily approach them ; but the use of that instrument being to appearance well known to them, they are very cautious in allowing a person having one to get near them.   Notwithstanding all their caution, however, many are shot by approaching them under cover of a tree, on horseback, or in a boat.   They do not possess the power of smelling gunpowder, as the crow and the raven are absurdly supposed to do ; nor are they aware of the effects of spring-traps, as I have seen some of them caught by these instruments. Their sight, although probably as perfect as that of any bird, is much affected during a fall of snow, at which time they may be approached without difficulty.

The White-headed Eagle seldom appears in very mountainous districts, but prefers the low lands of the sea-shores, those of our large lakes, and the borders of rivers. It is a constant resident in the United States, in every part of which it is to be seen. The roosts and breeding places of pigeons are resorted to by it, for the purpose of picking up the young birds that happen to fall, or the old ones when wounded. It seldom, however, follows the flocks of these birds when on their migrations.

When shot at and wounded, it tries to escape by long and quickly repeated leaps, and, if not closely pursued, soon conceals itself. Should it happen to fall on the water, it strikes powerfully with expanded wings, and in this manner often reaches the shore, when it is not more than twenty or thirty yards distant. It is capable of supporting life without food for a long period. I have heard of some, which, in a state of confinement, had lived without much apparent distress for twenty days, although I cannot vouch for the truth of such statements, which, however, may be quite correct. They defend themselves in the manner usually followed by other Eagles and Hawks, throwing themselves backwards, and furiously striking with their talons at any object within reach, keeping their bill open, and turning their head with quickness to watch the movements of the enemy, their eyes being apparently more protruded than when unmolested.

It is supposed that Eagles live to a very great age,—some persons have ventured to say even a hundred years. On this subject, I can only observe, that I once found one of these birds, which, on being killed, proved to be a female, and which, judging by its appearance, must have been very old. Its tail and wing-feathers were so worn out, and of such a rusty colour, that I imagined the bird had lost the power of moulting. The legs and feet were covered with large warts, the claws and bill were much blunted, it could scarcely fly more than a hundred yards at a time, and this it did with a heaviness and unsteadiness of motion such as I never witnessed in any other bird of the species. The body was poor and very tough. The eye was the only part which appeared to have sustained no injury. It remained sparkling and full of animation, and even after death seemed to have lost little of its lustre. No wounds were perceivable on its body.

The White-headed Eagle is seldom seen alone, the mutual attachment which two individuals form when they first pair seeming to continue until one of them dies or is destroyed. They hunt for the support of each other, and seldom feed apart, but usually drive off other birds of the same species. They commence their amatory intercourse at an earlier period than any other *land bird* with which I am acquainted, generally in the month of December. At this time, along the Mississippi, or by the margin of some lake not far in the interior of the forest, the male and female birds are observed making a great bustle, flying about and circling in various ways, uttering a loud cackling noise, alighting on the dead branches of the tree on which their nest is already preparing, or in the act of being repaired, and caressing each other. In the beginning of January incubation commences. I shot a female, on the 17th of that month, as she sat on her eggs, in which the chicks had made considerable progress.

The nest, which in some instances is of great size, is usually placed on a very tall tree, destitute of branches to a considerable height, but by no means always a dead one. It is never seen on rocks. It is composed of sticks, from three to five feet in length, large pieces of turf, rank weeds, and Spanish moss in abundance, whenever that substance happens to be near. When finished, it measures from five to six feet in diameter, and so great is the accumulation of materials, that it sometimes measures the same in depth, it being occupied for a great number of years in succession, and receiving some augmentation each season. When placed in a naked tree, between the forks of the branches, it is conspicuously seen at a great distance. The eggs, which are from two to four, more commonly two or three, are of a dull white colour, and equally rounded at both ends, some of them being occasionally granulated. Incubation lasts for more than three weeks, but I have not been able to ascertain its precise duration, as I have observed the female on different occasions sit for a few days in the nest, before laying the first egg. Of this I assured myself by climbing to the nest every day in succession, during her temporary absence,—a rather perilous undertaking when the bird is sitting.

I have seen the young birds when not larger than middle-sized pullets. At this time, they are covered with a soft cottony kind of down, their bill and legs appearing disproportionately large. Their first plumage is of a greyish colour, mixed with brown of different depths of tint, and before the parents drive them off from the nest, they are fully fledged. As a figure of the Young White-headed Eagle will appear in the course of the publication of my Illustrations, I shall not here trouble you with a description of its appearance. I once caught three young Eagles of this species, when fully fledged, by having the tree on which their nest was cut down. It caused great trouble to secure them, as they could fly and scramble much faster than any of our party could run. They, however, gradually became fatigued, and at length were so exhausted as to offer no resistance, when we were securing them with cords. This happened on the border of Lake Pontchartrain, in the month of April. The parents did not think fit to come within gun-shot of the tree while the axe was at work.

The attachment of the parents to the young is very great, when the latter are yet of a small size; and to ascend to the nest at this time would be dangerous. But as the young advance, and, after being able to take wing and provide for themselves, are not disposed to fly off, the old birds turn them out, and beat them away from them. They return to the nest, however, to roost, or sleep on the branches immediately near it, for several weeks after. They are fed most abundantly while under the care of the parents, which procure for them ample supplies of fish, either accidentally cast ashore, or taken from the Fish-Hawk, together with rabbits, squirrels, young lambs, pigs, opossums, or raccoons. Every thing that comes in the way is relished by the young family, as by the old birds.

The young birds begin to breed the following spring, not always in pairs of the same age, as I have several times observed one of these birds in brown plumage mated with a full-coloured bird, which had the head and tail pure white. I once shot a pair of this kind, when the brown bird (the young one) proved to be the female.

This species requires at least four years before it attains the full beauty of its plumage when kept in confinement. I have known two instances in which the white of the head did not make its appearance until the sixth spring. It is impossible for me to say how much sooner this state of perfection is attained, when the bird is at full liberty, although I should suppose it to be at least one year, as the bird is capable of breeding the first spring after birth.

The weight of Eagles of this species varies considerably. In the males, it is from six to eight pounds, and in the females from eight to twelve. These birds are so attached to particular districts, where they have first made their nest, that they seldom spend a night at any distance from the latter, and often resort to its immediate neighbourhood. Whilst asleep, they emit a loud hissing sort of snore, which is heard at the distance of a hundred yards, when the weather is perfectly calm. Yet, so light is their sleep, that the cracking of a stick under the foot of a person immediately wakens them. When it is attempted to smoke them while thus roosted and asleep, they start up and sail off without uttering any sound, but return next evening to the same spot.

Before steam-navigation commenced on our western rivers, these Eagles were extremely abundant there, particularly in the lower parts of the Ohio, the Mississippi, and the adjoining streams. I have seen hundreds going down from the mouth of the Ohio to New Orleans, when it was not at all difficult to shoot them. Now, however, their number is considerably diminished, the game on which they were in the habit of feeding, having been forced to seek refuge from the persecution of man farther in the wilderness. Many, however, are still observed on these rivers, particularly along the shores of the Mississippi.

In concluding this account of the White-headed Eagle, suffer me, kind reader, to say how much I grieve that it should have been selected as the Emblem of my Country. The opinion of our great Franklin on this subject, as it perfectly coincides with my own, I shall here present to you. " For my part," says he, in one of his letters, " I wish the Bald Eagle had not been chosen as the representative of our country. He is a bird of bad moral character ; he does not get his living honestly ; you may have seen him perched on some dead tree, where, too lazy to fish for himself, he watches the labour of the Fishing-Hawk ; and when that diligent bird has at length taken a fish, and is bearing it to his nest for the support of his mate and young ones, the Bald Eagle pursues him, and takes it from him. With all this injustice, he is never in good case, but, like those among men who live by sharping and robbing, he is generally poor, and often very lousy. Besides, he is a rank coward : the little King Bird, not bigger than a Sparrow, attacks him boldly, and drives him out of the district. He is, therefore, by no means a proper emblem for the brave and honest Cincinnati of America, who have driven all the *King Birds* from our country ; though exactly fit for that order of knights which the French call *Chevaliers d'Industrie*."

It is only necessary for me to add, that the name by which this bird is universally known in America is that of *Bald Eagle,* an erroneous denomination, as its head is as densely feathered as that of any other species, although its whiteness may have suggested the idea of its being bare.

FALCO LEUCOCEPHALUS, *Linn.* Syst. Nat. vol. i. p. 124.—*Lath.* Ind. Ornith. vol. i. p. 11.

BALD EAGLE, *Lath.* Synops. vol. i. p. 29.—*Wilson*, Americ. Ornith. vol. iv. p. 89. Pl. 36. Adult.

SEA EAGLE, FALCO OSSIFRAGUS, *Wils.* Amer. Ornith. vol. vii. p. 16. Pl. 55. fig. 2 Young.

Adult Male.   Plate XXXI.

Bill shortish, very deep, compressed ; upper mandible with the dorsal outline at first straight, curved towards the tip, rounded above, sloping and flattish on the sides, nearly straight, with an obtuse process, in the acute, overlapping edges ; the tip deflected, trigonal, acute, at its lower part nearly perpendicular to the gap line ; lower mandible slightly convex in its dorsal outline, with inflected acute edges, which are arched toward the end, the tip broadly rounded. A naked cere, in the fore part of which are the oblong, oblique, nearly dorsal, open nostrils, which have a process from the anterior margin. Head rather large, flat above. Neck robust, rather short. Body ovate. Feet with the leg long, the tarsus short, feathered in its upper third, rounded, anteriorly covered with transverse scutella, posteriorly with large, laterally with small tuberculous scales ; toes robust, free, scutellate above, papillar and scabrous beneath, with large tubercles ; claws curved, rounded, marginate beneath, very acute.

Plumage compact, imbricated, glossy ; feathers of the head, neck and breast, narrow and pointed ; of the back and breast acute, of the other parts broad and rounded. Space between the bill and eye barish, being sparsely covered with bristly feathers. Eyebrow bare and projecting. Wings long, second quill longest, first considerably shorter. Tail of ordinary length, much rounded, extending considerably beyond the tips of the wings ; of twelve, broad, rounded feathers.

Bill, cere, edge of eyebrow, iris, and feet, yellow ; claws bluish-black. The general colour of the plumage is deep chocolate, the head, neck, tail, abdomen, and upper and under tail-coverts, white.

Length 34 inches, extent of wings 7 feet ; bill along the back $2\frac{1}{4}$ inches, along the under mandible $2\frac{1}{4}$, in depth $1\frac{1}{12}$; tarsus 3, middle toe $3\frac{1}{2}$.

THE BLACK-BILLED CUCKOO.

COCCYZUS ERYTHROPHTHALMUS, CH. BONAP.

PLATE XXXII. MALE AND FEMALE.

I HAVE not met with this species in the State of Louisiana more than half a dozen times ; nor indeed have I seen it at all in the Western States, excepting that of Ohio, where I have occasionally observed an individual, apparently out of its usual range. Some of these individuals were probably bound for the Upper Lakes. The woody sides of the sea are the places to which this species usually resorts. It passes from the south early in March, and continues its route through Florida, Georgia, and all the other States verging on the Atlantic, beginning to rest and to breed in North Carolina, and extending its travels to the Province of Maine.

The flight of this species is swifter than that of its near relative, the Yellow-billed Cuckoo, for which bird it is easily mistaken by ordinary observers. It does not so much frequent the interior of woods, but appears along their margins, on the edges of creeks and damp places. But the most remarkable distinction between this species and the Yellow-billed Cuckoo is, that the former, instead of feeding principally on insects and fruits, procures fresh-water shellfish and aquatic larvæ for its sustenance. It is therefore more frequently seen on the ground, near the edges of the water, or descending along the drooping branches of trees to their extremities, to seize the insects in the water beneath them*.

The nest of this bird is built in places similar to those chosen by the other species, and is formed of the same materials, arranged with quite as little art. The females lay from four to six eggs, of a greenish-blue, nearly equal at both ends, but rather smaller than those of the Yellow-billed Cuckoo. It retires southward fully a fortnight before the latter.

It being so scarce a species in Louisiana, I have honoured it by placing a pair on a branch of Magnolia in bloom, although the birds represented were not shot on one of these trees, but in a swamp near some,

---

* After the summer showers, the ground is seen covered with multitudes of very small frogs, of a brownish-black colour, which many of the inhabitants foolishly suppose to have descended from the clouds. Some of these I have occasionally found in the stomach of the Black-billed Cuckoo.

where the birds were in pursuit of such flies as you see figured, probably
to amuse themselves.   The Magnolia has already been presented to
your view in another plate, where it was figured in seed.   Here you have
it arrayed in all the beauty of its splendid blossoms.

COCCYZUS ERYTHROPHTHALMUS, *Ch. Bonap.* Synops. of Birds of United States, p. 42.
BLACK-BILLED CUCKOO, CUCULUS ERYTHROPHTHALMA, *Wils.* Amer. Ornith. vol. iv.
p. 15. Pl. xxviii. fig. 2.

Adult Male.   Plate XXXII. Fig 1.

Bill as long as the head, compressed, slightly arched, acute, not more
robust than that of many Sylviæ; upper mandible carinated above, its
margins acute and entire; lower mandible carinated beneath, acute.
Nostrils basal, lateral, linear-elliptical, half-closed by a membrane. Head
and neck of ordinary size.   Body rather slender.   Feet short and small;
tarsus scutellate before and behind ; toes two before, separated ; two behind, one of which is versatile; the sole flat; claws slender, compressed,
arched.

Plumage blended, soft, slightly glossed.   Wings long, the first quill
short, the third longest.   Tail long, graduated, of ten feathers, which are
rather narrow and rounded.

Upper mandible brownish-black ; lower bluish.   Iris hasel.   A bare
space of a deep scarlet tint around the eye.   Feet dull blue.   The general colour of the upper parts is light greenish-brown.   Cheeks and forehead tinged with greyish-blue.   Tail-feathers, excepting the two middle
ones, tipped with white.   Under parts brownish-white.

Length 11¼ inches, extent of wings 15 ; beak along the ridge ⅚,
along the gap 1¼.

Adult Female.   Plate XXXII. Fig. 2.

The female differs very little in external appearance from the male,
and is nearly of the same dimensions.

THE GREAT MAGNOLIA.

MAGNOLIA GRANDIFLORA, *Wild.* Sp. Pl. vol. ii. p. 1255.

This plant has already been described at p. 28, the ripe fruit having
been represented in Plate V.

THE AMERICAN GOLDFINCH.

FRINGILLA TRISTIS, LINN.

PLATE XXXIII. Male and Female.

This species merely passes over the State of Louisiana in the beginning of January, and at that season is seen there for only a few days,
alighting on the highest tops of trees near water-courses, in small groups
of eight or ten, males and females together. They feed at that period on
the opening buds of Maples, and others that are equally tender and juicy.
In the month of November they are again seen moving southwards, and
for a few days only.

A few breed in Kentucky and the State of Ohio, but the Middle Districts are their principal places of resort during summer, although they
extend their migrations to a high latitude. They arrive in the State of
New York about the middle of April; and as they become very abundant in that State during the summer, I shall describe their habits as observed there.

The flight of the American Goldfinch is exactly similar to that of the
European Bird of the same name, being performed in deep curved lines, alternately rising and falling, after each propelling motion of the wings. It
scarcely ever describes one of these curves without uttering two or three
notes whilst ascending, such as its European relative uses on similar occasions. In this manner, its flight is prolonged to considerable distances,
and it frequently moves in a circling direction before alighting. Their
migration is performed during the day. They seldom alight on the
ground, unless to procure water, in which they wash with great liveliness and pleasure, after which they pick up some particles of gravel or
sand. So fond of each other's company are they, that a party of them
passing on the wing will alter its course at the calling of a single one
perched on a tree. This call is uttered with much emphasis: the bird
prolongs its usual note, without much alteration, and as the party approaches, erects its body, and moves it to the right and left, as if turning
on a pivot, apparently pleased at shewing the beauty of its plumage and
the elegance of its manners. No sooner has the flock, previously on
wing, alighted, than the whole party plume themselves, and then perform

a little sweet concert.　So much does the song of our Goldfinch resemble that of the European species, that whilst in France and England, I have frequently thought, and with pleasure thought, that they were the notes of our own bird which I heard.　In America again, the song of the Gold-finch recalled to my remembrance its transatlantic kinsman, and brought with it too a grateful feeling for the many acts of hospitality and kind-ness which I have experienced in the " old country."

The nest also is perfectly similar to that of the European bird, being externally composed of various lichens fastened together by saliva, and lined with the softest substances.　It is small and extremely handsome, and is generally fixed on a branch of the Lombardy Poplar, being some-times secured to one side of a twig only.　I have also found it in Alder bushes, a few feet above the ground, as well as in other trees.　The fe-male deposits from four to six eggs, which are white, tinged with blush, and marked at the larger end with reddish-brown spots.　They raise only one brood in a season.　The young follow the parents for a long time, are fed from the mouth, as Canaries are, and are gradually taught to ma-nage this themselves.　When it happens that the female is disturbed while on her nest, she glides off to a neighbouring tree, and calls for her mate, pivoting herself on her feet, as above described.　The male approaches, passes and repasses on the wing at a respectful distance from the intruder, in deeper curves than usual, uttering its ordinary note, and when the un-welcome visitant has departed, flies with joy to his nest, accompanied by the female, who presently resumes her occupation.

The food of the American Goldfinch consists chiefly of seeds of the Hemp, the Sun-flower, the Lettuce, and various species of Thistle.　Now and then, during winter, it eats the fruit of the Elder.

In ascending along the shores of the Mohawk river, in the month of August, I have met more of these pretty birds in the course of a day's walk than anywhere else ; and whenever a thistle was to be seen along either bank of the New York Canal, it was ornamented with one or more Goldfinches.　They tear up the down and withered petals of the ripening flowers with ease, leaning downwards upon them, eat off the seed, and allow the down to float in the air.　The remarkable plumage of the male, as well as its song, are at this season very agreeable ; and so familiar are these birds, that they suffer you to approach within a few yards, before they leave the plant on which they are seated.　For a considerable space along the Gennessee river, the shores of Lake Erie, Lake Ontario, and even Lake Superior, I have always seen many of them in the latter part of summer. They have then a decided preference for the vicinity of water.

It is an extremely hardy bird, and often remains the whole winter in the Middle Districts, although never in great numbers. When deprived of liberty, it will live to a great age in a room or cage. I have known two instances in which a bird of this species had been confined for upwards of ten years. They were procured in the market of New York when in mature plumage, and had been caught in trap-cages. One of them having undergone the severe training, more frequently inflicted in Europe than America, and known in France by the name of *galérien*, would draw water for its drink from a glass, it having a little chain attached to a narrow belt of soft leather fastened round its body, and another equally light chain fastened to a little bucket, kept by its weight in the water, until the little fellow raised it up with its bill, placed a foot upon it, and pulled again at the chain until it reached the desired fluid and drank, when, on letting go, the bucket immediately fell into the glass below. In the same manner, it was obliged to draw towards its bill a little chariot filled with seeds ; and in this distressing occupation was doomed to toil through a life of solitary grief, separated from its companions, wantoning on the wildflowers, and procuring their food in the manner in which nature had taught them. After being caught in trap-cages, they feed as if quite contented ; but if it has been in spring that they have lost their liberty, and they have thus been deprived of the pleasures anticipated from the previous connexion of a mate, they linger for a few days and die. It is more difficult to procure a mule brood between our species and the Canary, than between the latter and the European Goldfinch, although I have known many instances in which the attempt was made with complete success.

The young males do not appear in full plumage until the following spring. The old ones lose their beauty in winter, and assume the duller tints of the female. In fact, at that season, young and old of both sexes resemble each other.

There is a trait of sagacity in this bird and the Purple Finch (*Fringilla purpurea*), which is quite remarkable, and worthy of the notice of such naturalists as are fond of contrasting instinct with reason. When a Goldfinch alights on a twig imbued with bird-lime expressly for the purpose of securing it, it no sooner discovers the nature of the treacherous substance, than it throws itself backwards, with closed wings, and hangs in this position until the bird-lime has run out in the form of a slender thread considerably below the twig, when feeling a certain degree of security, it beats its wings and flies off, with a resolution, doubtless, never to alight in such a place again ; as I have observed Goldfinches that had escaped from me in this manner, when about to alight on any twig, whether smeared with bird-lime or not, flutter over it, as if to assure themselves of its being safe for them to perch upon it.

FRINGILLA TRISTIS, *Linn.* Syst. Nat. vol. i. p. 320.—*Lath.* Ind. Ornith. vol. i. p. 62.
—*Ch. Bonaparte*, Synopsis of Birds of the United States, p. 111.
AMERICAN GOLDFINCH, FRINGILLA TRISTIS, *Lath.* Synops. vol. iii. p. 288.—*Wils.*
Amer. Ornith. vol. i. p. 20. Pl. 1. fig. 2. Adult Male in Summer.—*Ch. Bonaparte*,
Amer. Ornith. vol. i. p. 57. Pl. 6. fig. 4. Female.

Adult Male in spring.   Plate XXXIII. Fig. 1.

Bill rather short, conical, very acute; upper mandible a little broader than the lower, very slightly declinate at the tip, rounded on the sides, as is the lower, which has the edges inflected and acute ; the gap line straight, not extending to beneath the eye.   Nostrils basal, roundish, concealed by the feathers.   Head rather large.   Neck short.   Body pretty full.   Legs of moderate length, slender ; tarsus longer than the middle toe, covered anteriorly with a few longish scutella ; toes scutellate above, free, the lateral ones nearly equal ; claws very slender, much compressed, acute, and slightly arched, that of the hind toe not much larger.

Plumage soft and blended.   Wings of ordinary length, the third and fourth quills longest, the second nearly as long.   Tail of ordinary length, forked, the lateral feathers curved outwards a little towards the tip.

Bill and feet yellowish-brown.   Iris dark brown.   The general colour of the plumage is a rich lemon-yellow, fading posteriorly into yellowish-white.   Fore and upper part of the head, wings, and tail, black ; quills externally margined, and the large coverts tipped, with yellowish-white ; inner webs of the tail white.

Length 4½ inches, extent of wings 8 ; bill along the ridge ⅓, along the gap ₁₆/₅.

Adult Female in spring.   Plate XXXIII. Fig. 2.

The female wants the black spot on the head, and in her the fine yellow of the male is changed into brownish-olive, fading posteriorly into yellowish-grey, the fore neck and breast greyish-yellow. The band formed by the tips of the large wing-coverts is dull white.

Length and other dimensions nearly as in the male.

THE COMMON THISTLE.

CNICUS LANCEOLATUS, *Willd.* Sp. Pl. vol. iii. p. 1666. *Pursh*, Flora Amer. vol. ii. p. 506. *Smith*, Engl. Bot. vol. iii. p. 388.—SYNGENESIA POLYGAMIA ÆQUALIS, *Linn.* CINAROCEPHALÆ, *Juss.*

This well known species of Thistle, common in the temperate and colder parts of both continents, it is unnecessary to describe.

THE WORM-EATING WARBLER.

SYLVIA VERMIVORA, LATH.

PLATE XXXIV. MALE AND FEMALE.

THE nest of this active little bird is formed of singular materials, being composed externally of dried mosses and the green blossoms of Hickories and Chestnut-trees, while the interior is prettily lined with fine fibrous roots, the whole apparently rather small for the size of the occupants. About the middle of May the female lays four or five eggs, which are cream-coloured, with a few dark red spots near the larger end, leaving a circular unspotted part at the extremity. The nest is usually placed between two small twigs of a bush, not more than eight or nine feet from the ground, and sometimes only four or five.

The flight of the Worm-eating Warbler resembles that of the Crested Titmouse, being of short duration, and accompanied with the same rustling noise, which is occasioned by the rather concave formation of their wings.

It merely passes through Louisiana in spring, appearing there as early as the beginning of April, and extends its migrations to the borders of Lake Erie, where I shot several in autumn. It is probable that it proceeds farther north. It returns through Louisiana about the end of October, only remaining a few days on its passage.

It is an inhabitant of the interior of the forests, and is seldom found on the borders of roads or in the fields. In spring they move in pairs, and, during their retrograde marches, in little groups, consisting each of a family, seven or eight in number ; on which account I am inclined to believe that they raise only a single brood in the year. They are ever amongst the decayed branches of trees or other plants, such as are accidentally broken off by the wind, and are there seen searching for insects or caterpillars. They also resort to the ground, and turn over the dried leaves in quest of the same kind of food. They are unsuspecting, and will suffer a person to approach within a few paces. When disturbed, they fly off to some place where withered leaves are seen. They have only a few weak notes, which do not deserve the name of song. Their industry, however, atones for this defect, as they are seen continually

M

moving about, rustling among the leaves, and scarcely ever removing from one situation to another until after they have made a full inspection of the part in which they have been employed.

This species reaches the Central Atlantic Districts in the middle of May, and breeds there, as well as farther northward. I have found them more numerous in the Jerseys than in any other portion of the Union. In Kentucky and Ohio I have seen only a few of them; nor have I ever found their nests in either of these States.

The plant on which you see a pair of Worm-eating Warblers is well known throughout the United States by the name of Poke-berry. It grows in every situation, from the tops of the most arid mountain-ridges to the lowest and richest valleys; and it is almost impossible to follow a fence for a hundred yards without seeing some of it. Its berries are food for numerous species of our birds, and produce a beautiful dark crimson juice, which is used instead of red ink by some of the country people, although it does not retain its original colour for many days. This plant grows to the height of four or six feet, and is eaten when it first shoots from the ground as a substitute for asparagus, quantities of it being not unfrequently exposed in the markets. The juice of the berries is taken in cases of ague and continued fever, but requires to be used with judgment, as too large a doze proves deleterious.

SYLVIA VERMIVORA, *Lath.* Ind. Ornith. vol. ii. p. 544.—*Ch. Bonaparte,* Synops. of Birds of the United States, p. 86.

WORM-EATING WARBLER, SYLVIA VERMIVORA, *Wils.* Americ. Ornith. vol. iii. p. 74. vol. xxiv. fig. 4.

Adult Male. Plate XXXIV. Fig. 1.

Bill longish, nearly straight, rather strong, elongated-conical, as deep as broad at the base, with sharp, nearly straight edges. Nostrils basal, oval, half concealed by the feathers. Head rather large, neck short. Body short and full. Feet of ordinary length, rather slender; tarsus compressed, covered anteriorly with a few long scutella, acute behind, longer than the middle toe; toes scutellate above, free; claws arched, slender, compressed, acute.

Plumage blended, soft and tufty. Wings of ordinary length, considerably curved, the second quill longest, the first little shorter. Tail rather short, a little rounded, of twelve rather narrow, obtuse feathers.

Bill blackish-brown above, greenish-grey beneath. Iris hazel. Feet flesh-colour. General colour of the upper parts deep green, tinged with brown. Head and lower parts light brownish-yellow, the former with four longitudinal black bands, of which one on each side proceeds from the middle of the upper mandible, the other from the inferior angle of its base. The lower part of the neck anteriorly, and the fore part of the breast are more yellow than the rest of the under parts; the abdomen and under tail-coverts nearly white.

Length 5½ inches, extent of wings 8½; bill along the ridge ₇⁷₈, along the gap ⅔; tarsus ⅚, middle toe ¾.

Adult Female. Plate XXXIV. Fig. 2.
The female hardly differs from the male in external appearance.

THE AMERICAN POKE-WEED.

PHYTOLACCA DECANDRA, *Willd.* Sp. Pl. vol. i. p. 822. *Pursh*, Fl. Amer. vol. i. p. 324.
—DECANDRIA DECAGYNIA, *Linn.* ATRIPLICES, *Juss.*

This species is distinguished by its elliptico-lanceolate leaves, and decandrous flowers, the other species differing in the number of stamina and one of them being diœcious. The berries, which are nearly globular, are disposed in an elongated, pendulous raceme, and are of a purplish-black colour. The flowers are white, their peduncles, partial and general, of a bright carmine-purple colour.

CHILDREN'S WARBLER.

SYLVIA CHILDRENII.

PLATE XXXV. Male and Female.

This little bird so much resembles the young of that called, I know not why, the Blue-eyed Yellow Warbler, that I was at first inclined to think it the same; but, recollecting that the latter acquires the full colouring of its plumage, in both sexes, before the return of spring, and finding some material differences in their habits, I have not hesitated in presenting it to you, kind reader, not only as a new species, but as one extremely rare in the United States.

I shot two of these birds in May 1821, near the town of Jackson, in the State of Louisiana. They were sitting amongst the stalks of the plant, on which they are represented. Their wings were constantly drooping by the sides of their body, their tail spread out like a fan, and they uttered a low *tweet* note, which was very soft and sweet. They now and then chased small insects on the wing, but more commonly searched for them amongst the leaves and blossoms of the plants on which they were. After a few minutes, I discovered their nest, which contained five young ones nearly fledged. It was attached by the sides to two twigs of the plant, and was formed of the dried bark of the same plant, mixed with skins of caterpillars and some silky substances. The lining consisted of goat's or deer hair, I think the former, as there were some tame goats in an adjoining pasture. I shot both the parents, and took the young under my care, but they would not receive any food, and died towards the end of the second day after their removal. I have never seen another of these birds since.

The scarcity of this species in the United States putting me in mind of that of true friendship among men, I have named it after my most esteemed friend, J. G. CHILDREN, Esq. of the British Museum, as a tribute of sincere gratitude for the unremitted kindness which he has shewn me.

The plant is known by the name of the *Wild Spanish Coffee.* It grows very abundantly in almost every field in the Uplands of Lower Louisiana. The smell of its flowers, as well as of its leaves, is extremely disagreeable, if not nauseous.

CHILDREN'S WARBLER, SYLVIA CHILDRENII.

Adult Male.   Plate XXXV. Fig. 1.

Bill longish, straight, subulato-conical, acute, the edges sharp, the gap line slightly deflected at the base.   Nostrils basal, lateral, elliptical, half closed by a membrane.   Head and neck of ordinary size.   Body rather slender.   Feet of ordinary length, slender; tarsus longer than the middle toe, covered anteriorly by a few scutella, the uppermost long; toes scutellate above, free, the hind toe of moderate size; claws slender, compressed, acute, arched.

Plumage soft, blended, tufty.   Wings of ordinary length, acute, the first quill longest.   Tail shortish, when closed nearly even.   A few short bristles at the base of the upper mandible.

Bill brown, lighter beneath.   Iris dark brown.   Feet flesh-coloured. The general colour of the upper parts is yellowish-green, tinged with brown.   Forehead, sides of the head, supra-ocular region, and under parts generally deep yellow.   Quills dusky on the inner webs.   Tail feathers dusky on the outer webs, yellow on the inner, excepting the two middle, which are dusky.

Length $4\frac{1}{4}$ inches, extent of wings $7\frac{1}{2}$; bill along the ridge $\frac{5}{12}$, along the gap $\frac{7}{12}$.

Adult Female.   Plate XXXV. Fig. 2.

The female is considerably smaller.   The distribution of its colouring is the same, but the tints are much lighter, the upper parts being pale yellowish-green tinged with grey; the sides of the head, supra-ocular and frontal spaces pale yellowish-grey, and the under parts of a tint approaching to lemon-yellow.

THE WILD SPANISH COFFEE.

CASSIA OCCIDENTALIS, *Willd.* Sp. Pl. vol. ii. p. 518.   *Pursh,* Flor. Amer. vol. i. p. 305.—DECANDRIA MONOGYNIA, *Linn.*   LEGUMINOSÆ, *Juss.*

This species is distinguished by its ovato-lanceolate, quinquejugate leaves, scabrous at the margin, the outer larger; its many-flowered axillar and somewhat panicled peduncles; and its linear, falciform legumes. It flowers through the summer, and grows chiefly in old fields, in the Southern States.

MEADVILLE.

THE incidents that occur in the life of a student of nature, are not all of the agreeable kind, in proof of which, I shall present you, good reader, with an extract from one of my journals.

My money was one day stolen from me by a person, who perhaps imagined that to a naturalist it was of little importance. This happened on the shores of Upper Canada. The affair was as unexpected as it well could be, and as adroitly managed as if it had been planned and executed in Cheapside. To have repined when the thing could not be helped, would certes not have been acting manfully. I therefore told my companion to keep a good heart, for I felt satisfied that Providence had some relief in store for us. The whole amount of cash left with two individuals fifteen hundred miles from home, was just seven dollars and a-half. Our passage across the lake had fortunately been paid for. We embarked and soon got to the entrance of Presque Isle Harbour, but could not pass the bar, on account of a violent gale which came on as we approached it. The anchor was dropped, and we remained on board during the night, feeling at times very disagreeable, under the idea of having taken so little care of our money. How long we might have remained at anchor I cannot tell, had not that Providence, on whom I have never ceased to rely, come to our aid. Through some means to me quite unknown, Captain JUDD of the United States Navy, then probably commandant at Presque Isle, sent a gig with six men to our relief. It was on the 29th of August 1824, and never shall I forget that morning. My drawings were put into the boat with the greatest care. We shifted into it, and seated ourselves according to directions politely given us. Our brave fellows pulled hard, and every moment brought us nearer to the American shore. I leaped upon it with elated heart. My drawings were safely landed, and for any thing else I cared little at the moment. I searched in vain for the officer of our navy, to whom I still feel grateful, and gave one of our dollars to the sailors to drink the " freedom of the waters ;" after which we betook ourselves to a humble inn to procure bread and milk, and consider how we were to proceed.

Our plans were soon settled, for to proceed was decidedly the best. Our luggage was rather heavy, so we hired a cart to take it to Meadville, for which we offered five dollars. This sum was accepted, and we set off. The country through which we passed might have proved favourable to our pursuits, had it not rained nearly the whole day. At night we alighted and put up at a house belonging to our conductor's father. It was Sunday night. The good folks had not yet returned from a distant meeting-house, the grandmother of our driver being the only individual about the premises. We found her a cheerful dame, who bestirred herself as actively as age would permit, got up a blazing fire to dry our wet cloths, and put as much bread and milk on the table as might have sufficed for several besides ourselves.

Being fatigued by the jolting of the cart, we asked for a place in which to rest, and were shewn into a room in which were several beds. We told the good woman that I should paint her portrait next morning for the sake of her children. My companion and myself were soon in bed, and soon asleep, in which state we should probably have remained till morning, had we not been awakened by a light, which we found to be carried by three young damsels, who having observed where we lay, blew it out, and got into a bed opposite ours. As we had not spoken, it is probable the girls supposed us sound asleep, and we heard them say how delighted they would be to have their portraits taken, as well as that of their grandmother. My heart silently met their desire, and we fell asleep, without farther disturbance. In our back woods it is frequently the case that one room suffices for all the sleepers of a family.

Day dawned, and as we were dressing we discovered that we were alone in the apartment, the good country girls having dressed in silence and left us before we had awakened. We joined the family and were kindly greeted. No sooner had I made known my intentions as to the portraits, than the young folks disappeared and soon after returned attired in their Sunday clothes. The black chalk was at work in a few minutes, to their great delight, and as the fumes of the breakfast that was meantime preparing reached my sensitive nose, I worked with redoubled ardour. The sketches were soon finished, and soon too was the breakfast over. I played a few airs on my flageolet, while our guide was putting the horses to the cart, and by ten o'clock we were once more under way towards Meadville. Never shall I forget MAXON RANDELL and his hospitable family. My companion was as pleased as myself, and as the weather was now beautiful, we enjoyed our journey with all that happy thoughtlessness best suited to our character. The country now became covered with heavy timber, principally evergreens, the Pines and

the Cucumber trees loaded with brilliant fruits, and the Spruces throwing
a shade over the land in good keeping for a mellow picture.   The lateness of the crops was the only disagreeable circumstance that struck us ;
hay was yet standing, probably, however, a second crop; the peaches
were quite small and green, and a few persons here and there, as we passed the different farms, were reaping oats.   At length we came in sight
of French Creek, and soon after reached Meadville.   Here we paid the
five dollars promised to our conductor, who instantly faced about, and
applying the whip to his nags, bade us adieu, and set off.

We had now only a hundred and fifty cents.   No time was to be lost.
We put our baggage and ourselves under the roof of a tavern-keeper
known by the name of J. E. SMITH, at the sign of the *Traveller's Rest*, and
soon after took a walk to survey the little village that was to be laid under contribution for our further support.   Its appearance was rather
dull; but, thanks to GOD, I have never despaired while rambling thus
for the sole purpose of admiring his grand and beautiful works.   I had
opened the case that contained my drawings, and putting my portfolio
under my arm, and a few good credentials in my pocket, walked up
Main Street, looking to the right and left, examining the different *heads*
which occurred, until I fixed my eyes on a gentleman in a store who
looked as if he might want a sketch.   I begged him to allow me to sit
down.   This granted, I remained purposely silent until he very soon
asked me what was " *in that portfolio.*"   These three words sounded
well, and without waiting another instant, I opened it to his view.   This
was a Hollander, who complimented me much on the execution of the
drawings of birds and flowers in my portfolio.   Shewing him a sketch of
the best friend I have in the world at present, I asked him if he would
like one in the same style of himself.   He not only answered in the affirmative, but assured me that he would exert himself in procuring as
many more customers as he could.   I thanked him, be assured, kind
reader ; and having fixed upon the next morning for drawing the sketch,
I returned to the *Traveller's Rest*, with a hope that to-morrow might
prove propitious.   Supper was ready, and as in America we have generally but one sort of *Table d'hôte*, we sat down, when, every individual
looking upon me as a Missionary priest, on account of my hair, which in
those days flowed loosely on my shoulders, I was asked to say grace,
which I did with a fervent spirit.

Daylight returned.   I visited the groves and woods around, with my

companion, returned, breakfasted, and went to the store, where, notwithstanding my ardent desire to begin my task, it was ten o'clock before the
sitter was ready. But, reader, allow me to describe the *artist's room*.
See me ascending a crazy flight of steps, from the back part of a store-room
into a large garret extending over the store and counting room, and
mark me looking round to see how the light could be stopped from obtruding on me through no less than four windows facing each other at
right angles. Then follow me scrutinizing the corners, and finding in
one a cat nursing her young, among a heap of rags intended for the
paper-mill. Two hogsheads filled with oats, a parcel of Dutch toys carelessly thrown on the floor, a large drum and a bassoon in another part,
fur caps hanging along the wall, and the portable bed of the merchant's
clerk swinging like a hammock near the centre, together with some rolls
of sole leather, made up the picture. I saw all this at a glance, and
closing the extra windows with blankets, I soon procured a *painter's light*.

A young gentleman sat, to try my skill. I finished his phiz, which
was approved of. The merchant then took the chair, and I had the good
fortune to please him also. The room became crowded with the gentry
of the village. Some laughed, while others expressed their wonder ; but
my work went on notwithstanding the observations that were made. My
sitter invited me to spend the evening with him, which I did, and joined
him in some music on the flute and violin. I returned to my companion
with great pleasure ; and you may judge how much that pleasure was increased, when I found that he also had made two sketches. Having
written a page or two of our journals, we retired to rest.

The following day was spent much in the same manner. I felt highly gratified that from under my grey coat my talents had made their way
and I was pleased to discover that industry and moderate abilities prove
at least as valuable as first-rate talents without the former of these qualities. We left Meadville on foot, having forwarded our baggage by
waggon. Our hearts were light, our pockets replenished, and we walked
in two days to Pittsburg, as happy as circumstances permitted us to be.

THE STANLEY HAWK.

FALCO STANLEII.

PLATE XXXVI. MALE AND FEMALE.

BEFORE entering upon the description of this interesting species, allow me to submit to your consideration a few observations respecting the flight of the different species of Hawks, which I have had occasion to examine both in America and in Europe.

All such species as are usually referred to the subgenus Astur, or are most nearly allied to it, and which consequently have shorter wings, as well as longer tails, than the true Falcons, sail less frequently and less continuously in circles, and embrace a smaller space in their gyrations, than the latter birds. Their general flight is low, sometimes only a few feet above the ground, and their velocity surpasses that of the true Falcons on such occasions. Their body is more compressed and elongated, and appears to be propelled through the air chiefly by the action of their long tail. None of these birds ever glide down on their prey from a great height, with closed wings, and the rustling noise produced by Eagles or other nobler tribes of the genus. The types of this group I would consider to be the Goshawk (*Falco palumbarius*) and the Stanley Hawk. For the type of the True Falcons, no species could answer better than the Great-footed Hawk (*Falco peregrinus*).

A distinct and intermediate kind of flight belongs to such Hawks as have both a long tail and long wings. These species are able to dive through the air, either when in pursuit of their prey, or for amusement or exercise, although with less firmness of action than the True Falcons; and they fly over the earth with less velocity than the Asturs, their motions then consisting of easy flappings, or loose protracted sailings. The Hen-harrier (*Falco cyaneus*), the Forked-tailed Hawk (*Falco furcatus*), and the White-tailed Hawk (*Falco dispar*), are of this tribe.

It may be remarked here, that most species of Shrikes bear a great resemblance in their flight to the Asturs. But, let us return to the Stanley Hawk.

On the 5th of December 1809, I made a drawing of the male of this species, in its matured state of colouring, at Louisville, in Kentucky, where I then resided. That drawing is now before me, and the bird which it represents is to this day undescribed. The figure would have been engraved and presented to your consideration, kind reader, had it not been as stiff, and as little indicative of life, as those usually seen in books on Natural History. The expectation of being able to procure another individual in precisely the same state of plumage, has, together with the above circumstance, induced me to content myself, for the present, with offering to your inspection a male, probably two years old, and an adult female. I have killed many of the latter in the course of my rambles, but I had not the good fortune to obtain an old male, although I have seen several on wing, and once wounded one whilst perched near its nest. In this article, I shall give you a full description of the three different figures, as they shew considerable diversity, especially in the colour of the eyes, the adult bird having the iris of a reddish-orange tint, while the young bird has it of a bright yellow. But as I am desirous of adhering to my plan, I shall speak of its habits before I trouble you with its description, remarking in the mean time, that I have honoured the species with the name of the President of the Linnean Society of London, the Right Honourable Lord STANLEY, a nobleman whose continued kindness to me I am happy in acknowledging.

The flight of the Stanley Hawk is rapid, protracted, and even. It is performed at a short height above the ground or through the forest. It passes along in a silent gliding manner, with a swiftness even superior to that of the Wild Pigeon (*Columba migratoria*), seldom deviating from a straight-forward course, unless to seize and secure its prey. Now and then, but seldom unless after being shot at, it mounts in the air in circles, of which it describes five or six in a hurried manner, and again plunging downwards, continues its journey as before.

The daring exploits performed by the Stanley Hawk, which have taken place in my presence, are very numerous, and I shall relate one or two of them. This marauder frequently attacks birds far superior to itself in weight, and sometimes possessed of courage equal to its own. As I was one morning observing the motions of some Parakeets near Bayou Sara, in the State of Louisiana, in the month of November, I heard a Cock crowing not far from me, and in sight of a farm-house. The Stanley Hawk the next moment flew past me, and so close that I might have touched it with the barrel of my gun, had I been prepared. Its wings struck with extraordinary rapidity, and its tail appeared as if closed. Not more than a few seconds elapsed before I heard the cackling of the Hens, and the war-cry of the Cock, and at the same time observed the Hawk rising, as if without effort, a few yards in the air, and again falling towards the ground with the rapidity of lightning.   I proceeded to the spot, and found the Hawk grappled to the body of the Cock, both tumbling over and over, and paying no attention to me as I approached. Desirous of seeing the result, I remained still, until perceiving that the Hawk had given a fatal squeeze to the brave Cock, I ran to secure the former ; but the marauder had kept a hawk's eye upon me, and, disengaging himself, rose in the air in full confidence.   The next moment I pulled a trigger, and he fell dead to the ground.   It proved a young male, such as you see, kind reader, represented in the Plate, pursuing a lovely Blue-bird nearly exhausted.   The Cock was also dead ; its breast was torn, and its neck pierced in several places by the sharp claws of the Hawk.

Some years afterwards, not far from the amed Falls of Niagara, in the month of June, one of these Hawks, which on being examined proved to be a female, attacked a brood of young chickens, yet under the care of their mother.   It had just struck one of the chickens, and was on the eve of carrying it off in its claws, when the hen, having perceived the murderous deed, flew against the Hawk with such force as to throw it fairly on its back, when the intrepid mother so effectively assailed the miscreant with feet and bill, as to enable me, on running up, to secure the latter.

This species frequently kills and eats the bird commonly called the Pheasant (*Tetrao Umbellus*).   Partridges and young hares are also favourite dainties.   It also follows the Wild Pigeons in their migrations, and always causes fear and confusion in their ranks.

It breeds in the mountainous districts of the Middle and Northern States, to which it returns early in spring from the Southern States, where it spends the winter in considerable numbers, and is known by the name of the *Great Pigeon Hawk*.   So rapidly must they travel from one extremity of the country to another, to reach the places to which they resort for the purpose of breeding, that I have seen them copulate in Louisiana, where they never breed, in the month of February, and have found their nest with eggs in which the chick was far advanced, in the State of Connecticut, on the 20th of April.

The nest is usually placed in the forks of the branch of an Oak-tree towards its extremity.   In its general appearance it resembles that of the Common Crow, for which I have several times mistaken it.   It is composed externally of numerous crooked sticks, and has a slight lining of grasses and a few feathers.   The eggs are three or four, almost globular, large for the size of the bird, of a dullish-white colour, strongly granulated, and consequently rough to the touch. It was on discovering one of these nests that I wounded the second adult male which I have seen, but which never returned to its nest, on which I afterwards shot the female represented in the Plate, in the act of pouncing. I have several times found other nests of birds of this species, but the owners were not in full plumage, and their eyes had not obtained the rich orange colouring of the adult birds.

Those which I have observed near the Falls of Niagara were generally engaged in pursuing Red-winged Starlings, over the marshes of the neighbourhood. When this Hawk is angry, it raises the feathers of the upper part of the head, so as to make them appear partially tufted. The cry at this time may be represented by the syllable *kee*, *kee*, *kee*, repeated eight or ten times in rapid succession, and much resembling that of the Pigeon Hawk (*Falco columbarius*) or the European Kestril. The young of this species bear no resemblance to those of the Goshawk, of which a figure will be given in the same Plate with the adult of the Stanley Hawk.

STANLEY HAWK, FALCO STANLEII.

Adult Male.

Bill short, robust, cerate; upper mandible with the dorsal outline curved from the base, the back rounded, the sides sloping at the base, convex toward the end, the margin sharp, overlapping, having an obtuse lobe, the tip trigonal, very acute, and curved downwards; lower mandible broadly rounded on the back, convex on the sides, acute in the edges, somewhat abrupt at the end. Nostrils oval, oblique, in the fore-part of the cere. Head rather large, flat above; eyebrow acute and projecting. Neck strong. Body rather elongated. Legs long; tarsi rather long, and with the toes somewhat slender, the former scutellate anteriorly, the latter scutellate above, papillar and tuberculate beneath; claws long, curved, roundish, rather slender, and extremely acute.

Plumage compact, imbricated, glossy. Space between the beak and eye sparsely covered with bristly feathers. Tibial feathers rather compact, and not much elongated. Wings long: fifth quill longest, sixth and fourth nearly equal, first very short. Tail long, straight, a little rounded, of twelve rather broad feathers.

Bill light blue at the base, black at the tip. Cere greenish-yellow. Iris reddish-orange. Tarsus and toes bright yellow; claws brownish-black. The general colour of the upper parts is dark greyish-brown. Quills barred with brownish-black. Tail with four bars of brownish-black, the terminal one broader; the tips of all the feathers white. The general colour of the lower parts is brownish-white. Sides of the head and the throat longitudinally lined with dark brown; fore-neck and breast marked with arrow-shaped spots of brownish-red, the shafts blackish. Legs similarly marked, the spots smaller, and transversely elongated. Abdomen and under tail-coverts nearly free of spots.

Length 20 inches, extent of wings 36; beak along the back 1¼, along the gap from the tip of the lower mandible 1½; tarsus 2¾, middle toe 2¼. Wings 4½ inches shorter than the tail.

Adult Female.   Plate XXXVI. Fig. 2.

Bill brownish-black above; the base of the upper mandible, and the greater part of the lower, light blue. Cere greenish. Iris yellow. Feet greenish-yellow; claws brownish-black. Head and neck brownish-white, each feather with a large reddish-brown spot near the end. General colour of the upper parts chocolate-brown; quills and tail wood-brown, barred as in the male. Under parts brownish-white. Throat and sides of the head marked as in the male; breast with guttiform spots of deep brown; legs with smaller, somewhat arrow-shaped spots of reddish-brown. Abdomen and under tail-coverts whitish.

Length 21¼ inches, extent of wings 38; bill along the back 1¼, along the gap 1½; tarsus 3, middle toe 2¾. Wings 5 inches shorter than the tail.

Young Male.   Plate XXXVI. Fig. 1.

Bill and feet coloured nearly as in the adult. Iris yellow, as in the female. The general colour of the upper parts is dark umber; several of the scapulars, wing-coverts and upper tail-coverts with a large spot of white. Quills and tail-feathers barred as in the adult, the last bar on the tail much narrower. Under parts light reddish-brown. Sides of the head, and the neck longitudinally streaked with deep brown; the markings on the breast and legs also longitudinal.

Length 19¾, extent of wings 34; beak 1¼; wings 5½ inches shorter than the tail.

The bird represented as about to be seized by the male is the Blue-bird, *Saxicola Sialis* of Bonaparte, *Sylvia Sialis* of other authors.

THE GOLDEN-WINGED WOODPECKER.

PICUS AURATUS, LINN.

PLATE XXXVII. MALE AND FEMALE.

It is generally agreeable to be in the company of individuals who are naturally animated and pleasant. For this reason, nothing can be more gratifying than the society of Woodpeckers in the forests. To prove this to you, kind reader, I shall give you a full account of the habits of the Golden-winged Woodpecker.

This species, which is usually called *Pique-bois jaune* by the French settlers in Louisiana, and receives the name of *High-holder*, *Yucker*, and *Flicker* in other parts of the Union, being seldom or never graced with the epithet *Golden-winged*, employed by naturalists, is one of the most lively of our birds, and is found over the whole of the United States.

No sooner has spring called them to the pleasant duty of making love, as it is called, than their voice, which, by the way, is not at all disagreeable to the ear of man, is heard from the tops of high decayed trees, proclaiming with delight the opening of the welcome season. Their note at this period is merriment itself, as it imitates a prolonged and jovial laugh, heard at a considerable distance. Several males pursue a female, reach her, and, to prove the force and truth of their love, bow their heads, spread their tail, and move sidewise, backwards and forwards, performing such antics, as might induce any one witnessing them, if not of a most morose temper, to join his laugh to theirs. The female flies to another tree, where she is closely followed by one, two, or even half a dozen of these gay suitors, and where again the same ceremonies are gone through. No fightings occur, no jealousies seem to exist among these beaux, until a marked preference is shewn to some individual, when the rejected proceed in search of another female. In this manner all the Golden-winged Woodpeckers are soon happily mated. Each pair immediately proceed to excavate the trunk of a tree, and finish a hole in it sufficient to contain themselves and their young. They both work with great industry and apparent pleasure. Should the male, for instance, be employed, the female is close to him, and congratulates him on the removal of every chip which his bill sends through the air. While he rests, he appears to be speaking to her on the most tender subjects, and when fatigued, is at once assisted by her. In this manner, by the alternate exertions of each, the hole is dug and finished. They caress each other on the branches, climb about and around the tree with apparent delight, rattle with their bill against the tops of the dead branches, chase all their cousins the Red-heads, defy the Purple Grakles to enter their nest, feed plentifully on ants, beetles and larvæ, cackling at intervals, and ere two weeks have elapsed, the female lays either four or six eggs, the whiteness and transparency of which are doubtless the delight of her heart. If to raise a numerous progeny may contribute to happiness, these Wood-peckers are in this respect happy enough, for they have two broods each season ; and as this might induce you to imagine Woodpeckers extremely abundant in America, I may at once tell you that they are so.

Even in confinement, the Golden-winged Woodpecker never suffers its naturally lively spirit to droop. It feeds well, and by way of amusement, will continue to destroy as much furniture in a day as can well be mended by a different kind of workman in two. Therefore, kind reader, do not any longer believe that Woodpeckers, I mean those of America, are such stupid, forlorn, dejected and unprovided for beings, as they have hitherto been represented. In fact, I know not one of the seventeen species found in our extensive woods, that does not exhibit quite as much mirth and gaiety as the present bird. They are serviceable birds in many points of view, and therefore are seldom shot at, unless by idlers, their flesh, moreover, not being very savoury. They have ample range, and wherever they alight, there is to be found the food to which they at all times give decided preference.

The flight of this species is strong and prolonged, being performed in a straighter manner than that of any other of our Woodpeckers. They propel themselves by numerous beats of the wings, with short intervals of sailing, during which they scarcely fall from the horizontal. Their migrations, although partial, as many remain even in the middle districts during the severest winters, are performed under night, as is known by their note and the whistling of their wings, which are heard from the ground, although by no means so distinctly as when they fly from a tree or from the earth, when suddenly alarmed. When passing from one tree to another on wing, they also fly in a straight line, until within a few yards of the spot on which they intend to alight, when they suddenly raise themselves a few feet, and fasten themselves to the bark of the trunk by their

1

claws and tail. If they intend to settle on a branch, which they as frequently do, they do not previously rise; but in either case, no sooner has the bird alighted, if it be not pursued or have suspicions of any object about it, than it immediately nods its head, and utters its well-known note, " *Flicker*." It easily moves sidewise on a small branch, keeping itself as erect as other birds usually do; but with equal ease does it climb by leaps along the trunk of trees or their branches, descend, and move sidewise or spirally, keeping at all times its head upwards, and its tail pressed against the bark as a support.

On the ground, where it frequently alights, it hops with great ease. This, however, it does merely to pick up a beetle, a caterpillar, a grain of corn dropt by a squirrel from the ear in the fields, or to enable it to examine the dead roots of trees, or the side of a prostrate log, from which it procures ants and other small insects. It is also fond of various fruits and berries. Apples, grapes, persimons and dogwood berries seem quite agreeable to it, and it does not neglect the young corn of the farmer's field. Even poke-berries or huckle-berries answer its purpose at times and during winter it is a frequenter of the corn-cribs.

In this species, as in a few others, there is a singular arrangement in the colouring of the feathers of the upper part of the head, which I conceive it necessary for me to state, that it may enable persons better qualified than myself to decide as to the reasons of such arrangement. The young of this species frequently have the whole upper part of the head tinged with red, which at the approach of winter disappears, when merely a circular line of that colour is to be observed on the hind part, becoming of a rich silky vermilion tint. The Hairy, Downy and Red cockaded Woodpeckers are subject to the same extraordinary changes, which, as far as I know, never reappear at any future period of their lives. I was at first of opinion that this change appeared only on the head of the male birds, but on dissection I found it equally affecting both sexes. I am induced to believe, that, in consequence of this, many young Woodpeckers of different species have been described and figured as forming distinct species themselves. I have shot dozens of young Woodpeckers in this peculiar state of plumage, which, on being shewn to other persons, were thought by them to be of different species from what the birds actually were. This occurrence is the more worthy of notice, as it is exhibited on all the species of this genus on the heads of which, when in full plumage, a very narrow line exists.

N

Raccoons and Black Snakes are dangerous enemies to this bird. The former frequently put one of their fore legs into the hole where it has nestled or retired to rest, and if the hole be not too deep, draw out the eggs and suck them, and frequently by the same means secure the bird itself. The Black Snake contents itself with the eggs or young. Several species of Hawks attack them on the wing, and as the Woodpeckers generally escape by making for a hole in the nearest tree, it is pleasing to see the disappointment of the Hawk, when, as it has just been on the point of seizing the terrified bird, the latter dives, as it were, into the hole. Should the Woodpecker not know of a hole near enough to afford it security, it alights on a trunk, and moves round it with such celerity as frequently to enable it to elude its pursuer.

Their flesh is esteemed good by many of the sportsmen of the Middle Districts, and is frequently eaten. Some are now and then exposed in the markets of New York and Philadelphia; but I look upon the flesh as very disagreeable, it having a strong flavour of ants.

The neck of this species is larger than that of any other with which I am acquainted, and consequently the skin of this bird is more easily pulled over the head, which it is difficult to do in the other species, on account of the slenderness of their neck, and the great size of the head.

PICUS AURATUS, *Linn.* Syst. Nat. vol. i. p. 174.—*Lath.* Ind. Ornith. vol. i. p. 242.—
    Ch. Bonaparte, Synopsis of Birds of the United States, p. 44.
GOLD-WINGED WOODPECKER *Lath.*. Synops. vol. ii. p. 597.—*Wils.* Americ. Ornith.
    vol. ii. p. 45. Pl. iii. fig. 1. Male.

Adult Male.   Plate XXXVII. Fig. 1, 1, 1.

Bill slightly arched, strong, nearly as long as the head, compressed at the tip, which is a little abrupt; upper mandible convex on the sides, with acute, overlapping edges; lower mandible with acute, inflected edges, the dorsal outline nearly straight, a little convex towards the end. Nostrils basal, lateral, oval, partly covered by recumbent feathers. Head of ordinary size. Neck shortish. Body ovate. Feet short, rather robust; tarsus scutellate before, compressed; two toes before, and two behind, scutellate above; claws compressed, arched, acute.

Plumage rather compact and imbricated, blended on the head and neck. Wings longish, the third and fourth quills longest, the second much shorter, the first very small. Tail of ordinary length, rounded, consisting of ten broad feathers, worn to an elongated tip by being rubbed against the bark of trees.

Bill brown above and at the tip, light blue beneath. Iris light brown. Feet greyish-blue. Upper part of the head and hind neck light purplish-grey ; a transverse band of scarlet on the lower part of the occiput. Upper parts generally light greenish-brown, spotted with black ; the lower back white, the tail-coverts of the same colour, spotted with black. Primaries brownish-black, their shafts, as are those of all the large feathers, orange. Tail brownish-black. Sides of the head and fore neck light brownish-red, tinged with grey. A black streak along each side of the throat, and a lunated patch of the same across the fore part of the breast. The rest of the breast reddish-white, spotted with black, as are the lighter coloured abdomen and under tail-coverts. Under surface of the wings and tail of a fine rich yellow.

Length 12½ inches, extent of wings 16 ; bill along the ridge 1½, along the gap 1¾ ; tarsus 1⅓, middle toe 1¼.

Adult Female. Plate XXXVII. Fig. 2, 2.

The female differs chiefly in wanting the black streaks on the throat, in having the lunulated spot on the breast smaller, and in being somewhat duller in the tints of the plumage generally.

Dimensions nearly the same.

THE KENTUCKY WARBLER.

SYLVIA FORMOSA, WILS.

PLATE XXXVIII. MALE AND FEMALE.

THIS beautiful species is the most common and abundant that visits the State of Louisiana and those situated on the borders of the Mississippi. In Kentucky it is much less common, and in the State of Ohio scarcer still. It is an extremely active and lively bird. It is found in all the low grounds and damp places near water-courses, and generally among the tall rank weeds and low bushes growing in rich alluvial soil. Continually in motion, it is seen hopping in every direction from stalk to stalk, or from one twig to another, preying upon insects and larvæ, or picking small berries, seldom, however, pursuing insects on wing. During spring, its agreeable notes are heard in every quarter. They are emphatic, and resemble the words *tweedle, tweedle, tweedle,* distinctly repeated. This little bird is seen at intervals of a few minutes on the skirts of the tall plants, peeping cunningly to discover whether any intruders may be near ; after which it immediately re-enters the thicket, and repeats its little ditty.

I never saw this bird fly farther than a few yards at a time. Its flight is low, and performed in a quick gliding manner, the bird throwing itself into the nearest bush or thicket of tall grass. It arrives in the Southern States, from Mexico, about the middle of March, and remains with us until the middle of September, during which time it rears two broods. Its nest is small, beautifully constructed, and usually attached to several stems of rank weeds. The outer parts are formed of the bark of stalks of the same weeds in a withered state, mixed with a finer kind and some cottony substances. It is beautifully lined with the cottony or silky substance that falls from the Cotton-wood tree. The eggs are from four to six, of a pure white colour, finely sprinkled with bright red dots.

This species destroys great numbers of spiders, which it frequently obtains by turning over the withered leaves on the ground. The young males do not attain the full beauty of their plumage until the first spring, and resemble the mother during their stay with us the first season

Young and old associate together, and live in great harmony. I have not seen this species farther eastward than North Carolina.

The branch on which two of these birds are represented, is that of the tree commonly called the White Cucumber, a species of Magnolia. It flowers as early in the season as the Dog-wood. The flowers open before the leaves are expanded, and emit an odour resembling that of a lemon, but soon becoming disagreeable, as the blossom fades. This tree seldom grows to the height of thirty feet, and is consequently disregarded as a timber-tree. I have met with it only in the States of Mississippi and Louisiana, where it grows on the grounds preferred by the Kentucky Warbler during its stay in those States.

KENTUCKY WARBLER, SYLVIA FORMOSA, *Wils.* Amer. Ornith. vol. iii. p. 85. Pl. xxv. Fig. 3.

SYLVIA FORMOSA, *Ch. Bonaparte*, Synops. of Birds of the United States, p. 34.

Adult Male.   Plate XXXVIII. Fig. 1.

Bill of ordinary length, nearly straight, subulato-conical, acute, the edges acute, the gap line a little deflected at the base. Nostrils basal, lateral, elliptical, half closed by a membrane. Head and neck of ordinary size. Body rather full. Feet of ordinary length, slender ; tarsus longer than the middle toe, covered anteriorly by a few scutella, the uppermost long ; toes scutellate above, the inner free, the hind toe of moderate size ; claws slender, compressed, acute, arched.

Plumage soft, blended, tufty. Wings of ordinary length, acute, the second quill longest. Tail of ordinary length, slightly forked when closed.

Bill brownish-black above, lighter beneath. Iris hazel. Feet pale flesh-colour. The general colour of the plumage above is deep yellowish-green, the crown of the head, and a broad patch under the eye, including the lore, black. Under parts, and a broad streak over the eye, bright yellow, tinged with green on the sides, abdomen, and under tail-coverts. Wings and tail yellowish-green, the inner webs only being dusky. Some spots of bluish-grey on the occiput.

Length 5$\frac{1}{4}$ inches, extent of wings 8 ; bill along the ridge $\frac{4}{12}$, along the gap $\frac{7}{12}$; tarsus $\frac{11}{12}$, middle toe $\frac{5}{6}$.

Adult Female.   Plate XXXVIII. Fig. 2.

The female resembles the male, but wants the black band under the eye, and has the black of the head less extended backwards.　The tints of the plumage generally are also lighter.

Dimensions nearly the same.

MAGNOLIA AURICULATA, *Wild.* Sp. Pl. vol. ii. p. 1268. *Pursh.* Flor. Amer. vol. ii. p. 482. *Mich.* Arbr. Forest. de l'Amer. Septentr. vol. iii. p. 94. Pl. 7.—POLYANDRIA POLYGYNIA, *Linn.* MAGNOLIÆ, *Juss.*

This species, which is remarkable for the beauty of its foliage, is known in America by the names of *White Cucumber Tree, Long-leaved Cucumber Tree,* and *Indian Physic.* The latter name it has obtained from the circumstance of its bark being used in intermittent fevers. It is characterized by its rhomboido-oboval acute leaves, which are narrowed and two-lobed at the base; and its ovate acute petals. The flowers are greenish-white.

THE CRESTED TITMOUSE.

PARUS BICOLOR, LINN.

PLATE XXXIX. MALE AND FEMALE.

ALTHOUGH this smart little bird breeds in the State of Louisiana and the adjacent districts, it is not there found in so great numbers as in the Middle States, and farther to the northward. It generally prefers the depth of the forests during summer, after which it approaches the plantations, and even resorts to the granaries for corn.

Its flight is short, the bird being seldom seen on the wing long enough to cross a field of moderate extent. It is performed by repeated flaps of the wings, accompanied by jerks of the body and tail, and occasions a rustling noise, as it takes place from one tree to another. It moves along the branches, searches in the chinks, flies to the end of twigs and hangs to them by its feet, whilst the bill is engaged in detaching a beech or hazel nut, an acorn or a chinquapin, upon all of which it feeds, removing them to a large branch, where, having secured them in a crevice, it holds them with both feet, and breaks the shell by repeated blows of its bill. They are to be seen thus employed for many minutes at a time. They move about in little companies formed of the parents and their young, eight or ten together, and escorted by the Nuthatch or the Downy Woodpecker. It is pleasing to listen to the sound produced by their labour, which in a calm day may be heard at the distance of twenty or thirty yards. If a nut or an acorn is accidentally dropped, the bird flies to the ground, picks it up, and again returns to a branch. They also alight on the ground or on dry leaves, to look for food, after the trees become bare, and hop about with great nimbleness, going to the margins of the brooks to drink, and when unable to do so, obtaining water by stooping from the extremity of a twig hanging over the stream. In fact, they appear to prefer this latter method, and are also fond of drinking the drops of rain or dew as they hang at the extremities of the leaves.

Their notes are rather musical than otherwise, the usual one being loud and mellow. They do not use the *tee-tee-tee* of their relative the Black-capped Titmouse, half so often as the latter does, but emit a considerable variety of sounds, many of which, if the bird from which they come does not happen to be known to the listener, are apt to induce disappointment in him, when on going up he finds it to be very different from what he expected. These sounds sometimes resemble a whistle, at another time a loud murmur, and seem as if proceeding from a bird at a much greater distance.

The crest of this species, which is generally erect, is a great improvement to its general appearance, the tints of the plumage being, as you perceive, kind reader, none of the most brilliant. The Crested Titmouse is of a rather vicious disposition, which sometimes prompts it to attack smaller birds, and destroy them by thumping their heads with its bill until it breaks the skull.

This species sometimes forms a nest by digging a hole for the purpose in the hardest wood, with great industry and perseverance, although it is more frequently contented with the hole of the Downy Woodpecker, or some other small bird of that genus. It fills the hole with every kind of warm materials, after which the female deposits from six to eight eggs, of a pure white, with a few red spots at the larger end. The eggs are laid about the beginning of April in the Southern States, and nearly a month later in the Middle Districts. As soon as the young are able to leave the nest, they are seen following the parent birds, and continue with them until the next spring.

I have met with this species in all parts of the United States which I have visited; and as my rambles have been extended over a very large portion of that country, I am surprised that I have not met with more than two species of Titmice, although I am of opinion that several others will yet be discovered.

The species of Pine, on a twig of which you see a pair these birds, is the *White Pine* (*Pinus Strobus*), a tree of great beauty, of which individuals have been observed of the enormous height of 180 feet, with a diameter at the base of from six to eight feet. The trunk is branchless for two-thirds of its height, and affords the most valuable wood perhaps of any tree in the United States.

Parus bicolor, *Linn.* Syst. Nat. vol. i. p. 544.—*Lath.* Ind. Ornith. vol. ii. p. 567. —*Ch. Bonaparte,* Synops. of Birds of the United States, p. 100.
Crested Titmouse, Parus bicolor, *Wils.* Amer. Ornith. vol. i. p. 137, Pl. 8. fig. 5. Toupet Titmouse, *Lath.* Synops. vol. iv. p. 544.

Adult Male.   Plate XXXIX.   Fig 1.

Bill short, straight, rather robust, compressed, acute; both mandibles, with the dorsal outline arched, the upper slightly declinate at the tip. Nostrils basal, roundish, concealed by the recumbent feathers. Head large. Neck and body robust. Feet of ordinary length, rather robust; tarsus compressed, anteriorly scutellate, a little longer than the middle toe; outer toe slightly united at the base, hind one much stronger; claws rather large, much compressed, arched, acute.

Plumage blended, tufty; feathers of the upper part of the head elongated into a crest. Wings of moderate length, the second, third, and fourth quills nearly equal and longest. Tail long, even, of ten rather narrow, rounded feathers.

Bill black. Iris dark brown. Feet lead-colour. The general colour of the upper parts is a dull leaden blue; the forehead black; sides of the head lighter, and tinged with brown. Under parts greyish-white, sides tinged with yellowish-brown.

Length 6½ inches, extent of wings 9; bill along the ridge ½, along the gap ½; tarsus ⅓, middle toe ⅗.

Adult Female.   Plate XXXIX.   Fig. 2.

The female hardly differs from the male in external appearance, being equally crested, and having the same tints.

THE WHITE PINE.

PINUS STROBUS, *Willd.* Sp. Plant. vol. iv. p. 501. *Pursh,* Flor. Amer. vol. ii. p. 644. *Mich.* Arb. Forest. de l'Amer. Sept. vol. i. p. 104. Pl. x.—MONŒCIA MONADELPHIA, *Linn.* CONIFERÆ, *Juss.*

This species, which is a true Pine, has the leaves very slender, five together, with very short sheaths, and is further characterized by its cylindrical, pendulous cones, which are longer than the leaves, and have their scales lax. It grows in rich soil, in all parts of the United States from Canada to Virginia, and affords the best timber for masts, as well as for other purposes. In Britain, where it has long been planted, it is generally known by the name of *Weymouth* Pine, or Lord Weymouth's Pine, from the name of the nobleman who introduced it.

THE AMERICAN REDSTART.

MUSCICAPA RUTICILLA, LINN.

PLATE XL. MALE AND FEMALE.

THIS is one of the most lively, as well as one of the handsomest, of our Fly-catchers, and ornaments our woods during spring and summer, when it cannot fail to attract the attention of any person who may visit the interior of the shady forests. It is to be met with over the whole of the United States, where it arrives, according to the different localities, between the beginning of March and the 1st of May. It takes its departure, on its way southward, late in September, and in the beginning of October.

It keeps in perpetual motion, hunting along the branches sidewise, jumping to either side in search of insects and larvæ, opening its beautiful tail at every movement which it makes, then closing it, and flirting it from side to side, just allowing the transparent beauty of the feathers to be seen for a moment. The wings are observed gently drooping during these motions, and its pleasing notes, which resemble the sounds of *Tetee-whee, T'etee-whee*, are then emitted. Should it observe an insect on the wing, it immediately flies in pursuit of it, either mounts into the air in its wake, or comes towards the ground spirally and in many zig-zags. The insect secured, the lovely Redstart reascends, perches, and sings a different note, equally clear, and which may be expressed by the syllables *wizz, wizz, wizz*. While following insects on the wing, it keeps its bill constantly open, snapping as if it procured several of them on the same excursion. It is frequently observed balancing itself in the air, opposite the extremity of a bunch of leaves, and darting into the midst of them after the insects there concealed.

When one approaches the nest of this species, the male exhibits the greatest anxiety respecting its safety, passes and repasses, fluttering and snapping its bill within a few feet, as if determined to repel the intruder. They now and then alight on the ground, to secure an insect, but this only for a moment. They are more frequently seen climbing along the trunks and large branches of trees for an instant, and then shifting to a branch, being, as I have said, in perpetual motion. It is also fond of giving chase to various birds, snapping at them without any effect, as if solely for the purpose of keeping up the natural liveliness of its disposition.

The young males of this species do not possess the brilliancy and richness of plumage which the old birds display, until the second year, the first being spent in the garb worn by the females; but, towards the second autumn, appear mottled with pure black and vermilion on their sides. Notwithstanding their want of full plumage, they breed and sing the first spring like the old males.

I have looked for several minutes at a time on the ineffectual attacks which this bird makes on wasps while busily occupied about their own nests. The bird approaches and snaps at them, but in vain; for the wasp elevating its abdomen, protrudes its sting, which prevents its being seized. The male bird is represented in the plate in this posture.

Its nest is generally made on a low bush or sapling, and has the appearance of hanging to the twigs. It is slight, and is composed of lichens and dried fibres of rank weeds or grape vines, nicely lined with soft cottony materials. The female lays from four to six white eggs, sprinkled with ash-grey and blackish dots. It rears only a single brood in a season. The old birds, I am inclined to think, leave the United States a month or three weeks before the young, some of which linger in the deep swamps of the States of Mississippi and Louisiana until the beginning of November.

MUSCICAPA RUTICILLA, *Linn.* Syst. Nat. vol. i. p. 336.—*Lath.* Ind. Ornith. vol. ii. p. 473.—*Ch. Bonaparte,* Synops. of Birds of the United States, p. 68.

AMERICAN REDSTART, MUSCICAPA RUTICILLA, *Wils.* Amer. Ornith. vol. i. p. 103, Pl. vi. fig. 6. adult male; vol. v. p. 119. Pl. 45, fig. 2, young.—*Lath.* Synops. vol. iv. p. 427.

Adult Male. Plate XL. Fig. 1.

Bill of ordinary length, depressed at the base, compressed toward the tip, acute; upper mandible slightly notched, and deflected at the tip; lower straight. Nostrils basal, lateral, linear. Head and neck of moderate size. Body rather slender. Feet moderately long, slender; tarsus covered with short scutella before, with a longitudinal keeled plate behind, longer than the middle toe; toes slender, free; claws small, weak, slightly arched, compressed, acute.

Plumage blended, soft, glossy. The bill margined at the base with long spreading bristles. Wings of moderate length, third quill longest, second and first little shorter. Tail rather long, rounded.

Bill brownish-black. Iris dark brown. Feet blackish. Head, neck, fore part of the breast, and upper parts, black, the head, neck, and back glossed with blue. Sides of the breast, and under wing-coverts reddish-orange ; abdomen white. Quills brownish-black, their anterior half orange, forming a broad transverse band on the wing. Two middle tail-feathers black, the rest black in their terminal half, yellow in the basal half.

Length 5 inches, extent of wings $6\frac{1}{2}$; bill along the ridge $\frac{9}{12}$, along the gap $\frac{1}{2}$; tarsus $\frac{3}{4}$, middle toe $\frac{7}{12}$.

Adult Female. Plate XL. Fig. 2.

Bill, feet and iris, as in the male. Head and upper parts brownish-grey, the former tinged with blue. Under parts greyish-white, the breast at the sides dull yellow. Band on the wings and at the base of the tail, pale yellow, tinged with green.

Dimensions nearly as in the male.

THE VIRGINIAN HORNBEAM, OR IRON-WOOD TREE.

OSTRYA VIRGINICA, *Willd.* Sp. Pl. vol. iv. p. 469. *Pursh*, Flor. Amer. vol. ii. p. 623.
—MONŒCIA POLYANDRIA, *Linn.* AMENTACEÆ, *Juss.*

This species is distinguished by its ovato-oblong leaves, which are somewhat cordate at the base, unequally serrated and acuminate, and its twin, ovate, acute cones. It is a small tree, attaining a height of from twenty to thirty feet, and a diameter of about one foot. The wood is white, and close-grained. The common name in America is *Iron-wood*, which it receives on account of the great hardness of the wood.

THE COUGAR.

THERE is an extensive Swamp in the section of the State of Mississippi which lies partly in the Choctaw territory. It commences at the borders of the Mississippi, at no great distance from a Chicasaw village, situated near the mouth of a creek known by the name of Vanconnah, and partly inundated by the swellings of several large bayous, the principal of which, crossing the swamp in its whole extent, discharges its waters not far from the mouth of the Yazoo River. This famous bayou is called False River. The swamp of which I am speaking follows the windings of the Yazoo, until the latter branches off to the north-east, and at this point forms the stream named Cold Water River, below which the Yazoo receives the draining of another bayou inclining towards the north-west, and intersecting that known by the name of False River, at a short distance from the place where the latter receives the waters of the Mississippi. This tedious account of the situation of the Swamp, is given with the view of pointing it out to all students of nature who may chance to go that way, and whom I would earnestly urge to visit its interior, as it abounds in rare and interesting productions: birds, quadrupeds and reptiles, as well as molluscous animals, many of which, I am persuaded, have never been described.

In the course of one of my rambles, I chanced to meet with a squatter's cabin on the banks of the Cold Water River. In the owner of this hut, like most of those adventurous settlers in the uncultivated tracts of our frontier districts, I found a person well versed in the chase, and acquainted with the habits of some of the larger species of quadrupeds and birds. As he who is desirous of instruction ought not to disdain listening to any one, who has knowledge to communicate, however humble may be his lot, or however limited his talents, I entered the squatter's cabin, and immediately opened a conversation with him respecting the situation of the swamp, and its natural productions. He told me he thought it the very place I ought to visit, spoke of the game which it contained, and pointed to some bear and deer skins, adding that the individuals to which they had belonged formed but a small portion of the number of those animals which he had shot within it. My heart swelled with delight, and on asking if he would accompany me through the great morass, and allow me to become an inmate of his humble but hospitable mansion, I was gratified to find that he cordially assented to all my proposals. So I immediately unstrapped my drawing materials, laid up my gun, and sat down to partake of the homely but wholesome fare intended for the supper of the squatter, his wife, and his two sons.

The quietness of the evening seemed in perfect accordance with the gentle demeanour of the family. The wife and children, I more than once thought, seemed to look upon me as a strange sort of person, going about, as I told them I was, in search of birds and plants; and were I here to relate the many questions which they put to me in return for those which I addressed to them, the catalogue would occupy several pages. The husband, a native of Connecticut, had heard of the existence of such men as myself, both in our own country and abroad, and seemed greatly pleased to have me under his roof. Supper over, I asked 'my kind host what had induced him to remove to this wild and solitary spot. " The people are growing too numerous now to thrive in New England," was his answer. I thought of the state of some parts of Europe, and calculating the denseness of their population compared with that of New England, exclaimed to myself, " How much more difficult must it be for men to thrive in those populous countries !" The conversation then changed, and the squatter, his sons and myself, spoke of hunting and fishing, until at length tired, we laid ourselves down on pallets of bear skins, and reposed in peace on the floor of the only apartment of which the hut consisted.

Day dawned, and the squatter's call to his hogs, which, being almost in a wild state, were suffered to seek the greater portion of their food in the woods, awakened me. Being ready dressed, I was not long in joining him. The hogs and their young came grunting at the well known call of their owner, who threw them a few ears of corn, and counted them, but told me that for some weeks their number had been greatly diminished by the ravages committed upon 'them by a large *Panther*, by which name the Cougar is designated in America, and that the ravenous animal did not content himself with the flesh of his pigs, but now and then carried off one of his calves, notwithstanding the many attempts he had made to shoot it. The *Painter*, as he sometimes called it, had on several occasions robbed him of a dead deer; and to these exploits the squatter added several remarkable feats of audacity which it had performed, to give me an idea of the formidable character of the beast. Delighted by his description, I offered to assist him in destroying the enemy, at which he was highly pleased, but assured me that unless some of his neighbours should join us with their dogs and his own, the attempt would prove fruitless. Soon after, mounting a horse, he went off to his neighbours, several of whom lived at a distance of some miles, and appointed a day of meeting.

The hunters, accordingly, made their appearance, one fine morning, at the door of the cabin, just as the sun was emerging from beneath the horizon. They were five in number, and fully equipped for the chase, being mounted on horses, which in some parts of Europe might appear sorry nags, but which in strength, speed and bottom, are better fitted for pursuing a cougar or a bear through woods and morasses than any in that country. A pack of large ugly curs were already engaged in making acquaintance with those of the squatter. He and myself mounted his two best horses, whilst his sons were bestriding others of inferior quality.

Few words were uttered by the party until we had reached the edge of the Swamp, where it was agreed that all should disperse and seek for the fresh track of the Painter, it being previously settled that the discoverer should blow his horn, and remain on the spot, until the rest should join him. In less than an hour, the sound of the horn was clearly heard, and, sticking close to the squatter, off we went through the thick woods, guided only by the now and then repeated call of the distant huntsmen. We soon reached the spot, and in a short time the rest of the party came up. The best dog was sent forward to track the Cougar, and in a few moments, the whole pack were observed diligently trailing, and bearing in their course for the interior of the Swamp. The rifles were immediately put in trim, and the party followed the dogs, at separate distances, but in sight of each other, determined to shoot at no other game than the Panther.

The dogs soon began to mouth, and suddenly quickened their pace. My companion concluded that the beast was on the ground, and putting our horses to a gentle gallop, we followed the curs, guided by their voices. The noise of the dogs increased, when, all of a sudden their mode of barking became altered, and the squatter, urging me to push on, told me that the beast was *treed*, by which he meant that it had got upon some low branch of a large tree to rest for a few moments, and that should we not succeed in shooting him when thus situated, we might expect a long chase of it. As we approached the spot, we all by degrees united into a body, but on seeing the dogs at the foot of a large tree, separated again and galloped off to surround it.

. Each hunter now moved with caution, holding his gun ready, and allowing the bridle to dangle on the neck of his horse, as it advanced slowly towards the dogs. A shot from one of the party was heard, on which the Cougar was seen to leap to the ground, and bound off with such velocity as to shew that he was very unwilling to stand our fire longer. The dogs set off in pursuit with great eagerness and a deafening cry. The hunter who had fired came up and said that his ball had. hit the monster, and had probably broken one of his fore-legs near the shoulder, the only place at which he could aim. A slight trail of blood was discovered on the ground, but the curs proceeded at such a rate that we merely noticed this, and put spurs to our horses, which galloped on towards the centre of the Swamp. One bayou was crossed, then another still larger and more muddy; but the dogs were brushing forward, and as the horses began to pant at a furious rate, we judged it expedient to leave them and advance on foot. These determined hunters knew that the Cougar being wounded, would shortly ascend another tree, where in all probability he would remain for a considerable time, and that it would be easy to follow the track of the dogs. We dismounted, took off the saddles and bridles, set the bells attached to the horses' necks at liberty to jingle, hoppled the animals, and left them to shift for themselves.

Now, kind reader, follow the group marching through the swamp, crossing muddy pools, and making the best of their way over fallen trees and amongst the tangled rushes that now and then covered acres of ground. If you are a hunter yourself, all this will appear nothing to you; but if crowded assemblies of " beauty and fashion," or the quiet enjoyment of your " pleasure-grounds," alone delight you, I must mend my pen before I attempt to give you an idea of the pleasure felt on such an expedition.

After marching for a couple of hours, we again heard the dogs. Each of us pressed forward, elated at the thought of terminating the career of the cougar. Some of the dogs were heard whining, although the greater number barked vehemently. We felt assured that the Cougar was treed, and that he would rest for some time to recover from his fatigue. As we came up to the dogs, we discovered the ferocious animal lying across a large branch, close to the trunk of a cotton-wood tree. His broad breast lay towards us; his eyes were at one time bent on us

2

and again on the dogs beneath and around him; one of his fore legs hung loosely by his side, and he lay crouched, with his ears lowered close to his head, as if he thought he might remain undiscovered. Three balls were fired at him, at a given signal, on which he sprang a few feet from the branch, and tumbled headlong to the ground. Attacked on all sides by the enraged curs, the infuriated Cougar fought with desperate valour; but the squatter advancing in front of the party, and almost in the midst of the dogs, shot him immediately behind and beneath the left shoulder. The Cougar writhed for a moment in agony, and in another lay dead.

The sun was now sinking in the west. Two of the hunters separated from the rest, to procure venison, whilst the squatter's sons were ordered to make the best of their way home, to be ready to feed the hogs in the morning. The rest of the party agreed to camp on the spot. The cougar was despoiled of its skin, and its carcass left to the hungry dogs. Whilst engaged in preparing our camp, we heard the report of a gun, and soon after one of our hunters returned with a small deer. A fire was lighted, and each hunter displayed his *pone* of bread, along with a flask of whisky. The deer was skinned in a trice, and slices placed on sticks before the fire. These materials afforded us an excellent meal, and as the night grew darker, stories and songs went round, until my companions, fatigued, laid themselves down, close under the smoke of the fire, and soon fell asleep.

I walked for some minutes round the camp, to contemplate the beauties of that nature, from which I have certainly derived my greatest pleasures. I thought of the occurrences of the day, and glancing my eye around, remarked the singular effects produced by the phosphorescent qualities of the large decayed trunks which lay in all directions around me. How easy, I thought, would it be for the confused and agitated mind of a person bewildered in a swamp like this, to imagine in each of these luminous masses some wondrous and fearful being, the very sight of which might make the hair stand erect on his head. The thought of being myself placed in such a predicament burst over my mind, and I hastened to join my companions, beside whom I laid me down and slept, assured that no enemy could approach us without first rousing the dogs, which were growling in fierce dispute over the remains of the cougar.

At daybreak we left our camp, the squatter bearing on his shoulder the skin of the late destroyer of his stock, and retraced our steps until we found our horses, which had not strayed far from the place where we

o

had left them.   These we soon saddled, and jogging along, in a direct course, guided by the sun, congratulating each other on the destruction of so formidable a neighbour as the panther had been, we soon arrived at my host's cabin.   The five neighbours partook of such refreshment as the house could afford, and dispersing, returned to their homes, leaving . me to follow my favourite pursuits.

THE RUFFED GROUSE.

TETRAO UMBELLUS, LINN.

PLATE XLI. MALE AND FEMALE.

YOU are now presented, kind reader, with a species of Grouse, which, in my humble opinion, far surpasses as an article of food every other land-bird which we have in the United States, except the Wild Turkey, when in good condition. You must not be surprised that I thus express an opinion contradictory to that of our Eastern epicures, who greatly prefer the flesh of the Pinnated Grouse to that of the present species, for I have had abundant opportunity of knowing both. Perhaps, after all, the preference may depend upon a peculiarity in my own taste; or I may give the superiority to the Ruffed Grouse, because it is as rarely met with in the Southern States, where I have chiefly resided, as the Pinnated Grouse is in the Middle Districts; and were the *bon-vivants* of our eastern cities to be occasionally satiated with the latter birds, as I have been, they might possibly think their flesh as dry and flavourless as I do.

The names of *Pheasant* and *Partridge* have been given to the present species by our forefathers, in the different districts where it is found. To the west of the Alleghanies, and on these mountains, the first name is generally used. The same appellation is employed in the Middle Districts, to the east of the mountains, and until you enter the State of Connecticut; after which that of *Partridge* prevails.

The Ruffed Grouse, although a constant resident in the districts which it frequents, performs partial sorties at the approach of autumn. These are not equal in extent to the peregrinations of the Wild Turkey, our little Partridge, or the Pinnated Grouse, but are sufficiently so to become observable during the seasons when certain portions of the mountainous districts which they inhabit become less abundantly supplied with food than others. These partial movings might not be noticed, were not the birds obliged to fly across rivers of great breadth, as whilst in the mountain lands their groups are as numerous as those which attempt these migrations; but on the north-west banks of the Ohio and Susquehanna rivers, no one who pays the least attention to the manners and habits of our birds, can fail to observe them. The Grouse approach the banks of

o 2

the Ohio in parties of eight or ten, now and then of twelve or fifteen, and, on arriving there, linger in the woods close by for a week or a fortnight, as if fearful of encountering the danger to be incurred in crossing the stream. This usually happens in the beginning of October, when these birds are in the very best order for the table, and at this period great numbers of them are killed. If started from the ground, with or without the assistance of a dog, they immediately alight on the nearest trees, and are easily shot. At length, however, they resolve upon crossing the river; and this they accomplish with so much ease, that I never saw any of them drop into the water. Not more than two or three days elapse after they have reached the opposite shore, when they at once proceed to the interior of the forests, in search of places congenial to the general character of their habits. They now resume their ordinary manner of living, which they continue until the approach of spring, when the males, as if leading the way, proceed singly towards the country from which they had retreated. The females follow in small parties of three or four. In the month of October 1820, I observed a larger number of Ruffed Grouse migrating thus from the States of Ohio, Illinois and Indiana into Kentucky, than I had ever before remarked. During the short period of their lingering along the north-west shore of the Ohio that season, a great number of them was killed, and they were sold in the Cincinnati market for so small a sum as 12½ cents each.

Although these birds are particularly attached to the craggy sides of mountains and hills, and the rocky borders of rivers and small streams, thickly mantled with evergreen trees and small shrubs of the same nature, they at times remove to low lands, and even enter the thickest cane-brakes, where they also sometimes breed. I have shot some, and have heard them *drumming* in such places, when there were no hills nearer than fifteen or twenty miles. The lower parts of the State of Indiana and also those of Kentucky, are amongst the places where I have discovered them in such situations.

The charming groves which here and there contrast so beautifully with the general dull appearance of those parts of Kentucky and Tennessee, to which the name of *Barrens* is given, are sought by the Ruffed Grouse. These groves afford them abundant food and security. The gentle coolness that prevails in them during the summer heat is agreeable and beneficial to these birds, and the closeness of their undergrowth in other spots moderates the cold blasts of winter. There this species breeds,

and is at all times to be found. Their *drumming* is to be heard issuing
from these peaceful retreats in early spring, at the same time that the
booming of their relative, the Pinnated Grouse, is recognised, as it reaches
the ear of the traveller, from the different parts of the more open country
around. In such places as the groves just mentioned, the species now before you, kind reader, is to be met with, as you travel towards the south,
through the whole of Tennessee and the Choctaw Territory ; but as you
approach the city of Natchez they disappear, nor have I ever heard of
one of these birds having been seen in the State of Louisiana.

The mountainous parts of the Middle States being more usually the
chosen residence of this species, I shall, with your permission, kind reader, return to them, and try to give you an account of this valuable Grouse.

The flight of the Ruffed Grouse is straight-forward, rather low, unless when the bird has been disturbed, and seldom protracted beyond a
few hundred yards at a time. It is also stiff, and performed with a continued beating of the wings for more than half its duration, after which
the bird sails and seems to balance its body as it proceeds through the air,
in the manner of a vessel sailing right before the wind. When this bird
rises from the ground at a time when pursued by an enemy, or tracked
by a dog, it produces a loud whirring sound, resembling that of the whole
tribe, excepting the Black Cock of Europe, which has less of it than any
other species. This whirring sound is never heard when the Grouse rises
of its own accord, for the purpose of removing from one place to another ;
nor, in similar circumstances, is it commonly produced by our little Partridge. In fact, I do not believe that it is emitted by any species of Grouse,
unless when surprised and forced to rise. I have often been lying on the
ground in the woods or the fields for hours at a time, for the express purpose of observing the movements and habits of different birds, and have
frequently seen a Partridge or a Grouse rise on wing from within a few
yards of the spot in which I lay unobserved by them, as gently and softly
as any other bird, and without producing any whirring sound. Nor even
when this Grouse ascends to the top of a tree, does it make any greater
noise than other birds of the same size would do.

I have said this much respecting the flight of Grouse, because it is a
prevalent opinion, both among sportsmen and naturalists, that the whirring sound produced by birds of that genus, is a necessary effect of their
usual mode of flight. But that this is an error, I have abundantly satisfied myself by numberless observations.

On the ground, where the Ruffed Grouse spends a large portion of its time, its motions are peculiarly graceful. It walks with an elevated firm step, opening its beautiful tail gently and with a well-marked jet, holding erect its head, the feathers of which are frequently raised, as are the velvety tufts of its neck. It poises its body on one foot for several seconds at a time, and utters a soft *cluck*, which in itself implies a degree of confidence in the bird that its *tout ensemble* is deserving of the notice of any bystander. Should the bird discover that it is observed, its step immediately changes to a rapid run, its head is lowered, the tail is more widely spread, and if no convenient hiding-place is at hand, it immediately takes flight with as much of the whirring sound as it can produce, as if to prove to the observer, that, when on wing, it cares as little about him as the deer pretends to do, when, on being started by the hound, he makes several lofty bounds, and erects his tail to the breeze. Should the Grouse, however, run into a thicket, or even over a place where many dried leaves lie on the ground, it suddenly stops, squats, and remains close until the danger is over, or until it is forced by a dog or the sportsman himself to rise against its wish.

The shooting of Grouse of this species is precarious, and at times very difficult, on account of the nature of the places which they usually prefer. Should, for instance, a covey of these birds be raised from amongst Laurels (*Kalmia latifolia*) or the largest species of Bay (*Rhododendron maximum*), these shrubs so intercept the view of them, that, unless the sportsman proves quite an adept in the difficult art of pulling the trigger of his gun at the proper moment, and quickly, his first chance is lost, and the next is very uncertain. I say still more uncertain, because at this putting up of the birds, they generally rise higher over the bushes, flying in a straight course, whereas at the second start, they often fly among the laurels, and rise above them in a circuitous manner, when to follow them along the barrel of the gun is considerably more difficult. Sometimes, when these birds are found on the sides of a steep hill, the moment they start, they dive towards the foot of the declivity, take a turn, and fly off in a direction so different from the one expected, that unless the sportsman is aware of the trick, he may not see them again that day. The young birds often prove equally difficult to be obtained, for as they are raised from amongst the closely tangled laurels, they only fly a few yards, and again drop among them. A smart cur-dog generally proves the best kind on these occasions; for no sooner does he start a covey of Ruffed Grouse than his barking alarms the birds as much as the report of a gun, and causes them to rise and alight on the nearest trees, on which they may be shot at with great success.

This leads me to remark, that the prevailing notion which exists in almost every district where these birds are numerous, that on firing at the lowest bird perched on a tree, the next above will not fly, and that by continuing to shoot at the lowest in succession, the whole may be killed, is contradicted by my experience; for on every attempt which I have made to shoot several in this manner on the same tree, my efforts have proved unsuccessful, unless indeed during a fall of snow, when I have killed three and sometimes four. The same cause produces the same effect on different birds. It may happen, however, that in districts covered with deep snow for several weeks, during severe winters, these birds, becoming emaciated and weak, may stand a repetition of shots from a person determined to shoot Grouse even when they are good for nothing; but, kind reader, this barbarous taste is, I hope, no more yours than it is mine.

During spring, and towards the latter part of autumn, at which times the Ruffed Grouse is heard *drumming* from different parts of the woods to which it resorts, I have shot many a fine cock by imitating the sound of its own wings striking against the body, which I did by beating a large inflated bullock's bladder with a stick, keeping up as much as possible the same *time* as that in which the bird beats. At the sound produced by the bladder and the stick, the male Grouse, inflamed with jealousy, has flown directly towards me, when, being prepared, I have easily shot it. An equally successful stratagem is employed to decoy the males of our little Partridge by imitating the call-note of the female during spring and summer; but in no instance, after repeated trials, have I been able to entice the Pinnated Grouse to come towards me, whilst imitating the *booming* sounds of that bird.

Early in spring, these birds are frequently seen feeding on the tender buds of different trees, and at that season are more easily approached than at any other. Unfortunately, however, they have not by this time recovered their flesh sufficiently to render them worthy of the attention of a true sportsman, although their flavour has already improved. When our mountains are covered with a profusion of Huckleberries and Whortleberries, about the beginning of September, then is the time for shooting this species, and enjoying the delicious food which it affords.

The Ruffed Grouse, on alighting upon a tree, after being raised from the ground, perches amongst the thickest parts of the foliage, and, assuming at once an erect attitude, stands perfectly still, and remains silent until all appearance of danger has vanished. If discovered when thus perched, it is very easily shot. On rising from the ground, the bird utters a cackling note repeated six or seven times, and before taking wing emits a lisping sort of whistle, which seems as if produced by the young of another bird, and is very remarkable.

When the ground is covered with snow sufficiently soft to allow this bird to conceal itself under it, it dives headlong into it with such force as to form a hole several yards in length, re-appears at that distance, and continues to elude the pursuit of the sportsman by flight. They are sometimes caught while beneath the snow. Many of them are taken alive in trap boxes during winter, although the more common method of catching or rather destroying them is by setting dead falls with a figure-of-four trigger.

Early in April, the Ruffed Grouse begins to *drum* immediately after dawn, and again towards the close of day. As the season advances, the drumming is repeated more frequently at all hours of the day; and where these birds are abundant, this curious sound is heard from all parts of the woods in which they reside. The drumming is performed in the following manner. The male bird, standing erect on a prostrate decayed trunk, raises the feathers of its body, in the manner of a Turkey-cock, draws its head towards it tail, erecting the feathers of the latter at the same time, and raising its ruff around the neck, suffers its wings to droop, and struts about on the log. A few moments elapse, when the bird draws the whole of its feathers close to its body, and stretching itself out, beats its sides with its wings, in the manner of the domestic Cock, but more loudly, and with such rapidity of motion, after a few of the first strokes, as to cause a tremor in the air not unlike the rumbling of distant thunder. This, kind reader, is the "*drumming*" of the Pheasant. In perfectly calm weather, it may be heard at the distance of two hundred yards, but might be supposed to proceed from a much greater distance. The female, which never drums, flies directly to the place where the male is thus engaged, and, on approaching him, opens her wings before him, balances her body to the right and left, and then receives his caresses.

The same trunk is resorted to by the same birds during the season, unless they are frequently disturbed. These trunks are easily known by the quantity of excrements and feathers about them. The males have the liberty of promiscuous concubinage, although not to such an extent as those of the Pinnated Grouse. They have frequent and severe battles at this season, which, although witnessed by the females, are never interrupted by them. The drumming sounds of these birds lead to their destruction, every young sportsman taking the unfair advantage of approaching them at this season, and shooting them in the act.

About the beginning of May, the female retires to some thicket in a close part of the woods, where she forms a nest. This is placed by the side of a prostrate tree, or at the foot of a low bush, on the ground, in a spot where a heap of dried leaves has been formed by the wind. The nest is composed of dried leaves and herbaceous plants. The female lays from five to twelve eggs, which are of a uniform dull yellowish colour, and are proportionate in size to the bird. The latter never covers them on leaving the nest, and in consequence, the Raven and the Crow, always on the look out for such dainties, frequently discover and eat them. When the female is present, however, she generally defends them with great obstinacy, striking the intruder with her wings and feet, in the manner of the Common Hen.

The young run about and follow the mother, the moment after they leave the egg. They are able to fly for a few yards at a time, when only six or seven days old, and still very small. The mother leads them in search of food, covers them at night with her wings, and evinces the greatest care and affection towards them on the least appearance of danger, trying by every art in her power to draw the attention of her enemies to herself, feigning lameness, tumbling and rolling about as if severely wounded, and by this means generally succeeding in saving them. The little ones squat at the least chuck of alarm from the mother, and lie so close as to suffer one to catch them in the hand, should he chance to discover them, which, however, it is very difficult to do. The males are then beginning to associate in small parties, and continue separated from the females until the approach of winter, when males, females, and young, mingle together. During summer, these birds are fond of dusting themselves, and resort to the roads for that purpose, as well as to pick up gravel. I have observed this species copulating towards autumn, but have not been able to account for this unseasonable procedure, as only one brood is raised in the season.

These birds have various enemies besides man. Different species of Hawks destroy them, particularly the Red-tailed Hawk and the Stanley

Hawk. The former watches their motions from the tops of trees, and falls upon them with the swiftness of thought, whilst the latter seizes upon them as he glides rapidly through the woods. Pole-cats, weasels, raccoons, oppossums, and foxes, are all destructive foes to them. Of these, some are content with sucking their eggs, while others feed on their flesh.

I have found these birds most numerous in the States of Pennsylvania and New York. They are brought to the markets in great numbers, during the winter months, and sell at from 75 cents to a dollar a-piece, in the eastern cities. At Pittsburg I have bought them, some years ago, for 12½ cents the pair. It is said that when they have fed for several weeks on the leaves of the *Kalmia latifolia*, it is dangerous to eat their flesh, and I believe laws have been passed to prevent their being sold at that season. I have, however, eaten them at all seasons, and although I have found their crops distended with the leaves of the Kalmia, have never felt the least inconvenience after eating them, nor even perceived any difference of taste in their flesh. I suspect it is only when the birds have been kept a long time undrawn and unplucked, that the flesh becomes impregnated with the juice of these leaves.

The food of this species consists of seeds and berries of all kinds, according to the season. It also feeds on the leaves of several species of evergreens, although these are only resorted to when other food has become scarce. They are particularly fond of fox-grapes and winter-grapes, as well as strawberries and dewberries. To procure the latter, they issue from the groves of the Kentucky Barrens, and often stray to the distance of a mile. They roost on trees, amongst the thickest parts of the foliage, sitting at some distance from each other, and may easily be smoked to death, by using the necessary precautions.

I cannot conclude this article, kind reader, without observing how desirable the acquisition of this species might be to the sportsmen of Europe, and especially to those of England, where I am surprised it has not yet been introduced. The size of these birds, the beauty of their plumage, the excellence of their flesh, and their peculiar mode of flying, would render them valuable, and add greatly to the interest of the already diversified sports of that country. In England and Scotland there are thousands of situations that are by nature perfectly suited to their habits, and I have not a doubt that a few years of attention would be sufficient to render them quite as common as the Grey Partridge.

Tetrao Umbellus, *Linn.* Syst. Nat. vol. i. p. 275.—*Lath.* Ind. Orn. vol. ii. p. 638.—
    Ch. Bonaparte, Synops. of Birds of the United States, p. 126.
Ruffed Grouse, Tetrao Umbellus, *Wils.* Amer. Ornith. vol. vi. p. 45. Pl. 49.
    Male.—*Lath.* Synops. vol. iv. p. 738.
Shoulder-knot Grouse.—*Lath.* Synops. vol. iv. p. 737.

Adult Male.   Plate XLI. Fig. 1, 2.

Bill short, robust, slightly arched, rather obtuse, the base covered by
feathers; upper mandible with the dorsal outline straight in the feathered
part, convex towards the end, the edges overlapping, the tip declinate;
under mandible somewhat bulging toward the tip, the sides convex.
Nostrils concealed among the feathers. Head and neck small. Body
bulky. Feet of ordinary length; tarsus feathered, excepting at the lower
part anteriorly, where it is scutellate, spurless; toes scutellate above, pectinated on the sides; claws arched, depressed, obtuse.

Plumage compact, glossy. Feathers of the head narrow and elongated into a curved tuft. A large space on the neck destitute of feathers,
but covered over by an erectile ruff of elongated feathers, of which the
upper are silky, shining, and curved forwards at the end, which is very
broad and rounded. Wings short, broad, much rounded and curved, the
third and fourth quills longest. Tail long, ample, rounded, of eighteen
feathers.

Bill horn-colour, brownish-black towards the tip. Iris hazel. Feet
yellowish-grey. Upper part of the head and hind part of the neck bright
yellowish-red. Back rich chestnut, marked with oblong white spots, margined with black. Upper wing-coverts similar to the back. Quills
brownish-dusky, their outer webs pale reddish, spotted with dusky. Upper
tail-coverts banded with black. Tail reddish-yellow, barred and minutely
mottled with black, and terminated by a broad band of the latter colour,
between two narrow bands of bluish-white, of which one is terminal. A
yellowish-white band from the upper mandible to the eye, beyond which
it is prolonged. Throat and lower part of the neck light brownish-yellow. Lower ruff feathers of the same colour, barred with reddish-brown,
the upper black with blue reflections. A tuft of light chestnut feathers
under the wings. The rest of the under parts yellowish-white, with broad
transverse spots of brownish-red; the abdomen yellowish-red; and the
under tail-coverts mottled with brown.

Length 18 inches, extent of wings 2 feet ; bill along the ridge $\frac{3}{4}$, along the gap $1\frac{1}{12}$; tarsus $1\frac{7}{12}$, middle toe $1\frac{3}{4}$.

Adult Female. Plate XLI. Fig. 3.

The plumage of the female is less developed and inferior in beauty. The feathers of the head and ruff are less elongated, the latter of a duller black. The tints of the plumage generally are lighter than in the male.

THE ORCHARD ORIOLE.

ICTERUS SPURIUS, BONAP.

PLATE XLII. MALE IN DIFFERENT STATES, ADULT FEMALE AND NEST.

THE plumage of many species of our birds undergoes at times very extraordinary changes. Some, such as the male Tanagers, which during the summer months exhibit the most vivid scarlet and velvety black, assume a dingy green before they leave the country, on their way southward. The Goldfinch nearly changes to the same colour, after having been seen in a gay apparel of yellow and black. The Rice Bird loses its lively brightness until the return of spring. Others take several years before they complete their plumage, so as to shew the true place which they hold amongst the other species, as is the case with the Ibis, the Flamingo, and many other Waders, as well as with several of our land birds, among which, kind reader, the species now under your consideration is probably that in which these gradual improvements are most observable by such persons as reside in the country inhabited by them.

The plumage of the young birds of this species, when they leave the nest, resembles that of the female parent, although rather less decided in point of colouring, and both males and females retain this colour until the approach of the following spring, when the former exhibit a portion of black on the chin, the females never altering. In birds kept in cages, this portion of black remains without farther augmentation for two years; but in those which are at liberty, a curious mixture of dull orange or deep chestnut peeps out through a considerable increase of black-coloured feathers over the body and wings, intermixed with the yellowish-green hue which the bird had when it left the nest. The third spring brings him nearer towards perfection, as at that time the deep chestnut colour has taken possession of the lower parts, the black has deepened on the upper parts, and over the whole head, as well as on the wings and tail-feathers. Yet the garb with which it is ultimately to be covered requires another return of spring before it is completed, after which it remains as exhibited in the adult male, represented in the plate.

These extraordinary changes are quite sufficient of themselves to lead naturalists abroad into error, as they give rise to singular arguments even

with some persons in America, who maintain that the differences of colour
are indicative of different species. But, since the *habits* of these birds
under all these singular changes of plumage are ascertained to be precisely the same, the argument no longer holds good. I shall now endeavour to describe these habits with all the accuracy supplied by long
observation,

The migration of the Orchard Oriole from south to north is performed
by day, and singly, as is that of its relative the Baltimore Oriole, the
males appearing a week or ten days sooner than the females. Their
flight is lower than that of the Baltimore, and considerably shorter in its
continuance, the Orchard Oriole alighting more frequently on the tops of
the trees, to rest or to feed. They exhibit a greater repetition of motions of
the wings, although sliding through the air for a few yards only at a time,
and whilst about to alight, as well as afterwards, perform strong and well
marked jettings of the tail. This the Baltimore seldom does. No sooner
have they reached the portion of the country in which they intend to remain during the time of raising their young, than these birds exhibit all
the liveliness and vivacity belonging to their nature. The male is seen
rising in the air for ten or twenty yards in an indirect manner, jerking
his tail and body, flapping his wings, and singing with remarkable impetuosity, as if under the influence of haste, and anxious to return to the
tree from which he has departed. He accordingly descends with the
same motions of the body and tail, repeating his pleasant song as he
alights. These gambols and carollings are performed frequently during
the day, the intervals being employed in ascending or descending along
the branches and twigs of different trees, in search of insects or larvæ.
In doing this, they rise on their legs, seldom without jetting the tail,
stretch their neck, seize the prey, and emit a single note, which is sweet
and mellow, although in power much inferior to that of the Baltimore.
At other times, it is seen bending its body downwards, in a curved posture, with the head greatly inclined upwards, to peep at the under parts
of the leaves, so as not to suffer any grub to escape its vigilance. It now
alights on the ground, where it has spied a crawling insect, and again
flies towards the blossoms, in which many are lurking, and devours
hundreds of them each day, thus contributing to secure to the farmer the
hopes which he has of the productiveness of his orchard.

The arrival of the females is marked with all due regard, and the
males immediately use every effort in their power to procure from them

a return of attention. Their singings and tricks are performed with redoubled ardour, until they are paired, when nidification is attended to
with the utmost activity. They resort to the meadows, or search along
the fences for the finest, longest, and toughest grasses they can find, and
having previously fixed on a spot either on an Apple Tree, or amidst
the drooping branches of the Weeping Willow, they begin by attaching
the grass firmly and neatly to the twigs more immediately around the
chosen place. The filaments are twisted, passed over and under, and interwoven in such a manner as almost to defy the eye of man to follow their
windings. All this is done by the bill of the bird, in the manner used
by the Baltimore Oriole. The nest is of a hemispherical form, and
is supported by the margin only. It seldom exceeds three or four
inches in depth, is open almost to the full extent of its largest diameter
at the top or entrance, and finished on all sides, as well as within, with
the long slender grasses already mentioned. Some of these go round
the nest several times, as if coarsely woven together. This is the manner in which the nest is constructed in Louisiana; in the Middle Districts
it is usually lined with soft and warm materials. The female lays from
four to six eggs of a bluish-white tint, sprinkled with dark brown, and
raises only a single brood in the season. The young follow the parents
for several weeks, and many birds congregate towards autumn, but the
males soon separate from the females, and set out by themselves as they
arrived in spring.

The sociality of the Orchard Oriole is quite remarkable, and in this
respect that bird differs widely from the Baltimore, which will not suffer
any other bird of its species to build a nest, or to remain within a considerable distance from the spot which it has selected for its own; whereas
many nests of the species now before you may be observed in the same
garden or orchard, and often within a few yards of the house. I have
counted as many as nine of these nests on a few acres of ground, and the
different pairs to which they belonged lived in great harmony.

Although the food of the Orchard Orioles consists principally of insects of various kinds, it is not composed exclusively of them. They are
fond of different sorts of fruits and berries. Figs are also much relished
by them, as well as mulberries and strawberries, but not to such a degree
as to draw the attention of the gardener or husbandman towards their
depredations.

This species makes its first appearance in Louisiana early in March, and remains until October, being seen for several weeks after the Baltimore Oriole has set out. In reaches the Middle Districts in the beginning of April. I have met with it as far as the province of Maine and the head waters of the Mississippi. It is fond of high ground and the neighbourhood of mountains during the breeding season, after which it removes to the meadows and prairies in considerable numbers. Whilst in these meadows, it feeds principally upon a small species of cricket, ground spiders and small grasshoppers. Their flesh is very good at that late season, and is much esteemed by the Creoles of Louisiana.

The French of that State give it the name of *Pape de Prairie*, while they designate the Baltimore Oriole by that of *Pape de Bois*, which arises no doubt from the marked preference which the former manifests to the plains in autumn, where a great number are shot or caught in trap cages. It is easily kept in cages, where it sings with all the liveliness which it shews in its wild state, and may be fed on rice and dry fruits, when fresh ones cannot be procured. I have known one of these birds, a beautiful male, kept for upwards of four years by a friend of mine at New Orleans. It had been raised from the nest, and having passed through the different changes of its plumage, had become perfect, was full of action, and sung delightfully.

The nest represented in the plate was drawn in Louisiana, and was entirely composed of grass. It may be looked upon as a sample of the usual form and construction. The branch of Honey Locust on which you see these birds belongs to a tree which sometimes grows to a great height, without much apparent choice of situation. It is more abundant to the west of the Alleghanies, and towards the Southern Districts, than in the Middle States. The wood is brittle and seldom used. The trunk and branches are frequently covered with innumerable long, sharp, and extremely hard spines, protruded in every direction, and in some instances placed so near to each other as to preclude the possibility of any person's climbing them. It bears a long pod, containing a sweet substance, not unlike that of the honey of bees, and which is eaten by children, when it becomes quite ripe. The spines are made use of by tobacconists for the purpose of fastening together the different twists of their rolls.

ICTERUS SPURIUS, *Ch. Bonaparte,* Synops. of Birds of the United States, p. 51.

ORIOLUS SPURIUS, *Gmel.* Syst. Nat. vol. i. p. 389.—*Lath.* Ind. Ornith. vol. i. p. 180.

BASTARD BALTIMORE, *Lath.* Synops. vol. ii. p. 433.

ORCHARD ORIOLE, ORIOLUS MUTATUS, *Wils.* Americ. Ornith. vol. i. p. 64. Pl. iv.
fig. 1, 2, 3, 4.

Male in complete plumage. Plate XLII. Fig. 1, 2.

Bill conical, slender, longish, compressed, a little curved, very acute, with inflected acute margins ; upper mandible obtuse above, lower broadly obtuse beneath. Nostrils oval, covered by a membrane above, basal. Head and neck of ordinary size. Body rather slender. Feet of ordinary length ; tarsus a little longer than the middle toe ; inner toe little shorter than the outer ; claws arched, compressed, acute, that of the hind toe twice the size of the others.

Plumage soft, blended, glossy. Wings of ordinary length, the second and third primaries longest. Tail long, rounded, of twelve rounded feathers.

Bill black above with light blue margins, light blue beneath. Iris reddish-brown. Feet light blue. Head, neck, and upper back black ; the rest of the body dusky orange-red, approaching to chestnut. Quills and larger coverts black, margined with yellow, the latter tipped with yellowish-white ; tail black.

Length 6¼ inches, extent of wings 9 ; bill along the ridge $\frac{7}{12}$, along the gap ¾ ; tarsus 1, middle toe ⅝.

Adult Female. Plate XLII. Fig. 5.

Bill, feet and iris, as in the male. Head and upper parts brownish-green. Wings and tail greenish-brown ; wing-coverts tipped with white ; throat white, sides of the neck and under parts generally greyish-yellow. The young of both sexes resemble the female.

Male, first autumn and spring. Plate XLII. Fig. 3.

A patch of black on the throat, continued upwards over the lore and forehead. Head and upper parts brownish-green ; fore part of the back orange ; a yellow band over the eye. Under parts light yellow. Wings and tail as in the female, but the coverts tipped with yellow.

P

Male in the second year.　Plate XLII. Fig 4.

Irregularly spotted with black, yellow, and reddish orange, on the head, neck, and back ; the other parts nearly as in the adult male.

The Honey Locust.

Gleditschia triacanthos, *Willd.* Sp. Pl. vol. iv. p. 1097. *Pursh,* Flor. Amer. vol. i. p. 221. *Mich.* Arbr. Forest. vol. iii. p. 164. Pl. 10.—Polygamia Diœcia, *Linn.* Leguminosæ, *Juss.*

This tree, when growing in situations most favourable to it, sometimes attains a height of sixty or eighty feet, and a diameter of three or four. The bark is detached in large plates, and the trunk is marked with several broad furrows.　The flowers, which are small and of a greenish colour, are succeeded by long, flat, pendent, generally tortuous pods, of a brown colour.　The wood is very hard, but porous and brittle.　This species is distinguished by its numerous, generally tripartite spines, its linear-oblong leaflets, and its many-seeded, compressed legumes.

THE CEDAR BIRD.

BOMBYCILLA CAROLINENSIS, BRISS.

PLATE XLIII. MALE AND FEMALE.

LOUISIANA affords abundance of food and pleasant weather to this species, for nearly four months of the year, as the Cedar Birds reach that State about the beginning of November, and retire towards the Middle Districts in the beginning of March. The Holly, the Vines, the Persimon, the Pride-of-China, and various other trees, supply them with plenty of berries and fruits, on which they fatten, and become so tender and juicy as to be sought by every epicure for the table. I have known an instance of a basketful of these little birds having been forwarded to New Orleans as a Christmas present. The donor, however, was disappointed in his desire to please his friend in that city, for it was afterwards discovered that the steward of the steamer, in which they were shipped, made pies of them for the benefit of the passengers.

The appetite of the Cedar Bird is of so extraordinary a nature as to prompt it to devour every fruit or berry that comes in its way. In this manner they gorge themselves to such excess as sometimes to be unable to fly, and suffer themselves to be taken by the hand. Indeed I have seen some which, although wounded and confined in a cage, have eaten of apples until suffocation deprived them of life in the course of a few days. When opened afterwards, they were found to be gorged to the mouth.

It is a beautiful bird, but without any song, even during the breeding season, having only a note which it uses for the purpose of calling or rallying others of its species. This note is feeble, and as it were lisping, yet perfectly effectual, for when uttered by one in a flock within hearing of another party, the latter usually check their flight, and alight pell-mell on the same tree.

Their flight is easy, continued, and often performed at a considerable height. The birds move in close bodies, sometimes amounting to large flocks, making various circumvolutions before they alight, and then coming down in such numbers together as to seem to be touching each other. At this particular moment, or while performing their evolutions, some

P 2

dozens may be killed at a single shot; but if this opportunity is lost, the next moment after they alight, the whole group is in motion, dispersing over every bough to pick the berries which attracted them from the air. Their crest is now erected, their wings are seen constantly moving, and so eagerly do they grasp at the berries that they suffer many of them to fall. Every flock passing within hearing is invited to join in the feast, and in a few hours the tree is entirely stripped of its fruit. In this manner they search the whole of the forests, and towards winter are even satisfied with the berries of the Dog-wood. As the cherries and mulberries ripen in the Middle Districts, the Cedar Bird pays them frequent visits, and when these are out of season, the blackberries and huckleberries have their turn. After this, the Cedars supply a new and favourite food. I think the name of *Fruit-devourers* would be more applicable to these birds than that of *Chatterers*, which they bear among naturalists.

They are excellent fly-catchers also, spending much of their time in the pursuit of winged insects. This is by way of dessert, and is not managed with the vivacity or suddenness of true Fly-catchers, but with a kind of listlessness. They start from the branches, and give chase to the insects, ascending after them for a few yards, or move horizontally towards them, perhaps rather farther than when ascending, and as soon as the prey is secured, return to the spot, where they continue watching with slow motions of the head. Towards evening, this amusement is carried on for half an hour, or an hour at a time, and is continued longer at the approach of autumn, the berries then becoming scarcer.

These birds come from the north, but the furthest place from which they have started I am unable to tell. They reach the Middle Districts about the beginning of April, and begin to pair in the beginning of June, when thousands of young birds of other species have already left the nest. Their favourite place for their nest is generally the branch of an Apple-tree in the Orchard, its horizontal direction being apparently best adapted for their taste, although here they are frequently very insecure, the nest being seldom higher than ten feet from the ground, and often so low as to be seen into. It is composed of coarse grasses externally, and is lined with a finer kind. The female usually lays four eggs, of a purplish white, marked with black spots, which are larger towards the great end. The young are at first fed on insects, but after a week the parents procure different kinds of fruits for them. The Cedar Bird nestles less frequently in the low lands than it does in the upper parts of the country, preferring the immediate neighbourhood of mountains. These birds are more careful of themselves during the intrusion of strangers to their nest, than perhaps any other species, and sneak off, in a very unparental manner, quite out of sight, without ever evincing the least appearance of sorrow on the occasion. I have not been able to ascertain whether they raise more than one brood in a season.

When wounded by a shot, they fall to the ground as if dead, and remain there in a stiffened posture, as if absolutely stupid. When taken up in the hand, they merely open their bill, without ever attempting to bite, and will suffer a person to carry them in the open hand, without endeavouring to make off. Their crest at such times is laid flat and close to the head. It is lowered or raised at the will of the bird, but more usually stands erect. Their plumage is silky. The females do not exhibit the waxen appendages on the wings so soon as the males; but these appendages form no criterion as to the sex. I have seen males and females with them, both at the extremities of the scapulars and tailfeathers, seldom more than two or three attached to the latter, whilst there were five or six at the former. Very few of these birds remain the whole winter in the Middle States.

Now, kind reader, can *you* give a reason why these birds are so tardy in laying their eggs and rearing their young? It cannot be through want of fruit for the food of their progeny, as the young birds, being at first fed on insects, might continue to be so, at a season when these abound, and as the old birds themselves evince pleasure at seizing them on the wing on all occasions.

BOMBYCILLA CAROLINENSIS, *Briss.* vol. ii. p. 337.—*Ch. Bonaparte*, Synops. of Birds of the United States, p. 59.

AMPELIS GARRULUS, var. *Linn.* Syst. Nat. vol. i. p. 297.—*Lath.* Ind. Ornith. vol. i. p. 364.

CHATTERER OF CAROLINA, *Lath.* Synops. vol. iii. p. 93.

CEDAR BIRD, AMPELIS AMERICANA, *Wils.* Amer. Ornith. vol. i. p. 107. Fig. 1.

Adult Male. Plate XLIII. Fig. 1.

Bill short, straightish, broader than deep at the base, compressed towards the end; upper mandible convex in its dorsal outline, with the edges sharp, overlapping, and marked with a notch close upon the declinate, acute tip; lower mandible nearly straight, a little bulging toward the end. Nostrils basal, oval, partially concealed by the recumbent feathers. Head and neck of ordinary size. Body bulky. Legs rather short; tarsus compressed, anteriorly scutellate; toes scutellate above, the outer toe united at the base to the middle one, the inner shorter than the outer; claws arched, compressed, acute.

Plumage blended, soft and silky; an erectile tuft on the head. Wings rather long, the first quill longest. Tail slightly rounded, of twelve straight, broad feathers.

Bill, eyes, and feet, brownish-black. A black band on the forehead, passing backwards, tapering behind the eye, to the occiput, and margined above and below by a narrow white band. Head, neck, and breast yellowish-brown, or fawn colour, fading into yellow on the abdomen, and yellowish-white under the tail. Chin black. Back and wing-coverts greyish-brown, passing on the lower back into light bluish-grey, of which colour are the tail-coverts. Quills brownish-black, some of the secondaries tipped with a small flat, oblong appendage, of the colour of red sealing-wax. Of these appendages there are also frequently some on the tail, which is greyish at the base, passing into brownish-black, and terminated by a band of pale yellow.

Length 6¾ inches, extent of wings 11; bill along the ridge $\frac{4}{12}$, along the gap $\frac{5}{8}$; tarsus $\frac{7}{8}$.

Adult Female. Plate XLIII. Fig. 2.

The female is slightly smaller, and in external appearance differs from the male only in being a little lighter in the tints of the plumage, and in having the crest shorter. The waxen appendages also occur in the female.

THE RED CEDAR.

JUNIPERUS VIRGINIANA, *Willd.* Sp. Pl. vol. iv. p. 863. *Mich.* Arbr. Forest. de l'Amer. Septent. vol. iii. p. 42. Pl. 5.—DIŒCIA MONADELPHIA, *Linn.* CONIFERÆ, *Juss.*

This plant is very generally distributed in the United States, and frequently attains a height of from forty to fifty feet, with a diameter of a foot or fifteen inches at the base. It is distinguished by its ternate leaves, which are adnate at the base, and imbricated. The berries are oval, small, and of a bluish colour. The wood is red, close-grained, very durable, and has a strong scent. Its growth is extremely slow, and this circumstance, together with the great destruction of the tree for various purposes, has rendered it difficult to procure cedar-wood of tolerable size in the more accessible parts of the country.

THE SUMMER RED BIRD.

TANAGRA ÆSTIVA, GMEL.

PLATE XLIV. ADULT MALE, YOUNG MALE, AND FEMALE.

THIS beautiful species is destitute of song, and is of solitary habits, preferring at all times the interior of the forests, but not the densest parts of them. I have observed that woods interspersed with what are called *scrubby* hickories or stunted oaks, are favourite resorts of the Summer Red Birds.

Their residence in the United States scarcely exceeds four months. None remain in any of the more southern parts of our districts. Indeed, by the middle of September, it would be difficult to see a single pair in the forests of Louisiana. So very tender do they seem to be in regard to cold, or even temperate weather, that they seldom go farther north than Boston, or the shores of Lake Erie, but prefer the sandy woodlands all along the eastern shores, as far as Massachusets.

Their flight is performed in a gliding manner when passing through the woods, generally amidst the top branches of trees. Whilst migrating, they rise high above the trees, and pursue their journeys only during the day, diving towards dusk into the thickest parts of the foliage of tall trees, from which their usual unmusical but well-known notes of *chicky-chucky-chuck* are heard, after the light of day has disappeared. This species feeds principally on insects, and especially coleoptera, some of which are often of larger size than a bird of the dimensions of the Summer Red Bird might be supposed capable of swallowing. It seldom alights on the ground, but prefers pursuing insects on the wing, which it frequently does from the dried twigs at the extremity of the branches.

The construction of the nest of this richly clad species is nearly the same in all parts of the Union in which it breeds. It is frequently fixed on a branch crossing a road, or an opening of some description, or, if in the woods, in some partially cleared space. It is usually placed low on a horizontal branch. It is composed externally of dried stalks of weeds, and is finished within with fine grass, arranged in a slovenly manner. It is so insecurely fastened to the branch, that it may be shaken off by striking the latter smartly. The female lays four or five eggs of a light blue colour. The male and female sit upon them alternately for twelve days, and are as anxious about their safety as most species. The young are seen about the beginning of June, and follow their parents until the time of the migration of the latter, which takes place a fortnight earlier than that of the young birds. They raise only one brood in a season.

The alterations of plumage which appear in the young birds between the period at which they leave the nest, and the ensuing spring, are as great as those of the Orchard Oriole. They are at first nearly of the colour of the female. The males become a little mottled with dull reddish-orange, towards the time of their departure for the south, the females only deepening their tints. The following spring, the male appears either spotted all over the body with bright red and yellowish-green, or only partially so, having sometimes one wing of a greenish hue, whilst the other is tinged all over with a dull vermilion tint. All these spots and shades of colour gradually disappear, giving place to vermilion, which, however, is yet dull; nor is it until the third spring that the full brilliancy of the plumage is attained.

I have several times attempted to raise the young from the nest, but in vain. Insects, fruits, and eggs, mixed with boiled meat of various kinds, always failed, and the birds generally died in a very few days, uttering a dull note, as if elicited by great suffering. The same note is emitted by the young in their state of freedom, when, perched on a branch, they await the appearance of their parents with their proper food.

I have represented an adult male, his mate, and a young bird in its singularly patched state, to enable you to judge how different a family of these birds must appear to the eye of a person unacquainted with the peculiarity of these differences and changes of plumage.

The Vine on which you see them is usually called the *Muscadine*. It grows everywhere in Louisiana, and the State of Mississippi, and that most luxuriantly. In those States you may see vines of this species fifteen inches in diameter near the roots, either entwined round the trunk of a large tree, and by this means reaching the top branches and extending over them and those of another tree, or, as if by magic, swinging in the air, from roots attached at once to some of the uppermost branches. In favourable seasons, they are laden with grapes, which hang in small clusters from every branch, from which, when they are fully ripe, a good shake will make them fall in astonishing quantity. The skin is thick and very tough, the pulp glutinous, but so peculiarly flavoured as to be very agreeable to the taste. These grapes are eaten by most people, although an idea prevails, in Lower Louisiana particularly, that the eating of them gives rise to bilious fevers. For my part, I can well say, that the more I have eaten of them the better I have found myself; and for this reason seldom lost an opportunity of refreshing my palate with some of them in all my rambles. I am equally confident, that their juice would make an excellent wine. Another absurd opinion prevails in Louisiana, which is, that the Common Blackberries, however ripe and pleasant, produce boils; although the country people make use of a strong decoction of the root as a cure for dysentery.

TANAGRA ÆSTIVA, *Gmel.* Syst. Nat. vol. i. p. 889.—*Lath.* Ind. Orn. vol. i. p. 422.—
    Ch. Bonaparte, Synops. of Birds of the United States, p. 105.
SUMMER TANAGER, *Lath.* Synops. vol. iii. p. 220.
SUMMER RED BIRD, TANAGRA ÆSTIVA, *Wils.* Amer. Ornith. vol. i. p. 95, Pl. vi.
    fig. 3. Male, fig. 4. Female.

Adult Male.   Plate XLIV. Fig. 1.

Bill rather short, robust, tapering, compressed, acute; upper mandible a little convex in its dorsal outline, convex on the sides, the acute edge slightly notched near the tip, which is a little declinate; lower mandible also a little convex in its dorsal outline, with the edges inflected. Nostrils basal, lateral, round. Head large. Body rather long. Feet shortish; tarsus compressed, anteriorly scutellate, about the length of the middle toe; outer toe united at the base to the middle one; claws arched, compressed, acute.

Plumage soft, blended, glossy. Wings of ordinary length, the second quill longest. Tail slightly emarginate, of twelve acute feathers.

Bill yellowish-brown above, bluish below. Iris hazel. Feet and claws light greyish-blue. The whole plumage is vermilion, brighter on the lower parts, excepting the tips and inner webs of the quills, which are tinged with brown.

Length $7\frac{1}{4}$ inches, extent of wings 11; bill along the ridge $\frac{7}{12}$, along the gap 1; tarsus $\frac{5}{8}$.

Adult Female. Plate XLIV. Fig. 3.

The general colour above is light brownish-green, the sides of the head and the under parts generally brownish-yellow ; larger wing-coverts dusky, edged with yellow ; quills deep brown, externally margined with yellowish-red ; tail-feathers of the same colour. The bill, eyes and legs are of the same tints as in the male.

Dimensions nearly the same.

Young Male. Plate XLIV. Fig. 2.
Dull vermilion, spotted with dull green.

THE WILD MUSCADINE.

VITIS ROTUNDIFOLIA, *Mich.* Flor. Amer. vol. ii. p. 231. *Pursh,* Flor. Amer. vol. i. p. 169.—PENTANDRIA MONOGYNIA, *Linn.* VITES, *Juss.*

Leaves between heart-shaped and kidney-shaped, nearly equally toothed, shining on both sides.

TRAILL'S FLY-CATCHER.

Muscicapa Traillii.

PLATE XLV. Male.

THIS is a species which, in its external appearance, is so closely allied to the *Wood Pewee,* and the small Green-crested Fly-catcher, that the most careful inspection is necessary to establish the real differences existing between these three species. Its notes, however, are perfectly different, as are, in some measure, its habits, as well as the districts in which it resides.

The notes of Traill's Fly-catcher consist of the sounds *wheet, wheet,* which it articulates clearly while on wing. It resides in the skirts of the woods along the prairie lands of the Arkansas river, where alone I have been able to procure it. When leaving the top branches of a low tree, this bird takes long flights, skimming in zigzag lines, passing close over the tops of the tall grasses, snapping at and seizing different species of winged insects, and returning to the same trees to alight. Its notes, I observed, were uttered when on the point of leaving the branch. The pair chased the insects as if acting in concert, and doubtless had a nest in the immediate neighbourhood, although I was unable to discover it. It being in the month of April, I suspected the female had not begun to lay. Five of the eggs in the ovary were about the size of green pease. I could not perceive any difference in the colouring of the plumage between the sexes, and I have represented the male in that inclined and rather crouching attitude which I observed the bird always to assume when alighted.

I have named this species after my learned friend Dr THOMAS STEWART TRAILL of Liverpool, in evidence of the gratitude which I cherish towards that benevolent gentleman for all his kind attentions to me.

The Sweet Gum, on a branch of which I have placed Traill's Fly-catcher, grows in almost every portion of the western and southern districts of the United States. It sometimes attains a great size, but is more commonly of moderate stature. Its wood is of little use. This tree is frequently found with a cork-like bark protruding in shreds from its branches.

Plate XLV. Adult Male.

Bill of ordinary length, depressed, tapering to a point, the lateral outlines a little convex, very broad at the base ; the gap reaching to nearly
under the eye ; upper mandible with the edges acute, slightly notched
close upon the tip, which is a little deflected and acute ; lower mandible
straight, acute. Nostrils basal, lateral, elliptical. Head and neck of
moderate size. Body rather slender. Feet of moderate length, slender ;
tarsus compressed, covered anteriorly with short scutella, and longer than
the middle toe ; toes free, scutellate above ; claws compressed, arched,
acute.

Plumage soft and tufty ; feathers of the head narrow and erectile.
Wings of moderate length, third quill longest. Tail longish, slightly
forked when closed, of twelve rather narrow, obtuse feathers.

Bill dark brown above, yellow beneath. Iris hazel. Feet brownish-
black. The general colour of the plumage above is dull brownish-olive,
the two rows of larger wing-coverts tipped with dull white. Throat
greyish-white, as is a very narrow space around the eye ; sides of the head
and neck, and fore part of the breast, coloured like the back, but lighter ;
the rest of the under parts dull yellowish-white.

Length 5¾ inches, extent of wings 8½ ; bill along the ridge ½, along
gap ¾ ; tarsus $\frac{7}{12}$.

As already mentioned, this species bears a very close resemblance to
Muscicapa acadica, and *M. virens*, more especially the former.

Muscicapa virens has the tail deeply emarginate, whereas in the present species that part is nearly even. The colouring is nearly the same
in both, but *M. virens* is considerably larger.

Muscicapa acadica is also similarly coloured, but in it the whitish
space about the eye is larger, the throat darker, the breast and abdomen
lighter. The tail also is quite even. A decided difference exists in the
bill, which, in place of being convex in its lateral outlines, is a little
concave.

The Sweet Gum.

Liquidambar styraciflua, *Willd.* Sp. Pl. vol. iv. p. 476. *Pursh,* Fl. Amer. vol. ii.
p. 635. *Mich.* Arbr. Forest. de l'Amer. Sept. vol. iii. p. 194, Pl. iv.—Monœcia
Polyandria, *Linn.* Amentaceæ, *Juss.*

This species, which is the only one that grows in the United States,
is distinguished by its palmate leaves, the lobes of which are toothed and
acuminate, the axils of the nerves downy.   In large individuals, the bark
is deeply cracked.   The wood is very hard and fine grained, but is now
little used, although formerly furniture of various kinds was made of it.
When the bark is removed, a resinous substance exudes, which has an
agreeable smell, but is only obtained in very small quantity.

THE EARTHQUAKE.

TRAVELLING through the Barrens of Kentucky (of which I shall give you an account elsewhere) in the month of November, I was jogging on one afternoon, when I remarked a sudden and strange darkness rising from the western horizon. Accustomed to our heavy storms of thunder and rain, I took no more notice of it, as I thought the speed of my horse might enable me to get under shelter of the roof of an acquaintance, who lived not far distant, before it should come up. I had proceeded about a mile, when I heard what I imagined to be the distant rumbling of a violent tornado, on which I spurred my steed, with a wish to gallop as fast as possible to the place of shelter; but it would not do, the animal knew better than I what was forthcoming, and, instead of going faster, so nearly stopped, that I remarked he placed one foot after another on the ground with as much precaution as if walking on a smooth sheet of ice. I thought he had suddenly foundered, and, speaking to him, was on the point of dismounting and leading him, when he all of a sudden fell a-groaning piteously, hung his head, spread out his four legs, as if to save himself from falling, and stood stock still, continuing to groan. I thought my horse was about to die, and would have sprung from his back had a minute more elapsed, but at that instant all the shrubs and trees began to move from their very roots, the ground rose and fell in successive furrows, like the ruffled waters of a lake, and I became bewildered in my ideas, as I too plainly discovered that all this awful commotion in nature was the result of an earthquake.

. ' I had never witnessed any thing of the kind before, although, like every other person, I knew of earthquakes by description. But what is description compared with the reality? Who can tell of the sensations which I experienced when I found myself rocking as it were on my horse, and with him moved to and fro like a child in a cradle, with the most imminent danger around, and expecting the ground every moment to open, and present to my eye such an abyss as might engulf myself and all around me? The fearful convulsion, however, lasted only a few minutes, and the heavens again brightened as quickly as they had become obscured; my horse brought his feet to the natural position, raised his head, and galloped off as if loose and frolicking without a rider.

I was not, however, without great apprehension respecting my family, from which I was yet many miles distant, fearful that where they were the shock might have caused greater havock than I had witnessed. I gave the bridle to my steed, and was glad to see him appear as anxious to get home as myself. The pace at which he galloped accomplished this sooner than I had expected, and I found, with much pleasure, that hardly any greater harm had taken place than the apprehension excited for my own safety.

Shock succeeded shock almost every day or night for several weeks, diminishing, however, so gradually as to dwindle away into mere vibrations of the earth. Strange to say, I for one became so accustomed to the feeling as rather to enjoy the fears manifested by others. I never can forget the effects of one of the slighter shocks which took place when I was at a friend's house, where I had gone to enjoy the merriment that, in our western country, attends a wedding. The ceremony being performed, supper over, and the fiddles tuned, dancing became the order of the moment. This was merrily followed up to a late hour, when the party retired to rest. We were in what is called, with great propriety, a *Log-house*, one of large dimensions, and solidly constructed. The owner was a physician, and in one corner were not only his lancets, tourniquets, amputating-knives, and other sanguinary apparatus, but all the drugs which he employed for the relief of his patients, arranged in jars and phials of different sizes. These had some days before made a narrow escape from destruction, but had been fortunately preserved by closing the doors of the cases in which they were contained.

As I have said, we had all retired to rest, some to dream of sighs and smiles, and others to sink into oblivion. Morning was fast approaching, when the rumbling noise that precedes the earthquake began so loudly, as to waken and alarm the whole party, and drive them out of bed in the greatest consternation. The scene which ensued it is impossible for me to describe, and it would require the humorous pencil of CRUICKSHANK to do justice to it. Fear knows no restraints. Every person, old and young, filled with alarm at the creaking of the log-house, and apprehending instant destruction, rushed wildly out to the grass enclosure fronting the building. The full moon was slowly descending from her throne, covered at times by clouds that rolled heavily along, as if to conceal from her view the scenes of terror which prevailed on the earth below. . On the grass-plat we all met, in such condition as rendered it next

to impossible to discriminate any of the party, all huddled together in a
state of almost perfect nudity.   The earth waved like a field of corn before the breeze : the birds left their perches, and flew about not knowing
whither ; and the Doctor, recollecting the danger of his gallipots, ran to
his shop-room, to prevent their dancing off the shelves to the floor.
Never for a moment did he think of closing the doors, but, spreading
his arms, jumped about the front of the cases, pushing back here and
there the falling jars ; with so little success, however, that before the
shock was over, he had lost nearly all he possessed.

The shock at length ceased, and the frightened females, now sensible
of their dishabille, fled to their several apartments.   The earthquakes
produced more serious consequences in other places.   Near New Madrid,
and for some distance on the Mississippi, the earth was rent asunder in
several places, one or two islands sunk for ever, and the inhabitants fled
in dismay towards the eastern shores.

THE BARRED OWL.

STRIX NEBULOSA, LINN.

PLATE XLVI. MALE.

SHOULD you, kind reader, find it convenient or agreeable to visit the noble forests existing in the lower parts of the State of **Louisiana**, about the middle of October, when nature, on the eve of preparing for approaching night, permits useful dews to fall and rest on every plant, with the view of reviving its leaves, its fruits, or its lingering blossoms, ere the return of morn; when every night-insect rises on buzzing wings from the ground, and the fire-fly, amidst thousands of other species, appears as if purposely to guide their motions through the sombre atmosphere; at the moment when numerous reptiles and quadrupeds commence their nocturnal prowlings, and the fair moon, empress of the night, rises peacefully on the distant horizon, shooting her silvery rays over the heavens and the earth, and, like a watchful guardian, moving slowly and majestically along; when the husbandman, just returned to his home, after the labours of the day, is receiving the cheering gratulations of his family, and the wholesome repast is about to be spread out for master and servants alike;—it is at this moment, kind reader, that were you, as I have said, to visit that happy country, your ear would suddenly be struck by the discordant screams of the Barred Owl. Its *whah, whah, whah, whah-aa* is uttered loudly, and in so strange and ludicrous a manner, that I should not be surprised were you, kind reader, when you and I meet, to compare these sounds to the affected bursts of laughter which you may have heard from some of the fashionable members of our own species.

How often, when snugly settled under the boughs of my temporary encampment, and preparing to roast a venison steak or the body of a squirrel, on a wooden spit, have I been saluted with the exulting bursts of this nightly disturber of the peace, that, had it not been for him, would have prevailed around me, as well as in my lonely retreat! How often have I seen this nocturnal marauder alight within a few yards of me, exposing his whole body to the glare of my fire, and eye me in such a curious manner that, had it been reasonable to do so, I would gladly

have invited him to walk in and join me in my repast, that I might have
enjoyed the pleasure of forming a better acquaintance with him.   The
liveliness of his motions, joined to their oddness, have often made me
think that his society would be at least as agreeable as that of many of
the buffoons we meet with in the world.   But as such opportunities of
forming acquaintance have not existed, be content, kind reader, with the
imperfect information which I can give you of the habits of this Sancho
Pança of our woods.

   Such persons as conclude, when looking upon owls in the glare of
day, that they are, as they then appear, extremely dull, are greatly mistaken.   Were they to state, like BUFFON, that Woodpeckers are miser-
able beings, they would be talking as incorrectly ; and, to one who might
have lived long in the woods, they would seem to have lived only in their
libraries.

   The Barred Owl is found in all those parts of the United States
which I have visited, and is a constant resident.   In Louisiana it seems
to be more abundant than in any other state.   It is almost impossible to
travel eight or ten miles in any of the retired woods there, without seeing
several of them even in broad day ; and, at the approach of night, their
cries are heard proceeding from every part of the forest around the
plantations.   Should the weather be lowering, and indicative of the approach of rain, their cries are so multiplied during the day, and especially
in the evening, and they respond to each other in tones so strange, that
one might imagine some extraordinary fête about to take place among
them.   On approaching one of them, its gesticulations are seen to be of
a very extraordinary nature.   The position of the bird, which is generally erect, is immediately changed.   It lowers its head and inclines its
body, to watch the motions of the person beneath, throws forward the
lateral feathers of its head, which thus has the appearance of being
surrounded by a broad ruff, looks towards him as if half blind, and
moves its head to and fro in so extraordinary a manner, as almost to
induce a person to fancy that part dislocated from the body.   It follows
all the motions of the intruder with its eyes ; and should it suspect any
treacherous intentions, flies off to a short distance, alighting with its back
to the person, and immediately turning about with a single jump, to recommence its scrutiny.   In this manner, the Barred Owl may be followed to a considerable distance, if not shot at, for to halloo after it does
not seem to frighten it much.   But if shot at and missed, it removes to a

considerable distance, after which its *whah-whah-whah* is uttered with considerable pomposity. This owl will answer the imitation of its own sounds, and is frequently decoyed by this means.

The flight of the Barred Owl is smooth, light, noiseless, and capable of being greatly protracted. I have seen them take their departure from a detached grove in a prairie, and pursue a direct course towards the skirts of the main forest, distant more than two miles, in broad daylight. I have thus followed them with the eye until they were lost in the distance, and have reason to suppose that they continued their flight until they reached the woods. Once, whilst descending the Ohio, not far from the well-known *Cave-in-rock*, about two hours before sunset, in the month of November, I saw a Barred Owl teased by several crows, and chased from the tree in which it was. On leaving the tree, it gradually rose in the air, in the manner of a Hawk, and at length attained so great a height that our party lost sight of it. It acted, I thought, as if it had lost itself, now and then describing small circles, and flapping its wings quickly, then flying in zigzag lines. This being so uncommon an occurrence, I noted it down at the time. I felt anxious to see the bird return towards the earth, but it did not make its appearance again. So very lightly do they fly, that I have frequently discovered one passing over me, and only a few yards distant, by first seeing its shadow on the ground, during clear moon-light nights, when not the faintest rustling of its wings could be heard.

Their power of sight during the day seems to be rather of an equivocal character, as I once saw one alight on the back of a cow, which it left so suddenly afterwards, when the cow moved, as to prove to me that it had mistaken the object on which it had perched for something else. At other times, I have observed that the approach of the grey squirrel intimidated them, if one of these animals accidentally jumped on a branch close to them, although the Owl destroys a number of them during the twilight. It is for this reason, kind reader, that I have represented the Barred Owl gazing in amazement at one of the squirrels placed only a few inches from him.

The Barred Owl is a great destroyer of poultry, particularly of chickens when half-grown. It also secures mice, young hares, rabbits, and many species of small birds, but is especially fond of a kind of frog of a brown colour, very common in the woods of Louisiana. I have heard it asserted that this bird catches fish, but never having seen it do so, and never having found any portion of fish in its stomach, I cannot vouch for the truth of the report.

About the middle of March, these Owls begin to lay their eggs. This they usually do in the hollows of trees, on the dust of the decomposed wood. At other times they take possession of the old nest of a Crow or a Red-tailed Hawk. In all these situations I have found their eggs and young. The eggs are of a globular form, pure white, with a smooth shell, and are from four to six in number. So far as I have been able to ascertain, they rear only one brood in a season. The young, like those of all other Owls, are at first covered with a downy substance, some of which is seen intermixed with and protruding from the feathers, some weeks after the bird is nearly fledged. They are fed by the parents for a long time, standing perched, and emitting a hissing noise in lieu of a call. This noise may be heard in a calm night, for fifty or probably a hundred yards, and is by no means musical. To a person lost in a swamp, it is, indeed, extremely dismal.

The plumage of the Barred Owl differs very considerably, in respect to colour, in different individuals, more so among the males. The males are also smaller than the females, but less so than in some other species During the severe winters of our Middle Districts, those that remain there suffer very much ; but the greater number, as in some other species, remove to the Southern States. When kept in captivity, they prove excellent mousers.

The antipathy shewn to Owls by every species of day bird is extreme. They are followed and pursued on all occasions ; and although few of the day birds ever prove dangerous enemies, their conduct towards the Owls is evidently productive of great annoyance to them. When the Barred Owl is shot at and wounded, it snaps its bill sharply and frequently, raises all its feathers, looks towards the person in the most uncouth manner, but, on the least chance of escape, moves off in great leaps with considerable rapidity.

The Barred Owl is very often exposed for sale in the New Orleans market. The Creoles make *gumbo* of it, and pronounce the flesh palatable.

Strix nebulosa, *Gmel.* Syst. Nat. vol. i. p. 291.—*Lath.* Ind. Ornith. vol. i. p. 21.—
　　Ch. Bonaparte, Synops. of Birds of the United States, p. 38.
Barred Owl, Strix nebulosa, *Lath.* Synops. vol. i. p. 133—*Wils.* Amer. Ornith.
　　vol. iv. p. 61. Pl. 33. fig. 2.

Adult Male.　Plate XLVI. Fig. 1.

Bill very short, compressed, curved, acute, with a small cere at the base; upper mandible with its dorsal outline curved from the base, the edges acute, the point trigonal, very acute, deflected, lower mandible with the edges acute and inflected, obtuse at the tip.　Nostrils roundish, in the fore part of the cere, concealed by the recumbent bristles.　Head disproportionably large, as are the eyes and external ears.　Body short. Legs long; tarsus feathered; toes feathered at the base, scutellate above, papillar and tubercular beneath; claws curved, slender, rounded, extremely sharp.

Plumage exceedingly soft and downy, somewhat distinct above, tufty and loose beneath.　Long bristly feathers at the base of the bill, stretching forwards.　Eyes surrounded by several circles of compact feathers; auricular feathers forming a ruff, and with those of the head and neck capable of being erected.　Wings ample, the fourth quill longest, the first short.　Tail long, large, rounded, of twelve broad, rounded feathers.

Bill yellow, the under mandible tinged with blue on the back.　Eyes black.　Toes yellow; claws bluish-black.　The general colour of the upper parts is light reddish-brown.　Face and greater part of the head brownish-white, the feathers of the latter broadly marked with brown, of which a narrow band passes from the bill along the middle of the head. Feathers of the back and most of the wing-coverts largely spotted with white.　Primary coverts, quills, and tail, barred with light brownish-red; wings and tail tipped with greyish-white.　Under parts pale brownish-red, longitudinally streaked with brown, excepting the neck and upper breast, which are transversely marked, the abdomen, which is yellowish-white, and the tarsal feathers, which are light reddish.

Length 18 inches, extent of wings 40.　Bill along the ridge $1\frac{1}{4}$; tarsus $2\frac{1}{2}$, middle toe 2.

THE GREY SQUIRREL.

SCIURUS CINEREUS, *Harlan*, Fauna Americana, p. 173.

The Grey Squirrel is too well known to require any description. It migrates in prodigious numbers, crossing large rivers by swimming with its tail extended on the water, and traverses immense tracts of country, in search of the places where food is most abundant. During these migrations, the Squirrels are destroyed in vast quantities. Their flesh is white, very delicate, and affords excellent eating, when the animals are young. " In 1749," says Dr HARLAN, in the work above referred to, " a premium of three pence a-head was offered for their destruction, which amounted in one year to L. 8000 Sterling, which is equal to about 1,180,000 individuals killed."

THE RUBY-THROATED HUMMING BIRD.

TROCHILUS COLUBRIS, LINN.

PLATE XLVII. MALE, FEMALE, AND YOUNG.

WHERE is the person who, on seeing this lovely little creature moving on humming winglets through the air, suspended as if by magic in it, flitting from one flower to another, with motions as graceful as they are light and airy, pursuing its course over our extensive continent, and yielding new delights wherever it is seen;—where is the person, I ask of you, kind reader, who, on observing this glittering fragment of the rainbow, would not pause, admire, and instantly turn his mind with reverence toward the Almighty Creator, the wonders of whose hand we at every step discover, and of whose sublime conceptions we everywhere observe the manifestations in his admirable system of creation?—There breathes not such a person; so kindly have we all been blessed with that intuitive and noble feeling—admiration!

No sooner has the returning sun again introduced the vernal season, and caused millions of plants to expand their leaves and blossoms to his genial beams, than the little Humming Bird is seen advancing on fairy wings, carefully visiting every opening flower-cup, and, like a curious florist, removing from each the injurious insects that otherwise would ere long cause their beauteous petals to droop and decay. Poised in the air, it is observed peeping cautiously, and with sparkling eye, into their innermost recesses, whilst the etherial motions of its pinions, so rapid and so light, appear to fan and cool the flower, without injuring its fragile texture, and produce a delightful murmuring sound, well adapted for lulling the insects to repose. Then is the moment for the Humming Bird to secure them. Its long delicate bill enters the cup of the flower, and the protruded double-tubed tongue, delicately sensible, and imbued with a glutinous saliva, touches each insect in succession, and draws it from its lurking place, to be instantly swallowed. All this is done in a moment, and the bird, as it leaves the flower, sips so small a portion of its liquid honey, that the theft, we may suppose, is looked upon with a grateful feeling by the flower, which is thus kindly relieved from the attacks of her destroyers.

The prairies, the fields, the orchards and gardens, nay, the deepest shades of the forests, are all visited in their turn, and everywhere the little bird meets with pleasure and with food.   Its gorgeous throat in beauty and brilliancy baffles all competition.   Now it glows with a fiery hue, and again it is changed to the deepest velvety black.   The upper parts of its delicate body are of resplendent changing green; and it throws itself through the air with a swiftness and vivacity hardly conceivable.   It moves from one flower to another like a gleam of light, upwards, downwards, to the right, and to the left.   In this manner, it searches the extreme northern portions of our country, following with great precaution the advances of the season, and retreats with equal care at the approach of autumn.

I wish it were in my power at this moment to impart to you, kind reader, the pleasures which I have felt whilst watching the movements, and viewing the manifestation of feelings displayed by a single pair of these most favourite little creatures, when engaged in the demonstration of their love to each other:—how the male swells his plumage and throat, and, dancing on the wing, whirls around the delicate female; how quickly he dives towards a flower, and returns with a loaded bill, which he offers to her to whom alone he feels desirous of being united; how full of ecstacy he seems to be when his caresses are kindly received; how his little wings fan her, as they fan the flowers, and he transfers to her bill the insect and the honey which he has procured with a view to please her; how these attentions are received with apparent satisfaction; how, soon after, the blissful compact is sealed; how, then, the courage and care of the male are redoubled; how he even dares to give chase to the Tyrant Fly-catcher, hurries the blue-Bird and the Martin to their boxes; and how, on sounding pinions, he joyously returns to the side of his lovely mate. Reader, all·these proofs of the sincerity, fidelity, and courage, with which the male assures his mate of the care he will take of her while sitting on her nest, may be seen, and have been seen, but cannot be portrayed or described.

Could you, kind reader, cast a momentary glance on the nest of the Humming Bird, and see, as I have seen, the newly-hatched pair of young, little larger than humble-bees, naked, blind, and so feeble as scarcely to be able to raise their little bill to receive food from the parents; and could you see those parents, full of anxiety and fear, passing and repassing within a few inches of your face, alighting on a twig not more than a yard from your body, waiting the result of your unwelcome visit in a state of the utmost despair,—you could not fail to be impressed with the deepest pangs which parental affection feels on the unexpected death of a cherished child. Then how pleasing is it, on your leaving the spot, to see the returning hope of the parents, when, after examining the nest, they find their nurslings untouched ! You might then judge how pleasing it is to a mother of another kind, to hear the physician who has attended her sick child assure her that the crisis is over, and that her babe is saved. These are the scenes best fitted to enable us to partake of sorrow and joy, and to determine every one who views them to make it his study to contribute to the happiness of others, and to refrain from wantonly or maliciously giving them pain.

I have seen Humming Birds in Louisiana as early as the 10th of March. Their appearance in that State varies, however, as much as in any other, it being sometimes a fortnight later, or, although rarely, a few days earlier. In the Middle Districts, they seldom arrive before the 15th of April, more usually the beginning of May. I have not been able to assure myself whether they migrate during the day or by night, but am inclined to think the latter the case, as they seem to be busily feeding at all times of the day, which would not be the case had they long flights to perform at that period. They pass through the air in long undulations, raising themselves for some distance at an angle of about 40 degrees, and then falling in a curve ; but the smallness of their size precludes the possibility of following them farther then fifty or sixty yards without great difficulty, even with a good glass. A person standing in a garden by the side of a Common Althœa in bloom, will be as surprised to hear the humming of their wings, and then see the birds themselves within a few feet of him, as he will be astonished at the rapidity with which the little creatures rise into the air, and are out of sight and hearing the next moment. They do not alight on the ground, but easily settle on twigs and branches, where they move sidewise in prettily measured steps, frequently opening and closing their wings, pluming, shaking and arranging the whole of their apparel with neatness and activity. They are particularly fond of spreading one wing at a time, and passing each of the quill-feathers through their bill in its whole length, when, if the sun is shining, the wing thus plumed is rendered extremely transparent and light. They leave the twig without the least difficulty in an instant, and appear to be possessed of superior powers of vision, making directly towards a Martin or a Bluebird when fifty or sixty yards from them, and reaching them before they are aware of their approach.   No bird seems to resist their attacks, but they are sometimes chased by the larger kinds of humble-bees, of which they seldom take the least notice, as their superiority of flight is sufficient to enable them to leave these slow moving insects far behind in the short space of a minute.

The nest of this Humming Bird is of the most delicate nature, the external parts being formed of a light grey lichen found on the branches of trees, or on decayed fence-rails, and so neatly arranged round the whole nest, as well as to some distance from the spot where it is attached, as to seem part of the branch or stem itself.   These little pieces of lichen are glued together with the saliva of the bird.   The next coating consists of cottony substance, and the innermost of silky fibres obtained from various plants, all extremely delicate and soft.   On this comfortable bed, as in contradiction to the axiom that the smaller the species the greater the number of eggs, the female lays only two, which are pure white and almost oval.   Ten days are required for their hatching, and the birds raise two broods in a season.   In one week the young are ready to fly, but are fed by the parents for nearly another week.   They receive their food directly from the bill of their parents, which disgorge it in the manner of Canaries or Pigeons.   It is my belief that no sooner are the young able to provide for themselves than they associate with other broods, and perform their migration apart from the old birds, as I have observed twenty or thirty young Humming Birds resort to a group of Trumpet-flowers, when not a single old male was to be seen.   They do not receive the full brilliancy of their colours until the succeeding spring, although the throat of the male bird is strongly imbued with the ruby tints before they leave us in autumn.

The Ruby-throated Humming Bird has a particular liking for such flowers as are greatly tubular in their form.   The Common Jimpson-weed or Thorn-apple (*Datura Stramonium*) and the Trumpet-flower (*Bignonia radicans*) are among the most favoured by their visits, and after these, Honeysuckle, the Balsam of the gardens, and the wild species which grows on the borders of ponds, rivulets, and deep ravines ; but every flower, down to the wild violet, affords them a certain portion of sustenance.   Their food consists principally of insects, generally of the coleopterous order, these, together with some equally diminutive flies, being commonly found in their stomach.   The first are procured within the flowers, but many of the latter on wing.   The Humming Bird might therefore be looked upon as an expert fly-catcher. The nectar or honey which they sip from the different flowers, being of itself insufficient to support them, is used more as if to allay their thirst. I have seen many of these birds kept in partial confinement, when they were supplied with artificial flowers made for the purpose, in the corollas of which water with honey or sugar dissolved in it was placed. The birds were fed on these substances exclusively, but seldom lived many months, and on being examined after death, were found to be extremely emaciated. Others, on the contrary, which were supplied twice a-day with fresh flowers from the woods or garden, placed in a room with windows merely closed with moschetto gauze-netting, through which minute insects were able to enter, lived twelve months, at the expiration of which time their liberty was granted them, the person who kept them having had a long voyage to perform. The room was kept artificially warm during the winter months, and these, in Lower Louisiana, are seldom so cold as to produce ice. On examining an orange-tree which had been placed in the room where these Humming Birds were kept, no appearance of a nest was to be seen, although the birds had frequently been observed caressing each other. Some have been occasionally kept confined in our Middle Districts, but I have not ascertained that any one survived a winter.

The Humming Bird does not shun mankind so much as birds generally do. It frequently approaches flowers in the windows, or even in rooms when the windows are kept open, during the extreme heat of the day, and returns, when not interrupted, as long as the flowers are unfaded. They are extremely abundant in Louisiana during spring and summer, and wherever a fine plant of the trumpet-flower is met with in the woods, one or more Humming Birds are generally seen about it, and now and then so many as ten or twelve at a time. They are quarrelsome, and have frequent battles in the air, especially the male birds. Should one be feeding on a flower, and another approach it, they are both immediately seen to rise in the air, twittering and twirling in a spiral manner until out of sight. The conflict over, the victor immediately returns to the flower.

If comparison might enable you, kind reader, to form some tolerably accurate idea of their peculiar mode of flight, and their appearance when on wing, I would say, that were both objects of the same colour, a large sphinx or moth, when moving from one flower to another, and in a direct line, comes nearer the Humming Bird in aspect than any other object with which I am acquainted.

Having heard several persons remark that these little creatures had been procured with less injury to their plumage, by shooting them with water, I was tempted to make the experiment, having been in the habit of killing them either with remarkably small shot, or with sand.   However, finding that even when within a few paces, I seldom brought one to the ground when I used water instead of shot, and was moreover obliged to clean my gun after every discharge, I abandoned the scheme, and feel confident that it can never have been used with material advantage.   I have frequently secured some by employing an insect-net, and were this machine used with dexterity, it would afford the best means of procuring Humming Birds.

I have represented ten of these pretty and most interesting birds, in various positions, flitting, feeding, caressing each other, or sitting on the slender stalks of the trumpet-flower and pluming themselves. The diversity of action and attitude thus exhibited, may, I trust, prove sufficient to present a faithful idea of their appearance and manners.   A figure of the nest you will find elsewhere.   The nest is generally placed low, on the horizontal branch of any kind of tree, seldom more than twenty feet from the ground.   They are far from being particular in this matter, as I have often found a nest attached by one side only to a twig of a rose-bush, currant, or the strong stalk of a rank weed, sometimes in the middle of the forest, at other times on the branch of an oak, immediately over the road, and again in the garden close to the walk.

TROCHILUS COLUBRIS, *Linn.* Syst. Nat. vol. i. p. 191.—*Lath.* Ind. Ornith. vol. i. p. 312.—*Ch. Bonaparte*, Synopsis of Birds of the United States, p. 98.

RED-THROATED HUMMING BIRD, *Lath.* Synops. vol. ii. p. 769.

HUMMING BIRD, TROCHILUS COLUBRIS, *Wils.* Amer. Ornith. vol. ii. p. 26. Pl. 10. fig. 3. Male; fig. 4. Female.

Adult Male.   Plate XLVII.   Fig. 1, 1, 1, 1.

Bill long, straight, subulate, depressed at the base, acute; upper mandible rounded, its edges overlapping.   Nostrils basal, linear.   Tongue very extensile, filiform, divided towards the end into two filaments.   Feet very short and feeble; tarsus slender, shorter than the middle toe, partly feathered; fore toes united at the base; claws curved, compressed, acute.

Plumage compact, imbricated above and on the throat, with metallic lustre, blended beneath.   Wings long, narrow, a little incurved at the tip, the first quill longest. Tail forked when closed, when spread even in the middle and laterally rounded, of ten broad feathers, the outer curved inwards.

Bill and feet black. Iris of the same colour. Upper parts generally, including the two middle tail-feathers, green, with gold reflections. Quills and tail purplish-brown. Throat, sides of the head, and fore neck, carmine-purple, spotted with black, varying to crimson, orange, and deep black. Sides of the same colour as the back ; the rest of the under parts greyish-white, mixed with green.

Length $3\frac{1}{2}$ inches, extent of wings $4\frac{1}{4}$; bill along the ridge $\frac{1}{2}$, along the gap $\frac{5}{8}$; tarsus $\frac{1}{8}$, toe $\frac{1}{4}$.

Adult Female. Plate XLVII. Fig. 2, 2, 2.

The female differs from the male in wanting the brilliant patch on the throat, which is white, as are the under parts generally, and in having the three lateral tail-feathers tipped with the same colour.

Dimensions the same.

Young Bird. Plate XLVII. Fig. 3, 3.

The young birds have the under parts brownish-white, the tail tipped with white, and are somewhat lighter in their upper parts. In autumn the young males begin to acquire the red feathers of the throat.

———————

THE TRUMPET-FLOWER.

BIGNONIA RADICANS, *Willd.* Sp. Pl. vol. iii. p. 301. *Pursh,* Flor. Amer. vol. ii. p. 420.—DIDYNAMIA ANGIOSPERMIA, *Linn.* BIGNONIÆ, *Jus.*

This splendid species of Bignonia, which grows in woods and on the banks of rivers in all the Middle and Southern States, climbing on trees and bushes, is distinguished by its pinnate leaves, with ovate, widely serrate, acuminate leaflets, and large scarlet flowers, of which the funnel-shaped tube of the corolla is thrice the length of the calyx. The pods are of a brown colour, from four to seven inches long, and contain a double row of kidney-shaped light brown seeds.

THE AZURE WARBLER.

SYLVIA AZUREA, STEPH.

PLATE XLVIII. MALE AND FEMALE.

So scarce is this bird in the Middle Districts, that its discovery in the State of Pennsylvania has been made a matter of much importance. Its habits are consequently very little known, even at the present day, and it would appear that only two individuals have been seen by our American ornithologists, one of which, a young female, has been figured by the Prince of Musignano.

It arrives in the lower parts of the State of Louisiana, in company with many other species of Warblers, breeds there and sets out again about the beginning of October. It is as lively as most species of its genus, possesses the same manner of flight, moves sidewise up and down the branches and twigs, frequently changing sides, and hangs to the extremities of bunches of leaves or berries, on which it procures the insects and larvæ of which its food is principally composed. The liveliness of its notes renders it conspicuous in those parts of the skirts of the forests which it frequents; and its song, although neither loud nor of long continuance, is extremely sweet and mellow.

I have no precise recollection of the time when I first made a drawing of this pretty little bird, but know this well, that a drawing which I had of it was one of the unfortunate collection destroyed by the rats at Henderson. In Louisiana, where it is as numerous as other Sylviæ, I have several times shot five or six during a single walk, towards the end of August, when the young are nearly full coloured.

The nest is placed in the forks of a low tree or bush, more frequently on a Dog-wood tree. It is partly pensile, projecting a little above the twigs to which it is attached, and extending below them for nearly two inches. The fibres of vines and of the stalks of rank herbaceous plants, together with slender roots, compose the outer part, being arranged in a circular manner. The lining consists entirely of the dry fibres of the Spanish Moss. The female lays four or five eggs, of a pure white colour, with a few reddish spots at the larger end. When the female is disturbed during incubation, she trails along the twigs and branches,

with expanded tail and drooping wings, and utters a plaintive note, resembling in all these circumstances the Blue-eyed Warbler. I am not
sure that they raise more than one brood in a season. When the young
abandon the nest, their plumage partakes of a greenish tinge, and no difference can be perceived between the sexes without dissection. The little
family move and hunt together, and exhibit much pleasure in pursuing
small insects on wing, which they seize without any clicking sound of
their bill. They seem at this period to evince a great partiality for
trees the tops of which are thickly covered by grape vines, amongst the
broad leaves of which they find ample supplies of food. They also sometimes alight on the tall weeds, and pick a few of their seeds. The males
or females do not assume the full brilliancy of their plumage until the
following spring.

I am inclined to think that this species is extremely abundant in the
Mexican dominions, as I have observed these birds more numerous towards Natchitochez and along the waters of the Red River. On the
other hand, I have not observed it eastward of the State of Tenessee.

The twig on which it is represented, belongs to a small tree or shrub,
which grows along the skirts of the forests in the State of Louisiana.
The bark is easily stripped off, when the wood shews a yellow, resinous
colour. It is brittle, and is not applied to any use. The berries are
eaten by different species of birds.

SYLVIA AZUREA, *Stephens*, Cont. Shaw's Zool. vol. i. p. 653.—*Ch. Bonaparte*, Synops.
     of Birds of the United States, p. 85; and Amer. Ornith. vol. ii. p. 27. Pl. xi.
     Fig. 2. Young female.
CŒRULEAN WARBLER, SYLVIA CŒRULEA, *Wilson*, Amer. Ornith. vol. ii. p. 141.
     Pl. xvii. fig. 5. Male.

Adult Male. Plate XLVIII. Fig. 1.

Bill of ordinary length, straight, much broader than deep at the base,
tapering, compressed toward the acute tip. Nostrils basal, oval, exposed.
Head of ordinary size. Body rather slender. Feet of ordinary length,
slender; tarsus compressed, covered anteriorly with a few long scutella,
acute behind, scarcely longer than the middle toe; toes free, scutellate
above; claws arched, slender, much compressed, acute.

Plumage soft and blended, glossy. Wings of ordinary length, the
first and second quills longest. Tail longish, even, of twelve rather nar-

row, obtuse feathers. Short bristle-pointed feathers at the base of the upper mandible.

Bill bluish-black. Iris blackish-brown. Feet blue. Head and upper parts generally, of a fine rich blue, the back marked with longitudinal streaks of blackish, and a narrow band of black from the forehead passing along the lore to behind the eye. Tips of the two rows of larger wing-coverts white, forming two conspicuous bands across the wing. Quills black, externally margined with blue. Tail of the same colour, each feather having a patch of white on the inner web, near the end, excepting the two middle ones; all externally margined with blue. Under parts white, as well as a streak over the eye, above which is a streak of blackish.

Length $4\frac{1}{2}$ inches, extent of wings 8; bill along the ridge $\frac{5}{12}$, along the gap $\frac{7}{12}$; tarsus $\frac{9}{12}$, middle toe $\frac{7}{12}$.

Adult Female. Plate XLVIII. Fig. 2.

The female differs from the male, chiefly in having the colours paler.

THE BEAR-BERRY.

ILEX DAHOON, *Mich.* Fl. Amer. vol. ii. p. 228. *Pursh.* Fl. Amer. vol. i. p. 117. —TETRANDRIA TETRAGYNIA, *Linn.* RHAMNI, *Juss.*

This species of Holly is distinguished by its elliptico-lanceolate leaves, which are thick, leathery, shining, and reflected at the margin, and its corymboso-paniculate, lateral and terminal peduncles. The berries are globular and bright red.

R

THE BLUE-GREEN WARBLER.

SYLVIA RARA, Wils.

PLATE XLIX. Male.

The Blue-green Warbler so resembles the young of the Azure Warbler, that were not the form of its bill, and some of its habits, considerably different, I should be tempted to consider it a mere variety of that
bird. It is equally rare in the Middle Districts, where I have shot only
a few, and these in the dark recesses of the Great Pine Swamp.

On its passage through the States, it is found in Louisiana, where it
appears in the beginning of April. This lateness of its arrival indicates
its coming from a great distance, most of the other species appearing
several weeks earlier. They seem to disperse soon after, as on their first
appearance several may be procured in one day, as well as during their
equally short stay in autumn, when, again, I have shot six or seven from
a single tree, on which they appeared as busily engaged as if so many Titmice. I have met with them singly and far apart in Kentucky, in Ohio,
upon the Missouri, and along Lake Erie, but I have never found their nest.

In spring it has a soft and mellow song, which is not heard beyond
the distance of a few paces. It is performed at intervals between the
times at which the bird secures an insect, which it does with great ex-
pertness, either on wing, or amongst the leaves of the trees and bushes.
The tops of trees, however, appear to please them best, the reverse being
the case with the Azure Warbler.

The Blue-green Warbler has a peculiar cunning manner of leaning
downwards to view a person, or while searching for an insect, and which
is very different from that of any other bird, although I am unable to
describe it. While thus leaning, it moves its head sidewise so very
slowly that the motion is hardly perceptible, unless much attention is
paid to it. After this, it either starts off and flies to some distance from
the observer, or darts towards the prey that had attracted its notice.
While catching an insect on the wing, it produces a slight clicking sound
with its bill, and in this respect approaches the Vireos. Like some of
them also, it descends from the highest tops of the trees to low bushes, and
eats small berries, particularly towards autumn, when insects begin to fail.

Its flight is performed in zigzag lines of a few yards, as if it were undetermined where to alight. I have found no difference between the sexes as to external appearance.

The plant on which I have figured a male is found in Louisiana, growing along the skirts of woods and by fences. It is called the *Spanish Mulberry*. It is a herbaceous perennial plant, attaining a height of from four to eight feet. The fruits are eaten by children, but are insipid.

SYLVIA RARA, BLUE-GREEN WARBLER, *Wils.* Amer. Ornith. vol. iii. p. 119. Pl. 27. fig. 2.—*Ch. Bonaparte*, Synops. of Birds of the United States, p. 82.

Adult Male.   Plate XLIX.

Bill longish, nearly straight, depressed at the base, tapering to a point. Nostrils basal, oval, half concealed by the feathers. Head and neck of ordinary size. Body ovate. Feet of ordinary length, rather slender; tarsus compressed, covered anteriorly with a few long scutella, acute behind, rather longer than the middle toe; toes scutellate above, free; claws arched, slender, much compressed, acute.

Plumage blended, soft and tufty. Wings longish, little curved, the first and second quills longest. Tail shortish, rounded, of twelve rather acute feathers.

Bill dark brown above, light blue beneath. Iris dark brown. Feet light blue. General colour of the upper parts light greenish-blue, of the under parts white. A white streak over the eyes. Tips of the two first rows of wing-coverts white, forming two bands across the wing. Quills blackish-brown, their outer margins blue. Tail blackish-brown, the outer feathers having a white patch on the inner web near the end.

Length 4¾ inches, extent of wings 8; bill along the ridge ⅓, along the gap ½; tarsus ⅔.

THE SPANISH MULBERRY.

CALLICARPA AMERICANA, *Willd.* Sp. Pl. vol. i. p. 619. *Pursh,* Fl. Amer. vol. i. p. 97.—TETRANDRIA MONOGYNIA, *Linn.* VITICES, *Juss.*

A perennial herbaceous plant, with oval, serrate leaves, which are downy beneath ; sessile cymes of red flowers, and globular red berries, arranged apparently in dense whorls. It grows in dry gravelly or sandy soil, in Virginia, Carolina, and Louisiana.

THE BLACK AND YELLOW WARBLER.

SYLVIA MACULOSA, LATH.

PLATE L. YOUNG MALE.

THIS little bird was by mistake engraved, and named after my friend W. SWAINSON, Esq., during my absence from London, one drawing having been accidentally substituted for another. It is in reality the young of the Black and Yellow Warbler, and was intended to form part of the Plate which will represent the adult male and female of that species. My good friend will, I know, excuse this mistake, as I have honoured a beautiful new species with his name.

It being more consistent with my present arrangement to give a full account of each species, as it is represented in the Plate allotted to it, and its different states of plumage, as much as this object can be attained, you will permit me, kind reader, to postpone the habits of this species until you see the whole group together. In the mean time, I shall confine myself to a description of the immature state of plumage as represented in my illustrations.

SYLVIA MACULOSA, *Lath.* Ind. Ornith. vol. ii. p. 536.—*Ch. Bonaparte*, Synops. of Birds of the United States, p. 78.

YELLOW-RUMPED WARBLER, *Lath.* Synops. vol. iv. p. 481.

BLACK AND YELLOW WARBLER, SYLVIA MAGNOLIA, *Wils.* Americ. Ornith. vol. iii. p. 63. Pl. 23. Male.

Young Male. Plate L.

Bill brown above, brownish-yellow beneath. Iris dark hazel. Feet brownish-yellow, claws yellow. Head and hind-neck light greyish-blue, blending into yellowish-green on the back, the lower part of which is spotted with black; a broad band across the rump yellow, the upper tail-coverts black. Wings bluish-grey when closed, the outer webs being of that colour, the inner brownish-black; tips of the two larger rows of coverts white, forming two bands of that colour. Tail black, with a broad band of white in the middle, on the inner webs, excepting on the two middle feathers, which are margined with blue, the outer webs of the other feathers being bluish-white; the under parts are ochre-yellow, the posterior part of the breast and sides spotted with black. Length 5 inches, extent of wings 7¼.

THE WHITE OAK.

QUERCUS PRINUS, *Willd.*, Sp. Pl. vol. iv. p. 439. *Pursh,* Fl. Amer. vol. ii. p. 633.— QUERCUS PRINUS PALUSTRIS, *Mich.* Arbr. Forest. de l'Amer. Sept. vol. ii. p. 51. Pl. 7.—MONŒCIA POLYANDRIA, *Linn.* AMENTACEÆ, *Juss.*

Leaves oblongo-oval, acute, largely toothed, the teeth nearly equal, dilated, and callous at the tip; cupule craterate, attenuated at the base; acorn ovate. This species grows in low shady woods, and along the margins of rivers, from Pennsylvania to Florida. The wood is porous, and of inferior quality.

THE HURRICANE.

VARIOUS portions of our country have at different periods suffered severely from the influence of violent storms of wind, some of which have been known to traverse nearly the whole extent of the United States, and to leave such deep impressions in their wake as will not easily be forgotten. Having witnessed one of these awful phenomena, in all its grandeur, I shall attempt to describe it for your sake, kind reader, and for your sake only, the recollection of that astonishing revolution of the etherial element even now bringing with it so disagreeable a sensation, that I feel as if about to be affected by a sudden stoppage of the circulation of my blood.

I had left the village of Shawaney, situated on the banks of the Ohio, on my return from Henderson, which is also situated on the banks of the same beautiful stream. The weather was pleasant, and I thought not warmer than usual at that season. My horse was jogging quietly along, and my thoughts were, for once at least in the course of my life, entirely engaged in commercial speculations. I had forded Highland Creek, and was on the eve of entering a tract of bottom land or valley that lay between it and Canoe Creek, when on a sudden I remarked a great difference in the aspect of the heavens. A hazy thickness had overspread the country, and I for some time expected an earthquake, but my horse exhibited no propensity to stop and prepare for such an occurrence. I had nearly arrived at the verge of the valley, when I thought fit to stop near a brook, and dismounted to quench the thirst which had come upon me.

I was leaning on my knees, with my lips about to touch the water, when, from my proximity to the earth, I heard a distant murmuring sound of an extraordinary nature. I drank, however, and as I rose on my feet, looked toward the south-west, where I observed a yellowish oval spot, the appearance of which was quite new to me. Little time was left me for consideration, as the next moment a smart breeze began to agitate the taller trees. It increased to an unexpected height, and already the smaller branches and twigs were seen falling in a slanting direction towards the ground. Two minutes had scarcely elapsed, when the whole forest before me was in fearful motion. Here and there, where one tree pressed against another, a creaking noise was produced, similar to that occasioned by the violent gusts which sometimes sweep over the country. Turning instinctively toward the direction from which the wind blew, I saw, to my great astonishment, that the noblest trees of the forest bent their lofty heads for a while, and unable to stand against the blast, were falling into pieces. First, the branches were broken off with a crackling noise ; then went the upper part of the massy trunks ; and in many places whole trees of gigantic size were falling entire to the ground. So rapid was the progress of the storm, that before I could think of taking measures to insure my safety, the hurricane was passing opposite the place where I stood. Never can I forget the scene which at that moment presented itself. The tops of the trees were seen moving in the strangest manner, in the central current of the tempest, which carried along with it a mingled mass of twigs and foliage, that completely obscured the view. Some of the largest trees were seen bending and writhing under the gale ; others suddenly snapped across ; and many, after a momentary resistance, fell uprooted to the earth. The mass of branches, twigs, foliage and dust that moved through the air, was whirled onwards like a cloud of feathers, and on passing, disclosed a wide space filled with fallen trees, naked stumps, and heaps of shapeless ruins, which marked the path of the tempest. This space was about a fourth of a mile in breadth, and to my imagination resembled the dried-up bed of the Mississippi, with its thousands of planters and sawyers, strewed in the sand, and inclined in various degrees. The horrible noise resembled that of the great cataracts of Niagara, and as it howled along in the track of the desolating tempest, produced a feeling in my mind which it were impossible to describe.

The principal force of the hurricane was now over, although millions of twigs and small branches, that had been brought from a great distance, were seen following the blast, as if drawn onwards by some mysterious power. They even floated in the air for some hours after, as if supported by the thick mass of dust that rose high above the ground. The sky had now a greenish lurid hue, and an extremely disagreeable sulphureous odour was diffused in the atmosphere. I waited in amazement, having sustained no material injury, until nature at length resumed her wonted aspect. For some moments, I felt undetermined whether I should return to Morgantown, or attempt to force my way through the wrecks of the tempest. My business, however, being of an urgent nature, I ventured into the path of the storm, and after encountering innumerable difficulties, succeeded in crossing it. I was obliged to lead my horse by the bridle, to enable him to leap over the fallen trees, whilst I scrambled over or under them in the best way I could, at times so hemmed in by the broken tops and tangled branches, as almost to become desperate. On arriving at my house, I gave an account of what I had seen, when, to my surprise, I was told that there had been very little wind in the neighbourhood, although in the streets and gardens many branches and twigs had fallen in a manner which excited great surprise.

Many wondrous accounts of the devastating effects of this hurricane were circulated in the country, after its occurrence. Some log houses, we were told, had been overturned, and their inmates destroyed. One person informed me that a wire-sifter had been conveyed by the gust to a distance of many miles. Another had found a cow lodged in the fork of a large half-broken tree. But, as I am disposed to relate only what I have myself seen, I shall not lead you into the region of romance, but shall content myself with saying that much damage was done by this awful visitation. The valley is yet a desolate place, overgrown with briars and bushes, thickly entangled amidst the tops and trunks of the fallen trees, and is the resort of ravenous animals, to which they betake themselves when pursued by man, or after they have committed their depredations on the farms of the surrounding district. I have crossed the path of the storm, at a distance of a hundred miles from the spot where I witnessed its fury, and, again, four hundred miles farther off, in the State of Ohio. Lastly, I observed traces of its ravages on the summits of the mountains connected with the Great Pine Forest of Pennsylvania, three hundred miles beyond the place last mentioned. In all these different parts, it appeared to me not to have exceeded a quarter of a mile in breadth.

THE RED-TAILED HAWK.

FALCO BOREALIS, GMEL.

PLATE LI. MALE AND FEMALE.

THE Red-tailed Hawk is a constant resident in the United States, in every part of which it is found. It performs partial migrations, during severe winters, from the Northern Districts towards the Southern. In the latter, however, it is at all times more abundant, and I shall endeavour to present you with a full account of its habits, as observed there.

Its flight is firm, protracted, and at times performed at a great height. It sails across the whole of a large plantation, on a level with the tops of the forest-trees which surround it, without a single flap of its wings, and is then seen moving its head sidewise to inspect the objects below. This flight is generally accompanied by a prolonged mournful cry, which may be heard at a considerable distance, and consists of a single sound resembling the monosyllable *Kae*, uttered in such a manner as to continue for three or four minutes, without any apparent inflection or difference of intensity. It would seem as if uttered for the purpose of giving notice to the living objects below that he is passing, and of thus inducing them to bestir themselves and retreat to a hiding-place, before they attain which he may have an opportunity of pouncing upon some of them. When he spies an animal, while he is thus sailing over a field, I have observed him give a slight check to his flight, as if to mark a certain spot with accuracy, and immediately afterwards alight on the nearest tree. He would then instantly face about, look intensely on the object that had attracted his attention, soon after descend towards it with wings almost close to his body, and dart upon it with such accuracy and rapidity as seldom to fail in securing it.

When passing over a meadow, a cotton-field, or one planted with sugar-canes, he performs his flight close over the grass or plants, uttering no cry, but marking the prey in the manner above described, and on perceiving it, ascending in a beautiful curved line to the top of the nearest tree, after which he watches and dives as in the former case. Should he not observe any object worthy of his attention, while passing over a meadow or a field, he alights, shakes his feathers, particularly those of the tail, and after spending a few minutes in pluming himself, leaves the perch, uttering his usual cry, and ascending in the air, performs large and repeated circular flights, carefully inspecting the field, to assure himself that there is in reality nothing in it that may be of use to him. He then proceeds to another plantation. At other times, as if not assured that his observations have been duly made, he rises in circles over the same field to an immense height, where he looks like a white dot in the heavens. Yet from this height he must be able to distinguish the objects on the ground, even when these do not exceed our little partridge or a young hare in size, and although their colour may be almost the same as that of surrounding bodies; for of a sudden his circlings are checked, his wings drawn close to his body, his tail contracted to its smallest breadth, and he is seen to plunge headlong towards the earth, with a rapidity which produces a loud rustling sound nearly equal to that of an Eagle on a similar occasion.

Should he not succeed in discovering the desired object in the fields, he enters the forest and perches on some detached tree, tall enough to enable him to see to a great distance around. His posture is now erect, he remains still and silent, moving only his head, as on all other oc-casions, to enable his keen eye to note the occurrences which may take place in his vicinity. The lively Squirrel is seen gaily leaping from one branch to another, or busily employed in searching for the fallen nuts on the ground. It has found one. Its bushy tail is beautifully curved along its back, the end of it falling off with a semicircular bend; its nimble feet are seen turning the nut quickly round, and its teeth are al-ready engaged in perforating the hard shell; when, quick as thought, the Red-tailed Hawk, which has been watching it in all its motions, falls upon it, seizes it near the head, transfixes and strangles it, devours it on the spot, or ascends exultingly to a branch with the yet palpitating vic-tim in his talons, and there feasts at leisure.

As soon as the little King-bird has raised its brood, and when its cour-age is no longer put in requisition for the defence of its young or its mate, the Red-tailed Hawk visits the farm-houses, to pay his regards to the poultry. This is done without much precaution, for, while sailing over the yard where the chickens, the ducklings, and the young turkeys are, the Hawk plunges upon any one of them, and sweeps it off to the nearest wood. When impelled by continued hunger, he now and then manages to elude the vigilance of the Martins, Swallows and King-birds, and watching for a good opportunity, falls upon and seizes an old fowl, the dying screams of which are heard by the farmer at the plough, who swears vengeance against the robber. He remembers that he has observed the Hawk's nest in the woods, and full of anger at the recollection of the depredations which the plunderer has already committed, and at the anticipation of its many visits during the winter, leaves his work and his horses, strides to his house, and with an axe and a rifle in his hands proceeds towards the tree, where the hopes of the Red-tailed Hawk are snugly nestled among the tall branches. The farmer arrives, eyes the gigantic tree, thinks for a moment of the labour which will be required for felling it, but resolves that he shall not be overreached by a Hawk. He throws aside his hat, rolls up his sleeves, and applies himself to the work. His brawny arms give such an impulse to the axe, that at every stroke large chips are seen to fall off on all sides. The poor mother-bird, well aware of the result, sails sorrowfully over and around. She would fain beg for mercy towards her young. She alights on the edge of the nest, and would urge her offspring to take flight. But the farmer has watched her motions. The axe is left sticking in the core of the tree, his rifle is raised to his shoulder in an instant, and the next moment the whizzing ball has pierced the heart of the Red-tailed Hawk, which falls unheeded to the earth. The farmer renews his work, and now changes sides. A whole hour has been spent in the application of ceaseless blows. He begins to look upwards, to judge which way the giant of the forest will fall, and having ascertained this, he redoubles his blows. The huge oak begins to tremble. Were it permitted to speak, it might ask why it should suffer for the deeds of another ; but it is now seen slowly to incline, and soon after with an awful rustling produced by all its broad arms, its branches, twigs and leaves, passing like lightning through the air, the noble tree falls to the earth, and almost causes it to shake. The work of revenge is now accomplished : the farmer seizes the younglings, and carries them home, to be tormented by his children, until death terminates their brief career.

Notwithstanding the very common occurrence of such acts of retribution between man and the Hawk, it would be difficult to visit a plantation in the State of Louisiana, without observing at least a pair of this species hovering about, more especially during the winter months. Early in February, they begin to build their nest, which is usually placed within the forest, and on the tallest and largest tree in the neighbourhood. The male and female are busily engaged in carrying up dried sticks, and other materials, for eight or ten days, during which time their cry is seldom heard. The nest is large, and is fixed in the centre of a triply forked branch. It is of a flattish form, constructed of sticks, and finished with slender twigs and coarse grasses or Spanish moss. The female lays four or five eggs, of a dull white colour, splatched with brown and black, with a very hard, smooth shell. The male assists the female in incubating, but it is seldom that the one brings food to the other while thus employed.

I have seen one or two of these nests built in a large tree which had been left standing in the middle of a field; but occurrences of this kind are rare, on account of the great enmity shewn to this species by the farmers. The young are abundantly supplied with food of various kinds, particularly grey squirrels, which the parents procure while hunting in pairs, when nothing can save the squirrel from their attacks excepting its retreat into the hole of a tree; for should the animal be observed ascending the trunk or branch of a tree by either of the Hawks, this one immediately plunges toward it, while the other watches it from the air. The little animal, if placed against the trunk, when it sees the Hawk coming towards it, makes swiftly for the opposite side of the trunk, but is there immediately dived at by the other Hawk, and now the murderous pair chase it so closely, that unless it immediately finds a hole into which to retreat, it is caught in a few minutes, killed, carried to the nest, torn in pieces, and distributed among the young Hawks. Small hares, or, as we usually call them, *rabbits*, are also frequently caught, and the depredations of the Red-tailed Hawks at this period are astonishing, for they seem to kill every thing, fit for food, that comes in their way. They are great destroyers of tame Pigeons, and woe to the Cock or Hen that strays far from home, for so powerful is this Hawk, that it is able not only to kill them, but to carry them off in its claws to a considerable distance.

The continued attachment that exists between Eagles once paired, is not exhibited by these birds, which, after rearing their young, become as shy towards each other as if they had never met. This is carried to such a singular length, that they are seen to chase and rob each other of their prey, on all occasions. I have seen a couple thus engaged, when one of them had just seized a young rabbit or a squirrel, and was on the eve of rising in the air with it, for the purpose of carrying it off to a place of greater security. The one would attack the other with merciless fury, and either force it to abandon the prize, or fight with the same courage as its antagonist, to prevent the latter from becoming the sole possessor. They are sometimes observed flying either one after the other with great rapidity, emitting their continued cry of *kae,* or performing beautiful evolutions through the air, until one or other of them becomes fatigued, and giving way, makes for the earth, where the battle continues until one is overpowered and obliged to make off. It was after witnessing such an encounter between two of these powerful marauders, fighting hard for a young hare, that I made the drawing now before you, kind reader, in which you perceive the male to have greatly the advantage over the female, although she still holds the hare firmly in one of her talons, even while she is driven towards the earth, with her breast upwards.

I have observed that this species will even condescend to pounce on wood-rats and meadow-mice; but I never saw one of these birds seize even those without first alighting on a tree before committing the act.

During the winter months, the Red-tailed Hawk remains perched for hours together, when the sun is shining and the weather calm. Its breast is opposed to the sun, and it then is seen at a great distance, the pure white of that portion of its plumage glittering as if possessed of a silky gloss. They return to their roosting-places so late in the evening, that I have frequently heard their cry after sun-set, mingling with the jovial notes of Chuck-will's-widow, and the ludicrous laugh of the Barred Owl. In the State of Louisiana, the Red-tailed Hawk roosts amongst the tallest branches of the *Magnolia grandiflora,* a tree which there often attains a height of a hundred feet, and a diameter of from three to four feet at the base. It is also fond of roosting on the tall Cypress-trees of our swamps, where it spends the night in security, amidst the mosses attached to the branches.

The Red-tailed Hawk is extremely wary, and difficult to be approached by any one bearing a gun, the use of which it seems to understand perfectly; for no sooner does it perceive a man thus armed than it spreads its wings, utters a loud shriek, and sails off in an opposite direction. On the other hand, a person on horseback, or walking unarmed, may pass immediately under the branch on which it is perched, when it merely watches his motions as he proceeds. It seldom alights on fences, or the low branches of trees, but prefers the highest and most prominent parts of the tallest trees. It alights on the borders of clear streams to drink. I have observed it in such situations, immersing its bill up to the eyes, and swallowing as much as was necessary to quench its thirst at a single draught.

I have seen this species pounce on soft-shelled tortoises, and amusing enough it was to see the latter scramble towards the water, enter it, and save themselves from the claws of the Hawk by immediately diving. I am not aware that this Hawk is ever successful in these attacks, as I have not on any occasion found any portion of the skin, head, or feet of tortoises in the stomachs of the many Hawks of this species which I have killed and examined. Several times, however, I have found portions of bull-frogs in their stomach.

All our Falcons are pestered with parasitic flying ticks. Those found amongst the plumage of the Red-tailed Hawk, like all others, move swiftly sidewise between the feathers, issue from the skin, and shift from one portion of the body to another on wing, and do not abandon the bird for a day or two after the latter is dead. These ticks are large, and of an auburn colour.

The body of the Red-tailed Hawk is large, compact, and muscular. These birds protrude their talons beyond their head in seizing their prey, as well as while fighting in the air, in the manner shown in the Plate. I have caught several birds of this species by baiting a steel-trap with a live chicken.

The animal represented as held in one of the feet of the female, is usually called a *rabbit* in all parts of the United States, but is evidently a true hare. It never burrows, but has a *form* to rest in, and to which it returns in the manner of the common hare of Europe. I may hereafter present you, kind reader, with a full account of this American species, which occurs in great abundance in the United States.

I have only here to add, that amongst the American farmers the common name of our present bird is the *Hen-hawk*, while it receives that of *Grand mangeur de poules* from the Creoles of Louisiana.

FALCO BOREALIS, *Gmel.* Syst. Nat. vol. i. p. 266.—*Lath.* Ind. Ornith. vol. i. p. 25.—
    Ch. Bonaparte, Synops. p. 32.
AMERICAN BUZZARD, *Lath.* Synops. vol. i. p. 50.
RED-TAILED HAWK, FALCO BOREALIS, *Wils.* Amer. Ornith. vol. vi. p. 75. Pl. 52.
    fig. 1. Adult.
AMERICAN BUZZARD, OR WHITE-BREASTED HAWK, FALCO LEVERIANUS, *Wils.*
    Amer. Ornith. vol. vi. p. 78. Pl. 51. fig. 3. Young.

Adult Male. Plate LI. Fig. 1.

Bill short, robust, at the base as broad as deep, compressed towards
the end, cerate; upper mandible, with the dorsal outline, convex from the
base, rounded on the sides, the edges with an obtuse lobe, the tip trigonal, descending obliquely, acute; lower mandible involute at the edges,
truncate at the end, broadly rounded on the back. Nostrils roundish,
nearly dorsal, in the fore part of the cere. Head large, flat above. Neck
shortish, robust. Body bulky. Legs rather long, very robust; tarsi
stout, scutellate before and behind, the sides covered with hexagonal
scales; toes scutellate above, scaly on the sides, scabrous and tubercular
beneath; claws roundish, strong, curved, very acute.

Plumage compact and firm; feathers of the head and neck rather narrow, of the other parts broad and rounded. Tarsus feathered anteriorly
about one-third down. Wings long, ample, rounded, the fourth quill
longest, the first short. Tail of twelve broad, rounded feathers, even, and
of ordinary length.

Bill light blue, blackish at the tip, greenish-yellow on the margin towards the base; cere greenish-yellow. Iris hazel. Tarsi and toes yellow; claws brownish-black. Upper part of the head light brownish-
grey. Loral space and under eyelid white. A broad band of dark
brown from the angle of the mouth backwards. Neck above and on the
sides reddish-yellow, with large deep brown spots. Back deep brown;
scapulars of the same colour, broadly margined and tipped with brownish-
white. Lesser wing-coverts chocolate-brown; larger lighter brown, tipped with white. Primary quills blackish-brown; secondaries lighter, tipped with brownish-white; all barred with blackish. Upper tail-coverts
whitish, barred with brown, and yellowish-red in the middle. Tail bright
yellowish-red, tipped with whitish, and having a narrow bar of black near
the end. Lower parts brownish-white; the fore part of the breast and
neck light yellowish-red, the former marked with guttiform, somewhat
sagittate brown spots: abdomen and chin white; feathers of the leg and
tarsus pale reddish-yellow, those on the outside indistinctly spotted.

Length 20½ inches, extent of wings 46; bill along the back 1¼, along
the gap 2; tarsus 3½, middle toe 2¾. Wings when closed reaching to
within two inches of the tip of the tail.

Adult Female. Plate LI. Fig. 2.

The female, which is considerably larger, agrees with the male in the
general distribution of its colouring. The upper parts are darker, and

the under parts nearly white, there being only a few narrow streaks on the sides of the breast ; the tibial and tarsal feathers as in the male. The tail is of a duller red, and wants the black bar.

Length 24 inches.

The American Hare.

LEPUS AMERICANUS, *Harlan*, Fauna Americana, p. 193.

The Rabbit, as this animal is named in the United States, has the habits of the European Hare, forming a flat, well-beaten, oblong space among the grass, on which it rests during the day. It never burrows like the Common Rabbit of Europe, although it resorts for safety to the hollows of fallen trunks, or those frequently existing at the roots of standing trees, as well as to cavities in rocks. It feeds principally towards the approach of night and early in the morning, and spends the greater part of the day in its form. When startled by a dog, it proceeds in a direct manner for a considerable way, and then returns nearly by the same course. When disturbed, if there be not a dog present, it runs to a short distance, stops, raises its head, erects its ears, and is then easily discovered and shot. When the period of parturition approaches, it forms a kind of nest of long grass, arranged in an oblong form. Its flesh is whiter than that of the European Hare, but resembles it in flavour. It gnaws the bark of young trees in the orchards as well as in the forests, and is in many parts very abundant.

CHUCK-WILL'S-WIDOW.

CAPRIMULGUS CAROLINENSIS, BRISS.

PLATE LII. MALE AND FEMALE.

OUR Goatsuckers, although possessed of great power of wing, are particularly attached to certain districts and localities. The species now under consideration is seldom observed beyond the limits of the Choctaw Nation in the State of Mississippi, or the Carolinas, on the shores of the Atlantic, and may with propriety be looked upon as the southern species of the United States. Louisiana, Florida, the lower portions of Alabama and Georgia, are the parts in which it most abounds ; and there it makes its appearance early in spring, coming over from Mexico, and probably still warmer climates.

About the middle of March, the forests of Louisiana are heard to echo with the well-known notes of this interesting bird. No sooner has the sun disappeared, and the nocturnal insects emerge from their burrows, than the sounds, " *chuck-will's-widow,*" repeated with great clearness and power six or seven times in as many seconds, strike the ear of every individual, bringing to the mind a pleasure mingled with a certain degree of melancholy, which I have often found very soothing. The sounds of the Goatsucker, at all events, forebode a peaceful and calm night, and I have more than once thought, are conducive to lull the listener to repose.

The deep ravines, shady swamps, and extensive pine ridges, are all equally resorted to by these birds ; for in all such places they find ample means of providing for their safety during the day, and of procuring food under night. Their notes are seldom heard in cloudy weather, and never when it rains. Their roosting places are principally the hollows of decayed trees, whether standing or prostrate, from which latter they are seldom raised during the day, excepting while incubation is in progress. In these hollows I have found them, lodged in the company of several species of bats, the birds asleep on the mouldering particles of the wood, the bats clinging to the sides of the cavities. When surprised in such situations, instead of trying to effect their escape by flying out, they retire backwards to the farthest corners, ruffle all the feathers of their body,

ɓ

open their mouth to its full extent, and utter a hissing kind of murmur, not unlike that of some snakes. When seized and brought to the light of day, they open and close their eyes in rapid succession, as if it were painful for them to encounter so bright a light. They snap their little bill in the manner of Fly-catchers, and shuffle along as if extremely desirous of making their escape. On giving them liberty to fly, I have found them able to proceed until out of my sight. They passed between the trees with apparently as much ease and dexterity as if it had been twilight. I once cut two of the quill-feathers of a wing of one of these birds, and allowed it to escape. A few days afterwards I found it in the same log, which induces me to believe that they, like many other birds, resort to the same spot, to roost or spend the day.

The flight of the Chuck-will's-widow is as light as that of its relative, the well-known *Whip-poor-will*, if not more so, and is more graceful as well as more elevated. It somewhat resembles the flight of the Hen-harrier, being performed by easy flappings of the wings, interspersed with sailings and curving sweeps, extremely pleasing to the bystander. At the approach of night, this bird begins to sing clearly and loudly, and continues its notes for about a quarter of an hour. At this time it is perched on a fence-stake, or on the decayed branch of a tree in the interior of the woods, seldom on the ground. The sounds or notes which it emits seem to cause it some trouble, as it raises and lowers its head in quick succession at each of them. This over, the bird launches into the air, and is seen sweeping over the cotton fields or the sugar plantations, cutting all sorts of figures, mounting, descending, or sailing, with so much ease and grace, that one might be induced to call it the *Fairy of the night.* If it passes close to one, a murmuring noise is heard, at times resembling that spoken of when the bird is caught by day. It suddenly checks its course, inclines to the right or left, secures a beetle or a moth, continues its flight over the field, passes and repasses hundreds of times over the same ground, and now and then alights on a fence-stake, or the tallest plant in the place, from which it emits its notes for a few moments with increased vivacity. Now, it is seen following a road or a path on the wing, and alighting here and there to pick up the beetle emerging from its retreat in the ground; again, it rises high in air, and gives chase to the insects that are flying there, perhaps on their passage from one wood to another. At other times, I have seen it poise itself on its wings opposite the trunk of a tree, and seize with its bill the insects crawling on the bark, in this manner inspecting the whole tree, with motions as light as those by which the Humming Bird flutters from one flower to another. In this manner Chuck-will's-widow spends the greater part of the night.

The greatest harmony appears to subsist between the birds of this species, for dozens may be observed flying together over a field, and chasing insects in all directions, without manifesting any enmity or envy. A few days after the arrival of the male birds, the females make their appearance, and the love season at once commences. The male pays his addresses to the female with a degree of pomposity only equalled by the Tame Pigeon. The female, perched lengthwise on a branch, appears coy and silent, whilst the male flies around her, alights in front of her, and with drooping wings and expanded tail advances quickly, singing with great impetuosity. They are soon seen to leave the branch together and gambol through the air. A few days after this, the female, having made choice of a place in one of the most retired parts of some thicket, deposits two eggs, which I think, although I cannot be certain, are all that she lays for the season. This bird forms no nest. A little space is carelessly scratched amongst the dead leaves, and in it the eggs, which are elliptical, dull olive, and speckled with brown, are dropped. These are not found without great difficulty, unless when by accident a person passes within a few feet of the bird whilst sitting, and it chances to fly off. Should you touch or handle these dear fruits of happy love, and, returning to the place, search for them again, you would search in vain ; for the bird perceives at once that they have been meddled with, and both parents remove them to some other part of the woods, where chance only could enable you to find them again. In the same manner, they also remove the young when very small.

This singular occurrence has as much occupied my thoughts as the equally singular manner in which the *Cow Bunting* deposits her eggs, which she does, like the *Common Cuckoo* of Europe, one by one, in the nests of other birds, of different species from her own. I have spent much time in trying to ascertain in what manner the Chuck-will's-widow removes her eggs or young, particularly as I found, by the assistance of an excellent dog, that neither the eggs nor the young were to be met with within at least a hundred yards from the spot where they at first lay. The Negroes, some of whom pay a good deal of attention to the habits of birds and quadrupeds, assured me that these birds push the eggs or young with their bill along the ground. Some farmers, without troubling themselves much about the matter, imagined the transportation to be performed under the wings of the old bird. The account of the Negroes appearing to me more likely to be true than that of the farmers, I made up my mind to institute a strict investigation of the matter. The following is the result.

When the Chuck-will's-widow, either male or female (for each sits alternately) has discovered that the eggs have been touched, it ruffles its feathers and appears extremely dejected for a minute or two, after which it emits a low murmuring cry, scarcely audible to me, as I lay concealed at a distance of not more than eighteen or twenty yards. At this time I have seen the other parent reach the spot, flying so low over the ground that I thought its little feet must have touched it, as it skimmed along, and after a few low notes and some gesticulations, all indicative of great distress, take an egg in its large mouth, the other bird doing the same, when they would fly off together, skimming closely over the ground, until they disappeared among the branches and trees. But to what distance they remove their eggs, I have never been able to ascertain; nor have I ever had an opportunity of witnessing the removal of the young. Should a person, coming upon the nest when the bird is sitting, refrain from touching the eggs, the bird returns to them and sits as before. This fact I have also ascertained by observation.

I wish I could have discovered the peculiar use of the *pectinated claw* which this bird has on each foot; but, reader, this remains one of the many desiderata in ornithology, and I fear, with me at least, will continue so.

The Chuck-will's-widow manifests a strong antipathy towards all snakes, however harmless they may be. Although these birds cannot in any way injure the snakes, they alight near them on all occasions, and try to frighten them away, by opening their prodigious mouth, and emitting a strong hissing murmur. It was after witnessing one of these occurrences, which took place at early twilight, that the idea of representing these birds in such an occupation struck me. The beautiful little snake, gliding along the dead branch, between two Chuck-will's-widows, a male and a female, is commonly called the *Harlequin Snake*, and is, I believe, quite harmless.

The food of the bird now under consideration consists entirely of all sorts of insects, among which the larger species of moths and beetles are very conspicuous. The long bristly feathers at the base of the mandibles of these birds no doubt contribute greatly to prevent the insects from escaping, after any portion of them has entered the mouth of the bird.

These birds become silent as soon as the young are hatched, but are heard again before their departure towards the end of summer. At this season, however, their cry is much less frequently heard than in spring. They leave the United States all of a sudden, about the middle of the month of August.

CAPRIMULGUS CAROLINENSIS, *Gmel.* Syst. Nat. vol. i. p. 1028.—*Lath.* Ind. Ornith. vol. ii. p. 584.—*Ch. Bonaparte*, Synops. of Birds of the United States, p. 61.

CAROLINA GOATSUCKER, *Lath.* Synops. vol. iv. p. 592.

CHUCK-WILL'S-WIDOW, CAPRIMULGUS CAROLINENSIS, *Wils.* Amer. Ornith. vol. vi. p. 95. Pl. 54. fig. 2.

Adult Male.   Plate LII. Fig. 1.

Bill extremely short, feeble, opening to beyond the eyes, making the mouth when open of enormous dimensions; upper mandible arched in its dorsal outline, very broad at the base, suddenly contracted towards the tip, which is compressed and rather obtuse; lower mandible a little decurved at the tip. Nostrils basal, oval, prominent, covered above by a membrane. Head disproportionately large. Eyes and ears very large. Neck short. Body rather slender. Feet very short; tarsus partly feathered, anteriorly scutellate below; fore toes three, connected to the second joint by membranes, scutellate above; claws depressed, arched, that of the middle toe with the inner edge expanded and pectinate.

Plumage blended, soft and silky, without much gloss. Upper mandible margined at the base with long, stiff bristles, extending forwards and outwards. Wings long, somewhat falcate, narrow, the second and third quills longest. Tail long, ample, even, of ten broad, rounded feathers.

Bill yellowish-brown, the tip black. Iris hazel. Feet yellowish-brown, tinged with purple. Head and back dark brown, minutely mottled with yellowish-red, and longitudinally streaked with black. Three lines of the latter colour from the upper mandible, diverging along the head. A yellowish-white line over the eye. Sides of the head and chin yellowish-red, mottled with black. Wings barred with yellowish-red and brownish-black, and minutely sprinkled with the latter colour, as are the wing-coverts, which, together with the scapulars, are largely

spotted with black, and tinged with bluish-grey. Tail similarly barred and
sprinkled, the inner webs of the three outer feathers white, and their extremities light yellowish-red, more minutely sprinkled, and without bars.
Under parts blackish, sprinkled with yellowish-red, the belly lighter, and
a slight band of whitish across the fore-neck.

Length 12¾ inches, extent of wings 26; bill along the back ½, along
the gap 2.

Adult Female.   Plate LII. Fig. 2.

The colouring of the female is similar to that of the male. The three
outer tail-feathers are brownish on their inner webs, yellowish-red, without dots, at the tip, with a distinct subterminal bar of black.

THE HARLEQUIN SNAKE.

This beautiful Snake is rather rare in the United States, where I
have observed it only in the south.   It glides through the grass with
ease, and ascends to the tops of bushes and among the branches of fallen
trees, to bask in the sun.   Children are fond of catching it on account of
its beauty.   It feeds principally on insects, such as flies and small
Coleoptera.   Its usual size is that represented in the plate.

THE PAINTED FINCH.

FRINGILLA CIRIS, TEMM.

PLATE LIII. MALE IN DIFFERENT STATES OF PLUMAGE, AND FEMALE.

ABOUT the middle of April, the orange groves of the lower parts of Louisiana, and more especially those in the immediate vicinity of the City of New Orleans, are abundantly supplied with this beautiful little Sparrow. But no sooner does it make its appearance than trap-cages are set, and a regular business is commenced in the market of that city. The method employed in securing the male Painted Finch is so connected with its pugnacious habits, that I feel inclined to describe it, especially as it is so different from the common way of alluring birds, that it may afford you, kind reader, some amusement.

A male bird in full plumage is shot and stuffed in a defensive attitude, and perched among some grass seed, rice, or other food, on the same platform as the trap-cage. This is taken to the fields or near the orangeries, and placed in so open a situation, that it would be difficult for a living bird of any species to fly over it, without observing it. The trap is set. A male Painted Finch passes, perceives it, and dives towards the stuffed bird, with all the anger which its little breast can contain. It alights on the edge of the trap for a moment, and throwing its body against the stuffed bird, brings down the trap, and is made prisoner. In this manner, thousands of these birds are caught every spring. So pertinacious are they in their attacks, that even when the trap has closed upon them, they continue pecking at the feathers of the supposed rival. The approach of man seems to allay its anger in a moment. The live bird is removed to the lower apartment of the cage, and is thereby made to assist in decoying others.

They feed almost immediately after being caught; and if able to support the loss of liberty for a few days, may be kept for several years. I have known some instances of their being kept in confinement for upwards of ten years. Few vessels leave the port of New Orleans during the summer months, without taking some Painted Finches, and through this means they are transported probably to all parts of Europe. I have seen them offered for sale in London and Paris, with the trifling differ-

ence of value on each individual, which converted the sixpence paid for
it at New Orleans to three guineas in London.

The pugnacious habits of this species are common in a great degree
to the whole family of Sparrows.   Like the most daring, the Common
House Sparrow of Europe, they may be observed in spring time, in little
groups of four, five or six, fighting together, moving round each other to
secure an advantageous position, pecking and pulling at each other's
feathers with all the violence and animosity to which their small degree
of strength can give effect.

A group thus occupied I have attempted to represent in the plate.   I
have at the same time endeavoured to save you the trouble of reading a
long description of the changes which take place in their plumage, from
the time at which the young leave the nest, until the fourth year following, when the males attain the full beauty of their brilliant livery.
Where in fact would be the necessity of telling you more, than that the
young, during the first summer, are similar in colouring to the female;
that the next spring, the head of the males only has become of a handsome blue; that, the spring following, the same bird is mottled more or
less with azure, carmine, yellow and green; and that it requires another
return of the warm season before all these colours are perfected and rendered permanent; when at a single glance you can determine all this at
once.   Long descriptions of this kind are only fit to be read to the blind.
Colours speak for themselves.

The flight of the *Pape*, by which name the Creoles of Louisiana
know this bird best, is short, although regular, and performed by a nearly
constant motion of the wings, which is rendered necessary by their concave form.   It hops on the ground, moving forward with ease, now and
then jetting out the tail a little, and, like a true Sparrow, picking up and
carrying off on wing a grain of rice or a crumb of bread to some distance, where it may eat in more security.   It has a sprightly song, often
repeated, which it continues even when closely confined.   When the bird
is at liberty, this song is uttered from the top branches of an orange-
tree, or those of a common briar, and although not so sonorous as that of
the Canary, or of its nearer relative, the Indigo Bunting, is not far from
equalling either.   Its song is continued during the greatest heats of the
day, which is also the case with that of the Indigo Bird.

The nest of this pretty bird is generally placed in a low situation, in
an orange-tree, frequently within a few paces of the house, or far from it

on the edge of the fences, where briars are convenient. It raises two broods each season. The eggs are four or five, of a beautiful pearly, rather bluish colour, speckled with blackish, and are deposited in a simply constructed nest, lined with fine fibrous roots or horse-hair, and externally formed of fine grass. They readily breed in confinement, if their prison is rendered tolerably comfortable. The young are fed at first in the manner of Canaries, but at the end of ten or twelve days are taught to swallow grains of rice, insects or berries. No sooner are figs or grapes ripe than these birds attack them, feeding for some time almost entirely upon them. Towards evening, they also pursue insects on wing.

Some persons give the name of *Nonpareil* to this species, but it is more commonly known by the name of *Pape*, which, in fact, is a general appellation given by the inhabitants of Louisiana to all the smaller species of thick-billed birds.

The Painted Finches do not proceed far eastward, nor, indeed, up the Mississippi, being seldom seen above the City of Natchez, on that river, or farther to the east than the Carolinas. It retires southward in the beginning of October.

The Chickasaw Wild Plum, on a twig of which I have represented a group of these birds, is found growing abundantly in the country where the birds occur. It is a small shrub, the fruit of which is yellow when ripe, and excellent eating.

FRINGILLA CIRIS, *Ch. Bonaparte*, Synopsis of Birds of the United States, p. 107.
EMBERIZA CIRIS, *Linn.* Syst. Nat. vol. p. 313.—*Lath.* Ind. Ornith. vol. i. p. 416.
PAINTED BUNTING, *Lath.* Synops. vol. iii. p. 206.—*Wils.* Amer. Ornith. vol. iii. p. 68.
Pl. xxiv. fig. 1. Male ; Fig. 2. Female.

Adult Male, in full plumage. Plate LIII. Fig 1.

Bill short, robust, conical, somewhat bulging, straight, acute ; upper mandible broader, slightly declinate at the tip ; gap-line a little declinate at the base. Nostrils basal, roundish, partly concealed by the frontal feathers. Head and neck rather large. Body full. Feet of moderate length ; tarsus a little longer than the middle toe ; toes free, the lateral ones nearly equal ; claws compressed, arched, acute.

Plumage blended, tufty, somewhat compact on the head and back. Wings of ordinary length, the third quill longest. Tail shortish, even, of twelve rounded feathers.

Bill dark brown above, light-blue beneath. Iris hazel. Feet light blue. Head and upper neck pure azure, a circle of carmine round the eye. Back and lesser wing-coverts yellowish-green. Lower back and under parts deep carmine. Quills and tail purplish-brown; secondary coverts green.

Length 5¼, extent of wings 7½; bill along the ridge ⅓, along the gap ½; tarsus ¾, middle toe ⅝.

Male in the third year. Plate LIII. Fig. 2.

Head and under parts as in the full-plumaged male. Back mottled with yellow and light green; upper wing-coverts patched with green, yellow and brown.

Male in the second year. Plate LIII. Fig. 4.

Bill and upper part of the head as in the adult. Upper parts generally olive-green; under parts dull orange, paler behind.

Male in the first year. Plate LIII. Fig. 3.

Under mandible blue; in other respects similar to the female.

Adult Female. Plate LIII. Fig. 5.

Bill brown. Feet light blue. Upper parts in general light olive green; under parts dull orange, paler behind.

THE CHICKASAW PLUM.

PRUNUS CHICASA, *Mich.* Flor. Amer. vol. i. p. 284. *Pursh*, Flor. Amer. vol. i. p. 332. —ICOSANDRIA MONOGYNIA, *Linn.* ROSACEÆ, *Juss.*

This species is distinguished by its oblongo-elliptical, acuminate, serrulate leaves; smooth spinescent branches; flowers in pairs, with very short pedicels, and glabrous calyces; and its broadly oval fruits. It flowers in April and May.

THE RICE BIRD.

ICTERUS AGRIPENNIS, CH. BONAP.

PLATE LIV. MALE AND FEMALE.

VERY few of these birds pass through Louisiana in spring, and still fewer, on their return, in autumn; for which reason I am inclined to think that they do not spend the winter months so much in the Southern parts of America as in some of the West India Islands. Indeed, I am the more inclined to believe this to be the case, that they seldom penetrate far into the interior, during their stay with us, but prefer the districts bordering upon the Atlantic, through which they pass and repass in incredible numbers.

In Louisiana, small detached flocks of males or of females appear about the middle of March and beginning of April, alighting in the meadows and grain-fields, where they pick up the grubs and insects found about the roots of the blades. I have heard it asserted, though I cannot give it as a fact, that the appearance of the Rice Bird in spring forebodes a bad harvest. The idea probably originates from the circumstance that these birds do not pass through Louisiana regularly every year, there being sometimes three or four springs in succession in which they are not observed.

The plumage of many of the males at this early season still resembles that of the females, but it changes in the course of their stay, which is seldom more than a fortnight. I have ascertained this fact by dissecting many at this period, when, notwithstanding the dull colour of their plumage, I found the sexual organs greatly developed, which is not the case in autumn, even in the old males. I had another clew to the discovery of this fact. No sooner did a flock of females make its appearance, than these dull-looking gentlemen immediately paid them such particular attention, and sang so vehemently, that the fact of their being of a different sex became undeniable.

Here they pass under the name of *Meadow Birds*. In Pennsylvania they are called *Reed Birds*, in Carolina *Rice Buntings*, and in the State of New York *Boblinks*. The latter appellation is given to them as far eastward as they are known to proceed for the purpose of breeding.

During their sojourn in Louisiana, in spring, their song, which is extremely interesting, and emitted with a volubility bordering on the burlesque, is heard from a whole party at the same time ; when, as each individual is, of course, possessed of the same musical powers as his neighbours, it becomes amusing to listen to thirty or forty of them beginning one after another, as if ordered to follow in quick succession, after the first notes are given by a leader, and producing such a medley as it is impossible to describe, although it is extremely pleasant to hear it. While you are listening, the whole flock simultaneously ceases, which appears equally extraordinary. This curious exhibition takes place every time that the flock has alighted on a tree, after feeding for a while on the ground, and is renewed at intervals during the day.

There is a very remarkable fact in the history of this species, which is, that while moving eastward, during their migration, in spring, they fly mostly at night ; whereas in autumn, when they are returning southward, their flight is diurnal. This, kind reader, is another puzzle to me.

About the middle of May, the Boblinks reach the State of New York, their stay in the intermediate States being of short duration at that season, although sufficient to enable them to cause great injury to the corn fields in Virginia, Maryland, and Pennsylvania, where it is said, although I can scarcely give credit to the assertion, that they cut the blade near the root. This is perhaps laid to their charge for the purpose of aggravating the real injury which they afterwards inflict on the farmers, by feeding on the grain when in a milky and tender state. However, they reach the States of New York and Connecticut, and extend their journey to the easternmost of our districts, proceeding also to the borders of Lake Champlain, Lake Ontario, and the St Laurence.

By this time, they have become so plentiful, and have so dispersed all over the country, that it is impossible to see a meadow or a field of corn, which does not contain several pairs of them. The beauty, or, perhaps more properly, the variety of their plumage, as well as of their song, attracts the attention of the bird-catchers. Great numbers are captured and exposed for sale in the markets, particularly in those of the city of New York. They are caught in trap-cages, and feed and sing almost immediately after. Many are carried to Europe, where the shipper is often disappointed in his profits, as by the time they reach there, the birds have changed their colours and seem all females.

Whilst the love season lasts, the males are more sprightly than ever. Their song is mostly performed in the air, while they are rising and fall-

ing in successive jerks, which are as amusing as the jingling of their vocal essays. The variety of their colours is at this juncture very remarkable. It is equally so, when, on rising from among the grass and flying
away from the observer, they display the pure black and white of their
wings and body.

The nest of the Rice Bunting is placed on the ground, without much
apparent care as to choice of situation, but always amongst the grass, or in
a field of wheat or barley. It is composed of coarse dried grasses and
leaves externally, and is lined with finer meadow grass. It appears large
for the size of the bird. The female lays from four to six eggs, of a
white colour, strongly tinged with dull blue, and irregularly spotted with
blackish. They raise only one brood in a season.

No sooner have the young left the nest, than they and their parents
associate with other families, so that by the end of July large flocks begin to appear. They seem to come from every portion of the Eastern
States, and already resort to the borders of the rivers and estuaries to
roost. Their songs have ceased, the males have lost their gay livery, and
have assumed the yellow hue of the females and young, although the
latter are more firm in their tints than the old males, and the whole begin to return southward, slowly and with a single *clink*, sufficient however to give intimation of their passage, as they fly high in long files during the whole day.

Now begin their devastations. They plunder every field, but are
shot in immense numbers. As they pass along the sea shores, and follow the muddy edges of the rivers, covered at that season with full
grown reeds, whose tops are bent down with the weight of the ripe seeds,
they alight amongst them in countless multitudes, and afford abundant
practice to every gunner.

It is particularly towards sunset, and when the weather is fine, that
the sport of shooting *Reed Birds* is most profitable. They have then
fully satiated their appetite, and have collected closely for the purpose of
roosting. At the discharge of a gun, a flock sufficient to cover several
acres rises *en masse*, and performing various evolutions, densely packed,
and resembling a sultry cloud, passes over and near the sportsman, when he
lets fly, and finds occupation for some time in picking up the dozens which
he has brought down at a single shot. One would think that every gun
in the country has been put in requisition. Millions of these birds are destroyed, and yet millions remain, for after all the havock that has been

made among them in the Middle Districts, they follow the coast, and reach the rice plantations of the Carolinas in such astonishing numbers, that no one could conceive their flocks to have been already thinned. Their flesh is extremely tender and juicy. The markets are amply supplied, and the epicures have a glorious time of it.

By the end of October, few are found remaining in the States of New York and Pennsylvania; and by the first of December they have left the United States.

The food of these birds varies according to the seasons, and consists of grubs, caterpillars, insects of various kinds, such as beetles, grasshoppers, crickets, and ground-spiders, and the seeds of wild oats, wheat, barley, rice, and other grasses. They cling or climb along the stalks of rank weeds, reeds, and corn, with great activity and ease, and when at roost place themselves as near the ground as possible.

ICTERUS AGRIPENNIS, *Ch. Bonaparte,* Synops. of Birds of the United States, p. 53.
EMBERIZA ORYZIVORA, *Linn.* Syst. Nat. vol. i. p. 311.—*Lath.* Ind. Ornith. vol. i. p. 408.
RICE BUNTING, *Lath.* Synops. vol. iii. p. 188.—*Wils.* Amer. Ornith. vol. ii. p. 48, Pl. xii. fig. 1, 2.

Plate LIV. Fig. 1.   Adult Male in summer.

Bill of ordinary length, robust, conical, compressed; upper mandible narrower, inflected at the edges, the dorsal outline a little convex, the ridge slightly prolonged on the forehead, the palate furnished with a hard tubercle; under mandible with the dorsal outline convex, as are the sides, the edges inflected; the gap line much deflected at the base, straight. Nostrils basal, oval, in a short deep grove, nearly concealed by the feathers. Head large, neck thick, body full. Feet of ordinary length, rather strong; tarsus compressed, anteriorly covered with six scutella, posteriorly acute; toes scutellate above, the outer united at the base; claws arched, compressed, acute, the hind one very long.

Plumage compact, glossy. Wings of ordinary length, the second quill longest. Tail of ordinary length, composed of twelve acuminate feathers.

Bill dark brown above, bluish-grey beneath. Iris hazel. Feet light reddish-brown. Upper and fore part of the head, cheeks, tail, quills, and the whole under parts, black. Back of the head and neck brownish-yellow. Fore part of the back black, the feathers margined with yellow, as are the secondary quills and coverts. Lower back, tail-coverts and scapulars, pure white.

Length 7 inches, extent of wings 11; bill along the ridge $\frac{7}{12}$, along the gap $\frac{8}{9}$; tarsus 1$\frac{1}{8}$, middle toe 1$\frac{1}{4}$.

Adult Female in summer. Plate LIV. Fig. 2.

The female is somewhat less than the male, and differs greatly in the colours of the plumage, the upper parts being light yellowish-brown, longitudinally streaked with blackish-brown, the under parts pale greyish-yellow, the sides longitudinally marked with dark brown. There is a broad band of dark brown on each side of the head, beneath which is a yellowish streak over the eye, and a blackish spot behind it. The quills and tail-feathers are wood-brown, the former, as well as the coverts, margined with yellowish.

Notwithstanding the somewhat greater length of the bill, this bird evidently approaches very nearly to the genus *Emberiza,* or is one of the connecting links between it and the genus *Icterus.* The female in colouring bears a striking resemblance to *Emberiza miliaria.*

THE RED MAPLE.

ACER RUBRUM, *Willd.* Sp. Plant. vol. iv. p. 984. *Pursh,* Flor. Amer. vol. i. p. 265. *Mich.* Arb. Forest. de l'Amer. Sept. vol. ii. p. 210. Pl. 14.—OCTANDRIA MONO-GYNIA, *Linn.* ACERINEÆ, *Juss.*

This species, which is known by the names of *Red Maple* and *Swamp Maple,* is distinguished by its five-lobed or three-lobed leaves, which are cordate at the base, unequally and deeply toothed, and glaucous beneath; its sessile umbels, elongated pedicels, and smooth germens. The flowers and seeds are red. It is very extensively distributed, and in the Swamps of Pennsylvania and New Jersey attains a height of from sixty to eighty feet. When young, the bark is smooth, and covered with large white spots, but it ultimately cracks and becomes brown. The wood is hard and close, and takes a good polish. It is extensively used for various purposes.

CUVIER'S REGULUS.

REGULUS CUVIERII.

PLATE LV. Male.

I HAVE named this pretty and rare species after BARON CUVIER, not merely by way of acknowledgment for the kind attentions which I have received at the hands of that deservedly celebrated naturalist, but more as a homage due by every student of nature to one at present unrivalled in the knowledge of General Zoology.

I shot the bird represented in the Plate, on my father-in-law's plantation of Fatland Ford, on the Skuylkill River in Pennsylvania, on the 8th June 1812, while on a visit to my honoured relative Mr WILLIAM BAKEWELL. The drawing which I then made I have kept to this date, without having described the bird from which it was taken. I killed this little bird, supposing it to be one of its relatives, the Ruby-crested Wren, whilst it was searching for insects and larvæ amongst the leaves and blossoms of the *Kalmia latifolia*, on a branch of which you see it represented, and was not aware of its being a different bird until I picked it up from the ground. I have not seen another since, nor have I been able to learn that this species has been observed by any other individual. It might, however, be very easily mistaken for the Ruby-crowned Wren, the manners of which appear to be much the same.

My excellent friend CHARLES LUCIAN BONAPARTE, to whom also I shewed my drawing of this bird in London, proposed naming it *Regulus Carbunculus*; and I should probably have introduced it to you, kind reader, under that appellation, had I not changed it for that of *Regulus Cuvierii*, on my fortunately becoming acquainted with the highly celebrated and equally kind Secretary of the Royal Institute of France.

The *Kalmia latifolia* grows in great profusion in the State of Pennsylvania, and along the range of the Alleghanies, in all rocky and hilly situations.

REGULUS CUVIERII.

Plate LV. Male.

2

Bill short, straight, subulate, very slender, compressed, with inflected edges; upper mandible nearly straight in its dorsal outline, the edges slightly notched close upon the slightly declinate acute tip; lower mandible straight, acute. Nostrils basal, elliptical, half closed above by a membrane, covered over by the feathers. The whole form slender. Legs rather long; tarsus slender, much compressed, longer than the middle toe, covered anteriorly with a few indistinct scutella; toes scutellate, the lateral ones nearly equal and free; hind toe stouter; claws weak, compressed, arched, acute.

Plumage very loose and tufty Bristles at the base of the bill; a small decomposed feather covering the nostril. Wings of ordinary length, the third and fourth primaries longest. Tail of twelve feathers, emarginate.

Bill black. Iris hazel. Feet yellowish-brown. The general colour of the upper parts is dull greyish-olive. Forehead, lore, and a line behind the eye, black. A semilunar band of the same on the top of the head, the middle space vermilion. Wings and tail dusky, edged with greenish-yellow. Secondary coverts tipped with greyish-white. Under parts greyish-white.

Length 4¼ inches, extent of wings 6; bill along the ridge nearly ⅓, along the gap nearly ½; tarsus ⅞.

THE BROAD-LEAVED KALMIA, OR LAUREL.

KALMIA LATIFOLIA, *Willd.* Sp. Pl. vol. ii. p. 600. *Pursh*, Fl. Amer. vol. L p. 296.—
DECANDRIA MONOGYNIA, *Linn.* RHODODENDRA, *Juss.*

This beautiful species is characterized by its scattered, petiolate, elliptical leaves, which are smooth, and nearly of the same colour on both sides; and its terminal, viscid, and pubescent corymbs. It is a middle-sized shrub, sometimes attaining a height of eight or ten feet. The leaves are evergreen, as in the other species, and the flowers of a delicate pink.

KENTUCKY SPORTS.

IT may not be amiss, kind reader, before I attempt to give you some idea of the pleasures experienced by the sportsmen of Kentucky, to introduce the subject with a slight description of that State.

Kentucky was formerly attached to Virginia, but in those days the Indians looked upon that portion of the western wilds as their own, and abandoned the district only when forced to do so, moving with disconsolate hearts farther into the recesses of the unexplored forests. Doubtless the richness of its soil, and the beauty of its borders, situated as they are along one of the most beautiful rivers in the world, contributed as much to attract the Old Virginians, as the desire so generally experienced in America, of spreading over the uncultivated tracts, and bringing into cultivation lands that have for unknown ages teemed with the wild luxuriance of untamed nature. The conquest of Kentucky was not performed without many difficulties. The warfare that long existed between the intruders and the Redskins was sanguinary and protracted; but the former at length made good their footing, and the latter drew off their shattered bands, dismayed by the mental superiority and indomitable courage of the white men.

This region was probably discovered by a daring hunter, the renowned DANIEL BOON. The richness of its soil, its magnificent forests, its numberless navigable streams, its salt springs and licks, its saltpetre caves, its coal strata, and the vast herds of buffaloes and deer that browsed on its hills and amidst its charming valleys, afforded ample inducements to the new settler, who pushed forward with a spirit far above that of the most undaunted tribes, which for ages had been the sole possessors of the soil.

The Virginians thronged towards the Ohio. An axe, a couple of horses, and a heavy rifle, with store of ammunition, were all that were considered necessary for the equipment of the man, who, with his family, removed to the new State, assured that, in that land of exuberant fertility, he could not fail to provide amply for all his wants. To have witnessed the industry and perseverance of these emigrants, must at once have proved the vigour of their minds. Regardless of the fatigue attending every movement which they made, they pushed through an unexplored region of dark and tangled forests, guiding themselves by the sun alone, and reposing at night on the bare ground. Numberless streams they had to cross on rafts, with their wives and children, their cattle and their luggage, often drifting to considerable distances before they could effect a landing on the opposite shores. Their cattle would often stray amid the rice pasturage of these shores, and occasion a delay of several days. To these troubles add the constantly impending danger of being murdered, while asleep in their encampments, by the prowling and ruthless Indians; while they had before them a distance of hundreds of miles to be traversed, before they could reach certain places of rendezvous called *Stations.* To encounter difficulties like these must have required energies of no ordinary kind; and the reward which these veteran settlers enjoy was doubtless well merited.

Some removed from the Atlantic shores to those of the Ohio in more comfort and security. They had their waggons, their Negroes, and their families. Their way was cut through the woods by their own axemen, the day before their advance, and when night overtook them, the hunters attached to the party came to the place pitched upon for encamping, loaded with the dainties of which the forest yielded an abundant supply, the blazing light of a huge fire guiding their steps as they approached, and the sounds of merriment that saluted their ears assuring them that all was well. The flesh of the buffalo, the bear, and the deer, soon hung in large and delicious steaks, in front of the embers; the cakes already prepared were deposited in their proper places, and under the rich drippings of the juicy roasts, were quickly baked. The waggons contained the bedding, and whilst the horses which had drawn them were turned loose to feed on the luxuriant undergrowth of the woods, some perhaps hoppled, but the greater number, merely with a light bell hung to their neck, to guide their owners in the morning to the spot where they might have rambled, the party were enjoying themselves after the fatigues of the day.

In anticipation all is pleasure; and these migrating bands feasted in joyous sociality, unapprehensive of any greater difficulties than those to be encountered in forcing their way through the pathless woods to the land of abundance; and although it took months to accomplish the journey, and a skirmish now and then took place between them and the Indians, who sometimes crept unperceived into their very camp, still did the Virginians cheerfully proceed towards the western horizon, until the various groups all reached the Ohio, when, struck with the beauty of that magnificent stream, they at once commenced the task of clearing land, for the purpose of establishing a permanent residence.

Others, perhaps encumbered with too much luggage, preferred descending the stream. They prepared *arks* pierced with port-holes, and glided on the gentle current, more annoyed, however, than those who marched by land, by the attacks of the Indians, who watched their motions. Many travellers have described these boats, formerly called *arks*, but now named *flat-boats*. But have they told you, kind reader, that in those times a boat thirty or forty feet in length, by ten or twelve in breadth, was considered a stupendous fabric; that this boat contained men, women and children, huddled together, with horses, cattle, hogs and poultry for their companions, while the remaining portion was crammed with vegetables and packages of seeds? The roof or deck of the boat was not unlike a farm-yard, being covered with hay, ploughs, carts, waggons, and various agricultural implements, together with numerous others, among which the spinning-wheels of the matrons were conspicuous. Even the sides of the floating-mass were loaded with the wheels of the different vehicles, which themselves lay on the roof. Have they told you that these boats contained the little all of each family of venturous emigrants, who, fearful of being discovered by the Indians under night moved in darkness, groping their way from one part to another of these floating habitations, denying themselves the comfort of fire or light, lest the foe that watched them from the shore should rush upon them and destroy them? Have they told you that this boat was used, after the tedious voyage was ended, as the first dwelling of these new settlers? No, kind reader, such things have not been related to you before. The travellers who have visited our country, have had other objects in view.

I shall not describe the many massacres which took place among the different parties of White and Red men, as the former moved down the Ohio; because I have never been very fond of battles, and indeed have always wished that the world were more peaceably inclined than it is; and shall merely add, that, in one way or other, Kentucky was wrested from the original owners of the soil. Let us, therefore, turn our attention to the sports still enjoyed in that now happy portion of the United States.

We have individuals in Kentucky, kind reader, that even there are considered wonderful adepts in the management of the rifle. To *drive a nail* is a common feat, not more thought off by the Kentuckians than to cut off a wild turkey's head, at a distance of a hundred yards. Others will *bark* off squirrels one after another, until satisfied with the number procured. Some, less intent on destroying game, may be seen under night *snuffing a candle* at the distance of fifty yards, off-hand, without extinguishing it. I have been told that some have proved so expert and cool, as to make choice of the eye of a foe at a wonderful distance, boasting beforehand of the sureness of their piece, which has afterwards been fully proved when the enemy's head has been examined!

Having resided some years in Kentucky, and having more than once been witness of rifle sport, I shall present you with the results of my observation, leaving you to judge how far rifle-shooting is understood in that State.

Several individuals who conceive themselves expert in the management of the gun, are often seen to meet for the purpose of displaying their skill, and betting a trifling sum, put up a target, in the centre of which a common-sized nail is hammered for about two-thirds of its length. The marksmen make choice of what they consider a proper distance, which may be forty paces. Each man cleans the interior of his tube, which is called *wiping* it, places a ball in the palm of his hand, pouring as much powder from his horn upon it as will cover it. This quantity is supposed to be sufficient for any distance within a hundred yards. A shot which comes very close to the nail is considered as that of an indifferent marksman; the bending of the nail is, of course, somewhat better; but nothing less than hitting it right on the head is satisfactory. Well, kind reader, one out of three shots generally hits the nail, and should the shooters amount to half a dozen, two nails are frequently needed before each can have a shot. Those who drive the nail have a further trial amongst themselves, and the two best shots out of these generally settle the affair, when all the sportsmen adjourn to some house, and spend an hour or two in friendly intercourse, appointing, before they part, a day for another trial. This is technically termed *Driving the Nail.*

Barking off squirrels is delightful sport, and in my opinion requires a greater degree of accuracy than any other. I first witnessed this manner of procuring squirrels, whilst near the town of Frankfort. The performer was the celebrated DANIEL BOON. We walked out together, and followed the rocky margins of the Kentucky River, until we reached a piece of flat land thickly covered with black walnuts, oaks and hickories. As

the general mast was a good one that year, squirrels were seen gambolling on every tree around us.   My companion, a stout, hale, and athletic
man, dressed in a homespun hunting-shirt, bare-legged and moccasined,
carried a long and heavy rifle, which, as he was loading it, he said had
proved efficient in all his former undertakings, and which he hoped
would not fail on this occasion, as he felt proud to shew me his skill.
The gun was wiped, the powder measured, the ball patched with six-
hundred-thread linen, and the charge sent home with a hickory rod. We
moved not a step from the place, for the squirrels were so numerous that
it was unnecessary to go after them.   Boon pointed to one of these animals which had observed us, and was crouched on a branch about fifty
paces distant, and bade me mark well the spot where the ball should hit.
He raised his piece gradually, until the *bead* (that being the name given
by the Kentuckians to the *sight*) of the barrel was brought to a line with
the spot which he intended to hit.   The whip-like report resounded
through the woods and along the hills, in repeated echoes.   Judge of my
surprise, when I perceived that the ball had hit the piece of the bark
immediately beneath the squirrel, and shivered it into splinters, the con-
cussion produced by which had killed the animal, and sent it whirling
through the air, as if it had been blown up by the explosion of a powder
magazine. Boon kept up his firing, and, before many hours had elapsed,
we had procured as many squirrels as we wished ; for you must know,
kind reader, that to load a rifle requires only a moment, and that if it
is wiped once after each shot, it will do duty for hours.   Since that first
interview with our veteran Boon, I have seen many other individuals
perform the same feat.

The *snuffing of a candle* with a ball, I first had an opportunity of
seeing near the banks of Green River, not far from a large pigeon-roost,
to which I had previously made a visit.   I heard many reports of guns
during the early part of a dark night, and knowing them to be those of
rifles, I went towards the spot to ascertain the cause.   On reaching the
place, I was welcomed by a dozen of tall stout men, who told me they
were exercising, for the purpose of enabling them to shoot under night at
the reflected light from the eyes of a deer or wolf, by torch-light, of
which I shall give you an account somewhere else.   A fire was blazing
near, the smoke of which rose curling among the thick foliage of the
trees.   At a distance which rendered it scarcely distinguishable, stood a
burning candle, as if intended for an offering to the goddess of night, but

which in reality was only fifty yards from the spot on which we all stood. One man was within a few yards of it, to watch the effects of the shots, as well as to light the candle should it chance to go out, or to replace it should the shot cut it across. Each marksman shot in his turn. Some never hit either the snuff or the candle, and were congratulated with a loud laugh; while others actually snuffed the candle without putting it out, and were recompensed for their dexterity by numerous hurrahs. One of them, who was particularly expert, was very fortunate, and snuffed the candle three times out of seven, whilst all the other shots either put out the candle, or cut it immediately under the light.

Of the feats performed by the Kentuckians with the rifle, I could say more than might be expedient on the present occasion. In every thinly peopled portion of the State, it is rare to meet one without a gun of that description, as well as a tomahawk. By way of recreation, they often cut off a piece of the bark of a tree, make a target of it, using a little powder wetted with water or saliva, for the bull's eye, and shoot into the mark all the balls they have about them, picking them out of the wood again.

After what I have said, you may easily imagine with what ease a Kentuckian procures game, or dispatches an enemy, more especially when I tell you that every one in the State is accustomed to handle the rifle from the time when he is first able to shoulder it until near the close of his career. That murderous weapon is the means of procuring them subsistence during all their wild and extensive rambles, and is the source of their principal sports and pleasures.

RED-SHOULDERED HAWK.

FALCO LINEATUS, GMEL.

PLATE LVI. MALE AND FEMALE.

ALTHOUGH we are informed that a *skin* of this species has long ago
been described in Europe, we are, in the same breath, told that nothing
is known of the life and habits of the individual on the body of which it
once shone in all its native glossiness. Nothing, kind reader :—the tar-
nished coat only has been transmitted abroad ; and, like that belonging
to many equally interesting species of the feathered tribe, has been exposed for sale in distant markets, where the purchaser has felt as little
concern about the life of the individual to which it belonged, as purchasers
of another kind usually feel about the former owners of the thread-bare
vestments which we see offered for sale by the old-clothes'-men of St Giles's.
Even Mr ALEXANDER WILSON himself, knew nothing respecting the
habits of this species ; and as other authors, ranking equally high with
that pleasing writer, have unwittingly confounded it with another species,
known in the United States by the name of the *Winter Hawk*, it is with
satisfaction that I find myself in some degree qualified to give an account
of the differences of *habit* between the two species.

The *Red-shouldered Hawk*, or, as I would prefer calling it, the *Red-
breasted Hawk*, although dispersed over the greater part of the United
States, is rarely observed in the Middle Districts, where, on the contrary,
the *Winter Falcon* usually makes its appearance from the north, at the
approach of every autumn, and is of more common occurrence. Kentucky, Tennessee, and other Western States, with the most Southern
Districts of our Union, are apparently best adapted for the constant residence of the Red-shouldered Hawk, as in all these latter districts it is met
with in greater numbers than in any other.

This bird is one of the most noisy of its genus, during spring especially, when it would be difficult to approach the skirts of woods bordering
a large plantation without hearing its discordant shrill notes, *ka-hee, ka-hee,*
as it is seen sailing in rapid circles at a very great elevation. Its ordinary flight is even and protracted, excepting when it is describing the

circles just mentioned, when it often dives and gambols. It is a more general inhabitant of the woods than most of our other species, particularly during the summer, and in autumn and winter; now and then only, in early spring, shewing itself in the open grounds, and about the vicinity of small lakes, for the purpose of securing Red-winged Starlings and wounded Ducks.

The interior of woods seems, as I have said, the fittest haunts for the Red-shouldered Hawk. He sails through them a few yards above the ground, and suddenly alights on the low branch of a tree, or the top of a dead stump, from which he silently watches, in an erect posture, for the appearance of squirrels, upon which he pounces directly and kills them in an instant, afterwards devouring them on the ground. If accidentally discovered, he essays to remove the squirrel, but finding this difficult, he drags it partly through the air and partly along the ground, to some short distance, until he conceives himself out of sight of the intruder, when he again commences feeding. The eating of a whole squirrel, which this bird often devours at one meal, so gorges it, that I have seen it in this state almost unable to fly, and with such an extraordinary protuberance on its breast as seemed very unnatural, and very injurious to the beauty of form which the bird usually displays. On all occasions, such as I have described, when the bird is so gorged, it is approached with the greatest ease. On the contrary, when it is in want of food, it requires the greatest caution to get within shooting distance of it.

At the approach of spring, this species begins to pair, and its flight is accompanied with many circlings and zigzag motions, during which it emits its shrill cries. The male is particularly noisy at this time. He gives chase to all other Hawks, returns to the branch on which his mate has chanced to perch, and caresses her. This happens about the beginning of March. The spot adapted for a nest is already fixed upon, and the fabric is half finished. The top of a tall tree appears to be preferred by this Hawk, as I have found its nest more commonly placed there, not far from the edges of woods bordering plantations. The nest is seated in the forks of a large branch, towards its extremity, and is as bulky as that of the Common Crow. It is formed externally of dry sticks and Spanish moss, and is lined with withered grass and fibrous roots of different sorts, arranged in a circular manner. The female usually lays four eggs, sometimes five. They are of a broad oval form, granulated all over, pale blue, faintly blotched with brownish-red at the smaller end.

When one ascends to the nest, which, by the way, is not always an easy matter, as our Beech-trees are not only very smooth, but frequently without any boughs to a considerable distance from the ground, as well as of rather large size, the female bird, if she happens to be sitting, flies off silently and alights on a neighbouring tree, to wait the result. But, should the male, who supplies her with food, and assists in incubation, be there, or make his appearance, he immediately sets up a hue and cry, and plunges towards the assailant with such violence as to astonish him. When, on several occasions, I have had the tree on which the nest was placed cut down, I have observed the same pair, a few days after, build another nest on a tree not far distant from the spot in which the first one had been.

The mutual attachment of the male and the female continues during life. They usually hunt in pairs during the whole year; and although they build a new nest every spring, they are fond of resorting to the same parts of the woods for that purpose. I knew the pair represented in the Plate for three years, and saw their nest each spring placed within a few hundred yards of the spot in which that of the preceding year was.

The young remain in the nest until fully fledged, and are fed by the parents for several weeks after they have taken to wing, but leave them and begin to shift for themselves in about a month, when they disperse and hunt separately until the approach of the succeeding spring, at which time they pair. The young birds acquire the rusty reddish colour of the feathers on the breast and shoulders before they leave the nest. It deepens gradually at the approach of autumn, and by the first spring they completely resemble the old birds. Only one brood is raised each season. Scarcely any difference of size exists between the sexes, the female being merely a little stouter.

This Hawk seldom attacks any kind of poultry, and yet frequently pounces on Partridges, Doves, or Wild Pigeons, as well as Red-winged Starlings, and now and then very young rabbits. On one or two occasions, I have seen them make their appearance at the report of my gun, and try to rob me of some Blue-winged Teals shot in small ponds. I have never seen them chase any other small birds than those mentioned, or quadrupeds of smaller size than the *Cotton Rat*; nor am I aware of their eating frogs, which are the common food of the Winter Falcon, an account of which you will find, kind reader, in another part of this the first volume of my Biography of the Birds found in the United States of America.

FALCO LINEATUS, *Gmel.* Syst. Nat. vol. i. p. 268.—*Lath.* Synops. vol. i. p. 27.— *Wils.*
Amer. Ornith. vol. vi. p. 86. Pl. 53, fig. 3. Young Male.
FALCO HYEMALIS, *Ch. Bonaparte,* Synops. of Birds of the United States, p. 33.

Adult Male. Plate LVI. Fig. 1.

Bill short, as broad as deep, the sides convex, the dorsal outline convex from the base ; upper mandible cerate, the edges blunt, slightly inflected, with an obtuse lobe towards the curvature, the tip trigonal, deflected, very acute ; lower mandible involute at the edges, a little truncate at the end. Nostrils round, lateral, with a soft papilla in the centre. Head rather large. Neck and body rather slender. Legs longish ; tarsus rather slender, anteriorly scutellate ; toes scutellate above, scaly on the sides, scabrous and tuberculate beneath ; middle and outer toe connected at the base by a small membrane ; claws roundish, slender, curved, very acute.

Plumage compact, imbricated ; feathers of the head and neck narrow towards the tip, of the back broad and rounded ; tibial feathers elongated behind. Wings long, third and fourth primaries longest, first short.

Bill light blue at the base, bluish-black at the tip ; cere, basal margin of the bill, edges of the eyelids, and the feet, bright yellow. Iris hazel. Claws black. Head, neck, and back, light yellowish-red, longitudinally spotted with dark brown. Tail brownish-black, banded with greyish-white, the tip of the latter colour. Lesser wing-coverts bright yellowish-red, spotted with brown ; larger coverts and secondary quills dusky, broadly barred with white ; primary quills brownish-black banded with white, the greater part of their inner webs being of the latter colour. Lower parts of the neck and under wing-coverts light yellowish-red, the former longitudinally lined with blackish ; breast reddish-white, marked with transverse hastate yellowish-red spots ; abdomen and under tail-coverts reddish-white. Tibial feathers yellowish, transversely barred with dull orange.

Length 18 inches ; bill along the back $1\frac{1}{4}$, along the gap from the tip of under mandible $1\frac{1}{4}$; tarsus $2\frac{3}{4}$.

Adult Female. Plate LVI. Fig. 1.

The female differs from the male in being a little larger, and in having the tints lighter.

THE LOGGERHEAD SHRIKE.

LANIUS LUDOVICIANUS, LINN.

PLATE LVII. MALE AND FEMALE.

THIS species may with great propriety be called an inhabitant of the
" Low Countries," as it is seldom or never met with even in the vicinity
of the mountains intersecting the districts in which it usually resides. It
is also confined to that portion of our country usually known under the
name of the Southern States, seldom reaching farther eastward than
North Carolina, or farther inland than the State of Mississippi, in which
latter, as well as in Louisiana, it appears only during the winter months.
Its residence may, therefore, be looked upon as confined to the Floridas,
Georgia, and the Carolinas. In these States, it is seen along the fences
and bushes about the rice plantations, at all seasons, and is of some service to the planter, as it destroys the field-mice in great numbers, as well
as many of the larger kinds of grubs and insects, upon which it pounces
in the manner of a Hawk.

The Loggerhead has no song, but utters a shrill clear creaking prolonged note, resembling the grating of a rusty hinge slowly moved to
and fro. This sound is heard only during the spring season, and whilst
the female is sitting. About the beginning of March these birds begin
to pair. They exhibit at this time few of those marks of the tender
affection which birds usually shew. The male courts the female without
much regard, and she, in return, appears to receive his haughty attentions
with merely just as much condescension as enables her to become the
mother of a family, whose feelings are destined to be of the same cold
nature.

The nest is fixed in a low bush, generally near the centre of a dwarf
hawthorn, and is so little concealed as to be easily discovered. It is
coarsely constructed of dry crooked twigs, and is lined with fibrous roots
and slender grasses. The eggs, which are of a greenish white, are from
three to five. Incubation is performed by the male as well as by the female, but each searches for its own food during the intervals of sitting.

The young are at first fed on crickets, grasshoppers, and other insects; but as they become larger and stronger, they receive portions of

mice, which form the principal food of the grown birds at all seasons. The Loggerheads rear only one brood in the season.

Whilst this species is on wing, its motions are very rapid and direct, its flight being produced by quick flutterings of the wings, without any apparent undulation. The bird alights in a sudden firm manner, like a Hawk, stands erect, silent and watchful, until it spies its prey on the ground, when it suddenly pounces upon it, striking it first *with its bill*, but seizing it with its claws so immediately after, that the most careful observation alone can enable one to decide as to the priority of either action. I have never seen it attack birds, nor stick its prey on thorns in the manner of the Great American Shrike.

This bird appears in Louisiana only at intervals, and seldom remains more than a few weeks in December or January. It never comes near houses, although it frequents the fields around them. It has no note at this period, and appears singly, alighting on the stacks and fences, where it stands perched for a considerable time, carefully looking around over the ground. As soon as the spot is thoroughly examined, it flies off to another, and there renews its search.

I have given you, kind reader, the representation of a pair of these Shrikes, contending for a mouse. The difference of plumage in the sexes is scarcely perceptible; but I have thought it necessary to figure both, in order to shew the quarrelsome disposition of these birds even when united by the hymeneal band.

LANIUS LUDOVICIANUS, *Linn.* Syst. Nat. vol. i. p. 134.—*Ch. Bonaparte*, Synops. of Birds of the United States, p. 72.

LOGGERHEAD SHRIKE, LANIUS CAROLINENSIS, *Wils.* Amer. Ornith. vol. iii. p. 57. Pl. 22. fig. 8.

Adult Male. Plate LVII. Fig. 1.

Bill of moderate length, straightish, robust, acute, compressed; upper mandible with the dorsal outline a little arched, the tip declinate, the edges acute and overlapping, with a sharp process near the tip; lower mandible with the dorsal line a little convex, the tip acute and ascending. Nostrils basal, lateral, half closed by an arched membrane. Head large. Neck and body robust. Feet of ordinary length; tarsus scutellate before, acute behind; toes free, the lateral ones nearly equal; claws arched, compressed, acute.

Plumage soft, blended. Long bristly feathers at the base of the bill. Wings of ordinary length, curved, the second quill longest, the first and fifth equal. Tail long, graduated, of twelve rounded feathers.

Bill black. Iris dark brown. Feet greyish-black. The general colour of the upper parts is dark grey, of the under greyish-white, the sides tinged with brown. Forehead and sides of the head included in a broad black band. Wings and tail black. Base of the primaries, and tips of the secondaries and six inner primaries, white. Tail-feathers, excepting the four middle ones, white towards the end, the outer ones nearly all of that colour.

Length 8½ inches, extent of wings 13 ; bill along the ridge $\frac{7}{12}$, along the gap nearly 1 ; tarsus 1, middle toe $\frac{1}{2}$.

Adult Female. Plate LVII. Fig. 2.

The female differs from the male only in being a little smaller and somewhat darker and duller in the plumage.

THE GREEN BRIAR, OR ROUND-LEAVED SMILAX.

SMILAX ROTUNDIFOLIA, *Willd.* Sp. Pl. vol. iv. p. 779. *Pursh*, Flor. Amer. vol. I. p. 250.—DIŒCIA HEXANDRIA, *Linn.* ASPARAGI, *Juss.*

This species of Smilax, which is common along fences, in old fields, and by the borders of woods, is characterized by its shrubby stem, round branches, roundish-ovate, acuminate, slightly cordate, five or seven-nerved leaves, and spherical berries. It flowers in May and June. The berries are of a dark purple colour.

THE FIELD MOUSE.

This species is found in all parts of the United States, living in the meadows and woods. It forms narrow subterranean passages, to which it resorts on the least appearance of danger, but from which it is easily driven, by thrusting a twig into them.

THE HERMIT THRUSH.

TURDUS MINOR, GMEL.

PLATE LVIII. MALE AND FEMALE.

THIS, kind reader, is another constant resident in the Southern States, more especially those of Mississippi and Louisiana, where it abounds during the winter months, and is found in considerable numbers during spring and summer. In the lower parts of Kentucky, Indiana and Tennessee, it is also observed during spring and summer; but it becomes scarcer as you advance towards the Middle Districts, where a few are occasionally seen about the low woodlands of the Atlantic shores.

Except during winter, this Thrush prefers the darkest, most swampy, and most secluded cane-brakes along the margins of the Mississippi, where it breeds and spends the summer, retiring to higher lands during the period when the alluvial grounds are covered with the water which, during freshets, generally inundates these low cane-brakes and swampy retreats.

The flight of the Hermit Thrush is performed low over the ground, and in a gliding manner, as the bird shifts from one place to another at a short distance. In this respect, it differs greatly from its relative, my great favourite, the Wood Thrush, the flight of which is more protracted, and is performed at a greater elevation.

The Hermit Thrush has no song, and only utters a soft plaintive note, seldom heard at a greater distance than twenty-five or thirty yards. It is most frequently seen on the ground, where it hops with the same movements employed by the well-known little *Red-breast* of Europe, in other words, before it hops its breast almost comes in contact with the ground, the tail is a little raised, the wings droop, and after hopping, it runs a few steps, erects its head, and looks around.

All the nests of the Hermit Thrush which I have found were in every instance placed lower on the branches of trees than those of the Wood Thrush, seldom above seven or eight feet from the ground, and sometimes so low that I could easily look into them. These nests were fixed to a horizontal bough, but were not *saddled* upon it so deeply as those of the Wood Thrush are. They were smaller, and had no mud or plaster of any kind, but were extremely compact, the outer parts being formed of coarse dry weeds, and here and there a withered leaf, the interior composed of a long delicate kind of grass, which is found growing along the edges of cane-brakes.. This grass is arranged in a circular manner, to the whole extent of its length, and gives the inner part of the nest of this bird a remarkable appearance of neatness and finish. The female lays from four to six eggs, of a light blue colour, sprinkled with dark dots towards the large end. The first set are laid early in April, the second about the middle of June; for, in Lower Louisiana, this species rears two broods in the year. The female is much attached to her nest, and glides off silently from it when closely approached, not, however, unless she thinks herself or her nest observed. The young run after the parents, on the ground, for several days after they leave the nest.

As soon as the waters of the Mississippi become so swelled as to over-flow the banks, the Hermit Thrush retires to the nearest hills, and mixes with many other birds, amongst which the Wood Thrush is pre-eminent. The former is, however, easily recognised at once, by its single plaintive note, heard from the boughs of low trees, on the berries of which it feeds. In fact, its food is altogether composed of different fruits and berries, which are at all seasons abundant in our woods.

The branches so thickly covered with dull red berries, and upon which two Hermit Thrushes are seen, belong to a shrub which grows in the swampy recesses preferred by these birds. Its leaves fall off at an early period, and are of an ovato-lanceolate form, thin consistence, and deep green colour, their under surface light grey. The common name of it is *Robin Wood*. It seldom grows taller than from seven to eight feet, and all the branches, in a favourable season, are thickly covered with the berries, on which many birds, besides the *Turdus migratorius*, from which it seems to have derived its common name, are seen to feed.

TURDUS MINOR, *Gmel.* Syst. Nat. vol. i. p. 809.—*Ch. Bonaparte*, Synops. of Birds of
the United States, p. 75.—*Lath.* Ind. Ornith. vol. i. p 328.

LITTLE THRUSH, *Lath.* Synops. vol. iii. p. 20.

HERMIT THRUSH, TURDUS SOLITARIUS, *Wils.* Amer. Ornith. vol. v. p. 95, Pl. 4S.
fig. 2.

Adult Male.   Plate LVIII. Fig. 1.

Bill of ordinary length, nearly straight, compressed towards the end; upper mandible with the dorsal outline a little convex, the tip slightly declinate, the margins acute, inflected towards the end, slightly notched close upon the tip; lower mandible slightly convex in its dorsal line, the tip rather obtuse. Head of ordinary size; neck and body rather slender. Feet rather long; tarsus longish, compressed, slender, anteriorly covered with a few elongated, indistinct scutella, posteriorly edged, longer than the middle toe; toes scutellate above, lateral ones almost equal, the outer connected as far as the second joint.

Plumage rather loose. A few longish bristles at the base of the upper mandible. Wings of ordinary length, the third quill longest, the first very short. Tail rather short, even, of twelve broad feathers, the shaft of which projects a little beyond the extremity of the webs, as is the case with the outer primaries.

Bill dark brown, yellowish towards the base of the lower mandible. Iris hazel. Feet flesh-colour. The general colour of the upper parts is light yellowish-brown, changing on the rump and tail into dull yellowish-red. Quills dusky, margined externally with yellowish-brown. Primary coverts yellowish-brown, dusky at the end; secondary coverts tipped with yellowish-red. Under parts greyish-white, the neck and breast spotted with dark brown.

Length 7 inches, extent of wings $10\frac{1}{2}$; bill along the ridge $\frac{7}{12}$, along the gap $\frac{6}{8}$; tarsus $1\frac{1}{8}$.

Adult Female. Plate LVIII. Fig. 2.

The female differs only in having the spots on the breast somewhat larger, and the tints of the upper parts rather deeper.

U

THE CHESTNUT-SIDED WARBLER.

SYLVIA ICTEROCEPHALA, LATH.

PLATE LIX. MALE AND FEMALE.

In the beginning of May 1808, I shot five of these birds, on a very cold morning, near Potts-grove, in the State of Pennsylvania. There was a slight fall of snow at the time, although the Peach and Apple trees were already in full bloom. I have never met with a single individual of this species since. They all had their wings drooping, as if suffering severely from the sudden change of the weather, and had betaken themselves to the lower rails of a fence, where they were engaged in searching after insects, particularly spiders. I procured every one of those which I met with that morning, and which were five in number, two of them males, and the rest females.

Where this species goes to breed I am unable to say, for to my inquiries on this subject I never received any answers which might have led me to the districts resorted to by it. I can only suppose, that if it is at all plentiful in any portion of the United States, it must be far to the northward, as I ransacked the borders of Lake Ontario, and those of Lakes Erie and Michigan, without meeting with it. I do not know of any naturalist who has been more fortunate, otherwise I should here quote his observations.

The females had the ovaries furnished with numerous eggs, about the size of the head of a common pin. The stomach of all the birds which I killed contained some grass seeds of the preceding year, and a few small black spiders; but the birds appeared half-starved. Having procured them near the ground, I have placed them on a plant which grows about the fields, and flowers in the beginning of May.

SYLVIA ICTEROCEPHALA, *Lath.* Ind. Ornith. vol. ii. p. 538.—*Ch. Bonaparte*, Synops. of Birds of the United States, p. 80.

MOTACILLA ICTEROCEPHALA, *Linn.* Syst. Nat. vol. i. p. 334.

QUEBEC WARBLER, *Lath.* Synops. vol. iv. p. 484.

CHESTNUT-SIDED WARBLER, *Wils.* Amer. Ornith. vol. i. p. 99. Pl. 14. fig. 5.

Adult Male. Plate LIX. Fig. 1.

Bill of ordinary length, nearly straight, subulato-conical, acute, nearly as deep as broad at the base, the edges acute, the gap-line slightly deflected at the base, Nostrils basal, lateral, elliptical, half-closed by a membrane. Head of ordinary size. Neck short. Body slender. Feet of ordinary length, slender; tarsus longer than the middle toe, covered anteriorly by a few scutella, acutely edged behind; toes scutellate above, the inner free, the hind toe of moderate size; claws slender, compressed, acute, arched.

Plumage soft, blended, tufty. Wings of ordinary length, acute, the second quill longest. Tail short, slightly notched.

Bill light blue, blackish above. Iris hazel. Feet dusky. Forehead white; upper part of the head bright yellow. Loral space, and two lines proceeding from it, one over and behind the eye, the other downwards, black. Back dusky green, spotted with black, as are the lesser wing-coverts, the larger broadly tipped with bright yellow, excepting those of the primary quills, which are dusky. Primaries dusky, edged externally with light blue, as is the tail. Under parts white; side of the lower neck and body under the wings deep chestnut.

Length $5\frac{1}{4}$ inches, extent of wings 8; bill along the ridge $\frac{4}{12}$, along the gap $\frac{7}{12}$; tarsus $\frac{3}{4}$.

Adult Female. Plate LIX. Fig. 2.

The female is considerably smaller, but is coloured nearly in the same manner as the male. The chestnut patch on the sides is of less extent, and the primaries are yellow, instead of blue, on their outer webs.

THE MOTH MULLEIN.

VERBASCUM BLATTARIA, *Willd.* Sp. Pl. vol. i. p. 1006. *Pursh.* Flor. Amer. vol. i. p. 142, *Smith.* Engl. Flor. vol. i. p. 513.—PENTANDRIA MONOGYNIA, *Linn.* SoLANEÆ, *Juss.*

A biennial plant, distinguished from the other species of the same genus by its amplexicaul ovato-oblong, rugose, serrated, glabrous leaves, and one-flowered solitary pedicels. The ordinary colour of the flowers is yellow, but the plant represented is of a variety with larger whitish or pale rose-coloured flowers. It grows in fields and by roads, and is of common occurrence.

THE CARBONATED WARBLER.

SYLVIA CARBONATA.

PLATE LX. MALE.

I shot the two little birds here represented, near the village of Henderson, in the State of Kentucky, in May 1811. They were both busily engaged in searching for insects along the branches and amongst the leaves of a Dog-wood tree. Their motions were those common to all the species of the genus *Sylvia*. On examination, they were found to be both males. I am of opinion, that they were both young birds of the preceding year, and not in full plumage, as they had no part of their dress seemingly complete, excepting the head. Not having met with any other individuals of the species, I am at this moment unable to say any thing more about them. They were drawn, like all the other birds which I have represented, immediately after being killed; but the branch on which you see them was not added until the following summer.

The common name of this plant is *Service Tree*. It seldom attains a greater height than thirty or forty feet, and is usually found in hilly ground of secondary quality. The berries are agreeable to the taste, and are sought after by many species of birds, amongst which the Red-headed Woodpecker is very conspicuous.

SYLVIA CARBONATA.

Young Male. Plate LX.

Bill of ordinary length, nearly straight, subulato-conical, acute, nearly as deep as broad at the base, the edges acute, the gap line slightly deflected at the base. Nostrils basal, lateral, elliptical, half-closed by a membrane. Head rather small. Neck short. Body slender. Feet of ordinary length, slender; tarsus longer than the middle toe, covered anteriorly by a few scutella, acutely-edged behind; toes scutellate above, the inner free, the hind toe of moderate size; claws slender, compressed, acute, arched.

Plumage, soft, blended, tufty. Wings of ordinary length, acute, the second quill longest. Tail short, notched.

Bill brownish-black above, light blue beneath. Iris hazel. Feet light flesh-colour. Upper part of the head black. Fore part of the back, lesser wing-coverts and sides dusky, spotted with black. Lower back dull yellowish-green, as is the tail, of which the outer web of the outer feather is whitish. Tips of the second row of coverts white, of the first row yellow; quills dusky, their outer webs tinged with yellow. A line from the lore over the eye, sides of the neck, and the throat, bright yellow. A dusky line behind the eye. The rest of the under parts dull yellow, excepting the sides.

Length 4¾ inches; bill along the ridge $\frac{5}{12}$, along the gap $\frac{7}{12}$; tarsus ¾.

THE MAY-BUSH OR SERVICE.

PYRUS BOTRYAPIUM, *Willd.* Sp. Pl. vol. ii. p. 1013. *Pursh,* Flor. Amer. vol. i. p. 339.
ICOSANDRIA PENTAGYNIA, *Linn.* ROSACEÆ, *Juss.*

This species is distinguished by its ovate, acuminate leaves, racemose flowers, linear-lanceolate petals, pubescent germens, and smooth calycine segments.

THE TRAVELLER AND THE POLE-CAT.

On a journey from Louisville to Henderson in Kentucky, performed during very severe winter weather, in company with a foreigner, the initials of whose name are D. T., my companion spying a beautiful animal, marked with black and pale yellow, and having a long and bushy tail, exclaimed, " Mr AUDUBON, is not that a beautiful squirrel ?" " Yes," I answered, " and of a kind that will suffer you to approach it, and lay hold of it, if you are well gloved." Mr D. T. dismounting, took up a dry stick, and advanced toward the pretty animal, with his large cloak floating in the breeze. I think I see him approach, and laying the stick gently across the body of the animal, try to secure it; and I can yet laugh almost as heartily as I then did, when I plainly saw the discomfiture of the traveller. The Pole-cat, (for a true Pole-cat it was, the *Mephitis americana* of zoologists), raised its fine bushy tail, and showered such a discharge of the fluid given him by nature as a defence, that my friend, dismayed and infuriated, began to belabour the poor animal. The swiftness and good management of the Pole-cat, however, saved its bones, and as it made its retreat towards its hole, it kept up at every step a continued ejectment, which fully convinced the gentleman that the pursuit of such squirrels as these was at the best an unprofitable employment.

This was not all, however. I could not suffer his approach, nor could my horse; it was with difficulty he mounted his own; and we were forced to continue our journey far asunder, and he much to leeward. Nor did the matter end here. We could not proceed much farther that night; as, in the first place, it was nearly dark when we saw the Pole-cat, and as, in the second place, a heavy snow-storm began, and almost impeded our progress. We were forced to make for the first cabin we saw. Having asked and obtained permission to rest for the night, we dismounted and found ourselves amongst a crowd of men and women who had met for the purpose of *corn-shucking*.

To a European who has not visited the western parts of the United States, an explanation of this corn-shucking may not be unacceptable.

Corn (or you may prefer calling it maize) is gathered in the husk, that is, by breaking each large ear from the stem. These ears are first thrown into heaps in the field, and afterwards carried in carts to the barn, or, as in this instance, and in such portions of Kentucky, to a shed made of the blades or long leaves that hang in graceful curves from the stalk, and which, when plucked and dried, are used instead of hay as food for horses and cattle. The husk consists of several thick leaves rather longer than the corn-ear itself, and which secure it from the weather. It is quite a labour to detach these leaves from the ear, when thousands of bushels of the corn are gathered and heaped together. For this purpose, however, and in the western country more especially, several neighbouring families join alternately at each other's plantations, and assist in clearing away the husks, thus preparing the maize for the market or for domestic use.

The good people whom we met with at this hospitable house, were on the point of going to the barn (the farmer here being in rather good condition) to work until towards the middle of the night. When we had stood the few stares to which strangers must accustom themselves, no matter where, even in a drawing-room, we approached the fire. What a shock for the whole party! The scent of the Pole-cat, that had been almost stifled on my companion's vestments by the cold of the evening air, now recovered its primitive strength. The cloak was put out of the house, but its owner could not be well used in the same way. The company, however, took to their heels, and there only remained a single black servant, who waited on us until supper was served.

I felt vexed at myself, as I saw the good traveller displeased. But he had so much good breeding as to treat this important affair with great forbearance, and merely said he was sorry for his want of knowledge in zoology. The good gentleman, however, was not only deficient in zoological lore, but, fresh as he was from Europe, felt more than uneasy in this out-of-the-way house, and would have proceeded towards my own house that night, had I not at length succeeded in persuading him that he was in perfect security.

We were shewn to bed. As I was almost a stranger to him, and he to me, he thought it a very awkward thing to be obliged to lie in the same bed with me, but afterwards spoke of it as a happy circumstance, and requested that I should suffer him to be placed next the logs, thinking, no doubt, that there he should run no risk.

We started by break of day, taking with us the frozen cloak, and after passing a pleasant night in my own house, we parted.   Some years after, I met my Kentucky companion in a far distant land, when he assured me, that whenever the sun shone on his cloak, or it was brought near a fire, the scent of the Pole-cat became so perceptible, that he at last gave it to a poor monk in Italy.

The animal commonly known in America by the name of Pole-cat is about a foot and a half in length, with a large bushy tail, nearly as long as the body.   The colour is generally brownish-black, with a large white patch on the back of the head; but there are many varieties of colouring, in some of which the broad white bands of the back are very conspicuous.   The Pole-cat burrows, or forms a subterranean habitation among the roots of trees, or in rocky places.   It feeds on birds, young hares, rats, mice, and other animals, and commits great depredations on poultry.   The most remarkable peculiarity of this animal is the power, alluded to above, of squirting for its defence a most nauseously scented fluid contained in a receptacle situated under the tail, which it can do to the distance of several yards.   It does not, however, for this purpose, sprinkle its tail with the fluid, as some allege, unless when extremely harassed by its enemies.   The Pole-cat is frequently domesticated.   The removal of the glands prevents the secretion of the nauseous fluid, and when thus improved, the animal becomes a great favourite, and performs the offices of the common cat with great dexterity.

THE GREAT HORNED OWL.

STRIX VIRGINIANA, GMEL.

PLATE LXI. MALE AND FEMALE.

IT is during the placid serenity of a beautiful summer night, when the current of the waters moves silently along, reflecting from its smooth surface the silver radiance of the moon, and when all else of animated nature seems sunk in repose, that the Great Horned Owl, one of the Nimrods of the feathered tribes of our forests, may be seen sailing silently and yet rapidly on, intent on the destruction of the objects destined to form his food. The lone steersman of the descending boat observes the nocturnal hunter, gliding on extended pinions across the river, sailing over one hill and then another, or suddenly sweeping downwards, and again rising in the air like a moving shadow, now distinctly seen, and again mingling with the sombre shades of the surrounding woods, fading into obscurity. The bark has now floated to some distance, and is opposite the newly cleared patch of ground, the result of a squatter's first attempt at cultivation, in a place lately shaded by the trees of the forest. The moon shines brightly on his hut, his slight fence, the newly planted orchard, and a tree, which, spared by the axe, serves as a roosting-place for the scanty stock of poultry which the new comer has procured from some liberal neighbour. Amongst them rests a Turkey-hen, covering her offspring with extended wings. The Great Owl, with eyes keen as those of any falcon, is now seen hovering above the place. He has already espied the quarry, and is sailing in wide circles meditating his plan of attack. The Turkey-hen, which at another time might be sound asleep, is now, however, so intent on the care of her young brood, that she rises on her legs and purs so loudly, as she opens her wings and spreads her tail, that she rouses her neighbours, the hens, together with their protector. The cacklings which they at first emit soon become a general clamour. The squatter hears the uproar, and is on his feet in an instant, rifle in hand ; the priming examined, he gently pushes open his half closed door, and peeps out cautiously, to ascertain the cause by which his repose has been disturbed. He observes the murderous Owl just alighting on the dead branch of a tall tree, when, raising his never-failing

rifle, he takes aim, touches the trigger, and the next instant sees the foe
falling dead to the ground.   The bird is unworthy of his farther attention, and is left a prey to some prowling opossum or other carnivorous
quadruped. Again, all around is tranquillity. In this manner falls
many a Great Horned Owl on our frontiers, where the species abounds.

Differences of locality are no security against its depredations, for it
occurs in the highest mountainous districts, as well as in the low alluvial
lands that border the rivers, in the interior of the country, and in the
neighbourhood of the sea-shore. Every where it finds abundance of food.
It is, moreover, an extremely hardy bird, and stands the severest winters
of our northernmost latitudes. It is consequently found dispersed over
all parts of the United States.

The flight of the Great Horned Owl is elevated, rapid and graceful.
It sails with apparent ease, and in large circles, in the manner of an eagle,
rises and descends without the least difficulty, by merely inclining its
wings or its tail, as it passes through the air. Now and then, it glides
silently close over the earth, with incomparable velocity, and drops, as if
shot dead, on the prey beneath. At other times, it suddenly alights on
the top of a fence-stake or a dead stump, shakes its feathers, arranges
them, and utters a skriek so horrid that the woods around echo to its dismal sound. Now, it seems as if you heard the barking of a cur-dog;
again, the notes are so rough and mingled together, that they might be
mistaken for the last gurglings of a murdered person, striving in vain to
call for assistance; at another time, when not more than fifty yards distant, it utters its more usual *hoo, hoo, hoo-e*, in so peculiar an under tone,
that a person unacquainted with the notes of this species might easily
conceive them to be produced by an Owl more than a mile distant. During the utterance of all these unmusical cries, it moves its body, and
more particularly its head, in various ways, putting them into positions,
all of which appear to please it much, however grotesque they may seem
to the eye of man. In the interval following each cry, it snaps its bill,
as if by way of amusement; or, like the wild boar sharpening the edges
of his tusks, it perhaps expects that the action will whet its mandibles.

The food of the Great Horned Owl consists chiefly of the larger species of gallinaceous birds, half-grown Wild Turkeys, Pheasants, and domestic poultry of all kinds, together with several species of Ducks.
Hares, young Opossums and Squirrels are equally agreeable to it, and

whenever chance throws a dead fish on the shore, the Great Owl feeds with peculiar avidity on it.

It is one of the most common species along the shores of the Ohio and Mississippi, where it is to be met with at all seasons, being fond of roosting amongst the thick-growing young cotton-wood trees and willows, that cover the muddy sand-bars of these noble streams, as well as in the more retired woody swamps, where the gloomy cypress spreads its broad arms, covered with dangling masses of Spanish beard, which give way to the gentlest breeze. In both such situations I have frequently met with this owl: its body erect, its plumage closed, its tufted head-feathers partially lowered, and its head half turned and resting on one shoulder.

When the sun shines brightly, the bird is easily approached; but if the weather be cloudy, it rises on its feet, at the least noise, erects the tufts of its head, gives a knowing kind of nod, flies off in an instant, and generally proceeds to such a distance that it is difficult to find it again. When disturbed while at roost on willows near a river, it sails off low over the stream, as if aware that by so doing it renders its pursuit more difficult. I once nearly lost my life by going towards one that I had shot on a willow-bar, for, while running up to the spot, I suddenly found myself sunk in quicksand up to my arm-pits, and in this condition must have remained to perish, had not my boatmen come up and extricated me, by forming a bridge of their oars and some driftwood, during which operation I had to remain perfectly quiet, as any struggle would soon have caused me to sink overhead.

I have related this occurrence to you, kind reader,—and it is only one out of many,—to shew you that every student of nature must encounter some difficulties in obtaining the objects of his research, although these difficulties are little thought of when he has succeeded. So much is this the case with me, that, could I renew the lease of my life, I could not desire to spend it in any other pursuit than that which has at last enabled me to lay before you an account of the *habits* of our birds.

Early in February the Great Horned Owls are seen to pair. The curious evolutions of the male in the air, or his motions when he has alighted near his beloved, it is impossible to describe. His bowings, and the snappings of his bill, are extremely ludicrous; and no sooner is the female assured that the attentions paid her by the beau are the result of a sincere affection, than she joins in the motions of her future mate. At this juncture both might be said to be *dancing mad*, little dreaming, like most owls on such occasions, of the possibility of their being one day *horn-mad*.

The nest, which is very bulky, is usually fixed on a large horizontal branch, not far from the trunk of the tree. It is composed externally of crooked sticks, and is lined with coarse grasses and some feathers. The whole measures nearly three feet in diameter. The eggs, which are from three to six, are almost globular in form, and of a dull white colour. The male assists the female in sitting on the eggs. Only one brood is raised in the season. The young remain in the nest until fully fledged, and afterwards follow the parents for a considerable time, uttering a mournful sound, to induce them to supply them with food. They acquire the full plumage of the old birds in the first spring, and until then are considerably lighter, with more dull buff in their tints. I have found nests belonging to this species in large hollows of decayed trees, and twice in the fissures of rocks. In all these cases, little preparation had been made previous to the laying of the eggs, as I found only a few grasses and feathers placed under them.

The Great Horned Owl lives retired, and it is seldom that more than one is found in the neighbourhood of a farm, after the breeding season ; but as almost every detached farm is visited by one of these dangerous and powerful marauders, it may be said to be abundant. The havock which it commits is very great. I have known a plantation almost stripped of the whole of the poultry raised upon it during spring, by one of these daring foes of the feathered race, in the course of the ensuing winter.

This species is very powerful, and equally spirited. It attacks Wild Turkeys when half-grown, and often masters them. Mallards, Guinea-fowls, and common barn fowls, prove an easy prey, and on seizing them it carries them off in its talons from the farm-yards to the interior of the woods. When wounded, it exhibits a revengeful tenacity of spirit, scarcely surpassed by any of the noblest of the Eagle tribe, disdaining to scramble away like the Barred Owl, but facing its enemy with undaunted courage, protruding its powerful talons, and snapping its bill, as long as he continues in its presence. On these occasions, its large goggle eyes are seen to open and close in quick succession, and the feathers of its body, being raised, swell out its apparent bulk to nearly double the natural size.

You have before you, kind reader, a male and a female of this species, which I hope will give you a more perfect idea of the size and form of the Great Horned Owl than any description could do.

STRIX VIRGINIANA, *Gmel.* Syst. Nat. vol. i. p. 287.—*Lath.* Ind. Ornith. vol. i. p. 52.—
   Ch. Bonaparte, Synops. of Birds of the United States, p. 37.
VIRGINIAN EARED OWL, *Lath.* Synops. vol. i. p. 119.
GREAT HORNED OWL, STRIX VIRGINIANA, *Wilson,* Americ. Ornith. vol. vi. p. 52.
   Pl. 50. fig. 1.

Adult Male. Plate LXI. Fig. 1.

Bill short, compressed, curved, acute, with a cere at the base ; upper mandible with its dorsal outline curved from the base, the edges acute, the point trigonal, very acute, deflected ; lower mandible with the edges acute and inflected, obtuse at the tip. Nostrils oval, in the fore part of the cere. Head disproportionately large, as are the eyes and external ears. Body short. Legs of ordinary length ; tarsus and toes feathered ; toes papillar and tuberculate beneath ; claws curved, rounded, long, extremely sharp.

Plumage very soft and downy, somewhat distinct above, tufty and loose beneath. Long bristly feathers at the base of the bill, stretching forwards. Eyes surrounded by circles of compact feathers ; auricular coverts forming a ruff. Two erectile tufts of feathers on the head, one on each side. Wings ample, the fourth quill longest, the first short. Tail of ordinary length, rounded, of twelve broad feathers.

Bill black. Iris yellow. Claws black. Upper part of the head brownish-black, mottled with light brown, the tufts or horns of the same colour, margined with brown. Face brownish-red, with a circle of blackish-brown. The upper parts are undulatingly banded and minutely mottled with brownish-black and brownish-red, the ground colour on the lower part of the back tinged with grey. Wings and tail light brownish-yellow, barred and mottled with blackish-brown and light brownish-red. Chin white, upper part of the throat light reddish, spotted with black, a band of white across the middle of the fore neck ; lower fore neck and breast light yellowish-red, barred with deep brown, as are the under parts generally, some of the feathers being nearly white, but barred ; several longitudinal brownish-black patches on the lower fore neck ; tarsal feathers light yellowish-red, obscurely barred.

Length 23 inches; extent of wings 56; bill along the ridge 2; tufts on the head 3.

Adult Female.　Plate LXVI. Fig. 2.

The female is considerably larger than the male, and is duller and lighter in colouring, although the distribution of the tints is similar. The white of the chin is less pure, and the broad band of the same colour on the fore neck is wanting.

THE PASSENGER PIGEON.

COLUMBA MIGRATORIA, Linn.

PLATE LXII. Male and Female.

THE Passenger Pigeon, or, as it is usually named in America, the Wild Pigeon, moves with extreme rapidity, propelling itself by quickly repeated flaps of the wings, which it brings more or less near to the body, according to the degree of velocity which is required. Like the Domestic Pigeon, it often flies, during the love season, in a circling manner, supporting itself with both wings angularly elevated, in which position it keeps them until it is about to alight. Now and then, during these circular flights, the tips of the primary quills of each wing are made to strike against each other, producing a smart rap, which may be heard at a distance of thirty or forty yards. Before alighting, the Wild Pigeon, like the Carolina Parrot and a few other species of birds, breaks the force of its flight by repeated flappings, as if apprehensive of receiving injury from coming too suddenly into contact with the branch or the spot of ground on which it intends to settle.

I have commenced my description of this species with the above account of its flight, because the most important facts connected with its habits relate to its migrations. These are entirely owing to the necessity of procuring food, and are not performed with the view of escaping the severity of a northern latitude, or of seeking a southern one for the purpose of breeding. They consequently do not take place at any fixed period or season of the year. Indeed, it sometimes happens that a continuance of a sufficient supply of food in one district will keep these birds absent from another for years. I know, at least, to a certainty, that in Kentucky they remained for several years constantly, and were nowhere else to be found. They all suddenly disappeared one season when the mast was exhausted, and did not return for a long period. Similar facts have been observed in other States.

Their great power of flight enables them to survey and pass over an astonishing extent of country in a very short time. This is proved by facts well known in America. Thus, Pigeons have been killed in the neighbourhood of New York, with their crops full of rice, which they must have collected in the fields of Georgia and Carolina, these districts being the nearest in which they could possibly have procured a supply of that kind of food. As their power of digestion is so great that they will decompose food entirely in twelve hours, they must in this case have travelled between three hundred and four hundred miles in six hours, which shews their speed to be at an average about one mile in a minute. A velocity such as this would enable one of these birds, were it so inclined, to visit the European continent in less than three days.

This great power of flight is seconded by as great a power of vision, which enables them, as they travel at that swift rate, to inspect the country below, discover their food with facility, and thus attain the object for which their journey has been undertaken. This I have also proved to be the case, by having observed them, when passing over a sterile part of the country, or one scantily furnished with food suited to them, keep high in the air, flying with an extended front, so as to enable them to survey hundreds of acres at once. On the contrary, when the land is richly covered with food, or the trees abundantly hung with mast, they fly low, in order to discover the part most plentifully supplied.

Their body is of an elongated oval form, steered by a long well-plumed tail, and propelled by well-set wings, the muscles of which are very large and powerful for the size of the bird. When an individual is seen gliding through the woods and close to the observer, it passes like a thought, and on trying to see it again, the eye searches in vain; the bird is gone.

The multitudes of Wild Pigeons in our woods are astonishing. Indeed, after having viewed them so often, and under so many circumstances, I even now feel inclined to pause, and assure myself that what I am going to relate is fact. Yet I have seen it all, and that too in the company of persons who, like myself, were struck with amazement.

In the autumn of 1813, I left my house at Henderson, on the banks of the Ohio, on my way to Louisville. In passing over the Barrens a few miles beyond Hardensburgh, I observed the pigeons flying from north-east to south-west, in greater numbers than I thought I had ever seen them before, and feeling an inclination to count the flocks that might pass within the reach of my eye in one hour, I dismounted, seated myself on an eminence, and began to mark with my pencil, making a dot for every flock that passed. In a short time finding the task which I had undertaken impracticable, as the birds poured in in countless multitudes,

2

I rose, and counting the dots then put down, found that 163 had been made in twenty-one minutes. I travelled on, and still met more the farther I proceeded. The air was literally filled with Pigeons; the light of noon-day was obscured as by an eclipse; the dung fell in spots, not unlike melting flakes of snow; and the continued buzz of wings had a tendency to lull my senses to repose.

Whilst waiting for dinner at YOUNG's inn, at the confluence of Salt-River with the Ohio, I saw, at my leisure, immense legions still going by, with a front reaching far beyond the Ohio on the west, and the beech-wood forests directly on the east of me. Not a single bird alighted; for not a nut or acorn was that year to be seen in the neighbourhood. They consequently flew so high, that different trials to reach them with a capital rifle proved ineffectual; nor did the reports disturb them in the least. I cannot describe to you the extreme beauty of their aerial evolutions, when a Hawk chanced to press upon the rear of a flock. At once, like a torrent, and with a noise like thunder, they rushed into a compact mass, pressing upon each other towards the centre. In these almost solid masses, they darted forward in undulating and angular lines, descended and swept close over the earth with inconceivable velocity, mounted perpendicularly so as to resemble a vast column, and, when high, were seen wheeling and twisting within their continued lines, which then resembled the coils of a gigantic serpent.

Before sunset I reached Louisville, distant from Hardensburgh fifty-five miles. The Pigeons were still passing in undiminished numbers, and continued to do so for three days in succession. The people were all in arms. The banks of the Ohio were crowded with men and boys, incessantly shooting at the pilgrims, which there flew lower as they passed the river. Multitudes were thus destroyed. For a week or more, the population fed on no other flesh than that of Pigeons, and talked of nothing but Pigeons. The atmosphere, during this time, was strongly impregnated with the peculiar odour which emanates from the species.

It is extremely interesting to see flock after flock performing exactly the same evolutions which had been traced as it were in the air by a preceding flock. Thus, should a Hawk have charged on a group at a certain spot, the angles, curves, and undulations that have been described by the birds, in their efforts to escape from the dreaded talons of the plunderer, are undeviatingly followed by the next group that comes up. Should the bystander happen to witness one of these affrays, and, struck

x

with the rapidity and elegance of the motions exhibited, feel desirous of seeing them repeated, his wishes will be gratified if he only remain in the place until the next group comes up.

It may not, perhaps, be out of place to attempt an estimate of the number of Pigeons contained in one of those mighty flocks, and of the quantity of food daily consumed by its members. The inquiry will tend to shew the astonishing bounty of the great Author of Nature in providing for the wants of his creatures. Let us take a column of one mile in breadth, which is far below the average size, and suppose it passing over us without interruption for three hours, at the rate mentioned above of one mile in the minute. This will give us a parallelogram of 180 miles by 1, covering 180 square miles. Allowing two pigeons to the square yard, we have One billion, one hundred and fifteen millions, one hundred and thirty-six thousand pigeons in one flock. As every pigeon daily consumes fully half a pint of food, the quantity necessary for supplying this vast multitude must be eight millions seven hundred and twelve thousand bushels per day.

As soon as the Pigeons discover a sufficiency of food to entice them to alight, they fly round in circles, reviewing the country below. During their evolutions, on such occasions, the dense mass which they form exhibits a beautiful appearance, as it changes its direction, now displaying a glistening sheet of azure, when the backs of the birds come simultaneously into view, and anon, suddenly presenting a mass of rich deep purple. They then pass lower, over the woods, and for a moment are lost among the foliage, but again emerge, and are seen gliding aloft. They now alight, but the next moment, as if suddenly alarmed, they take to wing, producing by the flappings of their wings a noise like the roar of distant thunder, and sweep through the forests to see if danger is near. Hunger, however, soon brings them to the ground. When alighted, they are seen industriously throwing up the withered leaves in quest of the fallen mast. The rear ranks are continually rising, passing over the main-body, and alighting in front, in such rapid succession, that the whole flock seems still on wing. The quantity of ground thus swept is astonishing, and so completely has it been cleared, that the gleaner who might follow in their rear would find his labour completely lost. Whilst feeding, their avidity is at times so great that in attempting to swallow a large acorn or nut, they are seen gasping for a long while, as if in the agonies of suffocation.

On such occasions, when the woods are filled with these Pigeons, they are killed in immense numbers, although no apparent diminution ensues. About the middle of the day, after their repast is finished, they settle on the trees, to enjoy rest, and digest their food. On the ground they walk with ease, as well as on the branches, frequently jerking their beautiful tail, and moving the neck backwards and forwards in the most graceful manner. As the sun begins to sink beneath the horizon, they depart *en masse* for the roosting-place, which not unfrequently is hundreds of miles distant, as has been ascertained by persons who have kept an account of their arrivals and departures.

Let us now, kind reader, inspect their place of nightly rendezvous. One of these curious roosting-places, on the banks of the Green River in Kentucky, I repeatedly visited. It was, as is always the case, in a portion of the forest where the trees were of great magnitude, and where there was little underwood. I rode through it upwards of forty miles, and, crossing it in different parts, found its average breadth to be rather more than three miles. My first view of it was about a fortnight subsequent to the period when they had made choice of it, and I arrived there nearly two hours before sunset. Few Pigeons were then to be seen, but a great number of persons, with horses and waggons, guns and ammunition, had already established encampments on the borders. Two farmers from the vicinity of Russelsville, distant more than a hundred miles, had driven upwards of three hundred hogs to be fattened on the pigeons which were to be slaughtered. Here and there, the people employed in plucking and salting what had already been procured, were seen sitting in the midst of large piles of these birds. The dung lay several inches deep, covering the whole extent of the roosting-place, like a bed of snow. Many trees two feet in diameter, I observed, were broken off at no great distance from the ground ; and the branches of many of the largest and tallest had given way, as if the forest had been swept by a tornado. Every thing proved to me that the number of birds resorting to this part of the forest must be immense beyond conception. As the period of their arrival approached, their foes anxiously prepared to receive them. Some were furnished with iron-pots containing sulphur, others with torches of pine-knots, many with poles, and the rest with guns. The sun was lost to our view, yet not a Pigeon had arrived. Every thing was ready, and all eyes were gazing on the clear sky, which appeared in glimpses amidst the tall trees. Suddenly there burst forth

x 2

a general cry of " Here they come!" The noise which they made, though yet distant, reminded me of a hard gale at sea, passing through the rigging of a close-reefed vessel. As the birds arrived and passed over me, I felt a current of air that surprised me. Thousands were soon knocked down by the pole-men. The birds continued to pour in. The fires were lighted, and a magnificent, as well as wonderful and almost terrifying, sight presented itself. The Pigeons, arriving by thousands, alighted everywhere, one above another, until solid masses as large as hogsheads were formed on the branches all round. Here and there the perches gave way under the weight with a crash, and, falling to the ground, destroyed hundreds of the birds beneath, forcing down the dense groups with which every stick was loaded. It was a scene of uproar and confusion. I found it quite useless to speak, or even to shout to those persons who were nearest to me. Even the reports of the guns were seldom heard, and I was made aware of the firing only by seeing the shooters reloading.

No one dared venture within the line of devastation. The hogs had been penned up in due time, the picking up of the dead and wounded being left for the next morning's employment. The Pigeons were constantly coming, and it was past midnight before I perceived a decrease in the number of those that arrived. The uproar continued the whole night ; and as I was anxious to know to what distance the sound reached, I sent off a man, accustomed to perambulate the forest, who, returning two hours afterwards, informed me he had heard it distinctly when three miles distant from the spot. Towards the approach of day, the noise in some measure subsided, long before objects were distinguishable, the Pigeons began to move off in a direction quite different from that in which they had arrived the evening before, and at sunrise all that were able to fly had disappeared. The howlings of the wolves now reached our ears, and the foxes, lynxes, cougars, bears, raccoons, oppossums and pole-cats were seen sneaking off, whilst eagles and hawks of different species, accompanied by a crowd of vultures, came to supplant them, and enjoy their share of the spoil.

It was then that the authors of all this devastation began their entry amongst the dead, the dying, and the mangled. The pigeons were picked up and piled in heaps, until each had as many as he could possibly dispose of, when the hogs were let loose to feed on the remainder.

Persons unacquainted with these birds might naturally conclude that such dreadful havock would soon put an end to the species. But I have satisfied myself, by long observation, that nothing but the gradual diminution of our forests can accomplish their decrease, as they not unfrequently quadruple their numbers yearly, and always at least double it. In 1805 I saw schooners loaded in bulk with Pigeons caught up the Hudson River, coming in to the wharf at New York, when the birds sold for a cent a piece. I knew a man in Pennsylvania, who caught and killed upwards of 500 dozens in a clap-net in one day, sweeping sometimes twenty dozens or more at a single haul. In the month of March 1830, they were so abundant in the markets of New York, that piles of them met the eye in every direction. I have seen the Negroes at the United States' Salines or Saltworks of Shawanee Town, wearied with killing Pigeons, as they alighted to drink the water issuing from the leading pipes, for weeks at a time; and yet in 1826, in Louisiana, I saw congregated flocks of these birds as numerous as ever I had seen them before, during a residence of nearly thirty years in the United States.

The breeding of the Wild Pigeons, and the places chosen for that purpose, are points of great interest. The time is not much influenced by season, and the place selected is where food is most plentiful and most attainable, and always at a convenient distance from water. Forest-trees of great height are those in which the Pigeons form their nests. Thither the countless myriads resort, and prepare to fulfil one of the great laws of nature. At this period the note of the Pigeon is a soft *coo-coo-coo-coo*, much shorter than that of the domestic species. The common notes resemble the monosyllables *kee-kee-kee-kee*, the first being the loudest, the others gradually diminishing in power. The male assumes a pompous demeanour, and follows the female whether on the ground or on the branches, with spread tail and drooping wings, which it rubs against the part over which it is moving. The body is elevated, the throat swells, the eyes sparkle. He continues his notes, and now and then rises on the wing, and flies a few yards to approach the fugitive and timorous female. Like the domestic Pigeon and other species, they caress each other by billing, in which action, the bill of the one is introduced transversely into that of the other, and both parties alternately disgorge the contents of their crop by repeated efforts. These preliminary affairs are soon settled, and the Pigeons commence their nests in general peace and harmony. They are composed of a few dry twigs, crossing each other, and are supported by forks of the branches. On the same tree from fifty to a hundred nests may frequently be seen :—I might say a much greater number, were I not anxious, kind reader, that however wonderful my account of the Wild Pigeon is, you may not feel disposed to refer it to the marvellous. The eggs are two in number, of a broadly elliptical form, and pure white. During incubation, the male supplies the female with food. Indeed, the tenderness and affection displayed by these birds towards their mates, are in the highest degree striking. It is a remarkable fact, that each brood generally consists of a male and a female.

Here again, the tyrant of the creation, man, interferes, disturbing the harmony of this peaceful scene. As the young birds grow up, their enemies, armed with axes, reach the spot, to seize and destroy all they can. The trees are felled, and made to fall in such a way that the cutting of one causes the overthrow of another, or shakes the neighbouring trees so much, that the young Pigeons, or *squabs*, as they are named, are violently hurried to the ground. In this manner also, immense quantities are destroyed.

The young are fed by the parents in the manner described above ; in other words, the old bird introduces its bill into the mouth of the young one in a transverse manner, or with the back of each mandible opposite the separations of the mandibles of the young bird, and disgorges the contents of its crop. As soon as the young birds are able to shift for themselves, they leave their parents, and continue separate until they attain maturity. By the end of six months they are capable of reproducing their species.

The flesh of the Wild Pigeon is of a dark colour, but affords tolerable eating. That of young birds from the nest is much esteemed. The skin is covered with small white filmy scales. The feathers fall off at the least touch, as has been remarked to be the case in the Carolina Turtle. I have only to add, that this species, like others of the same genus, immerses its head up to the eyes while drinking.

In March 1830, I bought about 350 of these birds in the market of New York, at four cents a piece. Most of these I carried alive to England, and distributed amongst several noblemen, presenting some at the same time to the Zoological Society.

COLUMBA MIGRATORIA, *Linn.* Syst. Nat. vol. i. p. 285.—*Lath.* Ind. Ornith. vol. ii. p. 612.—*Ch. Bonaparte,* Synops. of Birds of the United States, p. 120.

PASSENGER PIGEON, COLUMBA MIGRATORIA, *Lath.* Synops. vol. iv. p. 661—*Wils.* Amer. Ornith. vol. v. p. 102. Pl. 44. fig. 1. Male.

Adult Male. Plate LXII. Fig. 1.

Bill straight, of ordinary length, rather slender, broader than deep at the base, with a tumid fleshy covering above, compressed towards the end, rather obtuse; upper mandible slightly declinate at the tip; edges inflected. Head small, neck slender, body rather full. Legs short and strong; tarsus rather rounded, anteriorly scutellate; toes slightly webbed at the base; claws short, depressed, obtuse.

Plumage blended on the neck and under parts, compact on the back. Wings long, the second quill longest. Tail graduated, of twelve tapering feathers.

Bill black. Iris bright red. Feet carmine purple, claws blackish. Head above and on the sides light blue. Throat, fore-neck, breast, and sides, light brownish-red, the rest of the under parts white. Lower part of the neck behind, and along the sides, changing to gold, emerald green, and rich crimson. The general colour of the upper parts is greyish-blue, some of the wing-coverts marked with a black spot. Quills and larger wing-coverts blackish, the primary quills bluish on the outer web, the larger coverts whitish at the tip. The two middle feathers of the tail black, the rest pale blue at the base, becoming white towards the end.

Length 16¼ inches, extent of wings 25; bill along the ridge $\frac{4}{8}$, along the gap $1\frac{1}{12}$; tarsus 1¼, middle toe 1½.

Adult Female. Plate LXII. Fig. 2.

The colours of the female are much duller than those of the male, although their distribution is the same. The breast is light greyish-brown, the upper parts pale reddish-brown, tinged with blue. The changeable spot on the neck is of less extent, and the eye of a somewhat duller red, as are the feet.

Length 15 inches, extent of wings 23; bill along the ridge $\frac{4}{8}$, along the gap $\frac{4}{8}$.

THE WHITE-EYED FLY-CATCHER, OR VIREO.

VIREO NOVEBORACENSIS, CH. BONAP.

PLATE LXIII. MALE.

THIS interesting little bird enters the State of Louisiana often as early as the 1st of March. Indeed, some individuals may now and then be seen a week or ten days sooner, provided the weather be mild. It throws itself into the thickest part of the briars, sumachs, and small evergreen bushes, which form detached groves in abandoned fields, where its presence is at once known by the smartness of its song. This song is composed of many different notes, emitted with great spirit, and a certain degree of pomposity, which makes it differ materially from that of all other Fly-catchers. It is frequently repeated during the day.

These birds become at once so abundant, that it would be more difficult not to meet one, than to observe a dozen or more, during a morning walk. Their motions are as animated as their music. They pass from twig to twig, upwards or downwards, examining every opening bud and leaf, and securing an insect or a larva at every leap. Their flight is short, light, and easy. Their migrations are performed during the day, and by passing from one low bush to another, for these birds seldom ascend to the tops of even moderately tall trees. Like all our other visitors, they move eastward as the season opens, and do not reach the Middle States before the end of April, or the beginning of May. Notwithstanding this apparently slow progress, they reach and disperse over a vast expanse of country. I have met with some in every part of the United States which I have visited.

Many remain in Louisiana, where they rear two broods, perhaps sometimes three, in a season. Of this, however, I am not quite certain. I never saw them alight on the ground, unless for the purpose of drinking, or of procuring fibrous roots for their nests. They are fond of sipping the dew drops that hang at the extremities of leaves. Their sorties after insects seldom extend beyond the bushes.

About the first of April, the White-eyed Fly-catcher forms a nest of dry slender twigs, broken pieces of grasses, and portions of old hornets' nests, which have so great a resemblance to paper, that the nest appears as if studded with bits of that substance. It is lined with fine fibrous roots, and the dried filaments of the Spanish moss. The nest is of the form of an inverted cone, and is fastened to two or three twigs of a Green Briar, a species of Smilax abundant in the old fields and along the fences. The eggs are from four to six, of a pure white, with a few dark spots near the larger end. In those districts where the Cow-bird is found, it frequently drops one of its eggs among them. I have seen the first brood from the nest about the middle of May. Unless when disturbed while upon its nest, this bird is extremely sociable, and may be approached within a few feet; but when startled from the nest, it displays the anxiety common to almost all birds on such occasions. The difference of colour in the sexes is scarcely perceptible.

The figure of a male has been given on a branch of the tree called in Louisiana the *Pride of China*, an ornamental plant, with fragrant flowers. The wood is extremely valuable on account of its great durability, and is employed for making posts and rails for the fences. Being capable of receiving a beautiful polish, it is also frequently made into various articles of furniture. For these reasons, the planters have found it expedient to adopt measures for increasing the propagation of this tree. It bears a pulpy fruit inclosing a hard seed, which is swallowed by different birds during the winter months. It has been thought deleterious, but without reason. A decoction of the root is used by the planters as an effectual vermifuge.

VIREO NOVEBORACENSIS, *Ch. Bonaparte*, Synops. of Birds of the United States, p. 70.
MUSCICAPA NOVEBORACENSIS, *Gmel.* Syst. Nat. vol. i. p. 947.—*Lath.* Ind. Ornith. vol. ii. p. 489.
HANGING FLY-CATCHER, *Lath.* Synops. Suppl. p. 174.
WHITE-EYED FLY-CATCHER, MUSCICAPA CANTATRIX, *Wils.* Amer. Ornith. vol. ii. p. 266. Pl. 18. Fig. 6.

Adult Male. Plate LXIII.

Bill shortish, nearly straight, rather strong, conico-acuminate, compressed towards the end; upper mandible slightly notched, and a little deflected at the tip; lower mandible ascending at the tip. Nostrils basal, rounded. Head and neck of ordinary size; body rather slender. Feet of ordinary length, slender ; tarsus anteriorly scutellate ; lateral toes nearly equal.

Plumage blended, soft and tufty. Wings shortish, the third quill longest. Tail even, of twelve rounded feathers.

Upper mandible blackish blue, lower light blue. Iris white. Feet greyish-blue. The general colour of the upper parts is light olive, the head greener. Sides of the head, including a line above the eye, and the loral space, bright yellow. Quills, large coverts, and tail; wood-brown, the quills edged externally with greenish-yellow, the larger coverts tipped with white, forming two bands. Sides of the neck tinged with bluish-grey ; the under parts greyish-white, excepting the sides, which are yellow.

Length 5 inches, extent of wings 7 ; bill along the ridge $\frac{5}{12}$, along the gap $\frac{7}{12}$.

The female scarcely differs from the male in external appearance.

THE PRIDE OF CHINA, OR BEAD-TREE.

MELIA AZEDARACH, *Linn.* Sp. Plant. p. 550.—DECANDRIA MONOGYNIA, *Linn.* MELIÆ, *Juss.*

Distinguished by its bipinnate shining leaves, with ferruginous dots beneath. In the south of Europe, the nuts are bored and strung by the Roman Catholics.

THE SWAMP SPARROW.

FRINGILLA PALUSTRIS, WILS.

PLATE LXIV. MALE.

THE shores and such flat sand-bars as are overgrown with grasses and rank weeds, along the Mississippi, from its mouth to a great height, as well as the swamps that occur in the woods, within a short distance from the margins of that river, are the resorts of the Swamp Sparrow, during autumn and winter. Although these birds do not congregate in flocks, their numbers are immense. They form the principal food of the many Sparrow Hawks, Pigeon Hawks, and Hen-harriers, which follow them as well as several other species, on their return from the Middle Districts, where they go towards spring, for the purpose of breeding. In those districts they continue to prefer low swampy places, damp meadows, and the margins of creeks and rivers.

It is a timid species, destitute of song, and merely uttering a single *cheep*, which is now and then heard during the day, but more frequently towards evening. They skulk along the weeds with activity, and feed principally upon the seeds of grasses, with a few insects, sometimes wading in shallow water. When wounded and forced to fall in the stream, they swim off to the nearest tuft of grass and hide in it. Their flight is short, low, and assisted by strong jerking motions of the body and tail, accompanied by a rustling of the wings. They alight by dropping suddenly amongst the weeds, seldom making towards a high tree. They are rarely if ever met with in dry woodlands.

Their nest is placed on the ground, at the foot of a large bunch of tall grass. It is composed of dry weeds and finer fibres of the same, and is sometimes partially covered over. The eggs are four or five, of a dull white, speckled with reddish. They raise two, sometimes three, broods in a season.

I found these birds abundantly dispersed in the swamps of Cayaga Lakes, and those bordering the Illinois river, during summer, and far up the Arkansas River in the winter months. Their flesh is sedgy, which perhaps forms no objection to some people against its use. They become fat and tender, when the weeds have produced an abundance of seeds. Their note differs from that of all other species of Sparrow, being harsher in its tone. The young follow the parents on the ground, skulking among the grass for nearly a week before they are able to fly.

The plant on which you see this bird is called the *May-apple*. It shoots from the ground in great numbers, and grows very close. The flowers appear at an early season, and are succeeded by a pulpy yellowish fruit, about the size of a pullet's egg, and which, when ripe, is pleasant to the taste, being a little acid and very cooling.

FRINGILLA PALUSTRIS, *Ch. Bonaparte*, Synops. of Birds of the United States, p. 110.
SWAMP SPARROW, FRINGILLA PALUSTRIS, *Wils.* Amer. Ornith. vol. iii. p. 49, Pl. xxii. fig. 1. Male.

Adult Male. Plate LXIV.

Bill short, conical, acute, straight ; upper mandible nearly straight in its dorsal line, as is the lower; gap-line a little declinate at the base. Nostrils basal, roundish, partly concealed by the feathers. Feet of moderate length ; tarsus longer than the middle toe ; toes free, the lateral ones nearly equal ; claws compressed, arched, acute.

Plumage rather compact above, soft and blended beneath. Wings short, rounded, the third and fourth quills longest. Tail longish, slightly notched, the feathers broad and rather acute.

Bill dark brown above, paler and tinged with blue beneath. Iris hazel. Feet yellowish-brown. Upper part of the head reddish-brown, streaked with black. Loral space, and a broad streak over the eye, yellowish-grey ; a dark line behind the eye, and another from the commissure of the mandibles. Upper parts generally yellowish-brown, spotted with brownish-black. Primary quill-coverts dusky, as are the inner webs of the secondary coverts and quills, their outer webs being brownish-red. Tail-feathers dusky, their outer webs brownish-red. Sides of the neck and the breast light grey, the rest of the under parts greyish-white.

Length 5¼ inches, extent of wings 7¼ ; bill along the ridge ₁⁵₂, along the back ⅜; tarsus ₁₁₂.

THE MAY-APPLE.

PODOPHYLLUM PELTATUM, *Willd.* Sp. Pl. vol. ii. p. 1141. *Pursh*, Flor. Amer. vol. ii. p. 366.—POLYANDRIA MONOGYNIA, *Linn.* RANUNCULACEÆ, *Juss.*

Root of many large tubers. Stalks several, each divided at the top, and bearing two peltate leaves, composed of five or seven lobes, with a flower in the fork. Petals nine, white. Fruit when ripe of the size of a plum, yellow.

THE RATHBONE WARBLER.

SYLVIA RATHBONIA.

PLATE LXV. MALE AND FEMALE.

KIND reader, you are now presented with a new and beautiful little species of Warbler, which I have honoured with the name of a family that must ever be dear to me. Were I at liberty here to express the gratitude which swells my heart, when the remembrance of all the unmerited kindness and unlooked-for friendship which I have received from the RATHBONES of Liverpool comes to my mind, I might produce a volume of thanks. But I must content myself with informing you, that the small tribute of gratitude which alone it is in my power to pay, I now joyfully accord, by naming after them one of those birds, to the study of which all my efforts have been directed. I trust that future naturalists, regardful of the feelings which have guided me in naming this species, will continue to it the name of the *Rathbone Warbler*.

I met with the species now under consideration only once, when I procured both the male and the female represented in the plate. They were actively engaged in searching for food amongst the blossoms and leaves of the Bignonia on which I have placed them. All my endeavours to discover their nest, or to procure other individuals, having proved abortive, I am unable to say any thing of their habits and history; but should I be more fortunate at some future period, I shall not fail to record the result of my observations respecting this delicate little Warbler.

The Bignonia on which they are represented, grows abundantly in the low alluvial grounds of the States of Mississippi and Louisiana, sparingly in Tennessee, and about the mouth of the Ohio. It twines round the trunks of various trees, and produces beautiful flowers, in which Humming Birds are frequently seen to search for the minute insects which form their food. They are destitute of smell, but are seen both during spring and autumn.

SYLVIA RATHBONIA.

Adult Male.　Plate LXV. Fig. 1.

Bill of ordinary length, nearly straight, subulato-conical, acute, as deep as broad at the base, with sharp edges.　Nostrils basal, oval, half concealed by the feathers.　Head rather large, neck short, body ovate. Feet of ordinary length, slender; tarsus compressed, covered anteriorly with a few long scutella, acute behind, a little longer than the middle toe; toes free, scutellate above; claws arched, slender, compressed, acute.

Plumage blended, soft, and tufty.　Wings of ordinary length, the second quill longest.　Tail rather short, nearly even, of twelve obtuse feathers.

Bill yellowish-brown above, yellow beneath.　Iris hazel.　Feet flesh-colour.　The general colour is bright yellow, the upper parts olivaceous. Quills and tail wood-brown, the former yellow on the outer web, the latter margined externally with the same colour.

Length $4\frac{1}{2}$ inches; bill along the ridge $\frac{1}{3}$, along the gap $\frac{6}{12}$; tarsus $\frac{7}{12}$, middle toe $\frac{1}{2}$.

Adult Female.　Plate LXV. Fig. 2.

The female is almost precisely the same in external appearance.

THE RAMPING TRUMPET-FLOWER.

BIGNONIA CAPREOLATA, *Willd.* Sp. Pl. vol. iii. p. 297.　*Pursh,* Flor. Amer. vol. ii. p. 419.—DIDYNAMIA ANGIOSPERMIA, *Linn.* BIGNONIÆ, *Juss.*

This species is distinguished by its conjugate cirrhous leaves, with oblongo-lanceolate leaflets, which are somewhat cordate at the base, the lower leaves single.　The flowers are carmine.

DEER HUNTING.

THE different modes of destroying Deer are probably too well understood and too successfully practised in the United States; for, notwithstanding the almost incredible abundance of these beautiful animals in our forests and prairies, such havock is carried on amongst them, that, in a few centuries, they will probably be as scarce in America, as the Great Bustard now is in Britain.

We have three modes of hunting Deer, each varying in some slight degree, in the different States and Districts. The first is termed *Still Hunting*, and is by far the most destructive. The second is called *Fire-light Hunting*, and is next in its exterminating effects. The third, which may be looked upon as a mere amusement, is named *Driving*. Although many deer are destroyed by this latter method, it is not by any means so pernicious as the others. These methods I shall describe separately.

Still Hunting is followed as a kind of trade by most of our frontier men. To be practised with success, it requires great activity, an expert management of the rifle, and a thorough knowledge of the forest, together with an intimate acquaintance with the habits of the Deer, not only at different seasons of the year, but also at every hour of the day, as the hunter must be aware of the situations which the game prefers, and in which it is most likely to be found, at any particular time. I might here present you with a full account of the habits of our Deer, were it not my intention to lay before you, at some future period, in the form of a distinct work, the observations which I have made on the various Quadrupeds of our extensive territories.

Illustrations of any kind require to be presented in the best possible light. We shall therefore suppose that we are now about to follow the *true hunter*, as the Still Hunter is also called, through the interior of the tangled woods, across morasses, ravines, and such places, where the game may prove more or less plentiful, even should none be found there in the first instance. We shall allow our hunter all the agility, patience, and care, which his occupation requires, and will march in his rear, as if we were spies, watching all his motions.

His dress, you observe, consists of a leather hunting-shirt, and a

pair of trowsers of the same material.   His feet are well moccassined ; he
wears a belt round his waist ; his heavy rifle is resting on his brawny
shoulder ; on one side hangs his ball-pouch, surmounted by the horn of
an ancient Buffalo, once the terror of the herd, but now containing a
pound of the best gunpowder ; his butcher knife is scabbarded in the
same strap ; and behind is a tomahawk, the handle of which has been
thrust through his girdle.   He walks with so rapid a step, that probably few men, besides ourselves, that is, myself and my kind reader,
could follow him, unless for a short distance, in their anxiety to witness
his ruthless deeds.   He stops, looks at the flint of his gun, its priming,
and the leather cover of the lock, then glances his eye towards the sky,
to judge of the course most likely to lead him to the game.

The heavens are clear, the red glare of the morning sun gleams
through the lower branches of the lofty trees, the dew hangs in pearly
drops at the top of every leaf.   Already has the emerald hue of the foliage been converted into the more glowing tints of our autumnal months.
A slight frost appears on the fence-rails of his little corn-field.   As he
proceeds, he looks to the dead foliage under his feet, in search of the
well known traces of a buck's hoof.   Now he bends toward the ground,
on which something has attracted his attention.   See ! he alters his course,
increases his speed, and will soon reach the opposite hill.   Now, he moves
with caution, stops at almost every tree, and peeps forward, as if already
within shooting distance of the game.   He advances again, but how very
slowly !   He has reached the declivity, upon which the sun shines in all
its growing splendour ;—but mark him ! he takes the gun from his shoulder,
has already thrown aside the leathern cover of the lock, and is wiping
the edge of his flint with his tongue.   Now he stands like a monumental
figure, perhaps measuring the distance that lies between him and the
game, which he has in view.   His rifle is slowly raised, the report follows,
and he runs.   Let us run also.   Shall I speak to him, and ask him the
result of this first essay ?   Assuredly, reader, for I know him well.

" Pray, friend, what have you killed ?" for to say, " what have you
shot at ?" might imply the possibility of his having missed, and so might
hurt his feelings ? " Nothing but a Buck." " And where is it ?" " Oh,
it has taken a jump or so, but I settled it, and will soon be with it.   My
ball struck, and must have gone through his heart."   We arrive at the
spot, where the animal had laid itself down among the grass in a thicket
of grape-vines, sumachs, and spruce-bushes, where it intended to repose

during the middle of the day. The place is covered with blood, the hoofs of the deer have left deep prints in the ground, as it bounced in the agonies produced by its wound ; but the blood that has gushed from its side discloses the course which it has taken. We soon reach the spot. There lies the buck, its tongue out, its eye dim, its breath exhausted : it is dead. The hunter draws his knife, cuts the buck's throat almost asunder, and prepares to skin it. For this purpose he hangs it upon the branch of a tree. When the skin is removed, he cuts off the hams, and abandoning the rest of the carcass to the wolves and vultures, re-loads his gun, flings the venison, enclosed by the skin, upon his back, secures it with a strap, and walks off in search of more game, well knowing that, in the immediate neighbourhood, another at least is to be found.

Had the weather been warmer, the hunter would have sought for the buck along the *shadowy* side of the hills. Had it been the spring sea-son, he would have led us through some thick cane-brake, to the margin of some remote lake, where you would have seen the deer, immersed to his head in the water, to save his body from the tormenting attacks of moschettoes. Had winter overspread the earth with a covering of snow, he would have searched the low damp woods, where the mosses and lichens, on which at that period the deer feeds, abound, the trees being generally crusted with them for several feet from the ground. At one time, he might have marked the places where the deer clears the velvet from his horns by rubbing them against the low stems of bushes, and where he frequently *scrapes* the earth with his fore-hoofs ; at another, he would have betaken himself to places where persimons and crab-apples abound, as beneath these trees the deer frequently stops to munch their fruits. During early spring, our hunter would imitate the bleating of the doe, and thus frequently obtain both her and the fawn ; or, like some tribes of Indians, he would prepare a deer's head, placed on a stick, and creeping with it amongst the tall grass of the prairies, would decoy the deer within reach of his rifle. But kind reader, you have seen enough of the *still hunter*. Let it suffice for me to add, that by the mode pursued by him, thousands of deer are annually killed, many individuals shooting these animals merely for the skin, not caring for even the most valuable portions of the flesh, unless hunger, or a near market, induce them to carry off the hams.

The mode of destroying deer by *fire-light*, or, as it is named in some

Y

parts of the country, *forest-light*, never fails to produce a very singular
feeling in him who witnesses it for the first time.   There is something in
it which at times appears awfully grand.   At other times, a certain degree of fear creeps over the mind, and even affects the physical powers, of
him who follows the hunter through the thick undergrowth of our woods,
having to leap his horse over hundreds of huge fallen trunks, at one time
impeded by a straggling grape-vine crossing his path, at another squeezed
between two stubborn saplings, whilst their twigs come smack in his
face, as his companion has forced his way through them.   Again, he
every now and then runs the risk of breaking his neck, by being suddenly pitched headlong on the ground, as his horse sinks into a hole covered
over with moss.   But I must proceed in a more regular manner, and
leave you, kind reader, to judge whether such a mode of hunting would
suit your taste or not.

The hunter has returned to his camp or his house, has rested and
eaten of his game.   He waits impatiently for the return of night.   He
has procured a quantity of pine-knots filled with resinous matter, and has
an old frying-pan, that, for aught I know to the contrary, may have been
used by his great grandmother, in which the pine-knots are to be placed
when lighted.   The horses stand saddled at the door.   The hunter comes
forth, his rifle slung on his shoulder, and springs upon one of them,
while his son, or a servant, mounts the other, with the frying-pan and
the pine-knots.   Thus accoutred, they proceed towards the interior of
the forest.   When they have arrived at the spot where the hunt is to
begin, they strike fire with a flint and steel, and kindle the resinous
wood.   The person who carries the fire moves in the direction judged to
be the best.   The blaze illuminates the near objects, but the distant
parts seem involved in deepest obscurity.   The hunter who bears the gun
keeps immediately in front, and after a while discovers before him two
feeble lights, which are produced by the reflection of the pine-fire from
the eyes of an animal of the deer or wolf kind.   The animal stands
quite still.   To one unacquainted with this strange mode of hunting, the
glare from its eyes might bring to his imagination some lost hobgoblin
that had strayed from its usual haunts.   The hunter, however, nowise
intimidated, approaches the object, sometimes so near as to discern its
form, when raising the rifle to his shoulder, he fires and kills it on the
spot.   He then dismounts, secures the skin and such portions of the flesh
as he may want, in the manner already described, and continues his

search through the greater part of the night, sometimes until the dawn of day, shooting from five to ten deer, should these animals be plentiful. This kind of hunting proves fatal, not to the deer alone, but also sometimes to wolves, and now and then to a horse or a cow, which may have straggled far into the woods.

Now, kind reader, prepare to mount a generous, full blood Virginian Hunter. See that your gun is in complete order, for, hark to the sound of the bugle and horn, and the mingled clamour of a pack of harriers! Your friends are waiting you, under the shade of the wood, and we must together go *driving* the light-footed deer. The distance over which one has to travel is seldom felt, when pleasure is anticipated as the result: so, galloping we go pell-mell through the woods, to some well known place, where many a fine buck has drooped its antlers under the ball of the hunter's rifle. The servants, who are called the *drivers*, have already begun their search. Their voices are heard exciting the hounds, and unless we put spurs to our steeds, we may be too late at our stand, and thus lose the first opportunity of shooting the fleeting game, as it passes by. Hark again! The dogs are in chase, the horn sounds louder and more clearly. Hurry, hurry on, or we shall be sadly behind!

Here we are at last! Dismount, fasten your horse to this tree, place yourself by the side of that large yellow poplar, and mind you do not shoot me! The deer is fast approaching; I will to my own stand, and he who shoots him dead wins the prize.

The deer is heard coming. It has inadvertently cracked a dead stick with its hoof, and the dogs are now so near it that it will pass in a moment. There it comes! How beautifully it bounds over the ground! What a splendid head of horns! How easy its attitudes, depending, as, it seems to do, on its own swiftness for safety! All is in vain, however: a gun is fired, the animal plunges and doubles with incomparable speed. There he goes! He passes another stand, from which a second shot, better directed than the first, brings him to the ground. The dogs, the servants, the sportsmen are now rushing forward to the spot. The hunter who has shot it is congratulated on his skill or good luck, and the chase begins again in some other part of the woods.

A few lines of explanation may be required to convey a clear idea of this mode of hunting. Deer are fond of following and retracing the paths which they have formerly pursued, and continue to do so even after they have been shot at more than once. These tracks are discovered by persons on horseback in the woods, or a deer is observed crossing a road, a field, or a small stream. When this has been noticed twice, the deer may be shot from the places called *stands* by the sportsman, who is stationed there, and waits for it, a line of stands being generally formed so as to cross the path which the game will follow. The person who ascertains the usual pass of the game, or discovers the parts where the animal feeds or lies down during the day, gives intimation to his friends, who then prepare for the chase. The servants start the deer with the hounds, and by good management, generally succeed in making it run the course that will soonest bring it to its death. But, should the deer be cautious, and take another course, the hunters, mounted on swift horses, gallop through the woods to intercept it, guided by the sound of the horns and the cry of the dogs, and frequently succeed in shooting it. This sport is extremely agreeable, and proves successful on almost every occasion.

Hoping that this account will be sufficient to induce you, kind reader, to go *driving* in our Western and Southern Woods, I now conclude my chapter on Deer Hunting by informing you, that the species referred to above is the Virginian Deer, *Cervus virginianus ;* and that, until I be able to present you with a full account of its habits and history, you may consult for information respecting it the excellent *Fauna Americana* of my esteemed friend Dr HARLAN of Philadelphia.

THE IVORY-BILLED WOODPECKER.

PICUS PRINCIPALIS, LINN.

PLATE LXVI. MALE AND FEMALE.

I HAVE always imagined, that in the plumage of the beautiful Ivory-billed Woodpecker, there is something very closely allied to the style of colouring of the great VANDYKE. The broad extent of its dark glossy body and tail, the large and well-defined white markings of its wings, neck, and bill, relieved by the rich carmine of the pendent crest of the male, and the brilliant yellow of its eye, have never failed to remind me of some of the boldest and noblest productions of that inimitable artist's pencil. So strongly indeed have these thoughts become ingrafted in my mind, as I gradually obtained a more intimate acquaintance with the Ivory-billed Woodpecker, that whenever I have observed one of these birds flying from one tree to another, I have mentally exclaimed, " There goes a Vandyke !" This notion may seem strange, perhaps ludicrous, to you, good reader, but I relate it as a fact, and whether or not it may be found in accordance with your own ideas, after you have inspected the plate in which is represented this great chieftain of the Woodpecker tribe, is perhaps of little consequence.

The Ivory-billed Woodpecker confines its rambles to a comparatively very small portion of the United States, it never having been observed in the Middle States within the memory of any person now living there. In fact, in no portion of these districts does the nature of the woods appear suitable to its remarkable habits.

Descending the Ohio, we meet with this splendid bird for the first time near the confluence of that beautiful river and the Mississippi ; after which, following the windings of the latter, either downwards toward the sea, or upwards in the direction of the Missouri, we frequently observe it. On the Atlantic coast, North Carolina may be taken as the limit of its distribution, although now and then an individual of the species may be accidentally seen in Maryland. To the westward of the Mississippi, it is found in all the dense forests bordering the streams which empty their waters into that majestic river, from the very declivities of the Rocky Mountains. The lower parts of the Carolinas, Georgia, Allabama, Louisiana, and Mississippi, are, however, the most favourite resorts of this bird, and in those States it constantly resides, breeds, and passes a life of peaceful enjoyment, finding a profusion of food in all the deep, dark, and gloomy swamps dispersed throughout them.

I wish, kind reader, it were in my power to present to your mind's eye the favourite resort of the Ivory-billed Woodpecker. Would that I could describe the extent of those deep morasses, overshadowed by millions of gigantic dark cypresses, spreading their sturdy moss-covered branches, as if to admonish intruding man to pause and reflect on the many difficulties which he must encounter, should he persist in venturing farther into their almost inaccessible recesses, extending for miles before him, where he should be interrupted by huge projecting branches, here and there the massy trunk of a fallen and decaying tree, and thousands of creeping and twining plants of numberless species! Would that I could represent to you the dangerous nature of the ground, its oozing, spongy, and miry disposition, although covered with a beautiful but treacherous carpeting, composed of the richest mosses, flags, and water-lilies, no sooner receiving the pressure of the foot than it yields and endangers the very life of the adventurer, whilst here and there, as he approaches an opening, that proves merely a lake of black muddy water, his ear is assailed by the dismal croaking of innumerable frogs, the hissing of serpents, or the bellowing of alligators! Would that I could give you an idea of the sultry pestiferous atmosphere that nearly suffocates the intruder during the meridian heat of our dogdays, in those gloomy and horrible swamps! But the attempt to picture these scenes would be vain. Nothing short of ocular demonstration can impress any adequate idea of them.

How often, kind reader, have I thought of the difference of the tasks imposed on different minds, when, travelling in countries far distant from those where birds of this species and others as difficult to be procured are now and then offered for sale in the form of dried skins, I have heard the amateur or closet-naturalist express his astonishment that half-a-crown was asked by the person who had perhaps followed the bird when alive over miles of such swamps, and after procuring it, had prepared its skin in the best manner, and carried it to a market thousands of miles distant from the spot where he had obtained it. I must say, that it has at least grieved me as much as when I have heard some idle fop complain of the poverty of the Gallery of the Louvre, where he had paid nothing, or when I have listened to the same infatuated idler lamenting the loss of his shilling, as he sauntered through the Exhibition Rooms of the Royal Academy of London, or any equally valuable repository of art.   But, let us return to the biography of the famed Ivory-billed Woodpecker.

The flight of this bird is graceful in the extreme, although seldom prolonged to more than a few hundred yards at a time, unless when it has to cross a large river, which it does in deep undulations, opening its wings at first to their full extent, and nearly closing them to renew the propelling impulse.   The transit from one tree to another, even should the distance be as much as a hundred yards, is performed by a single sweep, and the bird appears as if merely swinging itself from the top of the one tree to that of the other, forming an elegantly curved line.   At this moment all the beauty of the plumage is exhibited, and strikes the beholder with pleasure.   It never utters any sound whilst on wing, unless during the love season ; but at all other times, no sooner has this bird alighted than its remarkable voice is heard, at almost every leap which it makes, whilst ascending against the upper parts of the trunk of a tree, or its highest branches.   Its notes are clear, loud, and yet rather plaintive.   They are heard at a considerable distance, perhaps half a mile, and resemble the false high-note of a clarionet.   They are usually repeated three times in succession, and may be represented by the monosyllable *pait, pait, pait.* These are heard so frequently as to induce me to say that the bird spends few minutes of the day without uttering them, and this circumstance leads to its destruction, which is aimed at, not because (as is supposed by some) this species is a destroyer of trees, but more because it is a beautiful bird, and its rich scalp attached to the upper mandible forms an ornament for the war-dress of most of our Indians, or for the shot-pouch of our squatters and hunters, by all of whom the bird is shot merely for that purpose.

Travellers of all nations are also fond of possessing the upper part of the head and the bill of the male, and I have frequently remarked, that on a steam-boat's reaching what we call a *wooding-place,* the *strangers* were very apt to pay a quarter of a dollar for two or three heads of this Woodpecker.   I have seen entire belts of Indian chiefs closely ornamented with the tufts and bills of this species, and have observed that a great value is frequently put upon them.

The Ivory-billed Woodpecker nestles earlier in spring than any other species of its tribe.   I have observed it boring a hole for that purpose in the beginning of March.   The hole is, I believe, always made in the trunk of a live tree, generally an ash or a hagberry, and is at a great height.　The birds pay great regard to the particular situation of the tree, and the inclination of its trunk ; first, because they prefer retirement, and again, because they are anxious to secure the aperture against the access of water during beating rains.　To prevent such a calamity, the hole is generally dug immediately under the junction of a large branch with the trunk.　It is first bored horizontally for a few inches, then directly downwards, and not in a spiral manner, as some people have imagined.　According to circumstances, this cavity is more or less deep, being sometimes not more than ten inches, whilst at other times it reaches nearly three feet downwards into the core of the tree.　I have been led to think that these differences result from the more or less immediate necessity under which the female may be of depositing her eggs, and again have thought that the older the Woodpecker is, the deeper does it make its hole.　The average diameter of the different nests which I have examined was about seven inches within, although the entrance, which is perfectly round, is only just large enough to admit the bird.

Both birds work most assiduously at this excavation, one waiting outside to encourage the other, whilst it is engaged in digging, and when the latter is fatigued, taking its place.　I have approached trees whilst these Woodpeckers were thus busily employed in forming their nest, and by resting my head against the bark, could easily distinguish every blow given by the bird.　I observed that in two instances, when the Woodpeckers saw me thus at the foot of the tree in which they were digging their nest, they abandoned it for ever.　For the first brood there are generally six eggs　They are deposited on a few chips at the bottom of the hole, and are of a pure white colour.　The young are seen creeping out of the hole about a fortnight before they venture to fly to any other tree.　The second brood makes its appearance about the 15th of August.

In Kentucky and Indiana, the Ivory-bills seldom raise more than one brood in the season.　The young are at first of the colour of the female, only that they want the crest, which, however, grows rapidly, and towards autumn, particularly in birds of the first breed, is nearly equal to that of the mother.　The males have then a slight line of red on the head, and do not attain their richness of plumage until spring, or their full size until the second year.　Indeed, even then, a difference is easily observed between them and individuals which are much older.

The food of this species consists principally of beetles, larvæ, and large grubs.　No sooner, however, are the grapes of our forests ripe than they are eaten by the Ivory-billed Woodpecker with great avidity. I have seen this bird hang by its claws to the vines, in the position so often assumed by a Titmouse, and, reaching downwards, help itself to a bunch of grapes with much apparent pleasure. Persimons are also sought for by them, as soon as the fruit becomes quite mellow, as are hagberries.

The Ivory-bill is never seen attacking the corn, or the fruit of the orchards, although it is sometimes observed working upon and chipping off the bark from the belted trees of the newly-cleared plantations. It seldom comes near the ground, but prefers at all times the tops of the tallest trees. Should it, however, discover the half-standing broken shaft of a large dead and rotten tree, it attacks it in such a manner as nearly to demolish it in the course of a few days. I have seen the remains of some of these ancient monarchs of our forests so excavated, and that so singularly, that the tottering fragments of the trunk appeared to be merely supported by the great pile of chips by which its base was surrounded. The strength of this Woodpecker is such, that I have seen it detach pieces of bark seven or eight inches in length at a single blow of its powerful bill, and by beginning at the top branch of a dead tree, tear off the bark, to an extent of twenty or thirty feet, in the course of a few hours, leaping downwards with its body in an upward position, tossing its head to the right and left, or leaning it against the bark to ascertain the precise spot where the grubs were concealed, and immediately after renewing its blows with fresh vigour, all the while sounding its loud notes, as if highly delighted.

This species generally moves in pairs, after the young have left their parents. The female is always the most clamorous and the least shy. Their mutual attachment is, I believe, continued through life. Excepting when digging a hole for the reception of their eggs, these birds seldom, if ever, attack living trees, for any other purpose than that of procuring food, in doing which they destroy the insects that would otherwise prove injurious to the trees.

I have frequently observed the male and female retire to rest for the night, into the same hole in which they had long before reared their young. This generally happens a short time after sunset.

When wounded and brought to the ground, the Ivory-bill immediately makes for the nearest tree, and ascends it with great rapidity and perseverance, until it reaches the top branches, when it squats and hides, generally with great effect. Whilst ascending, it moves spirally round the tree, utters its loud *pait, pait, pait*, at almost every hop, but becomes silent the moment it reaches a place where it conceives itself secure. They sometimes cling to the bark with their claws so firmly, as to remain cramped to the spot for several hours after death. When taken by the hand, which is rather a hazardous undertaking, they strike with great violence, and inflict very severe wounds with their bill as well as claws, which are extremely sharp and strong. On such occasions, this bird utters a mournful and very piteous cry.

PICUS PRINCIPALIS, *Linn.* Syst. Nat. vol. i. p. 173.—*Lath.* Ind. Ornith. vol. i. p. 225. —*Ch. Bonaparte,* Synops. of Birds of the United States, p. 44.
WHITE-BILLED WOODPECKER, *Lath.* Synops. vol. ii. p. 553.
IVORY-BILLED WOODPECKER, PICUS PRINCIPALIS, *Wils.* Amer. Ornith. vol. iv. Pl. 29, Fig. 1.

Adult Male.   Plate LXVI. Fig. 1.

Bill long, straight, strong, polyhedral, tapering, compressed and truncated at the tip ; mandibles nearly equal, both nearly straight in their dorsal outline. Nostrils basal, oval, partly covered by recumbent bristly feathers. Head large. Neck long and slender. Body robust. Feet rather short, robust ; tarsus strong, scutellate before, scaly on the sides ; two toes before and two behind, the inner hind toe shortest ; claws strong, arched, very acute.

Plumage compact, glossy. Feathers of the head elongated and erectile. Wings large, the third and fourth quills longest. Tail long, graduated, of twelve tapering stiff feathers worn to a point by being rubbed against the bark of trees.

Bill of an ivory-white, whence the common name of the bird. Iris bright yellow. Feet greyish blue. The general colour of the plumage is black, with violet reflections, more glossy above. The feathers of the middle and hind part of the head are of a vivid deep carmine. A broad band of white runs down the neck and back, on either side, commencing narrow under the ear, and terminating with the scapulars. The five outer primaries black, the rest white towards the end, the secondaries wholly white, so that when the wings are closed, the posterior part of the back seems white, although it is in reality black.   Lateral tail-feathers with a spot of white near the tip of each web.

Length 21 inches, extent of wings 30 ; bill along the back 2½, along the gap 3 ; tarsus 2.

Adult Female.   Plate LXVI.   Fig. 2, 3.

The female resembles the male in colouring, but wants the vivid patch on the crest, which is wholly black.

THE RED-WINGED STARLING, OR MARSH BLACKBIRD.

ICTERUS PHŒNICEUS, DAUD.

PLATE LXVII. Male in different states, Female and Young.

If the name of *Starling* has been given to this well-known species, with the view of assimilating it to the European bird of that name, it can only have been on account of the numbers of individuals that associate together, for in every other respect it is as distinct from the true Starlings as a Common Crow. But without speaking particularly of generic or specific affinities—a task which I reserve for another occasion—I shall here content myself with giving you, kind reader, an account of the habits of this bird.

The Marsh Blackbird is so well known as being a bird of the most nefarious propensities, that in the United States one can hardly mention its name, without hearing such an account of its pilferings as might induce the young student of nature to conceive that it had been created for the purpose of annoying the farmer. That it destroys an astonishing quantity of corn, rice, and other kinds of grain, cannot be denied; but that before it commences its ravages, it has proved highly serviceable to the crops, is equally certain.

As soon as spring makes its appearance, almost all the Redwings leave the Southern States, in small detached and straggling flocks, the males leading the way in full song, as if to invite the females to follow. Prodigious numbers make their appearance in the Eastern Districts, as winter recedes, and are often seen while piles of drifted snow still remain along the roads, under shelter of the fences. They frequently alight on trees of moderate size, spread their tail, swell out their plumage, and utter their clear and not unmusical notes, particularly in the early morning, before their departure from the neighbourhood of the places in which they have roosted; for their migrations, you must know, are performed entirely during the day.

Their food at this season is almost ·exclusively composed of grubs, worms, caterpillars, and different sorts of coleopterous insects, which they procure by searching with great industry, in the meadows, the orchards, or the newly ploughed fields, walking with a graceful step, but much quicker than either of their relatives, the Purple Grakle or the Boat-tail of the Southern States. The millions of insects which the Red-wings destroy at this early season, are, in my opinion, a full equivalent for the corn which they eat at another period; and for this reason, the farmers do not molest them in spring, when they resort to the fields in immense numbers. They then follow the ploughman, in company with the Crow Blackbird, and as if aware of the benefit which they are conferring, do not seem to regard him with apprehension.

The females being all arrived, the pairing season at once commences. Several males are seen flying in pursuit of one, until, becoming fatigued, she alights, receives the addresses of her suitors, and soon makes a choice that establishes her the consort of one of them. The " happy couple" immediately retire from the view of the crowds around them, and seek along the margins of some sequestered pond or damp meadow, for a place in which to form their nest. An Alder bush or a thick tuft of rank weeds answer equally well, and in such places a quantity of coarse dried weeds is deposited by them, to form the exterior of the fabric which is to receive the eggs. The nest is lined with fine grasses, and, in some instances, with horse-hair. The eggs are from four to six in number, of a regular oval form, light blue, sparsely spotted with dusky.

Now is the time, good-natured reader, to see and admire the courage and fidelity of the male, whilst assiduously watching over his beloved mate. He dives headlong towards every intruder that approaches his nest, vociferating his fears and maledictions with great vehemence, passing at times within a few yards of the person who has disturbed his peace, or alighting on a twig close to his nest, and uttering a plaintive note, which might well prevent any other than a mischievous person from interfering with the hopes and happiness of the mated Redwings.

The eggs are hatched, and the first brood has taken flight. The young soon after associate with thousands of other striplings, and shift for themselves, whilst the parent birds raise a second family. The first brood comes abroad about the beginning of June, the second in the beginning of August. At this latter period, the corn in the Middle Districts has already acquired considerable consistence, and the congregated Redwings fall upon the fields in such astonishing numbers as to seem capable of completely veiling them under the shade of their wings. The husbandman, anxious to preserve as much of his corn as he can, for his own use or for market, pursues every possible method of annoyance or destruction. But his ingenuity is almost exerted in vain. The Red-wings heed not his efforts further than to remove, after each report of his gun, from one portion of the field to another. All the *scarecrows* that he may choose to place about his grounds are merely regarded by the birds as so many *observatories*, on which they occasionally alight.

The corn becoming too hard for their bills, they now leave the fields, and resort to the meadows and the margins of streams thickly overgrown with the Wild Oat and other grasses, upon the seeds of which they feed with great avidity during the autumnal and winter months. They then associate partially with the Reed Birds, Grakles, and Cow-pen Buntings, and are seen to move from the Eastern to the Southern Districts, in such immense and thick flocks as almost to cloud the air.

The havock made amongst them is scarcely credible. I have heard that upwards of fifty have been killed at a shot, and am the more inclined to believe such accounts that I have myself shot hundreds in the course of an afternoon, killing from ten to fifteen at every discharge. Whilst travelling in different parts of the Southern States, during the latter part of autumn, I have often seen the fences, trees and fields so strewed with these birds, as to make me believe their number fully equal to that of the falling leaves of the trees in the places traversed by me.

Towards evening they alight in the marshes by millions, in compact bodies, settle on the reeds and rushes close above the water, and remain during the night, unless disturbed by the gunners. When this happens, they rise all of a sudden, and perform various evolutions in the air, now gliding low over the rushes, and again wheeling high above them, pre-serving silence for a while, but finally diving suddenly to the spot for-merly chosen, and commencing a general chuckling noise, after which they remain quiet during the rest of the night.

Different species of Hawks derive their principal sustenance from them at this season. The Pigeon Hawk is an adept in picking the fattest from their crowded flocks; and while they are in the Southern States, where millions of them spend the winter, the Hen-harriers are seen con-tinually hovering over them, and picking up the stragglers.

The Marsh Blackbird is easily kept in confinement, and sings there with as much vigour as when at full liberty. It is kept in good order with rice, wheat, or any other small grain. Attempts have been made

to induce these birds to breed in confinement, but in as far as I have
been able to ascertain, have failed.   As an article of food, they are little
better than the Starling of Europe, or the Crow Blackbird of the United
States, although many are eaten and thought good by the country people,
who make pot-pies of them.

I have represented a male and a female in the adult state, a male in
the first spring, and a young bird, and have placed them on the branch
of a Water Maple, these birds being fond of alighting on trees of that
kind, in early spring, to pick up the insects that frequent the blossoms.
This tree is found dispersed throughout the United States, and grows, as
its name indicates, in the immediate vicinity of water.   Its wood is soft,
and is hardly used for any other purpose than that of being converted
into common domestic utensils.

Icterus phœniceus, *Ch. Bonaparte,* Synops. of Birds of the United States, p. 52.
Oriolus phœniceus, *Linn.* Syst. Nat. vol. i. p. 161.—*Lath.* Ind. Ornith. vol. i. p. 178.
Red-winged Starling, Sturnus prædatorius, *Wils.* Amer. Ornith. vol. iv. p. 30.
    Pl. 30.   Male and Female.
Red-winged Oriole, *Lath.* Synops. vol. ii. p. 428.

Male in complete plumage.   Plate LXVII. Fig. 1.

Bill conical, rather slender, longish, compressed, nearly straight, very
acute, with inflected acute margins; upper mandible obtuse above, encroaching on the forehead, lower broadly obtuse beneath; gap-line deflected at the base.   Nostrils oval, basal.   Head and neck of ordinary
size.   Body full.   Feet of ordinary length; tarsus a little longer than
the middle toe; inner toe little shorter than the outer; claws arched,
acute, compressed, that of the hind toe twice the size of the rest.

Plumage soft, blended, glossy.   Wings of ordinary length, the second
and third quills longest.   Tail rather long, rounded, of twelve rounded
feathers.

Bill and feet black.   Iris dark brown.   The general colour of the
plumage is glossy black; the lesser wing-coverts scarlet, their lower row
bright yellow.

Length 9 inches, extent of wings 14; bill along the ridge $1\frac{1}{4}$, along
the gap 1.

Male, the first spring.   Plate LXVII. Fig. 2.

Bill, eyes and feet, as in the adult male. The general colour of the upper parts is dark-brown, the feathers edged with lighter. The shoulder is scarlet, but of a lighter tint; the second row of wing-coverts broadly margined with brownish-white; the larger coverts and quills margined with reddish-white. Quills and tail brownish-black. The under parts are dark greyish-brown, spotted with black.

Adult Female. Plate LXVII. Fig. 3.

The adult female resembles the male of the first spring in colouring. The bill is lighter; there is a broad streak of pale brown from the bill over each eye; the wing-coverts are less broadly margined, and the lesser wing-coverts are merely tinged with red. The size is greatly inferior to that of the adult male, the length being only 7¼ inches.

Young Bird. Plate LXVII. Fig. 4.

The young is similar to the female, lighter on the cheeks and throat, and having merely a slight tinge of red on the lesser wing-coverts.

THE RED MAPLE OR SWAMP MAPLE.

ACER RUBRUM, *Willd.* Sp. Pl. vol. iv. p. 984. *Pursh,* Flor. Amer. vol. i. p. 266. *Mich.* Abr. Forest. de l'Amer. Sept. vol. ii. p. 210, Pl. 14.—OCTANDRIA MONO-GYNIA, *Linn.* ACERINÆ, *Juss.*

This species having been represented in Plate LXVII in seed, has already been described at p. 287.

THE REPUBLICAN OR CLIFF SWALLOW.

HIRUNDO FULVA, VIEILL.

PLATE LXVIII. MALE, FEMALE, AND NESTS.

IN the spring of 1815, I for the first time saw a few individuals of this species at Henderson, on the banks of the Ohio, a hundred and twenty miles below the Falls of that river. It was an excessively cold morning, and nearly all were killed by the severity of the weather. I drew up a description at the time, naming the species *Hirundo republicana,* the *Republican Swallow,* in allusion to the mode in which the individuals belonging to it associate, for the purpose of forming their nests and rearing their young. Unfortunately, through the carelessness of my assistant, the specimens were lost, and I despaired for years of meeting with others.

In the year 1819, my hopes were revived by Mr ROBERT BEST, curator of the Western Cincinnati Museum, who informed me that a strange species of bird had made its appearance in the neighbourhood, building nests in clusters, affixed to the walls. In consequence of this information, I immediately crossed the Ohio to New Port, in Kentucky, where he had seen many nests the preceding season ; and no sooner were we landed than the chirruping of my long-lost little strangers saluted my ear. Numbers of them were busily engaged in repairing the damage done to their nests by the storms of the preceding winter.

Major OLDHAM of the United States' Army, then commandant of the garrison, politely offered us the means of examining the settlement of these birds, attached to the walls of the building under his charge. He informed us, that, in 1815, he first saw a few of them working against the wall of the house, immediately under the eaves and cornice; that their work was carried on rapidly and peaceably, and that as soon as the young were able to travel, they all departed. Since that period, they had returned every spring, and then amounted to several hundreds. They usually appeared about the 10th of April, and immediately began their work, which was at that moment, it being then the 20th of that month, going on in a regular manner, against the walls of the arsenal. They had about fifty nests quite finished, and others in progress.

z

About day-break they flew down to the shore of the river, one hundred yards distant, for the muddy sand of which the nests were constructed, and worked with great assiduity until near the middle of the day, as if aware that the heat of the sun was necessary to dry and harden their moist tenements. They then ceased from labour for a few hours, amused themselves by performing aerial evolutions, courted and caressed their mates with much affection, and snapped at flies and other insects on the wing. They often examined their nests to see if they were sufficiently dry, and as soon as these appeared to have acquired the requisite firmness, they renewed their labours. Until the females began to sit, they all roosted in the hollow limbs of the Sycamores (*Platanus occidentalis*) growing on the banks of the Licking River, but when incubation commenced, the males alone resorted to the trees. A second party arrived, and were so hard pressed for time, that they betook themselves to the holes in the wall, where bricks had been left out for the scaffolding. These they fitted with projecting necks, similar to those of the complete nests of the others. Their eggs were deposited on a few bits of straw, and great caution was necessary in attempting to procure them, as the slightest touch crumbled their frail tenement into dust. By means of a table spoon, I was enabled to procure many of them. Each nest contained four eggs, which were white, with dusky spots. Only one brood is raised in a season. The energy with which they defended their nests was truly astonishing. Although I had taken the precaution to visit them at sun-set, when I supposed they would all have been on the Sycamores, yet a single female happened to be sitting, and gave the alarm, which immediately called out the whole tribe. They snapped at my hat, body and legs, passed between me and the nests, within an inch of my face, twittering their rage and sorrow. They continued their attacks as I descended, and accompanied me for some distance. Their note may be perfectly imitated by rubbing a cork damped with spirit against the neck of a bottle.

A third party arrived a few days after, and immediately commenced building. In one week they had completed their operations, and at the end of that time thirty nests hung clustered like so many gourds, each having a neck two inches long. On the 27th July, the young were able to follow their parents. They all exhibited the white frontlet, and were scarcely distinguishable in any part of their plumage from the old birds. On they 1st of August, they all assembled near their nests, mounted about three hundred feet in the air, and at ten in the morning took their departure, flying in a loose body, in a direction due north. They returned the same evening about dusk, and continued these excursions, no doubt to exercise their powers, until the third, when, uttering a farewell cry, they shaped the same course at the same hour, and finally disappeared. Shortly after their departure, I was informed that several hundreds of their nests were attached to the Court-House at the mouth of the Kentucky River. They had commenced building them in 1815. A person likewise informed me, that, along the cliffs of the Kentucky, he had seen many *bunches*, as he termed them, of these nests attached to the naked shelving rocks overhanging that river.

Being extremely desirous of settling the long-agitated question respecting the migration or supposed torpidity of Swallows, I embraced every opportunity of examining their habits, carefully noted their arrival and disappearance, and recorded every fact connected with their history. After some years of constant observation and reflection, I remarked that among all the species of migratory birds, those that remove farthest from us, depart sooner than those which retire only to the confines of the United States ; and, by a parity of reasoning, those that remain later return earlier in the spring. These remarks were confirmed, as I advanced towards the south-west on the approach of winter, for I there found numbers of Warblers, Thrushes, &c. in full feather and song. It was also remarked that the *Hirundo viridis* of WILSON (called by the French of Lower Louisiana, *Le Petit Martinet à ventre blanc*) remained about the City of New Orleans later than any other Swallow. As immense numbers of them were seen during the month of November, I kept a diary of the temperature from the third of that month, until the arrival of *Hirundo purpurea.* The following notes are taken from my journal, and as I had excellent opportunities, during a residence of many years in that country, of visiting the lakes to which these Swallows were said to resort, during the transient frosts, I present them with confidence.

November 11.—Weather very sharp, with a heavy white frost. Swallows in abundance during the whole day. On inquiring of the inhabitants if this was a usual occurrence, I was answered in the affirmative by all the French and Spaniards. From this date to the 22d, the thermometer averaged 65°, the weather generally a drizzly fog. Swallows playing over the city in thousands.

November 25.—Thermometer this morning at 30°. Ice in New Orleans a quarter of an inch thick The Swallows resorted to the lee of the Cypress Swamp in the rear of the city. Thousands were flying in different flocks. Fourteen were killed at a single shot, all in perfect plumage, and very fat. The markets were abundantly supplied with these tender, juicy, and delicious birds. Saw Swallows every day, but remarked them more plentiful the stronger the breeze blew from the sea.

December 20.—The weather continues much the same. Foggy and drizzly mist. Thermometer averaging 63°.

January 14.—Thermometer 42°. Weather continues the same. My little favourites constantly in view.

January 28.—Thermometer at 40°. Having seen the *Hirundo viridis* continually, and the *H. purpurea* or Purple Martin beginning to appear, I discontinued my observations.

During the whole winter many of them retired to the holes about the houses, but the greater number resorted to the lakes, and spent the night among the branches of *Myrica cerifera*, the *Cirier*, as it is termed by the French settlers.

About sunset they began to flock together, calling to each other for that purpose, and in a short time presented the appearance of clouds moving towards the lakes, or the mouth of the Mississippi, as the weather and wind suited. Their aërial evolutions before they alight, are truly beautiful. They appear at first as if reconnoitring the place, when, suddenly throwing themselves into a vortex of apparent confusion, they descend spirally with astonishing quickness, and very much resemble a *trombe* or water-spout. When within a few feet of the *ciriers*, they disperse in all directions, and settle in a few moments. Their twittering, and the motions of their wings, are, however, heard during the whole night. As soon as the day begins to dawn, they rise, flying low over the lakes, almost touching the water for some time, and then rising, gradually move off in search of food, separating in different directions. The hunters who resort to these places destroy great numbers of them, by knocking them down with light paddles, used in propelling their canoes.

1

HIRUNDO FULVA, Vieill. Ois. de l'Amer. Sept. vol. i. p. 62. Pl. 32.—Ch. Bonaparte Synops. of Birds of the United States, p. 64.

FULVOUS or CLIFF-SWALLOW, HIRUNDO FULVA, Ch. Bonaparte, Amer. Ornith. vol. i. p. 63. Pl. 7. fig. 1.

Adult Male. Plate LXVIII. Fig. 1.

Bill short, feeble, much depressed and very broad at the base, compressed towards the tip; upper mandible nearly straight; gap as wide as the head, and extending to beneath the eye. Nostrils basal, lateral, roundish. Head of ordinary size. Neck short. Body rather slender. Feet very short and feeble; tarsus and toes scutellate anteriorly, lateral toes nearly equal, the outer united to the second joint; claws short, weak, arched, rather obtuse.

Plumage silky, shining, and blended; wings very long and slender, the first quill longest. Tail of ordinary length, the same length as the wings, even, of twelve straight, narrowish, rather abrupt feathers.

Bill black. Iris hazel. Feet dusky. Upper part of the head, the back, and the lesser wing-coverts black, with violet reflections. A line of black across the anterior part of the forehead, extending over the eyes. Forehead marked with a semilunar band of white, slightly tinged with red. Chin, throat, and sides of the head deep brownish-red, the band of each side narrowing and meeting the other at the back of the neck. Posterior part of the back and upper tail-coverts light yellowish-red. Breast pale reddish, the rest of the under parts greyish-white, tinged with red. Wings and tail brownish-black.

Length 5¼ inches, extent of wings 12; bill along the ridge ¼, along the gap $\frac{7}{12}$; tarsus ½, middle toe a little more than ½.

Adult Female. Plate LXVIII. Fig. 2.

The female in external appearance differs in no respect from the male.

THE BAY-BREASTED WARBLER.

SYLVIA CASTANEA, WILS.

PLATE LXIX. MALE AND FEMALE.

THIS species does not breed in the United States, or if it does, must spend the summer in some of the most remote north-western districts, so that I have not been able to discover its principal abode. It merely passes through the better known portions of the Union, where it remains for a very short time. There is something so very uncommon in its appearance in different States, that I cannot refrain from briefly mentioning it. It is sometimes found in Pennsylvania, or the State of New York, as well as in New Jersey, as early as the beginning of April, but is only seen there for a few days. I have shot some individuals at such times, when I observed them employed in searching for insects and larvæ along the fences bordering our fields. At other times I have shot them late in June, in the State of Louisiana, when the cotton-plant was covered with blossoms, amongst which they were busily searching for food. The Bay-breasted Warbler, however, has so far eluded my inquiries, that I am unable to give any further account of its habits.

SYLVIA CASTANEA, *Ch. Bonaparte*, Synops. of Birds of the United States, p. 80.
BAY-BREASTED WARBLER, SYLVIA CASTANEA, *Wils.* Amer. Ornith. vol. ii. p. 97. Pl. 14, fig. 4.

Adult Male. Plate LXIX. Fig. 1.

Bill of ordinary length, nearly straight, subulato-conical, acute, as deep as broad at the base, with sharp edges. Nostrils basal, oval, half concealed by the feathers. Head of ordinary size, neck short, body ovate. Feet of ordinary length, slender; tarsus compressed, covered anteriorly with a few long scutella, acute behind, a little longer than the middle toe; toes free, scutellate above; claws arched, slender, compressed, acute.

Plumage loose, tufty. Wings rather long, the second quill longest. Tail of ordinary length, slightly emarginate, of twelve rounded feathers.

Bill blackish above, greyish-blue beneath. Iris hazel. Feet greyish-blue, upper part of the head, the fore-neck, anterior part of the breast, and the sides, bright chestnut. Forehead and cheeks, including a small space over the eye, deep black, behind which is a transverse broad band of yellowish-white on the sides of the neck. Back and lesser wing-coverts yellowish-grey, spotted with blackish-brown. Larger coverts, quills and tail, blackish-brown, edged with light bluish-grey. Middle of the breast, abdomen, and under tail-coverts, white, tinged with reddish.

Length 5¼ inches, extent of wings 11 ; bill along the ridge nearly $\frac{7}{12}$, along the gap $\frac{7}{12}$; tarsus $\frac{5}{8}$, middle toe $\frac{3}{4}$.

Adult Female. Plate LXIX. Fig. 2.

The female is somewhat less. The colours are similar to those of the male, and have the same distribution, but are much fainter, especially the chestnut of the head and under parts, which are converted into light brownish-red.

The Highland Cotton-plant.

Gossipium herbaceum, *Linn.* Syst. Nat. vol. ii. p. 462.—Monadelphia Polyan-dria, *Linn.* Malvaceæ, *Juss.*

This species, commonly known in America, where it is cultivated, under the name of *Highland Cotton*, is distinguished by its five-lobed leaves and herbaceous stem.

.

HENSLOW'S BUNTING.

EMBERIZA HENSLOWII.

PLATE LXX.

I OBTAINED the bird represented in this plate opposite Cincinnati, in
the State of Kentucky, in the year 1820, whilst in the company of Mr
ROBERT BEST, then Curator of the Western Museum. It was on the
ground, amongst tall grass, and exhibited the usual habits of its tribe.
Perceiving it to be different from any which I had seen, I immediately
shot it, and the same day made an accurate drawing of it.

In naming it after the Rev. Professor HENSLOW of Cambridge, a
gentleman so well known to the scientific world, and who has permitted
me so to designate it, my object has been to manifest my gratitude for the
many kind attentions which he has shewn towards me. Its history and
habits are unknown. In appearance it differs so little from the Buntings,
that, for the present, I shall refer it to that genus.

EMBERIZA HENSLOWII.

Plate LXX.

Bill short, robust, conical, acute; upper mandible straight in the
dorsal outline, angular, and encroaching a little on the forehead, broader
than the lower, acute and inflected on the edges; lower mandible also inflected at the edges; the gap-line deflected at the base. Head rather
large, neck short, body full. Feet of ordinary length; tarsus scutellate
before, acute behind; toes free, scutellate above; claws slightly arched,
compressed, acute, that of the hind toe elongated.

Plumage compact, slightly glossed. Wings short, curved, the third
and fourth quills longest, the secondaries nearly as long as the primaries,
when the wing is closed. Tail short, graduated and deeply notched, of
twelve rather narrow very acute feathers.

Bill flesh-colour, darker above. Iris dark-brown. Feet flesh-colour.
The general colour of the upper parts is pale brown, the central part of
the feathers brownish-black, the margins of those of the back bright red.
Secondary coverts yellowish-red on the outer webs. Quills dark brown,

externally margined with light yellowish-brown. Tail-feathers dusky, margined externally with yellowish-brown. The under parts pale yellowish-grey, the breast, sides, and throat, spotted with brownish-black.

Length 5 inches, bill along the ridge ⅜, along the gap nearly ½; tarsus ⅔, middle toe ⅔, hind toe the same.

THE INDIAN PINK-ROOT OR WORM-GRASS.

SPIGELIA MARILANDICA, *Pursh*, Fl. Amer. vol. i. p. 139. Fig. 1. of the Plate.—
PENTANDRIA MONOGYNIA, *Linn.* APOCINEÆ, *Juss.*

Stem tetragonal, all the leaves opposite, ovate, acuminate. Flowers rich carmine, in a terminal spike. This plant is perennial, flowers in the summer months, and grows in rich soil by the margins of woods, in the Middle States. The roots are used as a vermifuge.

PHLOX ARISTATA, *Pursh*, Fl. Amer. vol. i. p. 130. Fig. 2. of the Plate.—PENTANDRIA MONOGYNIA, *Linn.* POLEMONIA, *Juss.*

This species is characterized by its erect, feeble stem, its linear-lanceolate leaves, lax fastigiate panicle, twin pedicels, oboval segments of the corolla, pubescent curved tube, and long subulate calycine teeth. The corolla is rose-coloured, but varies in tint, being sometimes nearly white, and sometimes deep red. It is perennial, flowers in the summer months, and occurs in the Middle and Atlantic States.

NIAGARA.

AFTER wandering on some of our great lakes for many months, I bent my course towards the celebrated Falls of Niagara, being desirous of taking a sketch of them. This was not my first visit to them, and I hoped it should not be the last.

Artists (I know not if I can be called one) too often imagine that what they produce must be excellent, and with that foolish idea go on spoiling much paper and canvas, when their time might have been better employed in a different manner. But digressions aside,—I directed my steps towards the Falls of Niagara, with the view of representing them on paper, for the amusement of my family.

Returning as I then was from a tedious journey, and possessing little more than some drawings of rare birds and plants, I reached the tavern at Niagara Falls in such plight, as might have deterred many an individual from obtruding himself upon a circle of well-clad and perhaps well-bred society. Months had passed since the last of my linen had been taken from my body, and used to clean that useful companion, my gun. I was in fact covered just like one of the poorer class of Indians, and was rendered even more disagreeable to the eye of civilized man, by not having, like them, plucked my beard, or trimmed my hair in any way. Had HOGARTH been living, and there when I arrived, he could not have found a fitter subject for a ROBINSON CRUSOE. My beard covered my neck in front, my hair fell much lower at my back, the leather dress which I wore had for months stood in need of repair, a large knife hung at my side, a rusty tin-box containing my drawings and colours, and, wrapped up in a worn-out blanket that had served me for a bed, was buckled to my shoulders. To every one I must have seemed immersed in the depths of poverty, perhaps of despair. Nevertheless, as I cared little about my appearance during those happy rambles, I pushed into the sitting-room, unstrapped my little burden, and asked how soon breakfast would be ready.

In America, no person is ever refused entrance to the inns, at least far from cities. We know too well how many poor creatures are forced to make their way from other countries in search of employment or to seek uncultivated land, and we are ever ready to let them have what they may call for. No one knew who I was, and the landlord looking at

me with an eye of close scrutiny, answered that breakfast would be on
the table as soon as the company should come down from their rooms.
I approached this important personage, told him of my avocations, and
convinced him that he might feel safe as to remuneration. From this
moment, I was, with him at least, on equal footing with every other person in his house. He talked a good deal of the many artists who had
visited the Falls that season, from different parts, and offered to assist me,
by giving such accommodations as I might require to finish the drawings I had in contemplation. He left me, and as I looked about the
room, I saw several views of the Falls, by which I was so disgusted, that
I suddenly came to my better senses. "What!" thought I, "have I
come here to mimic nature in her grandest enterprise, and add *my* cari-
cature of one of the wonders of the world to those which I here see? No.
—I give up the vain attempt. I shall look on these mighty cataracts
and imprint them, where alone they can be represented,—on my mind!"

Had I taken a view, I might as well have given you what might be
termed a regular account of the form, the height, the tremendous roar of
these Falls; might have spoken of people perilling their lives by going
between the rock and the sheet of water, calculated the density of the atmosphere in that strange position, related wondrous tales of Indians and
their canoes having been precipitated the whole depth;—might have told
of the narrow, rapid, and rockbound river that leads the waters of the
Erie into those of Ontario, remarking *en passant* the Devil's Hole and
sundry other places or objects;—but supposing you had been there, my
description would prove useless, and quite as puny as my intended view
would have been for my family; and should you not have seen them,
and are fond of contemplating the more magnificent of the Creator's
works, go to Niagara, reader, for all the pictures you may see, all the descriptions you may read, of these mighty Falls, can only produce in your
mind the faint glimmer of a glow-worm compared with the overpowering
glory of the meridian sun.

I breakfasted amid a crowd of strangers, who gazed and laughed at
me, paid my bill, rambled about and admired the Falls for a while, saw
several young gentlemen *sketching on cards* the mighty mass of foaming
waters, and walked to Buffalo, where I purchased new apparel and shear-
ed my beard. I then enjoyed civilized life as much as, a month before, I
had enjoyed the wildest solitudes and the darkest recesses of mountain
and forest.

THE WINTER HAWK.

FALCO HYEMALIS, GMEL.

PLATE LXXI.

EVERY species of bird is possessed of a certain, not always definable, cast of countenance, peculiar to itself. Although it undergoes changes necessary for marking the passions of the individual, its joy, its anger, its terror or despondency, still it remains the same *specific look*. Hawks are perhaps more characteristically marked in this manner than birds of any other genus, being by nature intended for deeds of daring enterprise, and requiring a greater perfection of sight to enable them to distinguish their prey at great distances. To most persons the *family-look* of particular species does not appear so striking as to the student of Nature, who examines her productions in the haunts which she has allotted to them. He perceives at a glance the differences of species, and when he has once bent his attention to an object, can distinguish it at distances which to the ordinary observer present merely a moving object, whether beast or bird. When years of constant observation have elapsed, it becomes a pleasure to him to establish the differences that he has found to exist among the various species of a tribe, and to display to others whose opportunities have been more limited the fruits of his research.

I hope, kind reader, you will not lay presumption to my charge, when I tell you that I think myself somewhat qualified to decide in a matter of this kind, or say that I go too far, when I assert that the Hawk which sails before me, at a distance so great that a careless observer might be apt to fancy it something else, I can distinguish and name with as much ease as I should recognise an old friend by his walk or his *tournure*. Independently of the cast of countenance so conspicuously distinctive of different species of birds, there are characters of separation in their peculiar notes or cries; and if you add to these the distinctions that exist in their habits, it will be easy for you, when you have looked at the Plate of the *Winter Falcon* and that of the *Red-shouldered Hawk,* and have been told that their notes and manners differ greatly, to perceive that these birds, although confounded by some, are truly distinct.

The Winter Hawk is not a constant resident in the United States,

but merely visits them, making its first appearance there at the approach
of winter. It extends over the whole Union, from the eastern to the
southernmost parts, but gives a decided preference to the Middle Districts,
where the greater number spend the winter. They come from the northern portions of the continent, where they breed, and from whence they
seem to be forced by the severity of the weather, to seek subsistence for
a time in milder climates. They return at the approach of spring, and
none, in as far as I have been able to discover, remain to breed in the
United States.

The flight of the Winter Hawk is smooth and light, although greatly
protracted, when necessity requires it to be so. It sails at times at a considerable elevation, and, notwithstanding the comparative shortness of its
wings, performs this kind of motion with grace, and in circles of more
than moderate diameter. It is a remarkably silent bird, often spending
the greater part of a day without uttering its notes more than once or
twice, which it does just before it alights to watch with great patience and
perseverance for the appearance of its prey. Its haunts are the extensive
meadows and marshes which occur along our rivers. There it pounces
with a rapid motion on the frogs, which it either devours on the spot, or
carries to the perch, or the top of the hay-stack, on which it previously
stood. If it seizes a small frog, it swallows it whole and at once ; but if
a large one, it first tears it to pieces. The appetite of the Winter Hawk
may be said to be ravenous. It seldom gives up eating, when food is
plentiful, until it has gorged itself so as to seem on the point of being
suffocated. At such times, it flies heavily, but removes farther at once
from a person who pursues it, than when its stomach is empty, as if at one
effort to ensure its safety, and afterwards enjoy the digestion of its food
in quiet.

When frogs are scarce during frosty weather, the Winter Hawk pursues the meadow mouse, but only in such cases, frogs being the favourite
food of this species. I have seen it when disappointed in seizing a large
bull-frog, which had saved itself by leaping into the water, stand on the
spot previously occupied by the reptile, and wait until it reappeared and
approached the shore, when the Hawk would strike at it with his talons,
although seldom successfully, as the frog would sink backward, and thus
escape.

Mr ALEXANDER WILSON has given a figure so unlike any bird of this
species, for one of the Winter Falcons, that although he has at the same

time briefly described the habits of the latter with accuracy, I cannot
think that the bird figured by him was of that species. My excellent
friend CHARLES LUCIAN BONAPARTE, has probably been led by Mr WIL-
SON's error to consider the Winter Hawk and the Red-shouldered Hawk
as identical. I have killed many individuals of both species, and knowing as I do that the Red-shouldered Hawk is a constant resident in the
Southern States, where I have often destroyed its nest and young, and
where very few Winter Hawks are ever seen, even during winter, I cannot hesitate a moment to pronounce them different and distinct species.

The Winter Hawk generally rests at night on the ground, amongst
the tall sedges of the marshes. From such places I have on several occasions started it, whilst in search of Ducks, and have shot it as it flew low
over the ground, attempting to escape unobserved. I have never seen
this Hawk in pursuit of any other birds than those of its own species,
each individual chasing the others from the district which it has selected
for itself.

The cry of the Winter Hawk is clear and prolonged, and resembles
the syllables kay-o. After uttering these notes, it generally alights.
Towards spring they associate in small parties of four or five, to perform
their migrations. In this respect the species resembles most of the Marsh
Hawks or Hen-harriers.

FALCO HYEMALIS, Gmel. Syst. Nat. vol. i. p. 274.—Lath. Ind. Ornith. vol. i. p. 34.—
    Ch. Bonaparte, Synops. of Birds of the United States, p. 33.
WINTER FALCON, FALCO HYEMALIS, Wils. Amer. Ornith. vol. iv. p. 73. Pl. 35.

Adult Male. Plate LXXI.

Bill short, as broad as deep at the base, the sides convex, the dorsal
outline convex from the base; upper mandible cerate, the edges blunt,
slightly inflected, with an obtuse lobe towards the curvature, the tip trigonal, deflected, very acute; lower mandible involute at the edges, a
little truncate at the end. Nostrils round, lateral, with a soft papilla in
the centre. Head rather large, neck and body rather slender. Tarsus
rather slender, anteriorly scutellate; toes scutellate above, scaly on the
sides, scabrous and tuberculate beneath; middle and outer toe connected at
the base by a small membrane; claws roundish, curved, slender, very acute.

Plumage compact, imbricated; feathers of the head and neck narrow
towards the tips, of the back broad and rounded; tibial feathers elongat-

ed behind. Wings long, third and fourth primaries longest, the first short.

Bill light blue, darker at the tip; cere, basal margin of the bill, edges of the eyelids, and the feet, yellow, tinged with green. Iris yellow. Claws black. Head, neck and back, pale brownish-red, longitudinally spotted with dark-brown, the sides and fore-part of the head greyish-white. Upper tail-coverts bluish-grey at the margins. Tail dull brown, banded with brownish-white, and tipped with white. Lesser wing-coverts brownish-red, spotted with dark brown; larger coverts and secondary quills umber, banded with brownish-white; primary quills light yellowish-red at the base, dull brown towards the end, barred with dark brown. Lower part of the neck, the sides and under wing-coverts, light brownish-red, the former longitudinally lined with brown. Breast greyish-white, sparsely marked with guttiform spots, abdomen white. Tibial feathers yellowish-white, marked with small roundish spots.

Length 22 inches; bill along the back $1\frac{1}{2}$; tarsus 3.

Compared with the adult male of the Red-shouldered Hawk, the present bird is much larger, and differs greatly in colouring; but the differences will be best understood by referring to the figures.

THE BULL-FROG, RANA TAURINA, *Cuv.*

The body olive-green, clouded with black; a yellow line along the back. Length ten or twelve inches. This Frog is found in all parts of the United States, but is more abundant in the Southern Districts. Its voice is louder than that of any other species, and may be distinctly heard at the distance of forty or fifty yards. It is particularly fond of such small pure streams of water as are thickly shaded by overhanging bushes. It sits for hours during the middle of the day, basking in the sun, near the margin of the water, to which it betakes itself by a great leap at the least appearance of danger, diving at once to the bottom, or swimming to the opposite side. In the Southern States, it is heard at all seasons, but principally during the spring and summer months. Its flesh is tender, white, and affords excellent eating. The hind legs, however, are the only parts used as food. They make excellent bait for the larger cat-fish. Some bull-frogs weigh as much as half a pound. I have generally used the gun for procuring them, shooting with very small shot.

THE SWALLOW-TAILED HAWK.

FALCO FURCATUS, LINN.

PLATE LXXII. MALE.

THE flight of this elegant species of Hawk is singularly beautiful and protracted. It moves through the air with such ease and grace, that it is impossible for any individual, who takes the least pleasure in observing the manners of birds, not to be delighted by the sight of it whilst on wing. Gliding along in easy flappings, it rises in wide circles to an immense height, inclining in various ways its deeply forked tail, to assist the direction of its course, dives with the rapidity of lightning, and, suddenly checking itself, reascends, soars away, and is soon out of sight. At other times a flock of these birds, amounting to fifteen or twenty individuals, is seen hovering around the trees. They dive in rapid succession amongst the branches, glancing along the trunks, and seizing in their course the insects and small lizards of which they are in quest. Their motions are astonishingly rapid, and the deep curves which they describe, their sudden doublings and crossings, and the extreme ease with which they seem to cleave the air, excite the admiration of him who views them while thus employed in searching for food.

A solitary individual of this species has once or twice been seen in Pennsylvania. Farther to the eastward, the Swallow-tailed Hawk has never, I believe, been observed. Travelling southward, along the Atlantic coast, we find it in Virginia, although in very small numbers. Beyond that State it becomes more abundant. Near the Falls of the Ohio, a pair had a nest and reared four young ones, in 1820. In the lower parts of Kentucky it begins to become numerous; but in the States farther to the south, and particularly in parts near the sea, it is abundant. In the large prairies of the Attacapas and Oppellousas, it is extremely common.

In the States of Louisiana and Mississippi, where these birds are abundant, they arrive in large companies, in the beginning of April, and are heard uttering a sharp plaintive note. At this period I generally remarked that they came from the westward, and have counted upwards of a hundred in the space of an hour, passing over me in a direct easterly course. At that season, and in the beginning of September, when they all retire from the United States, they are easily approached when they have alighted, being then apparently fatigued, and busily engaged in preparing themselves for continuing their journey, by dressing and oiling their feathers. At all other times, however, it is extremely difficult to get near them, as they are generally on wing through the day, and at night rest on the highest pines and cypresses, bordering the river-bluffs, the lakes or the swamps of that district of country.

They always feed on the wing. In calm and warm weather, they soar to an immense height, pursuing the large insects called *Musquito Hawks*, and performing the most singular evolutions that can be conceived, using their tail with an elegance of motion peculiar to themselves. Their principal food, however, is large grasshoppers, grass-caterpillars, small snakes, lizards, and frogs. They sweep close over the fields, sometimes seeming to alight for a moment to secure a snake, and holding it fast by the neck, carry it off, and devour it in the air. When searching for grasshoppers and caterpillars, it is not difficult to approach them under cover of a fence or tree. When one is then killed and falls to the ground, the whole flock comes over the dead bird, as if intent upon carrying it off. An excellent opportunity is thus afforded of shooting as many as may be wanted, and I have killed several of these Hawks in this manner, firing as fast as I could load my gun.

The Forked-tailed Hawks are also very fond of frequenting the creeks, which, in that country, are much encumbered with drifted logs and accumulations of sand, in order to pick up some of the numerous water-snakes which lie basking in the sun. At other times, they dash along the trunks of trees, and snap off the pupæ of the locust, or that insect itself. Although when on wing they move with a grace and ease which it is impossible to describe, yet on the ground they are scarcely able to walk.

I kept for several days one which had been slightly wounded in the wing. It refused to eat, kept the feathers of the head and rump constantly erect, and vomited several times part of the contents of its stomach. It never threw itself on its back, nor attempted to strike with its talons, unless when taken up by the tip of the wing. It died from inanition, as it constantly refused the food placed before it in profusion, and instantly vomited what had been thrust down its throat.

The Swallow-tailed Hawk pairs immediately after its arrival in the

A a

Southern States, and as its courtships take place on the wing, its motions are then more beautiful than ever. The nest is usually placed on
the top branches of the tallest oak or pine tree, situated on the margin of a stream or pond. It resembles that of the Common Crow externally, being formed of dry sticks, intermixed with Spanish moss, and
is lined with coarse grasses and a few feathers. The eggs are from four
to six, of a greenish-white colour, with a few irregular blotches of dark
brown at the larger end. The male and the female sit alternately, the
one feeding the other. The young are at first covered with buff-colour-
ed down. Their next covering exhibits the pure white and black of the
old birds, but without any of the glossy purplish tints of the latter. The
tail, which at first is but slightly forked, becomes more so in a few weeks,
and at the approach of autumn exhibits little difference from that of
the adult birds. The plumage is completed the first spring. Only one
brood is raised in the season. The species leaves the United States in
the beginning of September, moving off in flocks, which are formed immediately after the breeding-season is over.

Hardly any difference as to external appearance exists between the
sexes. They never attack birds or quadrupeds of any species, with the
view of preying upon them. I never saw one alight on the ground.
They secure their prey as they pass closely over it, and in so doing sometimes seem to alight, particularly when securing a snake. The common
name of the Snake represented in the plate is the Garter Snake.

FALCO FURCATUS, *Linn.* Syst. Nat. vol. i. p. 129.—*Lath.* Ind. Ornith. vol. i. p. 22.
    —*Ch. Bonaparte,* Synops. of Birds of the United States, p. 31.

SWALLOW-TAILED FALCON, *Lath.* Synops. vol. i. p. 60.

SWALLOW-TAILED HAWK, *Wils.* Amer. Ornith. vol. vi. p. 70. Pl. 51. Fig. 2.

Adult Male.   Plate LXXII.

Bill short, strong, curved, compressed towards the tip, opening to beneath the eye; upper mandible cerate, its dorsal outline curved from the
base, the edges acute and overlapping, the tip trigonal, very acute; lower
mandible rounded on the back, the edges acute, the tip rounded and declinate. Head large, neck short, body robust. Feet rather short; tarsus
very short, scaly all round; toes scaly, scutellate above, excepting at the
base; claws curved, very acute.

Plumage rather compact, blended, glossy. Wings very long and acute, the third quill longest, the first equal to the fifth, the primaries widely graduated, the secondaries comparatively very short. Tail very deeply forked, of twelve feathers, the lateral ones extremely elongated.

Bill bluish-black above, light blue on the cere, and the edges of both mandibles. Edges of the eyelids light blue; iris black. Feet light blue, tinged with green; claws flesh-coloured. The head, the neck all round, and the under parts, are white, tinged with bluish-grey; the shafts of the head, neck, and breast blackish. The rest of the plumage is black, with blue and purple reflections.

Length 25 inches, extent of wings 51½; beak along the back 1¼.

The female is similar to the male.

THE GARTER SNAKE.

This is one of our most abundant species, and is found everywhere in the meadows, the fields, the gardens, and the forests. It moves with ease, and now and then ascends low bushes. It is quite harmless.

THE WOOD THRUSH.

TURDUS MUSTELINUS, GMEL.

PLATE LXXIII. MALE AND FEMALE.

KIND reader, you now see before you my greatest favourite of the feathered tribes of our woods. To it I owe much. How often has it revived my drooping spirits, when I have listened to its wild notes in the forest, after passing a restless night in my slender shed, so feebly secured against the violence of the storm, as to shew me the futility of my best efforts to rekindle my little fire, whose uncertain and vacillating light had gradually died away under the destructive weight of the dense torrents of rain that seemed to involve the heavens and the earth in one mass of fearful murkiness, save when the red streaks of the flashing thunderbolt burst on the dazzled eye, and, glancing along the huge trunk of the stateliest and noblest tree in my immediate neighbourhood, were instantly followed by an uproar of crackling, crashing, and deafening sounds, rolling their volumes in tumultuous eddies far and near, as if to silence the very breathings of the unformed thought ! How often, after such a night, when far from my dear home, and deprived of the presence of those nearest to my heart, wearied, hungry, drenched, and so lonely and desolate as almost to question myself why I was thus situated, when I have seen the fruits of my labours on the eve of being destroyed, as the water, collected into a stream, rushed through my little camp, and forced me to stand erect, shivering in a cold fit like that of a severe ague, when I have been obliged to wait with the patience of a martyr for the return of day, trying in vain to destroy the tormenting moschettoes, silently counting over the years of my youth, doubting perhaps if ever again I should return to my home, and embrace my family !—how often, as the first glimpses of morning gleamed doubtfully amongst the dusky masses of the forest-trees, has there come upon my ear, thrilling along the sensitive cords which connect that organ with the heart, the delightful music of this harbinger of day !—and how fervently, on such occasions, have I blessed the Being who formed the Wood Thrush, and placed it in those solitary forests, as if to console me amidst my privations, to cheer my depressed mind, and to make me feel, as I did, that never ought man to de-

spair, whatever may be his situation, as he can never be certain that aid
and deliverance are not at hand.

The Wood Thrush seldom commits a mistake after such a storm as
I have attempted to describe; for no sooner are its sweet notes heard
than the heavens gradually clear, the bright refracted light rises in glad-
dening rays from beneath the distant horizon, the effulgent beams increase in their intensity, and the great orb of day at length bursts on the
sight. The grey vapour that floats along the ground is quickly dissi-
pated, the world smiles at the happy change, and the woods are soon
heard to echo the joyous thanks of their many songsters. At that moment, all fears vanish, giving place to an inspiriting hope. The hunter
prepares to leave his camp. He listens to the Wood Thrush, while he
thinks of the course which he ought to pursue, and as the bird approaches
to peep at him, and learn somewhat of his intentions, he raises his mind
towards the Supreme Disposer of events. Seldom, indeed, have I heard
the song of this Thrush, without feeling all that tranquillity of mind, to
which the secluded situation in which it delights is so favourable. The
thickest and darkest woods always appear to please it best. The borders of murmuring streamlets, overshadowed by the dense foliage of the
lofty trees growing on the gentle declivities, amidst which the sunbeams
seldom penetrate, are its favourite resorts. There it is, kind reader, that
the musical powers of this hermit of the woods must be heard, to be fully
appreciated and enjoyed.

The song of the Wood Thrush, although composed of but few notes, is
so powerful, distinct, clear, and mellow, that it is impossible for any person to hear it without being struck by the effect which it produces on the
mind. I do not know to what instrumental sounds I can compare these
notes, for I really know none so melodious and harmonical. They gradually rise in strength, and then fall in gentle cadences, becoming at
length so low as to be scarcely audible; like the emotions of the lover,
who at one moment exults in the hope of possessing the object of his af-
fections, and the next pauses in suspense, doubtful of the result of all his
efforts to please.

Several of these birds seem to challenge each other from different portions of the forest, particularly towards evening, and at that time nearly
all the other songsters being about to retire to rest, the notes of the
Wood Thrush are doubly pleasing. One would think that each individual is anxious to excel his distant rival, and I have frequently thought

that on such occasions their music is more than ordinarily effective, as it then exhibits a degree of skilful modulation quite beyond my power to describe. These concerts are continued for some time after sunset, and take place in the month of June, when the females are sitting.

This species glides swiftly through the woods, whilst on wing, and performs its migrations without appearing in the open country. It is a constant resident in the State of Louisiana, to which the dispersed individuals resort, as to winter quarters, from the different parts of the United States, to which they had gone to breed. They reach Pennsylvania about the beginning or middle of April, and gradually proceed farther north.

Their food consists of different kinds of berries and small fruits, which they procure in the woods, without ever interfering with the farmer. They also occasionally feed on insects and various lichens.

The nest is usually placed in a low horizontal branch of the Dogwood Tree, occasionally on smaller shrubs. It is large, well saddled on the branch, and composed externally of dry leaves of various kinds, with a second bed of grasses and mud, and an internal layer of fine fibrous roots. The eggs are four or five, of a beautiful uniform light blue. The nest is generally found in deep swampy hollows, on the sides of hills.

On alighting on a branch, this Thrush gives its tail a few jets, uttering at each motion a low chuckling note peculiar to itself, and very different from those of the Hermit or Tawny Thrush. It then stands still for a while, with the feathers of the hind part a little raised. It walks and hops along the branches with much ease, and often bends down its head to peep at the objects around. It frequently alights on the ground, and scratches up the dried leaves in search of worms and beetles, but suddenly flies back to the trees, on the least alarm.

The sight of a fox or raccoon causes them much anxiety, and they generally follow these animals at a respectful distance, uttering a mournful *cluck*, well known to hunters. Although, during winter, these birds are numerous in Louisiana, they never form themselves into flocks, but go singly at this period, and only in pairs in the breeding season. They are easily reared from the nest, and sing nearly as well in confinement as while free. Their song is occasionally heard during the whole winter, particularly when the sun reappears after a shower. Their flesh is extremely delicate and juicy, and many of them are killed with the blow-gun.

Having given you a description of the Dogwood before, when I presented that tree in bloom, I have only to say here, that you now see it in its autumnal colouring, adorned with its berries, of which the Wood Thrush is fond.

TURDUS MUSTELINUS, *Gmel.* Syst. Nat. vol. i. p. 817.—*Lath.* Ind. Ornith. vol. i. p. 331.—*Ch. Bonaparte*, Synops. of Birds of the United States, p. 75.

TAWNY THRUSH, *Lath.* Syn. vol. iii. p. 28.

WOOD THRUSH, TURDUS MELODIUS, *Wils.* Amer. Ornith. vol. i. p. 35. Pl. 2. fig. 1.

Adult Male. Plate LXXIII. Fig. 1.

Bill of ordinary length, nearly straight, compressed towards the end; upper mandible with the dorsal outline a little convex, the tip slightly declinate, the margins acute, inflected towards the end, slightly notched close upon the tip; lower mandible slightly convex in its dorsal line, the tip rather obtuse. Head of ordinary size; neck and body rather slender. Feet rather long; tarsus longish, compressed, slender, anteriorly covered with a few elongated scutella, posteriorly edged, longer than the middle toe; toes scutellate above, lateral ones almost equal, the outer connected as far as the second joint.

Plumage rather loose. A few longish bristles at the base of the upper mandible. Wings of ordinary length, the third quill longest, the first very short. Tail rather short, even, of twelve broad feathers.

Bill dark brown above, flesh-colour beneath. Iris dark brown. Feet pale flesh-colour. The general colour of the upper parts is light yellowish-brown, the tail and wings a little darker, the lower part of the back and the upper tail-coverts green. Eyes margined with a whitish circle. Under parts yellowish-white, spotted with blackish-brown, excepting the throat, the under tail-coverts, and the middle part of the breast and abdomen.

Length 8 inches, extent of wings 13; bill along the ridge $\frac{7}{12}$, along the gap 1; tarsus $1\frac{1}{2}$, middle toe $\frac{11}{12}$.

Adult Female. Plate LXXIII. Fig. 2.

The female scarcely differs from the male in external appearance.

The Dog-wood.

Cornus florida, *Willd.* Sp. Pl. vol. i. p. 661.   *Mich.* Arbr. Forest. de l'Amer. Sept. t. iii. p. 138. Pl. iii. *Pursh,* Fl. Amer. p. 108.—Tetrandria Monogynia, *Linn.* Caprifolia, *Juss.*

This plant has already been described at p. 45, a twig of it in flower having been represented in Plate VIII.

THE INDIGO BIRD.

FRINGILLA CYANEA, WILS.

PLATE LXXIV. MALE, FEMALE, AND YOUNG.

THE species here presented for inspection is best known to the Creoles of Louisiana by the name of *Petit Papebleu*. This is in accordance with the general practice of the first settlers of that State, who named all the Finches, Buntings, and Orioles, *Papes ;* and all the Warblers and Fly-catchers, *Grassets*. They made an exception, however, in favour of the Rice Bird, which they honoured with the name of *Ortolan*, an appellation given in the Island of St Domingo to the Ground Dove, which, however, is seldom seen near New Orleans.

The Indigo Bird arrives in the Southern States from the direction of Mexico, along with its relative the Painted Finch, and is caught in trap-cages, but with more difficulty than the latter bird. It spreads far and wide over the United States, extending from the borders of our Atlantic shores to those of our great lakes. It is not a forest bird, but prefers the skirts of the woods, the little detached thickets in and along the fields, the meadows, the gardens, and orchards, and is frequently seen hopping along, or perched on a fence, from which it does not disdain to send forth its pretty little song. The highest top of a detached tree is, however, preferred for this purpose, and the Indigo Bird is to be observed perched on this pinnacle, singing at short intervals for half an hour at a time. Its song is at first loud and clear, falling in cadences to a very low key. The whole consists of eight or ten notes. The bird now and then launches into the air, to cross a field, and sings until it has espied a favourite spot amongst the clover, when it immediately becomes silent and dives to the ground. The whole of this parade is performed by the male, which is alone to be seen, the female at this season keeping amongst the grass or the briars along the fields, where her humble plumage hides her in a great measure from observation. Some persons have thought that this practice was changed towards the latter part of summer, when, by a casual observer, only the females are to be seen. The true reason of this, however, is, that the young birds of both sexes resemble the mother during the first season.

The Indigo Bird is an active and lively little fellow, possesses much elegance in his shape, and also a certain degree of firmness in his make, which renders him equally a favourite with the Painted Finch, although he does not possess the variegated plumage of the latter. When the male of the species now before you is in full plumage, the richness of his apparel cannot fail to attract and please the eye of any observer. It is highly glossy, and changes from the brightest azure to green, when placed in a strong light. It requires three years to attain this perfect state. The female continues in the same very humble vesture which nature first accorded to her. The males, in the first spring, and not unfrequently during the first autumn, are mottled with dull light blue, interspersed among the original deep buff of their earlier stage. The blue increases in extent, and acquires a deeper tint, as the age of the bird advances. I have often seen males two years old which were still much inferior in the beauty of their plumage to those which had passed through three springs. Should the birds be caught when in full plumage, they gradually lose their brilliant tints, which at length become extremely dull. A similar alteration is observed to take place in Painted Finches which have been kept in cages for a certain period, as well as in the Baltimore and Orchard Orioles, and in the Bulfinch, Chaffinch, and other European birds.

The nest of the Indigo Bird is usually fixed amongst the rankest stalks of weeds or grass, now and then amongst the stems of a briar, or even in a small hollow in a decayed tree. In all cases its composition is the same; but when amongst grass, clover, or briars, it is attached to two or three of the stalks by its sides. It is formed of coarse grasses, hemp stalks, and flax, and is lined with slender grasses. The female lays from four to six eggs, which are blue, with a spot or two of purple at the larger end.

Towards fall, the young congregate into loose flocks or parties of eight or ten individuals, and proceed southward. I think their migration, at both periods of the year, is performed during night. Two broods are generally raised in a season. The food of the Indigo Bird consists of small seeds of various kinds, as well as insects, some of which it occasionally pursues on wing with great vigour. They are fond of basking and rolling themselves in the roads, from which they gather small particles of sand or gravel. I have frequently seen live birds of this species offered for sale in Europe.

I have represented an adult female, two young males of the first and second year, in autumn, and a male in the full beauty of its plumage.

They are placed on a plant usually called the *Wild Sarsaparilla.* It grows in Louisiana, on the skirts of the forests, in low damp places, and along the fields, where the Indigo Birds are to be found. It is a creeping plant, and is considered valuable on account of its medicinal properties.

FRINGILLA CYANEA, *Ch. Bonaparte,* Synops. of Birds of the United States, p. 107.
INDIGO BIRD, FRINGILLA CYANEA, *Wils.* Amer. Ornith. vol. i. p. 100. Pl. 4. fig. 5.
Male.—*Ch. Bonaparte,* Amer. Ornith. vol. ii. Pl. 2. fig. 3. Female.

Male in full plumage. Plate LXXIV. Fig. 1.

Bill short, robust, conical, a little bulging, straight, acute; upper mandible broader, slightly declinate at the tip; gap-line a little declinate at the base. Nostrils basal, roundish, partially concealed by the frontal feathers. Head rather large. Neck of ordinary size. Body ovate. Feet of ordinary length, rather slender; tarsus covered anteriorly with a few scutella, the uppermost long, posteriorly edged; toes free, scutellate above; claws slender, compressed, arched, acute.

Plumage glossy, somewhat silky, blended. Wings of ordinary length, the second and third quills longest. Tail of ordinary length, distinctly emarginate, of twelve obtuse feathers.

Bill brownish-black, light blue beneath. Iris dark brown. Feet yellowish-brown. The general colour is a rich sky-blue, deeper on the head, lighter beneath, and in certain lights changing to verdigris-green. The quills, larger wing-coverts, and tail-feathers, dark brown, margined externally with blue.

Length $5\frac{1}{4}$ inches, extent of wings $7\frac{1}{4}$; bill along the ridge $\frac{1}{2}$, along the gap nearly $\frac{1}{2}$; tarsus $\frac{7}{8}$.

Male in the second year. Plate LXXIV. Fig. 3.

Bill lighter, irides and feet as in the adult. Head, neck and body, blue, but of a lighter tint; tail as in the adult; wings, including the lesser coverts, dull brown, the secondary coverts and some of the quills margined with blue.

Male in the first autumn. Plate LXXIV. Fig. 2.

Bill, irides and feet as in the last. Head and body of a lighter and duller blue, interspersed with brown patches; wings brown, secondary coverts tipped with whitish.

Adult Female.   Plate LXXIV. Fig. 4.

Bill light brown, tinged with blue.   Iris hazel.   Feet yellowish-brown.   The general colour is light yellowish-brown, the under parts and the sides of the head lighter ; the wings deep brown, margined with lighter.   The female is also considerably smaller.

The Wild Sarsaparilla.

SCHISANDRA COCCINEA, *Mich.* Flor. Amer. vol. ii. p. 218.   *Pursh,* Flor. Amer. vol i. p. 212.—PENTANDRIA POLYGYNIA, *Linn.*

A climbing shrubby plant, distinguished by its carmine-coloured flowers, consisting of nine sepals ; its numerous, one-seeded berries, and elliptico-lanceolate leaves, acute at both ends, and supported upon a long petiole.

LE PETIT CAPORAL.

FALCO TEMERARIUS.

PLATE LXXXV.

THIS beautiful little Hawk appears to be nearly allied to the European Hobby (*Falco Subbuteo*, LINN.), and is not inferior to that species in spirit and activity. I procured the individual represented, in April 1812, near Fatland Ford in Pennsylvania, whilst in pursuit of a Dove, which it would doubtless have secured, had I not terminated its career. When I first discovered this species, the individual was standing perched on an old fence-stake, in the position in which it is figured. Never having met with another of the kind, I conclude that it is extremely rare in the United States. Of its nest or young I am unable to say any thing at present.

The name which I have given to this new and rare species was chosen at the time when NAPOLEON LE GRAND was in the zenith of his glory. Every body knows that his soldiers frequently designated him by the nickname of *Le Petit Caporal*, which I thought more suitable to to our *little* Hawk, than the names NAPOLEON or BONAPARTE, which I should have adopted, had I been so fortunate as to procure a new Eagle.

FALCO TEMERARIUS.

Plate LXXV.

Bill short, as broad as deep at the base, compressed towards the end, the dorsal outline convex from the base ; upper mandible cerate, with the edges acute, slightly inflected, and forming a sharp projecting process on each side, the tip trigonal, acute, descending ; lower mandible inflected at the edges, with a notch near the end on each side, abrupt at the tip. Nostrils roundish, with a central tubercle, perforated in the cere. Head rather large, neck short, body robust. Legs of ordinary length ; tarsus scutellate before and behind ; toes scutellate above, scaly on the sides, scabrous and tuberculate beneath ; middle toe much longer than the outer, which is connected with it at the base by a membrane; claws long, curved, roundish, very acute.

Plumage ordinary compact. Feathers of the head and neck narrow, of the back broad and rounded, of the breast oblong. Tibial feathers elongated externally. Space between the bill and eye covered with bristly feathers. Orbital spaces, and projecting edge of eyebrow bare. Wings nearly as long as the tail; the primary quills narrow and taper-ing, the second longest; the secondary quills short and rounded. Tail longish, nearly even.

Bill bluish-black above, yellow beneath. Cere, orbits and eyebrow greenish-yellow. Iris hazel. Feet pale orange. The general colour of the upper parts is light bluish-grey, darker on the head and wings, each feather with a black line along the shaft. Quills brownish-black. Tail marked with alternate broad bands of light ash-grey and brownish-black, the last black band much broader, the feathers tipped with white. Chin and throat yellowish-white; sides of the neck light yellowish-red, streaked with dark brown; lower part of the fore neck, the whole of the breast, and the sides, yellowish-white, with large spots of brown. Abdomen and under tail-coverts brownish-white; tibial feathers light reddish, each with a central line of blackish-brown.

Length $10\frac{3}{5}$ inches; bill along the back $\frac{3}{5}$; tarsus $1\frac{1}{4}$, middle toe $1\frac{7}{12}$.

HOSPITALITY IN THE WOODS.

HOSPITALITY is a virtue, the exercise of which, although always agreeable to the stranger, is not always duly appreciated. The traveller who has acquired celebrity, is not unfrequently received with a species of hospitality, which is so much alloyed by the obvious attention of the host to his own interest, that the favour conferred upon the stranger must have less weight, when it comes mingled with almost interminable questions as to his perilous adventures. Another receives hospitality at the hands of persons, who, possessed of all the comforts of life, receive the way-worn wanderer with pomposity, lead him from one part of their spacious mansion to another, and bidding him good night, leave him to amuse himself in his solitary apartment, because he is thought unfit to be presented to a party of *friends*. A third stumbles on a congenial spirit, who receives him with open arms, offers him servants, horses, perhaps even his purse, to enable him to pursue his journey, and parts from him with regret. In all these cases, the traveller feels more or less under obligation, and is accordingly grateful. But, kind reader, the hospitality received from the inhabitant of the forest, who can offer only the shelter of his humble roof, and the refreshment of his homely fare, remains more deeply impressed on the memory of the bewildered traveller than any other. This kind of hospitality I have myself frequently experienced in our woods, and now proceed to relate an instance of it.

I had walked several hundred miles, accompanied by my son, then a stripling, and, coming upon a clear stream, observed a house on the opposite shore. We crossed in a canoe, and finding that we had arrived at a tavern, determined upon spending the night there. As we were both greatly fatigued, I made an arrangement with our host to be conveyed in a light Jersey waggon a distance of a hundred miles, the period of our departure to be determined by the rising of the moon. Fair Cynthia, with her shorn beams, peeped over the forest about two hours before dawn, and our conductor, provided with a long twig of hickory, took his station in the fore-part of the waggon. Off we went at a round trot, dancing in the cart like pease in a sieve. The road, which was just wide enough to allow us to pass, was full of deep ruts, and covered here and there with trunks and stumps, over all which we were hurried. Our con-

ductor Mr FLINT, the landlord of the tavern, boasting of his perfect
knowledge of the country, undertook to drive us by a short-cut, and we
willingly confided ourselves to his management. So we jogged along,
now and then deviating to double the fallen timber. Day commenced
with promise of fine weather, but several nights of white frost having occurred, a change was expected. To our sorrow, the change took place
long before we got to the road again. The rain fell in torrents; the
thunder bellowed; the lightning blazed. It was now evening, but the
storm had brought perfect night, black and dismal. Our cart had no
cover. Cold and wet, we sat silent and melancholy, with no better expectation than that of passing the night under the little shelter the cart
could afford us.

To stop was considered worse than to proceed. So we gave the reins
to the horses, with some faint hope that they would drag us out of our
forlorn state. Of a sudden the steeds altered their course, and soon after
we perceived the glimmer of a faint light in the distance, and almost at
the same moment heard the barking of dogs. Our horses stopped by
a high fence, and fell a-neighing, while I hallooed at such a rate, that an
answer was speedily obtained. The next moment, a flaming pine torch
crossed the gloom, and advanced to the spot where we stood. The Negro
boy who bore it, without waiting to question us, enjoined us to follow
the fence, and said that Master had sent him to shew the strangers to the
house. We proceeded, much relieved, and soon reached the gate of a
little yard, in which a small cabin was perceived.

A tall fine-looking young man stood in the open door, and desired us
to get out of the cart and walk in. We did so, when the following conversation took place. " A bad night this, strangers; how came you
to be along the fence ? you certainly must have lost your way, for there
is no public road within twenty miles." " Aye," answered Mr FLINT,
" sure enough we lost our way; but, thank God ! we have got to a
house, and thank *you* for your reception." " Reception !" replied the
woodsman, " no very great thing after all; you are all here safe, and
that's enough.—Eliza," turning to his wife, " see about some victuals
for the strangers, and you, Jupiter," addressing the Negro lad, " bring
some wood and mend the fire. Eliza, call the boys up, and treat the
strangers the best way you can. Come, gentlemen, pull off your wet
clothes, and draw to the fire. Eliza, bring some socks and a shirt or
two."

For my part, kind reader, knowing my countrymen as I do, I was not much struck at all this; but my son, who had scarcely reached the age of fourteen, drew near to me, and observed how pleasant it was to have met with such good people. Mr FLINT bore a hand in getting his horses put under a shed. The young wife was already stirring with so much liveliness, that to have doubted for a moment that all she did was not a pleasure to her would have been impossible. Two Negro lads made their appearance, looked at us for a moment, and going out, called the dogs. Soon after the cries of the poultry informed us that good cheer was at hand. JUPITER brought more wood, the blaze of which illumined the cottage. Mr FLINT and our host returned, and we already began to feel the comforts of hospitality. The woodsman remarked that it was a pity we had not chanced to come that day three weeks; " for," said he, " it was our wedding-day, and father gave us a good house-warming, and you might have fared better; but, however, if you can eat bacon and eggs, and a broiled chicken, you shall have that. I have no whisky in the house, but father has some capital cider, and I'll go over and bring a keg of it." I asked how far off his father lived. " Only three miles, Sir, and I'll be back before Eliza has cooked your supper." Off he went accordingly, and the next moment the gallopping of his horse was heard. The rain fell in torrents, and now I also became struck with the kindness of our host.

To all appearance the united ages of the pair under whose roof we had found shelter did not exceed two score. Their means seemed barely sufficient to render them comfortable, but the generosity of their young hearts had no limits. The cabin was new. The logs of which it was formed were all of the tulip-tree, and were nicely pared. Every part was beautifully clean. Even the coarse slabs of wood that formed the floor looked as if newly washed and dried. Sundry gowns and petticoats of substantial homespun hung from the logs that formed one of the sides of the cabin, while the other was covered with articles of male attire. A large spinning-wheel, with rolls of wool and cotton, occupied one corner. In another was a small cupboard, containing the little stock of new dishes, cups, plates, and tin pans. The table was small also, but quite new, and as bright as polished walnut could be. The only bed that I saw was of domestic manufacture, and the counterpane proved how expert the young wife was at spinning and weaving. A fine rifle ornamented the chimney-piece. The fire-place was of such dimensions that it looked

B b

as if it had been purposely constructed for holding the numerous progeny expected to result from the happy union.

The black boy was engaged in grinding some coffee. Bread was prepared by the fair hands of the bride, and placed on a flat board in front of the fire. The bacon and eggs already murmured and spluttered in the frying-pan, and a pair of chickens puffed and swelled on a gridiron over the embers, in front of the hearth. The cloth was laid, and every thing arranged, when the clattering of hoofs announced the return of the husband. In he came, bearing a two-gallon keg of cider. His eyes sparkled with pleasure as he said, " Only think, ELIZA ; father wanted to rob us of the strangers, and was for coming here to ask them to his own house, just as if we could not give them enough ourselves ; but here's the drink—Come gentlemen, sit down and help yourselves." We did so, and I, to enjoy the repast, took a chair of the husband's making in preference to one of those called *Windsor*, of which there were six in the cabin. This chair was bottomed with a piece of deer's skin tightly stretched, and afforded a very comfortable seat.

The wife now resumed her spinning, and the husband filled a jug with the sparkling cider, and, seated by the blazing fire, was drying his clothes. The happiness he enjoyed beamed from his eye, as at my request he proceeded to give us an account of his affairs and prospects, which he did in the following words :—" I will be twenty-two next Christmas-day," said our host ; " My father came from Virginia when young, and settled on the large tract of land where he yet lives, and where with hard working he has done well. There were nine children of us. Most of them are married and settled in the neighbourhood. The old man has divided his lands among some of us, and bought others for the rest. The land where I am he gave me two years ago, and a finer piece is not easily to be found. I have cleared a couple of fields, and planted an orchard. Father gave me a stock of cattle, some hogs, and four horses, with two Negro boys. I camped here for most of the time when clearing and planting ; and when about to marry the young woman you see at the wheel, father helped me in raising this hut. My wife, as luck would have it, had a Negro also, and we have begun the world as well off as most folks, and, the Lord willing, may——but, gentlemen, you don't eat ; do help yourselves—ELIZA, maybe the strangers would like some milk." The wife stopped her work, and kindly asked if we preferred sweet or sour milk ; for you must know, reader, that sour milk is by some of our farmers considered a treat. Both sorts were produced, but, for my part, I chose to stick to the cider.

Supper over, we all neared the fire, and engaged in conversation. At length our kind host addressed his wife as follows :—" ELIZA, the gentlemen would like to lie down, I guess. What sort of bed can you fix for them ?" ELIZA looked up with a smile, and said : " Why, WILLY, we will divide the bedding, and arrange half on the floor, on which we can sleep very well, and the gentlemen will have the best we can spare them." To this arrangement I immediately objected, and proposed lying on a blanket by the fire ; but neither WILLY nor ELIZA would listen. So they arranged a part of their bedding on the floor, on which, after some debate, we at length settled. The Negroes were sent to their own cabin, the young couple went to bed, and Mr FLINT lulled us all asleep, with a long story intended to shew us how passing strange it was that he should have lost his way.

" Tired nature's sweet restorer, balmy sleep,"—and so forth. But Aurora soon turned her off. Mr SPEED, our host, rose, went to the door, and returning assured us that the weather was too bad for us to attempt proceeding. I really believe he was heartily glad of it ; but anxious to continue our journey, I desired Mr FLINT to see about his horses. ELIZA by this time was up too, and I observed her whispering to her husband, when he immediately said aloud, " To be sure, the gentlemen will eat breakfast before they go, and I will shew them the way to the road." Excuses were of no avail. Breakfast was prepared and eaten. The weather brightened a little, and by nine we were under way. WILLY on horseback headed us. In a few hours, our cart arrived at a road, by following which we at length got to the main one, and parted from our woodsman with the greater regret that he would accept nothing from any of us. On the contrary, telling Mr FLINT with a smile, that he hoped he might some time again follow the longest track for a short cut, he bade us adieu, and trotted back to his fair ELIZA and his happy home.

THE VIRGINIAN PARTRIDGE.

PERDIX VIRGINIANA, LATH.

PLATE LXXVI. MALE, FEMALE, AND YOUNG.

THE common name given to this bird in the Eastern and Middle Districts of our Union is that of *Quail*, but in the Western and Southern States, the more appropriate appellation of *Partridge* is bestowed upon it. It is abundantly met with in all parts of the United States, but more especially towards the interior. In the States of Ohio and Kentucky, where they are very abundant, they are to be seen in the markets, both dead and alive, in large quantities.

This species performs occasional migrations from the north-west to the south-east, usually in the beginning of October, and somewhat in the manner of the Wild Turkey. For a few weeks at this season, the northwestern shores of the Ohio are covered with flocks of Partridges. They ramble through the woods along the margin of the stream, and generally fly across towards evening. Like the Turkeys, many of the weaker Partridges often fall into the water, while thus attempting to cross, and generally perish ; for although they swim surprisingly, they have not muscular power sufficient to keep up a protracted struggle, although, when they have fallen within a few yards of the shore, they easily escape being drowned. I have been told by a friend that a person residing in Philadelphia had a hearty laugh on hearing that I had described the Wild Turkey as swimming for some distance, when it had accidentally fallen into the water. But be assured, kind reader, almost every species of land-bird is capable of swimming on such occasions, and you may easily satisfy yourself as to the accuracy of my statement by throwing a Turkey, a Common Fowl, or any other bird into the water. As soon as the Partridges have crossed the principal streams in their way, they disperse in flocks over the country, and return to their ordinary mode of life.

The flight of these birds is generally performed at a short distance from the ground. It is rapid, and is continued by numerous quick flaps of the wings for a certain distance, after which the bird sails until about to alight, when again it flaps its wings to break its descent. When chased by dogs, or started by any other enemy, they fly to the middle branches of trees of ordinary size, where they remain until danger is over. They walk with ease on the branches. If they perceive that they are observed, they raise the feathers of their head, emit a low note, and fly off either to some higher branch of the same tree, or to another tree at a distance. When these birds rise on wing of their own accord, the whole flock takes the same course; but when put up (in the sportsman's phrase), they disperse, after alighting call to each other, and soon after unite, each running or flying towards the well-known cry of the patriarch of the covey. During deep and continued snows, they often remain on the branches of trees for hours at a time.

The usual cry of this species is a clear whistle, composed of three notes; the first and last nearly equal in length, the latter less loud than the first, but more so than the intermediate one. When an enemy is perceived they immediately utter a lisping note, frequently repeated, and run off with their tail spread, their crest erected, and their wings drooping, towards the shelter of some thicket or the top of a fallen tree. At other times, when one of the flock has accidentally strayed to a distance from its companions, it utters two notes louder than any of those mentioned above, the first shorter and lower than the second, when an answer is immediately returned by one of the pack. This species has moreover a love-call, which is louder and clearer than its other notes, and can be heard at a distance of several hundred yards. It consists of three distinct notes, the two last being loudest, and is peculiar to the male bird. A fancied similarity to the words *Bob White* renders this call familiar to the sportsman and farmer; but these notes are always preceded by another, easily heard at a distance of thirty or forty yards. The three together resemble the words *Ah Bob White*. The first note is a kind of aspiration, and the last is very loud and clear. This whistle is seldom heard after the breeding season, during which an imitation of the peculiar note of the female will make the male fly towards the sportsman, who may then easily shoot it.

In the Middle Districts, the love-call of the male is heard about the middle of April, and in Louisiana much earlier. The male is seen perched on a fence-stake, or on the low branch of a tree, standing nearly in the same position for hours together, and calling *Ah Bob White* at every interval of a few minutes. Should he hear the note of a female, he sails directly towards the spot whence it proceeded. Several males may be heard from different parts of a field challenging each other, and should they meet on the ground, they fight with great courage and obstinacy, until the conqueror drives off his antagonist to another field.

The female prepares a nest composed of grasses, arranged in a circular form, leaving an entrance not unlike that of a common oven. It is placed at the foot of a tuft of rank grass or some close stalks of corn, and is partly sunk in the ground. The eggs are from ten to eighteen, rather sharp at the smaller end, and of a pure white. The male at times assists in hatching them. This species raises only one brood in the year, unless the eggs or the young when yet small have been destroyed. When this happens, the female immediately prepares another nest; and should it also be ravaged, sometimes even a third. The young run about the moment after they make their appearance, and follow their parents until spring, when, having acquired their full beauty, they pair and breed.

The Partridge rests at night on the ground, either amongst the grass or under a bent log. The individuals which compose the flock form a ring, and moving backwards, approach each other until their bodies are nearly in contact. This arrangement enables the whole covey to take wing when suddenly alarmed, each flying off in a direct course, so as not to interfere with the rest.

These birds are easily caught in snares, common dead-falls, traps and pens, like those for the Wild Turkey, but proportionate to the size of the bird. Many are shot, but the principal havock is effected by means of nets, especially in the Western and Southern States. The method employed is as follows:

A number of persons on horseback, provided with a net, set out in search of Partridges, riding along the fences or briar-thickets, which the birds are known to frequent. One or two of the party whistle in imitation of the second call-note above described, and as Partridges are plentiful, the call is soon answered by a covey, when the sportsmen immediately proceed to ascertain their position and number, seldom considering it worth while to set the net when there are only a few birds. They approach in a careless manner, talking and laughing as if merely passing by. When the birds are discovered, one of the party gallops off in a circuitous manner, gets in advance of the rest by a hundred yards or more, according to the situation of the birds, and their disposition to run, while the rest of the sportsmen move about on their horses, talking to each other, but at the same time watching every motion of the Partridges. The person in advance being provided with the net, dismounts, and at once falls to placing it, so that his companions can easily drive the Partridges into it. No sooner is the machine ready, than the net-bearer remounts and rejoins the party. The sportsmen separate to a short distance, and follow the Partridges, talking and whistling, clapping their hands, or knocking upon the fence-rails. The birds move with great gentleness, following each other, and are kept in the right direction by the sportsmen. The leading bird approaches and enters the mouth of the net, the others follow in succession, when the net-bearer leaps from his horse, runs up and secures the entrance, and soon dispatches the birds. In this manner, fifteen or twenty Partridges are caught at one driving, and sometimes many hundreds in the course of a day. Most netters give liberty to a pair out of each flock, that the breed may be continued.

The success of driving depends much on the state of the weather. Drizzly rain or melting snow are the best, for in such weather Partridges and Gallinaceous Birds in general will run to a great distance rather than fly; whereas if the weather be dry and clear, they generally take to wing the moment they discover an intruder, or squat so that they cannot be driven without very particular care. Again, when the flocks are found in the woods, they run off so briskly and so far, that it is difficult for the net-bearer to place his machine in time.

The net is cylindrical, thirty or forty feet in length, by about two in diameter, excepting at the mouth or entrance, where it is rather larger, and at the extremity, where it assumes the form of a bag. It is kept open by means of small wooden hoops, at a distance of two or three feet from each other. The mouth is furnished with a semicircular hoop, sharpened at both ends, which are driven into the ground, thus affording an easy entrance to the birds. Two pieces of netting called wings, of the same length as the cylindrical one, are placed one on each side of the mouth, so as to form an obtuse angle with each other, and are supported by sticks thrust into the ground, the wings having the appearance of two low fences leading to a gate. The whole is made of light and strong materials.

The Virginian Partridge is easily kept in cages or coops, and soon becomes very fat. Attempts at rearing them from the eggs have generally failed, probably for want of proper care, and a deficiency of insects, on which the young feed. The ordinary food of the species consists of seeds of various kinds, and such berries as grow near the surface of the ground, along with which they pick up a quantity of sand or gravel. Towards autumn, when the young have nearly attained their full size, their flesh becomes fat, juicy and tender, and being moreover white and extremely agreeable to the palate, is in much request. Twenty years ago, they were commonly sold at twelve cents the dozen; but now they are more commonly sold at fifty cents. They suffer greatly in the Middle Districts during severe winters, and are killed in immense numbers.

This bird has been introduced into various parts of Europe, but is not much liked there, being of such pugnacious habits as to drive off the common Grey Partridge, which is considered a better bird for the table.

In the Plate I have represented a group of Partridges attacked by a Hawk. The different attitudes exhibited by the former cannot fail to give you a lively idea of the terror and confusion which prevail on such occasions.

PERDIX VIRGINIANA, *Lath.* Ind. Ornith. vol. ii. p. 650.—*Ch. Bonaparte*, Synops. of Birds of the United States, p. 124.

TETRAO VIRGINIANUS, *Linn.* Syst. Nat. vol. i. p. 277.

QUAIL or PARTRIDGE, PERDIX VIRGINIANA, *Wils.* Americ. Ornith. vol. vi. p. 21. Pl. 47. fig. 2. Male.

Adult Male.   Plate LXXVI. Fig. 1, 1, 1, 1.

Bill short, robust, rather obtuse, the base covered by feathers; upper mandible with the dorsal outline curved, the sides convex, the edges overlapping, the tip declinate; under mandible nearly straight in its dorsal outline, arched on the edges, the sides convex. Nostrils concealed among the feathers. Head and neck of ordinary size. Body short and bulky. Feet of ordinary length; tarsus anteriorly scutellate, a little compressed, spurless; toes scutellate above, pectinate on the sides; claws arched, obtuse.

Plumage compact, glossy. Feathers of the upper part of the head erectile into a tuft. Wings short, broad, much curved and rounded, the fourth quill longest. Tail short, rounded, of twelve rounded feathers.

Bill dark brown. Iris hazel. Feet greyish-blue. The forehead, a broad line over each eye, and the throat and fore-neck, white. Lore, auricular coverts, and a broad irregular semilunar band on the fore-neck, more or less black. Upper part of the head, hind and lower part of the neck all round, reddish-brown. Upper back and wing-coverts bright brownish-red; the lower part of the back light red tinged with yellow. Primaries dusky, externally margined with blue; secondaries irregularly barred with light red. Tail greyish-blue, excepting the middle feathers, which are dull greyish-yellow, sprinkled with black. Sides of the neck spotted with white. Under parts white, streaked with brownish-red, transversely and undulatingly barred with black. Sides and under tail-coverts reddish.

Length 10 inches, extent of wings 15; bill along the back $\frac{1}{2}$, along the gap $\frac{7}{12}$; tarsus $\frac{1}{2}$, middle toe nearly the same.

Young Male. Plate LXXVI. Fig. 2, 2.

Similar to the adult male in the general distribution of the colours; but the white of the head and throat bright reddish-yellow, the black of the fore-neck and sides of the head deep brown, the under parts less pure and more dusky, and the tail of a duller grey.

Adult Female. Plate LXXVI. Fig. 3, 3, 3.

The female resembles the young male, but is more decidedly coloured, the bill darker, the head of a more uniform and richer reddish-yellow, the sides of the neck spotted with yellow and black.

Length $9\frac{1}{2}$ inches, extent of wings 14.

Young Female. Plate LXXVI. Fig. 4, 4. 4.

The young females are somewhat smaller and lighter in their tints than the yonng males.

Very Young Birds. Plate LXXVI. Fig. 5, 5, 5, 5, 5, 5, 5.

Bill brownish-yellow. Iris light hazel. The general colour of the upper parts light yellowish-brown, patched with grey; sides of the head dusky.

THE BELTED KINGSFISHER.

ALCEDO ALCYON, LINN.

PLATE LXXVII. MALE AND FEMALE.

You must not suppose, good-natured reader, that the lives which I try to write, are short or lengthy according to the natural dimensions of the objects themselves; for if with the representation of a large bird, I present you with a long history of its habits, it is merely because that bird, being perhaps more common, and therefore more conspicuous, I have had better and more frequent opportunities of studying them. This happens to be the case with the bird which I proceed to describe.

The Belted Kingsfisher!—Now, kind reader, were I infected with the desire of giving new names to well-known objects, you may be assured that, notwithstanding the partly appropriate name given to this bird, I should call it, as I think it ought to have been called, the *United States' Kingsfisher*. My reason for this will, I hope, become apparent to you, when I say that it is the only bird of its genus found upon the inland streams of the Union. Another reason of equal force might be adduced, which is, that, although the males of all denominations have, from time immemorial, obtained the supremacy, in this particular case the term Belted applies only to the female, the male being destitute of the belt or band by which she is distinguished. But names already given and received, whether apt or inapt, I am told, must not be meddled with. To this law I humbly submit, and so proceed, contenting myself with feeling assured that many names given to birds might, with much benefit to the student of nature, become the subjects of reform.

The Belted Kingsfisher is a constant resident in the States of Louisiana, Mississippi, Arkansas, and all the districts that lie to the south of North Carolina. Its inland migrations along the windings of our noble rivers extend far and wide, over the whole of the United States. In all those portions which I have visited it also breeds, although it returns to the south from many parts during severe winters.

The flight of this bird is rapid, and is prolonged according to its necessities, extending at times to considerable distances, in which case it is performed high in the air. When, for instance, the whole course of one of our northern rivers becomes frozen, the Kingsfisher, instead of skimming closely over the surface that no longer allows it to supply itself with food, passes high above the tallest trees, and takes advantage of every short cut which the situation of the river affords. By this means it soon reaches a milder climate. This is also frequently the case, when it seems tired of the kind of fish that occurs in a lake, and removes to another in a direct line, passing over the forests, not unfrequently by a course of twenty or thirty miles towards the interior of the country. Its motions when on wing consist of a series of flaps, about five or six in number, followed by a direct glide, without any apparent undulation. It moves in the same way when flying closely over the water.

If, in the course of such excursions, the bird passes over a small pool, it suddenly checks itself in its career, poises itself in the air, like a Sparrow-hawk or Kestril, and inspects the water beneath, to discover whether there may be fishes in it suitable to its taste. Should it find this to be the case, it continues poised for a few seconds, dashes spirally headlong into the water, seizes a fish, and alights on the nearest tree or stump, where it swallows its prey in a moment.

The more usual range of the Belted Kingsfisher, however, is confined to the rivers and creeks that abound throughout the United States ; all of which, according to the seasons, are amply supplied with various fishes, on the fry of which this bird feeds. It follows their course up to the very source of the small rivulets ; and it is not unusual to hear the hard, rapid, rattling notes of our Kingsfisher, even amongst the murmuring cascades of our higher mountains. When the bird is found in such sequestered situations, well may the angler be assured that trout is abundant. Mill-ponds are also favourite resorts of the Kingsfisher, the usual calmness of the water in such places permitting it to discover its prey with ease. As the freshets are proportionally less felt on the adjoining shores, the holes dug in the earth or sand by this species, in which it deposits its eggs, are generally found in places not far from a mill worked by water.

I have laid open to my view several of these holes, in different situations and soils, and have generally found them to be formed as follows. The male and female, after having fixed upon a proper spot, are seen clinging to the bank of the stream in the manner of Woodpeckers. Their long and stout bills are set to work, and as soon as the hole has acquired a certain depth, one of the birds enters it, and scratches out the

sand, earth or clay, with its feet, striking meanwhile with its bill to extend the depth. The other bird all the while appears to cheer the la-
bourer, and urge it to continue its exertions ; and, when the latter is fatigued, takes its place. Thus, by the co-operation of both, the hole is
dug to the depth of four, five, or sometimes six feet, in a horizontal direction, at times not more than eighteen inches below the surface of the
ground, at others eight or ten feet. At the Chicasaw Bluffs, on the Mississippi, I have seen some of these holes more than fifty feet below the
surface, but generally beyond reach of the highest freshets. The hole is
just large enough to admit the passage of a single bird at a time. The
end is rounded and finished in the form of a common oven, to allow the
pair or the whole brood to turn round in it at ease. Here, on a few
sticks and feathers, the eggs are deposited to the number generally of six.
They are pure white. Incubation continues for sixteen days. In the
Middle States, these birds seldom raise more than one brood in the year,
but in the southern usually two. Incubation is performed by both parents, which evince great solicitude for the safety of their young. The
mother sometimes drops on the water, as if severely wounded, and flutters and flounders as if unable to rise from the stream, in order to induce
the intruder to wade or swim after her, whilst her mate, perched on the
nearest bough, or even on the edge of the bank, jerks his tail, erects his
crest, rattles his notes with angry vehemence, and then springing off,
passes and repasses before the enemy, with a continued cry of despair.

I have not been able to ascertain whether or not the young are fed
with macerated food disgorged by the parents into their bills, but I have
reason to think so, and I have always observed the old ones to swallow
the fishes which they had caught, before they entered the hole. The
young are, however, afterwards fed directly on the entire fish ; and I
have frequently seen them follow the parent birds, and alight on the
same branch, flapping their wings, and calling with open bill for the food
just taken out of the water, when the petition was seldom denied.

The Kingsfisher resorts to the same hole, to breed and roost, for
many years in succession. On one occasion, when I attempted two evenings to seize one of these birds, long after night had closed, I tried in
vain the first time. I fitted a small net bag to the entrance, and returned home. Next morning the bird had scratched a passage under the
net, and thus escaped. The following evening I saw it enter the hole,
and having procured a stick that filled the entrance for upwards of a

foot, I felt certain of obtaining it ; but before I reached the place next day, it had worked its way out. After this, I abandoned my attempt, although the bird continued to repose in the same hole.

No superstitious notions exist in the United States respecting this species. The flesh is extremely fishy, oily, and disagreeable to the taste. On the contrary, the eggs are fine eating.

I was ready to put my pen aside, kind reader, when, on consulting my journals, all of which are now at hand, I happened to read, that I have seen instances of this bird's plunging into the sea after small fry, at Powles Hook, in the bay opposite to the City of New York. I am not aware that this is a common occurrence.

ALCEDO ALCYON, *Linn.* Syst. Nat. vol. i. p. 180.—*Lath.* Ind. Ornith. vol. i. p. 257.—
    Ch. Bonaparte, Synops. of Birds of the United States, p. 48.
BELTED KINGSFISHER, *Lath.* Synops. vol. ii. p. 637.—*Wils.* Amer. Ornith. vol. iii.
    p. 59, Pl. 23, fig. 1.

Adult Male. Plate LXXVII. Fig. 1, 2.

Bill long, straight, tetragonal, tapering to an acute point, compressed towards the end ; upper mandible keeled, with the dorsal line straight, the edges overlapping ; lower mandible with the dorsal line slightly convex, the tip ascending ; gap-line extending to beneath the eyes. Nostrils basal, dorsal, oblong, oblique, half-closed by a bare membrane. Head large, neck short, body robust. Feet very short; tarsus roundish, anteriorly scutellate, half the length of the middle toe ; outer and middle toes nearly equal, inner much shorter, hind toe small ; claws rather strong, arched, acute, channelled beneath.

Plumage compact. Feathers of the head long, narrow, rather loose, pointed, and erectile, in the form of a longitudinal crest, of which the anterior feathers are longest. Wings longish, the third primary longest. Tail short, even, of twelve broad rounded feathers.

Bill brownish-black, light greenish-blue at the base. Iris hazel. Feet greyish-blue ; claws black. Head, cheeks, hind neck and upper parts, generally light blue, the shaft of each feather blackish. A white spot before the eye, and a slight streak of the same colour on the under eyelid. Quills brownish-black, the base of the primaries barred with white, the secondaries blue on the outer web. Two middle tail-feathers blue, as are the outer edges of the rest, excepting the outermost ; all, excepting the two middle ones, brownish-black, barred with white. A broad band of white across the neck, broader anteriorly and including the chin and throat. A band of blue across the fore part of the breast. The rest of the under parts white, excepting the sides, which are mottled with blue.

Length 12½ inches, extent of wings 20 ; bill along the ridge 2, along the gap 2¼ ; tarsus ½, middle toe 1$\frac{1}{12}$.

Adult Female.   Plate LXXVII. Fig. 3.

The blue of the female is much duller. The band on the upper part of the breast is of dull greyish blue and light red intermixed ; below this is a narrow band of white, and across the middle of the breast a broad band of yellowish-red, of which colour also are the sides. The rest of the under parts are white, tinged with red.

THE GREAT CAROLINA WREN.

TROGLODYTES LUDOVICIANUS, CH. BONAPARTE.

PLATE LXXVIII. Male and Female.

PERMIT me to suggest, kind reader, that I think it always best to see and judge of individuals in their own country. There independence and ease are more commonly met with, and the observer is less attended to. This being admitted, I shall give you the history and life of the Great Carolina Wren, as studied in the State of Louisiana, where that bird is a constant resident.

Its flight is performed by short flappings of the wings, the concave under surfaces of which occasion a low rustling, as the bird moves to the. distance of a few steps only at each start. It is accompanied by violent jerks of the tail and body, and is by no means graceful. In this manner. the Carolina Wren moves from one fence-rail to another, from log to log, up and down among the low branches of bushes, piles of wood, and. decayed roots of prostrate trees, or between the stalks of canes. Its tail is almost constantly erect, and before it starts to make the least flight or leap, it uses a quick motion, which brings its body almost into contact with the object on which it stands, and then springs from its legs. All this is accompanied with a strong *chirr-up*, uttered as if the bird were in an angry mood, and repeated at short intervals.

The quickness of the motions of this active little bird is fully equal to that of the mouse. Like the latter, it appears and is out of sight in a moment, peeps into a crevice, passes rapidly through it, and shews itself at a different place the next instant. When satiated with food, or fatigued with these multiplied exertions, the little fellow stops, droops its tail, and sings with great energy a short ditty something resembling the words *come-to-me, come-to-me*, repeated several times in quick succession, so loud, and yet so mellow, that it is always agreeable to listen to them. During spring, these notes are heard from all parts of the plantations, the damp woods, the swamps, the sides of creeks and rivers, as well as from the barns, the stables and the piles of wood, within a few yards of the house. I have frequently heard these Wrens singing from the roof of an abandoned flat-boat, fastened to the shore, a small distance below the city of New Orleans. When its song was finished, the bird went on creeping from one board to another, thrust itself through an auger-hole, entered through the boat's side at one place, and peeped out at another, catching numerous spiders and other insects all the while. It sometimes ascends to the higher branches of a tree of moderate size, by climbing along a grape-vine, searching diligently amongst the leaves and in the chinks of the bark, alighting sidewise against the trunk, and moving like a true Creeper. It possesses the power of creeping and of hopping in a nearly equal degree. The latter kind of motion it employs when nearer the ground, and among piles of drifted timber. So fond is this bird of the immediate neighbourhood of water, that it would be next to impossible to walk along the shore of any of the islands of the Mississippi, from the mouth of the Ohio to New Orleans, without observing several on each island.

Amongst the many species of insects which they destroy, several are of an aquatic nature, and are procured by them whilst creeping about the masses of drifted wood. Their *chirr-up* and *come-to-me come-to-me* seldom cease for more than fifteen or twenty minutes at a time, commencing with the first glimpse of day, and continuing sometimes after sunset.

The nest of the Carolina Wren is usually placed in a hole in some low decayed tree, or in a fence-stake, sometimes even in the stable, barn or coach-house, should it there find a place suitable for its reception. I have found some not more than two feet from the ground, in the stump of a tree that had long before been felled by the axe. The materials employed in its construction are hay, grasses, leaves, feathers, and horse-hair, or the dry fibres of the Spanish moss ; the feathers, hair or moss forming the lining, the coarse materials the outer parts. When the hole is sufficiently large, the nest is not unfrequently five or six inches in depth, although only just wide enough to admit one of the birds at a time. The number of eggs is from five to eight. They are of a broad oval form, greyish-white, sprinkled with reddish-brown. Whilst at Oakley, the residence of my friend JAMES PERRIE, Esq. near Bayou Sara, I discovered that one of these birds was in the habit of roosting in a Wood Thrush's nest that was placed on a low horizontal branch, and had been filled with leaves that had fallen during the autumn. It was in the habit of thrusting his body beneath the leaves, and I doubt not found the place very comfortable.

They usually raise two, sometimes three broods in a season. The young soon come out from the nest, and in a few days after creep and hop about with as much nimbleness as the old ones. Their plumage undergoes no change, merely becoming firmer in the colouring.

Many of these birds are destroyed by Weasels and Minxes. It is, notwithstanding, one of the most common birds which we have as resident in Louisiana. They ascend along the shores of the Mississippi as high as the Missouri River, and along the Ohio nearly to Pittsburg, although they do not occur in great numbers in the neighbourhood of that city. They are common in Georgia, the Carolinas, Kentucky, Ohio and Indiana. A few are to be seen along the Atlantic shores as far as Pennsylvania and New Jersey. In the latter State I have found its nest, near a swamp, a few miles from Philadelphia. I never observed them farther to the eastward.

The Dwarf Buck-eye, on a blossomed twig of which you observe a pair of Great Carolina Wrens, is by nature as well as name a low shrub. It grows near swampy ground in great abundance. Its flowers, which are scentless, are much resorted to by the Humming Birds, on their first arrival, as they appear at a very early season. The wood resembles that of the Common Horse-chestnut, and its fruit is nearly the same in form and colour, but much smaller. I know of no valuable property possessed by this beautiful shrub.

TROGLODYTES LUDOVICIANUS, *Ch. Bonaparte*, Synops. of Birds of the United States, p. 93.

SYLVIA LUDOVICIANA, *Lath.* Ind. Ornith. vol. ii. p 548.

GREAT CAROLINA WREN, CERTHIA CAROLINIANA, *Wils.* Amer. Ornith. vol. ii. p. 61, Pl. 12. fig. 5.

Adult Male. Plate LXXVIII. Fig. 1.

Bill nearly as long as the head, subulato-conical, slightly arched, compressed towards the tip; upper mandible with the sides convex towards the end, concave at the base, the edges acute and overlapping; under mandible with the back and sides convex. Nostrils oblong, straight, basal, with a cartilaginous lid above, open and bare. Head oblong, neck of ordinary size, body ovate. Legs of ordinary length; tar-

c c

sus longer than the middle toe, compressed, anteriorly scutate, posteriorly edged ; toes, scutellate above, inferiorly granulate ; second and fourth
nearly equal, the hind toe almost as long as the middle one, third and
fourth united as far as the second joint ; claws long, slender, acute, arcuate, much compressed.

Plumage soft, lax, and tufty. Wings short, very convex, broad and
rounded, the first quill very short, the fourth longest. Tail rather long,
curved downwards, much rounded, of twelve narrowish, rounded feathers.

Bill wood-brown above, bluish beneath. Iris hazel. Legs flesh-colour. The general colour of the upper part is brownish-red. A yellowish-
white streak over the eye, extending far down the neck, and edged above
with dark brown. Quills, coverts and tail barred with blackish-brown ;
secondary and middle coverts tipped with white ; shafts of the scapulars
white. Throat greyish-white, under parts reddish-buff, paler behind.
Under tail-coverts white, barred with blackish.

Length 5¼ inches, extent of wings 7½ ; bill along the ridge ⅜, along
the gap 1½ ; tarsus ⅚.

Adult Female. Plate LXXVIII. Fig. 2.

The female differs from the male in being lighter above, tinged with
grey beneath, and in wanting the white tips of the wing-coverts.

This species and the Marsh Wren form the transition from Troglodytes to Certhia, resembling the former in habits and colouring, and the
latter in the form of the bill, as well as partly in habits.

THE DWARF BUCK-EYE.

ÆSCULUS PAVIA, *Willd.* Sp. Pl. vol. ii. p. 286. *Pursh,* Fl. Amer. vol. ii. p. 254.—
HEPTANDRIA MONOGYNIA, *Linn.* ACERA, *Juss.*

Leaves quinate, smooth, unequally serrated ; racemes lax ; generally
with ternate flowers ; corollas tetrapetalous, their connivent claws of the
length of the calyx ; stamens seven, shorter than the corolla. The flowers
are scarlet.

THE TYRANT FLY-CATCHER.

MUSCICAPA TYRANNUS, Briss.

PLATE LXXIX. Male and Female.

The Tyrant Fly-catcher, or, as it is commonly named, the Field Martin, or King Bird, is one of the most interesting visitors of the United States, where it is to be found during spring and summer, and where, were its good qualities appreciated as they deserve to be, it would remain unmolested. But man being generally disposed to consider in his subjects a single fault sufficient to obliterate the remembrance of a thousand good qualities, even when the latter are beneficial to his interest, and tend to promote his comfort, persecutes the *King Bird* without mercy, and extends his enmity to its whole progeny. This mortal hatred is occasioned by a propensity which the Tyrant Fly-catcher now and then shews to eat a honey-bee, which the narrow-minded farmer looks upon as exclusively his own property, although he is presently to destroy thousands of its race, for the selfish purpose of seizing upon the fruits of their labours, which he does with as little remorse as if nature's bounties were destined for man alone.

The Field Martin arrives in Louisiana, from the south, about the middle of March. Many individuals remain until the middle of September, but the greater number proceed gradually northwards, and are dispersed over every portion of the United States. For a few days after its arrival, it seems fatigued and doleful, and remains perfectly silent. But no sooner has it recovered its naturally lively spirits, than its sharp tremulous cry is heard over the fields, and along the skirts of all our woods. It seldom enters the forests, but is fond of orchards, large fields of clover, the neighbourhood of rivers, and the gardens close to the houses of the planters. In this last situation, its habits are best observed.

Its flight has now assumed a different manner. The love-season is at hand. The male and female are seen moving about through the air, with a continued quivering motion of their wings, at a height of twenty or thirty yards above the ground, uttering a continual, tremulous, loud shriek. The male follows in the wake of the female, and both seem panting for a suitable place in which to form their nest. Meanwhile, they

c c 2

watch the motions of different insects, deviate a little from the course of
their playful rounds, and with a sweeping dart secure and swallow the
prey in an instant. Probably the next sees them perched on the twig of
a tree, close together, and answering the calls of nature.

The choice of a place being settled by the happy pair, they procure
small dry twigs from the ground, and rising to a horizontal branch, arrange them as the foundation of their cherished home. Flakes of cotton,
wool or tow, and other substances of a similar nature, are then placed in
thick and regular layers, giving great bulk and consistence to the fabric,
which is finally lined with fibrous roots and horse-hair. The female then
deposits her eggs, which are from four to six in number, broadly ovate,
reddish-white, or blush colour, irregularly spotted with brown. No sooner has incubation commenced, than the male, full of ardour, evinces the
most daring courage, and gallantly drives off every intruder. Perched
on a twig not far from his beloved mate, in order to protect and defend
her, he seems to direct every thought and action to these objects. His
snow-white breast expands with the warmest feelings; the feathers of his
head are raised and spread, the bright orange spot laid open to the rays
of the sun; he stands firm on his feet, and his vigilant eye glances over
the wide field of vision around him. Should he spy a Crow, a Vulture,
a Martin, or an Eagle, in the neighbourhood or at a distance, he spreads
his wings to the air, and pressing towards the dangerous foe, approaches
him, and commences his attack with fury. He mounts above the enemy,
sounds the charge, and repeatedly plunging upon the very back of his
more powerful antagonist, essays to secure a hold. In this manner, ha-
rassing his less active foe with continued blows of his bill, he follows him
probably for a mile, when, satisfied that he has done his duty, he gives
his wings their usual quivering motion, and returns exulting and elated
to his nest, trilling his notes all the while.

Few Hawks will venture to approach the farm-yard while the King
Bird is near. Even the cat in a great measure remains at home; and,
should she appear, the little warrior, fearless as the boldest Eagle, plunges towards her, with such rapid and violent motions, and so perplexes
her with attempts to peck on all sides, that grimalkin, ashamed of herself,
returns discomfited to the house.

The many eggs of the poultry which he saves from the plundering
Crow, the many chickens that are reared under his protection, safe from
the clutches of the prowling Hawks, the vast number of insects which he

devours, and which would otherwise torment the cattle and horses, are benefits conferred by him, more than sufficient to balance the few raspberries and figs which he eats, and calculated to insure for him the favour and protection of man.

The King Bird fears none of his aërial enemies save the Martin ; and although the latter frequently aids him in protecting his nest, and watching over the farm-yard, it sometimes attacks him with such animosity as to force him to retreat, the flight of the Martin being so superior to that of the King Bird in quickness and power, as to enable it to elude the blows which the superior strength of the latter might render fatal. I knew an instance in which some Martins, that had been sole proprietors of a farm-yard for several seasons, shewed so strong an antipathy to a pair of King Birds, which had chanced to build their nest on a tree within a few yards of the house, that, no sooner had the female begun to sit on her eggs, than the Martin attacked the male with unremitting violence for several days, and, notwithstanding his courage and superior strength, repeatedly felled him to the ground, until he at length died of fatigue, when the female was beaten off in a state of despair, and forced to seek a new protector.

The King Bird is often seen passing on the wing over a field of clover, diving down to the very blossoms, and reascending in graceful undulations, snapping his bill, and securing various sorts of insects, now and then varying his mode of chase in curious zigzag lines, shooting to the right and left, up and down, as if the object which he is pursuing were manœuvring for the purpose of eluding him.

About the month of August, this species becomes comparatively mute, and resorts to the old abandoned fields and meadows. There, perched on a fence-stake or a tall mullein stalk, he glances his eye in various directions, watching the passing insects, after which he darts with a more direct motion than in spring. Having secured one, he returns to the same or another stalk, beats the insect, and then swallows it. He frequently flies high over the large rivers and lakes, sailing and dashing about in pursuit of insects. Again, gliding down towards the water, he drinks in the manner of various species of Swallow. When the weather is very warm, he plunges repeatedly into the water, alights after each plunge on the low branch of a tree close by, shakes off the water and plumes himself, when, perceiving some individuals of his tribe passing high over head, he ascends to overtake them, and bidding adieu to the country, proceeds towards a warmer region.

The King Bird leaves the Middle States earlier than most other species. While migrating southwards, at the approach of winter, it flies with a strong and continued motion, flapping its wings six or seven times pretty rapidly, and sailing for a few yards without any undulations, at every cessation of the flappings. On the first days of September, I have several times observed them passing in this manner, in detached parties of twenty or thirty, perfectly silent, and so resembling the *Turdus migratorius* in their mode of flight, as to induce the looker-on to suppose them of that species, until he recognises them by their inferior size. Their flight is continued through the night, and by the 1st of October none are to be found in the Middle States. The young acquire the full colouring of their plumage before they leave us for the south.

The flesh of this bird is delicate and savoury. Many are shot along the Mississippi, not because these birds eat bees, but because the French of Louisiana are fond of bee-eaters. I have seen some of these birds that had the shafts of the tail-feathers reaching a quarter of an inch beyond the end of the webs.

I have placed a male and a female Field Martin on a twig of the Cotton-wood Tree. This plant is very appropriately named, for not only are the grape-like bunches of seeds filled with a beautiful soft cottony substance, but the wood can scarcely be sawed on account of the looseness of its inner fibres. It grows to a great height and size, particularly along the shores of the Mississippi and Ohio, and in all alluvial grounds to the west of the Alleghany Mountains. It is principally used for firewood and fence-rails, but is of indifferent quality for either purpose.

MUSCICAPA TYRANNUS, *Briss.* vol. ii. p. 391.—*Ch. Bonaparte*, Synops. of Birds of the United States, p. 66.

LANIUS TYRANNUS, *Linn.* Syst. Nat. vol. i. p. 136.—*Lath.* Ind. Ornith. vol. i. p. 81.

TYRANT SHRIKE, *Lath.* Synops. vol. i. p. 184.

TYRANT FLY-CATCHER, MUSCICAPA TYRANNUS, *Wils.* Amer. Ornith. vol.i. p. 66. Pl. 13. fig. 1.

Adult Male. Plate LXXIX. Fig. 1.

Bill of moderate length, rather stout, subtrigonal, depressed at the base, straight; upper mandible with the dorsal outline nearly straight, and sloping to near the tip, which is deflected and acute, the edges sharp and overlapping; lower mandible with the back broad, the sides slanting, the end slightly declinate. Nostrils basal, lateral, roundish, partly covered by the bristly feathers. Head rather large, neck stout, body ovate. Feet rather short; tarsus covered anteriorly with a few scutella, compressed, acute behind, about the same length as the middle toe ; toes free, scutellate above ; claws arched, compressed, acute.

Plumage soft, blended, glossy. Basirostral bristles long, directed outwards. Feathers of the head narrow, elongated, and erectile, forming a short longitudinal tuft. Wings rather long, the second and third quills longest. Tail rather long, even, of twelve broadly acuminate feathers.

Bill black. Iris dark brown. Feet greyish-blue. The general colour of the upper parts is dark bluish-grey, the head darker. Feathers along the middle of the crown forming a rich flame-coloured patch, margined with yellow. Quills brownish-black, as are the coverts, which, together with the secondary quills, are externally margined and tipped with dull white. Tail brownish-black, deeper towards the end, each feather largely tipped with white, of which colour also is part of the outer web of the lateral feathers. Under parts greyish-white, throat and fore-neck pure white, the breast tinged with ash-grey.

Length $8\frac{1}{4}$ inches, extent of wings $14\frac{1}{2}$; bill along the ridge $\frac{7}{12}$, along the gap 1.

Adult Female. Plate LXXIX. Fig. 2.

The female is duller in colouring; the upper parts being lighter and tinged with brown, the under parts more dusky, the orange spot on the head smaller and not so bright, and the white tip of the tail less pure and not so extensive.

THE COTTON-WOOD.

POPULUS CANDICANS, *Willd.* Sp. Pl. vol. iv. p. 806. *Pursh.* Fl. Amer. vol. ii. p. 618. *Mich.* Arbr. Forest. de l'Amer. Sept. vol. iii. Pl. 13.—DIŒCIA OCTANDRIA, *Linn.* AMENTACEÆ, *Juss.*

This species of Poplar is distinguished by its broadly cordate, acuminate, unequally and obtusely serrated, venous leaves; hairy petioles, resinous buds, and round twigs. The leaves are dark green above, whitish beneath. The resinous substance with which the buds are covered has an agreeable smell. The bark is smooth, of a greenish tint.

THE PRAIRIE TITLARK.

ANTHUS PIPIENS.

PLATE LXXX. MALE.

I SHOT two of these birds whilst traversing one of the extensive prairies of our North-western States. Five of them had been running along the foot-path before me, for some time. I at first looked upon them as of the Common Brown Titlark species (*Anthus Spinoletta*), but as they rose on the wing, the difference of their notes struck me, and, shooting at them, I had the good fortune to kill two, which I discovered, on examination, to be of a new and distinct species, although in the general appearance of their plumage they were very nearly allied to the Brown Titlark. The rest I pursued in vain, and was forced to abandon the chase on account of the approach of night, and the necessity of preparing for rest after a long walk.

The flight of the Prairie Titlark is irregular, and performed by jerks, although greatly protracted, when the bird is pursued or frightened. At short intervals these birds plunged through the air, came towards the ground, and flew close over the prairie, as if about to alight, and again rising, made a large circuit. In this manner they continued all the time I saw them on wing. Whilst on the ground they ran briskly, vibrating their tail, whenever they stopped, and picking up the insects near them.

The notes of the Prairie Titlark are clear and sharp, consisting of a number of *tweets*, the last greatly prolonged. The two individuals which I procured proved to be males. They seemed to be in imperfect plumage, it being then the month of October, and the crescent on their breast not being so distinctly defined at the surface, as it was deeper among the feathers. Of their mode of nestling, and other habits, I can say nothing, as I never happened to meet with another individual of the species.

ANTHUS PIPIENS.

Male. Plate LXXX.

Bill straight, slender, compressed, acuminate; upper mandible carinated at the base, rounded on the sides, the edges inflected towards the

tip, which is slightly declinate and notched ; lower mandible ascending
in its dorsal outline.   Nostrils basal, lateral, elliptical, half closed above
by a membrane.   The general form slender.   Feet of ordinary length ;
tarsus slender, compressed ; toes free; claws of the fore toes arched, compressed; acute, of the hind toe very long, subulate-compressed, nearly
straight.

Plumage soft, blended.   Wings of ordinary length, first, second, and
third quills longest, the secondaries notched at the tip.   Tail long, emarginate.

Bill dark brown, the under mandible orange at the base.   Iris hazel.
Feet brownish-black.   The general colour of the upper parts is dull
olive-brown ; a brownish-white line over the eye ; auricular coverts
blackish.   Under parts pale yellowish-grey ; an obscure lunule of brownish-black on the fore neck, the lower part of which, and the sides, are
streaked with dark brown, and tinged with reddish-brown.

Length 6½ inches, bill along the ridge ½, along the gap ¾ ; tarsus ⅝,
middle toe ¾, hind toe ¾.

PHLOX SUBULATA, *Willd.* Sp. Pl. vol. i. p. 842. *Pursh*, Fl. Amer. vol. i. p. 151.—
PENTANDRIA MONOGYNIA, *Linn.* POLEMONIA, *Juss.*

Cæspitose, pubescent ; leaves linear, pungent, ciliate ; corymbs few-
flowered ; pedicels trifid ; divisions of the corolla wedge-shaped, emarginate ; teeth of the calyx subulate, scarcely shorter than the tube of the
corolla.   The flowers are pink, with a purple star in the centre.   It grows
in rocky places, and on barren, gravelly ground, flowering through the
summer.

THE ORIGINAL PAINTER.

As I was lounging one fair and very warm morning on the *Levee* at New Orleans, I chanced to observe a gentleman, whose dress and other accompaniments greatly attracted my attention. I wheeled about, and followed him for a short space, when, judging by every thing about him that he was a true original, I accosted him.

But here, kind reader, let me give you some idea of his exterior. His head was covered by a straw hat, the brim of which might cope with those worn by the fair sex in 1880; his neck was exposed to the weather; the broad frill of a shirt, then fashionable, flapped about his breast, whilst an extraordinary collar, carefully arranged, fell over the top of his coat. The latter was of a light green colour, harmonizing well with a pair of flowing yellow nankeen trowsers, and a pink waistcoat, from the bosom of which, amidst a large bunch of the splendid flowers of the Magnolia, protruded part of a young alligator, which seemed more anxious to glide through the muddy waters of some retired swamp, than to spend its life swinging to and fro among folds of the finest lawn. The gentleman held in one hand a cage full of richly-plumed Nonpareils, whilst in the other he sported a silk umbrella, on which I could plainly read " *Stolen from I,*" these words being painted in large white characters. He walked as if conscious of his own importance, that is, with a good deal of pomposity, singing " My love is but a lassie yet," and that with such thorough imitation of the Scotch emphasis, that had not his physiognomy brought to my mind a denial of his being from " within a mile of Edinburgh;" I should have put him down in my journal for a true Scot. But no:—his tournure, nay, the very shape of his visage, pronounced him an American, from the farthest parts of our eastern Atlantic shores.

All this raised my curiosity to such a height, that I accosted him with " Pray, Sir, will you allow me to examine the birds you have in that cage?" The gentleman stopped, straightened his body, almost closed his left eye, then spread his legs apart, and, with a look altogether quizzical, answered, " Birds, Sir, did you say birds?" I nodded, and he continued, " What the devil do you know about birds, Sir?"

Reader, this answer brought a blush into my face. I felt as if caught in a trap, for I was struck by the force of the gentleman's question; which, by the way, was not much in discordance with a not unusual mode of granting an answer in the United States. Sure enough, thought I, little or perhaps nothing do I know of the nature of those beautiful denizens of the air; but the next moment vanity gave me a pinch, and urged me to conceive that I knew at least as much about birds as the august personage in my presence. "Sir," replied I, "I am a student of nature, and admire her works, from the noblest figure of man to the crawling reptile which you have in your bosom." "Ah!" replied he, "a-a-a naturalist, I presume!" "Just so, my good Sir," was my answer. The gentleman gave me the cage; and I observed from the corner of one of my eyes, that his were cunningly inspecting my face. I examined the pretty finches as long as I wished, returned the cage, made a low bow, and was about to proceed on my walk, when this odd sort of being asked me a question quite accordant with my desire of knowing more of him: "Will you come with me, Sir? If you will, you shall see some more curious birds, some of which are from different parts of the world. I keep quite a collection." I assured him I should feel gratified, and accompanied him to his lodgings.

We entered a long room, where, to my surprise, the first objects that attracted my attention were a large easel, with a full length unfinished portrait upon it, a table with pallets and pencils, and a number of pictures of various sizes placed along the walls. Several cages containing birds were hung near the windows, and two young gentlemen were busily engaged in copying some finished portraits. I was delighted with all I saw. Each picture spoke for itself: the drawing, the colouring, the handling, the composition, and the keeping—all proved, that, whoever was the artist, he certainly was possessed of superior talents.

I did not know if my companion was the painter of the picture, but, as we say in America, I strongly guessed, and without waiting any longer, paid him the compliments which I thought he fairly deserved. "Aye," said he, "the world is pleased with my work, I wish I were so too, but time and industry are required as well as talents, to make a good artist. If you will examine the birds, I'll to my labour." So saying, the artist took up his pallet, and was searching for a rest-stick, but not finding the one with which he usually supported his hand, he drew the rod of a gun, and was about to sit, when he suddenly threw down his implements on the table, and, taking the gun, walked so me, and asked if "I had ever seen a percussion-lock." I had not, for that improvement was not yet in vogue. He not only explained the superiority of the lock in question, but undertook to prove that it was capable of acting effectually under water. The bell was rung, a flat basin of water was produced, the gun was charged with powder, and the lock fairly immersed. The report terrified the birds, causing them to beat against the gilded walls of their prisons. I remarked this to the artist. He replied, "The devil take the birds !—more of them in the market; why, Sir, I wish to shew you that I am a marksman as well as a painter." The easel was cleared of the large picture, rolled to the further end of the room; and placed against the wall. The gun was loaded in a trice, and the painter, counting ten steps from the easel, and taking aim at the supporting-pin on the left, fired. The bullet struck the head of the wooden pin fairly, and sent the splinters in all directions. "A bad shot, sir," said this extraordinary person, "the ball ought to have driven the pin farther into the hole, but it struck on one side ; I'll try at the hole itself." After reloading his piece, the artist took aim again, and fired. The bullet this time had accomplished its object, for it had passed through the aperture, and hit the wall behind. "Mr———, ring the bell and close the windows," said the painter, and turning to me, continued, "Sir, I will shew you the *ne plus ultra* of shooting." I was quite amazed, and yet so delighted, that I bowed my assent. A servant having appeared, a lighted candle was ordered. When it arrived, the artist placed it in a proper position, and retiring some yards, put out the light with a bullet, in the manner which I have elsewhere, in this volume, described. When light was restored, I observed the uneasiness of the poor little alligator, as it strove to effect its escape from the artist's waistcoat. I mentioned this to him. "True, true," he replied, "I had quite forgot the reptile, he shall have a dram ;" and unbuttoning his vest, unclasped a small chain, and placed the alligator in the basin of water on the table.

Perfectly satisfied with the acquaintance which I had formed with this renowned artist, I wished to withdraw, fearing I might inconvenience him by my presence. But my time was not yet come. He bade me sit down, and paying no more attention to the young pupils in the room than if they had been a couple of cabbages, said, "If you have leisure and will stay awhile, I will shew you how I paint, and will relate to you an incident of my life, which will prove to you how sadly situated an artist is at times." In full expectation that more eccentricities were to be witnessed, or that the story would prove a valuable one, even to a naturalist, who is seldom a painter, I seated myself at his side, and observed with interest how adroitly he transferred the colours from his glistening pallet to the canvas before him.   I was about to compliment him on his facility of touch, when he spoke as follows :

" This is, sir, or, I ought to say rather, this will be the portrait of one of our best navy officers, a man as brave as CÆSAR, and as good a sailor as ever walked the deck of a seventy-four.   Do you paint, Sir?" I replied " Not yet."   " Not yet ! what do you mean ?"   " I mean what I say : I intend to paint as soon as I can draw better than I do at present." " Good," said he, " you are quite right, to draw is the first object ; but, sir, if you should ever paint, and paint portraits, you will often meet with difficulties.   For instance, the brave Commodore, of whom this is the portrait, although an excellent man at every thing else, is the worst sitter I ever saw ; and the incident I promised to relate to you, as one curious enough, is connected with his bad mode of sitting.   Sir, I forgot to ask if you would take any refreshment—a glass of wine, or ——."   I assured him I needed nothing more than his agreeable company, and he proceeded.   " Well, Sir, the first morning that the Commodore came to sit, he was in full uniform, and with his sword at his side.   After a few moments of conversation, and when all was ready on my part, I bade him ascend this *throne*, place himself in the attitude which I contemplated, and assume an air becoming an officer of the navy."   He mounted, placed himself as I had desired, but merely looked at me as if I had been a block of stone.   I waited a few minutes, when, observing no change on his placid countenance, I ran the chalk over the canvas, to form a rough outline.   This done, I looked up to his face again, and opened a conversation which I thought would warm his warlike nature ; but in vain.   I waited and waited, talked and talked, until my patience—Sir, you must know I am not overburdened with phlegm—being almost run out, I rose, threw my pallet and brushes on the floor, stamped, walking to and fro about the room, and vociferated such calumnies against our navy, that I startled the good Commodore.   He still looked at me with a placid countenance, and, as he has told me since, thought I had lost my senses.   But I observed him all the while, and, fully as determined to carry my point, as he would be to carry off an enemy's ship, I gave my oaths additional emphasis, addressed him as a representative of the navy, and, steering somewhat clear of personal insult, played off my batteries against the craft.   The Commodore walked up to me, placed his hand on the hilt of his sword, and told me, in a resolute manner, that if I intended to insult the navy, he would instantly cut off my ears.   His features exhibited all the spirit and animation of his noble nature, and as I had now succeeded in rousing the lion, I judged it time to retreat.   So, changing my tone, I begged his pardon, and told him he now looked precisely as I wished to represent him.   He laughed, and returning to his seat, assumed a bold countenance.   And now, Sir, see the picture?"

At some future period, I may present you with other instances of the odd ways in which this admired artist gave animation to his sitters.   For the present, kind reader, we shall leave him finishing the Commodore, while we return to our proper studies.

THE FISH HAWK, OR OSPREY.

PLATE LXXXI. Male.

COMPARING the great size of this bird, its formidable character, its powerful and protracted flight, and the dexterity with which, although a land bird, it procures its prey from the waters of the ocean, with the very inferior powers of the bird named the Kingsfisher, I should be tempted to search for a more appropriate appellation than that of Fish-Hawk, and, were I not a member of a republic, might fancy that of *Imperial Fisher* more applicable to it.

The habits of this famed bird differ so materially from those of almost all others of its genus, that an accurate description of them cannot fail to be highly interesting to the student of nature.

The Fish Hawk may be looked upon as having more of a social disposition than most other Hawks. Indeed, with the exception of the Swallow-tailed Hawk (*Falco furcatus*), I know none so gregarious in its habits. It migrates in numbers, both during spring, when it shews itself along our Atlantic shores, lakes, and rivers, and during autumn, when it retires to warmer climes. At these seasons, it appears in flocks of eight or ten individuals, following the windings of our shores in loose bodies, advancing in easy sailings or flappings, crossing each other in their gyrations. During the period of their stay in the United States, many pairs are seen nestling, rearing their young, and seeking their food, within so short a distance of each other, that while following the margins of our eastern shores, a Fish Hawk or a nest belonging to the species, may be met with at every short interval.

The Fish Hawk may be said to be of a mild disposition. Not only do these birds live in perfect harmony together, but they even allow other birds of very different character to approach so near to them as to build their nests of the very materials of which the outer parts of their own are constructed. I have never observed a Fish Hawk chasing any other bird whatever. So pacific and timorous is it, that, rather than encounter a foe but little more powerful than itself, it abandons its prey to the White-headed Eagle, which, next to man, is its greatest enemy. It never forces its young from the nest, as some other Hawks do, but, on the contrary, is seen to feed them even when they have begun to procure food for themselves.

Notwithstanding all these facts, a most erroneous idea prevails among our fishermen, and the farmers along our coasts, that the Fish Hawk's nest is the best *scare-crow* they can have in the vicinity of their houses or grounds. As these good people affirm, no Hawk will attempt to commit depredations on their poultry, so long as the Fish Hawk remains in the country. But the absence of most birds of prey from those parts at the time when the Fish Hawk is on our coast, arises simply from the necessity of retiring to the more sequestered parts of the interior for the purpose of rearing their young in security, and the circumstance of their visiting the coasts chiefly at the period when myriads of water-fowl resort to our estuaries at the approach of winter, leaving the shores and salt-marshes at the return of spring, when the Fish Hawk arrives. However, as this notion has a tendency to protect the latter bird, it may be so far useful, the fisherman always interposing when he sees a person bent upon the destruction of his favourite bird.

The Fish Hawk differs from all birds of prey in another important particular, which is, that it never attempts to secure its prey in the air, although its rapidity of flight might induce an observer to suppose it perfectly able to do so. I have spent weeks on the Gulf of Mexico, where these birds are numerous, and have observed them sailing and plunging into the water, at a time when numerous shoals of flying-fish were emerging from the sea to evade the pursuit of the dolphins. Yet the Fish Hawk never attempted to pursue any of them while above the surface, but would plunge after one of them or a bonita-fish, after they had resumed their usual mode of swimming near the surface.

The motions of the Fish Hawk in the air are graceful, and as majestic as those of the Eagle. It rises with ease to a great height by extensive circlings, performed apparently by mere inclinations of the wings and tail. It dives at times to some distance with the wings partially closed, and resumes its sailing, as if these plunges were made for amusement only. Its wings are extended at right angles to the body, and when thus flying it is easily distinguishable from all other Hawks by the eye of an observer accustomed to note the flight of birds. Whilst in search of food, it flies with easy flappings at a moderate height above the water, and with an apparent listlessness, although in reality it is keenly observing the objects beneath. No sooner does it spy a fish suited to its taste, than it checks its course with a sudden shake of its wings and tail, which gives it the appearance of being poised in the air for a moment, after which it plunges headlong with great rapidity into the water, to secure its prey, or continue its flight, if disappointed by having observed the fish sink deeper.

When it plunges into the water in pursuit of a fish, it sometimes proceeds deep enough to disappear for an instant. The surge caused by its descent is so great as to make the spot around it present the appearance of a mass of foam. On rising with its prey, it is seen holding it in the manner represented in the Plate. It mounts a few yards into the air, shakes the water from its plumage, squeezes the fish with its talons, and immediately proceeds towards its nest, to feed its young, or to a tree, to devour the fruit of its industry in peace. When it has satisfied its hunger, it does not, like other Hawks, stay perched until hunger again urges it forth, but usually sails about at a great height over the neighbouring waters.

The Fish Hawk has a great attachment to the tree to which it carries its prey, and will not abandon it, unless frequently disturbed, or shot at whilst feeding there. It shews the same attachment to the tree on which it has built its first nest, and returns to it year after year.

This species arrives on the southern coasts of the United States early in the month of February, and proceeds eastward as the season advances. In the Middle Districts, the fishermen hail its appearance with joy, as it is the harbinger of various species of fish which resort to the Atlantic coasts, or ascend the numerous rivers. It arrives in the Middle States about the beginning of April, and returns southward at the first appearance of frost. I have occasionally seen a few of these birds on the muddy lakes of Louisiana, in the neighbourhood of New Orleans, during the winter months; but they appeared emaciated, and were probably unable to follow their natural inclinations, and proceed farther south.

As soon as the females make their appearance, which happens eight or ten days after the arrival of the males, the love-season commences, and soon after, incubation takes place. The loves of these birds are conducted in a different way from those of the other Falcons. The males are seen playing through the air amongst themselves, chasing each other in sport, or sailing by the side or after the female which they have selected, uttering cries of joy and exultation, alighting on the branches of the tree on which their last year's nest is yet seen remaining, and doubtless congratulating

each other on finding their home again. Their caresses are mutual.
They begin to augment their habitation, or to repair the injuries which it
may have sustained during the winter, and are seen sailing together towards the shores, to collect the drifted sea-weeds with which they line the
nest anew. They alight on the beach, search for the driest and largest
weeds, collect a mass of them, clench them in their talons, and fly towards
their nest with the materials dangling beneath. They both alight and
labour together. In a fortnight the nest is complete, and the female deposits her eggs, which are three or four in number, of a broadly oval
form, yellowish-white, densely covered with large irregular spots of reddish-brown.

The nest is generally placed in a large tree in the immediate vicinity
of the water, whether along the seashore, on the margins of the inland
lakes, or by some large river. It is, however, sometimes to be seen in
the interior of a wood, a mile or more from the water. I have concluded
that, in the latter case, it was on account of frequent disturbance, or attempts at destruction, that the birds had removed from their usual haunt.
The nest is very large, sometimes measuring fully four feet across, and is
composed of a quantity of materials sufficient to render its depth equal to
its diameter. Large sticks, mixed with sea-weeds, tufts of strong grass, and
other materials, form its exterior, while the interior is composed of sea-
weeds and finer grasses. I have not observed that any particular species
of tree is preferred by the Fish Hawk. It places its nest in the forks of
an oak or a pine with equal pleasure. But I have observed that the tree
chosen is usually of considerable size, and not unfrequently a decayed one.
I dare not, however, affirm that the juices of the plants which compose the
nest, ever become so detrimental to the growth of a tree as ultimately to
kill it. In a few instances, I have seen the Fish Crow and the Purple
Grakle raising their families in nests built by them among the outer
sticks of the Fish Hawk's nest.

The male assists in incubation, during the continuance of which the
one bird supplies the other with food, although each in turn goes in quest
of some for itself. At such times the male bird is now and then observed
rising to an immense height in the air, over the spot where his mate is
seated. This he does by ascending almost in a direct line, by means of
continued flappings, meeting the breeze with his white breast, and occasionally uttering a cackling kind of note, by which the bystander is
enabled to follow him in his progress. When the Fish Hawk has at-

tained its utmost elevation, which is sometimes such that the eye can no longer perceive him, he utters a loud shriek, and dives smoothly on half-extended wings towards his nest. But before he reaches it, he is seen to expand his wings and tail, and in this manner he glides towards his beloved female, in a beautifully curved line. The female partially raises herself from her eggs, emits a low cry, resumes her former posture, and her delighted partner flies off to the sea, to seek a favourite fish for her whom he loves.

The young are at length hatched. The parents become more and more attached to them, as they grow up. Abundance of food is procured to favour their development. So truly parental becomes the attachment of the old birds, that an attempt to rob them of those dear fruits of their love, generally proves more dangerous than profitable. Should it be made, the old birds defend their brood with great courage and perseverance, and even sometimes, with extended claws and bill, come in contact with the assailant, who is glad to make his escape with a sound skin.

The young are fed until fully fledged, and often after they have left the nest, which they do apparently with great reluctance. I have seen some as large as the parents, filling the nest, and easily distinguished by the white margins of their upper plumage, which may be seen with a good glass at a considerable distance. So much fish is at times carried to the nest, that a quantity of it falls to the ground, and is left there to putrify around the foot of the tree. Only one brood is raised each season.

The Fish Hawk seldom alights on the ground, and when it does so, walks with difficulty, and in an extremely awkward manner. The only occasions on which it is necessary for them to alight, are when they collect materials for the purpose of repairing their nest at the approach of autumn, or for building a new one, or repairing the old, in spring.

I have found this bird in various parts of the interior of the United States, but always in the immediate neighbourhood of rivers or lakes. When I first removed to Louisville in Kentucky, several pairs were in the habit of raising their brood annually on a piece of ground immediately opposite the foot of the Falls of the Ohio in the State of Indiana. The ground belonged to the venerable General CLARK, and I was several times invited by him to visit the spot. Increasing population, however, has driven off the birds, and few are now seen on the Ohio, unless during their migrations to and from Lake Erie, where I have met with them.

I have observed many of these birds at the approach of winter, sail-

ing over the lakes near the Mississippi, where they feed on the fish which
the Wood Ibis kills, the Hawks themselves being unable to discover
them whilst alive in the muddy water with which these lakes are filled.
There the Ibises wade among the water in immense flocks, and so trample
the bottom as to convert the lakes into filthy puddles, in which the fishes
are unable to respire with ease. They rise to the surface, and are instantly killed by the Ibises. The whole surface is sometimes covered in
this manner with dead fish, so that not only are the Ibises plentifully
supplied, but Vultures, Eagles and Fish Hawks, come to participate in
the spoil. Except in such places, and on such occasions, I have not observed the Fish Hawk to eat of any other prey than that which it had
procured by plunging headlong into the water after it.

I have frequently heard it asserted that the Fish Hawk is sometimes
drawn under the water and drowned, when it has attempted to seize a
fish which is too strong for it, and that some of these birds have been
found sticking by their talons to the back of Sturgeons and other large
fishes. But, as nothing of this kind ever came under my observation, I
am unable to corroborate these reports. The roosting place of this bird
is generally on the top-branches of the tree on which its nest is placed, or
of one close to it.

Fish Hawks are very plentiful on the coast of New Jersey, near
Great Egg Harbour, where I have seen upwards of fifty of their nests
in the course of a day's walk, and where I have shot several in the course
of a morning. When wounded, they defend themselves in the manner
usually exhibited by Hawks, erecting the feathers of the head, and trying to strike with their powerful talons and bill, whilst they remain prostrate on their back.

The largest fish which I have seen this bird take out of the water,
was a Weak-Fish, such as is represented in the plate, but sufficiently
large to weigh more than five pounds. The bird carried it into the air
with difficulty, and dropped it, on hearing the report of a shot fired at it.

FALCO HALIAETUS, *Linn.* Syst. Nat. vol. i. p. 129.—*Lath.* Ind. Ornith. vol. i. p. 17.
     Ch. Bonaparte, Synops. of Birds of the United States, p. 26.
CAROLINA OSPREY, *Lath.* Synops. vol. i. p. 74.
FISH HAWK, FALCO HALIAETUS, *Wils.* Amer. Ornith. vol. v. p. 13. Pl. 5. fig. 1.

Adult Male.   Plate LXXXI.

Bill short, as broad as deep at the base, the sides convex, dorsal outline straight at the base, curved towards the end; upper mandible cerate, the edges acute, with a festoon at the curvature, the tip trigonal, deflected, very acute; lower mandible inflected at the edges, which are slightly arched, the tip obtusely truncate, the dorsal line slightly concave at the base, convex towards the end. Nostrils oval, oblique, lateral, in the fore part of the cere. Head rather large. Body robust. Legs rather long; tarsus short, remarkably thick, covered all round with hexagonal scales; toes also remarkably thick, the outer versatile, covered anteriorly with broad, laterally with small hexagonal scales; claws curved, roundish, very acute.

Plumage compact, imbricated; feathers of the head and neck narrow, of the back broad and rounded, of the breast also rounded. Tibial feathers short, tarsus feathered anteriorly one-third down. Wings very long, acute, the third quill longest, the second and fourth equal, the first not much shorter. Tail rather long, of twelve broad, rounded feathers.

Bill brownish-black, blue at the base and margin; cere light-blue. Iris yellow. Feet pale greyish-blue, tinged with brown; claws black. The general colour of the upper parts is dusky brown; the tail barred with pale brown. The upper part of the head and neck white, the middle part of the crown dark brown. A broad band of the latter colour from the bill down the side of the neck on each side. Under parts of the neck brownish white, streaked with dark brown. Under parts generally white. Anterior tarsal feathers tinged with brown.

Length 23 inches, extent of wings 54; bill along the back 2; tarsus 2¼, middle toe 3.

THE WEAK FISH.

The Weak Fish makes its appearance along our eastern shores about the middle of April, and remains until autumn. It is caught in the seine, and sold in our markets, being a delicate well-flavoured fish. It seldom attains any remarkable size. It is particularly plentiful about Great Egg Harbour, in New Jersey.

WHIP-POOR-WILL.

CAPRIMULGUS VOCIFERUS, WILS.

PLATE LXXXII. MALE AND FEMALE.

THIS bird makes its appearance in most parts of our Western and Southern Districts, at the approach of spring, but is never heard, and indeed scarcely ever seen, in the State of Louisiana. The more barren and mountainous parts of the Union seem to suit it best. Accordingly, the open Barrens of Kentucky, and the country through which the Alleghany ridges pass, are more abundantly supplied with it than any other regions. Yet, wherever a small tract of country, thinly covered with timber, occurs in the Middle Districts, there the *Whip-poor-will* is heard during the spring and early autumn.

This species of Night-jar, like its relative the Chuck-will's-widow, is seldom seen during the day, unless when accidentally discovered in a state of repose, when, if startled, it rises and flies off, but only to such a distance as it considers necessary, in order to secure it from the farther intrusion of the disturber of its noon-day slumbers. Its flight is very low, light, swift, noiseless, and protracted, as the bird moves over the places which it inhabits, in pursuit of the moths, beetles and other insects, of which its food is composed. During the day, it sleeps on the ground, the lowest branches of small trees and bushes, or the fallen trunks of trees so abundantly dispersed through the woods. In such situations, you may approach within a few feet of it ; and, should you observe it whilst asleep, and not make any noise sufficient to alarm it, it will suffer you to pass quite near it, without taking flight, as it seems to sleep with great soundness, especially about the middle of the day. In rainy or very cloudy weather, it sleeps less, and is more on the alert. Its eyes are then kept open for hours at a time, and it flies off as soon as it discovers an enemy approaching, which it can do, at such times, at a distance of twenty or thirty yards. It always appears with its body parallel to the direction of the branch or trunk on which it sits, and, I believe, never alights *across* a branch or a fence-rail.

No sooner has the sun disappeared beneath the horizon, than this bird bestirs itself, and sets out in pursuit of insects. It passes low over the bushes, moves to the right or left, alights on the ground to secure its prey, passes repeatedly and in different directions over the same field, skims along the skirts of the woods, and settles occasionally on the tops of the fence-stakes or on stumps of trees, from whence it sallies, like a Fly-catcher, after insects, and, on seizing them, returns to the same spot. When thus situated, it frequently alights on the ground, to pick up a beetle.   Like the Chuck-will's-widow, it also balances itself in the air, in front of the trunks of trees, or against the sides of banks, to discover ants, and other small insects that may be lurking there.   Its flight is so light and noiseless, that whilst it is passing within a few feet of a person, the motion of its wings is not heard by him, and merely produces a gentle undulation in the air.   During all this time, it utters a low murmuring sound, by which alone it can be discovered in the dark, when passing within a few yards of one, and which I have often heard when walking or riding through the barrens at night.

Immediately after the arrival of these birds, their notes are heard in the dusk and through the evening, in every part of the thickets, and along the skirts of the woods.   They are clear and loud, and to me are more interesting than those of the Nightingale.   This taste I have pro-bably acquired, by listening to the Whip-poor-will in parts where Nature exhibited all her lone grandeur, and where no discordant din interrupted the repose of all around.   Only think, kind reader, how grateful to me must have been the cheering voice of this my only companion, when, fatigued and hungry, after a day of unremitted toil, I have planted my camp in the wilderness, as the darkness of night put a stop to my labours! I have often listened to the Nightingale, but never under such circum-stances, and therefore its sweetest notes have never awaked the same feeling.

The Whip-poor-will continues its lively song for several hours after sunset, and then remains silent until the first dawn of day, when its notes echo through every vale, and along the declivities of the mountains, until the beams of the rising sun scatter the darkness that overhung the face of nature.   Hundreds are often heard at the same time in different parts of the woods, each trying to out-do the others; and when you are told that the notes of this bird may be heard at the distance of several hundred yards, you may form an idea of the pleasure which every lover of nature must feel during the time when this chorus is con-tinued.

Description is incapable of conveying to your mind any accurate idea
of the notes of this bird, much less of the feelings which they excite.
Were I to tell you that they are, in fact, not strictly musical, you might
be disappointed. The cry consists of three distinct notes, the first and
last of which are emphatical and sonorous, the intermediate one less so:
These three notes are preceded by a low cluck, which seems preparatory
to the others, and which is only heard when one is near the bird. A
fancied resemblance which its notes have to the syllables *whip-poor-will*,
has given rise to the common name of the bird.

This species is easily shot, when the moon is shining, and the night
clear, as you may then approach it without much caution. It is, however,
difficult to hit it on wing, on account of the zig-zag lines in which it flies,
as well as the late hour at which it leaves its resting-place. It is seldom
killed, however, being too small to be sought as an article of food, although its flesh is savoury, and it is too harmless to excite dislike.

It deposits its eggs about the middle of May, on the bare ground, or
on dry leaves, in the most retired parts of the thickets which it frequents.
They are always two in number, of a short elliptical form, much rounded,
and nearly equal at both ends, of a greenish-white colour, spotted and
blotched with bluish-grey, and light brown. The young burst the
shell in fourteen days after the commencement of incubation, and look
at first like a mouldy and almost shapeless mass, of a yellowish colour. When first able to fly they are of a brown colour, interspersed
with patches of buff, the brown being already beautifully sprinkled
with darker dots and zig-zag lines. They attain their full plumage
before they depart, with their parents, for the south. I think their
southward migration, which is performed by night, must be very rapid,
as I have never found any of these birds in Louisiana at that season,
whereas they proceed slowly on their return in spring. Both birds sit
on the eggs, and feed the young for a long time after they are able to fly,
either on wing, in the manner of the Common House Swallow, or while
perched on the fences, wood-piles, or houses. The food of the young at
first consists of ants, and partially digested beetles and large moths,
which the parents disgorge; but at the end of a fortnight the parents
present the food whole to the young, which then swallow it with ease.

Much has been said respecting the difference existing between the
Whip-poor-will and the *Night Hawk*, for the purpose of shewing them
to be distinct species. On this subject I shall only say, that although

I have known both birds from my early youth, I have seldom seen a farmer or even a boy in the United States, who did not know the difference between them.

It is a remarkable fact that even the largest moths on which the Whip-poor-will feeds, are always swallowed tail foremost, and when swallowed, the wings and legs are found closely laid together, and as if partially glued by the saliva or gastric juice of the bird. The act of deglutition must be greatly aided by the long bristly feathers of the upper mandible, as these no doubt force the wings of the insects close together, before they enter the mouth.

I have represented a male and two females, as well as some of the insects on which they feed. The former are placed on a branch of Red Oak, that tree being abundant on the skirts of the Kentucky Barrens, where the Whip-poor-will is most plentiful.

CAPRIMULGUS VOCIFERUS, *Ch. Bonaparte*, Synops. of Birds of the United States, p. 62.

WHIP-POOR-WILL, CAPRIMULGUS VOCIFERUS, *Wils.* Amer. Ornith. vol. v. p. 71. Pl. 41. fig. 1. Male, fig. 2. Female, fig. 3. Young.

Adult Male.   Plate LXXXII. Fig. 1.

Bill extremely short, feeble, opening to beyond the eyes, making the mouth, when open, of enormous dimensions; upper mandible arched in its dorsal outline, very broad at the base, suddenly contracted at the tip, which is compressed and rather obtuse; lower mandible decurved. Nostrils basal, oval, prominent, covered above by a membrane. Head disproportionately large. Eyes and ears very large. Neck short. Body rather slender. Feet very short; tarsus partly feathered, anteriorly scutellate below; fore toes three, connected to the second joint by membranes, scutellate above; claws depressed, arched, that of the middle toe with the inner edge expanded and pectinate.

Plumage blended, soft and silky, without much gloss. Upper mandible margined at the base with stiff bristles, much longer than the bill, extending forwards and outwards. Wings long, narrow, the second and third quills longest. Tail rather long, ample, even, of ten broad rounded feathers.

Bill dark brown. Iris dark hazel. Feet reddish-purple, the scales and claws blackish. The general colour of the upper parts is dark brownish-grey, streaked and minutely sprinkled with brownish-black. Cheeks brownish-red. The quills and coverts are dark brown, spotted in bars with light brown, the tips of the former mottled with light and dark brown. Four middle tail-feathers like those of the back, the three lateral white in their terminal half, deep brown, spotted with light brown towards the base, the latter colours running along the outer web of the outermost to near the tip. Throat and breast similar to the back, with a transverse band of yellowish-white across the fore-neck; the rest of the under parts paler and mottled.

Length 9 inches, extent of wings 19; bill along the ridge $\frac{5}{12}$, along the gap $1\frac{7}{12}$.

Adult Female. Plate LXXXII. Fig. 2, 3.

The female resembles the male in colouring, but the lateral tail-feathers are reddish-white towards the tip only, and the band across the fore-neck is pale yellowish-brown.

BLACK OAK OR QUERCITRON.

QUERCUS TINCTORIA, *Willd.* Sp. Pl. vol. iv. p. 444. *Pursh,* Flor. Amer. vol. ii. p. 629. *Mich.* Abr. Forest. de l'Amer. Sept. vol. ii. p. 110. Pl. 2.—MONŒCIA POLYANDRIA, *Linn.* AMENTACEÆ, *Juss.*

Leaves obovato-oblong, sinuate, pubescent beneath, their lobes acuminate, obsoletely denticulate; the cup scutellato-turbinate; the acorn globular depressed. This is one of the largest trees of the United States, and attains a height from eighty to ninety feet, with a diameter of from four to five. The bark is deeply cracked, and of a black colour. The wood is reddish, coarse-grained, and not so much esteemed as that of the White Oak, and some other species. The bark is used for tanning, as well as for dyeing wool of a yellow colour. It is generally distributed, especially in the mountainous parts.

THE HOUSE WREN.

TROGLODYTES ÆDON, VIEILL.

PLATE LXXXIII. MALE, FEMALE, AND YOUNG.

ALTHOUGH Louisiana is supplied with thousands of the Great Carolina Wren, not a single individual of the present species is ever to be
found there. It appears, indeed, that the central districts of our Atlantic coasts are their principal places of resort, probably because certain
portions of the country are intended to be occupied by different species of
the same genus. Thus, I think it highly probable that the Great Carolina Wren has been intended for the Southern Districts, the House Wren
for the Middle States, Bewick's Long-tailed Wren for the regions of the
Rocky Mountains, and the Little Wren for our north-eastern territories,
along the St Lawrence, although it also breeds in the State of New
York, and even in that of Pennsylvania, where I have found it in the
Great Pine Swamp. I am induced to think that a fifth species of Wren
will yet be found within the limits of the United States. From this arrangement I exclude the bird called the Marsh Wren, which more properly belongs to the genus *Certhia*. But, as I have already said, I leave
all these matters to be discussed by the system-makers.

The opinion expressed by a former writer, that the House Wren
occurs in the United States, is as incorrect as the assertion of a subsequent author, that the Florida Jay is met with on the Mississippi and
Ohio. During a residence of twenty years in the different States through
which these great streams pass, I never saw either the one or the other
of these birds. These are errors, however, which are to be attributed to
the circumstance that one of the writers alluded to never visited the
Southern or Western States, while the other merely passed once through
them.

From whence the House Wren comes, or to what parts it retires
during winter, is more than I have been able to ascertain. Although it
is extremely abundant in the States of Pennsylvania, New Jersey, Virginia,
and Maryland, from the middle of April until the beginning of October, I
have never been able to trace its motions, nor do I know of any naturalist
in our own country, or indeed in any other, who has been more fortunate.

Its flight is short, generally low, and performed by a constant tremor
of the wings, without any jerks of either the body or tail, although the
latter is generally seen erect, unless when the bird is singing, when it is
always depressed. When passing from one place to another, during the
love-season, or whilst its mate is sitting, this sweet little bird flutters still
more slowly through the air, singing all the while. It is sprightly, active,
vigilant, and courageous. It delights in being near and about the gardens,
orchards, and the habitations of man, and is frequently found in abundance in the very centre of our eastern cities, where many little boxes are
put up against the walls of houses, or the trunks of trees, for its accom-
modation, as is also done in the country. In these it nestles and rears
its young. It is seldom, however, at a loss for a breeding place, it being
satisfied with any crevice or hole in the walls, the sill of a window, the
eaves, the stable, the barn, or the upper side of a piece of timber, under
the roof of a piazza. Now and then, its nest may be seen in the hollow
branch of an apple tree. I knew of one in the pocket of an old broken-
down carriage, and many in such an old hat as you see represented in the
plate, which, if not already before you, I hope you will procure, and
look at the little creatures anxiously peeping out or hanging to the side
of the hat, to meet their mother, which has just arrived with a spider,
whilst the male is on the lookout, ready to interpose should any intruder
come near. The same nest is often resorted to for several successive
years, merely receiving a little mending.

The familiarity of the House Wren is extremely pleasing. In Pennsylvania a pair of these birds had formed a nest, and the female was sitting in a hole of the wall, within a few inches of my (literally so-called)
drawing-room. The male was continually singing within a few feet of
my wife and myself, whilst I was engaged in portraying birds of other
species. When the window was open, its company was extremely agreeable, as was its little song, which continually reminded us of its happy
life. It would now and then dive into the garden at the foot of the window, procure food for its mate, return and creep into the hole where it
had its nest, and be off again in a moment. Having procured some flies
and spiders, I now and then threw some of them towards him, when he
would seize them with great alacrity, eat some himself, and carry the rest
to his mate. In this manner, it became daily more acquainted with us,
entered the room, and once or twice sang whilst there. One morning I
took it in to draw its portrait, and suddenly closing the window, easily

caught it, held it in my hand, and finished its likeness, after which I re-. stored it to liberty. This, however, made it more cautious, and it never. again ventured within the window, although it sang and looked at us as at first. It is it which you see placed on the hat.

The antipathy which the House Wren shews to cats is extreme. Although it does not attack puss, it follows and scolds her until she is out of sight. In the same manner, it makes war on the Martin, the Blue Bird and the House Swallow, the nest of any of which it does not scruple to appropriate to itself, whenever occasion offers. Its own nest is formed of dry crooked twigs, so interwoven as scarcely to admit entrance to any other bird. Within this outer frame-work grasses are arranged in a circular manner, and the whole is warmly lined with feathers and other equally soft materials. The eggs are five or six, of a regularly oval form, and uniform pale reddish colour. Two broods are raised in the season.

The male seems to delight in attempting to surpass in vocal powers others of his species, during the time of incubation; and is frequently seen within sight of another, straining his little throat, and gently turning his body from side to side, as if pivoted on the upper joints of his legs. For a moment he conceives the musical powers of his rival superior to his own, and darts towards him, when a battle ensues, which over, he immediately resumes his song, whether he has been the conqueror or not.

When the young issue from the nest, it is interesting to see them follow the parents amongst the currant bushes in the gardens, like so many mice, hopping from twig to twig, throwing their tail upwards, and putting their bodies into a hundred different positions, all studied from the parents, whilst the latter are heard scolding, even without cause, but as if to prevent the approach of enemies, so anxious are they for the safety of their progeny. They leave Pennsylvania about the 1st of October.

TROGLODYTES ÆDON, *Ch. Bonaparte*, Synops. of Birds of the United States, p. 92.
HOUSE WREN, SYLVIA DOMESTICA, *Wils.* Amer. Ornith. vol. i. p. 129, Pl. 8, fig. 3.

Adult Male.   Plate LXXXIII. Fig. 1.

Bill of ordinary length, nearly straight, slender, acute, subtrigonal at the base, compressed towards the tip; upper mandible with the ridge obtuse, the sides convex towards the end, concave at the base, the edges

acute and overlapping; under mandible with the back and sides convex.
Nostrils oblong, straight, basal, with a cartilaginous lid above, open and
bare. Head ovate, eyes of moderate size, neck of ordinary length, body
ovate, nearly equal in breadth and depth. Legs of ordinary length;
tarsus longer then the middle toe, compressed, covered anteriorly
with six scutella, posteriorly with a long plate forming an acute angle.
Toes scutellate above, inferiorly granulate, second and fourth nearly
equal, the hind toe almost equal to the middle one, third and fourth united as far as the second joint; claws long, slender, acute, arcuate, much
compressed.

Plumage soft, tufty, slightly glossed. No bristly feathers about the
beak. Wings shortish, broad, rounded: first quill half the length of the
second, which is very little shorter than the third and fourth. Tail of
ordinary length, of twelve narrow, lax feathers.

Bill dark brown above, yellowish-brown beneath. Iris hazel. Feet
flesh-colour. The general colour of the upper parts is reddish-brown,
darker on the head, brighter on the tail-coverts, indistinctly barred with
dark brown; wings and tail undulatingly banded, tips of the larger
wing-coverts whitish. A yellowish-grey line from the upper mandible
over the eye; cheeks of the same colour, mottled with brownish-red.
Under parts brownish-grey; sides barred with brown, as are the under
tail-coverts.

Length $4\frac{1}{4}$ inches, extent of wings $5\frac{1}{2}$; bill along the ridge $\frac{1}{4}$, along
the gap $\frac{3}{4}$; tarsus $\frac{2}{3}$, middle toe $\frac{7}{12}$.

Adult Female.   Plate LXXXIII. Fig. 2.
The female scarcely differs from the male in external appearance.

Young Birds.   Plate LXXXIII. Fig. 3.
The young are of a lighter brown, more indistinctly barred, but resemble the old birds in the general distribution of their colouring.

This species differs from the Winter Wren, chiefly in having the
bill a little stouter, the tail considerably longer, and the under parts
less distinctly barred.

THE BLUE-GREY FLY-CATCHER.

MUSCICAPA CŒRULEA, WILS.

PLATE LXXXIV. MALE AND FEMALE.

THIS diminutive lively bird is rendered peculiarly conspicuous by its being frequently the nurse or foster-parent of the young Cow Bunting, the real mother of which drops her egg in its nest. A few individuals of this species remain in Louisiana during spring and summer, and breed there ; but the greater number proceed far eastward, and spread over the United States, although they are not common in any part.

The Blue-grey Fly-catcher arrives in the neighbourhood of New Or-leans about the middle of March, when it is observed along the water-courses, flitting about and searching diligently, amidst the branches of the Golden Willow, for the smaller kinds of winged insects, devouring amongst others great numbers of moschettoes. Its flight resembles that of the Long-tailed Titmouse of Europe. It moves to short distances, vi-brating its tail while on wing, and, on alighting, is frequently seen hang-ing to the buds and bunches of leaves, at the extremities of the branches of trees. It seldom visits the interior of the forests, in any portion of our country, but prefers the skirts of woods along damp or swampy places, and the borders of creeks, pools, or rivers. It seizes insects on wing with great agility, snapping its bill like a true Fly-catcher, now and then making little sallies after a group of those diminutive flies that seem as if dancing in the air, and cross each other in their lines of flight, in a thousand various ways.

When it has alighted, its tail is constantly erected, its wings droop, and it utters at intervals its low and uninteresting notes, which resemble the sounds *Tsee, Tsee*. It seldom if ever alights on the ground, and when thirsty prefers procuring water from the extremities of branches, or sips the rain or dewdrops from the ends of the leaves.

Its nest is composed of the frailest materials, and is light and small in proportion to the size of the bird. It is formed of portions of dried leaves, the husks of buds, the silky fibres of various plants and flowers, and light grey lichens, and is lined with fibres of Spanish Moss or horse-

hair. I have found these nests always attached to two slender twigs of
Willow. The eggs are four or five, pure white, with a few reddish dots
at the larger end. Two broods are reared in a season. The young and
old hunt and migrate together, passing amongst the tops of the highest
trees, from one to another. They leave the State of Louisiana in the beginning of October, the Middle States about the middle of September.
I have seen some of these birds on the border line of Upper Canada,
along the shores of Lake Erie. I have also observed them in Kentucky,
Indiana, and along the Arkansas River.

In the plate is represented, along with a pair of these delicate birds, a
twig of one of our most valuable trees, with its pendulous blossoms.
This tree, the Black Walnut, grows in almost every part of the United
States, in the richest soils, and attains a great height and diameter. The
wood is used for furniture of all sorts, receives a fine polish, and is extremely durable. The stocks of muskets are generally made of it. The
Black Walnut is plentiful in all the alluvial grounds in the vicinity of
our rivers. The fruit is contained in a very hard shell, and is thought
good by many people.

SYLVIA CŒRULEA, *Lath.* Ind. Ornith. vol. ii. p. 540.—*Ch. Bonaparte*, Synops. of Birds
    of the United States, p. 85.
MOTACILLA CŒRULEA, *Linn.* Syst. Nat. vol. i. p. 337.
CŒRULEAN WARBLER, *Lath.* Synops. vol. iv. p. 460.
BLUE-GREY FLY-CATCHER, MUSCICAPA CŒRULEA, *Wils. Amer.* Ornith, vol. ii.
    p. 164. Pl. 18. fig. 5.

Adult Male.   Plate LXXXIV. Fig. 1.

Bill of ordinary length, straight, subulato-conical, depressed at the base,
acute; upper mandible with the edges acute and overlapping, notched close
to the end, the tip slightly declinate. Head rather large. Neck short, body
ovate. Legs of ordinary length ; tarsus slender, compressed, scutellate before, acute behind ; toes free, scutellate ; claws arched, compressed, acute.

Plumage soft, blended, tufty. Basirostral bristles distinct. Wings
short, much curved, the third quill longest. Tail longish, rounded, of
twelve rounded feathers.

Bill bluish-black. Iris hazel. Feet greyish-blue. The general colour of the upper parts is bright blue, approaching to ultramarine, deeper
on the head, and fading on the tail-coverts. Quills and primary coverts

brownish-black, margined externally with blue ; secondary coverts slightly tipped with greyish. Tail blackish, the lateral feathers nearly all white, the two next tipped with the same colour. A narrow band of black on the forehead, extending over the eyes. Under parts greyish-white, the sides of the neck bright blue, the sides greyish-blue.

Length $4\frac{1}{4}$ inches, extent of wings $6\frac{1}{4}$; bill along the ridge $\frac{1}{2}$, along the gap a little more than $\frac{1}{2}$; tarsus $\frac{7}{12}$.

Adult Female. Plate LXXXIV. Fig. 2.

The female is much duller in colouring, the bright blue of the male being in her light greyish-blue. The black band on the forehead is also wanting.

THE BLACK WALNUT.

JUGLANS NIGRA, *Willd.* Sp. Pl. vol. iv. p. 456. *Pursh,* Flor. Amer. vol. ii. p. 636. *Mich.* Arbr. Forest. de l'Amer. Sept. vol. i. p. 157. Pl. 1.—MONŒCIA POLYANDRIA, *Linn.* TEREBINTHACEÆ, *Juss.*

This species belongs to the division with simple, polyandrous male catkins, and is distinguished by its numerous ovato-lanceolate, subcordate, serrated leaflets, narrowed towards the end, somewhat downy beneath, as are the petioles ; its globular scabrous fruits, and wrinkled nuts. The leaves have seven or eight nearly opposite pairs of leaflets. The male catkins are pendent. The fruits are sometimes from six to eight inches in circumference, the kernel brown and corrugated, and, although eaten, inferior to the Common Walnut. The bark of the trunk is thick, blackish, and cracked ; the wood of a very dark colour.

THE YELLOW-THROATED WARBLER.

SYLVIA PENSILIS, LATH.

PLATE LXXXV. MALE.

THIS beautiful bird absents itself from the State of Louisiana only for two months in the year, December and January. When they return in the beginning of February, they throw themselves by thousands into all the cypress woods and cane-brakes, where they are heard singing from the first of March until late in autumn, sometimes in November.

Their habits are very different from those of the Warblers, and are more in general accordance with those of the Certhiæ. They move up and down, sidewise and spirally, along the trunks, branches, and even twigs of the tallest and largest Cypresses, or such other trees as are found intermingled with them. They are extremely active, in fact, fully as much so as the little Brown Creeper itself. Like it, they suddenly leave the uppermost branches or higher parts of the trunks, and diving downwards alight on the roots, and renew their search after small insects and larvæ. I never saw any of them pursue insects on wing.

The nest of this species is prettily constructed. Its outer parts are composed of grey lichens and soft mosses, the interior of silky substances and a few fibres of the Spanish moss. The female lays four pure white eggs, having two or three purple dots near the larger end. I think they raise two broods during their stay in Louisiana, but cannot speak of this as certain. The nest is placed on a horizontal branch of a Cypress, twenty, thirty, or even fifty feet above the ground, and is with difficulty discovered from below, as it resembles a knot or a tuft of moss.

The song of the Yellow-throated Warbler would please you, kind reader. Of this I have not a doubt, as it is soft and loud, and is continued for two or three minutes at a time, not unlike that of the Painted Finch, or Indigo Bird. As it is heard in all parts of our most dismal Cypress Swamps, it contributes to soothe the mind of a person whose occupation may lead him to such places. I never saw this species on the ground. The male and the female are nearly alike in plumage, but the young birds, which hunt for insects in company, in the manner of Creepers or Titmice, do not acquire the yellow on the throat, nor the full brilliancy of their plumage, until the first spring.

These birds confine themselves to the Southern States, seldom moving farther towards the Middle Districts than North Carolina. They do not even ascend the Mississippi farther than the Walnut Hills. They are abundant in the neighbourhood of the Red River, and probably do not go farther south than Mexico, during their short absence from the United States.

Happening to shoot several of these birds on a large Chinquapin tree, growing on the edge of a hill close to a swamp, I have put a male on one of its twigs, which is furnished with a few fruits quite ripe and ready to leave their husks. In the Southern States this tree is rare. It generally prefers elevated places, and rocky declivities, with an arid soil. The wood resembles that of the Chestnut, but the trees being generally small, little use is made of it as timber. The fruit is eaten by children. This tree is abundant along the greater part of the range of the Alleghanies and its branches.

SYLVIA PENSILIS, *Lath.* Ind. Ornith. vol. ii. p. 520.—*Ch. Bonaparte,* Synops. of Birds of the United States, p. 79.

PENSILE WARBLER, *Lath.* Synops. vol. iv. p. 441.

YELLOW-THROATED WARBLER, SYLVIA FLAVICOLLIS, *Wils.* Amer. Ornith. vol. ii. p. 64. Pl. 4. fig. 6.

Adult Male. Plate LXXXV.

Bill shortish, nearly straight, subulato-conical, acute, as deep as broad at the base, the edges acute, the gap line a little deflected at the base. Nostrils basal, elliptical, lateral, half-closed by a membrane. Head rather small. Neck short. Body slender. Feet of ordinary length, slender; tarsus longer than the middle toe, covered anteriorly by a few scutella, the uppermost long; toes scutellate above, the inner free, the hind toe of moderate size; claws slender, compressed, acute, arched.

Plumage soft, blended, tufty. Wings of ordinary length, acute, the second quill longest. Tail longish, slightly emarginate.

Bill brownish-black. Iris dark-brown. Feet yellowish-brown. The general colour of the upper parts is light greyish-blue, the head darker. A white line from the base of the upper mandible over the eye. Forehead, loral space, a line behind the eye, and a patch including the ear-

E e 2

coverts, descending along the neck, and terminating acutely, black. Under eyelid white. Wing-coverts dusky, tipped with white. Quills blackish, externally margined with light greyish-green. Tail-feathers black, the middle ones edged with greenish-blue, the outer white along the outer margin, and with the next two having a white patch on the inner web towards the end. Throat and fore-neck bright yellow, as is a spot before the eye. The rest of the under parts white, the sides mottled with dusky.

Length 5½ inches, extent of wings 8¼; bill along the ridge nearly ½, along the gap $\frac{7}{12}$; tarsus ⅚, middle toe ⅜.

The female is similar to the male, but has the colours somewhat duller.

THE CHINQUAPIN.

CASTANEA PUMILA, *Willd.* Sp. Pl. vol. iv. p. 461. *Pursh,* Flor. Amer. vol. ii. p. 625. *Mich.* Arbr. Forest. de l'Amer. Sept. vol. ii. p. 166. Pl. 7.—MONŒCIA POLY-ANDRIA, *Linn.* AMENTACEÆ, *Juss.*

This species of Chestnut is characterized by its oblong, acute, sharply-serrated leaves, which are whitish and downy beneath. The fruit is very agreeable, and is a favourite food of Squirrels, and birds of different species, such as Pigeons, Jays, Turkeys, and Woodpeckers.

LOUISVILLE IN KENTUCKY.

Louisville in Kentucky has always been a favourite place of mine. The beauty of its situation, on the banks of *La Belle Rivière*, just at the commencement of the famed rapids, commonly called the Falls of the Ohio, had attracted my notice, and when I removed to it, immediately after my marriage, I found it more agreeable than ever. The prospect from the town is such that it would please even the eye of a Swiss. It extends along the river for seven or eight miles, and is bounded on the opposite side by a fine range of low mountains, known by the name of the Silver Hills. The rumbling sound of the waters, as they tumble over the rock-paved bed of the rapids, is at all times soothing to the ear. Fish and game are abundant. But, above all, the generous hospitality of the inhabitants, and the urbanity of their manners, had induced me to fix upon it as a place of residence; and I did so with the more pleasure when I found that my wife was as much gratified as myself, by the kind attentions which were shewn to us, utter strangers as we were, on our arrival.

No sooner had we landed, and made known our intention of remaining, than we were introduced to the principal inhabitants of the place and its vicinity, although we had not brought a single letter of introduction, and could not but see, from their unremitting kindness, that the Virginian spirit of hospitality displayed itself in all the words and actions of our newly-formed friends. I wish here to name those persons who so unexpectedly came forward to render our stay among them agreeable, but feel at a loss with whom to begin, so equally deserving are they of our gratitude. The Croghans, the Clarks (our great traveller included), the Berthouds, the Galts, the Maupins, the Tarascons, the Beals, and the Booths, form but a small portion of the long list which I could give. The matrons acted like mothers towards my wife, the daughters proved agreeable associates, and the husbands and sons were friends and companions to me. If I absented myself on business or otherwise, for any length of time, my wife was removed to the hospitable abode of some friend in the neighbourhood until my return, and then, kind reader, I was several times obliged to spend a week or more with these good people, before they could be prevailed upon to let us return to our own residence. We lived for two years at Louisville, where we enjoyed many of the best pleasures which this life can afford ; and whenever we have since chanced to pass that way, we have found the kindness of our former friends unimpaired.

During my residence at Louisville, much of my time was employed in my ever favourite pursuits. I drew and noted the habits of every thing which I procured, and my collection was daily augmenting, as every individual who carried a gun, always sent me such birds or quadrupeds as he thought might prove useful to me. My portfolios already contained upwards of two hundred drawings. Dr W. C. GALT, being a botanist, was often consulted by me, as well as his friend Dr FERGUSON. M. GILLY drew beautifully, and was fond of my pursuits. So was my friend, and now relative, N. BERTHOUD. As I have already said, our time was spent in the most agreeable manner, through the hospitable friendship of our acquaintance.

One fair morning, I was surprised by the sudden entrance into our counting-room of Mr ALEXANDER WILSON, the celebrated author of the " American Ornithology," of whose existence I had never until that moment been apprised. This happened in March 1810. How well do I remember him, as he then walked up to me ! His long, rather hooked nose, the keenness of his eyes, and his prominent cheek-bones, stamped his countenance with a peculiar character. His dress, too, was of a kind not usually seen in that part of the country ; a short coat, trowsers, and a waistcoat of grey cloth. His stature was not above the middle size. He had two volumes under his arm, and as he approached the table at which I was working, I thought I discovered something like astonishment in his countenance. He, however, immediately proceeded to disclose the object of his visit, which was to procure subscriptions for his work. He opened his books, explained the nature of his occupations, and requested my patronage.

I felt surprised and gratified at the sight of his volumes, turned over a few of the plates, and had already taken a pen to write my name in his favour, when my partner rather abruptly said to me in French, " My dear AUDUBON, what induces you to subscribe to this work ? Your drawings are certainly far better, and again you must know as much of the habits of American birds as this gentleman." Whether Mr WILSON understood French or not, or if the suddenness with which I paused, disappointed him, I cannot tell; but I clearly perceived that he was not pleased. Vanity and the encomiums of my friend prevented me from subscribing. Mr WILSON asked me if I had many drawings of birds. I rose, took down a large portfolio, laid it on the table, and shewed him, as I would shew you, kind reader, or any other person fond of such subjects, the whole of the contents, with the same patience with which he had shewn me his own engravings.

His surprise appeared great, as he told me he never had the most distant idea that any other individual than himself had been engaged in forming such a collection. He asked me if it was my intention to publish, and when I answered in the negative, his surprise seemed to increase. And, truly, such was not my intention; for, until long after, when I met the Prince of Musignano in Philadelphia, I had not the least idea of presenting the fruits of my labours to the world. Mr WILSON now examined my drawings with care, asked if I should have any objections to lending him a few during his stay, to which I replied that I had none: he then bade me good morning, not, however, until I had made an arrangement to explore the woods in the vicinity along with him, and had promised to procure for him some birds, of which I had drawings in my collection, but which he had never seen.

It happened that he lodged in the same house with us, but his retired habits, I thought, exhibited either a strong feeling of discontent, or a decided melancholy. The Scotch airs which he played sweetly on his flute made me melancholy too, and I felt for him. I presented him to my wife and friends, and seeing that he was all enthusiasm, exerted myself as much as was in my power, to procure for him the specimens which he wanted. We hunted together, and obtained birds which he had never before seen; but, reader, I did not subscribe to his work, for, even at that time, my collection was greater than his. Thinking that perhaps he might be pleased to publish the results of my researches, I offered them to him, merely on condition that what I had drawn, or might afterwards draw and send to him, should be mentioned in his work, as coming from my pencil. I at the same time offered to open a correspondence with him, which I thought might prove beneficial to us both. He made no reply to either proposal, and before many days had elapsed, left Louisville, on his way to New Orleans, little knowing how much his talents were appreciated in our little town, at least by myself and my friends.

Some time elapsed, during which I never heard of him, or of his work. At length, having occasion to go to Philadelphia, I, immediately after my arrival there, inquired for him, and paid him a visit. He was then drawing a White-headed Eagle. He received me with civility, and took me to the Exhibition Rooms of REMBRANDT PEALE, the artist, who had then portrayed NAPOLEON crossing the Alps. Mr WILSON spoke not of birds or drawings. Feeling, as I was forced to do, that my company was not agreeable, I parted from him; and after that I never saw him again. But judge of my astonishment some time after, when on reading the thirty-ninth page of the ninth volume of American Ornithology, I found in it the following paragraph :—

" *March 23d*, 1810.—I bade adieu to Louisville, to which place I had four letters of recommendation, and was taught to expect much of every thing there; but neither received one act of civility from those to whom I was recommended, one subscriber, nor one new bird; though I delivered my letters, ransacked the woods repeatedly, and visited all the characters likely to subscribe. Science or literature has not one friend in this place."

THE BLACK WARRIOR.

FALCO HARLANI.

PLATE LXXXVI. MALE AND FEMALE.

LONG before I discovered this fine Hawk, I was anxious to have an opportunity of honouring some new species of the feathered tribe with the name of my excellent friend Dr RICHARD HARLAN of Philadelphia. This I might have done sooner, had I not waited until a species should occur, which in its size and importance should bear some proportion to my gratitude toward that learned and accomplished friend.

The Hawks now before you were discovered near St Francisville, in Louisiana, during my late sojourn in that State, and had bred in the neighbourhood of the place where I procured them, for two seasons, although they had always eluded my search, until, at last, as I was crossing a large cotton field, one afternoon, I saw the female represented in the Plate standing perched on the top of a high belted tree in an erect and commanding attitude. It looked so like the Black Hawk (*Falco niger*) of WILSON, that I apprehended what I had heard respecting it might prove incorrect. I approached it, however, when, as if it suspected my evil intentions, it flew off, but after at first sailing as if with the view of escaping from me, passed over my head, when I shot at it, and brought it winged to the ground. No sooner had I inspected its eye, its bill, and particularly its naked legs, than I felt assured that it was, as had been represented by those persons who had spoken to me of its exploits, a new species. I drew it whilst alive; but my intentions of preserving it and carrying it to England as a present to the Zoological Society were frustrated by its refusing food. It died in a few days, when I preserved its skin, which, along with those of other rare birds, I have since given to the British Museum, through my friend J. G. CHILDREN, Esq. of that Institution.

A few days afterwards I saw the male bird perched on the same tree, but was unable to approach him so long as I had a gun, although he frequently allowed me and my wife to pass close to the foot of the tree when we were on horseback and unarmed. I followed it in vain for nearly a fortnight, from one field to another, and from tree to tree. until our physician, Dr JOHN B. HEREFORD, knowing my great desire to obtain it, shot it in the wing with a rifle ball, and sent it alive to me. It was still wilder than the female, erected the whole of the feathers of its head, opened its bill, and was ever ready to strike with its talons at any object brought near it. I made my drawing of the male also while still alive.

This species, although considerably smaller than the Red-tailed Hawk, to which it is allied, is superior to it in flight and daring. Its flight is rapid, greatly protracted, and so powerful as to enable it to seize its prey with apparent ease, or effect its escape from its stronger antagonist, the Red-tail, which pursues it on all occasions.

The Black Warrior has been seen to pounce on a fowl, kill it almost instantly, and afterwards drag it along the ground for several hundred yards, when it would conceal it, and return to feed upon it in security. It was not observed to fall on Hares or Squirrels, but at all times evinced a marked preference for common Poultry, Partridges, and the smaller species of Wild Duck.

I was told that the young birds appeared to be of a leaden-grey colour at a distance, but at the approach of winter became as dark as the parents. None of them were to be seen at the time when I procured the latter. Of its nest or eggs nothing is yet known. My friends Messrs JOHNSON and CARPENTER frequently spoke of this Hawk to me immediately after my return to Louisiana from Europe, which took place in November 1829. I have a skin of this bird in my possession. Should its nest be discovered, and should I have an opportunity of becoming more acquainted with its habits, I shall not fail to give you an account of my observations.

FALCO HARLANI.

Adult Male. Plate LXXXVI. Fig. 1.

Bill short, robust, as broad as deep at the base, compressed towards the end; upper mandible nearly straight, and sloping in its dorsal outline, curved towards the tip, which is declinate, trigonal, acute, the sides convex, the edges acute, overlapping, with a rounded process on each side; lower mandible convex in its dorsal outline and on the sides, the tip rounded. Nostrils oval, oblique, in the fore part of the cere. Head very large, neck short, body robust. Feet of ordinary length; tarsus a little compressed, scutellate before and behind, reticularly scaly on the sides; toes scutellate above, scaly on the sides, tubercular and scabrous beneath; claws curved, roundish, very acute.

Plumage compact, feathers of the head and neck short and rounded, tibial feathers elongated and loose at the tips. Wings long; first quill short, fourth longest, third and fifth equal, the first primaries cut out on the inner web towards the end. Tail longish, ample, of twelve broad, rounded feathers.

Bill light blue, black towards the end; cere and angles of the mouth yellowish-green. Iris light yellowish-brown. Feet dull greenish-yellow, claws black.

The general colour of the plumage is deep chocolate-brown, the under parts lighter, the feathers there being margined with light brown. Tail lighter than the back, and rather narrowly barred with brownish-black, the tips brownish-red. Under wing-coverts whitish, spotted with deep brown.

Length 21 inches, extent of wings 45; bill along the back 1½, along the gap, from the tip of the lower mandible, 1½; tarsus 1¾.

Adult Female. Plate LXXXVI. Fig. 2.

The female resembles the male in external appearance.

Length 22 inches; bill along the back 1½.

This species bears a strong resemblance to the Common Buzzard (*Falco Buteo*) of Europe, from which, however, it differs in having the head broader, the legs stouter, and the general colour of the plumage darker. It is also considerably larger.

THE FLORIDA JAY.

CORVUS FLORIDANUS, BARTRAM.

PLATE LXXXVII. MALE AND FEMALE.

THIS beautiful and lively bird is a constant resident in the south-western parts of Florida, from which country it seldom if ever removes to any great distance. It is never seen in the State of Louisiana, far less in that of Kentucky, and when CHARLES BONAPARTE asserts that it occurs in these districts, we must believe that he has been misinformed. It is so confined to the particular portions of Florida which it inhabits, that even on the eastern shores of that peninsula few are to be seen. I have never observed it in any part of Georgia, or farther to the eastward.

The flight of the Florida Jay is generally performed at a short distance from the ground, and consists either of a single sailing sweep, as it shifts from one tree or bush to another, or of continuous flappings, with a slightly undulated motion, in the manner of the Magpie (*Corvus Pica*) or of the Canada Jay (*Corvus canadensis*). Its notes are softer than those of its relative the Blue Jay (*Corvus cristatus*), and are more frequently uttered. Its motions are also more abrupt and quicker. It is seen passing from one tree to another with expanded tail, stopping for a moment to peep at the intruder, and hopping off to another place the next minute. It frequently descends to the ground, along the edges of oozy or marshy places, to search for snails, of which, together with berries of various kinds, fruits and insects, its food consists. It is easily approached during the breeding season, but is more shy at other times. It is a great destroyer of the eggs of small birds, as well as of young birds, which it chases and kills by repeated blows of its bill on their heads, after which it tears their flesh with avidity.

The Florida Jay is easily kept in a cage, where it will feed on recent or dried fruits, such as figs, raisins, and the kernels of various nuts, and exhibits as much gaiety as the Blue Jay does in a similar state. Like the latter, it secures its food between its feet, and breaks it into pieces before swallowing it, particularly the acorns of the Live Oak, and the snails which it picks up among the Sword Palmetto. No sooner have the seeds of that plant become black, or fully ripe, than the Florida Jay makes them almost its sole food for a time, and wherever a patch of these troublesome plants are to be seen, there also is the Jay to be met with. I have called the Palmetto a troublesome plant, because its long, narrow, and serrated leaves are so stiff, and grow so close together, that it is extremely difficult to walk among them, the more so that it usually grows in places where the foot is seldom put without immediately sinking in the mire to a depth of several inches.

The nest of the Florida Jay is sparingly formed of dry sticks, placed across each other, and, although of a rounded shape, is so light that the bird is easily seen through it. It is lined with fibrous roots, placed in a circular manner. The eggs are from four to six, of a light olive colour, marked with irregular blackish dashes. Only one brood is raised in the season.

I had a fine opportunity of observing a pair of these birds in confinement, in the city of New Orleans. They had been raised out of a family of five, taken from the nest, and when I saw them had been two years in confinement. They were in full plumage, and extremely beautiful. The male was often observed to pay very particular attentions to the female, at the approach of spring. They were fed upon rice, and all kinds of dried fruit. Their cage was usually opened after dinner, when both immediately flew upon the table, fed on the almonds which were given them, and drank claret diluted with water. Both affected to imitate particular sounds, but in a very imperfect manner. These attempts at mimicry probably resulted from their having been in company with parrots and other birds. They suffered greatly when moulting, becoming almost entirely bare, and requiring to be kept near the fire. The female dropped two eggs in the cage, but never attempted to make a nest, although the requisite materials were placed at her disposal.

I have represented a pair of Florida Jays on a branch of the Persimon tree, ornamented with its richly coloured fruits. This tree grows to a moderate height as well as girth. The wood is hard and compact. The leaves drop off at an early period. The fruit, when fully ripe, is grateful to the palate. The Persimon occurs in all parts of the United States, but abounds in the low lands of Florida and Louisiana, probably more than in any other portion of the Union.

CORVUS FLORIDANUS, *Ch. Bonaparte*, Synops. of Birds of the United States, p. 58.
FLORIDA JAY, *Ch. Bonaparte*, Amer. Ornith. vol. II. Pl. 13. fig. 1.

Adult Male. Plate LXXXVII. Fig. 1.

Bill short, strong, straight, compressed, acute; upper mandible with the dorsal outline nearly straight, the sides sloping, the edges sharp and overlapping, the tip slightly declinate; lower mandible with the back narrow, the sides sloping. Nostrils basal, open, covered by the reversed bristly feathers. Head rather large, neck short, body robust. Feet of ordinary length; tarsus about the same length as the middle toe, anteriorly scutellate, compressed, acute behind; toes free, scutellate, the inner shorter than the outer; claws arched, compressed, acute.

Plumage soft, blended, glossy. A tuft of reflected bristly feathers over the nostril on each side, and several bristle-pointed feathers at the base of the upper mandible. Wings short, third and fourth quills longest, first short. Tail long, much rounded, of twelve rounded feathers.

Bill and feet brownish-black. Iris hazel. Upper part of the head, the cheeks, side, and back part of the neck, the wings and tail, of a bright purplish-azure. Back light yellowish-brown. A band of white on the forehead, extending over the eyes. The under parts brownish-white. The upper tail-coverts are blue, and the tail-feathers are indistinctly barred with deeper lines.

Length 11¼ inches; bill along the ridge ⅟₁, along the gap nearly 1⅛; tarsus 1₁₂, middle toe nearly the same.

Adult Female. Plate LXXXVII. Fig. 2.

The female presents the same colours as the male, the difference in tint being hardly perceptible.

THE PERSIMON TREE.

DIOSPYROS VIRGINIANA, *Willd.* Sp. Pl. vol. iv. p. 1107. *Pursh*, Flor. Amer. vol. i. p. 265. *Mich.* Abr. Forest. de l'Amer. Sept. vol. ii. p. 195. Pl. 12.—POLYGAMIA DIŒCIA, *Linn.* GUAIACANÆ, *Juss.*

Leaves ovato-oblong, acuminate, smooth, venous; petioles downy; buds smooth. The flowers are pale yellow, and the fruits, which are of the size of a plum, are of a globular form, and when mature, of a dull yellowish colour. The bark of old trees is cracked, and of a dark colour. The wood is employed for various purposes, being fine-grained, hard and durable.

THE AUTUMNAL WARBLER.

SYLVIA AUTUMNALIS, WILS.

PLATE LXXXVIII. MALE AND FEMALE.

THE Autumnal Warbler was so named by Mr WILSON, on account of its appearing in the neighbourhood of Philadelphia, where only it was seen by that writer, during its migration from the Northern States, where it breeds, to the confines of Mexico, its winter residence.

This species makes its appearance in great numbers, in the lower parts of Louisiana, early in March, and remains there for a few days along with many others. At this season, it passes from the high top of one tree to that of another, with great activity. In about a week after its first appearance, none are to be seen. It moves towards the northernmost of our Eastern Districts, as the season advances, and does not stop until it reaches the remote parts of the State of New York, many individuals, however, forcing their way still farther.

I have found it breeding in the immediate vicinity of the Cayuga Lakes, and on the borders of Lake Champlain, in retired parts of the woods, which it seems to prefer during the summer months. I have also found it in the lofty forests of that portion of Pennsylvania usually called the Great Pine Swamp. The nest, like that of many other *Sylviæ*, is partially conical and pensile, and is formed of the soft bark of vines, lined with the down of various plants. The eggs are from four to six, of a white colour, tinged with red, and sprinkled with brownish dots at the larger end. The nest is usually placed in the slender fork of a low bush. I have found the female sitting as late as the 20th of August, and therefore conclude that this species raises two broods in the season, although I have had no opportunity of finding the nest and eggs at an earlier period.

The food of the Autumnal Warbler consists of small insects, many of which it procures whilst on wing. It also searches with great industry among the leaves and along the twigs. Its habits are precisely similar to those of other Warblers. Its flight is short, unequal, and yet quick. It rises in the air to some distance, and returns towards the spot which it has left, in zigzag lines, as if it were afraid to venture out of the thickets which it inhabits.

No sooner have these birds reared their young than they assemble in large loose parties of fifty or more, and return towards the south, throwing themselves amongst the Willows and Birch-trees that margin the streams, as well as into orchards and the scattered trees in cultivated fields. Its common note is a simple *tweet*, but the male, in spring and during the period of incubation, repeats at short intervals a soft and pleasing variety of notes, scarcely, however, deserving the name of song.

These birds are so plentiful, and so easily found, from the middle of September to that of October, that while in the Great Pine Forest I sometimes shot more than a dozen in a day. I have never observed them in the Southern States at that season.

I have represented a pair of these plain-looking Warblers on a twig of the Canoe Birch, a tree too well known, from the use to which its bark is applied by the Indians in the construction of their light and beautiful boats, to require any particular description here.

SYLVIA AUTUMNALIS, *Ch. Bonaparte*, Synops. of Birds of the United States, p. 74.
AUTUMNAL WARBLER, SYLVIA AUTUMNALIS, *Wils.* Amer. Ornith. vol. iii. p. 65. Pl. 23. fig. 4.

Adult Male.   Plate LXXXVIII. Fig. 1.

Bill of ordinary length, nearly straight, slender, tapering, acute. Nostrils basal, lateral, elliptical, half-closed above by a membrane. Head and neck of ordinary size. Body slender. Feet longish, slender; tarsus longer than the middle toe, covered anteriorly with a few scutella, the uppermost long; toes scutellate above, the inner free, the hind toe of moderate size; claws slender, compressed, acute, arched.

Plumage loose, blended. Short bristly feathers at the base of the bill. Wings rather short, the first quill longest. Tail even.

Bill brown, the lower mandible yellowish towards the base. Iris hazel. Feet dusky. The general colour of the upper parts is light olive-green. The tail-coverts greyish. A pale line over the eye, which is encircled by a narrow line of whitish. Fore neck dull yellow; under parts generally yellowish-white. Quills and larger coverts dusky on their inner webs, the former margined, the latter tipped with white, so as to present two bands of that colour across the wing. Tail dusky, margined with dull white, the three outer feathers white on the greater part of their inner web.

Length 4½, extent of wings 8 ; bill along the ridge ½, along the gap $\frac{7}{12}$; tarsus ⅔.

Adult Female.   Plate LXXXVIII. Fig. 2.

The female resembles the male in external appearance.

CANOE BIRCH OR PAPER BIRCH.

BETULA PAPYRACEA, *Willd.* Sp. Pl. vol. iv. p. 464.   *Pursh,* Flor. Amer. vol. ii. p. 621.   *Mich.* Arbr. Forest. de l'Amer. Sept. vol. ii. p. 133. Pl. 1.—MONŒCIA POLYANDRIA, *Linn.* AMENTACEÆ, *Juss.*

Leaves ovate, acuminate, doubly serrated, the veins hairy beneath, the petiole smooth.   The female catkins pedunculate, pendent.   This tree is most abundant in the Northern States, where it sometimes attains a height of from seventy to eighty feet, and a diameter of three feet,

THE NASHVILLE WARBLER.

SYLVIA RUBRICAPILLA, WILS.

PLATE LXXXIX. MALE AND FEMALE.

I HAVE shot only three or four birds of this species, and these were all that I ever met with. I found them in Louisiana and Kentucky. A few specimens belonging to Mr TITIAN PEALE of Philadelphia, and which he, with his usual kindness, lent me for a few days, to compare their colouring with my drawings and notes, were the only others that I have seen. It is probable he had procured them in Pennsylvania, al-though I cannot now recollect if this was really the case.

The flight of this little bird is short, light, and entirely similar to that of the numerous species of Sylvia already described. Its food con-sists of insects and larvæ, which it procures by searching diligently and actively amongst the leaves and buds of low trees. It does not pursue insects on wing. With the exception of a few low, eagerly repeated, creaking notes, I have not heard any sounds from them. While uttering these notes, which are all the species seem to have in lieu of song, the male stands erect and still. I am not aware of its nest having been dis-covered or described by any naturalist.

The plant on a twig of which two Nashville Warblers are repre-sented, is usually called the *Swamp Spice*. It is a low bush, grows in the water, in swampy and muddy ground, and occurs from Georgia to New York. The berries, which are seldom eaten by birds, have little pulp, and consequently a large seed.

SYLVIA RUBRICAPILLA, *Ch. Bonaparte* Synops. of Birds of the United States, p. 87.
SYLVIA RUBRICAPILLA, NASHVILLE WARBLER, *Wils.* Amer. Ornith. vol. iii. p. 120.
PL. 27, fig. 3.

Bill rather short, slender, tapering, nearly straight, as deep as broad at the base. Nostrils basal, lateral, elliptical, half-closed by a membrane. Head of ordinary size, neck short, body full. Feet of ordinary length, slender; tarsus longer than the middle toe, anteriorly scutellate; toes free, scutellate above; claws slender, compressed, acute, arched.

Adult Male.   Plate LXXXIX. Fig. 1.

Plumage soft, blended, tufty.   Wings short, curved, the first and second quills longest.   Tail short, forked, of twelve rounded feathers.

Bill greenish-brown.   Iris dark brown.   Feet yellowish-green.   Head and cheeks brownish-grey, the upper part of the head dark red.   A circle of white round the eye.   The general colour of the upper parts is brownish-green, of the under greenish-yellow, brighter on the throat and breast.   Inner webs of the wing and tail-feathers dusky, the outer brownish-green, and of the primaries bright yellow.

Length 4½ inches, extent of wings 7 ; bill along the ridge ⅓, along the gap ½ ; tarsus ¾.

Adult Female.   Plate LXXXIX. Fig. 2.

The female is much duller ; the head and hind-neck dark brownish-grey, tinged with green, the former without the red patch, the under parts more mixed with grey, the sides olivaceous, and the yellow of the wings less pure.

THE SWAMP SPICE.

ILEX PRINOIDES, *Willd.* Sp. Pl. vol. L. p. 709.   *Pursh,* Flor. Amer. vol. 1. p. 118.—
TETRANDRIA TETRAGYNIA, *Linn.*   RHAMNI, *Juss.*

Leaves lanceolate, attenuated at the base, slightly serrated ; peduncles one-flowered.   The leaves of this species are deciduous, the berries bright red.

THE BLACK-AND-WHITE CREEPER.

CERTHIA VARIA, Wils.

PLATE XC. Male.

A more appropriate name has seldom been given to a bird than that by which the present species is designated. Notwithstanding the approximation of the bill in form to that of the *Sylvia*, I am decidedly inclined to place this species among the *Creepers* or *Certhia*. To convince you of the propriety of such an arrangement, I shall now lay before you an account of its habits.

The Black-and-white Creeper appears in the State of Louisiana as soon as the buds on the trees begin to expand, which happens about the middle of February. It throws itself into the forests, where it breeds, and remains until the beginning of November. It is usually seen on the largest trees of our woods. It has a few notes, consisting of a series of rapidly enunciated *tweets*, the last greatly prolonged. It climbs and *creeps* along the trunks, the branches, and even the twigs of the trees, without intermission, and so seldom perches, that I do not remember ever having seen it in such a position. It lives principally on small ants and their larvæ, which it secures as it ascends or descends in a spiral direction, sidewise, with the head either uppermost or beneath. It keeps its feet close together, and moves by successive short hops with a rapidity equalling even that of the Brown Creeper. It dives from the tops of the trees to their roots, and again ascends. At other times, it alights on a decayed fallen tree, and searches the bark for food, peeping into the crevices. It has only a very short flight, and moves directly from one tree to the nearest.

In this manner the Black-and-white Creeper reaches the Northern Districts. It always prefers the most uncultivated tracts, and is especially fond of the pines and hemlock-trees of the mountain-glens. I have met with it on the borders of Canada, round Lake Champlain, in the country far to the north-west, on the banks of the Illinois, in Ohio, Kentucky, and all the wooded districts of the Arkansas and Red River.

In Louisiana, its nest is usually placed in some small hole in a tree, and is composed of mosses in a dry state, lined with cottony substances. The eggs are from five to seven, of a short oval form, white, with a few brownish-red spots chiefly at the large end.

Two broods are raised in the season. The young go about in company, following the parents, and it is not unusual to see nine or ten of these birds scrambling with great activity along the trunk of a tree. I have not found its nest in the Middle States, where, however, I am convinced many breed.

The young are similar in colouring to the females. The young males do not acquire their full plumage until the following spring.

A male of this species is represented on a twig of the tree commonly called the Black Larch.

SYLVIA VARIA, *Lath.* Ind. Ornith. vol. ii. p. 539.—*Ch. Bonaparte*, Synopsis of Birds of the United States, p. 81.

WHITE-POLL WARBLER, *Lath.* Synops. vol. iv. p. 488.

BLACK-AND-WHITE CREEPER, CERTHIA VARIA, *Wils.* Amer. Ornith. vol. iii. p. 22. Pl. xix. fig. 3.

Adult Male. Plate XC.

Bill rather long, slightly arched, compressed, extremely slender, acute; nostrils basal, narrow, half-closed by a membrane. General form slender. Feet of ordinary length, slender; tarsus longer than the middle toe, scutellate before; toes free, scutellate, the hind one proportionally larger; claws compressed, very acute, arched.

Plumage soft and blended. Wings of ordinary length, third quill longest, secondaries short. Tail nearly even, of twelve narrow, rounded feathers.

Bill black. Iris hazel. Feet dusky yellow. Middle of the head longitudinally white, bordered on each side by a broad stripe of black, beneath which, on each side, over the eye, is a line of white. Ear-coverts and chin black. Back and breast streaked with white and black. Wings black, the outer margins of the quills greyish-white, the tips of the larger coverts, excepting the primary ones, white, forming two broad bands of that colour across the wing. Tail black, tinged with bluish-grey externally, the ends of the inner webs of the three outer feathers on each side white. Abdomen white; sides and under tail-coverts white, spotted with black.

Length 5¼ inches, extent of wings 7½; bill along the ridge ¼.

I

THE BLACK LARCH.

PINUS PENDULA, *Pursh*, Flor. Amer. vol. ii. p. 645.—MONŒCIA POLYANDRIA, *Linn.* CONIFERÆ, *Juss.*

Leaves fasciculate, deciduous; cones oblong, the margins of the scales inflected; bracteoles panduriform, with an attenuated tip. This species, which grows in cedar swamps, in the Northern States, attains a great size, and resembles the European Larch in appearance.

THE ECCENTRIC NATURALIST.

" What an odd looking fellow !" said I to myself, as while walking by the river, I observed a man landing from a boat, with what I thought a bundle of dried clover on his back; " how the boatmen stare at him ! sure he must be an original !" He ascended with a rapid step, and approaching me asked if I could point out the house in which Mr Audu-bon resided. " Why, I am the man," said I, " and will gladly lead you to my dwelling."

The traveller rubbed his hands together with delight, and drawing a letter from his pocket, handed it to me without any remark. I broke the seal and read as follows : " My dear Audubon, I send you an odd fish, which you may prove to be undescribed, and hope you will do so in your next letter. Believe me always your friend B." With all the simplicity of a woodsman I asked the bearer where the odd fish was, when M. de T. (for, kind reader, the individual in my presence was none else than that renowned naturalist) smiled, rubbed his hands, and with the greatest good humour said, " I am that odd fish I presume, Mr Audubon." I felt confounded and blushed, but contrived to stammer an apology.

We soon reached the house, when I presented my learned guest to my family, and was ordering a servant to go to the boat for M. de T.'s luggage, when he told me he had none but what he brought on his back. He then loosened the pack of weeds which had first drawn my attention. The ladies were a little surprised, but I checked their critical glances for the moment. The naturalist pulled off his shoes, and while engaged in drawing his stockings, not up, but down, in order to cover the holes about the heels, told us in the gayest mood imaginable that he had walked a great distance, and had only taken a passage on board the *ark*, to be put on this shore, and that he was sorry his apparel had suffered so much from his late journey. Clean clothes were offered, but he would not accept them, and it was with evident reluctance that he performed the lavations usual on such occasions before he sat down to dinner.

At table, however, his agreeable conversation made us all forget his singular appearance; and, indeed, it was only as we strolled together in the garden that his attire struck me as exceedingly remarkable. A

long loose coat of yellow nankeen, much the worse of the many rubs it had
got in its time, and stained all over with the juice of plants, hung loosely
about him like a sac. A waistcoat of the same, with enormous pockets,
and buttoned up to the chin, reached below over a pair of tight panta-
loons, the lower parts of which were buttoned down to the ankles. His
beard was as long as I have known my own to be during some of my
peregrinations, and his lank black hair hung loosely over his shoulders.
His forehead was so broad and prominent that any tyro in phrenology
would instantly have pronounced it the residence of a mind of strong
powers. His words impressed an assurance of rigid truth, and as he directed the conversation to the study of the natural sciences, I listened to
him with as much delight as Telemachus could have listened to Mentor.
He had come to visit me, he said, expressly for the purpose of seeing my
drawings, having been told that my representations of birds were accompanied with those of shrubs and plants, and he was desirous of knowing
whether I might chance to have in my collection any with which he was
unacquainted. I observed some degree of impatience in his request to be
allowed at once to see what I had. We returned to the house, when I
opened my portfolios and laid them before him.

He chanced to turn over the drawing of a plant quite new to him.
After inspecting it closely, he shook his head, and told me no such plant
existed in nature ;—for, kind reader, M. de T. although a highly scientific man, was suspicious to a fault, and believed such plants only to exist
as he had himself seen, or such as, having been discovered of old, had, according to Father MALEBRANCHE's expression, acquired a " venerable
beard." I told my guest that the plant was common in the immediate
neighbourhood, and that I should shew it him on the morrow. " And
why to morrow, Mr AUDUBON? let us go now." We did so, and on
reaching the bank of the river, I pointed to the plant. M. de T. I thought
had gone mad. He plucked the plants one after another, danced, hug-
ged me in his arms, and exultingly told me that he had got not merely a
new species, but a new genus. When we returned home, the naturalist
opened the bundle which he had brought on his back, and took out a
journal rendered water-proof by means of a leather case, together with a
small parcel of linen, examined the new plant, and wrote its description.
The examination of my drawings then went on. You would be pleased,
kind reader, to hear his criticisms, which were of the greatest advantage

to me, for, being well acquainted with books as well as with nature, he was well fitted to give me advice.

It was summer, and the heat was so great that the windows were all open. The light of the candles attracted many insects, among which was observed a large species of Scarabæus. I caught one, and, aware of his inclination to believe only what he should himself see, I shewed him the insect, and assured him it was so strong that it would crawl on the table with the candlestick on its back. " I should like to see the experiment made, Mr AUDUBON," he replied. It was accordingly made, and the insect moved about, dragging its burden so as to make the candlestick change its position as if by magic, until coming upon the edge of the table, it dropped on the floor, took to wing, and made its escape.

When it waxed late, I shewed him to the apartment intended for him during his stay, and endeavoured to render him comfortable, leaving him writing materials in abundance. I was indeed heartily glad to have a naturalist under my roof. We had all retired to rest. Every person I imagined was in deep slumber save myself, when of a sudden I heard a great uproar in the naturalist's room. I got up, reached the place in a few moments, and opened the door, when, to my astonishment, I saw my guest running about the room naked, holding the handle of my favourite violin, the body of which he had battered to pieces against the walls in attempting to kill the bats which had entered by the open window, probably attracted by the insects flying around his candle. I stood amazed, but he continued jumping and running round and round, until he was fairly exhausted, when he begged me to procure one of the animals for him, as he felt convinced they belonged to " a new species." Although I was convinced of the contrary, I took up the bow of my demolished Cremona, and administering a smart tap to each of the bats as it came up, soon got specimens enough. The war ended, I again bade him good night, but could not help observing the state of the room. It was strewed with plants, which it would seem he had arranged into groups, but which were now scattered about in confusion. " Never mind, Mr AUDUBON," quoth the eccentric naturalist, " never mind, I'll soon arrange them again. I have the bats, and that's enough."

Several days passed, during which we followed our several occupations. M. de T. searched the woods for plants, and I for birds. He also followed the margins of the Ohio, and picked up many shells, which he greatly extolled. With us, I told him, they were gathered into

heaps to be converted into lime.   " Lime ! Mr AUDUBON ; why, they are
worth a guinea a piece in any part of Europe."   One day, as I was returning from a hunt in a cane-brake, he observed that I was wet and
spattered with mud, and desired me to shew him the interior of one of
these places, which he said he had never visited.

The Cane, kind reader, formerly grew spontaneously over the greater
portions of the State of Kentucky and other Western Districts of our
Union, as well as in many farther south.   Now, however, cultivation, the
introduction of cattle and horses, and other circumstances connected with
the progress of civilization, have greatly altered the face of the country,
and reduced the cane within comparatively small limits.   It attains a
height of from twelve to thirty feet, and a diameter of from one to two,
and grows in great patches resembling osier-holts, in which occur plants of
all sizes.   The plants frequently grow so close together, and in course of
time become so tangled, as to present an almost impenetrable thicket.   A
portion of ground thus covered with canes is called a *Cane-brake.*

If you picture to yourself one of these cane-brakes growing beneath
the gigantic trees that form our western forests, interspersed with vines
of many species, and numberless plants of every description, you may
conceive how difficult it is for one to make his way through it, especially
after a heavy shower of rain or a fall of sleet, when the traveller, in forcing his way through, shakes down upon himself such quantities of water,
as soon reduce him to a state of the utmost discomfort.   The hunters
often cut little paths through the thickets with their knives, but the usual
mode of passing through them is by pushing one's self backward, and
wedging a way between the stems.   To follow a bear or a cougar pursued
by dogs through these brakes, is a task, the accomplishment of which
may be imagined, but of the difficulties and dangers accompanying which
I cannot easily give an adequate representation.

The canes generally grow on the richest soil, and are particularly
plentiful along the margins of the great western rivers.   Many of our
new settlers are fond of forming farms in their immediate vicinity, as the
plant is much relished by all kinds of cattle and horses, which feed upon
it at all seasons, and again because these brakes are plentifully stocked
with game of various kinds.   It sometimes happens that the farmer
clears a portion of the brake.   This is done by cutting the stems, which
are fistular and knotted, like those of other grasses, with a large knife or
cutlass.   They are afterwards placed in heaps, and when partially dried

set fire to. The moisture contained between the joints is converted into steam, which causes the cane to burst with a smart report, and when a whole mass is crackling, the sounds resemble discharges of musquetry. Indeed, I have been told that travellers floating down the rivers, and unacquainted with these circumstances, have been induced to pull their oars with redoubled rigour, apprehending the attack of a host of savages, ready to scalp every one of the party.

A day being fixed, we left home after an early breakfast, crossed the Ohio, and entered the woods. I had determined that my companion should view a cane-brake in all its perfection, and after leading him several miles in a direct course, came upon as fine a sample as existed in that part of the country. We entered, and for some time proceeded without much difficulty, as I led the way, and cut down the canes which were most likely to incommode him. The difficulties gradually increased, so that we were presently obliged to turn our backs to the foe, and push ourselves on the best way we could. My companion stopped here and there to pick up a plant and examine it. After a while, we chanced to come upon the top of a fallen tree, which so obstructed our passage that we were on the eve of going round, instead of thrusting ourselves through amongst the branches, when, from its bed in the centre of the tangled mass, forth rushed a bear, with such force, and snuffing the air in so frightful a manner, that M. de T. became suddenly terror-struck, and, in his haste to escape, made a desperate attempt to run, but fell amongst the canes in such a way, that he looked as if pinioned. Perceiving him jammed in between the stalks, and thoroughly frightened, I could not refrain from laughing at the ridiculous exhibition which he made. My gaiety, however, was not very pleasing to the savant, who called out for aid, which was at once administered. Gladly would he have retraced his steps, but I was desirous that he should be able to describe a cane-brake, and enticed him to follow me, by telling him that our worst difficulties were nearly over. We proceeded, for by this time the bear was out of hearing.

The way became more and more tangled. I saw with delight that a heavy cloud, portentous of a thunder gust, was approaching. In the mean time, I kept my companion in such constant difficulties, that he now panted, perspired, and seemed almost overcome by fatigue. The thunder began to rumble, and soon after a dash of heavy rain drenched us in a few minutes. The withered particles of leaves and bark attached

to the canes stuck to our clothes. We received many scratches from
briars, and now and then a twitch from a nettle. M. de T. seriously inquired if we should ever get alive out of the horrible situation in which
we were. I spoke of courage and patience, and told him I hoped we
should soon get to the margin of the brake, which, however, I knew to
be two miles distant. I made him rest, and gave him a mouthful of
brandy from my flask; after which, we proceeded on our slow and painful march. He threw away all his plants, emptied his pockets of the
fungi, lichens, and mosses which he had thrust into them, and finding
himself much lightened, went on for thirty or forty yards with a better
grace. But, kind reader, enough—I led the naturalist first one way,
then another, until I had nearly lost myself in the brake, although I was
well acquainted with it, kept him tumbling and crawling on his hands
and knees, until long after mid-day, when we at length reached the edge
of the river. I blew my horn, and soon shewed my companion a boat
coming to our rescue. We were ferried over, and, on reaching the house,
found more agreeable occupation in replenishing our empty coffers.

M. de T. remained with us for three weeks, and collected multitudes
of plants, shells, bats, and fishes, but never again expressed a desire of
visiting a cane-brake. We were perfectly reconciled to his oddities, and,
finding him a most agreeable and intelligent companion, hoped that his
sojourn might be of long duration. But, one evening when tea was
prepared, and we expected him to join the family, he was nowhere to be
found. His grasses and other valuables were all removed from his room.
The night was spent in searching for him in the neighbourhood. No
eccentric naturalist could be discovered. Whether he had perished in a
swamp, or had been devoured by a bear or a gar-fish, or had taken to
his heels, were matters of conjecture; nor was it until some weeks after,
that a letter from him, thanking us for our attention, assured me of his
safety.

THE BROAD-WINGED HAWK.

FALCO PENNSYLVANICUS, WILS.

PLATE XCI. MALE AND FEMALE.

ONE fine May morning, when nature seemed to be enchanted at the sight of her own great works, when the pearly dew-drops were yet hanging at the point of each leaf, or lay nursed in the blossoms, gently rocked, as it were, by the soft breeze of early summer, I took my gun, and, accompanied by my excellent brother-in-law, WILLIAM G. BAKEWELL, Esq. at that time a youth, walked towards some lovely groves, where many songsters attracted our attention by their joyous melodies. The woods were all alive with the richest variety, and, divided in choice, we kept going on without shooting at any thing, so great was our admiration of every bird that presented itself to our view. As we crossed a narrow skirt of wood, my young companion spied a nest on a tree of moderate height, and, as my eye reached it, we both perceived that the parent bird was sitting in it. Some little consultation took place, as neither of us could determine whether it was a Crow's or a Hawk's nest, and it was resolved that my young friend should climb the tree, and bring down one of the eggs. On reaching the nest, he said the bird, which still remained quiet, was a Hawk and unable to fly. I desired him to cover it with his handkerchief, try to secure it, and bring it down, together with the eggs. All this was accomplished without the least difficulty. I looked at it with indescribable pleasure, as I saw it was new to me, and then felt vexed that it was not of a more spirited nature, as it had neither defended its eggs nor itself. It lay quietly in the handkerchief, and I carried it home to my father-in-law's, shewed it to the family, and went to my room, where I instantly began drawing it. The drawing which I then made is at this moment before me, and is dated " Fatland Ford, Pennsylvania, May 27, 1812."

I put the bird on a stick made fast to my table. It merely moved its feet to grasp the stick, and stood erect, but raised its feathers, and drew in its neck on its shoulders. I passed my hand over it, to smooth the feathers by gentle pressure. It moved not. The plumage remained

as I wished it. Its eye, directed towards mine, appeared truly sorrow-
ful, with a degree of pensiveness, which rendered me at that moment
quite uneasy. I measured the length of its bill with the compass, began
my outlines, continued measuring part after part as I went on, and
finished the drawing, without the bird ever moving once. My wife sat
at my side, reading to me at intervals, but our conversation had frequent
reference to the singularity of the incident. The drawing being finished,
I raised the window, laid hold of the poor bird, and launched it into the
air, where it sailed off until out of my sight, without uttering a single
cry, or deviating from its course. The drawing from which the plate is
taken, was subsequently made, as I had to wait until I should procure a
male, to render it complete.

The above incident you will doubtless consider as extraordinary as I
myself did, and perhaps some may feel disposed to look upon it as a specimen of travellers' tales ; but as I have resolved to present you with the
incidents as they occurred, I have felt no hesitation in relating this.

The Broad-winged Hawk is seldom seen in Louisiana, and I believe
never except during the severe winters that occasionally occur in our
Middle and Eastern Districts. I have observed that its usual range seldom extends far west of the Alleghany Mountains; but in Virginia,
Maryland, and all the States to the eastward of these, it is by no means
a rare species. I have shot several in the Jerseys, the State of New
York, near the Falls of Niagara, and also in the Great Pine Forest.

Its flight, which is easy and light, is performed in circles. When
elevated in the air, it is fond of partially closing its wings for a moment,
and thus gliding to a short distance, as if for amusement. It seldom
chases other birds of prey, but is itself frequently teased by the Little
Sparrow-hawk, the King-bird, or the Martin. It generally attacks birds
of weak nature, particularly very young chickens and ducklings, and
during winter feeds on insects and other small animals. It flies singly,
unless during the breeding season, and after feeding retires to the top of
some small tree, within the woods, where it rests for hours together. It
is easily approached. When wounded by a shot so as to be unable to fly,
it, like most birds of its tribe, throws itself on its back, opens its bill,
protrudes its tongue, utters a hissing sound, erects the top-feathers of its
head, and defends itself by reiterated attempts to lay hold with its talons.
If a stick is presented to it in this state, it will clench it at once, and allow itself to be carried hanging to it for some distance, indeed until

the muscles become paralyzed, when it drops, and again employs the same means of defence.

When feeding, it generally holds its prey with both feet, and tears and swallows the parts without much plucking. I must here remark, that birds of prey never cover their victims by extending the wings over them, unless when about to be attacked by other birds or animals, that evince a desire to share with them or carry off the fruit of their exertions. In the stomach of this bird I have found wood-frogs, portions of small snakes, together with feathers, and the hair of several small species of quadrupeds. I do not think it ever secures birds on the wing, at least I never saw it do so.

The nest, which is about the size of that of the Common Crow, is usually placed on pretty large branches, and near the stem or trunk of the tree. It is composed externally of dry sticks and briars, internally of numerous small roots, and is lined with the large feathers of the Common Fowl and other birds. The eggs are four or five, of a dull greyish-white, blotched with dark brown. They are deposited as early as the beginning of March, in low places, but not until a fortnight later in the mountainous parts of the districts in which the bird more frequently breeds.

The tree on which I have placed a pair of these birds is known nearly throughout the Union by the name of *Pig-nut Hickory*. I have represented it along with them, not because the birds themselves feed on the nuts, as some people have supposed on seeing the drawing, but because it occurs abundantly in those States where the Broad-winged Hawk resides, and, again, because I have found the nest of that bird more frequently placed on its branches than on those of any other tree. The nuts have an excessively hard shell. The kernel is sweet, but as it is of small size, the nuts are seldom gathered for any other purpose than that of feeding tame squirrels. The hogs which run at large in our woods feed on them, as do all our different species of squirrels, and sometimes the raccoon. The wood of this tree is perhaps tougher than that of most of its genus; but as the trunk is seldom either very straight or very high, it is not used so much as some other hickories, for the purposes of husbandry. Its average height may be estimated at about fifty feet, and its diameter at from eighteen inches to two feet.

FALCO PENNSYLVANICUS, *Ch. Bonaparte,* Synops. of Birds of the United States, p. 29.
BROAD-WINGED HAWK, FALCO PENNSYLVANICUS, *Wils.* Amer. Orn. vol. vi. p. 92.
PL 54. fig. 1. Male.

Adult Male.   Plate XCI. Fig. 1.

Bill shortish, as broad as long, the sides convex, the dorsal outline convex from the base; upper mandible with the edges slightly inflected, waved with a broad rounded lobe, the tip trigonal, descending obliquely, acute; lower mandible inflected at the edges, rounded at the tip. Nostrils oval, oblique. Head rather large, flattened above. Neck shortish. Body ovate, broad anteriorly. Wings rather long, Legs longish, rather robust, roundish; tarsi covered before and behind with scuta; toes covered above with scuta, scabrous and tuberculate beneath; middle toe much the longest, outer connected at the base by a membrane, and shorter than the inner; claws long, curved, roundish, very acute.

Plumage ordinary, compact. Feathers of the head narrow, of the back broad and rounded, of the neck oblong. Space between the bill and eye covered with bristly feathers. Wing very broad, the primary quills broad, slightly narrowed toward the end, rounded, the fourth longest, the secondary quills curved inwards, broadly obtuse. Tail longish, nearly even, the feathers rather broad, truncated and rounded.

Bill bluish-black at the tip, blue towards the base; cere and margin yellow. Iris hazel. Feet gamboge-yellow; claws brownish-black. The general colour of the upper parts is dark umber; the forehead with a slight margin of whitish, the quills blackish-brown, the tail with three bands of dark brown, alternating with two whitish bands, and a narrower terminal band of greyish, the tips white. Throat whitish; cheeks reddish-brown, with a dark brown mystachial band; the under parts generally light reddish, marked with guttiform, umber spots along the neck, and sagittiform larger spots of the same colour on the breast and sides. Tibial feathers of the same colour, with numerous smaller spots.

Length 14 inches, extent of wings 32; bill $\frac{1}{4}$ along the ridge, $1\frac{1}{4}$ along the gap.

Adult Female.   Plate XCI. Fig. 2.

Colouring generally similar to that of the male, lighter above, more tinged with red beneath, where the spots are larger and more irregular.

Length 16 inches, extent of wings 35; bill 1 along the ridge, 1¼ along the gap.

This species is referred to the division *Astures* of the genus Falco.

THE PIG-NUT HICKORY.

JUGLANS PORCINA, *Mich.* Arbr. Forest. de l'Amer. Sept. t. i. p. 206. Pl. 9. *Pursh,* Flor. Amer. vol. ii. p. 638.—MONŒCIA POLYANDRIA, *Linn.* TEREBINTHACEÆ, *Juss.*

Leaves pinnate, with seven, five, or three ovato-lanceolate, smooth leaflets, attenuated at both ends; male catkins filiform; fruit globose; nut small, smoothish, very hard. The leaves on the twig represented in the plate are not serrated on the edges, although they are generally so in this species. This, however, is merely an occasional variety.

THE PIGEON HAWK.

FALCO COLUMBARIUS, LINN.

PLATE XCII. MALE AND FEMALE.

IT is when the whole of the shores of our eastern rivers are swarming with myriads of Rice Buntings, Red-wings, Soras, and other migratory birds,—when all the sportsmen of those parts of our country are induced to turn out in the expectation of full bags of game, that the daring feats of the little spirited Falcon now before you are displayed.

Imagine yourself, good-natured reader, with a gun on your shoulder, following the windings of one of those noble streams which embellish our country and facilitate its commerce, having constantly within your view millions of birds on their way to the south, and which in the evenings fall thick as the drops of a hail-shower on the bordering marshes, to spend the night there in security, and by rest to restore the vigour necessary for their gaining the distant regions, whence half of them had emerged the preceding spring. Well, as you are proceeding, full of anxiety, and gazing in astonishment at the multitudes of feathered travellers, all of a sudden a larger bird attracts your eye. It sweeps along in the stillness of the autumnal evening with a rapidity seldom equalled, creating confusion, terror, and dismay along the whole shores. The flocks rise *en masse* with a fluttering sound which comes strangely on your ear, double and double again, turn and wind over the marsh, agitated and fearful of imminent danger. And now, closely crowded, they would fain escape, but alas! one has been singled out, and in the twinkling of an eye, the Pigeon Hawk, darting into the middle of the flock, seizes and carries him off. Now is your time. Hundreds of sportsmen are dispersed over the marsh, paddling their canoes, or splashing among the reeds. Pull your trigger, and let fly, for it is impossible, should you be ever so inexpert, not to bring down several birds at a shot.

But, leaving you to your sport, I must follow the little marauder, as he makes toward the nearest shore, where he alights and devours his prey, and then, with unsatiated appetite, and bent on foul deeds, returns to the scene of action.

When the Reed-birds, the Redwings, and Soras, shall have become

so scarce as to be searched for with the same interest as our little Partridges already are; when the margins of our rivers shall have been
drained and ploughed to the very tide-mark; when the Grouse shall have
to be protected by game-laws; when Turkeys shall no longer be met with
in the wild state;—how strange will the tale which I now tell sound in
the ears of those who may walk along the banks of these rivers, and over
the fields which have occupied the place of these marshes!

The Pigeon Hawk does not, I believe, raise its young within the
United States, but somewhere farther to the north. At least, I am inclined to think so, for in all my wanderings I never found its nest, nor
saw the bird at any other season than late in summer, during the autumnal months, or in the winter. Its migration, or rather its pursuit of migrating birds, extends to the southernmost parts of our country; for I
have killed it not only in Louisiana, but high up the Arkansas River, in
regions bordering upon the Mexican territory.

The daring spirit which it displays exceeds that of any other Hawk
of its size. It seizes the Red-breasted Thrush, the Wild Pigeon, and
even the Golden-winged Woodpecker, on land; whilst along the shores
it chases several species of Snipes, as well as the Green-winged Teal. The
latter bird, however, dives at the approach of the Hawk, and thus eludes
his gripe; while the little plunderer, having descended to the surface of
the water with the velocity of an arrow, passes onwards, ascending again,
without seeming to move its wings, the impulse which it acquired in the
descent carrying it onwards, as a carriage, after being whirled down a
steep declivity, surmounts the next eminence, without additional propulsion. Even the presence of the tyrant man he little heeds, and in Pennsylvania one of this species came almost right upon me while in pursuit
of a dove, which found safety in my bosom from its persecutor.

When not in full chase, the Pigeon Hawk flies with an unsteady and
undetermined motion, flapping its wings frequently, while it rises in spiral
curves. This parade is of short duration, for, as if it remembered that
it was losing time, it again approaches the ground, and skims swiftly over
the streams, across the fields, along the fences, or by the skirts of the
woods, as if intending to frighten all the little birds in its way. Should
it unexpectedly meet a man, it darts upwards, and quickly passes over to
continue its search. I have known these Hawks attack birds in cages,
hanging against the walls of houses, in the very streets of our eastern
ities.   G g 2

When wounded in the wing, it shakes the other as it falls, describing the spiral curves of a screw; and, if no person is near to secure it, makes its way by long leaps to the thickets, where it is very difficult to find it. But if the gunner is at hand, and attempts to lay hold of it, the little ruffian erects his feathers, screams shrilly and piercingly, and, like the rest of his tribe, throws himself on his back, to be ready to clutch his enemy.

FALCO COLUMBARIUS, *Linn* Syst. Nat. p. 128.—*Lath.* Ind. Ornith. vol. i. p. 44.—*Ch. Bonaparte,* Synops. of Birds of the United States, p. 28.

PIGEON HAWK, *Lath.* Synops. vol. i. p. 101.—*Wils.* Amer. Ornith. vol. ii. p. 107. Pl. 25. fig. 3.

Adult Male.   Plate XCII. Fig. 1.

Bill shortish, as broad as long, the sides convex, the dorsal outline convex from the base; upper mandible with the edges slightly inflected, and forming a projecting process, the tip trigonal, acute, descending obliquely; lower mandible inflected at the edges, with a notch near the end, abrupt at the tip. Nostrils roundish, with a central tubercle, perforated in the short cere. Head rather large, flattened above. Neck shortish. Body ovate. Legs short, roundish; tarsi covered before with transverse scuta, on the sides with scales; toes scutellate above, scabrous and tuberculate beneath; middle toe much longer than the outer, which is connected with it at the base by a membrane; claws long, curved, roundish, very acute.

Plumage ordinary, compact on the upper and fore parts, lax beneath. Feathers of the head and neck narrow, of the back rather short, broad and rounded, of the breast oblong. Space between the beak and eye covered with bristly feathers. Orbital spaces bare. Wings nearly as long as the tail; the primary quills narrow, tapering, cut out on the inner web towards the end, rounded, the second longest; the secondary quills short, obtuse. Tail longish, nearly even. Tibial feathers long, forming a large tuft externally.

Bill bluish-black at the tip, blue towards the base; cere, margin, and bare orbital space greenish-yellow. Iris dark brown. Feet greenish-yellow; claws brownish-black. The general colour of the upper parts is deep chocolate ; a line above the eyes, the tips of the first row of wing-coverts, the outer margins and tips of the secondaries, and the inner margins and tips of the primaries, whitish. The inner webs of the quills

marked with pale brown spots. Tail banded with brownish-white transverse spots, which do not reach the outer margin of the feathers, and
tipped with the same. Throat white, cheeks whitish, patched and streaked with brown. A broad mystachial band of the same colour. Under
parts generally light reddish-brown, marked with guttiform spots. Tibial
feathers marked with more elongated spots. Under tail-coverts nearly
spotless.

Length 13 inches, extent of wings 28 ; bill $\frac{7}{12}$ along the ridge, $\frac{11}{12}$
along the gap.

Adult Female. Plate XCII. Fig. 2.

The colouring of the female is generally similar to that of the male,
somewhat lighter above, with the spots of the lower parts broader.

Length 14½ inches, extent of wings 30 ; bill $\frac{3}{4}$ along the ridge, $\frac{7}{8}$
along the gap, measured from the tip of the lower mandible.

THE SEA-SIDE FINCH.

FRINGILLA MARITIMA, WILS.

PLATE XCIII. MALE AND FEMALE.

THE monotonous chirpings which one hears in almost every part of our
maritime salt-marshes, are produced by this bird and another nearly allied to it. The Sea-side Finch may be seen at any hour of the day, during the months of May and June, mounted on the tops of the rankest
weeds which grow by the margins of tide-waters along the greater portion of our Atlantic coast, whence it pours forth with much emphasis the
few notes of which its song is composed. When one approaches it, it
either seeks refuge amongst the grass, by descending along the stalks and
blades of the weeds, or flies off to a short distance, with a continued
flirting of its wings, then alights with a rapid descent, and runs off with
great nimbleness. I am inclined to believe that it rears two broods in
the season, as I have found birds of this species sitting on their eggs early
in May, and again in the beginning of July. The nest is placed so close
to the ground that one might suppose it partly sunk in it, although this
is not actually the case. It is composed of coarse grasses externally, and
is lined with finer kinds, but exhibits little regularity in its structure.
The eggs are from four to six, of an elongated oval form, greyish-white,
freckled with brown all over. The male and the female sit alternately,
and will not fly off at the sight of man, unless he attempts to catch them
on the nest, when they skulk off as if badly wounded. Many nests may
be found in the space of a few acres of these marshes, where the land is
most elevated, and where small shrubs are seen. They select these spots,
because they are not liable to be overflowed by high floods, and because
there are accumulated about them drifted sand, masses of sea-weed, and
other castings of the sea, among which they find much food of the kind
which they seem to prefer. This consists of marine insects, small crabs
and snails, as well as the green sand beetle, portions of all of which I
have found in their stomach.

It is very difficult to shoot them unless when they are on wing, as
their movements while they run up and down the weeds are extremely
rapid ; but their flight is so direct and level, that a good marksman can

easily kill them before they alight amongst the grass again. After the young are well grown, the whole of these birds betake themselves to the ditches or sluices by which the salt-marshes are intersected, fly along them, and there find abundant food. They enter the larger holes of crabs, go into every crack and crevice of the drying mud, and are then more difficult to be approached, as the edges of these ditches are usually over-grown with taller and ranker sedges. Having one day shot a number of these birds, merely for the sake of practice, I had them made into a pie, which, however, could not be eaten, on account of its fishy savour.

The Rose on which I have drawn these birds is found so near the sea, on rather higher lands than the marshes, that I thought it as fit as any other plant for the purpose, more especially as the Finches, when very high tides overflow the marshes, take refuge in these higher grounds. It is sweetly scented, and blooms from May to August. I have never met with it elsewhere than on the small sea islands and along the coasts, where it grows in loose sandy sail.

FRINGILLA MARITIMA, *Ch. Bonoparts*, Synops. of Birds of the United States, p. 110.
SEA-SIDE FINCH, FRINGILLA MARITIMA, *Wils.* Amer. Ornith. vol. iv. p. 68, Pl. 34. Fig. 2.

Adult Male. Plate XCIII. Fig. 1.

Bill shortish, robust, conical, acute; upper mandible broader than the lower, slightly declinate at the tip; the edges of both mandibles slightly arched, and a little deflected at the base. Nostrils basal, roundish, open, partially concealed by the feathers. Head rather large. Neck shortish. Body rather robust. Legs of moderate length, slender; tarsus longer than the middle toe, covered anteriorly with a longitudinal plate above, and a few large scuta below; toes scutellate above, free, the lateral ones nearly equal; claws slender, slightly arched, compressed, acute, that of the hind toe larger.

Plumage ordinary, compact above, soft and blended beneath. Wings short, and much curved, third and fourth quills longest, first much shorter. Tail of ordinary length, much rounded, the feathers narrow and rather pointed.

Bill dark brown above, light blue beneath. Iris hazel. Feet and claws greyish-blue. Crown of the head deep brown, surrounded by a line of greyish-blue. Upper part of the back, wings, and tail, olive-brown mixed with pale blue. Lesser wing-coverts reddish-brown, larger coverts edged and tipped with brownish-white, the edge of the wing-joint yellow. Outer margins of the tail-feathers paler. A broad yellow streak from the base of the bill over the eye. Throat and fore-neck greyish-white, with a streak of greyish-blue on each side. Breast and sides dull greyish-blue, the abdomen paler.

There is very little difference between the sexes as to colour or size.

Length 8 inches, extent of wings 11 ; bill along the ridge ⅚, along the gap 1.

The Carolina Rose.

Rosa Carolina, *Pursh*, Flor. Amer. p. 345.—Icosandria Polygynia, *Linn.* Rosaceæ, *Juss.*

This beautiful species, which attains a height of five or six feet, is generally characterized by its globose germens, which, with the peduncles, are more or less hispid ; its hairy petioles, slightly curved prickles, and oblongo-lanceolate, acute, serrated leaflets, which are glaucous beneath. It varies greatly, however, like many other species of the same genus.

THE GRASS FINCH, OR BAY-WINGED BUNTING.

FRINGILLA GRAMINEA, GMEL.

PLATE XCIV. MALE.

I HAVE never seen the Bay-winged Bunting in any portion of Louisiana, Missouri, Kentucky, or Ohio, and am therefore inclined to look upon it as a resident of the country lying to the eastward of the range of the Alleghanies. It there occurs from Georgia to Massachusets, both along the shores and inland, as far as the base of the mountains, and here and there on the mountains themselves, but seldom in places to which cultivation has not extended. I have thought it prepossessed in favour of sandy ground, and dry barren soils. It sings sweetly, and at times for half-an-hour, without changing its place, either from the tops of the Sassafras or Sumach bushes which grow along the fences, or from the upper bar or stake of a fence itself. During this little serenade, it is easily approached, but when on the ground, where it runs nimbly and with grace, it is rather shy. It is fond of scratching in the warm and dry sand, and of wallowing in it, to cleanse its body. Its flight, which is easy, consists of a succession of gentle undulations, and, when it is chased, sometimes extends over the whole of a field. It is a solitary bird, and is rather pugnacious, for when two males or two females happen to meet, little skirmishes frequently ensue. The nest, which is placed among the grass, and partly sunk in the ground, little attention being paid to its concealment, is prettily constructed. It is formed externally of leaves and fine grass, and is well lined with horse hair, so as to look neat and comfortable. The female lays from four to six eggs, about the middle of April, in favourable seasons, and generally rears two broods each year. I have shot these birds during winter, in the neighbourhood of Lancaster in Pennsylvania, where but few are seen. At the same period of the year they were found numerous along the sea-coast of Virginia and Carolina. Their food consists principally of the seeds of grasses and other plants, although they sometimes run after insects and eat them also. Their flesh is juicy, tender and savoury.

Having drawn the figure which you will see on referring to the plate, near the sea-shores of New Jersey, where the bird which it represents was shot while walking among little groups of the plant there vulgarly called the Prickly Pear, I have represented it also. It shoots up its fleshy stems from among the driest sand, and there flourishes in the greatest perfection and abundance. The flower is destitute of scent, but the fruit is agreeably acid, and is often eaten by children. I have observed a plant of the same genus about the sterile cliffs of the Kentucky River, and in particular near the town of Frankfort, as well as in Louisiana on Alexander's Creek, at which place it grows to a great size. This is probably a distinct species. I have not observed Cactuses growing in a wild state in any other part of the Union.

FRINGILLA GRAMINEA, *Gmel.* Syst. Nat. vol. i. p. 922.—*Lath.* Ind. Ornith. vol. i. p. 445.—*Ch. Bonaparte,* Synops. of Birds of the United States, p. 108.

GRASS FINCH, *Lath.* Synops. vol. iii. p. 273.

EMBERIZA GRAMINEA, BAY-WINGED BUNTING, *Wils.* Amer. Ornith. vol. iv. p. 51. Pl. 31. fig. 5.

Adult Male.   Plate XCIV.

Bill shortish, robust, conical, acute; upper mandible broader than the lower, slightly declinate at the tip, the edges of both mandibles straight to near the base, where they are a little deflected. Nostrils basal, roundish, open, partially concealed by the feathers. Head rather large. Neck short. Body robust. Legs of moderate length, slender; tarsus of the same length as the middle toe, covered anteriorly with a longitudinal plate above, and a few transverse scuta below; toes scutate above, free, the lateral ones nearly equal; claws slender, arched, compressed, acute, that of the hind toe largest.

Plumage ordinary, compact. Wings of ordinary length, third and fourth quills longest, first and second little shorter. Tail longish, nearly equal, or slightly forked.

Bill dark brown on the back of the upper mandible, pale on the sides and below. Iris hazel. Tarsi, toes, and claws, flesh-colour. The general colour of the upper parts is light brown, streaked and mottled with darker. Lesser wing-coverts bright reddish-brown or bay, the larger deep brown, edged with pale brown; quills also deep brown, the first margined externally with white. Tail-feathers dark brown, the outer marked with an oblique band of white, including the outer web and part of the inner towards the tip, the next three margined externally with white, changing into pale brown on the other. A narrow circle of white around the eye. Throat and breast yellowish-white, the latter and the fore part of the cheeks streaked with dark brown. Sides and abdomen very pale yellowish-brown, the former sparsely streaked with dark brown; the posterior abdominal region and under tail-coverts white.

There is no perceptible difference as to colour or size between the male and the female.

Length 5¾ inches, extent of wings 10; bill ½ along the ridge, ½ along the gap.

This species has been variously classed, some considering it as a Fringilla, others as an Emberiza. It seems to me to be more in its true place in the former genus, while in its habits, colouring and form, it also approaches closely to some species of Alauda.

The Prickly Pear, or Indian Fig.

Cactus Opuntia, *Willd.* Sp. Pl. vol. ii. p. 943. *Pursh,* Fl. Amer. p. 323.—Icosandria Monogynia, *Linn.* Cacti, *Juss.*

This species has an articulated fleshy stem, with ovate, compressed joints, sparsely covered with setaceous prickles; large yellow flowers, and red, acidulous, eatable berries. It flowers in June and July, and grows in sandy fields and dry barren soil.

THE YELLOW-POLL WARBLER.

SYLVIA ÆSTIVA, GMEL.

PLATE XCV. MALE.

As soon as the welcome note of the Purple Martin is heard in spring, on its return to the United States, which, in Louisiana, sometimes takes place early in March, the little Warbler here presented to your inspection follows, and is seen gaily moving from tree to tree, feeding on the smaller insects, and tuning its pipe, which, however, is not the most melodious. It approaches the gardens and orange-groves, and again flies off to the willows, along the margins of the pools and lagoons. Its sojourn is of short duration in Louisiana, for it moves gradually eastward as the season advances, leaving nothing but the recollection of its passage through the land. Its migration, in as far as I have been able to ascertain, is principally performed during the night. I have observed many in the course of one day in a place, which, next day, if the weather had become warm, scarcely contained a single individual. It never breeds in the district mentioned above, nor even in the State of Mississippi. A few breed in Kentucky, more in Ohio, and their nests in this manner increase the farther you proceed eastward. I have seen many of these birds, as well as their nests, on the Genessee River ; but in the States of New York, Connecticut, Pennsylvania, Maryland, and Virginia, they may be found in every orchard and garden, and even in the streets, among the foliage of our trees.

The males chase each other with great courage, and fight for a few moments, to establish their claim to any particular spot or tree, after which they are seen climbing up and down among the twigs and smaller branches, looking keenly among the leaves and blossoms for insects. Careless of the presence of man, the Blue-eyed Warbler is easily approached. The same carelessness makes it build its little nest almost always within reach of the latter. The parents are very assiduous in the discharge of their duties. They construct a nest about the middle of May, in the forked branches of a small tree, often within a few paces of a house. The nest is strongly fastened to the twigs, is formed externally of hemp, flax, or woolly substances, and is well lined with different kinds of hair, intermixed with softer materials. It breeds twice during the summer, and returns southward in the beginning of autumn, in small parties, shifting chiefly by night. During the breeding-season, this little bird, when approached, shews great anxiety for the preservation of its eggs or young, and tries, with all the artifices employed by many other species, to entice the aggressor away from its nest. They are seen, on their return to the south, passing through Louisiana in October.

I made my drawing of this species near Natchez, and having killed the specimen while it was searching for insects among the flowers of a large climbing plant, I have figured part of the latter also. This plant I have never seen, excepting in low, damp or marshy places. It there runs over decayed trees, spreading in the form of a bower, and hanging in graceful festoons. The long pendulous clusters of pale purple flowers are destitute of odour.

SYLVIA ÆSTIVA, *Gmel.* Syst. Nat. vol. i. p. 996.—*Lath.* Ind. Ornith. vol. ii. p. 551.— *Ch. Bonaparte,* Synops. of Birds of the United States, p. 83.

YELLOW-POLL WARBLER, *Lath.* Syn. vol. iv. p. 515.

BLUE-EYED WARBLER, SYLVIA CITRINELLA, *Wils.* Amer. Ornith. vol. ii. p. 111. Pl. 15. fig. 6.

Bill about as long as the head, slender, straight, subulate, as deep as broad at the base. Nostrils basal, lateral, elliptical, half closed by a membrane. Head rather small. Neck short. Body ovate, rather slender. Feet of ordinary length, slender; tarsus longer than the middle toe, covered anteriorly with a few scutella, the uppermost long; toes scutellate above, the inner free, the hind toe of moderate size; claws slender, compressed, acute, arched.

Plumage soft, blended, tufty, a few bristles at the base of the bill. Wings of ordinary length, acute. Tail longish, slightly forked.

Bill dark blue, the lower mandible edged with yellow. Iris brown. Feet and claws pale brown. Hind head and upper parts generally pale yellowish-green, the tail-coverts more yellow. The fore part of the head, the cheeks, the throat, and the sides of the neck, pure golden-yellow; the rest of the lower parts yellow, the breast and sides streaked with brownish-red. Quills and alula deep brown, their outer webs yellowish, as are the margins of the large coverts.   Tail-feathers deep brown, with yellow margins.

Length 5¼ inches, extent of wings 10; bill $\frac{5}{12}$ along the ridge, $\frac{3}{4}$ along the gap.

The female differs from the male only in having the colours less bright, and the streaks on the breast somewhat broader and fewer.

SCIPIO AND THE BEAR.

THE Black Bear (*Ursus americanus*), however clumsy in appearance,
is active, vigilant, and persevering ; possesses great strength, courage, and
address ; and undergoes with little injury the greatest fatigues and hard-
ships in avoiding the pursuit of the hunter.   Like the Deer, it changes
its haunts with the seasons, and for the same reason, namely, the desire
of obtaining suitable food, or of retiring to the more inaccessible parts,
where it can pass the time in security, unobserved by man, the most dangerous of its enemies.   During the spring months, it searches for food in
the low rich alluvial lands that border the rivers, or by the margins of
such inland lakes as, on account of their small size, are called by us ponds.
There it procures abundance of succulent roots, and of the tender juicy
stems of plants, upon which it chiefly feeds at that season.   During the
summer heat, it enters the gloomy swamps, passes much of its time in
wallowing in the mud, like a hog, and contents itself with crayfish, roots,
and nettles, now and then, when hard pressed by hunger, seizing on a
young pig, or perhaps a sow, or even a calf.   As soon as the different
kinds of berries which grow on the mountains begin to ripen, the Bears
betake themselves to the high grounds, followed by their cubs.   In such
retired parts of the country where there are no hilly grounds, it pays visits
to the maize fields, which it ravages for a while.   After this, the various
species of nuts, acorns, grapes, and other forest fruits, that form what in
the Western Country is called *mast*, attract its attention.   The Bear is
then seen rambling singly through the woods to gather this harvest, not
forgetting meanwhile to rob every *Bee-tree* it meets with, Bears being, as
you well know, expert at this operation.   You also know that they are
good climbers, and may have been told, or at least may now be told, that
the Black Bear now and then *houses* itself in the hollow trunks of the larger trees for weeks together, when it is said to suck its paws.   You are
probably not aware of a habit in which it indulges, and which, being curious, must be interesting to you.

At one season, the Black Bear may be seen examining the lower part
of the trunk of a tree for several minutes with much attention, at the same
time looking around, and snuffing the air, to assure itself that no enemy
is near.   It then raises itself on its hind legs, approaches the trunk, em-

braces it with its fore legs, and scratches the bark with its teeth and claws for several minutes in continuance. Its jaws clash against each other, until a mass of foam runs down on both sides of the mouth. After this it continues its rambles.

In various portions of our country, many of our woodsmen and hunters who have seen the Bear performing the singular operation just described, imagine that it does so for the purpose of leaving behind it an indication of its size and power. They measure the height at which the scratches are made, and in this manner can, in fact, form an estimate of the magnitude of the individual. My own opinion, however, is different. It seems to me that the Bear scratches the trees, not for the purpose of shewing its size or its strength, but merely for that of sharpening its teeth and claws, to enable it better to encounter a rival of its own species during the amatory season. The Wild Boar of Europe clashes its tusks and scrapes the earth with its feet, and the Deer rubs its antlers against the lower part of the stems of young trees or bushes, for the same purpose.

Being one night sleeping in the house of a friend, I was wakened by a Negro servant bearing a light, who gave me a note, which he said his master had just received. I ran my eye over the paper, and found it to be a communication from a neighbour, requesting my friend and myself to join him as soon as possible, and assist in killing some Bears at that moment engaged in destroying his corn. I was not long in dressing, you may be assured, and, on entering the parlour, found my friend equipt and only waiting for some bullets, which a Negro was employed in casting. The overseer's horn was heard calling up the Negroes from their different cabins. Some were already engaged in saddling our horses, whilst others were gathering all the cur-dogs of the plantation. All was bustle. Before half an hour had elapsed, four stout Negro men, armed with axes and knives, and mounted on strong nags of their own (for you must know, kind reader, that many of our slaves rear horses, cattle, pigs and poultry, which are exclusively their own property), were following us at a round gallop through the woods, as we made directly for the neighbour's plantation, a little more than five miles off.

The night was none of the most favourable, a drizzling rain rendering the atmosphere thick and rather sultry; but as we were well acquainted with the course, we soon reached the house, where the owner was waiting our arrival. There were now three of us armed with guns, half a dozen servants, and a good pack of dogs of all kinds. We jogged on towards the detached field in which the Bears were at work. The owner told us that for some days several of these animals had visited his corn, and that a Negro who was sent every afternoon to see at what part of the enclosure they entered, had assured him there were at least five in the field that night. A plan of attack was formed : the bars at the usual gap of the fence were to be put down without noise ; the men and dogs were to divide, and afterwards proceed so as to surround the Bears, when, at the sounding of our horns, every one was to charge towards the centre of the field, and shout as loudly as possible, which it was judged would so intimidate the animals, as to induce them to seek refuge upon the dead trees with which the field was still partially covered.

The plan succeeded. The horns sounded, the horses galloped forward, the men shouted, the dogs barked and howled. The shrieks of the Negroes were enough to frighten a legion of Bears, and those in the field took to flight, so that by the time we reached the centre they were heard hurrying towards the tops of the trees. Fires were immediately lighted by the Negroes. The drizzling rain had ceased, the sky cleared, and the glare of the crackling fires proved of great assistance to us. The Bears had been so terrified, that we now saw several of them crouched at the junction of the larger boughs with the trunks. Two were immediately shot down. They were cubs of no great size, and being already half dead, we left them to the dogs, which quickly dispatched them.

We were anxious to procure as much sport as possible, and having observed one of the Bears, which from its size we conjectured to be the mother, ordered the Negroes to cut down the tree on which it was perched, when it was intended the dogs should have a tug with it, while we should support them, and assist in preventing the bear from escaping by wounding it in one of the hind legs. The surrounding woods now echoed to the blows of the axemen. The tree was large and tough, having been girded more than two years, and the operation of felling it seemed extremely tedious. However, it began to vibrate at each stroke ; a few inches alone now supported it; and in a short time it came crashing to the ground, in so awful a manner that Bruin must doubtless have felt the shock as severe as we should feel a shake of the globe produced by the sudden collision of a comet.

The dogs rushed to the charge, and harassed the Bear on all sides. We had remounted, and now surrounded the poor animal. As its life depended upon its courage and strength, it exercised both in the most

energetic manner. Now and then it seized a dog, and killed him by a
single stroke.   At another time, a well administered blow of one of its
fore-legs sent an assailant off yelping so piteously, that he might be looked
upon as *hors de combat*.   A cur had daringly ventured to seize the Bear
by the snout, and was seen hanging to it, covered with blood, whilst a
dozen or more scrambled over its back.   Now and then, the infuriated
animal was seen to cast a revengeful glance at some of the party, and we
had already determined to dispatch it, when, to our astonishment, it suddenly shook off all the dogs, and before we could fire, charged upon one
of the Negroes, who was mounted on a pied horse.   The Bear seized the
steed with teeth and claws, and clung to its breast.   The terrified horse
snorted and plunged.   The rider, an athletic young man, and a capital
horseman, kept his seat, although only saddled on a sheep's skin tightly
girthed, and requested his master not to fire at the Bear.   Notwithstanding his coolness and courage, our anxiety for his safety was raised to the
highest pitch, especially when in a moment we saw rider and horse come
to the ground together ; but we were instantly relieved on witnessing the
masterly manner in which SCIPIO dispatched his adversary, by laying
open his skull with a single well-directed blow of his axe, when a deep
growl announced the death of the Bear, and the valorous Negro sprung
to his feet unhurt.

Day dawned, and we renewed our search. Two of the remaining
Bears were soon discovered, lodged in a tree about a hundred yards from
the spot where the last one had been overpowered.   On approaching them
in a circle, we found that they manifested no desire to come down, and
we resolved to try *smoking*. We surrounded the tree with a pile of
brushwood and large branches.   The flames ascended and caught hold
of the dry bark.   At length the tree assumed the appearance of a pillar
of flame.   The Bears mounted to the top branches.   When they had
reached the uppermost, they were seen to totter, and soon after, the
branch cracking and snapping across, they came to the ground, bringing
with them a mass of broken twigs.   They were cubs, and the dogs soon
worried them to death.

The party returned to the house in triumph. SCIPIO's horse, being
severely wounded, was let loose in the field, to repair his strength by
eating the corn.   A cart was afterwards sent for the game.   But before
we had left the field, the horses, dogs, and bears, together with the fires,
had destroyed more corn within a few hours, than the poor Bear and her
cubs had during the whole of their visits.

THE COLUMBIA JAY.

CORVUS BULLOCKII.

PLATE XCVI. Adult.

The genus *Corvus* consists of birds which differ considerably in their appearance and manners. This circumstance has given rise to various separations and groupings. It may, in fact, be considered analogous to the great genera *Falco*, *Psittacus* and *Columba*, which, although the species composing them exhibit great diversity, may be allowed to retain their integrity, because the gradations between the species are so minute that each group presents an uninterrupted series. Were one to compare the Golden Eagle with the Swallow-tailed Hawk, the Red Macaw with the Ground Parrot of New Holland, or the Great Crested Pigeon with the Turtle Dove, he might doubtless find reasons for separating these birds into genera, could he but forget that the intermediate gradations are to be seen. It is so with the Crows and Jays. The former are characterized by a certain gravity of aspect; their flight is regular, protracted, and performed by easy flappings and sailings; they frequent open places, and feed on almost all kinds of food indiscriminately; their cry is a dull croak or scream. The latter are much smarter in their appearance, more lively in their motions; their flight is less protracted, and performed by short flappings; they frequent woods and thickets, and live chiefly on fruits; and their notes are emitted in noisy chatterings. The bill of the Crows is large, robust, cultriform, covered at the base with long, stiff, closely adpressed, reversed, bristly feathers; that of some of the Jays is much smaller, not robust, and approaching to the form of that of Thrushes and Nutcrackers, and the basirostral feathers are diminished in size and rigidity. The Crows have shortish, even or rounded tails, with long and sometimes rather sharp wings. The Jays have the tail often greatly elongated and cuneiform or graduated, with short, much rounded, concave wings. Numerous other contrasts are afforded, the Crows, for example, being generally dull and uniform in their colours, the Jays variegated and often brilliant. All these circumstances I intend to discuss in another work, and in the mean time retain the usual generic name for the present splendid species, which has the bill of nearly the same form as the true Crows, combined with the elongated tail, and lively colouring of the Jays.

Were I to relate to you, good reader, the various accounts which I have heard respecting this splendid bird, I should have enough to say; but as I have resolved to confine myself entirely to the results of my own observation, I must for the present remain silent on the subject.

The specimen from which the drawings were taken was presented to me by a friend who had received it from the Columbia River, and is the only individual represented in the volume which I did not myself procure on the spot. However, as I expect to ramble again through our vast forests and extensive territories, I may yet be enabled to give you a full account of this beautiful bird, which, from the splendour of its plumage, deserves all the attention of the naturalist. In the mean time I adjoin a notice respecting it, with which I have lately been favoured by my friend, the Prince of Musignano. " Le superbe geai, dont vous me parlez, est sans doute l'oiseau que WAGLER a fait connâitre le premier, sous le nom de *Pica Bullockii*, et que TEMMINCK a figuré dans ses planches coloriées, sous cellui de *Garrula Gubernatrix*. Son nom legitime, suivant mes principes, sera *Garrulus Bullockii*, mais vous avez raison de dire qu'il ne se trouve pas dans mon Synopsis : ce n'est que par votre lettre que j'ai appris qu'il se trouvait dans le territoire des Etats-unis. Jusqu'a présent on ne l'avait trouve qu'au Mexique et à la Californie. Il n'est pas etonnant qu'il se retrouve sur la rivière Columbia. Mais comment l'avez-vous obtena et avez-vous pu le dessiner vivant? Trois autres especes de geais, qui ne sont pas dans mon Synopsis, habitent l'extremité nord de l'Amerique, et il est probable, qu' outre votre superbe *geai commandeur*, plusieurs autres des especes Mexicaines se retrouvent dans sa partie occidentale."

CORVUS BULLOCKII, *Wagler.*

Bill of ordinary length, straight, robust, compressed; upper mandible with the dorsal outline straightish at the base, declinate and convex towards the tip, which is deflected, the sides convex, the edges rather sharp; lower mandible with the dorsal outline slightly concave towards the base, convex and ascending towards the tip. Nostrils basal, oval, partly concealed by short bristly feathers. Proportions of parts ordinary. Feet of ordinary length, rather strong; tarsus compressed, about the length of the middle toe, anteriorly scutellate, covered behind with two longitudinal plates, meeting at an acute angle; toes free, scutellate above ; claws of ordinary size, arched, convex above, canaliculate beneath.

Plumage compact, glossy. Feathers of the head elongated into a crest, the posterior ones recurvate. Wings longish, the third and fourth quills longest, the first short. Tail very long, graduated, of twelve feathers, of which the two central are slightly curved, and greatly exceed the rest in length.

Bill and feet brownish-black. Iris hazel. The general colour of the plumage is bright blue, with purple reflections. The fore neck and anterior part of the breast black ; the rest of the under parts white. The inner webs of the quills dusky, the four outer feathers of the tail white towards the tip.

Length 31 inches, extent of wings 26 ; bill along the ridge 1½, tarsus 2, middle toe 2.

THE LITTLE SCREECH OWL.

STRIX ASIO, LINN.

PLATE XCVII. ADULT AND YOUNG.

THIS Owl, although found in the Southern States, is there very rare. During a long residence in Louisiana, I have not met with more than two individuals. On advancing towards the confluence of the Ohio and Mississippi, we find them becoming rather more numerous; above the Falls of the former, they increase in number; and as the traveller advances towards the sources of that noble river, their mournful notes are heard in every quarter during mild and serene nights. In Virginia, Maryland, and all the Eastern Districts, the bird is plentiful, particularly during the autumnal and winter months, and is there well known under the name of the *Screech Owl.*

You are presented, kind reader, with three figures of this species, the better to shew you the differences which exist between the young and the full-grown bird. The contrast of colouring in these different stages I have thought it necessary to exhibit, as the *Red Owl* of WILSON and other naturalists is merely the young of the bird called by the same authors the *Mottled Owl*, and which, in fact, is the adult of the species under consideration. The error committed by the author of the " American Ornithology," for many years misled all subsequent students of nature; and the specific identity of the two birds which he had described as distinct under the above names, was first publicly maintained by my friend CHARLES LUCIAN BONAPARTE, although the fact was long before known to many individuals with whom I am acquainted, as well as to myself.

The flight of the Mottled Owl is smooth, rapid, protracted and noiseless. It rises at times above the top branches of the highest of our forest trees, whilst in pursuit of large beetles, and at other times sails low and swiftly over the fields, or through the woods, in search of small birds, field-mice, moles or wood-rats, from which it chiefly derives its subsistence. On alighting, which it does plumply, the Mottled Owl immediately bends its body, turns its head to look behind it, performs a curious nod, utters its notes, then shakes and plumes itself, and resumes its flight.

in search of prey. It now and then, while on wing, produces a *clicking* sound with its mandibles, but more frequently when perched near its mate or young. This I have thought is done by the bird to manifest its courage, and let the hearer know that it is not to be meddled with, although few birds of prey are more gentle when seized, as it will suffer a person to touch its feathers and caress it, without attempting to bite or strike with its talons, unless at rare intervals. I carried one of the young birds represented in the Plate, in my coat pocket, from Philadelphia to New York, travelling alternately by water and by land. It remained generally quiet, fed from the hand, and never attempted to escape. It was given me by my good friend Dr Richard Harlan, of Philadelphia, and was lost at sea, in the course of my last voyage to England.

The notes of this Owl are uttered in a tremulous, doleful manner, and somewhat resemble the chattering of the teeth of a person under the influence of extreme cold, although much louder. They are heard at a distance of several hundred yards, and by some people are thought to be of ominous import.

The little fellow is generally found about farm-houses, orchards, and gardens. It alights on the roof, the fence or the garden gate, and utters its mournful ditty at intervals for hours at a time, as if it were in a state of great suffering, although this is far from being the case, the song of all birds being an indication of content and happiness. In a state of confinement, it continues to utter its notes with as much satisfaction as if at liberty. They are chiefly heard during the latter part of winter, that being the season of love, when the male bird is particularly attentive to the fair one which excites his tender emotions, and around which he flies and struts much in the manner of the Common Pigeon, adding numerous nods and bows, the sight of which is very amusing.

The nest is placed in the bottom of the hollow trunk of a tree, often not at a greater height than six or seven feet from the ground, at other times so high as from thirty to forty feet. It is composed of a few grasses and feathers. The eggs are four or five, of a nearly globular form, and pure white colour. If not disturbed, this species lays only one set of eggs in the season. The young remain in the nest until they are able to fly. At first they are covered with a downy substance of a dull yellowish-white. By the middle of August, they are fully feathered, and are then generally of the colour exhibited in the plate, although considerable differences exist between individuals, as I have seen some of a deep chocolate colour, and others nearly black. The feathers change their colours as the pairing season advances, and in the first spring the bird is in its perfect dress.

After nearly thirty years of observation, I may say, hardly interrupted, I may be allowed to draw your attention to the following fact as highly curious. I have observed that every species of Owl which breeds in the Northern and Middle States is considerably more deficient in its powers of vision during the day or on moonlight nights, when the ground is covered with snow, than the species that breed in, and consequently may be considered as residents of, more northern countries, such as the Snow Owl, the Forked-tailed Owl, and the Hawk Owl, all of which shew no material difference in their power of vision, be the sun or moon shining ever so brightly on the snow. I have frequently approached the Great Horned Owl, as well as every other species that breeds in the United States, during what I call *glaring* snows, whilst, on the same day, my attempts to approach the Snow Owl or the Hawk Owl were ineffectual. Yet on examining the structure of the eyes of all these species, I have found little or no difference in them. I wish some competent anatomist would investigate this singular fact, and communicate the result of his inquiries, for the benefit of the scientific world, and that of the author of the Biography of the Birds of the United States.

The Mottled Owl rests or spends the day either in a hole of some decayed tree, or in the thickest part of the evergreens which are found so abundantly in the country, to which it usually resorts during the breeding season as well as in the depth of winter.

The branch on which you see three individuals of this species, an adult bird and two young ones, is that of the Jersey Pine (*Pinus inops*), a tree of moderate height and diameter, and of a scrubby appearance. The stem is generally crooked, and the wood is not considered of great utility. It grows in large groves in the state from which it has derived its name, and is now mostly used for fuel on board our steam-vessels. The Mottled Owl is often observed perched on its branches.

STRIX ASIO, *Linn.* Syst. Nat. vol. i. p. 132.—*Lath.* Ind. Ornith. vol. i. p. 54.— *Ch. Bonaparte,* Synopsis of Birds of the United States, p. 36.

RED EARED OWL, *Lath.* Synops. vol. i. p. 123.

MOTTLED OWL, STRIX NÆVIA, *Wils.* Amer. Ornith. vol. iii. p. 16. Pl. 19. fig. 1. Adult.

RED OWL, STRIX ASIO, *Wils.* Americ. Ornith. vol. v. p. 83. Pl. 42. fig. 1. Young.

Adult. Plate XCVII. Fig. 1.

Bill very short, compressed, curved, acute, with a small cere at the base; upper mandible with its dorsal outline curved from the base, the edges acute, the point trigonal, very acute, deflected; lower mandible with the edges acute and inflected, obtuse at the tip. Nostrils roundish, in the fore part of the cere, concealed by the recumbent bristles. Head disproportionally large, as are the eyes and external ears. Body short. Legs of ordinary length, tarsus feathered; toes scutellate and sparsely covered with bristles, papillar and tubercular beneath; claws curved, slender, rounded, extremely sharp.

Plumage very soft and downy, somewhat distinct on the head and back, tufty and loose beneath. Long bristly feathers at the base of the bill, stretching forwards and outwards; auricular feathers forming a ruff. Two tufts of erectile feathers on the head, one over each eye. Wings ample, the fourth quill longest, the first short. Tail short, even, of twelve broad, rounded feathers.

Bill yellowish-green. Iris gold-yellow. Feet greenish-yellow. The general colour of the upper parts pale brown, spotted and sprinkled with brownish-black. A pale grey line from the base of the upper mandible over each eye. Primaries light brownish-grey, barred with brownish-black. Primary coverts dark brown, secondary coverts white at the tip. Throat yellowish-grey, under parts light grey, patched and sprinkled with brownish-black. Tarsal feathers tinged with red.

Length 10 inches, extent of wings 22.

Young birds fully pledged. Plate XCVII. Fig. 2, 3.

Bill and feet pale greenish-yellow. Iris light yellow. The general colour of the upper parts is light brownish-red, each feather with a blackish-brown line in the centre, the tail and quills barred with dull brown. A reddish-white line over each eye, the tips of the secondary coverts of the same colour. Breast and sides light yellowish grey, spotted and lined with brownish-black and bright reddish-brown, the rest of the under parts very uniform yellowish-grey, the tarsal feathers pale yellowish-red.

THE JERSEY PINE.

PINUS INOPS, *Pursh*, Fl. Amer. vol. ii. p. 641. *Mich.* Arbr. de l'Amer. Sept. vol. i.
p. 58. pl. iv.—MONŒCIA MONADELPHIA, *Linn.* CONIFERÆ, *Juss.*

Leaves short, in pairs; cones recurved, oblongo-conical, of the length of the leaves; prickles of the scales subulate, straight. It is also named the *Pitch Pine* and *Scrub Pine*. It grows in dry sterile ground, from New Jersey to Carolina.

THE WHITE-BELLIED SWALLOW.

HIRUNDO BICOLOR, VIEILL.

PLATE XCVIII. MALE AND FEMALE.

THIS Swallow often spends the winter months in the State of Louisiana, resorting principally to the neighbourhood of the marshes that border the lakes of Pont Chartrain and those of Bayou St John, near the city of New Orleans, an account of which I have already given when speaking of the Republican Swallow. At the beginning of spring, it spreads widely over the country, and may be observed skimming over the streets of our cities, as well as along the meadows in their neighbourhood.

Its flight is easy, continued, and capable of being greatly protracted. It is seen sailing, circling, turning, and winding in all directions, during the greater part of the day. Like all other Swallows, it feeds on the wing, unceasingly pursuing insects of various kinds, and in seizing them producing a snapping noise which may be heard at some distance. So quarrelsome is this Swallow, that it is almost continually fighting with its own species. Yet they remain in flocks at all seasons, and many pairs are often seen to breed within a short distance of each other. It also attacks the House Swallow, and frequently takes possession of its nest.

It generally prefers the hollow of a tree for its nest, which is of a globular form, composed of slender grasses, and abundantly lined with feathers of various kinds. The eggs are from four to six, of a pure white colour, strongly tinged with blush, occasioned by the transparency of the shell, and are deposited about the end of May. It breeds twice during the season.

No sooner have the young of the second brood acquired their full power of flight, than parents and offspring assemble in large flocks, and resort to the roofs of houses, the tops of decayed trees, or the sandy beaches of our rivers, from whence they take their departure for the south. They fly in a close body, and thus continue their journey, until they reach the places adapted for their winter residence, when they again resume by day the habits which they exhibit during their summer so-

journ in the Middle and Northern States, but collect at night and resort
to the sedges and tall plants of the marshes.

HIRUNDO BICOLOR, *Ch. Bonaparte*, Synops. of Birds of the United States, p. 65.
GREEN-BLUE OR WHITE-BELLIED SWALLOW, HIRUNDO VIRIDIS, *Wils.* Amer. Ornith. vol. iii. p. 44. Pl. 38. fig. 3.

Adult Male. Plate XCVIII. Fig. 1.

Bill short, feeble, much depressed and very broad at the base, compressed at the tip ; upper mandible slightly arched in its dorsal outline ;
gap as wide as the head, and extending to beneath the eye. Nostrils basal, lateral, roundish. Head large, flattened above. Neck short. Body
rather slender. Feet very short and feeble ; tarsus and toes scutellate
anteriorly ; lateral toes nearly equal, the outer united to the second
joint ; claws short, weak, arched.

Plumage silky, shining, and blended. Wings very long, acute, the
first quill longest. Tail of ordinary length, deeply emarginate, of twelve
rounded feathers.

The general colour of the upper parts is steel-blue with green reflections. Quills and tail-feathers brownish-black. The under parts are
white.

Length $5\frac{1}{4}$ inches, extent of wings 10 ; bill along the back $\frac{1}{3}$, along
the gap $\frac{6}{8}$; tarsus $\frac{5}{8}$, middle toe $\frac{6}{8}$.

Adult Female. Plate XCVIII. Fig. 2.
The female resembles the male in size and colour.

THE COW-PEN BIRD.

ICTERUS PECORIS,

PLATE XCIX. Male and Female.

The works of Nature are evidently perfect in all their parts. From the manifestations of consummate skill everywhere displayed, we must infer that the intellect which planned the grand scheme, is infinite in power; and even when we observe parts or objects which to us seem unnecessary, superfluous, or useless, it would be more consistent with the ideas which we ought to have of our own feeble apprehension, to consider them as still perfect, to have been formed for a purpose, and to execute their intended function, than to view them as abortive and futile attempts.

The seed is dropped on the ground. It imbibes moisture, swells, and its latent principle of life receiving an impulse, slowly unfolds. Its radicle shoots down into the earth, its plumule rises toward the sky. The first leaflets appear, and as we watch its progress, we see it assuming size and strength. Years pass on, and it still enlarges. It produces flowers and fruits, and gives shelter to multitudes of animated beings. At length it stands the glory of the forest, spreading abroad its huge arms, covering with its dense foliage the wild animals that retreat to it for protection from the sun and the rain. Centuries after its birth, the stately tree rears its green head to the sky. At length symptoms of decay begin to manifest themselves. The branches wither, the core dies and putrefies. Grey and shaggy lichens cover its trunk and limbs. The Woodpecker resorts to it for the purpose of procuring the insects which find shelter beneath its decayed bark. Blackness spreads over the heavens, the muttering of the thunder is heard. Suddenly there comes on the ear the bickering noise of the whirlwind, which scatters the twigs and the foliage around, and meeting in its path the patriarch of the forest, lays him prostrate on the ground. For years the massy trunk lies extended on the earth; but it is seen gradually giving way. The summer's sun and the winter's frost crumble it into dust, which goes to augment the soil. And thus has it finished its course.

Look again at the egg of the bird, dropped on its curious bed, the construction of which has cost the parent bird many labours and anxieties.

It also is a seed, but it gives rise to a very different object. Fostered by the warmth imparted by the parent bird, the germ which it contains swells into life, and at length bursting its fragile enclosure, comes tottering into existence. To sustain the life and contribute to the development of this helpless being, the mother issues in quest of food, which she carefully places in its open throat. Day after day it acquires new development under the fostering care of its nurse, until at length, invested with all the powers which Nature intended to bestow upon it, it spreads its pinions to the breeze, and sallies forth to perform the many offices for which it is destined.

How often have I watched over the little bird in its nest, and marked the changes which day after day it exhibited : the unfolding of its first scanty covering of down, the sprouting of its plumelets, the general enlargement of all its parts ! With what pleasure have I viewed the development of its colouring and the early manifestations of its future habits !

Amid these wonderful operations of Nature, there is one which has occasionally engaged my attention, and occupied my thoughts, ever since I first became acquainted with the bird of which I now proceed to speak.

The Cow Bird, which in form and character is allied to the Crow Blackbird, the Redwing, the Orchard Oriole, and other species, together with some of which it forms the genus *Icterus*, differs from these birds in one important circumstance, which approximates it to the Cuckoo of Europe, a bird entirely different in habits and appearance. Like that bird, it makes no nest of its own, but deposits its eggs, one at a time, in the nests of other birds, leaving them to the care of a foster-parent.

In the State of Louisiana, the Cow-pen Bird, or as it is also called, the Cow Blackbird, or Cow Bunting, is seen only at long intervals. Some years pass without the appearance of a single individual there. At other times immense flocks are observed mixing with the Redwings, Crow Blackbirds and Robins, searching about the farm-yards, the fields, and the meadows with great diligence for food. At such times they are easily approached, and are shot in great numbers, being considered more delicate and better flavoured than the species with which they associate, excepting the Robin. Like the Redwings, they seek the swamps and the margins of lakes and rivers, where they roost among the tall sedges, flags, and other aquatic plants. When disturbed in these retreats, they rise in a dense mass, perform various evolutions in the air, and alight again to resume their repose. At daybreak, they return to the cultivated parts of the country to search for food. In Georgia and South Carolina, they occur in great abundance every winter. Some also spend the winter in Virginia and Maryland, as well as in the States of Kentucky and Indiana, where I have observed them lingering about farm-houses and cow-pens during severe weather. Great flocks, however, retire much farther south. I have seen many of these birds passing high in the air, at mid-day, in the month of October, pursuing their course steadily, as if bent upon a long journey.

The Cow-pen Bird, after passing the winter in the Southern States, or in regions nearer the equator, makes its appearance in the Middle States about the end of March or beginning of April, arriving in small parties. Their flight is performed chiefly under night; and during the day they are seen resting on the trees, or frequenting the banks of streams in quest of food. They continue to be seen in small flocks until the beginning of June, when they disappear, the various flocks having successively passed northward.

Its flight is similar to that of the Redwing, with which it frequently associates in its rambles. During spring and summer it feeds on insects, larvæ and worms, frequenting the cornfields, meadows and open places.

The males and females arrive together; but contrary to the general practice among the feathered tribes, these birds do not pair. The males seem to regard the females with little interest. The numberless acts of endearment, the many carrollings, joyous flights, and bursts of ecstatic feeling, which other birds display at the commencement of the breeding season, are entirely dispensed with. When a particular intimacy takes place between two individuals of different sexes, it soon ceases, and the same individuals mate with others. The sexual attachment intended for the benefit of the young brood does not take place, because in this species the young are not to be reared by their parents, but to be left to the care of birds of other kinds. The Cow-pen Buntings, in fact, like some unnatural parents of our own race, send out their progeny to be nursed.

When the female is about to deposit her eggs, she is observed to leave her companions, and perch upon a tree or fence, assuming an appearance of uneasiness. Her object is to observe other birds while engaged in constructing their nests. Should she not from this position discover a nest, she moves off and flies from tree to tree, until at length, having found a

ı

suitable repository for her egg, she waits for a proper opportunity, drops
it, flies off, and returns in exultation to her companions.

The birds in whose nests the eggs of the Cow Bunting are thus deposited, are all smaller than itself. That which is most frequently favoured with the unwelcome gift is the Maryland Yellow-throat. The
other species in which I have found the egg of the Cow Bird are the
Chipping Sparrow, the Blue Bird, the Yellow Bird, several Fly-catchers,
especially the Blue-grey and the White-eyed, and the Golden-crowned
Thrush. The nests of these birds are very different in form, size and
materials, as well as in position, some being placed high on trees, others
in low bushes, and that of the Thrush on the ground.

It is also a very remarkable circumstance, that although the Cow-
Bird is larger than the species in the nests of which it deposits its eggs,
the eggs themselves are not much superior in size to those of their
intended foster-parents. This is equally the case with the European
Cuckoo, which selects, for the purpose of depositing its egg, the nest of
the Titlark, Hedge-Sparrow, or some other small bird. And here, as in
so many other cases, may we observe the adaptation of means to ends
which nature has so admirably made. The egg of the Cuckoo, in fact,
is not so large as that of the Skylark, a bird which, to the other, hardly
bears the proportion of one to six. The intention here has not been by
a similarity in size and colouring, to deceive the bird in whose nest the
egg is placed, for, on all occasions, the individuals on which the gift
have been bestowed, receive it unwillingly, and, in fact, manifest great
alarm and resentment. On the contrary, the object has been to secure
the development of the embryo, by adapting the size of the egg to the
capability of imparting heat to it.

Should the Cow-Bird deposit its egg in a nest newly finished, and as
yet empty, the owners of the nest not unfrequently desert it; but, when
they have already deposited one or more eggs, they generally continue
their attachment to it. There is reason for believing, however, that, on
all occasions, they are aware of the intrusion that has been effected.

The Cow-Bird never deposits more than one egg in a nest, although
it is probable it thus leaves several in different nests, especially when we
consider the vast numbers of the species that are to be seen on their return southward. It does not make a forcible entrance, but watches its
opportunity, and when it finds the nest deserted by its guardians, slips
to it like one bent on the accomplishment of some discreditable project.

When the female returns, and finds in her nest an egg which she immediately perceives to be different from her own, she leaves the nest, and perches on a branch near it, returns and retires several times in succession, flies off, calling loudly for her mate, who soon makes his appearance, manifesting great anxiety at the distress of his spouse. They visit the nest together, retire from it, and continue chattering for a considerable time. Nevertheless, the obnoxious egg retains its position, the bird continues to deposit its eggs, and incubation takes place as usual. The egg of the Cow Bird is of a regular oval form, pale greyish-blue, sprinkled with umber-brown dots and short streaks, which are more numerous at the larger end.

Incubation has been continued for nearly a fortnight, and the young Cow Bird bursts the shell. Another remarkable occurrence now takes place. The eggs of the foster-bird are yet unhatched, and soon after disappear. In every case the Cow Bird's egg is the first hatched, and herein also is manifested the wisdom of Nature; for the parent-birds finding a helpless object, for whose subsistence it behoves them to provide, fly off to procure food for it. The other eggs are thus neglected, and the chicks which they contain necessarily perish. Birds have probably the means of knowing an addle egg, for, when any such remain after the hatching of the others, they always remove them from the nest; and, in the present case, the remaining eggs are soon removed, and may sometimes be seen strewn about in the vicinity of the nest. In the case of the Cuckoo matters are differently managed, for the young bird of that species very ungratefully jostles out of the nest all his foster-brothers and sisters, that he may have room enough for himself. If we are fond of admiring the wisdom of Nature, we ought to mingle reason with our admiration; and here we might be tempted to suspect her not so wise as we had imagined, for why should the poor Yellow-throat have been put to the trouble of laying all these eggs, if they are, after all, to produce nothing? This is a mystery to me; nevertheless, my belief in the wisdom of Nature is not staggered by it.

As the young Cow-Bird grows up, its foster-parents provide for it with great assiduity, and manifest all the concern and uneasiness at the intrusion of a stranger, that they would do were their own offspring under their charge. When fully fledged, the young bird is of a sooty-brown colour. Long after it has left the nest, it continues to be fed by its affectionate guardians, until it is at length able to provide for itself.

Towards the end of September, the old and young Cow Birds congregate in vast numbers, and are seen wending their way southward, sometimes by themselves, more frequently intermingled with other species, such as the Purple Grakles and the Redwings, which they join in their plundering expeditions. They are to be seen in the Middle States until near the end of October, although unusually severe weather sometimes forces them southward at an earlier period.

This species derives its name from the circumstance of its frequenting cow-pens. In this respect it greatly resembles the European Starling. Like that bird it follows the cattle in the fields, often alights on their backs, and may be seen diligently searching for worms and larvæ among their dung. In spring, the cattle in many parts of the United States are much infested with intestinal worms, which they pass in great quantities, and on these the Cow-bird frequently makes a delicious repast.

It has no song properly so called, but utters a low muttering sort of chuckle, in performing which, it is seen to swell out its throat, and move the feathers there in succession, in a manner very much resembling that of the European Starling.

ICTERUS PECORIS, *Ch. Bonaparte*, Synops. of Birds of the United States, p. 53.

STURNUS JUNCETI, *Lath.* Ind. Ornith. vol. i. p. 326. Male.

FRINGILLA PECORIS, *Gmel.* Syst. vol. i. p. 910.—*Lath.* Ind. Ornith. vol. i. p. 443.

COW-BUNTING, EMBERIZA PECORIS, *Wils.* Amer. Ornith. vol. ii. p. 145. Pl. 18. fig. 1. Male, fig. 2. Female, fig. 3. Young.

Adult Male. Plate XCIX. Fig. 1.

Bill conical, robust, very acute, compressed towards the end; upper mandible obtuse above, rounded on the sides, encroaching a little on the forehead with an angle, the margins acute and overlapping; lower mandible with the sides inflected; gap-line much deflected at the base. Nostrils basal, lateral, oval, covered above by a membrane. Head of ordinary size. Neck rather short. Body rather robust. Feet of ordinary length; tarsus compressed, acute behind, anteriorly covered with seven longish scutella; toes free, scutellate, lateral ones nearly equal; claws arched, compressed, acute.

Plumage blended, glossy. Wings longish, curved, somewhat rounded, the second quill longest. Tail shortish, rounded, a little emarginate, of twelve straight, rounded feathers.

Bill and feet brownish-black. Iris dark hazel. Head and neck sooty brown, the general colour of the other parts is brownish-black, the fore part of the breast glossed with blue, the upper parts with green and blue reflections.

Length 7 inches, extent of wings $11\frac{1}{2}$; bill along the ridge $\frac{7}{12}$, along the gap $\frac{5}{8}$, tarsus $1\frac{1}{12}$, middle toe $1\frac{1}{12}$.

Adult Female. Plate XCIX. Fig. 2.

The female is somewhat less than the male. Bill, eyes, and feet of the same colour as the male. The general colour of the plumage is dusky brown, resembling that of the head and neck of the male, the under parts somewhat lighter, as are the tips of the quills and larger wing-coverts.

THE MARSH WREN.

TROGLODYTES PALUSTRIS, CH. BONAP.

PLATE C. MALE, FEMALE, AND NEST.

THE haunts of this interesting little bird are, in the Middle Districts, the margins of rivers at their confluence with the sea, and the adjoining marshes of our Atlantic shores. In such places, the Marsh Wren is found in great numbers, from the beginning of April to the middle of October, when it retires southward, many individuals wintering on the south-western shores of the Floridas, and along the mouths of the Mississippi.

It is a homely little bird, and is seldom noticed, unless by the naturalist, when searching for other species, or by children, who in all countries are fond of birds. It lives entirely amongst the sedges, flags, and other rank plants that cover the margins of the rivers, and the inlets of the sea. Its flight is very low and short, and is performed by a continued flirting of the wings, but without the motions of the tail employed by the Great Carolina Wren. Its song, if song I can call it, is composed of several quickly repeated notes, resembling the grating of a rusty hinge, and is uttered almost continuously during the fore part of the day, the performer standing perched on the top of a tall weed, from which, on the appearance of an intruder, it instantly dives into the thickest part of the herbage, but to which it returns the moment it thinks the danger over, and renews its merry little song.

The males are extremely pugnacious, and chase each other with great animosity, until one or other has been forced to give way. This disposition is the more remarkable, as these birds build their nests quite close to each other. I have seen several dozens of these nests in the course of a morning ramble, in a piece of marsh not exceeding forty or fifty acres.

The nest is nearly of the size and shape of a cocoa-nut, and is formed of dried grasses, entwined in a circular manner, so as to include in its mass several of the stems and leaves of the sedges or other plants, among which it is placed. A small aperture, just large enough to admit the birds, is left, generally on the south-west side of the nest. The interior is composed of small dry grasses, and is nearly of the depth and width of a common bottle. The eggs, which are from six to eight, are of a regular oval form, and deep chocolate colour, and, from their small size, resemble so many beads. The Marsh Wren raises two broods in the season, and on each occasion forms a new nest. In consequence of this practice, the deserted nests of the year, and those remaining since the preceding season, may be seen in the marshes in every direction, there being scarcely a tuft of tall weeds that is not adorned with one of them.

The food of the Marsh Wren principally consists of minute aquatic insects, and equally diminutive mollusca, which it procures by moving along the blades of the grasses, or the twigs of other plants, which it does with great activity. Indeed, so rapid are its movements among the weeds, that one might easily mistake it for a mouse, did he not observe its tail now and then raised over its back, so as to allow the white under-coverts of the former to become conspicuous.

Although I have shot and examined many birds of this species, I have not found any remarkable differences in the plumage of the sexes.

The young birds assume their full colouring so soon after they leave their nest, that by the time the species departs from the Middle Districts on its way southward, it is hardly possible to distinguish them from the old birds.

In the plate, the last of my first volume of the BIRDS OF AMERICA, you have, *kind* reader (as I hope I may now with confidence call you), three figures of this little inhabitant of our marshy shores, together with the representation of its nest.

TROGLODYTES PALUSTRIS, *Ch. Bonaparte,* Synops. of Birds of the United States, p. 93.
MARSH WREN, TROGLODYTES PALUSTRIS, *Wils.* Amer. Ornith. vol. iii. p. 58. Pl. 12. fig. 4.

Adult Male. Plate C. Fig. 1.

Bill longish, slightly arched, slender, acute, subtrigonal at the base, compressed towards the tip; upper mandible with the ridge obtuse, the sides convex towards the end, concave at the base, the edges acute and overlapping; under mandible with the sides and back convex. Nostrils oblong, direct, basal, with a cartilaginous lid above, open and bare. Head ovate, eyes rather large, neck of ordinary length, body short and full. Legs of ordinary length; tarsus longer than the middle toe, compressed, covered anteriorly with six scutella, posteriorly with a long plate, forming an acute edge; toes scutellate above, the second and fourth nearly equal, the hind toe almost equal to the middle one, the third and fourth united as far as the second joint; claws rather long, slender, acute, arched, much compressed.

Plumage soft, tufty, slightly glossed. No bristly feathers about the bill. Wings short, broad, rounded: first quill half the length of the second, which is very little shorter than the third and fourth. Tail of ordinary length, much rounded, of twelve rounded feathers.

Bill dark brown above, yellow beneath. Iris hazel. Feet light brown. The general colour of the upper parts is dark brown, the sides of the head deeper, the fore part of the back brownish-black, longitudinally streaked with white, the quills externally margined with lighter brown, the tail barred with dark brown. A white line over the eye, extending down the neck; the sides of the latter mottled with light brown and grey; the under parts of a silvery greyish-white; the abdominal feathers and under tail-coverts tipped with brown.

Length 5 inches, extent of wings $6\frac{1}{4}$; bill along the ridge nearly $\frac{7}{12}$, along the gap $\frac{3}{4}$; tarsus $\frac{5}{6}$, middle toe nearly $\frac{3}{4}$.

Adult Female. Plate C. Fig. 2, 3.

The female differs very little in external appearance from the male. The black of the back is less deep, and the white lines are less conspicuous; the under parts, also, are of a duller white.

COLONEL BOON.

DANIEL BOON, or, as he was usually called in the Western Country, COLONEL BOON, happened to spend a night with me under the same roof, more than twenty years ago. We had returned from a shooting excursion, in the course of which his extraordinary skill in the management of the rifle had been fully displayed. On retiring to the room appropriated to that remarkable individual and myself for the night, I felt anxious to know more of his exploits and adventures than I did, and accordingly took the liberty of proposing numerous questions to him. The stature and general appearance of this wanderer of the western forests approached the gigantic. His chest was broad and prominent; his muscular powers displayed themselves in every limb; his countenance gave indication of his great courage, enterprise, and perseverance; and when he spoke, the very motion of his lips brought the impression that whatever he uttered could not be otherwise than strictly true. I undressed, whilst he merely took off his hunting shirt, and arranged a few folds of blankets on the floor, choosing rather to lie there, as he observed, than on the softest bed. When we had both disposed of ourselves, each after his own fashion, he related to me the following account of his powers of memory, which I lay before you, kind reader, in his own words, hoping that the simplicity of his style may prove interesting to you.

" I was once," said he, " on a hunting expedition on the banks of the Green River, when the lower parts of this State (Kentucky) were still in the hands of nature, and none but the sons of the soil were looked upon as its lawful proprietors. We Virginians had for some time been waging a war of intrusion upon them, and I, amongst the rest, rambled through the woods in pursuit of their race, as I now would follow the tracks of any ravenous animal. The Indians outwitted me one dark night, and I was as unexpectedly as suddenly made a prisoner by them. The trick had been managed with great skill; for no sooner had I extinguished the fire of my camp, and laid me down to rest, in full security, as I thought, than I felt myself seized by an indistinguishable number of hands, and was immediately pinioned, as if about to be led to the scaffold for execution. To have attempted to be refractory, would have proved useless and dangerous to my life; and I suffered myself to be removed from my camp to theirs, a few miles distant, without uttering even a word of complaint. You are aware, I dare say, that to act in this manner was the best policy, as you understand that by so doing, I proved to the Indians at once, that I was born and bred as fearless of death as any of themselves.

" When we reached the camp, great rejoicings were exhibited. Two squaws and a few papooses appeared particularly delighted at the sight of me, and I was assured, by very unequivocal gestures and words, that, on the morrow, the mortal enemy of the Red-skins would cease to live. I never opened my lips, but was busy contriving some scheme which might enable me to give the rascals the slip before dawn. The women immediately fell a searching about my hunting-shirt for whatever they might think valuable, and, fortunately for me, soon found my flask filled with *monongahela* (that is, reader, strong whisky). A terrific grin was exhibited on their murderous countenances, while my heart throbbed with joy at the anticipation of their intoxication. The crew immediately began to beat their bellies and sing, as they passed the bottle from mouth to mouth. How often did I wish the flask ten times its size, and filled with aqua-fortis ! I observed that the squaws drank more freely than the warriors, and again my spirits were about to be depressed, when the report of a gun was heard at a distance. The Indians all jumped on their feet. The singing and drinking were both brought to a stand, and I saw, with inexpressible joy, the men walk off to some distance and talk to the squaws. I knew that they were consulting about me, and I foresaw that in a few moments the warriors would go to discover the cause of the gun having been fired so near their camp. I expected that the squaws would be left to guard me. Well, Sir, it was just so. They returned ; the men took up their guns, and walked away. The squaws sat down again, and in less than five minutes had my bottle up to their dirty mouths, gurgling down their throats the remains of the whisky.

" With what pleasure did I see them becoming more and more drunk, until the liquor took such hold of them that it was quite impossible for these women to be of any service. They tumbled down, rolled about, and began to snore : when I, having no other chance of freeing myself from the cords that fastened me, rolled over and over towards the fire, and, after a short time, burned them asunder. I rose on my feet, stretched my stiffened sinews, snatched up my rifle, and, for once in my life, spared that of Indians. I now recollect how desirous I once or twice felt to lay open the skulls of the wretches with my tomahawk ; but when I again thought upon killing beings unprepared and unable to defend themselves, it looked like murder without need, and I gave up the idea.

" But, Sir, I felt determined to mark the spot, and walking to a thrifty ash sapling, I cut out of it three large chips, and ran off. I soon reached the river, soon crossed it, and threw myself deep into the cane-brakes, imitating the tracks of an Indian with my feet, so that no chance might be left for those from whom I had escaped to overtake me.

" It is now nearly twenty years since this happened, and more than five since I left the Whites' settlements, which I might probably never have visited again, had I not been called on as a witness in a law-suit that was pending in Kentucky, and which I really believe would never have been settled, had I not come forward, and established the beginning of a certain boundary line. This is the story, Sir.

" Mr ———— moved from Old Virginia into Kentucky, and having a large tract granted to him in the new State, laid claim to a certain parcel of land adjoining Green River, and as chance would have it, took for one of his corners the very Ash tree on which I had made my mark, and finished his survey of some thousands of acres, beginning, as it is expressed in the deed, ' at an Ash marked by three distinct notches of the tomahawk of a white man.'

" The tree had grown much, and the bark had covered the marks; but somehow or other, Mr ———— heard from some one all that I have already said to you, and thinking that I might remember the spot alluded to in the deed, but which was no longer discoverable, wrote for me to come and try at least to find the place or the tree. His letter mentioned that all my expenses should be paid, and not caring much about once more about going back to Kentucky, I started and met Mr ————. After some conversation, the affair with the Indians came to my recollection. I considered for a while, and began to think that after all I could find the very spot, as well as the tree, if it was yet standing.

"Mr ———— and I mounted our horses, and off we went to the Green River Bottoms. After some difficulties, for you must be aware, Sir, that great changes have taken place in those woods, I found at last the spot where I had crossed the river, and waiting for the moon to rise, made for the course in which I thought the Ash tree grew. On approaching the place, I felt as if the Indians were there still, and as if I was still a prisoner among them. Mr ———— and I camped near what I conceived the spot, and waited until the return of day.

" At the rising of the sun, I was on foot, and after a good deal of musing, thought that an Ash tree then in sight must be the very one on which I had made my mark. I felt as if there could be no doubt of it, and mentioned my thought to Mr ———. " Well, Colonel Boon," said he, " if you think so, I hope it may prove true, but we must have some witnesses ; do you stay here about, and I will go and bring some of the settlers whom I know." I agreed. Mr ——— trotted off, and I, to pass the time, rambled about to see if a deer was still living in the land. But ah ! Sir, what a wonderful difference thirty years makes in the country ! Why, at the time when I was caught by the Indians, you would not have walked out in any direction for more than a mile without shooting a buck or a bear. There were then thousands of buffaloes on the hills in Kentucky ; the land looked as if it never would become poor ; and to hunt in those days was a pleasure indeed. But when I was left to myself on the banks of Green River, I dare say for the last time in my life, a few *signs* only of deer were to be seen, and, as to a deer itself, I saw none.

"Mr ——— returned, accompanied by three gentlemen. They looked upon me as if I had been WASHINGTON himself, and walked to the Ash tree, which I now called my own, as if in quest of a long lost treasure. I took an axe from one of them, and cut a few chips off the bark. Still no signs were to be seen. So I cut again until I thought it was time to be cautious, and I scraped and worked away with my butcher knife, until I *did* come to where my tomahawk had left an impression in the wood. We now went regularly to work, and scraped at the tree with care, until three hacks as plain as any three notches ever were, could be seen. Mr ——— and the other gentlemen were astonished, and, I must allow, I was as much surprised as pleased myself. I made affidavit of this remarkable occurrence in presence of these gentlemen. Mr —— gained his cause. I left Green River for ever, and came to where we now are ; and, Sir, I wish you a good night."

I trust, kind reader, that when I again make my appearance with another volume of Ornithological Biography, I shall not have to search in vain for the impression which I have made, but shall have the satisfaction of finding its traces still unobliterated. I now withdraw, and, in the words of the noted wanderer of the western wilds, " WISH YOU A GOOD NIGHT."

INDEX.

NEILL & CO. PRINTERS,
Old Fishmarket, Edinburgh.

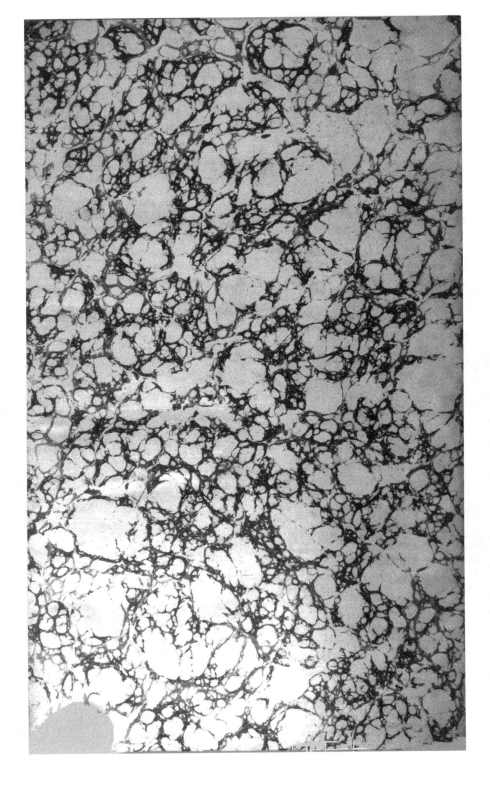

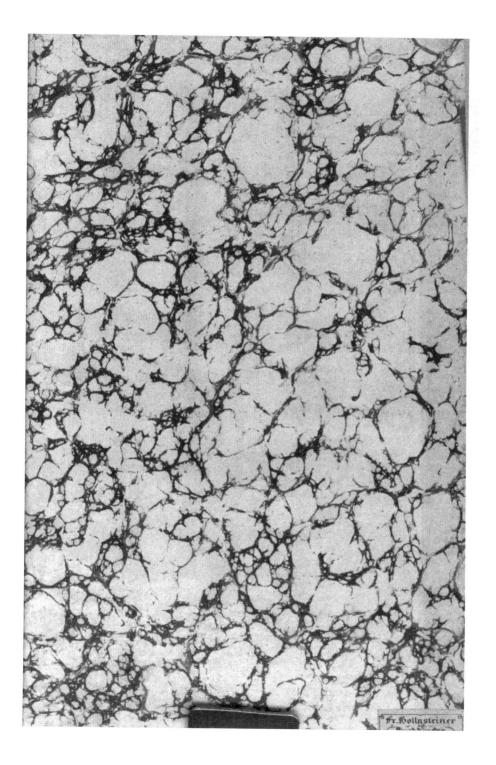

CPSIA information can be obtained
at www.ICGtesting.com
Printed in the USA
BVHW041221010821
613366BV00012B/685